HEALTH INSURANCE AND CANADIAN PUBLIC POLICY

CANADIAN PUBLIC ADMINISTRATION
SERIES
COLLECTION ADMINISTRATION PUBLIQUE
CANADIENNE

J. E. Hodgetts, *General Editor/Rédacteur en chef*

The Institute of Public Administration of Canada
L'Institut d'administration publique du Canada

This series is sponsored by the Institute of Public
Administration of Canada as part of its constitutional
commitment to encourage research on contemporary
issues in Canadian public administration and public
policy, and to foster wider knowledge and understanding amongst practitioners and the concerned citizen.
There is no fixed number of volumes planned for the
series, but under the supervision of the Research
Committee of the Institute and the General Editor,
efforts will be made to ensure that significant areas
will receive appropriate attention.

L'Institut d'administration publique du Canada
commandite cette collection dans le cadre de ses
engagements statutaires. Il se doit de promouvoir la
recherche sur des problèmes d'actualité portant sur
l'administration publique et la détermination des poli-
tiques publiques ainsi que d'encourager les praticiens
et les citoyens intéressés à les mieux connaître et à les
mieux comprendre. Il n'a pas été prévu de nombre de
volumes donné pour la collection mais, sous la direction du Rédacteur en chef et du Comité de recherche
de l'Institut, l'on s'efforce d'accorder l'attention voulue
aux questions importantes.

Canada and Immigration:
Public Policy and Public Concern
Freda Hawkins

The Biography of an Institution:
The Civil Service Commission of Canada, 1908–1967
J. E. Hodgetts, William McCloskey, Reginald
Whitaker, V. Seymour Wilson

An edition in French has been published under the
title *Histoire d'une institution: La Commission de la
Fonction publique du Canada, 1908–1967*,
by Les Presses de l'Université Laval.

Old Age Pension and Policy-Making in Canada
Kenneth Bryden

Provincial Governments as Employers:
A Survey of Public Personnel Administration
in Canada's Provinces
J. E. Hodgetts and O. P. Dwivedi

Transport in Transition:
The Reorganization of the Federal Transport Portfolio
John W. Langford

Initiative and Response:
The Adaptation of Canadian Federalism to
Regional Economic Development
Anthony G. S. Careless

Canada's Salesman to the World:
The Department of Trade and Commerce, 1892–1939
O. Mary Hill

Health Insurance and Canadian Public Policy:
The Seven Decisions that Created the Canadian
Health Insurance System
Malcolm G. Taylor

Health Insurance and Canadian Public Policy

The Seven Decisions that Created The Canadian Health Insurance System

MALCOLM G. TAYLOR

The Institute of Public Administration of Canada
L'Institut d'administration publique du Canada

McGill–Queen's University Press
Montreal

© The Institute of Public Administration of Canada /
    L'Institut d'administration publique du Canada 1978
ISBN 0–7735–0307–2 (cloth)
ISBN 0–7735–0308–0 (paper)

Legal deposit fourth quarter 1978
Bibliothèque Nationale du Québec

Design by Anthony Crouch MGDC
Printed in Canada by Hignell Printing Limited

For Audrey, Deanne, and Burke

Contents

Tables

Preface

THIS IS A STUDY OF the development of the Canadian health insurance system. It is also a study of the policy-making process in federal and provincial governments that, over a period of thirty years, brought the system into being.

Because hospital insurance and medical care insurance were introduced a decade apart, each province made two decisions, for a total of twenty. The federal government made three separate decisions, the first in 1945 in the famous Green Book Proposals, which was aborted, the second on hospital insurance in 1956, and the third on medical care insurance in 1966. While all of these were large and complex decisions for the governments making them, and all worthy of analysis, it was simply impossible to include all of them in this study. It was necessary, therefore, to select those decisions which were *determinative*, in that they launched the system and created the program design. Careful analysis indicates that there were six determinative decisions: the three by the federal government, that of Saskatchewan for hospital insurance in 1946 and similarly of Ontario in 1955, and Saskatchewan's decision on medicare in 1959. There was one other that, although not determinative, was of such importance as to warrant inclusion. Quebec's decision on medicare in 1970 reveals the extraordinary difficulties of government decision making in a federal state, and especially under the turbulent conditions that led to the October Crisis, with its simultaneous withdrawal of services by the Federation of Specialists. It is a graphic illustration of the problems created for provinces by federal initiatives in fields of provincial jurisdiction.

There were, of course, earlier decisions by provincial governments that contributed to the evolution of health insurance in this country.

British Columbia passed a health insurance act in 1935, only to have the program cancelled three weeks before it was to go into operation. I have examined that attempt elsewhere in some detail[1] but since it was aborted it cannot be considered as having been a determinative decision. Nor can the statutes passed by Alberta in 1935, Saskatchewan in 1944, Ontario in 1944, or Manitoba in 1945. All of these, and the legislative inquiries and royal commissions that preceded them, undoubtedly advanced the cause of health insurance in Canada but shaped the outcomes only marginally.

Seven decisions, therefore, are analyzed for the contribution they made to the Canadian health insurance system and the light they shed on the governmental process. The purpose of the analysis is to identify and examine the impact of ideas, public opinion, interest groups, and political forces as they came to bear on the perceived problems, caused the decisions to be made, and shaped the design of the proposed solutions. This is followed by a summary of the short-term results (i.e., to about the end of 1971) of the policies and programs that were adopted.

As an aid to understanding the policy-making process, I have adopted (and adapted) the *systems analysis* construct of David Easton[2] and of elaborations by such others as Daniel Katz, Robert L. Kahn,[3] and Ira Sharkansky.[4] In Easton's conceptual framework, the political system, like all social systems, is characterized by "boundaries." The system receives "inputs" from the environment in the form of demands and support. These are then subjected to the "conversion process"—the dynamic "withinputs" of political leaders and the bureaucracy. The results are the "outputs" of policy in the form of legislation, regulations, and taxes, and in the strategies developed to implement the program. These outputs of policies and strategies have effects on the environment that are characterized as "outcomes." Information about these is returned to the political system as further inputs in the form of "feedback," enabling the system to make new adjustments in the policy or strategy to improve the quality of the outcomes. It is a continuous, cyclical process with the system responding to the stress that is both imposed upon it from without and generated from within.

The political system differs from all other systems in that it is, as Easton says, "predominantly oriented toward the authoritative allocation of values in a society."[5] It is the only system having a monopoly of the legitimate use of coercion. This fundamental characteristic of government is profusely illustrated in the analysis that follows, for the history of health insurance in Canada is largely about conflicts in values held by the medical profession, the insurance industry, labour unions, farmers' associations, political parties, and provincial governments, and about the decisions made by governments in their allocations of values that would be authoritative.

I have adapted the Easton conceptual framework by organizing each case study to answer the following questions; with the headings used in the text in parentheses.

1. Why was the decision made? (The Action Imperatives)
2. What were the constraints limiting the policy choices? (The Constraints)
3. What were the risks? (The Uncertainties)
4. What were the contributions of external forces to the content and timing of policies? (The External Contributions)

The answers to these four questions comprise the *inputs.*

The fifth question relates to the governmental process.

5. What were the contributions of the bureaucracy and the government ministers, Cabinet, caucus and Legislature, or Parliament? (Internal Contributions)

These are the *withinputs.*

The next two questions are concerned with what emerged from the "conversion process."

6. What kind of program was created? (The Policy)
7. How did the government introduce the program? (The Strategy of Implementation)

These are the *outputs.*

The final question relates to the environment.

8. What were the results of the program?

These are the *outcomes.*

Diagramatically, the analytic frame of reference appears as follows:

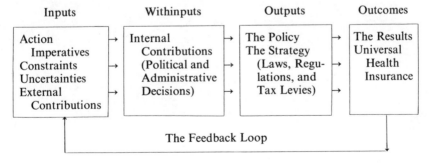

Figure 1. The Policy-Making Process

It would be comforting to believe that the governmental process follows so neat and logical a course, but, obviously, it does not. Unforeseen obstacles appear, unpredictable events (such as an election defeat) occur, and feedback from the environment warns of the need for changes in policy or strategy. With each of these decisions taking from two to six years to bring to conclusion, new inputs and withinputs appear at different times, and in some of the cases, therefore, several stages in the strategy of implementation can be discerned before the objective is reached.

This study, like a number of recent works,[6] focuses on the interaction of federal-provincial relations as well as on government-interest group relations, highlighting how extraordinarily complex the Canadian governmental system has become in the post-war era. The more one examines the roles of interest groups and national and provincial political parties in the formulation of policies, and the increasing interdependence of the federal and provincial governments, the less the two-tier federal system resembles the traditional "layer-cake" concept and the more it exhibits the idiosyncratic confusion of a marble cake. It is hoped that the following analyses will enhance our understanding of the complexities of the system, but I would not claim to have fully probed or discovered all its labyrinthine ways.

Acknowledgements

It is a pleasure to acknowledge the many contributions by others to this study. I am especially indebted to the Hon. Jack Pickersgill, literary executor of the Mackenzie King estate, for access to the Mackenzie King Diary, the Mackenzie King *Papers*, and the Brooke Claxton *Papers*; to Mr. T. C. Douglas for access to his *Papers*; to Mrs. Woodrow Lloyd, for permission to use her late husband's *Papers*; to Dr. H. D. Dalgleish for access to the extraordinary collection of press clippings in the library of the Saskatchewan College of Physicians and Surgeons; to Dr. W. I. Smith, archivist of the Public Archives of Canada; to Mr. Ian Wilson, Saskatchewan Provincial Archivist; and to Miss M. Smigarowski, librarian of the Saskatchewan Department of Health. I should like also to express my appreciation to the many officials who generously granted interviews: ministers and deputy ministers of health, chairmen of hospital and medical care commissions, executive directors of the provincial divisions of the Canadian Medical Association and of the provincial Hospital Associations, and of their national bodies.

I was also saved from many errors by the following who read one or more chapters in draft form and most of whom also granted interviews: Dr. J. F. C. Anderson, Saskatoon; Dr. Robert Armstrong, Ottawa; Dr. E. W. Barootes, Regina; Mrs. Isobel Brown, Toronto; Mr. Robert Bryce, Ottawa; Mr. Claude Castonguay, Montreal; Dr. Kenneth Charron, Toronto; Dr. H. D. Dalgleish, Saskatoon; Mr. T. C. Douglas, Ottawa; Mr. George Gathercole, Toronto; the Hon. Walter Gordon, Toronto; Dr. Gerard Hamel, Montreal; Dr. C. J. Houston, Yorkton; Mrs. Frances Ireland, Toronto; Dr. Arthur D. Kelly, Toronto; Mr. Tom Kent, Sidney; Mr. Tim Lee, Toronto; the Hon. Paul Martin, London, England; Mr. Stanley Martin, Toronto; Dr. J. T. McLeod, Toronto; Dr. T. H. McLeod,

Ottawa; Dr. Frederick D. Mott, Pittsford, New York; the Rt. Hon. Lester Pearson, Ottawa; the Hon. J. E. Pickersgill, Ottawa; Dr. Raymond Robillard, Montreal; Dr. Leonard Rosenfeld, Chapel Hill, North Carolina; Dr. F. Burns Roth, Toronto; Mr. John E. Sparks, Windsor; Dr. Ian Urquhart, Toronto; Mr. Ronald Verbrugge, Toronto; Mr. Carman Feader, Regina; and the editor of this series, Dr. J. E. Hodgetts. Their comments have been invaluable but, needless to say, they bear no responsibility for the interpretations I have presented.

I have also been greatly assisted by Miss Christa Wypkema, Mrs. Carol Raemer, and Miss Diane Surplis, who served as my research assistants, and by Mrs. Irene Wensley, Ms. Pauline Geldart, Miss Rosalie Still, and Ms. Rea Wilmshurst who typed the drafts and the final manuscript. I am especially grateful for the support and encouragement of my colleagues, James Gillies, William Dimma, Wally Crowston, and Don Daly and for the contribution of Maurice Demers and Joe Galimberti of the Institute of Public Administration of Canada. My deepest debt is to my wife, Audrey, who with unfailing patience has done so much in so many ways to help me in the preparation of this book.

The travel and research were made possible by generous grants from the Canada Council, the Ford Foundation, and the Institute of Public Administration of Canada, for which I am most grateful.

Chapter One

The 1945 Health Insurance Proposals:
Policymaking for Post-war Canada

IT WAS 10 A.M. ON AUGUST 6, 1945 and in the House of Commons Chamber —borrowed for the occasion—all was ready. Months of feverish activity —of committee meetings piled upon meetings, of draft reports mutilated and revised, torn apart and revised again—had reached their climax. There on the conference table, fresh from the King's Printer in their green covers, neatly arranged in front of the four federal ministers and the nine provincial premiers, were copies of the Dominion government's design for a new post-war world for Canada—the famous "Green Book Proposals."[1]

The delegates were there as the spokesmen for ten governments to consider the future of Canada, and the differences among them were as varied as the regions from which they came. There were the representatives of the central government grown both powerful and confident in the exercise of wartime authority, the representatives of large provinces with great resources, and the premiers of small and less wealthy provinces with the depression economy still vividly impressed on their minds. They were leaders of ten political parties bearing five different labels, some fresh from new electoral mandates, some allied with the federal Liberal party, and others committed to its frustration and embarrassment.

They were the main players about to enter into a new bargaining game in which the stakes were extraordinarily high: restructuring of the tax system, millions of dollars of revenues for new programs, the future balance of forces in the scale of federal-provincial relations, political party fortunes, and, not least, personal political careers—all, and more, hung on the outcomes.

It was a pregnant moment as Prime Minister Mackenzie King intoned his welcoming statement and sought the cooperation of the provinces in the strategies of a new war against ancient foes:

> The enemies we shall have to overcome will be on our own Canadian soil. They will make their presence known in the guise of sickness, unemployment and want. It is to plan for a unified campaign in Canada against these enemies of progress and human well-being that we have come together at this time. This may well be the most important Canadian Conference since Confederation. It is ours to make it worthy of the place which Canada holds today in the eyes of the world.[2]

The mood was not lost on the premiers or the 150 advisers. The dreams, hopes, and aspirations of the Canadian people were focused now on their leaders who had the power and authority to convert those dreams into the realities of policies, agreements, legislation, and operating programs. The realities, even at their best, could never, of course, match the hopes engendered by the frustrations and deprivations of ten years of depression and six years of war. There was a mood of rebellion against the universal risks of unemployment and sickness, disability and old age, widowhood and poverty, a pervasive dissatisfaction with precarious minimum wages, drought-stricken farms, grudgingly-granted relief payments, and a suspiciously-administered, means-tested old age pension.

It is impossible for anyone under the age of forty today, protected as we now are with a full panoply of social insurance programs, to appreciate, or perhaps even to comprehend, the threats to individual and family independence and integrity that characterized the thirties and extended, to a declining degree, into the forties and the fifties. But to millions the threats had been real and, for hundreds of thousands, had come to pass. The hopes of a nation—ambivalently balanced between the confidence born of a magnificent war effort and the fear of the return of a depression —were focused on these key actors in the unfolding drama.

The Hon. Louis St. Laurent, minister of justice, took over as acting chairman and introduced the proposals in these words:

> In familiar terms, our objectives are high and stable employment and income, and a greater sense of public responsibility for individual economic security and welfare. Realization of these objectives for all Canadians, as Canadians, is a cause in which we hope for national enthusiasm and unity.

The Government has clear and definite views on how these objectives can be attained;

First, to facilitate private enterprise to produce and provide employment;

Secondly, to promote bold action by the state in those fields in which the public interest calls for public enterprise in national development;

Thirdly, to provide, through public investment, productive employment for our human and physical resources when international and other conditions adversely affect employment; and

Fourthly, to provide, on the basis of small regular payments against large and uncertain individual risks, for such hazards and disabilities as unemployment, sickness, and old age.[3]

These, then, were the goals and the means, as formulated by the federal government and, it was hoped, to be accepted by the provinces. They were broad in scope and called for new thrusts and initiatives as well as federal-provincial cooperation on a scale never before envisaged. High on the list of priorities was health insurance which is our concern here. The health proposals, too, were bold, imaginative, and comprehensive, offering four types of financial assistance to the provinces: 1. Grants for Planning and Organization; 2. Health insurance grants for a wide range of benefits; 3. Health Grants; 4. Financial Assistance in the Construction of Hospitals.

No one who reflects on the travails of introducing hospital insurance in the fifties and medical care insurance in the sixties can examine these proposals with other than amazement at their audacity. Our purpose here is to analyze why and how decisions of such magnitude were made.

In a proposal as complex as national health insurance, and especially when it is being considered for adoption in a federal state, there are literally scores of actors and decision makers, playing their roles both individually and in groups. Moreover, as individuals or groups they make their appearances over extended periods of time, and on various stages or venues and, of course, may and indeed do change their views and positions with consequently different effects on the outcomes. In addition, the same roles are sometimes taken by different actors as, for example, when Brooke Claxton succeeded Ian Mackenzie as health minister and, naturally, altered the scenario in keeping with his different perception of goals, policies, programs, and strategies.

In the development of the 1945 proposals, there were four main stages on which the actors performed. The first was the Department of Pensions and National Health (hereafter called the Health Department) and the Interdepartmental Committee (usually referred to as the Heagerty Committee) which functioned from February 1942 to December 1944. The main action then shifted to the second arena—the House of Commons Special Committee on Social Security which met in 1943 and again in 1944. The third was the Cabinet and its Committee on Dominion-Provincial Relations which was formed in 1944. The fourth arena was the 1945–46 Dominion-Provincial Conference which extended over nine months, meeting either in Conference or as the Coordinating Committee with its various sub-committees.

We shall examine first why the decision was made.

THE ACTION IMPERATIVES

1. *The depression.* The experience of the 1930s was disastrous for the hundreds of thousands "on relief" as well as for many who managed to escape what was then considered that ignominious fate. Our heritage of the Elizabethan Poor Law had placed responsibility for the sick poor on local government but many cities, towns, and especially rural munici-palities in Canada quickly reached the point of near or actual bankruptcy from the combination of declining revenues and expanding relief pay-ments for food, clothing, and shelter. Medical care, except in the direst emergency conditions, was a luxury that only few individuals or munici-palities could afford.

The danger to health was matched only by the indignities suffered by individuals forced to appeal to municipal relief officers for authorization to be admitted to hospital. A growing conviction at the grass-roots was often expressed as, "Never again will I crawl on my hands and knees to a municipal official before I can be admitted to hospital." A survey con-ducted by the Canadian Medical Association (CMA) in 1933 revealed only a few municipalities able to meet part of the costs. Most of the provinces, too, found the burden of medical services beyond their financial capacity. The medical profession thus bore the brunt of providing medical care to the indigent and their stacks of unpaid bills would be empty legacies for their heirs. So serious was the situation in Saskatche-wan, for example, that in December 1932, the provincial government through its Relief Commission made a grant of $75.00 a month to doctors in fifty-six rural municipalities in Relief Area "A" and $50.00 a month in 103 rural municipalities in Relief Area "B."[4] It is little wonder that in 1933 the Saskatchewan Medical Association endorsed health insurance.

The provincial medical associations did their utmost to persuade pro-vincial governments not only to meet a more reasonable share of costs but also to induce them to persuade the Dominion government that medical care was as essential to survival as food, clothing, and shelter in which the national government was sharing. The CMA also lobbied the

Dominion government, but to no avail. At a meeting the CMA Executive was finally able to obtain with Prime Minister R. B. Bennett, he brusquely told them: "While I have every sympathy with the point of view you have expressed, you really have no contact with me; the matters which you have presented are strictly the business of the provinces."[5]

2. *Health status.* There were not available in the 1940s the comprehensive data on the extent of illness in the population or of its economic impact that were to become accessible to analysts in the 1950s with the publication of the results of the Sickness Survey of 1950–51, but the information at hand reinforced what everyone knew, that Canadians were not a healthy people.

According to the Dominion Bureau of Statistics, the most sensitive indicator, infant mortality rates, showed Canada ranking seventeenth among developed nations in 1937, the most recent year for which international comparisons could be made in 1941.[6] In 1940, there were 13,783 infant deaths, with rates of thirty-eight per 1,000 live births in British Columbia to seventy per 1,000 in Quebec and eighty per 1,000 in New Brunswick. Part of the cause was the number of births outside hospital. In the four eastern provinces an average of only twenty percent of births occurred in hospital, and even in the five western provinces, an average of only two-thirds of maternity cases was hospitalized.

Maternal mortality rates which had dropped from 5.7 per 1,000 live births in 1926 to 4.0 per 1,000 in 1940 for Canada as a whole were still high, ranging from 2.9 per 1,000 in Prince Edward Island, to 4.8 in New Brunswick.

Equally shocking, despite improvements, were the deaths from communicable diseases. Tuberculosis was the most serious, with 5,789 deaths in 1940, but others were also high: influenza, 2,789; whooping cough, 628; typhoid, 224; diphtheria, 213; and measles, 168.

A summary report of a meeting of the Dominion Council of Health in 1941 gave these highlights of the health situation in Canada.

The situation in regard to mortality from tuberculosis is unsatisfactory. In the field of control of venereal diseases Canada is backward. The maternal mortality rate in Canada is high, and when compared to other countries with a similar standard of living, may be considered excessively so. The situation in regard to mental disease in Canada is grave. Canada has lost, on an average, 15,000 children under one year of age each year during the last ten years. These deaths are due to causes which are preventable or controllable. Noteworthy advances have been made in the control of communicable diseases and particularly those of childhood during recent years, but there remains much to be done in this field. Generally, the health of people in rural areas does not compare favourably with that in urban districts. In a recent health survey of rural Manitoba youth covering 3,146 young people between the ages of 13 and 30, it was found that 70 percent had one or more remediable defects or conditions which require medical attention.[7]

A report of the Canadian Medical Association's Committee on Economics summed up the situation in 1934 in these words: "Many [of our people] are going without adequate medical care, some are overwhelmed with the cost and losses due to illness; preventable diseases and postponable deaths are still common, comparatively few physicians have the opportunity to practise preventive medicine, while, at the same time, physicians in general are not adequately remunerated."[8]

3. *Organized action.* There had been a number of organized developments, going back a decade or more, generated by the mutual discontent of most of the public and many in the medical profession, as well as by the concerns of government. One such was the municipal doctor system in which a physician provided general practitioner services for a basic salary. This operated in sixty-seven municipalities in Saskatchewan, five in Manitoba, and three in Alberta.

In British Columbia a Royal Commission on State Health Insurance recommended in 1932 a health insurance program for that province. In 1935 the Government acted on its recommendations and presented a draft bill for public discussion which, after amendments demanded by the medical profession and the Manufacturers' Association, both of which opposed it, was passed in March 1936, to go into effect in March 1937. On February 19, 1937, the plan was indefinitely postponed and, despite an affirmative vote in a plebiscite conducted during the election on June 1, 1937, that plan was never again introduced. But at least one government had tried and the public demand was evident.[9] In 1940 the British Columbia Medical Association sponsored a prepayment plan (MSA) which was highly successful from the beginning, confirming public need and interest.

In Alberta, two Commissions of Inquiry had reported in favour of health insurance, one in 1929 and the other in 1933. In 1935 a Health Insurance Act was passed, but on the defeat of the government later in the year, it was not implemented.[10]

In 1935 a program of major importance was established in Ontario when the Government signed an agreement with the Ontario Medical Association providing for a contribution by the Government of thirty-five cents per month on behalf of each person in receipt of relief to the Medical Welfare Board created by the OMA. From this fund payments were made to Ontario doctors for office and home calls. This was the first social assistance public medical care plan in Canada and after the war was adopted, with modifications, by four other provinces.[11]

4. *The Royal Commission on Dominion-Provincial Relations.* The Rowell-Sirois Royal Commission, appointed in 1937, carefully avoided recommendations on substantive policies other than Dominion-provincial financial relations. But its exploration of social insurance did envisage action to provide "state medicine and state hospitalization or health insurance."[12] It emphasized the chaotic financial results on business if some provinces, acting independently on health insurance, levied taxes on employers that placed them in a less competitive position with respect to businesses in provinces that did not. The commission was equally concerned about employees who, by moving from one province to another, would lose their entitlement to benefits, and also with the possibility that employees would move to provinces that offered the advantages of health insurance protection. Its conclusion favoured some form of national action: "The balance of advantage lies in some degree of uniformity throughout Canada, and, therefore, in the collection of contributions by the Dominion."[13]

Its examination of social insurance systems in other countries underscored the lack of such a system in Canada, and its general conclusion that it was impossible to establish a wage that would allow every worker and his family to meet the heavy liabilities of serious illness, prolonged unemployment, accident, and premature death, contributed to public thinking about collective solutions to the obvious social problems.

5. *Public opinion.* There were other compelling arguments for action, reasons that were intangible but which became more pervasive throughout the country as the war dragged on. These derived from the growing conviction that the sacrifice and toil of war could be justified only if the goals were positive. Ian Mackenzie, the minister of pensions and national health, had expressed it in these terms: "Few today can regard war as an adventure and therefore it only becomes tolerable as a crusade with social and economic reform as a banner under which we fight." President Roosevelt had proclaimed the "four freedoms" including freedom from fear and from want. Anthony Eden had declared that social security must be the first object of policy abroad not less than at home. Winston Churchill and Franklin Roosevelt had galvanized the free world with the Atlantic Charter in which the Fifth Article declared "the desire to bring about the fullest collaboration between all nations in economic fields with the object of securing for all improved labour standards, economic advancement, and social security."

No government in Canada could ignore the ground swell of public opinion casting off the pessimism of depression, or the evidence of a maturing nation becoming aware of undreamed-of strengths and daily growing in resolve that there *could* be, there *must* be, a better way of life than that of the 1930s.

6. *Party rivalry.* The impact of party rivaly in the political environment is well illustrated by a letter received by Mackenzie King in December 1942 from a Liberal back-bencher. H. B. Mckinnon, M. P. from Kenora, Ontario, wrote to the prime minister expressing his concern about the hostile attitude of organized labour towards the government.

> I find that this feeling [of hostility] is quite prevalent even among the railroad men of this country. . . . The late by-election in North Centre Winnipeg in which the CCF member, Stanley Knowles, was re-elected by a 2–1 majority over the Liberal candidate, reflects, in my opinion, a feeling that is largely held, and I believe the same result might occur in a good many constituencies in Canada if an election was held in Canada in the near future. Through the Atlantic Charter and through the reception of the Beveridge Report in the Old Country and through repeated utterances in Canada and the United States, the workers of Canada have, as I see it, come to expect that a good many reforms on their behalf will be put into effect after the war. I feel that an indication of positive action along this line would be of assistance in securing further cooperation from workers in war-time production. It seems to me that immediate thought should be given to (a) extension of Old Age Pensions, (b) Health Insurance, (c) plans for post-war employment.[14]

Mackenzie King replied:

> I share all your concern over the attitude of labour, and you may be sure I am not less interested in seeing that the right steps are taken to give wage earners and others that security with respect to their fundamental needs which must be made the first consideration in all post-war policies. . . . Meanwhile, I am bringing some of [your] representations before my colleagues in the Cabinet for consideration by the government as a whole.[15]

But Stanley Knowles' election was not an isolated example of the growing strength of the depression-born party, the Cooperative Commonwealth Federation (CCF). In August 1943, it became the official opposition in Ontario and in June 1944, formed the Government in Saskatchewan. If the challenge of this new party was to be successfully met, the Liberal government would have to be more responsive to Canadians' needs and desires.

7. *The views of Prime Minister Mackenzie King.* In the initiation of any governmental proposal, the personal objectives and commitment of the party leader who occupies the position of premier or prime minister at a particular juncture in history is frequently the most crucial factor in the decision to act or not to act.

In 1943 and 1944, as public opinion in the allied nations grew more confident in the ultimate winning of the war, there began a wave of rising expectations for a better post-war world. Despite the demands on his time to coordinate the war effort and meet a number of political crises, Mackenzie King became increasingly aware that the thrust of a number of forces was beginning to provide an opportunity favourable to the philosophy he had espoused in his book, *Industry and Humanity*, written at the end of World War I. But it would be a race with time, for as he indicated in his diary, he had tentatively set August 7, 1944, the twenty-fifth anniversary of his leadership, as the date for his retirement.[16]

On January 10, 1943, he read a speech by Sir William Beveridge which referred to Lloyd George as having been responsible for introducing old age pensions in Britain, and noted in his diary that Winston Churchill, who had introduced unemployment insurance, might round out his career by putting through health insurance, or an entire social security program. King went on to record, "That program I made very much my own from the days I was Deputy Minister of Labour. It is all set out in my *Industry and Humanity*. I should be happy indeed if I could round out my career with legislation in the nature of social security."[17]

On January 12, 1943, he pointed out to the Cabinet the need for social security legislation at the forthcoming session of Parliament or, if not legislation, consideration of a future program.[18]

On January 24 he noted in his diary, "I had this morning worked out a good part of the speech on social insurance, speaking on the need of a charter for social insurance in Canada. Made use of my *Industry and Humanity*. Indeed was impressed to find how completely the whole out-line was to be found there. It looks as if I am to have the privilege of completing the circle of federal social security measures which, with the exception of the Annuities Bill, I was responsible for beginning. . . . It should really help to mark an epoch in development of Liberal policy in Canada."[19]

Later, in the summer of 1943, he listened to a speech by Sir William Beveridge and "was inspired by the parallels in his life interest with my own." . . . and felt that in his book he had "anticipated very much the program Sir William is putting forward today ... Our lives have been given over very largely to life-long study of social problems."[20]

Again, as he was drafting the 1944 Speech from the Throne, he took pride in the fact that his early ideas were now to be spoken from the Throne as Government policy.

It is difficult to assess the importance he really attached to pushing the program through. In his diary covering 1944–45 the references to health insurance are rare, as other issues captured the time he might have preferred to direct to the social security problems. But that his views were a powerful force in incorporating health insurance and other social security measures in the post-war reconstruction proposals is clear.

THE CONSTRAINTS

In any thrust in a political system, no matter how strong the imperatives for innovation may be, there are constraints on action, limitations that set boundaries which must be accepted or within which ingenuity must operate. These constraints are always more confining in a federal system than in a unitary state. Indeed, because the constitutions of federal states are of a vintage predating the problems of contemporary society, it has often been necessary for leaders attempting to solve those problems either to dramatize the issues so successfully that constitutional amendment is possible or to find elastic clauses in the constitution within which effective accommodation can be made. Such was the dilemma facing those concerned with developing a solution to the economic problems of health care in Canada in 1940.

In 1940, the Canadian constitutional terrain had been reported upon by the Rowell-Sirois Royal Commission on Dominion-Provincial Relations in probably the most thorough examination of any federal state ever undertaken. Its major recommendations were the transfer of jurisdiction over income tax, corporation income tax, and succession duties to the federal government, and "to replace the chaotic and illogical subsidy system now existing and, to provide for balanced budgets and average standards of services in every province ... a National Adjustment Grant [must be given to] certain provinces."[21]

The commission observed that although the BNA Act did not expressly allocate jurisdiction in public health, it did allocate marine hospitals and quarantine to the federal government, and hospitals, asylums, charities, and eleemosynary institutions to the provinces. But it has been construed that the power over generally all matters of a merely local or private nature assigned to the provinces was probably, as the commission observed, "deemed to cover health matters."[22]

Accordingly, in its proposed division of responsibilities, the commission recommended that the provinces should accept responsibility for "policy as to the method [e.g., whether by health insurance or by state medicine and state hospitalization] of providing state medical services for indigents or low-income groups."[23] The commission also observed that "the desirability of co-ordinating all medical services within the provinces under provincial control is a strong argument against the establishment of any scheme which would remove any large group [i.e., the general population or non-indigents] within the province from provincial responsibility, as a Dominion health insurance scheme would do."[24]

On the financing of health insurance the commission noted:

Ordinarily Health Insurance contributions are assessed against employers and employees though the State may contribute part of the cost. If income groups whose incomes are too low to enable them to pay part or all of their contributions are included in the scheme, the State may contribute the necessary additional amounts for these groups, or heavier contributions may be exacted from higher income groups. One method is that of exacting contributions from workers in proportion to earnings rather than on a per capita basis. . . . In the event of a province instituting a scheme for Health Insurance providing for taxes on wages and wage bills, it might be found convenient to entrust the Dominion with the collection. If the Dominion were also levying taxes on wages and wage bills for other Social Insurance schemes [unemployment insurance and/or contributory old age pensions] it would appear to be highly desirable in the interests of economies and tax collections and tax compliance that the collection be made by a single authority, and the Dominion is obviously the appropriate authority.[25]

It went on to say, "In recommending provincial jurisdiction over Health Insurance we are aware of the possibility incidental to any Social Insurance scheme put into effect province by province that it may result in inequalities of taxes on industry as between provinces. We think, however, that regional differences in Canada militate against an acceptable national scheme."[26]

The commission also made clear its conception of the differences among various types of social security programs:

We have concluded that two types of Social Insurance—Unemployment Insurance and contributory Old Age Pensions—are inherently of a national character, but Health Insurance and Workmen's Compensation are not, and that in view of Canadian conditions, these can be financed and efficiently administered by the provinces. There is also the possibility that if certain provinces should desire a uniform scheme, administered by the Dominion, they could delegate to the Dominion the authority to institute such a scheme provided that our recommendation for general power of delegation, which we deal with elsewhere, is implemented.[27]

A related recommendation that was to have important implications for health insurance was that "the Dominion be given exclusive jurisdiction over the two services, Unemployment Insurance and contributory Old Age Pensions. . . . It is not improbable that, in the course of time . . . conditions would warrant national Health Insurance or a national system of Workmen's Compensation. It would, therefore, seem desirable that rigidity in the matter of jurisdiction should be avoided."[28]

At the same time, the commission took strong exception to the device of conditional grants: "The experience with conditional grants leads us to doubt whether joint administration of activities by the Dominion and a province is ever a practical way of surmounting constitutional difficulties. Where legislative power over a particular subject is divided it is ordinarily desirable that these powers should be pooled under the control of a single government in order to secure unified efforts in administration."[29] As Professor Donald Smiley has observed, "On the grounds both of its general formulation of a viable Federal system and administrative effectiveness, the Commission assigned the conditional grant to a very restricted role in its recommendations."[30]

In summary, health insurance was a matter for provincial policy. The choices were health insurance and state medicine, although these were not defined. Regional differences reinforced the desirability of provincial programs. Presumably the national adjustment grants would be adequate to enable low-income provinces to finance health services. But the use of conditional grants for such purposes was rejected. The commission had drawn narrow boundaries within which any federal policy could be created. It was clear that even if the provinces agreed to the Rowell-Sirois proposals, the kind of role—if any—for the federal government in the provision of health services for Canadians was very much in doubt.

The Dominion-Provincial Conference to consider the Rowell-Sirois proposals was held on January 14–15, 1941, and quickly came to an end because of the opposition of Ontario, Quebec, and British Columbia to the taxation proposals. Mackenzie King was sanguine about the outcome, feeling that wartime was "not the time to permanently settle these matters, but I feel equally strongly that not to have held a Conference in advance, to make the situation clear, would have occasioned more trouble in the end."[31] He was, therefore, not at all disturbed when the conference broke up with no agreement on a permanent settlement but with an acknowledgement from all the provincial leaders that the wartime financial requirements of the federal government must be given the highest priority.

Accordingly, the federal government proposed to the provinces that they should, for the duration of the war and one year after, renounce their rights to collect personal and corporation income taxes, and that the Dominion, in return, compensate them according to one of two alternative formulae. These proposals were adopted through federal and provincial legislation in 1942, each province selecting the more advantageous alternative. Mackenzie King noted in his diary, "What is now being done will last until a year after the war which may mean that, at that time, the provinces will have come to see that the Sirois Report is, after all, what is best for them as well as for us. It is a bold and far-reaching policy that will, I believe, succeed."[32]

Timing. The issue of the timing of national action, if any, was one about which there were strong differences of opinion. Ian Mackenzie saw both health and unemployment insurance as justifiable, even necessary, wartime measures. But Mackenzie King, albeit alert to the growing threat from the CCF and aware of the need for positive action, was more influenced by the financial exigencies of the war. After the Liberal caucus meeting on March 24, 1942, he recorded in his diary: "I spoke for about half an hour very emphatically on the questions of elections and social security matters. They [the caucus] must realize the real nature of what was involved in a social security program. It was social revolution . . . but this could not be done in a day, but would take years . . . it was wrong to think of increased outlays on anything that could be avoided until victory was won. Important, however, to keep everything in readiness for the peace."[33]

Timing was, therefore, one of the major constraints, as well as, in the earlier stages, one of the important uncertainties.

Financial constraints. As with any social measure of large magnitude, sheer cost was a major constraint. But in a federal system, in a country just shifting from a depression economy to an unpredictable war economy, the financial constraint was further magnified by the unequal capacity of the provinces to finance health insurance, the fact that unemployment insurance on a national scale was coming into being, and that demands for old age pensions were being increasingly heard. The basic question was the capacity of the economy to underwrite such programs. The 1941 census had revealed that sixty-two percent of wage earners had incomes of less than $950 per year. Given such low levels of income, could all three programs—or even two—be financed? The financial constraints as we shall see later were not only large, they were also very complex.

THE UNCERTAINTIES

There are uncertainties in all political decisions but the enormity of the task of insuring the total population of Canada was, for the time, akin to a flight into outer space. There was little experience to go on, and no certitude about the outcomes. Among the major uncertainties were the following.

1. *The costs of the program.* No one really knew what a comprehensive public health insurance program would cost. Data were available on doctors' incomes and it would be possible from hospital statistics collected by the Dominion Bureau of Statistics to obtain a reasonable estimate of costs of hospital services. But there was no way of knowing what utilization would be if the total population were insured or if services were brought up to adequate standards. New data were becoming available from the Associated Medical Services in Toronto, Windsor Medical Services, Medical Services Associated in British Columbia, and the Manitoba Blue Cross Plan. But these plans were all limited in one way or another and were enrolling those who were the healthier members of the population. Their experience would be helpful but not conclusive.

2. *Revenue collection.* If an "insurance approach" were to be taken, then everyone in each province would have to be registered and pay a registration fee or premium—in other words, a poll tax. It would be possible to collect from employees through their employers but what would be the response of the self-employed, the migratory workers, and the farmhands to a premium form of tax? How would one collect from the unemployed and if they could not pay who could pay on their behalf? Should the program have an upper income ceiling as the Canadian Medical Association had been proposing?

3. *Program linkages.* Would it be possible to launch the health insurance program as an independent program or would it be necessary that it be designed so that unemployment insurance and old age security could be combined with it simultaneously or added subsequently?

4. *Response of the profession.* What would be the response of the medical profession? The executive of the Canadian Medical Association had concluded at its 1939 meeting that it could not speak for the profession with respect to health insurance because not enough of the members were familiar with such a program and its potential consequences.

5. *Response of business and industry.* What would be the response of business and industry to a new tax? Their reaction to the British Columbia

1936 proposals had been total opposition and, in fact, in concert with the British Columbia Medical Association, the B.C. Manufacturers' Association had successfully aborted the plan just as it was about to go into effect. Would such a tax have an inhibiting effect on exports? Would it be realistic to assume that farmers would pay an employers' contribution on behalf of farmhands?

6. *Financing.* Given the uneven fiscal capacity of the provinces, how could a program be designed that could be financed by all provinces? And if that were not possible, would that mean that it should be a national program, financed and administered from Ottawa? If that were the only realistic alternative, would it be possible to get a constitutional amendment?

7. *Administration.* If it were not to be a federally-administered program, but required large conditional grants to the provinces, how could these be administered in such a way as to overcome the very strong objections to, and the shortcomings of, conditional grants as viewed by the Rowell-Sirois Commission?

These were among the major uncertainties as the director of Public Health Services began his studies of ways by which the national government could participate in the provision of prepaid health services within the framework of the Canadian federal system.

INITIATING THE POLICY

To this point we have considered the external factors that would lead to some type of action, taking into consideration the limitations on what could be done and the uncertainties surrounding any choice of alternative courses. We turn now to examine the roles and contributions of political leaders and senior public officials as they gathered their information, expanded and sharpened their analyses, considered options, interacted with each other and with various public groups, and gradually began to formulate a policy that could be moved from department to Cabinet, to Parliament, and to the statute books.

These activities, in the terminology of systems analysis, are the "within-puts" or what others have called "the conversion process." The process occurs within the apparatus of government, a complex structure of hierarchically arranged departments, boards, and commissions. All are headed by officials of senior (usually deputy minister) rank, having different personalities, skills, influence, and power. All are responsible to ministers, also varying in their personalities, skills, influence, and power. Each

15

agency maintains a network of relationships with other agencies and especially with Treasury Board and the Finance Department. All these forces come together and find their resolution in the Cabinet. From this "web of government" emerges the Government's decisions on objectives, policies, and programs. But within the web are waged some of the most fascinating struggles in contemporary society. The decision on health insurance in Ottawa, in the early 1940s, was no exception.

Ian MacKenzie was minister of defence when the war broke out but it became clear that "though he was one of the outstanding debaters in Parliament, he lacked administrative capacity . . . needed in war time."[34] Because of his close ties with Mackenzie King it was with great reluctance that King replaced him at the Defence Department and transferred him on September 19, 1939, when a number of portfolio changes were made, to the relatively tranquil ministry of Pensions and National Health. But MacKenzie's ebullient and eclectic spirit seemed undampened. There were new campaigns to be fought, greener fields to conquer, new terrain to be occupied.

On December 27, 1939, he wrote to Mackenzie King urging that unemployment and health insurance be introduced as war measures, arguing that "Unemployment insurance will be indispensable in coping with the reestablishment problem . . . and a demand for a national health system is inevitable. These, together with the St. Lawrence Seaway, National Housing Plan, the Municipal Assistance Scheme, Land Settlement, Reforestation, and National Highways will be necessary features of a national program for the aftermath of the war."[35] One of his reasons for early action was that he felt that the reforms were possible only when eight of the nine provincial governments were Liberal. The war was only four months along but Ian Mackenzie had already outlined the planning agenda for post-war Canada.

Mackenzie King replied that he would take the matter up with the Cabinet, which he did, but that body had more pressing priorities, and the proposal was rejected.[36] In response, the minister acted on his own, laying his plans carefully. First, he requested Dr. J. J. Heagerty, director of Public Health Services, to expand the activities of his division in its study of health insurance. He then considered ways in which to involve the provincial health officials and the leaders of the health professions. The opportunity presented itself in the form of the regular meeting of the Dominion Council of Health. That body was chaired by the deputy minister of pensions and national health and was composed of the provincial deputy ministers of health and representatives of the Canadian Medical Association, labour, farmers, and urban and farm women. To that meeting, held on June 13 and 14, 1941, the health minister suggested that the subject of health insurance be discussed with the objective of assisting the provinces in formulating comprehensive health plans. The discussion which followed supported in principle the need for health insurance, and opinions were expressed that the people desired it and that the medical profession was willing to grant every assistance needed for the formulation of a health insurance plan.[37]

With this meeting, for the first time, overtures with respect to health insurance had been made by a federal minister of health to the provinces and the professions. The effect of the meeting was to further stimulate the work undertaken by Dr. Heagerty and, more importantly, to alert the health professions and the provinces of the need to establish their own policies.

The next step in Mackenzie's strategy was to have Dr. Heagerty request the health professions and various other organizations to form health insurance committees which could meet with him and discuss the problems to be faced in drawing up a suitable plan for health insurance in Canada.[38] It was evident, however, from the amount of statistical and financial information needed, that the undertaking would require a great deal of assistance, particularly from the Dominion Bureau of Statistics. On February 5, 1942, therefore, Ian Mackenzie obtained Cabinet approval to expand the Heagerty studies by appointing by order-in-council an Inter-Departmental Advisory Committee on Health Insurance.[39] The committee was composed of Dr. Heagerty, one economist, one legal adviser, six members of the Dominion Bureau of Statistics, and an actuary from the Department of Trade and Commerce. There was thus created what would now be called an internal "task force" which, in the short space of a year, was to create the first blueprint ever drawn for a national health insurance plan for Canada.

Shortly after the appointment of the committee, there appeared a document that was to receive international acclaim and have a major impact on all western nations—the report of Sir William Beveridge on social insurance for Britain.[40] So comprehensive was its review and so innovative and farsighted were its concepts that it provided a ready-made base for the committee's deliberations, although many of its recommendations would have to be fundamentally altered for application in a federal state.

One of the members of the Interdepartmental Committee was Dr. Leonard Marsh who, as a graduate student, had worked with Professor Beveridge. He was now commissioned by the parallel Committee on Post-War Reconstruction (chaired by Dr. Cyril James, principal of McGill University) to prepare a comprehensive survey of social security. His report, submitted a year later, is a remarkable document, particularly when assessed in the light of the short time available for its preparation. In twenty-two sections he examined the nature of social security programs, existing social welfare legislation in Canada, the "universal risks" of sickness, invalidity, and old age, and specific matters to be considered in establishing a social security system for Canada, including extensive analysis of desirable principles for a health insurance program.[41]

Meanwhile, Dr. Heagerty was meeting with the representatives of the fourteen associations invited to cooperate with him, and most frequently with those from the Canadian Medical Association, known as the "Committee of Seven." Finally, in December 1942, approximately nine months after its formal appointment, the committee submitted to the minister the most comprehensive report on health services (558 pages) ever prepared in Canada prior to the report of the Royal Commission in 1964. It included an historical survey of health insurance in other countries and in Canada. It analyzed the administration, financing, scope, and benefits of six countries in which plans were voluntary and thirty-three others in which they were compulsory; it reviewed the public health agencies operating in Canada and presented a 150-page statistical survey on the health status of Canadians; it examined the hospital facilities in each of the provinces. It presented a forty-page analysis of the economic status of Canadians, including statistical tables on national income, sources of national income, and distribution by income classes and provinces, and it then gave estimates of the costs of the health insurance plan it was proposing.

After analyzing the constitutional constraints, the extensive information it had collected, and the various submissions received from professional and voluntary associations, the committee concluded that six basic principles should govern any federal proposal: 1. That no scheme of health insurance can be successful without a comprehensive public health program of a preventive nature; 2. That a real health program as distinguished from a policy of cash benefits can be effective only if it embraces the entire population; 3. That the principle of compulsory contributions should be embodied in any plan of health insurance to the greatest possible extent; 4. That public opinion and efficiency demand to the greatest possible extent a national plan; 5. That the Constitution, as at present understood and interpreted, prevents the Dominion Parliament from adopting a single comprehensive national Health Insurance Act; 6. That, for practical reasons, a constitutional amendment is not desirable.

On the basis of these principles, the committee prepared two draft bills, one for the Canadian Parliament and the other a model bill for the provinces. Despite the strong views of the Rowell-Sirois Commission against the use of the grant-in-aid device, the committee recommended it as the only feasible policy.

Almost three years to the day when he had first proposed health insurance to the prime minister, Mackenzie was armed with specific proposals, draft legislation, and backup information. He was now ready to act.

The first weeks of January 1943 were crucial for Mackenzie's objectives. The proposal, including the draft legislation, was presented to Cabinet on January 8. The Cabinet made no decision but referred the proposal to the Economic Advisory Committee chaired by W. C. Clark, the deputy minister of finance, for an examination of its financial implications. Mackenzie, however, still wanted an immediate decision by Cabinet to introduce the legislation in the House of Commons and early in the morning of January 20 he forwarded a letter to the prime minister, stating that he "would be glad to have the decision of Cabinet on the Health Insurance proposals on Friday."[42] Later in the same morning, however, he received the report of Clark's Economic Advisory Committee which reflected Clark's conviction that the three social insurance programs of unemployment insurance, old age security, and health insurance should be administered and financed in the same manner: "If social security is to be established on a sound basis, it is undesirable to set up so important a part of it as health insurance on a pattern which is objectionable if applied to other phases of a comprehensive plan [and] . . . which was found objectionable in the case of Unemployment Insurance."[43]

With respect to the financial proposals, Clark's committee concluded: "It is doubtful if costs of approximately $7.00 per head can be carried by the provinces. [Moreover] provinces would have a strong case for resisting any such financial rearrangement as that recommended by the Sirois Commission. . . . The Committee recommends that the Bill . . . be deferred for further study."[44]

Mackenzie responded immediately with a second letter to the prime minister later the same day in which he characterized Clark's report as "just a stalling by a financial group of two years' work done in the Health Department."[45] He was clearly distressed, saying, "If it is not possible to introduce this Bill at the present session, I shall have to consider the matter very seriously." But recognizing that the judgement of the Finance department would likely prevail, he offered a compromise:

The only other possible alternative would be that if a particular measure is not mentioned in the Speech from the Throne, at least that speech should mention the setting up of a Select Special Committee of Parliament to consider the whole question of health insurance. To that Committee could be submitted our Departmental draft proposals.

He then added a special plea:

It seems to me we should certainly offer something definite and constructive to Parliament at the present session. Yesterday as Chairman of the business committee of the Cabinet, I recommended to Council the passing of $229 million for eleven war contracts. Last year we gave $1 billion to England. . . . Now, when it is sought to help the health of the Canadian people, financial arguments are brought forward to retard the legislation. I wish to assure you that I regard this matter as a very serious one and if it is felt by Council that it should not be accepted, then I should like to have a personal discussion with you on all the issues involved.

On Friday, January 22, Mackenzie again laid the health proposals before Cabinet, this time backed up by Dr. Heagerty and Mr. A. D. Watson (actuary on the Interdepartmental Committee). As King wrote in his diary: "Both [Heagerty and Watson] made an excellent presentation," but then he added, "Clark [finance deputy minister] gave arguments against. What was said by both parties bore out what I had previously said to the Cabinet, namely, that the matter could only be considered by reference to a Committee of the House of Commons in the first instance."[46]

On January 28, the Throne Speech announced Ian Mackenzie's compromise alternative, that a comprehensive scheme of social insurance should be worked out at once, which would constitute a charter for social security for the whole of Canada, and the intention of the Government to appoint a committee of the House to consider these matters and to submit for study and consideration the establishment of a national system of health insurance. The proposals of the Heagerty Committee and the minister were thus to be submitted to a parliamentary committee. This represented progress of a sort, but it fell far short of Mackenzie's objectives of specific legislation.

The House of Commons Special Committee on Social Security was composed of forty-one members, of whom thirty-one were Liberals, six Conservatives, two CCF, and two Social Credit. It included Health Minister Mackenzie and Dr. Cyrus MacMillan, who was elected chairman. The terms of reference of the committee were:

To examine and study the existing social insurance legislation of the Parliament of Canada and of the several provincial legislatures; social insurance policies of other countries; the most practicable measures of social insurance for Canada, including health insurance, and the steps which will be required to effect their inclusion in a national plan; the constitutional and financial adjustments which will be required for the achievement of a nation-wide plan for social security; and other related matters.[47]

Three documents were presented to the committee at its first meeting on March 16, 1943: the report on social security by Dr. Marsh; the Heagerty Report on Physical Fitness;[48] and, the draft copy of a bill entitled "An Act Respecting Health Insurance, Public Health, the Conservation of Health, the Prevention of Disease and other matters relating thereto."

The first witness was the Hon. Ian MacKenzie, who explained the constitutional situation with respect to health insurance, outlined health insurance programs in other parts of the world, discussed the relevance of the Beveridge Report to Canada, enumerated the steps by which the current proposals had been developed, and stressed the six basic principles upon which they had been based. The major features of the proposals were outlined above, but it will be useful to note some of the details.

The federal government would provide direct grants for six health purposes: tuberculosis, mental health, venereal disease, physical fitness, special investigations in public health, and professional training for physicians, engineers, nurses, and sanitary inspectors.

The financial requirements were based on a single contributor paying three percent of income to a maximum of $26, a contributor with one dependant paying 3.7 percent of income to a maximum of $52, and with two dependants paying 4.3 percent of income to a maximum of $78. Employers would contribute the amount by which three percent of an employee's income fell short of $26 and the province would contribute such sums in respect of unemployed and self-employed individuals.

The Advisory Committee had estimated that on the basis of the 1939 population, the total cost of the program would be $232,896,000. The proposed tax rates were estimated to yield:

Employees and their dependants	$ 63,500,000
Employers	$ 24,200,000
Assessed Contributors	$ 37,000,000
Total:	$124,700,000

The balance of $132,000,000 would be shared by the Dominion and provincial governments and the committee submitted calculations based on alternative proportions that the Dominion might contribute, ranging from $40,000,000 to $107,000,000. Whatever Dominion contributions would be decided upon would be in addition to the annual health grants for public health purposes estimated to total $6.5 million.

In selecting the means by which the contribution of the insured contributors would be collected, the Advisory Committee wholeheartedly recommended the stamp system, indicating that in their view, as used for unemployment insurance, it had no near competitor.

Free choice of doctor would be assured, and he would be responsible for referrals to specialists and hospitals and for prescribed medicines. In discussing this provision, the minister indicated that while the profession had been disposed to insist upon fees, "I am advised that there is now a swing on the part of the doctors towards capitation and I would suggest that, from a public health standpoint, the capitation system is preferable, because it will encourage the physician to counsel and urge preventive measures."[49]

The committee's proposals envisaged the organization of administrative health regions to make certain that preventive and treatment services would be available outside large urban centres, and the salaried municipal doctor system that operated in the prairie provinces was also favoured.

The committee recommended provincial administration by a commission representative of all the professions rendering services, as well as of insured persons, workers in industry, farmers, employers, and such other groups as might be deemed appropriate, with a medical doctor as full time chairman, and the deputy minister of health an *ex officio* member.

The House of Commons Committee thus had before it for consideration a statement of objectives and a detailed outline of proposals for a program to achieve those objectives. It was now time for the concerned interest groups to make their respective cases in the public forum of the committee. These external forces with their demands, support, opposition, and criticism that would help to shape the policy are referred to in the terminology of systems analysis as "the inputs." In this instance there was little in the public testimony that was new to the minister or Dr. Heagerty since each of the organizations testifying had already made known its views to Dr. Heagerty. But for the House of Commons Committee and the public generally, it was the first time that they had been exposed to such a range of information and opinion.

THE EXTERNAL CONTRIBUTIONS

The Dominion Council of Health. The council was not, of course, a typical interest group since most of its members were provincial deputy ministers of health. But its testimony was important for it focused on the issue of administration of health insurance by the Health Department or by an independent commission as demanded by organized medicine. Speakers for the council emphasized that they did not speak either for the Dominion Council of Health as a whole or for their respective provincial governments.[50]

Approving the general provisions of the program and especially the public health grants and the emphasis on preventive services, the group felt, nevertheless, that the proposed integration of preventive and treatment services could best be achieved by administering the act through the medium of the Department of Health or by means of a commission responsible to the Legislature through the medium of the Department of Health. If the first alternative were chosen, there should be established within the department a division of health insurance—obviously responsible to the deputy minister. There should also be a provincial health insurance advisory council, with the deputy minister as chairman, and with representatives of the professions and other involved interest groups.

If the second alternative were to be adopted, the spokesmen proposed that the commission should consist of three members, with the chairman a medical doctor, and with the deputy minister of health an *ex officio* member. An advisory council would also be appointed.

The group strongly endorsed the involvement of the general practitioner in the provision of preventive services but did observe that it was realized that certain preventive services might be brought into play in a more effective and economical way under provincial, regional, and municipal auspices.

The Canadian Medical Association (CMA). Without question, the most important influences in the formulation of the report of the House of Commons Special Committee were those of the Canadian Medical Association. This resulted from the unusually close collaboration of the CMA's Committee of Seven with the Heagerty Committee and the acceptance by the latter of most of the CMA "principles." Because of the significance of the CMA's contribution, it is necessary to outline the evolution of its policies.

In 1934, after two years of work, the CMA's Committee on Economics released a 50,000 word report on the economics of medical practice,[51] including a review of health insurance programs in Germany, Britain, France, and South Africa, and of the recent reports of the U.S. Committee on the Costs of Medical Care. The document was remarkably comprehensive and objective. Its survey of Canadian conditions, worsened by the depression, is a clinical record of the malaise of economic man in the thirties as experienced by the medical profession.

The committee reviewed findings and recommendations of the Royal Commissions in British Columbia and Alberta and, as well, the reports of various provincial association committees that had been examining economic problems and health insurance as a solution.

The general view of the report was that government health insurance was necessary and, in view of the obvious interest of the public in it, probably inevitable. It was imperative, in its judgement, that the views of the profession should be heard. Accordingly, the committee believed it essential that the CMA should design a plan if the profession desired to direct the development of health insurance along the lines which to its members appeared to be best. This would be strategically very important for "in this as in other matters, it is the body which has prepared a concrete proposal which may expect this proposal, with modifications, to be accepted and to provide the basic plan for the final scheme."[52] And with disarming confidence in its own objectivity and wisdom, the committee observed, "This is not a selfish motive, because what is best for the medical profession must be best for the public. Passive opposition gets nowhere."[53]

One of the most impressive attributes of the committee was its wide-ranging interest in the subject and the homespun wisdom of its observations—some of which, in hindsight, one might wish had had more opportunity to prevail in the future. For example:

> We are not making full use of the knowledge we do possess as evidenced by the number of preventible diseases which continue to occur.

> Medical services in their medical aspects should be under the control of the medical profession. The business part of any such organized services will naturally be controlled by those who pay for the services.

> The most serious ill result which could grow out of health insurance would be its being considered as a "cure-all".... There is grave danger in overselling all forms of social insurance as panaceas for the ills of mankind.

> The [proposed] plan supports the principle of a state insurance fund with the elimination of other insurance carriers. In no other way does it seem possible to avoid the conflicts between the insurance carriers and the medical profession which have had such unfortunate results in many countries.

> Arguments are advanced in favour of requiring some payment by the insured for each illness, to prevent abuse of the medical benefit. This is not viewed sympathetically, because the main objective is to remove any economic barrier which now keeps doctor and patient apart.

> Despite what may be said as to the need for a complete service, it is not to be forgotten that it is the public who, as consumers, have to decide what they are prepared to pay for. It is not the responsibility of the medical profession to attempt to force upon the public a service for which the people are unwilling to pay, nor is it the responsibility of the medical profession to provide services which the public are able,

but unwilling, to pay for. However, the medical profession should not, by opposing the plan, seek to deprive the public of medical services for which the public are willing to pay through state health insurance.

There does not appear to be any reason why a uniform system of payments should be advocated. It seems much more reasonable to allow the medical practitioners of each area to choose which system they desire to use. There is a sum for distribution; the method used will neither decrease nor increase it, otherwise the fund would not be solvent.[54]

The main contribution of the report, however, was a series of nineteen "principles" to guide the development of any Canadian plan of health insurance. In brief, the major principles were that health insurance should be administered by a commission, the majority of whose members should be representative of organized medicine; that the plan be compulsory for persons having up to a specified level of income (usually set at $2,500); that all indigents, as well as the dependants of insured persons, be included; that contributions to the insurance fund should be made by the insured, employers, and the government; that physicians be remunerated by the method or methods they select; that the schedule of fees be under the complete control of the organized profession in each province; that no economic barrier be imposed between patient and doctor; that the plan be periodically actuarially approved; that a pension plan for practitioners be provided; and a number of others of lesser consequence.[55]

Despite the general approval of the principles, and increasing discussion of health insurance, the executive felt that the profession was in no position to promulgate an official policy.

With the imminent release of the report of the Heagerty Advisory Committee in 1943, however, the executive concluded that an official policy must be declared. Accordingly, it took the unprecedented step of convoking a Special Meeting of General Council, the "parliament" of the profession, on January 18 and 19, 1943, eight weeks before the hearings of the House of Commons Committee.

There can have been no other meeting of the CMA Council, before or since, so marked with idealism and harmony. Each member had copies of the two draft bills, and a copy of the CMA principles. In addition, the Committee on Economics had replies from a survey of all the provincial committees on economics. Moreover, the meeting was attended by Dr. J. J. Heagerty, and by Mr. W. G. Gunn, the departmental attorney and legal draftsman of the proposed legislation, as well as by the CMA's solicitor, Mr. Arthur Fleming. The special meeting was obviously intended to grapple with details as well as with broad principles.

In speaking to the council on the progress of discussions with the Advisory Committee on Health Insurance, Dr. R. I. Harris said, "changes [in the draft legislation] have been made easy so far by the magnificent cooperation between Dr. Heagerty's committee and the representatives of the CMA. I would like to pay tribute to Dr. Heagerty's work which I think is blazing a trail for democratic nations."[56] The Hon. Ian Mac-Kenzie and the Hon. J. L. Ralston, minister of national defence, paid a brief visit to the council and both were generous in their praise of the profession's cooperation. This was reciprocated by a formal resolution passed by the council expressing its appreciation to the ministers and to Dr. Heagerty. It was an extraordinary example of cooperation and good feeling based on mutual trust between the profession and the government.

The council then went to work on every detail of the draft bills and most of the discussion was an elucidation of the provisions by members of the Committee of Seven for those who had not been privy to the discussions with the Heagerty Committee. Few changes in the draft bill were proposed. Among the most significant issues were the following.

1. There must be an income ceiling above which coverage would not be available and below which all, including indigents, would be compulsorily covered.

2. Every person must designate his physician so that every general practitioner would have a list of patients for whom he was responsible. This would accord with the expanded role foreseen for the general practitioner as a public health officer, in line with the emphasis on the integration of preventive and treatment services.

3. There was a good deal of discussion on methods of remuneration, with such leaders as Dr. G. F. Strong of Vancouver stating emphatically, "Many of the points [of difficulty] that have been touched upon will be smoothed out automatically if the general practitioner has a capitation fee and the specialists fee-for-service. I think it is a physical impossibility to have a satisfactory system on fee-for-service for both general practitioners and specialists."[57]

4. Yet another major issue was the structure and locus of the administrative authority. Mindful of the generally low state of provincial civil service administration, and the prevalence of patronage in many appointments, there was reluctance to place in the Department of Health sole authority for an agency that would have such intrinsic power to influence medical practice and therefore their professional careers. It was recognized, too, that the "consumers" of medical services had two vital interests: quality of services and their insurance premiums. Administration should therefore be directed by a tripartite body representing the govern-

ment, the profession, and the interest groups of employees, employers, and agriculture.

The overwhelming impression one gains is that the elected representatives of organized medicine in Canada were fully reconciled to, if not enthusiastic about, a new system of medical financing which would have a major impact on medical practice: Dr. G. F. Strong: "It is inconceivable that [the practice of medicine] will not be changed . . . it is up to us to see that the public get the best form of health insurance that they can possibly have, and that the doctors get a fair return for their services."[58] Dr. Harris McPhedran: "There are two things we should bear in mind. One, that this is a revolution in the practice of medicine. The other is that instead of thinking about what we are going to get out of it we should also think what we are going to put into it . . . no matter what the method of payment, we should keep in mind rendering the best service possible for the people."[59]

So out of ten years of independent analysis and study, and a year of collaboration with the Advisory Committee on Health Insurance, there had come agreement of organized medicine not only on the principle of health insurance but on the details of a national and a model provincial bill which incorporated, in extraordinary degree, the CMA principles. The wisdom of the observation in the 1934 Economics Committee Report that he who presents the first draft generally wins the day was once again confirmed, but that the health of the nation and expansion and up-grading of the medical profession were the central and over-riding objectives, there could be no doubt.

The climax of the Special Meeting was the unanimous endorsement of these two historic resolutions:

1. The Canadian Medical Association approves the adoption of the principle of health insurance.

2. The Canadian Medical Association favours a plan of health insurance which will secure the development and provision of the highest standard of health services, preventative and curative, if such plan be fair both to the insured and to all those rendering the services.[60]

These resolutions which presaged the CMA's positive brief to the House of Commons Committee on Social Security eased the task of the Government as no other single act by any other organization could have done. Although the resolutions approved no specific plan, it was reasonably certain that any program that met substantially the so-called principles would receive the profession's support.

With its public declaration of these two resolutions, the CMA presentation to the committee concentrated on two major points: a call for a comprehensive health plan for Canadians with emphasis on preventive medicine and removal of any economic barrier to treatment services, and a statement of those features of a health insurance plan that would make it truly successful, and of others that should be avoided. "We visualize for Canada a system of health insurance which will be more all-inclusive, efficient and sound than any which has ever been devised and operated elsewhere."[61] It then drew upon its studies of about forty plans in other countries and on on-site studies of several of them by the general secretary, Dr. T. C. Routley, to list a number of "weaknesses" noted in other plans. These included limited range of services, exclusion of dependants and indigents, intermediate agencies (such as the Friendly Societies in Britain) as carriers, inadequate payment for services, inadequate provision of diagnostic services, lack of emphasis on preventive medicine, and lack of democratic principles in the administration of some plans. "From the viewpoint of administration a multiplicity of local arrangements, perhaps overlapping in the one community, creates a situation so chaotic that efficient operation becomes very difficult. If Canada is to have health insurance, let its actions be not hamstrung by lack of vision or courage."[62]

It then examined the voluntary plans which had begun to expand in Canada and listed their inadequacies: none provided complete range of services, some did not cover dependants, and although "these plans deserve great credit for their pioneering service ... it is in the public interest to have all these plans absorbed."[63]

The features to be included in any plan were as follows: adequate preventive and public health services ("As years pass the cost of curative services can be expected to materially decrease as disease is controlled and physical fitness increased."); general practitioner services; hospitalization; specialists and consultants; diagnostic services, visiting nurse service; drugs and applicances; dental services; and rehabilitation services. There should also be some form of federal control to achieve a degree of uniformity, administration by independent commissions, inclusion of those of low or no income; personal contributions, and payment of general practitioners by fee-for-service, capitation, or salary as decided by the profession and each provincial commission. Although it did not restate its earlier policy of an income ceiling for compulsory participation, it did visualize what would now be referred to as "opted-out" doctors servicing private patients under "any arrangements which are agreeable to themselves and their patients, provided these arrangements are not contrary to the public interest."[64] Yet another positive approach was its statement that "we can foresee the creation of 'health centres' such as have been envisioned by the British Medical Planning Commission in its constructive report of 1942," and its elaboration of how these health centres would be used by general practitioners, consultant specialists, health visitors, and public health nurses.[65]

The statement ended on a ringing note of cooperation: "The CMA desires to assure the Committee that our entire organization, stretching from sea to sea, stands ready to render any assistance in its power towards the solution of one of the country's most important problems, namely, the safeguarding of the health of our people."[66]

It was Canadian organized medicine's finest hour.

The Canadian Hospital Council (CHC). The CHC was not then the democratic body that, as an association, it was later to become. Dr. Harvey Agnew, the former assistant secretary of the Canadian Medical Association in charge of hospital relations, was the chief leader in the formation of the CHC. He and the council had given a great deal of thought to the economic situation of hospitals which, in the depression, had bordered on disaster, and to the impact that a health insurance program would have.

Because of its unique combination of constituents which included not only provincial hospital associations but the Catholic Hospital Associations, the provincial departments of health, and the federal Health Department, the CHC could not give to the health insurance proposal the unanimous (or ringing) endorsement that the Canadian Medical Association had done. The submission simply said that "the CHC is generally in favour of the principle of health insurance. This is not necessarily the opinion of individual Boards of Trustees or Sisters' Councils nor the governmental departments cooperating in the work of the Canadian Hospital Council. Nor does it imply approval of any particular plan."[67]

The brief first pointed out what it considered the points of excellence in the existing hospital system. These included wide-spread availability of hospitals to most of Canada's scattered population, the fact that the hospitals take good care of the poor, that provincial grants and municipal payments were of great assistance, that hospitals were predominantly "public," only a few being proprietary, service was maintained at a high level of quality, and, finally, both public and private patients were cared for in the same hospitals. On the other hand, there were some weaknesses. These included the fact that costs were a severe handicap to patients of moderate means, that some communities lacked hospital facilities, that the lack of coordinated planning resulted in gaps and in duplication, and that the current system of paying for indigents was a frequent cause of strained relations between hospitals and municipalities.

It then presented what it considered the essential principles of a governmental hospital insurance program and these, as one would expect, were similar to those enunciated by the Canadian Medical Association.

The brief stated that voluntary hospitals should be utilized and not be taken over by the state; hospitalization should be through public, and only in exceptional circumstances, through proprietary hospitals; hospital benefits should be reasonably complete; facilities should be made available to all types of patients; hospitalization of indigents should be provided for; the dependants of the insured should be included; remuneration should be fair to all parties concerned; hospitals should retain the right to determine their own medical staffing privileges; insured persons should have the privilege of taking higher priced accommodation by paying the difference in charges; health insurance should be on a provincial basis but under federal coordination; direction of the plan should be strictly non-political; hospitals should be represented on the commission or advisory council; and the health insurance fund should be a contributory one.

It concluded its presentation, emulating the CMA, by stating that the Canadian Hospital Council on behalf of the hospitals of Canada, wished to record its desire and willingness to be of any service possible in the working out of any plan of health care which would be of lasting benefit to the sick and promote better national health.[68]

The Canadian Dental Association (CDA). The Canadian Dental Association had been one of the groups which had submitted a plan to the advisory committee. Its brief to the Common's committee was strongly positive on the need for organized action but, acutely conscious of the disparity between dental needs and trained personnel resources, was understandably cautious about the part of the dental health problem that could be realistically attacked. The evidence was that the "backlog" of needs was overwhelming. Twenty-three percent of the available manpower for the armed services was discovered to be unfit for enlistment due to dental defects. "The ravages of dental caries among the children of the nation is a well known condition among all public health officials, often spoken of as a national disgrace."[69] Given the limited resources, the greatest benefits would be gained by a program directed to children only. The CDA concluded therefore that in the event that health insurance were enacted in Canada, "the profession advocates the institution of a compulsory dental health insurance plan for all children up to age sixteen."[70] Since not all provinces would be able to undertake even this obligation, the age limit should be set by each province.

The CDA also favoured administration by a commission on which they would be directly represented. Looking at basic needs, the CDA argued strongly that the proposed health grants should include grants for dental research, dental public health education, as well as for university education of more dentists.

In sum, the brief reflected a strong desire to contribute to a program of dental benefits combined with a realistic assessment of what the inadequate numbers of dental personnel could accomplish.

The Canadian Life Insurance Officers' Association (CLIOA). The resolutions of the Canadian Medical Association in January 1943 had been not only a dramatic boon for the government but a major force on public opinion favouring the proposition. But it must have been equally gratifying and no less surprising to receive endorsement of a national health insurance program from so important a section of the business community as the Canadian Life Insurance Officers' Association.

Viewed in the light of later attitudes of the insurance industry—attributable to the spectacular growth of sickness and accident policy sales in the 1950s—the document was almost heretical, for in unequivocal terms the brief declared that "with the inauguration of a comprehensive and efficient health and rehabilitation service, we as a life insurance organization, are also heartily in accord."[71]

On the other hand it criticized strongly the proposal that the public health grants should be contingent upon the inauguration of health insurance: "Preventive measures of various kinds can and should be set up as fully and as completely as possible without waiting for the working out of the health insurance scheme."[72] It then went on to say that the association concurred "that the full objective of preventive measures cannot be attained until the practising physician becomes in effect a public health officer in respect to the families for whose health he is responsible."[73]

As one would expect from the insurance spokesmen, there was presented a strong case for financing the program by personal contributions that met the full cost without any government subsidy from general tax revenues. It also expressed a regret that the advisory committee had not made known its methods for making an accurate forecast of costs rather than basing its estimates on current expenditures under the existing system of supplying medical care.

It quarrelled, further, with the proposal that each province must assume financial responsibility for those unable to pay the full amount with the disturbing result that "the provinces on which the burden would be relatively high would be the very provinces least able to meet such a cost."[74] Rather, the federal government should establish one fund with grants of almost the total (ninety to ninety-five percent) average national *per capita* costs to the provinces for them to administer. A province's costs would not be increased, therefore, by the inability to pay of a large proportion of the population, or by a disproportionately large number of children in the population.

On a major recommendation urged by the CMA, that there be an income ceiling for participation in the program, the CLIOA admitted that there was a difference of opinion among its members, but listed six problems that such a policy would encounter, including the "in-and-out" status created by fluctuating incomes, as well as the fact that "insofar as the health of the individual is affected by the health of his fellow citizens, the success of health insurance may be impaired by the intermingling of insured and uninsured individuals."[75]

It was a highly constructive presentation and although, under questioning, spokesmen did not deny that the industry had a financial interest in prolonging insured lives, they indicated that this objective clearly coincided with that of every individual.

Trades and Labour Congress (TLC). The Labour movement in Canada was then organized nationally in two organizations: The Trades and Labour Congress and the Canadian Congress of Labour. Mr. Percy Bengough, the president of the Trades and Labour Congress, was probably the best informed about health insurance of any leader in the labour movement for he had been not only a strong advocate of health insurance in British Columbia but had actually been a member of the B.C. Health Insurance Commission. He spoke therefore with knowledge, experience, and passion. Mindful of the major fact that had defeated the British Columbia proposal—that British Columbia was acting alone—the Trades and Labour Congress took the view that the program should be national rather than provincial but, bowing to the realities of provincial jurisdiction, acquiesced in the basic proposal for national aid to provincial plans provided that they achieved the maximum uniformity possible. There should also be, the TLC insisted, a close tie-up with the newly enacted unemployment insurance plan and provision for sickness cash benefits. But there were strong expressions of opposition to any notion that on any health insurance commission the representatives of consumers and particularly of labour should be accorded anything less than majority representation. "Labour needs to be assured," said Mr. Bengough, "that the primary purpose of a Health Insurance Act is to operate for the benefit of the contributors and not entirely in the interests of the medical profession."[76] The proposal that a medical man should be chairman of the commission was opposed for the same reason, that it placed too much control in the hands of the profession. With all other ideas, that the program should be universal, contributory, and comprehensive, the Trades and Labour Congress agreed.

The Canadian Congress of Labour (CCL). The views of the Canadian Congress of Labour, as expected, were very similar, stressing particularly the importance of financing the program nationally rather than provincially and by a progressive income tax levy. It was equally adamant about the composition of the commission, stressing the importance of majority taxpayer representation. Once again there was strong emphasis on the primacy of public health preventive services, an emphasis as strong, indeed, as that made by the Federation of Agriculture.[77]

The Canadian Federation of Agriculture (CFA). Discussions with the Canadian Federation of Agriculture were extremely useful, for that organization had published in 1942 a booklet entitled "Health on the March" in which were outlined eight "principles" of a national plan of health insurance. This document had served as a focal point for thousands of meetings and many discussions on the national radio forum network of the CBC. Mr. H. H. Hannam, president of the federation, was unusually well informed, articulate, and persuasive. The principles favoured a national plan, based primarily on the fact that the selective service call-up of young men had resulted in a rejection rate of forty-four percent— clearly indicating a nation-wide problem. A national plan called for administration by a representative commission at Ottawa with a majority being lay people. The national legislation should provide that the central commission function through parallel provincial commissions. The total financing should be from Dominion revenues since, through the wide range of tax fields open to it, "the national taxation touches every income earner and no new machinery need be devised." The plan should include all citizens and there should be absolutely no income ceiling, to avoid the unnecessary administrative confusion resulting from fluctuating incomes, and to achieve financial soundness and equity. But there was a more important reason: "Health is moving rapidly from the field of thinking of a service or a charity for some to be given by the better privileged to others . . . into the field of thinking of it as an integral part of the life of every Canadian. In other words, the people are thinking of health as a right of citizenship, of even greater importance than education or police protection, which are taken for granted."[78]

Finally, said the CFA, "To make the plan fully effective, it must borrow from the experience of some of the municipal doctor plans of the western provinces which were successful from both a preventive and treatment point of view because of total community involvement. The dynamics of the rural community must be utilized in a program for better health."[79] Many of these ideas were to have major impacts on the draft measures.

Sir William Beveridge. Although not a spokesman for a Canadian interest group, nor posing as an expert in Canadian social security, Sir William Beveridge's appearance was one, if not the major, highlight of the committee hearings. He did not concern himself with details of the proposed program, other than to praise Dr. Marsh's report. He emphasized that the objective was not social insurance, but, rather, social progress. And this could be achieved by attacking what he called the five "giant evils" of Want, Disease, Ignorance, Squalor, and Idleness.[80]

The question period elicited an interesting observation by Sir William on the importance of the individual contributing directly to the social insurance system. "Every insured person," he said, "should make a flat contribution of about one-quarter of the cost [in contrast to a graduated income tax] . . . I am quite certain that is what the people of Britain want. It adds to their sense of self respect to make a contribution irrespective of means. . . . if you have [such] a system people will realize that they cannot get unlimited benefits without paying for them; and I believe that is an element of sound finance."[81]

The appearance of Sir William Beveridge had provided few technical answers, but his presence had clearly inspired the committee with a vision of a brighter future and enhanced its conviction that it was engaged in one of the most important policy decisions ever to come before the Canadian Parliament.

On July 23, 1943, after more than four months of hearings and deliberations, during which it had held thirty-two meetings and examined 117 witnesses representing thirty-two organizations, the Special Committee submitted its report. It had also approved a bill for the establishment of a National Council for Physical Fitness and had reported it to the House.

The committee approved the general principles enunciated in the Heagerty Report and embodied in the draft legislation. It recommended that before the bill was finally reported, senior officials should visit the provinces to provide them with full information, a conference of Dominion and provincial representatives should be held, and study of the bill should be continued by a Committee of the House and by the Interdepartmental Advisory Committee.[82]

THE POLICY RE-EXAMINED

With the report of the House of Commons Committee supported by the testimony of the various interest groups, the minister and the departmental officials had now to re-examine the policy and consider the strategy to obtain Cabinet endorsement.

During the summer recess of Parliament, Health Minister Mackenzie gave a good deal of thought to his proposed program and to his strategy in persuading the prime minister and the Cabinet. In a letter written on August 19, 1943, he reminded the prime minister of the very encouraging paragraphs in the Throne Speech and of the recommendations of the Committee on Social Security. He indicated his concern about the future of the Liberal government:

> There is no doubt that our government is unpopular. That is very largely the result of inescapable war conditions. The restrictions that have been found necessary are generally hated by the people. . . . It is not Tory-ism under its new guise that is killing us; it is the unnatural, un-Liberal regimentation we have been constrained to adopt and, worse still, to defend. This situation cannot, I fear, be corrected until the Armistice. What are the other causes? What of the rise of socialism all across Canada? It was for years a British Columbia and a Saskatchewan freak but it is now definitely a national political menace. Why?

He then listed a number of discontents: those on small fixed allowances from the state, the small increase in the old age pension, the low rates of war veterans' allowances, the selective service experiments, even beer regulations. He reminded the prime minister that the Committee on Social Security had recommended a Dominion-Provincial Conference to deal with the financial and constitutional features of the Health Bill:

> I believe such a Conference to be unavoidable . . . say about the end of November. I believe, however, that the Conference should deal with the whole field of Social Security. . . . I suppose we cannot escape a discussion of the Sirois proposals . . . or at least of the financial and taxation structure. We can then make such amendments to the Health Bill as we decide are necessary, and refer it again to the Parliamentary committee, introduce it into the House in February or March, 1944 and have it through by June.[83]

This was the time-table and scenario visualized by Mackenzie. He also recommended that his department be split into a Department of Veterans' Affairs and a Department of Health and Social Security, believing that a separate ministry would increase the momentum.

It will be recalled that in January 1943, the Economic Advisory Committee chaired by W. C. Clark, the deputy minister of finance, had been highly critical of the financial proposals drafted by the Interdepartmental

Committee dominated by officials of the Health Department and DBS. Similar criticisms had been expressed by the House of Commons Committee.

Accordingly, on November 19, 1943, Mackenzie appointed a Committee on Health Insurance Finance consisting of one representative each from the Departments of Finance and Revenue, the Bank of Canada, the Unemployment Insurance Commission, and the Dominion Bureau of Statistics, to re-examine the whole financing question. The new committee concurred in the criticisms of the earlier proposals and recommended that (1) the annual personal contribution (to be collected by the provinces) be reduced from $26 to $12; (2) there be an income tax levy (i) for a single person of three percent of income over $660 with a maximum of $30; (ii) for a married person, five percent of income over $1200 per year with a maximum of $50, this to be collected by the Dominion along with the income tax. In addition, the Dominion would contribute to each province according to a formula designed to take account of some degree of fiscal need. One effect of the formula was that the federal contribution would bear the full cost of all children under sixteen years of age. The provinces would carry the costs of administration, and the amount by which *per capita* costs in any province exceeded the Dominion average.

The Finance Committee also expressed doubts as to the reliability of the cost estimates, based, as they were, on inadequate data on both incomes and health care costs. It stressed that health insurance would be expensive and that the formula it was recommending would entail much larger federal contributions than those originally contemplated by the Advisory Committee. "The Committee feels that this is inevitable if health insurance is to be soundly financed and generally applied throughout the Dominion."[84]

It then dealt with one issue that has been heatedly debated ever since:

It is clearly undesirable that one government should raise a large amount of funds which another government . . . is spending. Consequently [these] recommendations will offend against this canon of good practice and the principle of direct political responsibility for expenditures. Nevertheless it seems clear that the provinces cannot finance health insurance themselves . . . and that a purely national scheme . . . is at present considered constitutionally and politically impracticable.[85]

The committee concluded with a recommendation that was without doubt the most extreme suggestion for federal intervention in provincial administration to be made in the six and a half years of discussions of the entire proposal.

It would help to overcome the inherent difficulties of the Dominion financing provincial schemes if the Dominion required as a condition of making grants to the provinces for health insurance, that the province appoint one or more nominees of the Dominion Government, for example, an officer of the Department of National Health and an officer of the Department of Finance, to the [provincial Health Insurance Commission].[86]

On the basis of its revised recommendations, the Finance Committee estimated the costs and sources of revenue of the program as follows:

Total Cost (at $21.60 per person)	$250,000,000
Contributions by adults ($12 *per capita*)	100,000,000
Collected by Dominion through the Income Tax	50,000,000
Contributed by the Dominion from general revenues	100,000,000

With these various recommendations coming from the influential finance group, the Interdepartmental Committee revised the draft legislation for presentation to the House of Commons Committee.

The House of Commons Special Committee on Social Security was reconstituted and held its first meeting on February 24, 1944. Because of the delay in formulating the new financial proposals, the recommended visit by federal officials to the provinces had not taken place and Mackenzie's recommendation for a Dominion-provincial conference had been ignored. Several of the opposition members of the committee were highly critical that they were considering a draft bill that was not a government-sponsored measure and about which the provinces had not been consulted. With the assurance of the minister that a conference would be held and a government decision taken as soon as possible, the committee continued its examination of the proposed changes, questioned the expert witnesses, and heard major presentations from a small number of organizations.

During the committee's deliberations in the week of May 8, a conference of the provincial ministers of health and their deputies was convened to discuss the health insurance proposals, and a joint meeting was arranged with the House of Commons Committee, the Advisory Committee, and the Finance Committee.

All the provincial ministers approved the principle of health insurance and favoured its early adoption, but stressed that each province should be permitted to introduce each benefit in its own time as it became feasible to do so, and should also be permitted to raise the funds in any way it saw fit.[87]

These issues were of such importance that the committee agreed that it would be necessary to leave the question of the financial arrangements to the forthcoming Dominion-Provincial Conference.

At its last meeting on July 28, the committee completed its final report to the House of Commons, approving, with minor amendments, the two draft bills prepared by the Advisory Committee and the Finance Committee.

The House of Commons received the report of its Social Security Committee but since no government bill had been introduced, and the entire proposal depended upon the outcome of negotiations with the provinces, the only major reference in the House was in the Speech from the Throne in January 1945.

The Government had now to come to grips with a specific proposal, to evaluate the policy recommendations from the civil service, and the myriad demands, recommendations, and suggestions that had come from the Royal Commission, the Marsh and Beveridge reports, a host of interest groups representing consumers and the professions, the preliminary views of the provinces expressed by the ministers of health at their May meeting in Ottawa, and the draft legislation approved by the House of Commons Committee on Social Security. On few, if any other, major governmental policy proposals to that date had there been such a copious supply of both information and advice. There were many opposing points of view among the various interest groups with respect to highly important details, especially on financing and on the nature of the responsible administrative agency at the provincial level. But there was unprecedented agreement on the main objective that a national plan was both necessary and desirable. The provinces, too, appeared to agree in principle but their decisions to participate would depend ultimately on hard bargaining with premiers and finance ministers rather than on favourable responses by ministers of health.

THE STRATEGY OF IMPLEMENTATION (FIRST STAGE)

The time had now come for the Cabinet to agree on the final policy and to design a strategy for its implementation including the question of timing. Obviously the two "outputs" of policy and strategy are interrelated. Strategy is clearly dictated by policy but there are many policies that are altered by the exigencies of the strategy necessary to implement them.

As we have seen, the Commons Committee on Social Security in July, and Ian Mackenzie in his letter to the prime minister in August, had urged a Dominion-provincial conference to obtain agreement on the health measure. On the other hand, W. C. Clark, the deputy minister of finance and chairman of the Economic Advisory Committee, believed that health insurance should be linked to old age pensions, both contingent upon a reordering of financial relationships with the provinces. The expiry of the taxation rental agreements one year after the cessation of hostilities would require a conference with the provinces but other issues and more immediate problems had delayed a decision on a date.

The Cabinet had recognized that a conference was inevitable, but were also aware that even the calling of a meeting, and especially its timing— quite apart from its substantive negotiations—was attended by grave uncertainties and hazardous political risks. Further procrastination was abruptly ended, however, with the arrival of an unexpected letter from Premier George Drew of Ontario on January 7, 1944, urging that a Dominion-provincial conference be called at the earliest possible moment to consider post-war planning.[88]

The immediate reaction to Drew's request was suspicion of his motives. "It may be assumed," said Claxton, "that the Premier of Ontario would not have proposed a conference unless he hoped to derive some political advantage for himself or his party from the proposal."[89]

The political risks, as seen by Claxton, could be summarized as follows: 1. The obvious danger of a conference was that it would create a breach between the Liberals at Ottawa and those at Quebec (then led by Premier Adelard Godbout). Godbout could not agree to the financial and constitutional readjustments which were essential to place any federal government in a position to deal effectively with employment and social policies; 2. The federal government, in its turn, could not afford to embark on any schemes which would involve tremendous grants-in-aid or, alternatively, would leave all the poorer provinces fiscally incapable of performing essential services; 3. It would be a great advantage to the Conservatives and especially to Mr. Drew, to have this divergence brought out into the open. Mr. Drew's one hope of getting power federally was to lead a crusade against Quebec. The Ontario government had already tried to show that Ottawa was yielding to Quebec in face of a common front of the other eight provinces.

In addition, there was uncertainty and risk even in the timing of the conference. In view of Drew's phrasing of his letter, it should probably be held as soon as possible. However, if it were held while Parliament was in session, there would be a good deal of debate and unnecessary controversy in the House, as well as provincial pressures on federal members. The Easter recess therefore appeared best. That date might, on the other hand, conflict with the Imperial War Conference to be held in London, and because of their own legislative sessions, some provincial governments, particularly in the Maritimes, might not be able to attend even then. There would have to be an enormous amount of preparation. Unlike the 1941 Conference when the subject matter was the Report of the Royal Commission, the subject matter for this conference would have to be organized from the beginning and would take, in Claxton's view, at least four months to prepare background material as well as to make a great many policy decisions. But, if the conference were postponed until after the session, (i.e., in August or September), it would mean that legislation incorporating the results of the conference would have to be held over, and the blame for the delay (in an election year) would rest on the Liberals.

It was finally agreed that sometime between April 11 and 22 would be the least disadvantageous time, depending upon the provinces' responses.

Accordingly, letters were sent by the clerk of the privy council, A. D. P. Heeney, referring to Premier Drew's letter, and suggesting a conference on post-war employment, reconstruction, and the financial relationship between the Dominion and the provinces.

In the Speech from the Throne on January 27, 1944 the Government stated:

> The working out of a comprehensive national scheme [of social security] in which federal and provincial activities will be integrated and which will embody nation-wide health insurance, will require further consultation and close cooperation with the provinces. My ministers will welcome opportunities for such consultation.

> When suitable arrangements are reached with the provinces, my ministers will be prepared to recommend measures to provide for federal assistance in a nation-wide system of health insurance, and for a national scheme of contributory old age pensions on a more generous basis than that at present in operation.[90]

During the week of January 17, 1944, Claxton prepared a memorandum proposing the organization of committees to undertake preparations for the conference. He suggested a Cabinet committee and, responsible to it, an interdepartmental committee of officials chaired by a member of the Cabinet committee. The subjects to be considered were: (a) financial arrangements; (b) economic controls in the post-war period; (c) unemployment assistance, children's allowances, contributory old age pensions, and health insurance.[91]

Three weeks later, on February 14, the Cabinet appointed the Committee on the Dominion-Provincial Conference. It included the minister of mines and resources, Mr. Crerar (chairman), the minister of finance, Mr. Ilsley, the minister of justice, Mr. St. Laurent, the minister of agriculture, Mr. Gardiner, the secretary of state, Mr. McLarty, and the minister of labour, Mr. Mitchell.

A Supervisory Committee of Parliamentary Assistants was appointed to oversee the work of officials and to be responsible to the Cabinet committee, with Brooke Claxton as chairman. There was also appointed an Advisory Committee of officials representing twelve departments, with W. C. Clark, the deputy minister of finance, as chairman. And, to make certain that all these committees were coordinated, Mr. Alex Skelton from the Bank of Canada was appointed secretary to all committees.[92]

By the middle of February all the provinces had replied, all had accepted the invitation, and none had proposed subjects or conditions other than that most provinces wanted to wait until their legislative sessions were over.

On February 17, the Cabinet Committee held its first meeting, with most of it a free-wheeling discussion centring on the scope of the agenda. Claxton had prepared a draft agenda based on recommendations of the Rowell-Sirois Commission, on recent social security proposals, and on post-war employment needs, and attached to it an extensive memorandum analyzing the major items.

The major issues were three: How extensive should the proposals be? What preparations and strategies should be employed? What were the likely outcomes?

Claxton's memorandum indicated that he wanted a broad agenda, with his primary item being the patriation of the constitution and agreement on a clear-cut method of amending it. His other subjects and recommendations were:

(a) continuation of exclusive Dominion income corporation tax collection

(b) addition of succession duties to exclusive Dominion field

(c) assumption by Dominion of responsibility for relief to able-bodied unemployed

(d) assumption by Dominion of responsibility for old age pensions when put on a contributory basis

(e) assumption by Dominion of major portion of health insurance costs

(f) full Dominion power to implement bona fide treaties and international agreements even when dealing with subjects which are normally matters of provincial jurisdiction.[93]

Despite the case for Claxton's far-reaching proposals for constitutional revision, the general feeling of the Cabinet committee was that such proposals should be kept to an absolute minimum. Mr. St. Laurent, in particular, thought that Quebec would not be prepared to accept any important changes regardless of their apparent merit or reasonableness. He questioned whether continuation of *de facto* occupation of tax fields by the Dominion depended upon continuation of the agreements or some equivalent constitutional adjustment. It was argued that, while existing Dominion rates might bar the provinces from re-entering the personal income tax field, this could not be relied on in the case of corporation income taxes and that a return to double taxation in that field would have serious repercussions on any program to provide employment after the war. Mr. Crerar also pointed out that if the allocation of tax powers were not clearly and finally settled, endless Dominion-provincial controversy would result which would be extremely harmful to national unity. Mr. St. Laurent stressed that the emphasis must be on changes which were necessary to put the Dominion in a position to pursue full employment and high income policies, and great care must be taken to avoid the appearances of attempting to increase Dominion revenues at the expense of the provinces.

With extraordinary political insight, Mr. Ilsley observed that the provinces would make very large demands for financial assistance in one form or another but that they would not be prepared to surrender the proposed tax fields to the Dominion and that the conference would consequently result in a stalemate.

All the members agreed that the Dominion's position would be greatly strengthened if it were able, at the time of the conference, to outline its general intentions in the field of public works, including public investment, reforestation, rural electrification, mining, and other developmental roads, and, in particular, to assure the provinces that the Dominion was taking seriously the responsibility for developing full employment and high income policies.[94]

Meanwhile, the Secretariat had invited all the provinces to send a Treasury official to assist federal finance officers in bringing together national and provincial financial statistics on a uniform basis. But even at the technical level, the first signs of difficulties to come had appeared. Despite six requests to Premier Drew between February 28 and April 15, no official had been sent from Ontario and it was not until May that Mr. Harold Chater arrived to round out the full complement of finance officials. It was an ill omen.

In addition to these financial and statistical analyses, a second group of studies, on full employment, was undertaken under the direction of Dr. W. A. Mackintosh. A third group of studies was assumed by committees involving various departments: unemployment relief, health insurance, children's allowances, old age pensions, veterans' reestablishment, price control, and a nutrition program. A fourth group was assigned studies on public finance policy and a fifth on constitutional and legal studies. By May, the Secretariat was able to report substantial progress in all areas.[95]

But that was the only level at which events were moving. The stalling of Ontario in dispatching Mr. Chater, the various provincial legislative sessions, the prospects of two provincial elections, and the proposal for a conference of prime ministers in London were all delaying the calling of the conference itself. The longer the delay, of course, the more questionable became a decision to hold the conference before a general election.

The pressures from Premier Drew in Ontario and, particularly, from the opposition in the Commons, continued to mount, and all of King's dexterous political footwork came into play as he parried questions in the House. On twenty-nine different days of sittings, between February 2 and August 14, 1944, questions were asked of the prime minister about the timing of the conference.

Finally, on Saturday, July 22, Mackenzie King was told that Premier Drew had said on the radio the previous evening that "what he was living for most was to get the Government at Ottawa out of office." Wrote King in his diary, "It gave me just what I needed. . . . I decided not to have the Conference for the reason that I knew this would be his attitude. I had not expected him to say so in the open, but it is like Drew."[96]

As far as can be ascertained, he did not then inform anyone else of his decision.

On August 3, 1944, the Cabinet Committee met again for another general review. Mr. Crerar said that neither the Dominion nor the provinces could plan their reconstruction programs until the tax situation was clarified and that the two problems of reconstruction and Dominion-provincial relations were inseparable. Mr. McLarty said that the question of whether the Dominion needed exclusive jurisdiction in the tax fields depended in part on the desirability of the Dominion expanding its social welfare activities. Mr. St. Laurent thought that the federal position would be such that exclusive possession of the income and corporation tax fields was desirable in any case. Succession duties, currently yielding only $39 million a year to both levels of government, while desirable, were not essential. The Dominion's present commitments and the requirements of the national economy would be such that the Dominion would need to raise very large revenues. If the provinces were to compete in taxing the same sources there was danger of killing the goose. Mr. Mitchell observed that we were taxing ourselves into socialism.

Mr. St. Laurent suggested that while universal old age pensions had clear administrative advantages it might be necessary to restrict them by some form of means test at the start. He noted that we were already committed to family allowances, and health insurance was on the horizon. Mr. Ilsley said that the first thing to settle was whether the Dominion should make every effort to acquire exclusive possession of the proposed

43

tax fields. He himself strongly supported this. Mr. Crerar thought that these proposals would precipitate acrimonious dispute with some provinces. Mr. St. Laurent noted that this was inevitable with Quebec in any case, and that the Quebec campaign to alter or at least reinterpret the terms of Confederation was already well under way. He thought that the Quebec government's ambition was to retain and expand autonomous powers and that no matter how financially advantageous a proposal might be, it would be rejected if it involved the surrender of any existing prerogatives. Mr. Crerar thought that in a conflict the majority of the people would support provincial governments against the Dominion. Mr. St. Laurent observed that this was so because people were made constantly aware of the services which provincial governments rendered while they tended to think of the central government as the one imposing burdens such as taxation and conscription. He thought that such measures as family allowances would tend to correct this.[97]

The parliamentary session was drawing to a close and on August 14 Mackenzie King made his statement in the Commons on the timing of the conference. There were, he indicated, several reasons for the delays: (1) the provincial legislative sessions; (2) the elections in six of the nine provinces since August 1943; (3) the defeat of the incumbent government in two of these; (4) the fact that the conference must not fail, that Canada could not afford a repetition of 1941. "There is an additional reason why, if the Conference is to be a success, it should be held only after a general election. What above all else is required to make the Conference a success is a cooperative attitude on the part of all governments concerned. How far that attitude has thus far been in evidence may be judged from the [tabled] correspondence."[98]

He then made his surprise announcement, quoting from Premier Drew's radio broadcast. "Such being the declared aim of the Premier of Ontario, it must be apparent that any conference held before a Federal election would have little or no hope of success. . . . Preparations for the Conference can and will be continued so that it will be possible to have the Conference held immediately following a general election."[99]

The political uncertainties assessed eight months earlier had matured into risks too great to take. Public opinion would have to be tested and mobilized in support of the federal government's objectives. In the meantime, the work of the committees of officials went on.

Ian Mackenzie's four and a half year campaign to achieve a health program for Canada had produced a conceptual design for federal-provincial cooperation, draft legislation, cost estimates, assurances of professional cooperation, provincial government interest and study, and a much better-informed public opinion resulting from the two sessions of the House of Commons Committee. But, like Moses, he was not to lead the movement to the promised land. On June 13, 1944 the Cabinet approved the establishment of a new department which was later named National Health and Welfare, to which Claxton was named minister on October 13, with Mackenzie becoming minister of veterans' affairs.[100]

One other decision had an important influence on Mackenzie's dream. At the Cabinet meeting on July 18, King had Council "give final decision on no further legislation on health at this session . . . ; that we had gone as far as we should on public expenditures and on social security matters, and that to announce further large new expenditures in view of outlay for family allowances, would only alarm one side of the electorate in the matter of taxation, and no further thanks from the other."[101]

Family allowances had been given priority. The effect was to terminate consideration of health insurance as a single program to be developed on its own merits. It was now only a part of that complex post-war design for Canada, its prospects conditional on a massive reorganization of the financial underpinnings of the federal system.

The committee on health insurance of the Interdepartmental Committee continued its work. It consisted of Dr. Heagerty, R. B. Bryce of Finance, and J. E. Howes of the research staff of the Bank of Canada, these latter two having been members of the Committee on Finance which had recommended the changes in the financing formula in the draft legislation. These changes, as we have seen, had been accepted in principle by the House of Commons Committee on Social Security which also recognized that a Dominion-Provincial Conference would have to agree on the finance proposals.

But now, with Claxton as the new minister of health and chairman of the Interdepartmental Committee, and health insurance being considered not as an independent program but as part of what was being developed as a broad range of reconstruction proposals and financial changes, the strategy for achieving health insurance was drastically altered. The original policy had implied substantial intervention in provincial decision making by requiring uniform legislation by the provinces based on the model bill. With the inclusion of health insurance in a comprehensive package of proposals, that strategy could no longer be followed. The offer must appear more attractive and less interventionist. Strategy had dictated a change in policy.

The major decision was to abandon the entire concept of a model act for the provinces and, particularly, any precondition of any specific method of provincial financing. It was decided that the full range of health services would be provided by the provinces in two stages and that the federal share would be set at a maximum of sixty percent of the estimated cost of each service. This federal share and a federal contribution to old age pensions could be financed from a four or five percent income levy.

The planning and organization and other health grants remained, as did loans for hospital construction.

It was an abandonment of a whole series of positions that had been built up over more than four years by the Health Department. It would obviously be a serious disappointment to the Canadian Medical Association for now the battles for its principles, particularly administration by independent commissions, would have to be fought on nine separate fronts.

On the other hand, the new flexibility should make the proposals more attractive to the provinces and that, as King repeatedly said to the Cabinet, and reiterated in his diary, was crucial for the success of the conference. But in advance of the conference—as he had decided in 1944—must come the election which was crucial to everything.[102]

The timing of the election was extraordinarily complex; if it were held before the war ended (and King had optimistic confidential information on that eventuality), then the Progressive Conservatives would capitalize on the conscription and reinforcement issue; there were the San Francisco Conference and the Victory Loan campaign; and then there was the Ontario election which, King was aware, Premier Drew wanted to hold in advance of the federal election in order to strengthen his own position at the conference. King's preference was for June 11 but just before he could announce it, Premier Drew announced the Ontario election on that date. Finally, after discussions on strategy, King announced the national election on the same date, whereupon Mr. Drew advanced the Ontario date to June 4.

For King it was a bitter election campaign, with the growing threat of the CCF on the one hand (until June 4 when the Ontario CCF lost heavily to the Conservatives) and the strident attacks of the well-organized and well-financed Progressive Conservatives. The conscription issue, the charges of pandering to Quebec, the accumulated resentments against six years of wartime restrictions, and even after V-E Day, the opposition to the need to extend the war effort to the Pacific, were more than enough to discredit any government. Moreover, the party fortunes looked dim, with the earlier defeats of Liberal governments in Quebec and Saskatchewan compounded by the defeat of General McNaughton in the Grey North by-election on February 5, 1945. Equally disturbing as the campaign progressed were the reports of declining support for Mackenzie King in his own riding of Prince Albert. Nevertheless, despite the references in his diary to his trials and tribulations, King remained confident that with victory in Europe he could defuse the conscription issue and emphasize "winning the peace" as he had stressed "winning the war" in 1940.

He was wary, however, in his campaign rhetoric, torn in his strategy for the election. He needed to make a ringing appeal to the Canadian voters but he had also to consider the high stakes for which, if re-elected, he would be bargaining at the Dominion-Provincial Conference with highly sensitive provincial governments. Extracts from some of his campaign statements reveal his moderate tone. In Prince Albert on May 19, "We are prepared as soon as the elections are over, if we are returned to power, to hold a Dominion-Provincial Conference to see if we cannot effect agreements with the different provinces of Canada whereby on matters pertaining to health our several governments may be able to establish a minimum standard of well-being for the people of all Canada."[103] At Winnipeg on May 24, "A main task of the Canadian government from now on will be to seek to maintain full employment and to provide social security for the people of our country."[104] In London, May 30, "The Liberal program looks beyond family allowances to the early establishment of other great social measures. . . . The government also believes that a substantial improvement in national health could be achieved through Dominion-Provincial cooperation. We have accordingly pledged ourselves to support a measure for Federal assistance in a nation-wide system of health insurance, to include assistance to the provinces for preventive medicine. If the present government is returned to office we shall proceed with these measures as soon as agreements with the provinces can be concluded."[105]

The Conservative party ran under a new name—Progressive Conservative—and under a new leader, Mr. John Bracken of Manitoba. The P-C platform also revealed the impact of post-war aspirations and under the title, *Bracken's Charter for a Better Canada*, promised bold action. On health services it said: "We will set up a positive health insurance programme including improved nutritional standards, an efficient preventive health service and a contributory health insurance scheme."[106]

The CCF, sparked by the victory of its Saskatchewan division, outlined a comprehensive social security program of which health services were the central thrust: "The CCF will establish a socialized health service, aimed at providing a national standard of health care in every province of Canada. It will provide all citizens with complete preventive and remedial services."

The Social Credit party, endeavoring to extend its influence beyond Alberta (and finding some unexpected support in Quebec), promised "the best possible health services available to all" and its candidates pointed to the Alberta Maternity Hospitalization Plan established in 1944.

Even the Communist party, under the name of Labor-Progressive, pledged that it would introduce "National Health Insurance to provide medical services, doctors' and nurses' care, hospitalization, and sick pay."

Health insurance had become a major issue of public concern, the declarations of political parties matching the citizens' responses in the public opinion polls. A poll taken in March 1944, reported an eighty percent affirmative response to the question, "Would you contribute to a national hospital-medical insurance plan?"[107]

The election results were: Liberals 125 (a loss of fifty-three); Progressive Conservatives, sixty-seven (a gain of twenty-eight); CCF, twenty-eight (a gain of ten); Social Credit, thirteen; Others, twelve. It was a slim majority, but at least the Liberals would form the government. There were two major casualties, however, both Mackenzie King and General Mac-Naughton losing their seats in Saskatchewan, where the CCF increased its representation from five to eighteen.

Still mindful of the upcoming conference, even in the Government's victory King was both modest and moderate: "The mandate the government has received today is a mandate to strive, above all else, for full employment and social security in our country, and for a new world order based on international understanding, on mutual aid, on friendship and good will—an era of world security and world peace."[108]

FINAL PREPARATIONS

With the election over, the scene shifted back to the Government, to the interactions of the bureaucratic and political actors as they grappled with the final details of the policy and refined the strategy of gaining the provinces' support for the proposals. All of the committees increased the tempo of preparation. The invitations to the provinces and the attendant publicity stressed the limited objectives of the conference. The Cabinet committee meeting on June 20 felt that it would be "extremely important to emphasize that no attempt would be made to reach agreement on either general principles or details, without giving provinces full opportunity to consider the proposals submitted at that time by the Dominion. Otherwise, there would be the danger that provincial leaders might, on receipt of the invitation, before proceeding to the Conference, commit themselves to an uncooperative position in advance. The main objective to be stressed should be to reach agreement to consider the Dominion's proposals and any alternatives, and to provide for the appointment of continuing Dominion-Provincial committees to work over these proposals. When they were in a position to report, the full Conference could be reassembled with the intention of trying to reach a specific agreement. The intervening time would have the additional advantage of allowing public opinion to formulate."[109]

The opening date of the conference had been set for August 6, but a great deal of work remained for the two major Cabinet committees—Reconstruction, and Dominion-Provincial Relations. Following the election, the latter committee was reconstituted on June 20, with the addition of Howe, Mckinnon, and Claxton as members, and the appointment of St. Laurent as chairman.[110]

On July 26 the full Cabinet began to consider the proposals and it was decided to hold daily meetings beginning July 30.[111] It was evident, however, at the July 26 meeting, with the conference little more than a week away, that there was still disagreement within the Cabinet committee on the overall strategy. The issue centred on the financing of health insurance and old age pensions. There was general agreement that health insurance and old age pensions should be on a contributory basis, the contribution coming from a special tax of four or five percent. Some members of the committee felt that this levy should be called a "contribution" and definitely ear-marked for social security. But Mr. St. Laurent thought that an ear-marked contribution would be legal only if provided for by constitutional amendment. Claxton, the minister who would be responsible for both programs, was so concerned that on July 27 he asked for a special meeting with the prime minister to settle the question. He pointed out that:

If we had gone to the provinces and asked for an amendment for family allowances, they would not have given it and there would be no family allowances today. It took five years to get an amendment to provide for unemployment insurance. There can be little doubt that Ontario and British Columbia would quickly refuse to consent to an amendment for these purposes. . . . Consequently, putting this tax or levy in a form requiring a constitutional amendment practically insures a turn down of the whole plan as regards social security. It means that we will never have a Dominion-wide system of health insurance and old age pensions on a contributory basis. It means moreover that the wealthier provinces will institute advanced social services of their own which will further widen the gaps between the wealthy and the the poorer provinces. Moreover, your great achievements in Canadian unity will not be the foundation stone of an enduring system of social welfare. . . . I believe that it is no exaggeration to say that the whole scheme of social welfare and the success of the Conference will turn on our treatment of this single question.

Mackenzie King finally decided; in the margin of Claxton's memorandum he wrote, "no ear-marking."[112]

On the night before the conference Mackenzie King read aloud the speech prepared for him to deliver the following morning. He wrote in his diary: "I feel that it is worthy of the occasion but it is God's mercy indeed that the material has been brought together in time. . . . It is very important. The Conference may well prove, with the material we have prepared, to be the instrument of completely changing the emphasis of administration and legislation on social problems from the Provinces to the Dominion."[113]

And that was clearly what some provincial governments came to fear.

THE POLICY

To this point we have traced the long evolution of a social idea to the stage of specific and elaborate government proposals. One could say that the process had covered a quarter century but it was only in the last five years that unprecedented attention had been given to health insurance. Even that was a long time as the issue proceeded along its tortuous route from department to Cabinet, to inter-departmental committee, to the House of Commons Committee and the public, to finance committee, to Cabinet, to committee, and back to Cabinet. And all along there had been the questions, statements, and debates in the House of Commons. Both the policy and the strategy were now decided upon. What were the "outputs" of this long gestation in terms of specific proposals?

They were now to be revealed, for the curtain was about to go up on the fourth stage, in the magnificent setting of the House of Commons chamber, where thirteen main actors, representing ten governments, would grapple with the challenge of a post-war design for Canada. Health insurance was one of the important issues, but whether it would become a reality, as its supporters hoped, depended, in the new strategy, on the outcome of the conference proposals as a whole.

And so on August 6, 1945 Prime Minister King welcomed the delegates to what he said "may well be the most important Canadian Conference since Confederation."[114]

The federal government set forth the basic principles underlying its proposals:

> In familiar terms, our objectives are high and stable employment and income, and a greater sense of public responsibility for individual economic security and welfare. Realization of these objectives for all Canadians, as Canadians, is a cause in which we would hope for national enthusiasm and unity.
> The Government has clear and definite views on how these objectives can be attained [including the provision] on the basis of small regular payments against large and uncertain individual risks, for such hazards, and disabilities as unemployment, sickness and old age.
> Because Canada is a federal state these responsibilities are shared by the federal and provincial governments. This division of responsibilities

should not be permitted to prevent any government, or governments in cooperation, from taking effective action. To devise a working cooperative arrangement to a common end, in harmony with our Federal system, is the main purpose of this Conference.

It is with these considerations in mind, and in search of common ground for agreement, that the Government presents its proposals. These proposals assume a broad federal responsibility, in co-operation with provincial governments, for establishing the general conditions and framework for high employment and income policies, and for support of national minimum standards of social services. They also assume that provincial governments should be in a financial position to discharge their responsibilities adequately.[115]

Federal ministers, in turn, presented the Government's proposed policies with respect to veterans' re-establishment, housing, community planning, industrial conversion from wartime to peacetime production, agriculture, wage controls, and public investment. Because of delays arising from a long procedural wrangle and King's announcement to the conference of the dropping of the atomic bomb, it was not until late evening of that long Monday that the health proposals item on the agenda was reached (and news of MacKenzie King's re-election in Glengarry arrived to refresh his spirits).

After presenting both social and economic arguments for a social security program, Mr. Claxton outlined the specific proposals.[116]

1. *Planning and organization grant.* This was to be a grant to enable each provincial government as soon as possible to establish a full-time planning staff to prepare for and organize health insurance benefits within the province and make provision for the training of necessary personnel. The grants ranged from $10,000 in Prince Edward Island to $194,000 in Ontario.

2. *Health insurance.* This proposal was designed to put provincial governments in a financial position to develop and administer a comprehensive health insurance program worked out by progressive stages on an agreed basis. The various health benefits were classified, as outlined in Table 1.

The proposed federal contribution to the cost of each benefit was (1) a basic grant of one-fifth of the *estimated* cost of each service as shown in the table, and (2) one-half the additional actual cost incurred by each provincial government for each benefit, provided that the total federal contribution did not exceed the amount stated in the table for each service. The maximum would therefore be $12.96 per person when the complete

TABLE 1

BASIS OF FEDERAL CONTRIBUTIONS FOR HEALTH INSURANCE
(DOLLARS PER CAPITA)

Service Provided	Estimated Average Cost of Service[a]	% of Total Cost	Basic Dominion Grant (20% of total est.)	Maximum Additional Dominion Grant (50% of additional actual cost to maximum)
First Stage				
General practitioner service	6.00	28	1.20	2.40
Hospital care	3.60	17	0.72	1.44
Visiting nursing service	0.60	3	0.12	0.24
Total first stage	10.20	48	2.04	4.08
Later Stages				
Other medical services (consultant, specialist and surgical)	3.50	16	0.70	1.40
Other nursing services (including private duty)	1.15	5	0.23	0.46
Dental care	3.60	16	0.72	1.44
Pharmaceutical (drugs, serums, and surgical appliances)	2.55	12	0.51	1.02
Laboratory services (blood tests, x-rays, etc.)	0.60	3	0.12	0.24
	21.60	100	4.32	8.64

[a]Estimated cost to be revised on basis of actual costs after three years.
SOURCE: Dominion-Provincial Conference, 1945, *Proceedings*, p. 90.

program was in operation, i.e., for each benefit, the federal government contribution could reach sixty percent.

For the first three years the cost of each benefit would be taken to be the amounts shown in the table. These figures would be replaced after each three years by the actual average cost of providing each benefit. Given, as we have seen, the extraordinary difficulty, indeed the impossibility, of obtaining accurate estimates of costs, it was clearly a trial and error method in which the errors of the federal government would become the provinces' trials.

A complete health insurance service for all the people of Canada would obviously take a number of years to introduce. The cost to the federal and provincial governments would depend on the health benefits provided at any given time. For the full health insurance program, when finally realized, the total estimated cost, for the population shown in the 1941 Census and for benefits as shown in Table 1, would be $250 million per annum. On this basis the federal government's share would be $150 million and the provincial governments' share $100 million.

On the same assumptions, the estimated payments by the federal government for the various stages are shown in table 2:

3. *Health grants.* The health grants were substantially those which have already been discussed but the government had removed the condition that they would be available only if the province introduced health insurance. It therefore stated that it was giving consideration to providing a series of grants without waiting for the inauguration of health insurance.

4. *Financial assistance in the construction of hospitals.* This offer was entirely new. The proposal was that the federal government should provide loans to the provincial governments for necessary expansion of hospital facilities at a rate of interest equal to or only slightly above the cost of such loans to the Dominion, and that the interest and amortization would

TABLE 2

COST TO THE FEDERAL GOVERNMENT OF INITIAL BENEFITS UNDER
HEALTH INSURANCE (IN THOUSANDS OF DOLLARS)

Province	General practitioner service	Hospital care	Visiting nursing service	Total
Prince Edward Island	342	206	34	582
Nova Scotia	2,081	1,248	208	3,587
New Brunswick	1,646	988	165	2,799
Quebec	11,995	7,197	1,199	20,391
Ontario	13,636	8,181	1,363	23,180
Manitoba	2,627	1,576	263	4,466
Saskatchewan	3,256	1,935	323	5,514
Alberta	2,866	1,720	287	4,873
British Columbia	2,944	1,767	294	5,005
Total cost to *federal* government	41,393	24,818	4,136	70,347

SOURCE: Federal-Provincial Conference, 1945, *Proceedings*, p. 91.

be payable out of the hospital care benefit under the health insurance grant, or out of the tuberculosis or the mental health grant, as the case might be. No estimate of the total to be available in this loan fund was presented.

With this extraordinary range of proposals and program strategies for post-war reconstruction occupying all of the first day, the conference adjourned at 10:45 p.m. The price to be paid by the provinces was to be announced the next morning.

The second day's agenda dealt with the tax-sharing proposals. The Dominion government stated that new financial arrangements should meet four requirements if they were to be acceptable to the Canadian people.

First, they should make possible the reorganization of the taxation system carefully designed to encourage rather than restrict enterprise, investment, and employment.

Second, the Dominion should have the financial resources to finance, when necessary, substantial deficits with unquestionable credit. The counterpart of this was that the provincial governments should be assured of more stable revenues.

Third, they should make possible at least an adequate minimum standard of services in all provinces while not denying to any province the advantages which its resources give to it nor the freedom to establish its own standards.

Fourth, the Dominion-provincial financial arrangements must be such as to strengthen, not weaken, the federal system established by the Constitution. They must be such as to give to the provincial governments a dependable financial basis on which to operate and assure them the freedom to make the decisions for which they were responsible, independently of the Dominion.

The federal government thereupon proposed:

1. That after the war-time agreements the provincial governments should by agreement forego the imposition of personal income taxes, corporation taxes and succession duties, leaving the Dominion government full and exclusive access to these revenue sources.

2. As a condition of such agreement the Dominion would substantially expand its present payments to the provincial governments under an arrangement which would ensure stable revenues and provide for their growth in proportion to increases in population and per capita national production.

3. There should be an agreement under which the provincial govern-

ments would commit themselves not to withdraw before an initial trial period of, say, three years.[117]

The minister of finance pointed out that by the Dominion's assuming responsibility for unemployment assistance and for old age pensions, by giving priority to provincial governments in the revenue field of taxation of mining and logging profits, by increasing the sums to be transferred from the current $125 million to as much as an estimated $215 million on the basis of 1944 per capita incomes, the net result would be to assure each provincial government of a surplus, in some cases a large surplus, on current account under average post-war conditions. "To sum up," he said, "it is the belief of the Dominion government that the proposed financial arrangements, in conjunction with the other measures recommended, would strengthen the Federal system under which all ten governments here represented function. They would give to each government an assured basis of financial responsibility and freedom of decision in the matters entrusted to it by the Constitution."[118]

With the completion of the federal proposals, presentations were made by each of the premiers, several of which were primarily courtesy replies, but from Nova Scotia, Manitoba, Prince Edward Island, and Saskatchewan there were substantial briefs, those of Manitoba and Saskatchewan being highly consistent with the federal viewpoint.

The policy had been announced and the offers made. Now all efforts were focused on the strategy of winning acceptance.

STRATEGY (SECOND STAGE)

On the third day of the conference (August 8), the Steering Committee composed of the prime minister and the nine provincial premiers met in the morning and agreed to set up a Continuing Coordinating Committee of the same membership. The functions of the committee were to supervise and coordinate the work of six continuing committees of civil servants, responsible respectively for (1) financial arrangements, (2) public investment, (3) social security, (4) agriculture, (5) labour, (6) housing. The Coordinating Committee met again on Friday, August 10, and agreed that it would reconvene about three months later on November 26; that in the meantime each provincial government would study the Dominion proposals and those of other governments; that further details of the proposals of the respective governments would be circulated; that the secretary of the Coordinating Committee, Mr. Alex Skelton, would be responsible for keeping all the governments informed of all relevant matters that developed, and supplying such additional information as might be required.

The conference adjourned at 3:20 p.m. on Friday, August 10.

The six continuing committees maintained a flow of information among the several governments, but at the end of October it was decided that Alex Skelton should tour the provinces and obtain a first hand report on the initial provincial responses to so vast a range of proposals. posals.

His major findings were:

1. It is likely that all provinces, except Quebec, will have more or less elaborately prepared statements.

2. Mr. Drew expressed an official desire to cooperate and emphasized the necessity of reaching an agreement. The province appears ready to accept the transfer of tax fields but will strongly oppose the per capita subsidy and will press as an alternative method of redistribution for some formula based on tax collections in each province. They do not like the proposed 20 percent timing grant or the health insurance plan; they would much prefer to see an extension of public health grants.

3. Mr. Duplessis was not prepared to commit himself in respect to any of the major proposals, although he did indicate that he had no fundamental objections to the tax transfers in the manner proposed provided the constitution was not changed and that the deal was financially favourable to Quebec. It would not seem likely that there would be any counter-proposals from Quebec or even prepared criticisms of the Dominion proposals but that Mr. Duplessis will adopt a fence-sitting, wait-and-see position.

4. It was apparent after the talks with Ontario and Quebec that British Columbia's position may be of critical importance. While neither Ontario nor Quebec like the Proposals, it seems clear that neither wishes to take the responsibility of directly opposing them. If British Columbia should flatly oppose them as being completely unacceptable, Ontario and Quebec could support British Columbia without the same onus. If British Columbia should not oppose the Proposals, it would appear likely that while Ontario and Quebec would quibble and stall they would at least have to go through the motions of giving them further consideration.

In general, the national Old Age Pension Proposals are popular, but the joint Dominion-Provincial Old Age Assistance Plan is less so. Opinion was more divided on the health proposals. The four western provinces all officially favour, Manitoba and Saskatchewan enthusiastically, the earliest possible introduction of health insurance. All provinces would welcome increased health grants. . . . Immediate introduction of the Planning Grant with no strings attached would be very popular.[119]

The Coordinating Committee (the committee of first ministers) met, as scheduled, in Ottawa on November 26, 1945. Prime Minister King opened the Conference by stating:

As tangible evidence of the Federal government's desire to achieve cooperation with the provincial governments and to speed up the work of reconstruction, it is our intention to appropriate necessary funds at this session of Parliament to provide at January 1, 1946 the planning grants for Health Insurance and the planning grants for public works as outlined in the Dominion Proposals [and] to make the grants available on January 1st without requiring any commitment other than an undertaking to report in an approved manner on the expenditure and the findings.[120]

As a result of a number of specific criticisms and counter-proposals it was agreed that the situation had moved beyond the technical level and needed detailed consideration at the ministerial level. Accordingly, the Coordinating Committee constituted an "Economic Committee" of three representatives (including one Cabinet minister) from each province, and three from the federal government, including Brooke Claxton as chairman. It agreed to reconvene on January 28, 1946.

The Economic Committee held meetings from December 4 to 14 and again from January 8 to 18. It examined in great detail the cost estimates, the financial proposals, and especially the impact on provinces of the latter. On December 13 and 14, it turned its attention to the health proposals. There was general agreement that the *per capita* cost of hospitalization would be at least $6.00. On the question of federal financing, Chairman Claxton indicated that a three to five percent income tax, possibly with a maximum of $125 for a single person and $200 for a married person, might be introduced.

Some of the provinces argued that it would be disadvantageous to them in their efforts to raise health insurance revenues if this tax were described as a health insurance levy. It was noted by Claxton that a major portion of the revenue from the tax would be required for old age pensions.

As a result of the various provincial representations, and the discussions in the Economic Committee, it was necessary for the federal government again to reconsider some aspects of its health insurance offer. Accordingly, the Cabinet Working Committee on Health Insurance met on January 4. It was agreed that the Dominion would not regard acceptance by every province of the health insurance proposals as essential to a financial agreement. The committee was of the opinion that it would require five years for any province to complete the first stage of health insurance and that the earlier proposal calling for the provision of those services within two years was unrealistic. It therefore recommended that the federal proposals be amended to read, "A province's participation in health insurance would begin upon its making an agreement with the federal government to provide the initial services in the First Stage within a period to be stated in the agreement. The agreement should provide for a registration fee to be paid by or on behalf of every person, who has attained his sixteenth birthday and whose normal place of residence is in the province or area where benefits are provided, for a registration, accounting and reporting system, for the cost of administration within the province to be paid out of money provided by the provincial government, and such other provisions and conditions that may be agreed to between the Provincial government and the Federal government. The provision of the services in the Later Stages may be provided in the light of the reports of the Provincial Planning and Organization staffs on the requirements of the provinces in the field of essential medical, hospital and related services."[121]

To this point, apart from a general hostility on the part of Premier Drew and a seeming lack of cooperation (Ontario was the only province not to be represented by a minister in the Economic Committee), there had been little indication of the Ontario response. But on January 8, the waiting ended as Ontario submitted its brief to the Economic Committee and simultaneously released it to the press, making clear that the federal proposals were unacceptable in principle.

Stressing that the 1942 rental of income tax, corporation tax, and succession duties had been for a wartime emergency period only, the brief emphasized the post-war necessity for provincial governments to increase their expenditures very greatly:

If the provincial governments, and in turn the provincial legislatures, were to abandon their most important sources of direct taxation in return for an annual payment on a fixed basis, they would place themselves in a legislative strait-jacket from which they could only escape by abandoning still further powers in return for added payments at some date in the future. If the provincial governments placed themselves in such a position that they were only able to expand their activity with the approval of the Dominion Government, they would become little more than local administrative commissions of the Dominion Government, and the provincial legislatures would cease to possess anything but the form of administrative responsibility.

No matter what the intention may be, the almost inevitable result which would follow the acceptance of such an arrangement would be the ultimate abandonment of the Federal System in favour of a Unitary System of government in Canada. The steady whittling down of provincial rights of taxation would produce a limitation of legislative independence which could only have the effect of rapidly increasing the centralized power of the Dominion Government.[122]

There followed a list of eleven objections to the federal proposals, the chief being that the payment of large unconditional subsidies to the provinces violated the principle that a government which is autonomous within its assigned jurisdiction should be charged with the responsibility of raising the money which it spends, subject to the approval of the legislative body. The objection to the health financing proposals was that "The Dominion government . . . proposes that the provinces finance their share of the cost of health insurance by the collection of a fee or tax to be paid by every person over sixteen years of age . . . the provinces would experience the utmost difficulty in underwriting health insurance services financed by such an unsatisfactory form of taxation."[123]

The brief then presented a number of alternative proposals, the most important being (1) that the Dominion government return the fields of personal and corporate income taxes and the succession duties to the provinces, withdraw from six tax fields completely (succession duties, gasoline, amusement, race-track paramutuel, security transfers, and electricity); and (2) that there be established a National Adjustment Fund to which all provinces would contribute ten percent of its revenues from the personal and corporation income taxes and succession duties, to be apportioned among provinces unable to maintain a national minimum of social services. It would have been difficult to design a set of proposals more at variance with those of the Dominion.

On the following day, January 9, the brief of the Saskatchewan government was released. It was highly detailed, covering fifty-six pages of the printed proceedings.[124] On the financial proposals, Saskatchewan objected to the fact that the principle of the national adjustment grant proposed in the Rowell-Sirois Royal Commission Report had been abandoned and that, therefore, the principle of fiscal need did not obtain in the new proposals. But, for our purposes here, the section on health insurance was the most interesting. Its salient points were the following:

1. Although health is clearly a matter of provincial jurisdiction, we recognize that a proper equalization of resources for health services can be achieved only through Federal assistance to the provinces. So essential do we consider Dominion-Provincial cooperation in this field,

that we strongly urge full consideration of the health proposals irrespective of whether agreement is reached on the other Dominion
Proposals.

2. The concept of two stages should be modified. It seems to us that
the Federal government should be prepared to contribute to the cost
of these later-stage services whenever they are ready to be introduced.
... we suggest that if a service can be introduced for a restricted
geographical area, it should also be possible to introduce it for a
restricted group in the population.

3. The suggestion that a portion of the Federal contributions might
be financed by a "Social Security Tax" raises peculiar administrative
problems. ... in the eyes of the taxpayer one of these taxes will be
regarded as duplication, and the public will feel that it is paying twice
for the same service. We submit that the Dominion is the logical
authority to collect the tax, since it will be the only authority collecting
income tax under the fiscal proposals, but the proceeds of the tax
should be shared by the provinces. [Because of the unreliability of the
cost estimates] the Federal government is, in fact, asking the provinces
to bear 100 percent of the risks arising out of the miscalculation in the
estimates. We feel that the Dominion should, in fairness, share the
risks with the provinces by assuming at least 50 percent of any excess
in actual provincial costs over the general Canadian estimate.[125]

The brief also raised the question of financial assistance in the construction of hospitals and recommended that the federal government
adopt a proposal then in the United States Congress (the Wagner-
Murray-Dingell Bill) which would make available to the states loans and
grants for hospital construction. The two briefs of Ontario and Saskatchewan revealed in stark terms the persistent dilemma for the national
government of a federal system composed of "have" and "have-not"
provinces.

The committee of experts immediately went to work to analyze the
implications of Premier Drew's brief for a meeting of the Cabinet on
January 23, in anticipation of the reconvening of the Coordinating
Committee on January 28, 1945.

The complexity, indeed in the minds of the federal experts, the un-
workability, of the Drew proposals boded ill for the conference, depending
on the degree of Mr. Drew's commitment to them. It was also clear—
especially to Clark, MacKintosh, and Skelton—that it would be necessary
to increase the *per capita* grant offer to the provinces from $12 to $15.[126]

The turn of events obviously distressed MacKenzie King who wrote
in his diary, "I voiced again my feeling of concern at the method of

Federal proposed finances which made one government the taxing power and the other governments the spending power. From the Federal government's point of view this was a double concern as taxing business is the unpopular end. From the point of view of economic and public finance I do not see how this system can be defended."[127] He seemed, nevertheless, to admit to himself the impossibility of changing the course of those events: "The experts seem to think that Drew will have to yield his point of view to pressure from the provinces. I am pretty sure that Drew will follow Duplessis in opposing the other provinces. It will mean the whole business will fall through, if he does."[128]

The Coordinating Committee met on January 18. It had before it the Economic Committee's analyses of the federal and various provincial proposals, the most important, of course, being those of Ontario.

The alternatives in meeting the needs of both the Dominion and the provinces, as MacKenzie King outlined them in his opening statement, were three:

1. By double taxation, as before the War, with both levels of government levying income, corporation, inheritance, and a number of other, taxes.

2. By increasing provincial taxes and by transferring taxes collected in one province to another [the Drew proposals].

3. By extending and adapting to peacetime conditions the wartime arrangements [the Dominion proposals].

As the meetings progressed, it appeared that the provinces were coming close to agreement on the income and corporation taxes. Premier Drew did not press his proposals but both he and Duplessis remained adamant on the succession duties.

In the strategy meetings of Cabinet and meetings of King with individual ministers, it became clear that there was a widening cleavage between King's views and those of Finance Minister Ilsley and his advisers. Of the succession duties, King observed, "I think we could afford to let the provinces collect. I also think they are right in seeking to get an undertaking [that we] would not invade the direct tax fields ... beyond what we have already gone and I should think that we might well afford to [let them] have certain definite taxes exclusively. It [the federal stance] was a line shaped out pretty much by Clark ... and Towers [the governor of the Bank of Canada] ... [who] feel that they could not map out the budget unless we had absolute control of the whole field of taxation."[129]

"It is," he added, "quite apparent neither Ontario nor Quebec will give up this field. Personally I do not blame them. I find myself very strongly of the position that Ontario and Nova Scotia are taking, namely, that provinces should be left with certain definite fields of taxation, the Dominion ditto, and subsidies reduced to as small a margin as possible. The Finance Department, behind which is the Bank of Canada, have completely changed the generally accepted procedure which has been to keep as largely as possible the spending authority responsible for the tax-raising."[130]

It was clear that the proposals from the bureaucracy ran counter to King's political instincts.[131]

The meeting of the Coordinating Committee (composed of first ministers) ended without decisions except that it would meet again on April 25.

In the subsequent weeks, the positions of Ontario and Quebec on the one hand and the finance group in Ottawa on the other were apparently becoming firmer. In addition, Finance Minister Ilsley was becoming increasingly alarmed at the growing magnitude of the post-war budgetary requirements and this imposed additional constraints on any suggestion for making the financial proposals more attractive to the provinces.

The meeting opened on Thursday, April 25, and Duplessis, for the first time, presented a formal brief. It offered little comfort to the federal government. Basing his case, as Premier Drew had done, on the "contract theory" of Confederation, Premier Duplessis argued that the sources of revenue requested by the federal government, "by their very nature, fall within the jurisdiction of the province, are required by the province and are subject to a Constitutional right of priority which belongs to the province."[132] He also insisted that the succession duties were solely the prerogative of the provinces since estates come within the scope of civil law. If the federal proposals were accepted, the budgetary deficit of Quebec for the years 1945–46 would amount to approximately $45 million. He concluded that:

> the financial proposals of the Dominion government tend to replace the system of fiscal autonomy of the provinces in the field of taxation, with a system of grants which would allow the Dominion government to exercise over them a financial tutelage control. Such a system is incompatible with their sovereignty.
>
> [With respect to health insurance] the Government of the Province of Quebec has concerned itself and will continue to concern itself with the problem of health insurance. It realizes, however, that the plan proposed by the Federal authorities is, by common consent, imperfectly elaborated, that it cannot be carried into execution in its present form and that it contains principles that are incompatible with the autonomy of the province. . . . legislation of this type, assigned ex-

clusively to the central government, would inevitably lead to Federal interference in all these fields [of hospitals, charitable institutions, education, regulation of the professions] which ought to be free of Dominion authority.

The Federal Minister of National Health and Welfare stated that the government would levy, to defray part of the necessary expenses, a five percent additional tax on the income of all taxpayers without exception. Such a measure, besides increasing the percentage of the national income absorbed by Federal taxation, will reduce still more the financial possibilities of the province of Quebec.[133]

Quebec had now rejected both the financial and the social security proposals.

Premier Drew refused to state any changes in the Ontario position until the conference reconvened in public session. On Friday the Coordinating Committee decided that it should report to the full-scale Dominion-Provincial Conference on Monday.

The Cabinet took advantage of the weekend adjournment to hold a special meeting on Saturday. King reiterated his view that the "Provinces ought to be given some fields of taxation for themselves. That we should lessen the amounts we were giving to them as payments for the fields they had surrendered or cause them to give us an amount of payment for the fields of taxation we were allowing them to take and to work a settlement on that basis. . . . That we were going far too rapidly with some of our social legislation. . . . the family allowances was right but all these grants to provinces for different health measures, etc., were simply handing from the Federal Treasury so much money to provinces to spend in ways which were helping them to fight us politically and were not economical. Howe made a very good proposal that the amusement tax be left to the provinces. They, to surrender the health grants. I favoured that."[134]

The Cabinet decided:

1. To increase the guaranteed minimum annual payment from $12 to $15 *per capita*.

2. The provinces would undertake not to levy income, corporation, or succession duty taxation.

3. If a province wished to continue to levy succession duties . . . the total annual payments to the province by the Dominion would be reduced by the amount of such credits. The Dominion would undertake not to enter the fields of real estate taxation and automobile licenses.

4. The Dominion would also undertake not to increase its special excise taxes on gasoline, amusements, or pari-mutuel betting. The Dominion would be prepared to consider withdrawing from any tax field in return for an adequate financial equivalent. It would be prepared to withdraw from the amusement tax field in consideration of its not paying the public health grants.[135]

These four changes and the other proposals with respect to public investment, health, and old age pensions were presented to the Conference on Monday.

Mr. Drew then restated the Ontario government position. His government was prepared to vacate and rent for an annual cash payment, as proposed by the Dominion government, the fields of corporation and personal income taxes for the term of a transitional tax agreement. In return, the Dominion government would vacate and undertake not to re-enter during the term of the agreement the fields of taxation (named above) and would recognize priority of provincial taxation with respect to mining and logging operations. The Dominion government would assume the full cost of relief for unemployed employables and the full cost of old age pensions and pensions for the blind. The statutory subsidies payable to the provinces under the BNA Act would continue to be paid.[136]

Mr. Drew then presented for the first time an algebraic formula for the calculation of the rental to be paid by the Dominion government, which related the amount of payment in accordance with increases in the gross national product and population, this to be multiplied by "X" dollars. It was not possible to calculate the total cost to the federal government because at this point, Premier Drew attached no dollar value to "X."

On Wednesday afternoon, Mr. Ilsley summed up the situation from his perspective as finance minister.

1. All provinces appear to believe that some agreement is essential, indeed urgent.

2. All provinces are willing for appropriate compensation and under certain conditions to allow the Dominion exclusive use of the personal and corporate income tax fields; six provinces are willing similarly to vacate the succession duty field, a seventh is willing to do so if there is substantial agreement, and two provinces have, to say the least, a strong preference for sole possession of this field by themselves.

3. Three provinces [Manitoba, Saskatchewan, and Alberta] have agreed to accept the Dominion Proposals as they stand. Only one province [Ontario] has submitted what might be called an alternative

to the Dominion's proposals. This proposal does not differ very greatly in kind from the Dominion Proposals, but its effect would be to throw so great a net increase in obligations upon the Dominion that it could not be accepted by the Dominion. Nor has any other province expressed the view that it would be acceptable to it.

4. The remaining five provinces expressed a desire to see some changes in the Dominion Proposals, most of which would be of some benefit to themselves at the expense of the Dominion.[137]

At the end of Wednesday's session, a few ministers met in King's office to review the deadlock. King felt that Ilsley now

saw that what I had been telling him all along was only too true. That it was a mistake to hold on to all those little taxes; that we should have come out and tried to give the provinces at least two or three small fields of their own. . . . I am perfectly sure . . . that public feeling in all the provinces would be against centralization . . . but you cannot get Clark, whose mind is wholly academic, to realize that no matter how theoretically accurate you may be or in accord with strict financial rules that what you are doing is no good unless you can get the public to understand and support it.[138]

On Thursday, Premier Drew finally stated his proposed value of "X," namely, $12. Quick calculations by Ilsley's experts indicated that it would cost the Dominion government in the neighbourhood of $100 million more per year.[139]

On Friday morning Ilsley produced a more accurate calculation of the costs of the Ontario proposal, prepared by the finance experts overnight, and these raised the additional cost above the Dominion proposals to a minimum of $134 million and, conceivably, as much as $200 million. At this stage the discussions became quite acrimonious and despite valiant efforts by Premiers Garson and Douglas to work out realistic compromises, it was clear that the conference was ending. Mr. Duplessis left at noon for Quebec City and did not attend the afternoon session. At that session the Hon. Mr. Claxton commented on the Ontario proposals, reviewed the Dominion's proposals for old age pensions and health insurance, and then added:

I mention these points to indicate that the Dominion plan was not only a plan for an adjustment with regard to taxes but it was a plan which was comprehensive and which aimed to deal with the main needs and desires of the Canadian people. Unfortunately, in the discussion too much emphasis has been allowed to be placed on the tax provisions. They are important, very important to everyone, including the Treasurers of the provinces but they are by no means the whole story.[140]

The conference adjourned, *sine die* at 5:33 p.m.[141] In his diary, MacKenzie King wrote that night,

Claxton made a speech of some length presenting the social legislation side of which earlier mention had been made by those who had spoken and which is now in a way being cast to the winds. . . . Claxton being on one of the Committees has pushed the social legislation to make too many commitments in the matter of social reform, particularly any commitments for legislation involving more in the way of taxation by a levy on all classes. . . . the public simply will not stand for it at this time and it is not right. We have done enough. . . . and [must] allow these social measures to follow on later.[142]

More than six and a half years had passed since Ian MacKenzie's first memorandum on health insurance to MacKenzie King, almost five years since the Cabinet had authorized by order-in-council the appointment of the Inter-Departmental Committee on Health Insurance.

In the policy-making process health insurance had been moved from abstract idea to specific form with the publication of the Heagerty report with its model bills. The proposal had come under intense analysis and discussion, with vast attendant publicity in the House of Commons Committee. It had been favourably considered by a conference of provincial health ministers and their deputies, and its financial provisions had been modified by a Finance Committee.

Then it had been moved out of the direct control of the Health Department to become part of the Dominion post-war design for Canada, developed by the Cabinet Committee on Dominion-Provincial Relations. There it had gained acceptance as it had not before, as Government policy, but the gain was partly offset by its becoming dependent upon other parts of a complex negotiating package.

The final stage of the policy development process—the strategy of implementation—was the Dominion-Provincial Conference. There, health insurance was always one of the major proposals, especially attractive to the western provinces, but, in the hard bargaining over revenue sources, it, like retirement pensions, came to take a secondary place, a desirable program that could be postponed.

As Claxton ruminated, in the dying moments of the conference, "At times it was made to appear as if the gasoline tax alone stood in the way of an agreement."[143]

With the collapse of the conference, the health insurance proposals were, if not dead, at least, in limbo. And, yet, it is necessary to consider the positive results that six years of analysis, creative design, and protracted negotiations had produced. What were the outcomes?

THE OUTCOMES

1. The health status of Canadians had been brought into public focus as never before. The rejection rates, for physical and mental reasons, of potential recruits to the armed forces had generated a shocking impact on public awareness. High infant and maternal mortality rates, and mortality and morbidity rates from preventable diseases were equally alarming.

2. The disparity among Canadian provinces and between urban and rural populations in availability of and access to medical and hospital services became, for the first time, a matter of national awareness and concern.

3. The economic barrier to needed health services for individuals was highlighted as never before, and the concomitant economic effects on medical practitioners and hospital financing were revealed in their stark and shameful reality.

4. There began to develop a new appreciation among politicians, health professions, and scores of public associations of the potentialities of what Winston Churchill had once called: "The magic of insurance."

5. A governmental planning group had been established under the direction of the dedicated and imaginative Dr. J. J. Heagerty which had brought together, for the first time, the statistical and financial data and the practical administrative concepts for using the insurance mechanism to solve the economic problems of health services.

6. The health professions, and especially the medical profession (and many of its members not unwillingly), had been forced to come to grips with the prospect of the people acting through their governments to introduce an entirely new relationship of doctor to patient: an end to assessment of an individual patient's capacity to pay, an end to mediocre incomes because of practice in economically depressed communities, an end to unpaid bills, but on the other hand, the beginning of the need to accept a wholly new situation—the participation of a third party in the financial nexus between patient and provider of service.

7. The majority of provincial governments, previously relatively unconcerned with the economic and health problems of their citizens, had now to face both an aroused public opinion and, for the first time, the prospects of the compelling pressures of federal grants inducing them to action in an area clearly of provincial constitutional jurisdiction, and despite the fact that for some of them there was neither ideological commitment nor political party rivalry justifying the political, administrative, and financial hazards.

8. Most important of all, there had been developed, and enunciated for all to ponder, a national initiative that might be postponed, but not permanently ignored, to act in behalf of the average citizen who daily faced the potentially catastrophic physical and financial consequences of unpredictable illness, accident, and disability.

Although the collapse of the conference had delayed action for the time being, all the other outputs were positive. Only a propitious concatenation of political forces was necessary for the next act in the drama of health insurance. In fact, the next act had already begun.

Chapter Two

The Saskatchewan Hospital Services Plan:
The Policy Decision To Go It Alone

THE FIRST ACT of the drama of health insurance had witnessed the failure of the Dominion-Provincial Conference to agree on the reallocation of tax resources and, with its collapse, the crumbling of the foundations of the hoped-for edifice of a national program of social security.

For the second act, the scene shifted to western Canada, a new cast of actors came on stage, and the action began in what seemed at the time to be merely a sub-plot but which, in the perspective of hindsight, came to be seen as the first decisive action in the long chain of events leading to our present system. Shortly after the opening of the conference in August 1945, and long before its demise, the Government of Saskatchewan had decided to launch one part of the health insurance program on its own initiative.

In retrospect, it was, paradoxically, the last province to be expected to act independently and, at the same time, and for the same reasons, the one in which planned and concerted public action was most necessary. As a result, the Saskatchewan decision not only accelerated the timetable but had a major influence in shaping the course of the development of health insurance in Canada. We shall first examine the background against which the decision was taken.

BACKGROUND

The social and economic characteristics of the province and people of Saskatchewan, and the special problems attendant upon pioneering the flat prairie lands to develop a one-crop or "wheat economy" are well known. In 1946, sixty percent of the population was rural, scattered over vast distances, with an average population density of three people per square mile.

The sparse population, the limited resources, and the high risk and uncertainty of a single export agricultural commodity inspired the pioneers to group action both in the development of efficient agencies for the marketing of their wheat and in providing essential social services. As a result the cooperative movement flourished in Saskatchewan on a scale unknown in other Canadian provinces. Professor S. M. Lipsett reported that in 1945 the average farmer belonged to four or five cooperatives.[1] Moreover, as we shall now see, the institution of local government was used to develop health services also to a degree unmatched elsewhere in Canada. Three different but related programs were created.

1. *The municipal doctor system.* Although the "municipal doctor system" was superseded in 1962 by the province-wide medical care program, in its time it fulfilled a major role in the medical economy of Saskatchewan and, to a lesser extent, in Alberta and Manitoba. The idea received both national and international publicity when the United States Committee on the Costs of Medical Care published a monograph on the system prepared by Dr. C. Rufus Rorem.[2] In its main report the committee recommended the adoption of the system in similar areas of the United States.

The origin of the municipal doctor system is almost a legend in Saskatchewan. In 1914, the rural municipality of Sarnia was about to lose its physician and, as an inducement for the doctor to stay, the rural municipal council, without legislative authority, offered the doctor an annual retainer fee of $1,500.[3] In 1916, the Rural Municipality Act[4] was amended by the provincial Legislature to grant authority to rural municipal councils to levy for this purpose. Following the war, rural areas found it difficult to attract doctors and, in 1919, the act was further revised to allow a municipality to pay a doctor a maximum salary of $5,000 for basic "general practitioner service." With the municipal doctor system thus legally launched, further amendments between 1919 and 1925 granted authority to villages and towns to enter into similar agreements[5] and in 1932, enabling parts of municipalities or two or more municipalities to cooperate in engaging the services of a physician.[6]

The terms of the contracts varied but the majority required the provision of a general medical service including minor surgery, maternity care, and general public health work. In certain circumstances, if the physician were qualified, major surgery was also included, and in 1937 the act was amended to require a separate contract if major surgery were provided.[7]

70

As a result of initiatives by the rural and urban municipal associations, there was passed at the 1939 session of the Legislature the Municipal Medical and Hospital Services Act.[8] The act permitted a municipality or a group of rural municipalities, villages, or towns to provide medical or hospital services by levying either a land or a personal tax or a combination of the two, such annual tax not to exceed $50 per family. Municipal councils were thus enabled to obtain some contribution from non-property owners toward the cost of medical services.

As attested to by its consistent expansion in terms of the number of municipalities, people, and doctors involved, it can be concluded that within certain inherent limitations the municipal doctor system had been reasonably successful. The comprehensive list of changes and amendments shows that its history was one of experimentation in the development of a service increasingly satisfactory to all parties concerned. Its chief advantage was that it served as a substantial inducement to a doctor to settle in a rural area in that it provided a new medical graduate a fairly sure means of rapidly establishing a practice and obtaining an assured income. Nonetheless, the system had a number of shortcomings and, in comparison with prepaid medical care obtainable in urban areas after World War II, left much to be desired.[9]

2. *The union hospital system.* As early as 1916 legislative provision was made for the combining of towns, villages, and rural municipalities in union hospital districts to establish local authorities for the purpose of erecting and maintaining a hospital.[10] Over the years the UHD system steadily expanded. By 1920 there were ten UHD's; by 1930 there were twenty. Only three were established in the 1930s and three more in the early 1940s to bring the total to twenty-six. In 1945 and 1946, with the incentives of the new CCF government's hospital construction grants, thirty-three new UHD's were created and steps were being taken to organize eleven more in 1947 for a total of seventy-eight. These districts covered more than one-third of the settled area of the province, included approximately one-third of the population, and provided about three-eighths of all of the province's hospital beds.[11]

3. *Municipal hospital care plans.* Less widely known than either the union hospital system or the municipal doctor system was the method of providing for payment for hospital care by the municipalities from general tax revenues.

Under the original Rural Municipalities Act passed in 1909, one of the duties of a municipal council was to pass bylaws for the purpose of granting "aid or relief to any needy person who is a resident of the municipality."[12]

In addition to providing hospital care for indigents, a number of municipalities began paying the hospital bills for all their ratepayers and collecting the necessary revenue through the general land tax. So far as can be determined, by 1927 at least ten were providing prepaid hospital care to their residents in this manner, although there was no statutory authority for such an arrangement.[13]

The first legislation in Canada to provide for a municipal hospital care plan for all residents of an area was the passage in 1919 of a special act to establish the Lloydminster Union Hospital District. While all other districts had been established by order-in-council under authority of the Union Hospital Act, a special act was required in this instance because, since Lloydminster straddles the Alberta-Saskatchewan border, joint action was required by both provincial legislatures. The act provided that "the Council of the Town of Lloydminster, the Rural Municipality of Britannia and the Rural Municipality of Wilton may enter into agreement with each other to provide money for the maintenance and extension of the said hospital *and for the payment of the expenses of their respective ratepayers and residents when patients in the said hospital.*"[14]

With the Lloydminster Act as an example, and in view of the number of other municipalities that were adopting similar programs, it was decided in 1927 to amend the Union Hospital Act and the Rural Municipality Act to provide legislative authority for these municipal hospital care plans.[15] In 1936 this arrangement was extended to towns and villages.[16]

As in the municipal doctor plans, the sole source of revenue for the support of these plans was the general land tax. In 1934 the Rural Municipality Act was amended to empower the council to fix an annual tax for non-rate-payers.[17] This appears to be the first instance in which statutory authority was granted for the levying of a personal tax for health services in Saskatchewan and, indeed, in Canada.

By 1942, eighty-eight municipalities provided their residents hospital services at municipal expense, with twelve obtaining the necessary funds through a personal tax under the Municipal Medical and Hospital Services Act, but with the vast majority providing services under the provisions of the Rural Municipality Act with its more restricted coverage by virtue of its tax on property.[18]

The early organization and development of these three systems—the construction and maintenance of hospital facilities and the prepayment of medical and hospital services through municipal tax levies—are a tribute to local initiative and the understanding of the importance of health services. Although each system had its limitations and obvious weaknesses, together they constituted a remarkable development not duplicated elsewhere in Canada.

But the local government programs were not the only pioneering thrusts; in several cities and towns voluntary, "mutual" plans were being proposed. In 1938, the Mutual Medical and Hospital Benefit Association Act was passed enabling any ten or more persons to incorporate a health insurance plan for its members.[19] Under this act, the Societies Act, and the Companies Act, thirteen different voluntary associations were set up. Not all were successful and in 1951 the Health Survey Committee reported on only four that were still active.[20]

Two other developments both reinforced this local experience and raised it to the provincial level. The first was the Saskatchewan Anti-Tuberculosis League which was a rare combination of governmental and voluntary action. Its most significant feature had again resulted from municipal initiatives. As with all other indigents in need of medical or hospital care, indigent tuberculosis patients were the responsibility of the municipalities. The differences from almost all other illnesses were both the cost of such long term illness and its indiscriminate distribution, with only a few municipalities bearing the brunt of the cost. To overcome this inequity, the municipalities agreed in 1920 to a pooling arrangement whereby, by contributing $100 to The Anti-T. B. League, each municipality in effect purchased insurance against a potentially catastrophic drain on its limited tax resources.

The other program was developed to meet the special requirements for cancer treatment. As a result of a report by a committee of the Saskatchewan College of Physicians and Surgeons in 1929, the Government passed the Cancer Commission Act in 1930. It provided for a Cancer Commission and the concentration of diagnostic and treatment facilities in two clinics located in Regina and Saskatoon. Until 1944, charges were nominal, but in the spring session of the Legislature in 1944, the Cancer Act was amended to provide that all costs of diagnosis, treatment, and hospitalization of cancer patients were to be borne by the provincial government. The clinics were staffed by full-time salaried personnel, including specialists in diagnostic and therapeutic radiology, and became recognized as leading cancer centres in all of Canada. A roster of qualified surgeons in private practice was maintained and any of these who provided treatment were eligible for payment by the commission.

Both programs bore witness to provincial acceptance of the concept of organized governmental action to solve medical economic problems beyond the capacity of the individual, involving both the provision of facilities and services and the removal of the direct financial cost to the individual.

As would be expected in such an environment, there had also been a great deal of discussion about a comprehensive province-wide health insurance program. Both the rural and urban municipal associations had long taken a strong stand favouring provincial action. In 1933, for example, the Urban Municipalities Association resolved "that the Provincial Government immediately institute a plan providing for state hospital treatment and state medical and allied services for the people of the Province."[21]

On June 6, 1933, a conference of representatives of the rural and urban municipal associations, the Saskatchewan Hospital Association, the College of Physicians and Surgeons, and the departments of Municipal Affairs and of Public Health was held for the purpose of finding some solution to their mutual health service problems. The meeting decided to recommend the principle of compulsory contributory health insurance and the continuation of a study of the application of such a system to Saskatchewan through local, provincial, and Dominion sources of support.[22] However, little interest was forthcoming from the provincial government, already heavily in debt as a result of its expenditures for relief services, or from the Dominion government which, at the time, as we have seen, maintained that the provision of health services was a provincial responsibility.[23]

The problems continued, however, as did the demands from various sources that the provincial government act to relieve the municipal governments of their heavy burden. At the annual meeting in January 1936, the Association of Rural Municipalities overwhelmingly endorsed a resolution urging the Dominion and provincial governments to inaugurate state medicine at the earliest possible date.[24]

Such a wide-spread demand for a solution to the problem of providing medical and hospital services to the population, half of which was in receipt of relief, could not be entirely ignored by the provincial government. The return of the Liberals to power in 1934 brought the announcement by Dr. J. M. Uhrich, the new minister of public health, that his department intended to compile a report similar to that prepared by the British Columbia Royal Commission.[25] So far as action was concerned, the minister stated that he was inclined to move slowly. Concluding his address in the Budget Debate, he stated: "It is all very well to talk glibly of these things but after all, when consideration is given to the amount of money at stake, the amount of taxation it would mean, the number of the people in the province who could not, under present conditions, meet the additional costs, members will agree it is incumbent upon us to move carefully and certainly not before all the facts are available."[26]

Dr. Uhrich was undoubtedly correct in his assessment of the financial capacity of the province to do more than it was doing. As we have seen, the depression of the thirties, accompanied by widespread drought, had in all of Canada its most devastating effects in Saskatchewan. Average annual cash income *per capita* declined in 1933 to $135. By 1937, expenditures for direct and agricultural relief exceeded combined provincial and municipal revenues by sixty-three percent. As the Royal Commission said, "the conditions in Saskatchewan were nothing short of disastrous."[27]

It was in this economic and social environment that the Cooperative Commonwealth Federation (CCF) movement began to develop. In the 1934 elections which returned the Saskatchewan Liberals to power, after a Conservative interlude of four years, the CCF obtained five seats in the fifty-five-seat Legislature and became the official opposition.

In the 1938 election the protest vote was split by the vigorous Social Credit campaign. The results: Liberals thirty-six, CCF ten, Social Credit two, and Independent two, Conservatives 0, with the Liberals having only a plurality instead of the majority of the votes it had enjoyed in 1934. With an increase in the support of the national party in the 1940 federal elections, the CCF waged "an intensive and persistent campaign to break down the Liberal supremacy in the province and to prepare the people for CCF government."[28]

By 1942, economic conditions in the province had improved to such an extent that it was possible to discontinue the grants to doctors and dentists in the former relief areas.[29] The issue of health insurance, however, remained before the Legislature. In a full-dress debate on the issue in 1942, the CCF opposition succeeded in getting a resolution passed that the Legislature "favoured a further extension of state-aided hospitalization and medical services in the province," but not until the minister had insisted on adding the words "as soon as the finances of the province and of the municipalities permit."[30]

With the CCF strength apparently greater than its small minority of members in the Legislature indicated, and with its clarion call for far-reaching reforms, the Patterson government felt under increasing pressure. Its main problem was that its five-year mandate expired in 1943 and that date appeared not to be a propitious time for an election. Two things were needed: more time, and a major issue on which it could campaign.

To meet the first requirement, the Government decided to use the fact that the nation was at war as an excuse to extend the life of the Legislature for one more year.

The announcement by the federal government that it would establish a Special Committee on Social Security fortuitously provided the Government the issue on which it could mount a counter-attack against the CCF which was stressing its commitment to health insurance.

Accordingly, Premier Patterson announced the appointment of a select committee to inquire into "practical measures of further social security and health services for Saskatchewan, the means by which the revenues for such services might be raised, and constitutional limitations affecting joint Dominion-Provincial arrangements."[31] The twenty-five-member

Select Special Committee on Social Security and Health Services conducted public hearings over a period of five weeks, during which it held twenty-three meetings and heard representations from thirty-eight organizations.[32]

The public response at the committee hearings was overwhelming, and because of the short legislative session, the committee was unable to complete its assignment. Furthermore, the committee was uncertain as to the direction its recommendations on health services should take, since the Social Security Committee of the House of Commons had not yet given any indication as to its intentions respecting the draft proposals. The provincial committee felt that its recommendations should lead to the adoption of a system of health services which could easily be integrated into a national system. With a sense of futility, the committee recommended the appointment of an inter-sessional committee which would, it was hoped, have time to come to grips with the issue.[33]

The Government agreed and appointed an intersessional committee[34] but at its meeting held in November 1943, the committee decided that it was "in no better position to recommend a final report inasmuch as members were not yet aware what the Federal Committee proposed to do."[35] It thereupon discussed and agreed upon a number of recommendations to be offered at the beginning of the next session.

The Select Committee on Social Security was re-appointed on February 18, 1944, for the purpose of completing, if possible, the task assigned to the original 1943 committee.[36]

In its final report, the committee observed that representations before the committee had advocated two different types of programs: (1) a system of state medicine financed from taxation in which members of the medical profession would be salaried civil servants; (2) a system of health insurance financed by contributions and with doctors being paid by fee-for-service, by capitation, or by salary. The committee was of the opinion that since federal assistance was a prerequisite to the adoption of a scheme of health services in Saskatchewan, and inasmuch as the Dominion government would probably determine which of the two systems it would support, the choice for Saskatchewan was not theirs to make.

The committee had, however, received a copy of the revised model act prepared by the Heagerty Committee and, on the basis largely of that draft proposal, recommended that the Assembly endorse the principle of health insurance for all the people of the province, (including all the benefits set forth in the proposed draft bill) and that, pending enactment of federal legislation, a commission be appointed to make necessary preparations, including the extension of existing municipal medical and hospital schemes and the possibility of making such schemes compulsory in all municipalities.[37]

Accordingly, on Friday, March 31, 1944, the Government introduced "A Bill Respecting Health Insurance," and gave it first and second reading on the same day.[38]

The bill provided for the appointment of a commission to administer the operation of the proposed Dominion government health insurance program in Saskatchewan. Duties were to include the investigation and consideration of conditions in the province with relation to the benefits, to make inquiries for the purpose of establishing public health and health insurance regions, to make tentative arrangements with hospital boards and professional bodies, and to make reports concerning the administration of health insurance to the minister.

The College of Physicians and Surgeons was taken by surprise. No one had anticipated that an act of such consequence would be introduced so late in the session. A hastily gathered delegation of eight doctors descended on the minister and persuaded him not to proceed to third reading of the bill the same day in order to give them an opportunity "to register a protest and make representations."[39] This was agreed to.

The same delegation again met on Saturday morning with the minister and protested the "startling and embarrassing" manner in which the bill had been introduced without warning and, particularly, a bill which provided neither for medical representation on the commission nor for representative advisory committees. They protested that such an act would "be held up as an example in other parts of the Dominion, and as such, it had its dangerous aspects." What was worse, added one senior member, the fear is that "if the Bill is in effect *when a dangerous element may be forming the Government*, it could have disastrous results." Another member said that if this bill were presented to the College, "not a single member would accept it."[40]

The minister, Dr. Uhrich, reviewed the background of the legislation, and explained that it was only an initiating, enabling bill and, as such, was quite innocuous. Only after action by the federal government would definite decisions be made. The delegation reiterated its objections and the meeting ended.

On Sunday, the entire twenty-one-member Health Insurance Committee met. A protest telegram was sent to Premier Patterson, and a long letter of objections to the minister. Copies of the telegram and the letter were sent to all members of the College.[41]

Despite the College's protests, the bill was passed unanimously, receiving royal assent on April 1, 1944, in the dying days of this last session of the Ninth Legislature. The Liberal government obviously realized that its prospects of administering a program of health insurance depended not only upon prior action by the Dominion government but, more decisively, on the results of the election to be held on June 15, 1944.[42]

The election of 1944 was one of the most bitterly contested in Saskatchewan history. With the exception of the five-year period from 1930 to 1934, the Liberal party had been in power since the formation of the province in 1905. Party standings in the Legislature at the time of dissolution were Liberals, thirty-three, Cooperative Commonwealth Federation, eleven, others, three, vacant, five. When final election returns were in, the CCF had elected a total of forty-seven, the Liberals had been reduced to five. In addition, under special wartime legislation, three representatives of the armed services were elected.[43]

It was against this background that the new government launched, two and one-half years later, the first universal hospital services plan in North America. We shall now examine the reasons why it acted.

THE ACTION IMPERATIVES

Why did Saskatchewan act at this time, on its own, in the face of what was becoming by early 1946 an almost certain deadlock in Dominion-provincial negotiations on health insurance and related issues? The reasons were numerous and complex: economic realities, the legacy of history, and the thrust of new political forces.

1. *The inadequacy of resources.* The shortage of medical doctors in the province had reached near emergency proportions by 1943 by which time the number of civilian doctors had dropped from a pre-war high of 600 to 408.[44] The depression-engendered exodus to other provinces, normal attrition, and more recent military enlistments had dropped Saskatchewan to the second lowest physician-population ratio of any province in Canada (1:2078, as compared to a national average of 1:1261).[45] The dental manpower situation was even more serious, with only 147 dentists in 1943, a decrease from 210 in 1938. But the average figures for the province as a whole obscured the gravity of the situation resulting from unequal distribution between rural and urban areas. The two major urban centres had physician-population ratios of 1:1096 and 1:1343 respectively, but the two most rural regions had ratios of 1:3016 and 1:3430.[46]

In only slight contrast to the deteriorating supply of medical personnel, there had been, even through the depression and continuing through the war, a gradual increase in the number of hospital beds. In 1932, Saskatchewan had 3.59 public hospital beds per 1,000 population, excluding mental hospitals and tuberculosis sanatoria. From 1932 to the end of the war another 700 beds were added and these, with a declining population, resulted in a ratio of 4.75 beds per thousand. However, the data were misleading for even with the construction added in 1945 and 1946,

102 of 133 public hospitals had fewer then twenty-five beds, ten more averaged thirty-six, and the four largest averaged 350. Even so, the supply of available beds was lower in Saskatchewan than in either of the adjoining provinces with their similar problems of sparse settlement and difficult transportation.[47]

The nurse supply situation was also serious. In Ontario, the population per registered nurse in 1942 was 320; in Canada as a whole, 461, but in Saskatchewan it was 696.[48] Public health nurses were even more scarce, with the 1939 population ratio in Saskatchewan 1:30,200 compared with 1:5,914 in Ontario and 1:7,670 in Canada as a whole,[49] or, only one-fifth that of Ontario and one-fourth of the national average. Clearly the situation with respect to health facilities and personnel was deplorably inadequate.

2. *The inadequacies of the municipal hospital plans.* The shortcomings were of three kinds: (i) Of the over 300 rural municipalities, fewer than one-third had introduced hospital insurance plans. Thus residents of more than two-thirds of the rural municipalities, of most of the villages, and all of the towns and cities, except those few insured in the voluntary plans, were not protected at all. (ii) The benefits under all the existing plans were limited. (iii) Many of the municipalities with programs were facing serious difficulty in financing them. A related financial problem was the burden carried by all local governments in meeting the costs of hospital care for indigents.

3. *The climate of opinion.* More than in any other province, with the possible exception of British Columbia, health insurance was, as we have seen, a pervasive subject of public discussion. The College of Physicians and Surgeons had endorsed it, the municipal associations had urged it, and the CCF party had itself contributed to the demand. The proceedings in Ottawa and the passage of a Health Insurance Act by the Saskatchewan Liberal government in its dying days had created mass expectations that something would be done.

4. *Personal and party commitment.* It is a commonplace observation that democratic government is a reactive mechanism, that it acts only (and belatedly) in response to pressures from the external environment. But this deterministic mode is frequently belied when, as we have already seen in the case of the combination of the Hon. Ian Mackenzie and Dr. J. J. Heagerty, political actors decide that there are alternative futures and that political choices can be made as to which one should be pursued. This policy decision was no exception. Tommy Douglas, holding the twin

portfolios of premier and of health minister, was now in a position to make choices about the future, and there was no question about his commitment. As he was to say later in the Legislature:

> I made a pledge with myself long before I ever sat in this House, in the years when I knew something about what it meant to get health services when you didn't have the money to pay for it. I made a pledge with myself that someday if I ever had anything to do with it, people would be able to get health services just as they are able to get educational services, as an inalienable right of being a citizen of a Christian country.[50]

This personal commitment on the part of the leader had, of course, also become a party commitment. The CCF opposition had been instrumental in persuading the Liberal government to set up the Committee on Social Security in 1943. In the election it had stressed its determination to act. Now that it was in power it had to deliver—preferably something dramatic.

5. *Provincial-federal strategy.* There was one new imperative in the balance—what would emerge from the Dominion-Provincial Conference. True, an offer had been made when it opened on August 6, 1945, but there was certain to be tough bargaining ahead. As Mr. Douglas observed, "We had to demonstrate the feasibility of the Plan before the Dominion-Provincial Conference if we were ever going to get federal participation."[51]

Taken together, there was an overwhelming case for a government decision to move forward.

THE CONSTRAINTS

The constraints on action presented a dilemma in that reasons for acting were at the same time reasons for not acting. With the glaring inadequacies of both facilities and personnel, how would it be possible to introduce a universal plan that could result only in unprecedented and perhaps overwhelming demand on the scarce resources? How would the health services system respond to such shock treatment?

A second major constraint was the matter of revenue. Although 1944 was the year of highest farm income in Saskatchewan's history, the need for new farm machinery, and the debts—both private and governmental—remaining from the depression years seriously restrained any idea of imposing new taxes. With the expected release of pent-up demands for a host of public services, the new government faced extraordinary pressures on a seriously limited budget. Not only were provincial revenue sources constricted, there was the additional, serious problem that the capacity of people to bear any additional taxes varied widely from one part of the province to another. Any province-wide program should take such regional disparities into consideration.

Finally, there was the constraint of time. A health services program, or even a major part of it, would be an enormous undertaking, indeed, the largest ever launched by a provincial government in terms of its costs, its organization, and the numbers of people it would affect. Moreover, since many new resources—including administrative capability—would have to be created, or organized, lead time before a program could be operating successfully even under the most favourable conditions would obviously be extremely close to the next election. Given that it would be a pioneering experiment, serious mismanagement or failure of any part of the program could lead to an electoral disaster. Action would need to be swift, but it would also need to be almost immediately and demonstrably successful.

THE UNCERTAINTIES

The first major uncertainty was obviously the question of costs. It was true that about 100 municipalities, villages, and towns were providing their residents with some degree of hospital insurance protection, but these varied widely in the range and extent of benefits.

Studies conducted in 1947 revealed that in 1946 the costs of these programs ranged up to $8.50 *per capita*.[52] The Dominion government estimates at the time (1944) indicated that hospitalization costs would average $4.60 *per capita* but, as we have seen, those estimates were admittedly of dubious validity.

A second uncertainty, given the extreme shortages of facilities and personnel, was whether—even with the now hoped for early end of the war— facilities could be expanded, and personnel recruited and trained rapidly enough, to meet the unleashed demand for services that universal insurance would bring.

But the major uncertainty, as time went on, was whether the federal government would, in fact, adopt a national program and begin to provide federal contributions to provincial programs. And if it did not, could the province, by any reasonable financial and political calculations, "go it alone"?

Finally, there was the uncertainty about cooperation of the medical profession and the hospitals. True, both had indicated a positive attitude toward health insurance. But that had been at a time when a long established party was in control of the government. The response might be quite different when the government was under the control of the socialist CCF.

For the new government of a province whose population had declined by nearly 100,000 in the preceding ten years, which had been struck harder by the depression than any other, and where most incomes depended on the vagaries of weather and international markets, all of these constituted risks and uncertainties of the highest order. In addition, the highest stake of all—political survival to achieve other and equally important objectives—lay in the balance.

The action imperatives were thus overwhelming: both health facilities and personnel were seriously inadequate and only strong publicly organized action could improve them; the economic barriers to needed health services were, for most of the population, individually insurmountable; there was a long tradition of cooperative and local government action pointing the way; and there was now a firm election commitment to be honoured.

THE EXTERNAL CONTRIBUTIONS AND INFLUENCES

There were a number of external factors (or inputs) that impacted on the governmental decision-making process and contributed to the final policy, shaping the program and its administration.

We have seen how the network of municipal medical and hospital services had constituted a partial solution, for part of the population, to the problem of inadequate health services, and how the precarious financial base of the municipal programs had provided one of the major imperatives for action on a province-wide scale. But, of course, these local experiences did more than spur provincial action; they also influenced the shape of the provincial response.

The first contribution was simply the *idea* of insuring by united action, primarily through government agencies, against the economic hazards of illness. This clearly influenced all parties in the enterprise. Past experience had shown that: 1. Individuals through their governments could tax themselves to provide funds for essential health services; 2. these funds could be used to build hospitals, pay doctors, and pay hospitals; 3. municipalities could combine on a province-wide basis to insure against catastrophic costs to any one of them (for example, T.B.); 4. in the case of a specific disease (cancer), provincial government action could mobilize expensive resources and pay for services provided to individuals; 5. municipalities could serve as efficient tax collection agencies for health services.

These were part of the positive legacy of the past in Saskatchewan in the mid-forties. But, equally important were the views and demands of a number of organized interest groups.

1. *The Saskatchewan College of Physicians and Surgeons (CP&S)*. As we have noted, many in the medical profession in Saskatchewan had suffered economic disaster along with the rest of the population during the 1930s, and many physicians received payments of $50 or $75 per month from the Saskatchewan Relief Commission.[53]

In February 1933, a meeting of the college was held to receive the report of its Special Committee on Health Insurance which recommended that "in Saskatchewan the principle of health insurance should be followed, the patient should have free choice of doctor, and the doctor should be paid for services rendered."[54]

With the invitation, in 1941, by Dr. Heagerty to the CMA to form a committee to advise him in the preparation of his report, the Saskatchewan division, like the others, began an intensive study of health insurance. The result of these deliberations was the adoption, at its annual meeting in Regina in September 1942, of the following resolution:

> Resolved that the College of Physicians and Surgeons of Saskatchewan inform the Government of Saskatchewan that we are in favour of state-aided Health Insurance on a reasonable fee-for-service-rendered-basis provided that the administration of such an arrangement is put into the hands of a non-political independent commission on which the medical profession is adequately represented by its own representatives elected by and responsible only to the College of Physicians and Surgeons.[55]

It was against this background that the College submitted its brief to the Select Committee of the Legislature in 1943. The College acknowledged that for a considerable section of the population provision of adequate medical care and hospitalization from their own individual resources was impracticable. "Some organized scheme or plan, state aided, appears to be essential. . . . voluntary benefits and co-operative associations have their place but they cannot reach the masses. . . . these associations service a class of salaried and higher wage-earners, enabling them to spread the costs of services which they, as a class, could provide in the main from their own resources."[56]

The brief repeated the profession's opposition to state medicine "[which] would in the main exclude freedom of action by the doctor and freedom of choice by the patient." It then strongly recommended to the committee that it consider a program "along the lines sketched at Ottawa and on the Principles endorsed by the CMA." The brief concluded with a strong note of cooperation: "You have our assurance that if a plan of health insurance along the lines indicated in our submission is eventually adopted, we will co-operate with the Legislature or with any body set up to work out details."[57] With this brief, the College had injected into the Saskatchewan decision process ideas similar to those introduced by the CMA to the Heagarty Committee.

2. *The Saskatchewan Hospital Association.* The Saskatchewan Hospital Association had never been able to achieve the closely-knit organization of the College of Physicians and Surgeons. Strapped for funds and limited to a part-time secretary, its main activities were two: the annual conference; and an intermittent campaign by letters, resolutions, and submissions by delegations to obtain increases in the provincial government's *per diem* grants.

Even during the depression, the association had managed to convene the annual conference to discuss mutual problems, appoint committees to examine specific issues, and communicate on their relationships with the provincial and municipal governments, particularly on the problems of municipal hospital contracts. Generally, the highlight of the conference was the participation of, and at least one major address by, Dr. Harvey Agnew, executive director of the Canadian Hospital Council and, occasionally, by the incumbent president of that body.

In 1935, spurred on by the Royal Commissions and legislative activities in Alberta and British Columbia, the superintendent of the Saskatoon City Hospital, Lemont Shaw, presented a paper to the conference on "The Possible Effect of a Health Insurance Plan on Our Hospitals."[58] This led to the appointment of a committee which reported the following year. It considered various alternatives: state medicine; a disease-by-disease approach; and, finally, a case for state hospitalization only, "which would leave people with sufficient income to pay their own medical expenses."[59]

Each year there was some reference to hospital insurance, and although there were discussions of the emerging Blue Cross plans in the USA, and of the various voluntary plans elsewhere in Canada, no parallel action was initiated by the association.

Given this past interest in and concern with hospital insurance, and the comprehensive brief prepared for the Ottawa committee by the Canadian Hospital Council, the Saskatchewan Association's brief was disappointing. It did not touch on the issue of hospital insurance but concentrated solely on the financial plight of the hospitals and the need for an increase in the *per diem* grants.

The major contributions of the Saskatchewan Hospital Association to the program were to come later.

3. *The Saskatchewan Association of Rural Municipalities* (SARM). The Saskatchewan Association of Rural Municipalities (SARM) was one of

Saskatchewan's strongest political forces, representing as it did 302 rural municipalities. Its brief to the committee reviewed the impact of provincial legislation that held the municipalities responsible for both the medical and hospital costs of the indigent. In addition, much of the burden of basic relief costs had fallen upon the municipalities during the depression. Despite these responsibilities, more than one-third of the 303 rural municipalities had developed, as we have seen, medical and/or hospital care plans, all of which were financed by a property tax until 1939, when personal taxes were authorized. But, said the SARM, "neither the tax on land nor the *per capita* tax has proven capable of providing sufficient revenue to give complete medical and hospital services."[60] All of the plans were restricted in some ways. Moreover, a basic weakness was the extreme range in *per capita* property assessments among the municipalities on which taxes were levied. As a consequence, the SARM believed that any health unit must be larger than a single municipality in order to secure a proper spread of risk, and that the cost of services rendered should be met by a direct personal tax on the individual and contributions by the provincial and Dominion governments.

It reminded the Legislative Committee that prior to 1940 the Association had consistently urged the inauguration of a system of state medicine, but since then had concluded that contributory health insurance was desired rather than state medicine, and that it should be under the control of a health commission in which the Government, the medical profession, the municipalities, and the public at large were represented.

The SARM then added what was to be a most significant contribution: "the municipalities should make their services available for the purpose of collecting the personal tax from their residents and should assume some measure of responsibility in this respect."[61]

4. *The State Hospital and Medical League.* The League was an organization unique to Saskatchewan; in no other province had such a pressure group been formed. It was also unique in Saskatchewan, for it was a confederation of other organizations, both voluntary and governmental. Started in 1936, by 1944 its affiliated membership included homemakers clubs, fraternal societies, church and farm organizations, Saskatchewan Teachers' Federation, cooperative groups, 120 rural municipalities, six cities, twenty-four towns and fifty-six villages.[62] Its organizer and secretary was E. R. Powell who had studied health service organization in the USSR and the Henry Kaiser program on the west coast. Reports of these studies and an analysis of Saskatchewan's needs and recommendations for a system of socialized medicine had been published in a widely circulated booklet entitled *The Medical Quest.*[63]

Its brief to the committee recommended that all available medical services be made accessible to all, regardless of the patient's ability to pay, by extending the municipal medical and hospital plans to all municipalities, villages, towns, and cities; by the setting up of diagnostic clinics; development of a medical school in Saskatchewan, and provision of educational grants and scholarships.

It criticized the fee-for-service method of payment with its emphasis on curative rather than preventive services and suggested that there was an apparent tendency to restrict the number of students allowed to take medical degrees.[64]

Another external source having great influence was, of course, the ideas generated by the Heagerty Committee, particularly those that had been incorporated in the model bill drafted for the provinces. As noted earlier, these ideas had received extensive consideration in Saskatchewan through the hearings conducted by the Select Committee in 1943 and 1944. Among the concepts and proposals emanating from the federal level, the most important were those relating to administration by a commission, universal coverage, registration of the total population, cost estimates, methods of raising revenue, a separate fund for health services, and regional organization. All were considered in the formative stages.

It was an especially creative period in Saskatchewan history, with an extraordinarily high level of dialogue among concerned citizens, interest group spokesmen, the newspapers, the legislators, and the Government.

THE GOVERNMENT'S CONTRIBUTION TO POLICY

When the new government took office in June 1944, only eight of the members had ever been in the Legislature and none had ever held a Cabinet post. The leader, T. C. Douglas, became premier and, in order to signal the primacy his government would allocate to health services, he also assumed the portfolio of health minister.

It was now, at the policy level, a very different situation from that in the spring of 1944. True, the external environment remained essentially unchanged: the same one-crop economy, the same shortages of facilities and personnel, the same budget constraints. But the political situation had been drastically altered: fifty-three percent of the electorate—a clear majority over three other parties—had voted for the reform government. Political demands had also changed: the CCF had campaigned on "security and progress" and there were no doubts that in the expectations of supporters, "progress" in the health field had a high priority.

On the other hand, as the Government contemplated the prospective contribution of the bureaucracy over which it was now presiding, there were two causes for concern. The first was the lack of experts within the

Health Department knowledgeable about programs beyond the traditional services of public health. The second was the patronage-ridden character of the Saskatchewan civil service. It would be a continuing problem for the entire Cabinet, as it dealt with a civil service notorious for its appointment on the basis of loyalty and obligation to the Liberal party.[65] The CCF leaders were fully aware of the problem and T. C. Douglas in a pre-election speech had made clear his insistence on having sympathetic experts at the top.[66]

With its broad health objectives in mind, its awareness of its own lack of expertise, and its chary attitude to the senior permanent officials, the Government decided on three courses of action: 1. It would seek external experts to serve as the nucleus of a permanent health planning group; 2. It would reinforce this planning group by appointing an *ad hoc* commission to make an immediate health survey and provide recommendations for new programs and the strategy for their introduction; 3. It would embark immediately on a broad range of health services for those whom the premier characterized as "the marginal class of people who have so little money that in many cases they cannot bear the costs of health services at all   the old age pensioners and their dependents, the blind and their dependents, those who receive mother's allowances and their dependents."[67] Action on these three decisions was undertaken immediately.

The Planning Staff. The first appointment, as assistant to the minister, was Dr. Mindel Sheps. An economist, Mr. Thomas H. McLeod, then special assistant to the premier, was seconded to work with Dr. Sheps.

The Social Assistance Medical Care Plan. Meetings were held with the negotiating committee of the College of Physicians and Surgeons on August 23, 1944 and with various other health professions and the Hospital Association immediately thereafter to obtain agreement for the introduction of a comprehensive health services program for all individuals receiving regular social assistance payments, a total of approximately 28,000 people. The proposal was that each beneficiary should be insured for the costs of the authorized health services. Since the health care of these people was, in general, the responsibility of the municipalities, and payment was made only when authorized in advance, their becoming "insured" under a new program would be a major advance for both them and the providers of service, as well as an important relief measure for the municipalities.

It was decided that the program should be administered by the Medical Services Division of the Department of Public Health which had been responsible for medical relief payments. The program with its comprehensive range of benefits was launched on January 1, 1945, six months after the Government's election to office.[68]

The Health Commission. It was decided that a survey should accomplish two goals: 1. to provide a series of explicit objectives and priorities, and 2. to dramatize the new government's thrust in health services. Accordingly, a physician of international reputation was selected to direct the survey. Dr. Henry Sigerist, of John Hopkins Medical School, was appointed commissioner with power to appoint technical experts.[69] After consultation, members of the medical, dental, and nursing professions, and a hospital administrator were appointed.[70]

Dr. Mindel Sheps was assigned the role of secretary to the commission and began her duties on August 14. The commissioner arrived on September 6 and met daily in various centres of the province from then until September 23, hearing and accepting submissions from about 100 groups and individuals. The commission also made full use of the submissions to and the reports of the 1943–44 Select Special Committee on Social Security.[71]

The goal enunciated by the commissioner was to provide complete medical services to all the people of the province, irrespective of their economic status or of whether they lived in town or country.

He observed that a promising beginning had already been made and that further steps could be taken without delay by using and extending the existing facilities. But, he warned, the final steps might have to wait until the province could count on subsidies from the Dominion, or on other sources of revenue.

He called for the development of health regions headed by a medical officer of health, not only to carry out general public health measures but, in addition, to supervise and coordinate all medical services. New hospitals would be necessary and some existing hospitals might be more readily used as convalescent homes, hospitals for chronic patients, or old folks homes. The regional hospital would provide major surgery and other specialized treatments. The surgeons should be appointed on a full-time basis, and approved by the Royal College of Physicians and Surgeons. A full-time dentist, an otolaryngologist, and other specialists should be appointed on a full-time basis according to need. The offices of the local doctors should be in the hospital so that they could use its facilities in their daily practice.

The commissioner concluded that the municipal doctor system had stood the test of time and therefore should be maintained and developed. The provincial government should set a minimum salary to be paid municipal doctors, the salary should be increased with years of service, and the programs should be subsidized by the provincial government.

The rural health programs should be carried out with the active participation of the population. Each rural health unit should have its health services commission consisting of representatives of the health personnel, the teachers, and representatives of the rural municipalities, towns, and villages involved. Representatives of these commissions and of the district hospitals should constitute the District Health Services Commission.

The commissioner believed that the problem of providing health services to the inhabitants of the cities was less difficult and less urgent. A number of voluntary plans were available but he felt that the most practical policy might be the gradual extension of public services so as to include maternity care and hospitalization, supplemented by a system of compulsory health insurance. With respect to hospitals, he recommended that free hospitalization for the entire population should be the goal.

A most important recommendation was that there should be established a permanent Health Services Planning Commission (HSPC) to obtain necessary data and information and to begin the required planning to achieve the major goals.

The commissioner's report received a good deal of attention but it did not, in fact, provide much more than a rough sketch rather than a blueprint for which the Government had been seeking. It did, however, accomplish the objective of providing province-wide publicity for the Government's health objectives.

At the direction of the minister, Dr. Sheps and T. H. McLeod immediately began the drafting of a health services act to be passed at a special session of the Legislature in November. Its two main provisions were, (1) the creation of the Health Services Planning Commission, the members to be appointed by the lieutenant governor in council, and, (2) authorization for the minister of public health to pay part or the whole of the cost of providing health services for such classes of persons as might be designated by the lieutenant governor in council.[72]

The act was passed and the commission established. Because no outstanding medical doctor was available for the position, a chairman was not immediately appointed, but the other members included three of those who had served with Dr. Sigerist: Mr. T. H. McLeod, Mr. C. C. Gibson, and Dr. Mindel Sheps, secretary. The deputy minister of health, Dr. C. F. W. Hames, was a member *ex officio*. Shortly thereafter, the Government appointed a twenty-one-member advisory committee to the commission composed of representatives of the professions, the public, and the government.

The small commission staff began drafting alternative policy proposals along the lines of the Sigerist Commission recommendations. The first major policy memorandum considered a maternity hospitalization program. In 1943, over 4,000 births—twenty-two percent of the total—occurred outside hospital; the maternal mortality rate among these was five times the rate among those hospitalized. There would be advantages to hospitals in being paid their costs, and standards could be expected to rise. The total costs for such a program were estimated to be under $600,000.

The memorandum also included the first consideration to be given to a problem that would become much greater in 1945, and continue to be difficult for years after that: how to pay the hospitals. It was suggested that hospitals be classified into "A," "B," and "C" categories, and paid a flat differential rate per case. The memorandum shed light on how serious this problem would be under a complete hospitalization program when it acknowledged that the hospitals division had not the necessary knowledge of conditions in the province's hospitals to classify them according to a point system or even according to the simpler system suggested above.

The memorandum concluded with a summary of the Alberta Maternity Hospitalization Act which had come into operation on April 1, 1944. Although such a limited program would solve part of a serious problem, and have a certain amount of public appeal, the fact that the Alberta program had been introduced by a Social Credit government probably detracted from its political appeal for the CCF in Saskatchewan.

During the summer of 1945, the commission began the task of organizing two demonstration regions: Health region No. 1 based in Swift Current and No. 3, based in Weyburn. The initial stages were contacts with municipal officials, public meetings with citizens, and arrangements for voting. These organizational developments proceeded with no more than normal opposition, and by November 26 both regions were established. Both boards began planning for public health services and regionally-administered hospital services and, in addition, the Swift Current board began the planning for a medical service. For the hospital and medical services, both boards set a target date of July 1, 1946.

In the remaining month of 1945, the commission pressed forward in its efforts to organize health regions for public health services, but there was developing a consensus that a province-wide hospitalization program should now have the highest priority.

With all the various activities of the commission, (only some of which have been documented here), it was not until the end of August 1945, that a policy memorandum on a hospitalization program was finally prepared.

The August memorandum first emphasized the shortages of all types of hospitals, the chaotic state of development (1,000 new beds were in the planning or construction stage), the lack of standards, and the shortage of personnel—professional, technical, and administrative.

The memorandum therefore proposed a comprehensive survey of hospitals by a committee which would make recommendations regarding (a) minimum standards of operation, nursing care, equipment, and diagnostic facilities for different types of hospitals and health centres; (b) the criteria to be used in the grading of such institutions for purposes of payment; (c) a hospital construction program; (d) administration, especially of smaller hospitals; and (e) related matters.[73]

The survey was agreed to by formal resolution of the commission. A committee was appointed, and the long and complex task of evaluating the hospitals was immediately begun.

The development of the program required decisions on a broad range of issues and problems that, taken together, would constitute the Government's policy to meet the twin objectives of ensuring the availability of hospital resources and of removing the economic barriers to their essential use.

That special relationship between political ministers and senior officials now intensified as policy goals, program concepts, administrative ideas, financial and bureaucratic constraints, questions of political feasibility and pay-off, and conflicting interest group demands were analyzed, assessed, weighed, projected, and "traded off" in countless committee meetings, and emerged, eventually, in specific proposals for legislative and administrative action.

Faced, as the HSPC was, with a unique challenge—the design of the first universal hospital insurance program in Canada (indeed, in North America)—the interchange between the new political leaders and the new and old bureaucrats was both innovative and highly productive. Among the issues and problems were (a) beneficiaries; (b) benefits; (c) costs; (d) sources of revenue; (e) tax collection; and (f) methods of paying hospitals. Each of these will be considered in turn, although in the actual planning process, of course, there were no such orderly stages.

Beneficiaries. There seems never to have been any other thought than that the program should be universal and compulsory. Although the CMA had half-heartedly argued for an income ceiling above which coverage would be either voluntary or unavailable, the Saskatchewan College of Physicians and Surgeons had specifically rejected this notion. The premise on which the commission operated was that all should be covered and everyone who could, should pay. On examination, it became evident that certain groups were already entitled to hospital services from other governmental agencies and should be excluded. There were others, in the far north of the province, who could not easily avail themselves of hospital services, and who should not, therefore, be required to pay a hospitalization tax, although they should be able to join voluntarily.

Altogether, eleven categories of individuals were exempted, including members of the armed forces, recently discharged veterans, Treaty Indians, patients in mental hospitals and T.B. sanatoria, inmates of prisons, members of the RCMP, and all those who were already entitled to hospital benefits under the Health Services Act.

It was also decided that any newborn child should be automatically insured, at no cost, for the balance of the year.

The benefits. The principle underlying the decision on the range of benefits was not dissimilar to that of universal coverage: within reasonable limits, all the essential services of the hospital should be included. This meant services at the standard ward level, and as many of the other services that, in the Blue Cross Plans, were designated as "extras"— i.e., operating room, anaesthetic services, radiology, laboratory services, drugs, etc.—as could be reasonably justified. The same principle obtained in the decision on benefit days. It was finally decided that there should be no limit on the number of days of care to which an insured resident would be entitled other than that of medical necessity. It was assumed that hospitals would continue their practice of making additional charges for semi-private and private accommodation but it would be desirable to ensure that a majority of beds was available at standard rates.

The estimates of costs. Although it would be possible to make more refined estimates of costs as the data on hospitals financing for the calendar year 1945 became available in 1946, it was necessary, for decision making by the Cabinet, to obtain a reasonable first estimate as soon as possible.

The problem of estimating the total cost of a universal hospital services plan with almost unlimited benefits was an especially difficult task, and involved dealing with many unknown factors. There was no other plan of such scope in North America whose experience could be used. In the voluntary hospitalization plans, a limit was normally placed on both the *per diem* payment and the number of days' care permitted and, as in the plans insuring medical care, the poorer risks were largely excluded. The unknown factors included the effect of the removal of the economic barrier on the demand for hospitalization; the effect on the average length of stay in hospital of the type of cases represented in the enormous "backlog" of unmet health needs for which it was believed there would be immediate demand; the effect of newly-developed techniques in medical and surgical treatment which tended to reduce the average length of stay in hospital but increased *per diem* costs; the effect on the hospitalization rate of an increase in facilities; and the unpredictable effect on costs of operation of the end of wartime controls on wages and prices. Another factor rendering the task even more difficult was the lack of uniformity in the accounting systems of the hospitals. But it was essential that a reasonable estimate be made.

Although there were many unknown factors, certain data were available. In the annual reports of Saskatchewan government-aided hospitals, the following trends were apparent: 1. An absolute increase in the number of patients hospitalized annually from 54,042 in 1934 to 96,465 in 1944; 2. An increase in the percentage of persons hospitalized from 5.5 percent of the population in 1934 to 11.7 percent in 1944; 3. An increase in average expenditure per patient from $34.63 in 1934 to $46.25 in 1944; 4. An increase in *per capita* expenditure for hospitalization from $1.93 in 1934 to $5.20 in 1944; 5. An increase in total expenditure for hospitalization in the province from $1,861,740 in 1934 to $4,282,864 in 1944.

In summary, the data revealed in the eleven-year period an increase of over 100 percent in the rate of hospitalization; an increase of 169 percent in the *per capita* cost of hospital services; an increase of 33 percent in the per patient cost of hospitalization; and an increase of 130 percent in the total cost of hospitalization to the people of the province, although in the same period there had been an estimated decrease of twelve percent in the population. Even more significant was the ten percent increase in the number of patients in 1944 over the preceding year, and an eighteen percent increase in costs in 1944 over 1943.

Certain other information shed additional light on the problem:

1. A survey of fifty-four of the municipal hospitalization programs indicated that 12.9 percent of the covered population were hospitalized as compared with the 11.7 percent of the general population.

2. The same survey showed, however, that the average length of stay was 8.6 days, compared with 9.9 days in the province generally.

3. It was generally agreed at the Dominion-Provincial Conference held in 1945 that a province-wide hospitalization scheme would result in an annual hospitalization rate of 1.5 days *per capita*.

Although, as noted in chapter 1, there had been serious reservations about the reliability of the Heagerty Committee estimates (and not least by Saskatchewan), the Saskatchewan planning group apparently concluded that given its own crude data, it could not do much better. It therefore accepted the 1.5 days estimate and multiplied that by its newly-calculated average *per diem* cost in Saskatchewan hospitals, and multi-plied that by an estimated 850,000 population to yield a preliminary estimate of $4,400,000. Part of this total cost would be met by payments for private and semi-private ward service, from persons not eligible under the government program, from workmen's compensation, etc., leaving an estimated total cost in the first year of $4,000,000 for the government plan. With this initial, and as time would reveal, conservative estimate, it was necessary to consider the methods of financing.

The sources of revenue. Certain factors or principles governed the determining of the amount of taxes necessary to finance the program and the manner in which the revenues were to be raised.

1. The provincial government should continue to contribute to hospitalization costs an amount at least as great as it was currently paying from general revenues under its system of grants to hospitals.

2. The provincial government should continue to pay the actual costs of hospitalization of those persons (old age and blind pensioners, mothers' allowance recipients, wards of the province, etc.) whose health services were being provided under the Health Services Act.

3. Except for the contributions, the hospitalization program should, so far as possible, be self-supporting.

With these considerations in mind, the first tentative estimate prepared in 1945 was that revenue of $4 *per capita* would meet actual costs, though not establish any reserve. As reports of increased costs in 1945 appeared, it became evident that the *per capita* revenues required would be closer to $5.00.

Although the municipal health programs had been financed mainly by municipal property taxes, the major influence on the choice of revenue source to finance the program was the requirement in the Dominion offer that the provinces provide for a registration fee to be paid by or on behalf of every person. A registration fee of any size was, in effect, an insurance premium, with the implication that non-payment disqualified one from entitlement to benefits. Apparently, in expectation of action by the Dominion government, no other alternative was seriously considered, and the premiums or personal tax system was decided upon.

The effect of a flat rate fee for every person (i.e., including every dependant) is a seriously regressive tax structure, as a single adult would pay $X and a head of a family of ten would pay $10X. (About twelve percent of Saskatchewan households had more than four members and these accounted for just under one-third of the population.)[74] The HSPC considered that a reasonable maximum should be established to reduce the burden on large families and it prepared alternative premium structures to raise the estimated required amount of revenue.

Registration and tax collection. From subsequent experience it is evident that planning for the task of registering the entire population of the province and collecting the tax from over 300,000 heads of families and single persons scattered over the vast area of Saskatchewan was not begun as early as would have been desirable.

In collecting the taxes, it was decided to accept the offer of the municipal associations that their members serve as registration and collection agencies. There were approximately 900 municipal secretaries and clerks in Saskatchewan, constituting a ready-made administrative structure. But it would require a good deal of training in new procedures, and the potential for administrative foul-ups through clerical error was great. A training manual and training program would be essential.

Paying the hospitals. How to pay the hospitals of the province equitably for services rendered to beneficiaries constituted the most difficult of the many complex problems associated with the introduction of the plan. The hospitals varied in size from five beds to over five hundred. Public ward rates ranged from $2 to $4 per day. Many of the hospitals made no distinction between private, semi-private, and public ward service. In those which did, the added charges for private ward services ranged from $2.50 to $6 per day above the public ward rate. In only a few hospitals was a system of accounting in effect that would supply adequate information concerning actual costs of operation. There was no correlation between size of hospital and the rates charged, nor could it be said that variations in rates were indicative of quality of service.

As in other problems, certain guiding principles were decided upon that should be observed regardless of the method of payment:

1. With the inauguration of the program, the Hospital Services Plan would become the chief source of income for all hospitals in the province. If the rates established were too low, only rarely would other sources of revenue be sufficient to overcome any substantial deficit.

2. Because of the essentiality of most hospitals, it would be impossible to permit a hospital to close its doors through lack of funds.

3. The earning of a large surplus by any hospital (a non-profit enterprise) would be as undesirable (financially, politically, and in principle) as the incurring of serious deficits.

95

4. A system of payment should be one which would encourage efficient operation and promote improvement in services. It must not subsidize inefficiency, waste, or extravagance.

5. Payments to hospitals should be all-inclusive; additional payments by patients for "extras" should be kept at an absolute minimum.

6. Payment should cover operating costs only. Capital costs were to be borne by the community served, supplemented by provincial construction grants.

The simplest answer to the problem of payment was that hospitals should be paid their costs of operation, but, as noted, the main obstacle in the way of this solution was the lack of uniform accounting and, in certain cases, of any intelligible accounting record in the hospitals of the province. It appeared that for the first year, at least, or until the installation of a uniform accounting system could provide sufficient reliable data on cost, some method of payment other than one based on costs of operation would have to be utilized.

A second proposal given consideration was a system of graduated payments based on size (number of beds). While there were some merits in this proposal, it appeared not to be equitable as it tended to penalize the small hospital which might be rendering efficient service but in which costs of operation might be unavoidably high for any number of reasons. It was rejected on the basis that it could not be demonstrated that there was a high correlation between size and cost.

In 1943 another method of payment of hospitals, referred to as the "units of credit" system, had been proposed by Dr. Harvey Agnew, the secretary of the Canadian Hospital Council, and had been approved in principle by that organization of which the Saskatchewan Hospital Association was a member.[75] The system may best be explained in the words of Dr. Agnew:

> In essence, the proposal is to grade hospitals according to the facilities and services provided. The *per diem* payment for each patient would be based on the number of "points" credited to each hospital and would be multiplied, of course, by the number of patient days recorded to give the total amount to be paid.
>
> Each hospital would be credited with so many points, according to the extent to which it provides laboratory services, X-ray, etc. The hospital would be paid so many mills for each unit, or point, credited to it. The mill rather than the cent is selected because it would lessen the use of decimals. . . . For example: One hospital might warrant 400

units and another 500 units. If the rate be, say 7 mills ($0.007), the first hospital would receive $2.80 per patient day and the other $3.50.

Dr. Agnew claimed a number of advantages for the system:

1. All hospitals would be paid according to their ability to provide services.

2. The plan would stimulate improvement in equipment and in expert personnel.

3. Size alone would not be a factor, as it would be in a system in which larger hospitals were paid a higher *per diem* rate.

4. By using different monetary values for the "unit of credit," varying amounts of payment adapted to varying cost situations (for example, as indicated by the cost-of-living index) could be calculated.

While the claimed advantages were generally accepted, there were certain causes for doubt about the result of the system in actual operation.

No matter what reasonable monetary value was assigned to the unit of credit (e.g. 6, 7, or 8 mills), one group of hospitals would probably find their costs of operation roughly equal to their revenues under the point system, a second would show a varying range of surpluses, but a third would show a varying range of deficits. In other words, the chief advantage of the point system was also the chief defect. While it encouraged economical provision of good service because the grants were not tied to cost of operation, yet it might result in substantial deficits for some if the grants were not sufficient to cover costs.

In short, the Government would probably be forced into paying at least a part of deficits incurred by any hospital unless these were clearly assignable to mismanagement, and the effect of this would be to undermine the principles of the point system.[76]

Despite the doubt and misgivings naturally accompanying any proposed departure from customary practice, there appeared sufficient merit and advantage to the units of credit system to propose to the Saskatchewan Hospital Association that it be studied by their members as a possible basis of payment for the first year.

On each of these issues, planning briefs with alternative solutions were presented for Cabinet decision.

THE STRATEGY OF IMPLEMENTATION

The second major task of the Planning Commission, in cooperation with the minister, and he with the Cabinet, was to design the strategy for executing the policy. The strategy in the case of the Saskatchewan Hospital Services Plan differs from the other cases examined in this study in that there was a minimum of conflict within the province and there were no protracted negotiations with the federal government although, as already noted, it was considered essential that the plan be designed to meet the federal requirements. The strategy was directed, accordingly, primarily to creating the administrative organization and eliciting the cooperation of all the affected groups who must make the system work: the municipalities, the hospitals, and the health professions. Moreover, the strategy had to be executed in such a way as to overcome, or at least reduce, the opposition—both within the interest groups and a segment of the public—to anything about to be "perpetrated by a socialist government."

The first stage of the strategy had begun very early, in the attempts to disarm the suspicions of the medical profession and the hospital associations. The first thrust, already discussed, were Premier Douglas's efforts to reassure the medical profession that he would not act without consultation and by demonstrating his good intentions throughout the negotiations on the social assistance medical care program.

The first approach to the hospitals also occurred early when the premier accepted an invitation to give the key-note address at the Hospital Association's annual meeting on October 30, 1944. There he attempted to allay certain fears and to direct the course of the members' thinking about the future. His main points were: (1) an assurance of the continuation of ownership of hospitals by municipalities, religious orders, and other voluntary groups; (2) the regional concept of hospital development; (3) proposals for provincial grants to assist in financing hospital construction (the first such program in Canada); (4) the need for chronic care hospitals; and (5) the desire of the Government to assist in the development of a comprehensive hospitals system. These efforts were directed to the creation of a climate of confidence essential to the success of the program.

The most critical decision concerned the question of timing. As has already been stressed, the decision to go it alone without certainty of Dominion government cost-sharing was fraught with major financial uncertainties and extraordinary political risks. To go it alone was to bear responsibility alone and time was running out for the successful introduction of so large, complex, and expensive an operation.

The question revolved around the juxtaposition of the introduction of the program and the timing of the next election. There were only two choices: before the election, or after. An election would be required in 1949 but, desirably, should be held in 1948. If the program were to be introduced before the election it must be seen to be operating successfully not later than the spring of 1948. But time was required (a) to create the administrative structure and procedures; (b) to complete as many as possible of 1,000 hospital beds approved for construction; and after the introduction of the program, (c) to correct any major defects that would inevitably appear before the voter evaluation in the election would take place.

The alternative was to postpone the introduction of the program until after the election. That would give time for more thorough preparation both in creating the administrative organization and in expanding facilities. It would thus greatly reduce the risk of foul-ups that might prove embarrassing in an election. On the other hand, it had grave political disadvantages in that the Government would certainly be accused of failing to fulfill its election platform. It was decided, therefore, that the program must begin on January 1, 1947, which would require passage of the legislation during the legislative session beginning about the first of February 1946. It was a very tight schedule.

With the launching date set, the most crucial stage in the strategy was the establishment of joint committees with the College of Physicians and Surgeons, the Hospital, Pharmaceutical, and Nurses' associations to reach agreement on benefits, methods of paying doctors for diagnostic services, a pharmaceutical formulary, a method of paying hospitals, and a host of similar details.

A parallel action in the strategy was to appoint a joint committee with the two municipal associations to establish the procedures for registering the population and collecting the premiums. Unfortunately, this committee was not appointed until June 1946, although the collection of premiums would have to begin in September. The committee quickly agreed upon the following principles and procedures:

1. In view of the striking population changes which had taken place since the 1941 census, it seemed essential that the entire population be pre-registered.

2. The Hospital Services (registration) cards should be prepared by the central administration and issued by the municipal collectors upon payment of tax due.

3. Partial or instalment payments of taxes should be accepted from those owing the larger amounts. However, to keep administrative costs low, the number of instalment payments permitted in a year should be kept to a minimum.

4. With respect to persons in receipt of public assistance the tax should be paid on their behalf by that agency of government, municipal or provincial, responsible for their medical and hospital care and treatment.

5. The commission should give assistance to municipal collectors in the collection of delinquent taxes.

6. Collectors should receive as remuneration for their services a fixed percentage of taxes collected.

7. In order to reduce the cost and burden of registering the population, it was decided that in cities and towns registration should coincide with the annual preparation of voters' lists and that the official enumerators should act as registrars for the hospital plan.

The function of the municipal council would thus become similar to that of the agent of an insurance company, responsible for collecting the premiums and delivering the policy. The nearly nine hundred municipal secretaries and town and city clerks would be key persons, responsible for interpreting the purposes, methods, and rulings of the plan to its thousands of beneficiaries.

Yet another problem, which could be decided only by the Cabinet, was the question of which agency should be responsible for the administration of this new, large, and politically vulnerable program. The premier had made a commitment to the College of Physicians and Surgeons to administer health insurance through an independent commission, but this program, in the view of the Cabinet, was hospital insurance and on this question the Hospital Association had presented no views. That left the Department of Health or, perhaps, the Health Services Planning Commission, which could in no way be considered an independent, representative commission. The relationships between these two bodies—the one staffed mainly by hold-overs from the preceding Liberal administration, and the other staffed by new recruits sympathetic to the government's health program—had not been without strain. In an early protest by the deputy minister of health over apparent encroachments on the department's territory, the premier had issued a memorandum reaffirming that the commission had been established as "solely a research and advisory group. . . . it cannot be considered an administrative body."[77] Accordingly, although the commission had designed and negotiated the contracts for the Social Assistance Health Services Program, the administration of the program was assigned to the Health Department. That was also true of the health regions which the commission was organizing and which, once established, came under the direction of the Health Department.

But no one in the Health Department had had any experience with either an insurance system or a program of such magnitude. Moreover, there were still reasons to doubt the wholeheartedness of the commitment of the permanent civil servants to the objectives of the new Government's health program, and all of the approximately 200 employees required to administer the Hospital Services Plan would have to be recruited through the newly-created Public Service Commission in any event.

The final step in the strategy of achieving the cooperation of the various associations was taken in January 1946, when the draft legislation was presented by the committees to their respective principals, the executives of the various associations. The municipal and hospital associations accepted the arrangements without change. The chairman of the Medical Advisory Committee reported that his committee was concerned about the supply of hospital beds, the need for special institutions for care of the aged, the chronically ill, and the convalescent, the need to reduce average length of stay, and restrictions on admissions for diagnostic purposes only. On the whole, the response was favourable: "The authors of the draft legislation are to be complimented on their approach to the problem....the provision of free hospitalization to all the citizens of the province is a principle which is most commendable. We endorse the method of administration provided in the bill."[78]

THE POLICY

The final stage of the policy process had now been reached, the passing into law of the statute that embodied the policy choices made, and the myriad decisions taken. For the policy makers, that is, the Cabinet and the CCF majority in the Legislature, it was the climax of a long and hard-fought battle that gave promise of fulfilling age-old aspirations and more recent political commitments. For the administrative officials it was partly climax, for they had participated in the decision making, but it was also for them a beginning for they would be charged with and committed to the responsibility of making a complicated system function, to bring those aspirations to the reality of an effective and efficiently operating program.

The legislation—the output of the governmental process—was introduced in the Legislature on March 12, 1946, received Royal Assent on April 4, 1946, and was scheduled to make the benefits of the program available on January 1, 1947.

What were the salient points of the policy?

1. The act established a universal, compulsory hospital care insurance system. In that benefits were to be conditional upon prior payment of the tax, the program followed established practices of social insurance. In that eligible residents were liable to wage garnishee or prosecution for failure to pay the tax, it was compulsory.

101

2. It provided for an almost complete range of hospital services as benefits at the standard ward level with no limitation on entitlement days as long as in-patient care was medically necessary.

3. The payment system was also all-inclusive, with no distinction between basic services and the so-called "extras" then common in Blue Cross and other voluntary or commercial coverage. The rates of payment were based, for the first year, on the Agnew "point system" in which hospitals were graded and paid according to the facilities and services provided.

4. The "premium" or tax structure was set at a uniform rate of five dollars to be paid by or on behalf of each adult and child with a maximum of $30 per family.

5. There was a commitment to subsidize the insurance system from general revenues by an amount equal to existing *per diem* grants to hospitals plus the actual costs of the cancer and social assistance programs, and to provide a loan fund to meet any deficit. Later, this loan provision was rescinded and the necessity of a non-repayable subsidy accepted.

6. Tax collection was assigned to the municipal councils, with payment of a commission of five percent of taxes collected to the council (which was generally passed on to the secretary-treasurer).

7. Administration was assigned to the HSPC—composed of a full-time chairman and four other civil servants. Thus the Government had decided against assigning the program either to the Department of Public Health or to an "independent, non-political" commission. The deputy minister of public health was appointed a member of the commission to achieve the desired coordination with public health services.

As a result, the commission became both a line agency and a staff agency. To it were transferred from the Health Department the Medical Services Division administering the Social Assistance Medical Care program, and the Hospital Planning Division. The commission created a regional services division responsible for regional development, a research division, and a division known as the Saskatchewan Hospital Services Plan.[79]

The government had been unable to find a suitable candidate for chairman of the commission until March 23, 1946 when Dr. Cecil Sheps (husband of the secretary, Dr. Mindel Sheps) was appointed acting chairman. Negotiations were underway with Dr. Frederick D. Mott, a senior officer in the United States Public Health Services, who was a graduate of McGill Medical School. On September 1, the Doctors Sheps resigned to accept fellowships for post-doctoral study in the United States, and Dr. Mott became chairman. He, in turn, appointed Dr. Leonard R. Rosenfeld, also an officer of the U.S. Public Health Service, as vice-chairman of the commission and executive director of the Hospital Services Plan, and the work of the commission and "the plan" went into high gear.

The new uniform hospital accounting system was finalized under G. W. Myers;[80] the point system evaluation was completed, the tax collection procedures agreed upon with the municipalities; and the organization of SHSP decided upon; scores of clerical, secretarial, and tabulating personnel were appointed and trained, and a massive publicity program was mounted to encourage early registration and tax payment.

It was a period of feverish activity, reminiscent of mobilization in 1939. The only office space available was in an ancient, vacated store building; clerical desks were long rows of plywood-on-trestles, with clerks sitting elbow-to-elbow, processing the registration and tax collection payments according to a system that, although using mechanical tabulating equipment, was quite primitive.[81]

As January 1, 1947 approached, the feelings of excitement—mixed with apprehension—accelerated, with hospital personnel and doctors waiting for the onslaught of increased demand, and Premier Douglas, his Cabinet and the CCF caucus hoping that the policy decision to "go it alone" would have positive rather than negative political results.

Apart from those already in hospital on December 31, the first patients to be admitted to hospital under the program were Mrs. Hunt, wife of a Regina doctor, who gave birth to a baby boy at fifteen seconds past midnight, January 1, Mrs. Joseph Safazakas, whose child was born at 5:45 a.m., and Mrs. Charles Reid, whose baby was born at 8:20 p.m. All three children automatically became insured beneficiaries for the year 1947.

A social idea had been translated into an operating reality; the first universal hospital insurance program in North America had been launched. For Saskatchewan there was no turning back.

THE OUTCOMES

1. From the political point of view, the gamble to introduce a program before the federal policy had been decided upon, "paid off." Although there were strains in the system resulting from the shortage of hospital beds, and much criticism in the anti-government press, the minor crises were weathered, and by the time of the election in 1948, the plan could be said to be operating successfully.

2. With hospital operating revenue assured by the SHSP, communities throughout the province began to develop new, or to expand existing, facilities. They were assisted in this endeavour by provincial hospital con-

struction grants for approved projects. With the planning, design, and controls introduced by the commission there began to emerge a coordinated system of community, district, and regional hospitals based on the two main centres of Saskatoon and Regina. The ratio of hospital beds to population increased from 4.8 per 1,000 in 1946 to 6.5 per 1,000 in 1951.[82]

3. The hospital utilization rate increased rapidly until it was the highest of any prepayment plan in Canada. This resulted from many factors: the shortage of physicians and a consequent pattern of practice that provided few home calls; the difficulties of transportation in rural Saskatchewan;[83] the combination of large families, low incomes, and poor housing; the failure (or impossibility in the early stages) to introduce out-patient benefits; the almost total lack of alternative chronic care hospitals, nursing homes, or home care programs; and, the fact that, unlike the voluntary plans, SHSP insured all recipients of social assistance and the aged.

4. The costs of the plan and, therefore, the provincial subsidy, were considerably in excess of estimates.

5. The tax collection system was successful to a degree unexpected for a regressive "poll" tax. The public reaction to tax increases has been silent consent if not approval, but there seems little doubt that it was the most widely endorsed program the government introduced in its first twenty years of office.[84]

6. All of Canada benefited from the Saskatchewan experience. From its inception until the Quebec Hospital Plan came into effect in 1961, no provincial government failed to send its officials to Regina to learn at first hand how the program operated, and what policies and procedures could be adapted to their home provinces. In the educational process through which Canadian governments learned how to administer universal hospital insurance, Saskatchewan paid most of the tuition fees.

7. With the resounding success of the hospital insurance program, and with public health, mental health, and the development of the hospitals system progressing rapidly, it was clearly only a matter of time and the obtaining of sufficient financial resources until the Government would move to fulfil its commitment to provide medical care as one of the insured services. In fact, the delay was to be longer than the Government had anticipated.

Chapter Three

Ontario Hospital Insurance:
The Decision Not To Go It Alone*

As the curtain went up on the next major act of the drama of health insurance, at first glance the stage seemed remarkably similar to that of the first act in 1945. The time: ten years later; the setting: a committee room of the House of Commons; the scene: a federal provincial conference; the characters: the same, the prime minister and the provincial premiers, with one additional player, Mr. Joey Smallwood, the premier of Newfoundland.

One felt a sense of *déjà vu*, but that was quickly dispelled, for between 1945 and 1955 there had been a remarkable change of actors. There were only three whose contracts had been consistently renewed: Duplessis of Quebec, Manning of Alberta, and Douglas of Saskatchewan. The prime minister, Mr. St. Laurent, had been present in 1945 but in the role of minister of justice. Some of the others had attended the 1950 conference on the tax agreements, but there were four who were making their first appearance on the national stage: Mr. Hicks of Nova Scotia, Mr. Fleming of New Brunswick, Mr. Matheson of Prince Edward Island, and Mr. Bennett of British Columbia.

More than faces, personalities, and political roles had changed, however; the 1945 scenario or "plot" appeared to have been completely reversed. Here was Prime Minister St. Laurent opening the conference

---

*Since I served as consultant to the Ontario government during the development of the Ontario Hospital Services Plan, it has been necessary to write part of this chapter in the first person.

by saying: "We believe that the proposals of 1945 are no longer suitable for our agenda in 1955 our conference is most likely to succeed if we plan to consider only a limited number of subjects of primary importance.... the first ... is that of future Federal-Provincial fiscal relations ... and [the second is] the question of assistance to the unemployed."[1]

Then it was the turn of the leading actor from Ontario to speak. He, too, had attended the 1945 conference as provincial treasurer and the 1950 conference in the role of premier. Mr. Frost agreed that fiscal relations and unemployment were key items but, he emphasized, there was another:

> This very important subject [of health insurance] deserves the consideration of the Conference. It is a matter which has been widely discussed and this Conference can do a great deal to clarify the issues involved. It is generally recognized that any health insurance plan of a broad nature should have both federal and provincial participation. We suggest that the whole question be intensively studied.... Health insurance has many important financial implications, not only for the provinces and the federal government but for the individual; and since it is one of the great objectives in the field of human betterment, it should be placed on the agenda for study, with a view to producing a sound, workable plan with which we could proceed.[2]

Mr. Frost's words were music to the ears of the premiers of British Columbia, Alberta, Saskatchewan, and Newfoundland, already involved in hospital insurance programs of varying scope. Among the federal actors, however, the reactions were mixed; some alarm on the part of the prime minister, but quiet satisfaction behind the calm countenance of the minister of national health and welfare, the Hon. Paul Martin.

How had this reversal of positions come about? Why did the federal government view the unfinished agenda of 1945 as "no longer suitable" in 1955? Had not that agenda been addressed to what Leonard Marsh had called "the universal risks"? Were they no longer risks? Nor universal? And how did it happen that a Conservative provincial premier was taking the health policy initiative from the Liberals? Surely this was a reversal of position. Something or someone had tampered with the script. In 1945 the federal government proposed—and the rich provinces had disposed. Now the richest province was proposing. Why? And who would now dispose and what would the disposition be?

The scenario had become extraordinarily complex. Not only did it involve rivalry between political parties, and conflict between the federal and provincial governments, but the interest groups—the medical profession, the hospital associations, and the insurance industry—had drastically altered their positions and thereby introduced discord rather than cooperation into the drama. But it was not simply an Alice-in-Wonderland scene; that was the first impression, but it was also the reality. *The fact was that almost everything had changed.* New political leaders had come on stage with new ideas; there were new inputs, new objectives, new constraints, new uncertainties, and a widening consensus among Canadians that a now proven solution must be effectively applied to a nation-wide, genuine, and serious problem.

THE BACKGROUND

Because the legacy of the past is part of every political issue, it is helpful to look back for beginnings to some earlier, unfinished agenda. In this case, that reference point was the collapse of the 1945–46 Dominion-Provincial Conference on Reconstruction.

It will be recalled that in the interplay of political forces in 1945 that were shaping the design of post-war Canada, for the first time since its 1919 party platform statement, a Liberal government had proposed a nation-wide health insurance program. That offer, however, had been inextricably bound up with the proposals for the transfer of major tax fields to the federal treasury. The rejection of the latter had automatically cancelled the former.

Between 1945 and 1955, although the federal government did not renew its health insurance offer, there were, nevertheless, a number of important developments that were slowly building up pressure for some larger action.

1. As we have seen, six months after the collapse of the conference, Saskatchewan introduced a universal hospital services plan that adhered fairly faithfully to the concepts enunciated in the Green Book proposals of 1945.

2. Two years later, British Columbia introduced a similar program. But the problems encountered were far greater than in Saskatchewan and maladministration of the program was a major cause of the Government's defeat in the election of 1952.

3. Alberta introduced a provincially-subsidized municipal hospital insurance program in 1950 but it covered only a part of the population.

4. In 1949, Newfoundland became a province of Canada and brought with it its famous cottage hospital system that covered a majority of the population outside the few urban centres. (The B.C., Alberta, and Newfoundland experience will be examined more fully in the next chapter.)

5. In May 1948, Prime Minister King announced the national health grants program (that is, the non-health insurance part of the 1945 proposals) which included a health survey grant that all provinces utilized.[3]

6. In June 1949, the Canadian Medical Association abandoned completely its 1943 policy of endorsing governmental health programs by announcing a new policy statement favouring the extension of voluntary plans to cover all Canadians with governments paying the premiums for those unable to provide for themselves.[4] The statement also recommended that "the first and most urgent stage [of health services] is the meeting of the costs of hospitalization for every citizen of Canada." The rejection of the governmental approach also became firm policies of the Canadian Hospital Association and the commercial insurance industry.[5]

There was mounting evidence to support these new attitudes in the rapid expansion of voluntary insurance enrolment. By 1952, almost 5.5 million Canadians were insured for hospital benefits through voluntary plans and commercial insurance and nearly four million were insured for medical and/or surgical benefits.

7. There was one other reversal of policy, this one by the federal government. In the 1953 election campaign, reflecting Mr. St. Laurent's conservative views, the Liberal party platform rejected further federal initiatives by announcing that "The Liberal party is committed to support a policy of contributory health insurance to be administered by the provinces when most of the provinces are ready to join in a nationwide scheme." "That," as the pundits said, "put the ball in the provinces' court."

The combination of all these developments had created a totally different environment from that of 1945. One person whose role both enabled and required him to be alert to such changes as they might affect government policy was Mr. George Gathercole, provincial economist for Ontario, who had become one of Premier Frost's closest official advisers. On a number of occasions during the winter of 1953–54, Mr. Gathercole and I talked about health insurance, the conversations ranging over the entire field including speculation on the significance for Ontario of the change in federal government policy. Mr. Gathercole's primary concern was the lack of a comprehensive information base on which a rational government policy could be formulated. His concern was conveyed to Mr. Frost. The result was a meeting in Mr. Frost's office on April 7, 1954, during which I was asked to prepare an analysis of the situation with respect to hospitals and physicians, the methods of financing health services with emphasis on insurance, and an analysis of alternative methods of extending health insurance to all residents of Ontario, together with estimates of costs of so doing.

The study was begun at the end of the academic term. An outline of the approach to be taken was discussed with Mr. Gathercole who assigned Mr. Ronald Verbrugge (a senior economist on his staff) and statistical and secretarial personnel to assist in the project.

A 186-page report was submitted on August 31.[6] The report (hereafter called the Taylor Report) analyzed the economics of hospital and medical care in Ontario, reviewed the services desirable in a comprehensive system, and the effects of introducing them in stages. It examined current expenditures and the costs of providing each stage of a health service to all residents, and explored alternative methods of administration and financing. Major emphasis was placed on the desirability of providing as much medical care as possible through group practice clinics, on the dangers of introducing hospital care insurance alone, and on the importance of preserving professional freedom.

Three sections analyzed the programs of British Columbia, Alberta, and Saskatchewan. The report made no recommendations but, in the letter of transmittal, highlighted four areas in which developments were considered imperative, quite apart from the issue of extending health insurance. These were: the creation of a health services planning agency, grants for the development of rehabilitation hospitals or departments of general hospitals, grants for the immediate development of home care programs, and grants to hospitals with schools of nursing to increase the educational component in the training of nurses and decrease the demands of the then widespread system of "contributed services."

The major premises on which the report was based were stated as follows: that all the costs of sickness and injury are borne by society in two ways, negatively through misery, disability, and premature death, and positively through the costs of preventive and treatment services; that it is in the interests of society as well as of the individual to reduce the negative costs by improving and expanding health care services; that increasing costs will inevitably fall on the provincial treasury; that wise planning and leadership on the part of the Government could contain the size of that financial burden by preventing the lop-sided development of certain health services; that the introduction of universal hospital insurance would necessitate strict controls to prevent the overbuilding of facilities; that professional and hospital services flourish best in an environment of freedom, including freedom from bureaucratic control; that government and private activity in the field of health are neither incompatible nor mutually exclusive since there is more to be done than both together can do; that it is easier for members of the community to pay more for health services while they are well than if only the sick pay for them; that in the words of the World Health Organization Charter, "informed opinion and active cooperation on the part of the public are of the utmost importance in the improvement of the health of the people."[7]

The report was distributed to all members of Cabinet and to senior officials in the Departments of Health, Treasury, Welfare, and Municipal Affairs. Premier Frost considered it a confidential government document, and it was not, therefore, released to the Legislature.

It was against this background of political party pronouncements, federal-provincial relations, the expanding voluntary insurance movement, and the financial position of hospitals that the Ontario government decision to press for a nation-wide program was slowly made. Why was it made?

THE ACTION IMPERATIVES

The Ontario policy to pressure the federal government to honour at least part of its 1945 proposals was a far more complex decision than that made by the Saskatchewan government in 1946. In weighing the imperatives in Ontario, one is dealing with less starkly obvious reasons, with grays rather than blacks and whites, with marginal increments rather than with total gains, with much greater opposition, and, obviously, with a government elected by a party committed to free enterprise and having no strong philosophical commitment to a government health program as a matter of principle. The policy emerged as an amalgam of financial realities, organizational limitations, interest group pressures, political rivalry, federal-provincial gamesmanship, and, perhaps most important, a concept of what Mr. Frost called, simply, "human betterment."

1. *The state of hospital resources.* As a result of the minimal investments in social capital during the depression and the war, the province was still short of what were generally considered to be adequate standards of hospital bed capacity. The Ontario Health Survey Report in 1951 had set as a minimum requirement 5.5 active-treatment beds per 1,000 population. By the end of 1954, the province was short of that goal by 5,500 beds, with a ratio of 4.4 beds per 1,000; the population increase alone required 800 new beds annually. The only provinces reaching or exceeding the Survey Committee standard were those three which had government-sponsored plans. It was evident that the supply of beds rested not only on the provision of capital funds but also on effective demand, on the ability of hospitals to obtain sufficient income to meet their operating costs.

A related problem was the imbalance in the kinds of hospital beds available. There were few rehabilitation facilities. There were few convalescent beds. The Survey Report had indicated a need of 7,500 chronic beds by the end of 1954, but there were only 4,000.

2. *The financial position of the hospitals.* Hospital operating costs in Ontario as in every other province and in the United States had been increasing at unprecedented rates. In the eight-year period since the war, total hospital expenditures had increased by 250 percent, hospital wages and salaries by 300 percent. But what was equally significant was that the costs per patient day in the two provinces having universal coverage had increased no more—in fact, in British Columbia, less—rapidly than in Ontario. In 1946, costs per patient day in British Columbia were twenty-four percent higher than in Ontario, but, in 1951, they were only twenty percent higher. Despite all the propaganda, it appeared that the costs of a government program could be responsibly controlled.

What was alarming, however, was the increasing frequency and size of hospital deficits in Ontario. Despite the fact that the provincial government made *per diem* grants to the hospitals (as did most of the other provinces), in 1952 six Class "A" hospitals had deficits averaging $2.46 per public ward day; twenty Class "B" hospitals had deficits averaging $1.92 per public ward day; and forty-six Class "C" hospitals had deficits averaging $1.26 per public ward day. A total of seventy-two hospitals had deficits amounting to $3.5 million. These deficits were incurred despite charges for public ward accommodation ranging from $9.30 per day at St. Michael's Hospital in Toronto to $14.43 per day in Oshawa. Semi-private charges were thirty percent higher and private ward charges sixty percent higher, on average, and any surpluses from these simply kept the deficits from being greater.

Part of the financial problem associated with hospitals was the increasing burden on both provincial and municipal governments for the care of indigent patients. Municipalities were required by provincial law to pay $6.00 per patient day on behalf of any indigent patient for whom it was responsible. This municipal payment was supplemented by two provincial payments: (a) a "maintenance" grant of $2.35 for each patient day in public ward beds (whether the patient was indigent or self-paying) and (b) an additional payment of $1.95 per patient day on behalf of indigent patients. Payments by governments were therefore an important source of funds supporting hospital solvency, as Table 3 indicates.

From these data, it is evident that nearly one-fifth (18.7 percent) of all hospital revenues came from provincial and municipal governments. Of this amount, 3.4 percent represented deficit payments by municipalities. Many hospitals, mainly those operated under church auspices, had no access to such sources. It was therefore significant that an additional

TABLE 3

PAYMENTS TO HOSPITALS IN ONTARIO BY PROVINCIAL AND MUNICIPAL
GOVERNMENTS, EXCLUSIVE OF WORKMEN'S COMPENSATION, 1954

	Payments	Percent of Hospitals' Income
Provincial Maintenance Grant	$5,937,000	7.8
Provincial payments on behalf of indigents: Provincial goverment in respect of indigents in unorganized territory	144,600	.2
On behalf of all indigents	1,501,600	2.0
Municipal government payments on behalf of indigents	4,043,700	5.3
Municipal deficit payments	2,573,400	3.4

SOURCE: Taylor Report.

$3,357,100 or 4.4 percent of all hospital revenues came from donations, interest, and miscellaneous sources.

3. *The role of insurance in the hospital economy of Ontario.* In Ontario, as in all but two of the provinces of Canada, voluntary insurance available through Blue Cross, commercial insurance, and cooperatives had become important sources of revenue for hospitals as well as providers of varying degrees of protection for patients. The Ontario Blue Cross Hospital Plan, a subsidiary of the Ontario Hospital Association, had enrolled by the end of 1954 a total of 1,921,607 participants. In addition, approximately 1,560,000 Ontario residents had some form of group or individual coverage through insurance companies and another 250,000 had coverage through cooperatives and other agencies. Some proportion of these people had more than one kind of coverage and this duplication was estimated by the Joint Committee (of the Insurance Companies) on Health Insurance to be approximately 250,000. With this estimated duplication removed, approximately 3,281,000 or sixty-seven percent of Ontario residents had some degree of protection against the costs of hospital bills.

It was clear, however, that the success of the voluntary method correlated highly with the degree of industralization of the population and therefore the numbers in large employee groups. Even in Ontario the earlier optimism that the voluntary system would embrace the total population, except for welfare recipients and a small additional group who could not afford premiums, began to fade. The reason was the rapid decline in the annual rates of growth from an increase in 1951 of 17.2 percent to 7.5 percent in 1952 and to 4.9 percent in 1953. Individual coverage had actually declined in absolute terms, from a high of 504,000 in 1952 to 437,000 in 1953.[8]

These data indicated that the voluntary system flourished only when insuring employee groups where the collection of premiums could be administered through pay-roll deduction, and it appeared that even in Ontario the outer limits were being approached. Approximately one-third of the population of Ontario did not have available a satisfactory system of budgeting their unpredictable hospital costs.

There were two additional questions about the voluntary system. The first was the degree of protection that the insurance available actually provided, and the second was the added costs that the insurance mechanism imposed. These questions were addressed in two separate studies in the Taylor Report.

The first study was conducted with the collaboration of the Dominion Bureau of Statistics and the Ontario Hospital Association in which a randomly selected sample of 14,000 hospital accounts was analyzed to ascertain the size of the account, by whom it was paid, and if paid by an insurance agency, what proportion of the bill was in fact "insured." The sample was drawn from hospitals in urban centres having a population of 25,000 or over where, it was assumed, the impact of insurance would be most visible.

The results of the survey indicated what would be expected, that the proportion of the hospital account paid by the insuring agency varied inversely with the size of the account, and with the proportion declining according to whether it was paid by Blue Cross, commercial group insurance, commercial individual insurance, or a cooperative.[9]

What was evident was that with respect to the larger accounts, when protection was most needed, even Blue Cross began to falter and the other types of coverage fell even further behind. In short, having two-thirds of the population insured did not mean that two-thirds of the population were fully protected. It also showed that the protection began to fall off when it was most needed—for the long-term illness and the serious accident.

The second special study centred on the question of the costs of "protection," or on how much the insurance system added to the costs of health services. In simplest terms, what was the difference between the premiums that insured subscribers paid and the benefits that insuring agencies paid out? This study was based on the annual reports of the

superintendent of insurance. The analysis showed the following relationships between benefits and premiums:

Type of Insurer	Benefits as Percent of Premiums	Premiums as Percent of Benefits
Blue Cross	85	118
Commercial (Group)	76.5	130
Commercial (Individual)	58.2	170
Cooperatives	85.8	116

The costs of the insurance mechanism, therefore, added to the costs
of hospital services, eighteen percent in the case of Blue Cross, thirty
percent in commercial group contracts, seventy percent in commercial
individual contracts, and sixteen percent in the case of cooperatives. The
data confirmed the much higher cost of selling and servicing individual
policies which, as shown earlier, also provided the least degree of protection.[10]

Despite these high overhead costs (compared with 5.7 percent for the
British Columbia plan and 5.0 percent for the Saskatchewan plan), the
increase in importance of voluntary insurance had been, as shown, almost
spectacular. Two-thirds of the population of Ontario had some insurance
for hospital benefits, and their insurance payments provided 47.4 percent
of all Ontario hospital revenues, or 56.6 percent of all non-governmental
sources. Self-paying patients provided 25.1 percent of all revenues and
35 percent of all non-governmental revenue.[11]

Four factors had accounted for this success: first, the needs of hospitals
for more assured sources of revenue that motivated the Blue Cross movement; second, the demands of labour unions for health insurance as part
of their packages of fringe benefits; third, aggressive marketing on the
part of commercial insurance; and fourth, the organized activities of
consumers in establishing the cooperative plans. But the success—and
in some cases, the failure, real and assumed—also had a self-defeating
effect. Whereas in 1945 only a small proportion of the population had
had any direct experience with it, now almost everyone was aware of it,
and two-thirds had taken advantage of it. But to a large proportion of the
remaining one-third, it was either unavailable, or not available on terms
which they could meet. And for some of those having coverage, the
protection was inadequate and the terms unsatisfactory, but the policies
were the only ones available.

Most of the problems faced by the insuring agencies are inherent in
the nature of the task of insuring health services, some of them character-

istic of both compulsory and voluntary systems while others are more typical of the voluntary approach. The special difficulties arise from the contrast between health insurance and other forms of both commercial and social insurance. In almost all other forms, the insured has a strong interest in avoiding the contingency against which he has insured. Life insurance is perhaps the best example; fire insurance is also obvious. Moreover, except for the occasional murderer or arsonist, normally no third party has a financial or other interest in the transaction.

But the *need* for health services is a less precisely determinable "contingency" than is death or conflagration except at extremes such as serious injury or illness. The demand for the insured benefits is initiated by the insured person on the basis of his perceived need, and that need is determined by a third party who also, therefore, is in a position to influence demand. A hospital administrator has high "readiness-to-serve" costs whether there are patients or not. It is as prudent for him to see that the beds are filled as it is for an inn-keeper with high fixed costs. It is also in the interest of the physician to see that, within ethical limits, the beds are filled. A version of Parkinson's law operates: occupancy rises to fill the beds available.

Accordingly, for the insuring agency, apart from monitoring excessive demand by review of records, the only apparently feasible means of assuring a reasonable relationship between revenues and expenditures was to define strictly those who were considered "insurable," to screen out the physically impaired, the chronically ill, the aged, and other high risks or "uninsurables." Blue Cross did not accept individual applications, although it would continue on an individual basis those who had left insured employment. Some companies insured only groups.

Both types of voluntary agencies were forced to set maximum limits on the benefits: Blue Cross usually in terms of numbers of days for each unrelated illness, and the commercial plans in terms of both days and payments per day. Individual contracts were also subjected to waiting periods, to exclusions for pre-existing conditions, and to cancellation for over-use and at retirement age.

The net impact of the unavoidable underwriting safeguards was that those most in need of an insuring or budgeting system, but outside its protection, were the chronically ill, the less physically robust, the low income groups, and the aged. And, of course, even those under its umbrella could through serious illness or injury find the protection minimal.

4. *Inequity of access to care.* One other element in the overall health care picture in the province was the difference in hospital use by the insured and the uninsured. Calculation of these rates was made by assuming that the utilization of hospitals by those persons insured through commercial

insurance or cooperatives was the same as that of Blue Cross subscribers, whose rates were known. The resulting estimates are shown in Table 4:

These data demonstrated that in 1953 the insured were admitted to hospital forty percent more frequently than were the uninsured. But the average length of stay of the latter was forty percent longer, attesting, one could assume, to their more serious conditions and, possibly, to their delay in seeking care.

These data, combined with the results of the Canadian Sickness Survey, published in 1953, confirming the higher rates of illness among lower income groups, reinforced with hard evidence the circular effects of low incomes and illness, and the preferred position of those with insurance.

5. *The idea of progress.* There were, in addition to the economic realities sketched above, two other factors of a different order, but powerful, nonetheless. The first of these might be termed "the idea of progress," a sense that the 1945 agenda for a better life in Canada had not yet been completed, that there were next steps to be taken along the road to what Premier Frost came to describe as "human betterment." It was linked to the growing public belief that health insurance worked, and that the goal of universal coverage was as attainable as it was desirable. This will be enlarged upon, later.

6. *The political realities.* The second of these factors was the increasing public attention being devoted to health insurance. Despite the easy return of the Progressive Conservatives in 1951, Mr. Donald MacDonald, leader of the CCF, never allowed the Legislature to forget the success of the Saskatchewan Hospital Services Plan, nor that a much less wealthy province had introduced its program without federal subsidy.

With the overwhelming Conservative majority, the sallies of the opposition parties might easily be disposed of, but as the year 1954 was ending, the issue had become more serious. The reason was that if the traditional four-year electoral cycle were to be followed, an election must be held at the most propitious time in 1955. The Ontario Liberals and the CCF had both campaigned strongly for health insurance in 1951. With the St. Laurent election campaign strategy in 1953 that had transferred the onus for initiative to the provinces, it could be anticipated that both parties would emphasize that the most significant provincial decision would be that of Ontario, and that, if elected, each would be committed to make the choice. From Mr. Frost's point of view the time might not be ripe for a decision; but it was time to remove the blame for delay from his government and return it to Mr. St. Laurent and the Liberal party that had held out the vague promise of health insurance since 1919.

TABLE 4

HOSPITAL ADMISSION RATES, AVERAGE DAYS' STAY, AND TOTAL PATIENT DAYS, INSURED AND NON-INSURED PATIENTS, ACTUAL, 1948–53; ESTIMATED 1954.

Year	Pop. in 1000's	Admissions per 1,000 Population			Average Days' Stay		Total Pop.	Total Patient Days
		Insured	Non-Insured	All Residents	Insured	Non-Insured		
1948	4,275	120	94.6	107.3	7.9	13.8	10.2	4,811,276
1949	4,378	122	97.8	109.9	8.9	12.4	10.2	5,023,544
1950	4,471	124	97.2	110.6	9.1	12.6	10.3	5,252,566
1951	4,598	127	98.5	115.6	9.0	13.0	10.1	5,510,301
1952	4,766	136	101.3	122.1	8.8	12.6	9.8	5,857,258
1953	4,897	139	98.0	122.6	8.3	13.3	10.2	6,141,000
1954	5,000	145	107.5	130.0	8.8	12.4	10.0	6,500,000

SOURCE: Taylor Report, p. 104.

7. *A national viewpoint.* There seems to have been one further factor that motivated Mr. Frost's actions. That was his vision of Canada as a whole and not simply as a collection of competing provinces. This view obliged him to help shape events as much as possible in a way that would contribute to the development of the Canadian nation. His biographer no doubt will cite other examples but one is relevant here. He made it explicit at the October 1955 Federal-Provincial Conference:

> All the provinces are now engaged in various projects which could be integrated into a national plan....it is properly a federal-provincial matter, and it should be brought out into the open and placed before this conference for study and action. If this is not done, we can look forward to more misunderstanding and confusion. The federal government and the ten provinces will continue to move in different directions, creating a hodge-podge that no one will be able to disentangle; and a national plan will never be achieved simply because of the impossibility of finding common ground upon which to act. A few years more and an integrated plan becomes an impossibility.[12]

This assessment of his motives is reinforced by the fact that, as the provincial treasurer, he was aware, probably more than anyone else, that the cost to the citizens of Ontario of a national plan would be greater than if Ontario, like the western provinces, decided to develop a program on its own.

As a result of all these factors, and reluctant though he may have been to embark on a policy that would be constrained, uncertain, and even, possibly, hazardous, the moment of truth had arrived. There were economic, political, and humanitarian reasons to act; there were financial and political reasons to delay. At some point in the near future, some kind of decision would have to be made.

To this point we have been examining the reasons why some action needed to be taken. But no matter what the problem, or how obvious the solution, every government is limited by various factors in the choices it can make. These constraints affecting a decision on health insurance will now be examined.

THE CONSTRAINTS

1. *The Conservative party.* One of the constraints on the Government's decision making was basic: whether a policy should be developed at all; and, if it were, whether it could be sold to the caucus, and other key party supporters. The latter were obviously ardent supporters of free enterprise and non-government intervention in principle, and many of them oppo-

nents of government health insurance in particular. Within the party, and beamed to it from many outside the party, was the ubiquitous claim that the voluntary system could do the job totally, if only government would fulfill its restricted but legitimate function of subsidizing those who needed help.

A key factor militating against action by this particular government was that its legislative majority was large and its future optimistic. Even if health insurance enjoyed the public demand that its supporters claimed, it would be sound political strategy to postpone action until its appeal was really needed. Given this political posture of the leading party supporters, an acceptable solution would necessarily be restricted to one that interfered as little as possible with the voluntary insurance system. Moreover, the degree to which it did interfere must be explainable in terms acceptable to a basically hostile, or at least divided, party leadership.

2. *The need for new revenues.* Of the alternative policies that might be available, for example, subsidies of hospitals, or doctors, or individuals, or of the insurance system itself, the preferred choice would have to be one that provided commensurate new revenues. With the rapid expansion of population and urban and industrial development, the increasing demands for social capital for roads, highways, and education, there were simply too many other priorities making claims on projected revenues from existing sources.

3. *The federal political constraint.* Given that Mr. Frost was determined not to move without federal cost sharing, a resulting constraint would be that an Ontario program might well have to be restricted to the limits within which the federal government determined that it could move. That meant, in turn, that the ultimate program must be acceptable to most, if not all, of the provinces. And in that design, the province of Quebec could well have an over-riding influence. Quebec might, possibly, be neutral. It might also oppose. It had traditionally been the "last man in" on every federal social service program. Four provinces—already involved in hospital insurance—could be counted upon in the support column. But for all the others, even fifty-percent sharing by the federal government was not necessarily attractive; there still remained for them the problem of financing the other fifty percent, and the imposition of taxes to raise that matching sum might well be beyond their political and financial capacity to achieve. Ontario would have to move warily here.

4. *Administrative requirements.* The administrative complexities of a government health insurance program were yet another major constraint on policy choices. Saskatchewan had had the advantage of a uniform, prov-

ince-wide, municipal system that was close to the people, and municipal spokesmen had publicly declared themselves, in advance of any action, prepared to participate in the vital function of assuring universal coverage. Ontario had no such ready-made premiums collection system. The cities were too large; the rural municipalities uncommitted. If a decision were made, the administrative task must be undertaken gradually, with sureness of touch, with no possibility of public reaction against it. The experience of British Columbia's precipitate and disastrous plunge into an administrative morass, with its fatal political consequences, had to be avoided at all costs. Careful planning, deliberate steps, and consummate political finesse must characterize any action. There was a vast difference in complexity in dealing with the one million people in each of the western provinces and the six millions in Ontario.

5. *The established pattern of hospital insurance.* Here, again, the situation differed from that of Saskatchewan. There, the Government started from an almost clean slate in that there had been no Blue Cross Plan and little commercial insurance coverage. In Ontario, on the other hand, a system was already in being, with established policies and standard operating procedures with respect to benefits and their pricing, conditions of entitlement, control mechanisms, and revenue collecting. If the Government were to displace that system partly or totally, there were limits to the extent to which it could change the established patterns or norms unless such changes were clearly perceived by all participants—hospitals, physicians, patients, subscribers—as important, if not major, improvements.

At the same time, of course, to the extent that these policies and procedures were judged by the Government to be effective and desirable, they would be perceived not as constraints to its decision making but, rather, as precedents to be used to advantage. The precedent of financing the system by individual responsibility for payment of premiums was clearly such an advantage. It was, in fact, a ready-made revenue system, a personal tax that had been voluntarily self-imposed. Despite the British Columbia experience with premiums and its switch to sales tax financing, here was a tax source not to be abandoned lightly, especially if the rate of "taxation" could be reduced by the fact of federal contributions.

There were other, lesser limitations on policy choices, but these were the major constraints within which the major decisions would have to be made.

THE UNCERTAINTIES

In general, the uncertainties were those characteristics of any political decision. Despite all the economic analyses, the projections, the forecasts, the preliminary bargaining with powerful interest groups, no political leader can ever be sure of the outcomes of a political decision of such magnitude. Etched in his mind is Murphy's Law: "If things can go wrong; they will; if they can't go wrong, they will anyway!" And the defeat of the British Columbia government in 1952 was a constant reminder, if one were needed. What were the most relevant uncertainties?

1. *Costs.* As in all such ventures, the primary uncertainty was the question of costs, and especially costs in the long run. The Taylor Report had analyzed the trends in hospital utilization, *per diem* costs, and rates of population increase. Reasonably accurate estimates could be made on the assumption of the continuation of those trends, with revisions for new hospital construction being completed, initiated, or in the approval stage. Estimates based on these data and analyses could reasonably be relied upon for, say, three years. But then new factors affecting demand and unit costs would almost certainly begin to have a major impact. Insured persons were admitted to hospital forty percent more often than were the uninsured. But the uninsured patients remained in hospital forty percent longer. How could one forecast the hospital days required once a universal plan with unlimited benefit-days came into effect? In three years their demands could be translated into a rapid expansion of hospital capacity. Improved staff-patient ratios could be expected; new and expensive technology would be introduced; demands for equality in pay of hospital workers with similar occupations in the community generally were to be expected; but the total financial impact of such demands was not predictable very far into the future.

2. *The shortage of facilities.* The question of the adequacy of facilities was complex. Despite the Saskatchewan and British Columbia experience, no one really knew what universal coverage and unlimited benefit days might produce in terms of demand in a population as large as that of Ontario. The shortage of auxiliary facilities—convalescent and chronic care beds and nursing homes—was serious. No one really knew the pent-up demand for long-term treatment. Once people had paid premiums for a policy that promised unlimited benefit-days, the demand might, indeed, be overwhelming. The Sickness Survey had revealed far more long-term disabling conditions than had previously been recognized.

3. *The ability to achieve universal enrolment.* A government system, no less than a commercial operation, could not avoid extraordinarily high costs (and therefore taxes) if only those needing care enrolled. It is the perennial problem of the free loader. To obtain the advantages of univer-sal participation—the healthy as well as the less healthy—universal cover-

age must be achieved. But that would mean compulsion, and not simply compulsion for large employee groups, but for individuals. Compulsion meant legal proceedings to enforce payment, which meant resentment, and resentment meant political recrimination at the polls. That might be acceptable in socialist Saskatchewan but not, in the view of the Progressive-Conservative premier, in Ontario. How many, then, might be enrolled? Without compulsion no one knew.

4. *The interest group response.* The fourth area of uncertainty embraced the reactions of three powerful groups: the medical profession, the hospital association, and the insurance industry. That all would oppose a government plan modelled on that of Saskatchewan or British Columbia was predictable. What was uncertain was the nature and vigour of that opposition and the impact it would have on public opinion and on the degree of cooperation that would be forthcoming if, despite their opposition, the Government went ahead. Negotiations with, and the political influence and power of, these groups would create outcomes that were as unpredictable as they were crucial to the shape and the success of any plan.

5. *The federal policies.* All of these uncertainties were exacerbated by the unpredictable political outcomes of bargaining with the federal government. The most extreme result would arise if the St. Laurent Cabinet decided not to participate at all. Ontario would then have to abandon any intentions to proceed or finance any program by itself. But if it were assumed that the federal government would do *something*, then whatever it chose would have unpredictable effects on Ontario. How far Ottawa might go and the concomitant demands it might make created uncertainties of a high order.

6. *The voters.* And, then, there were the citizens. What would be their response? Could the plan be made more attractive than the coverage already held by two-thirds of them? If it were to be a compulsory plan, what would be the reaction to that? What if a majority of them accepted the view of the insurance companies and prepayment spokesmen that government's role was simply to help those who could not afford voluntary plan premiums?

It would be, indeed, a risky venture. For a government with strong majority support, there was a great deal to be lost in the event of any foul-ups and, in terms of political credit, no one could be certain of the gains.

To this point we have examined briefly the historical background, the reasons why some action seemed necessary, and the constraints and uncertainties surrounding a policy decision of such magnitude. It is, of course, one thing for a policy analyst, with the advantage of hindsight, to lay out these many factors in their relatively neat compartments; they never appear that way to the political decision maker in the midst of the fray, dealing with a vast array of other problems, pressures, and objectives.

As a result of the experiences of the western provinces, the studies he had commissioned, and the discussions he had with Mr. Gathercole, Mr. Frost now had more information on which to develop a policy than had any of the provincial premiers who had taken the leap before him. But he had not yet made a decision. Finally, on March 23, 1955, a couple of hours before the evening session of the Legislature when he was to give his budget address, he asked George Gathercole to prepare a few remarks on health insurance for him to incorporate in his speech.[13] This Mr. Gathercole did.

Mr. Frost began his comments on health insurance in the budget speech by saying that he agreed with Mr. St. Laurent who had stated as recently as January 20, that his government could not undertake the establishment of any program while facilities were still too few to assure every citizen of hospital space which could be demanded under the contractual obligations of a health plan.[14] He then went on:

> Health insurance for the people of Ontario is inevitable, but lack of assurance of federal participation and overwhelming cost make it impossible at the present time. ... Whether the Federal government will contribute to such a plan is conjecture. So far, they have not undertaken to pay for any portion of the cost of hospital insurance plans operating in three other provinces, and it is unlikely they will make any contribution until health insurance is established on a national basis.
>
> However, the question is not one of whether health insurance will come—come it must and will. The only question is—when is the right time for it?[15]

He estimated that a hospital plan would cost $112,000,000 and the addition of physicians' services would increase the total to $189,000,000. To raise such amounts without a federal contribution would require premiums of up to $55 for a household of three plus a three percent retail sales tax. However, he observed that with a federal-provincial conference approaching, this was not the time to be making decisions.[16]

Two government members had spoken on health matters prior to Mr. Frost. The minister of health, the Hon. MacKinnon Philips, had given a review of the health situation in the province and had recited, among other accomplishments, the expansion of hospital accommodation in Ontario since 1946. Mr. Alfred Cowling, Progressive Conservative member for High Park, had stressed the rising demand for a health insurance system that did not involve state medicine. "Private insurance companies," he said, "working in cooperation with the medical profession can do a better job of protecting the health of our people than any government can."[17]

Whether the premier knew in advance of his colleague's decision to express his views publicly is not known, but Mr. Cowling's statement confirmed what many suspected, that neither the caucus nor the Cabinet had come to agreement on a health insurance policy.

Clearly, there was not yet a decision to act, but whatever the outcome might be, there was now a beginning. The premier had said that a program would come, but that it was impossible without federal participation and whether that eventuality would happen was a matter of conjecture.

Acutely aware of the federal Liberal strategy that placed the onus for action on provincial initiatives, and that Ontario had been handed the starter's gun, Mr. Frost began the planning of his strategy for the upcoming Federal-Provincial Conference in April which would decide upon the agenda for the full-scale conference later in the year.

The fact that the process of developing and introducing the program spanned five years inordinately complicates the presentation of this analysis. Far more than in the two preceding cases, the factors contributing to the policy—the inputs of interest groups, political parties, the federal government, withinputs of the bureaucracy and the governmental process, the outputs of legislation, and the decisions taken in the strategy of implementation—impacted in anything but nice, neat, easily perceived or described categories of a conceptual framework. Accordingly, in this chapter, the reader is forewarned that because of the long chronology of events, it has been necessary to move back and forth among the classifications that have been adopted.

For example, in the first two chapters, the "strategy of implementation" logically followed the final formulation of the policy or the legislative authorization of the program. In this case, however, it is necessary to consider the strategy at a number of points, the first being immediately after Mr. Frost's decision that the entire issue must be brought into the open and seriously studied by the two senior levels of government.

STRATEGY I

In the words of his former adviser, Mr. George Gathercole, Mr. Frost, "although inherently cautious, was a reformer, albeit a moderate reformer. Strategy and timing were the art of good government. He believed in gradualism, growth and development, betterment, not radical transformation. He took pleasure in planning improvements that would make Ontario and Canada a better place in which to live....he constantly admonished his colleagues not to make up their minds until all alternatives had been explored and assessed. He was thus in an unrivalled position to defend the policy adopted."[18]

His approach to the question of health insurance was wholly in character with this description. He was not committed to health insurance. He was keenly aware that in any attempt to bring a program to fruition in Ontario, he would find his most serious opposition within his own party caucus and from important Conservative party supporters, as well as from the insurance industry, probably from the medical profession and, even, possibly, from the Hospital Association and its Blue Cross organization. If a program were to be introduced, it would be essential, on the political level, to introduce it with the highest degree of public consensus and the largest possible federal contribution, and on the administrative level to bring it in smoothly and effectively. All these considerations, combined with his predilection for caution, dictated a gradualist approach. There must be no mistakes from undue haste.

As we have seen, he had decided that the issue should be raised at the forthcoming federal-provincial "agenda" conference. That decision was reinforced by an episode involving the Hon. J. W. Pickersgill. Mr. Pickersgill, then minister of citizenship and immigration, made a speech in Kitchener, Ontario, on April 4, 1955, and was quoted in the *Toronto Globe and Mail* as saying that national health insurance would come "only if there was a change of government in Ontario."[19]

On April 6, he was questioned in the House of Commons by Mr. George Hees, Progressive Conservative M. P. from Toronto. "[Did the Minister say] in Kitchener the other evening that the province of Ontario could only receive a hospitalization plan if it changed the government of that province?"[20]

Mr. Pickersgill replied: "What I said was this: Health is constitutionally a provincial matter but the policy of the Liberal party is to assist in provincially administered hospital insurance when the provinces generally are in accord, and that could not happen until the Ontario government adopted a new attitude."[21]

Mr. Frost was angered by the incident and although it was in itself insignificant, it did, however, add an emotional overtone to Mr. Frost's determination that responsibility for delay should be placed where it belonged—on the federal Liberals.

The assembly of federal and provincial delegates in Ottawa on April 29 was called a "preliminary meeting." Its purpose, the first time such a procedure had been used, was to agree upon an agenda for the main

125

conference to be convened later. As noted in the opening pages of this chapter, Prime Minister St. Laurent's strategy was to limit the agenda to two main items: federal-provincial fiscal agreements, and the question of assistance to the unemployed.[22] But, as we have seen, this did not satisfy Mr. Frost, the first of the provincial spokesmen. He agreed on the two points specified by Mr. St. Laurent and then stated that "health insurance deserves the consideration of this Conference [which] can do a great deal to clarify the issues involved." "We suggest," he said, "that the whole question be intensively studied, with a view to arriving at the following:

1. A health insurance plan in which there would be both federal and provincial participation and in which the fullest details of the extent of the coverage to the individual would be given.

2. Estimates as accurate as possible of the cost of such a plan and how that cost would be shared—(i) by the individual or family; (ii) by the provincial government; (iii) by the federal government.

3. How the monies to support such a plan would be raised.

4. In what manner and under what conditions a health plan could be proceeded with in stages in accordance with the medical and hospital organization and the financial position of each province.

5. In the stages suggested in (4), what priority could be given to meeting the crippling financial burdens imposed on the individual and family by prolonged illness and affliction.

6. In what way the plans established by individual provinces could be integrated into a federal-provincial health insurance plan.[23]

The responses of the other premiers were as might have been predicted: strong support from Mr. Douglas and Mr. Bennett, and no references by any of the others in their public, opening-day statements. But on Wednesday, when the conference met *in camera*, the constraints of speaking for the public record were removed. Only the formal overlay of parliamentary courtesy thinly veiled the tough political battle being waged as Mr. Frost pressed (with the support of Douglas and Bennett), and Mr. St. Laurent resisted.

In fact, as so frequently happens in such confrontations, increasing pressure generated increased resistance which in turn increased the pressure. Following a lunch-time consultation of federal ministers, in the afternoon session the prime minister finally conceded that health insurance should be on the agenda but only under the non-committal compromise heading of "Health and Welfare Services." Newspaper reporters were aware of the political struggle behind the closed doors and the headlines announced: "Provinces Win!"

A good beginning had been made by Mr. Frost in his strategy of dealing with the national government. It was now necessary to turn to the domestic part of the strategy, to contend with the opposition parties in the election, and to have the Office of the Provincial Economist and the Health Department begin the preparations for the October Conference on Federal-Provincial Relations.

THE GOVERNMENT CONTRIBUTION

Under this heading are grouped those ideas, analyses, and proposals generated by the interaction of senior officials and the ministers, as all the elements of proposed solutions to a problem are moulded into a program design that becomes enunciated finally as government policy. Until the final draft of the legislation is sent to the Queen's Printer and the last draft of a minister's statement is mimeographed, it is a complex and fluid process as the affected ministers, departments, treasury officials, and the legislative draftsmen react to the continuing demands, proposals, and criticisms from interest groups, press, caucus, and opposition parties, as well as to new ideas generated within the governmental process itself. These are the activities that in systems analysis terms are called the "with-inputs" and whose meaning can be encapsulated in the term, "to govern."

In the process that yielded the final form of the Ontario hospital insurance plan, the first contributions were the results of the discussions of Mr. Frost and Mr. Gathercole. These led, as noted, to the Taylor Report of 1954 which had analyzed the existing system of voluntary insurance and outlined alternative methods of achieving a universal program.

Six major alternatives were considered and the advantages and disadvantages of each examined and weighed in substantial detail. They were:

1. Administration by a government agency. Under this option, four methods of organizing the central agency were examined:

   (a) Administration by the Department of Health
   (b) Establishment of an independent commission
   (c) Government department and Advisory Council
   (d) Creation of PSI and Blue Cross as crown corporations.

2. The establishing of a contractual arrangement with the Ontario Blue Cross and Physicians Service, Inc. (PSI), to cover all Ontario residents.

3. Government subsidy of all insuring plans and companies.

4. Provincial subsidy of local or regional government programs.

5. Government subsidy of hospitals and physicians.

6. Government subsidy of patients.

Among the criteria used in evaluating each alternative were the following:

1. The importance of the cooperation of hospitals and the health professions to the success of any program.

2. The effectiveness of each proposal in achieving universal coverage.

3. The implications of different types of subsidies, i.e., of hospitals, medical doctors, insuring agencies, or of individual patients.

4. Administrative efficiency and costs.

5. Ministerial and legislative responsibility for the program and for the expenditure of public funds.

This analysis served as the basis for extensive discussion by the planning group with the three ministers most concerned. Only gradually did the choices emerge.

I had worked briefly with Mr. Gathercole in the preparation of materials for Mr. Frost prior to the April conference and, with the main conference scheduled for October, I was again asked to serve as consultant during the summer of 1955, working with Mr. Gathercole and Dr. J. T. Phair, deputy minister of health. Mr. Ronald Verbrugge continued to work on the financial aspects.

As Mr. Frost discussed with his planning group the political situation vis-à-vis Ottawa, he viewed it as still very much an open-ended political bargaining situation. Not all the provinces had spoken favourably or with enthusiasm in the closing sessions of the April meeting, and Mr. Duplessis had been totally non-commital. Mr. St. Laurent's personal opposition could be anticipated but his about-face at the April conference suggested that Mr. Paul Martin's support in the Cabinet was increasing. It was obvious, therefore, that if anything were to happen, and the maximum federal contribution to be obtained in the event that it did, it would be necessary to have maximum support from a maximum number of provinces. Because none of the provinces was yet certain what new revenues would be available following the up-coming tax agreement negotiations, some provinces might be able to go only part way towards a comprehensive plan and some, even, not be able to go any distance at all. It would be necessary to provide alternative proposals, one or more of which might be acceptable. Accordingly, the general strategy that emerged to guide Ontario's planning was (1) the most desirable plan for Ontario, modified by (2) the kind of program or programs that would be acceptable to Ottawa, which in turn would be influenced by (3) the program or programs acceptable to a majority of the provinces.[24]

The next step would be to make certain that there would be no working at cross purposes among politicians and officials. I therefore prepared a draft of a statement of objectives. Following discussion and modification these were agreed to be:

1. To make available to all the population more extensive hospital benefits than those currently available, regardless of age, health condition, or status of employment.

2. To meet the full costs of care, enabling the hospitals to eliminate their deficits and provide services of improved quality.

3. To remove, as far as possible, any artificial financial or administrative distinctions between acute, convalescent, or chronic care, or care for mental illness and tuberculosis.

4. To remove, as far as possible, any inducement to enter or remain in hospital for services that could be provided more economically elsewhere.

5. To meet to the fullest extent possible the aspirations of the people in this area of need, consistent with the prudent use of public funds, while disturbing existing patterns of practice or insurance arrangements as little as possible.[25]

The alternatives posed by the Taylor Report were analyzed and debated, and gradually a consensus of the ministers began to emerge. I was then asked to prepare drafts of a series of proposals which could be laid before the conference, together with a statement for each setting forth the purpose, description, method of administration, estimated costs, and method(s) of financing. The draft of each alternative was thoroughly analyzed and discussed by the committee and the ministers and, after several revisions, finally agreed upon.

The alternatives were as follows:

1. Diagnostic services, estimated to cost Ontario $18,000,000, or $3.00 *per capita*.

2. A home care program, estimated to cost $1.00 *per capita*.

3. Assistance toward extraordinary hospital costs. This was a reduced version of a catastrophic insurance program (what the insurance com-

panies had termed "major medical" but, in this proposal, restricted to hospital costs only)

4. Maternal and newborn hospital care. This resembled the Alberta program and was estimated to cost $12,500,000.

5. A comprehensive hospital services plan; estimated to cost for 1956, $106,000,000.[26]

It was assumed that the first four programs would be administered by the Government but three alternative methods of administration were listed under the comprehensive plan: (a) through voluntary plans and commercial insurance companies: (b) by the Blue Cross; (c) by a government agency.

To emphasize that these five proposals were to be considered by the other provincial governments as alternatives, each program proposal was separately bound, and copies were prepared for all members of the conference.

As a result of a meeting held on September 28 by the premier with the executive of the Ontario Hospital Association, Mr. Stanley Martin, associate secretary-treasurer of the OHA, and Mr. David Ogilvie, executive director of Blue Cross, joined the Ontario delegation to the conference.

STRATEGY II

The Federal-Provincial Conference re-convened in Ottawa on October 3, 1955. Its primary purpose was to reach consensus on a revised formula for the tax agreements. Health insurance was a separate item, but it was not unrelated for, as already noted, the capacity of some of the provinces to finance their share of a health services program depended very much upon the additional revenues forthcoming from any new fiscal formula.

Having dealt with the fiscal issue in his introductory statement to the conference, Mr. St. Laurent then set the stage for the health insurance item on the agenda by posing two questions:

What are the stages by which further action by the provinces in the field of health insurance might be considered as feasible; what agreement can be reached among the provinces themselves as to the order of priority of the various services?
Under what circumstances would the federal government be justified in offering to assist provincial activities in the health insurance field?[27]

The first he tentatively answered by saying that "It has been suggested that . . . the next logical step to be taken might well be the provision of radiological and laboratory services."

The second he answered by repeating what he had said on other occasions, that "if it can be reasonably shown that the national rather than merely local or sectional interest is thereby being served. . . . If there were a substantial majority of the Canadian people prepared to embark upon provincially administered schemes, then the Federal government would be justified in participating."[28]

Following Mr. St. Laurent's extensive introduction, Mr. Frost also spoke at length on the fiscal issue, and then turned to "the second main point to which I should like to refer, the matter of health and hospital insurance."[29] He reminded the conference of the length of time that health insurance had been proposed, of the 1945 federal commitment, and particularly of the necessity for this conference to bring the subject "out into the open for study and action."

He then made the point, quoted earlier, that in the absence of concerted action, the federal and provincial governments would continue to move in different directions, creating a hodge-podge that no one would be able to disentangle. A few years more and an integrated plan would become an impossibility.

He then outlined the five alternative proposals, and distributed copies of each to all the members. The primary objective of the Ontario initiative was to gain acceptance of the comprehensive hospital services plan; the others were submitted for consideration should there be failure to achieve the major objective.

The four elements in a comprehensive plan would include, said the document:[30]

1. In-patient and out-patient diagnostic services; 2. In-patient care in general, convalescent, and chronic care hospitals; 3. In-patient care in mental hospitals and tuberculosis sanatoria; 4. Home care services.

In concluding, Mr. Frost stated that Ontario was prepared to come into a national plan along the lines elaborated, and he suggested that a committee be set up to proceed with intensive studies of health insurance and report back to the conference at a later date.

The Frost statement, with its specific alternative proposals, had an almost electrifying effect on the conference. The negotiation of new and (for the provinces) more favourable tax agreements was still the main item on the agenda. But never before had there been such a specific health proposal from the largest province, with alternatives designed to elicit maximum support from the other provinces. Even so, their responses were mixed. Mr. Maurice Duplessis made no reference to health insurance. The others reacted as expected: those having programs, with strong endorsement; those not, with promises or indication of cooperation if requisite finances were forthcoming.

The rest of the conference was held *in camera* and at its conclusion the prime minister announced the appointment of a special committee on health insurance, composed of two ministers and two deputy ministers from the federal government and from each province, to make a comprehensive study.

GOVERNMENT PLANNING CONTINUED

Within the Government, the planning and development process was accelerated and, as he discussed the administrative alternatives with his advisers, Mr. Frost concluded that in order to meet the legislative timetable, the substantive decision he must now make concerned the nature of the agency to be responsible for the over-all program. That, he decided, should be a representative commission, established as soon as legislation could be passed. Given the increasing demand for hospital construction that could be expected once an insurance program was announced, there would need to be an agency responsible for making certain that the right facilities in the right amount were available in the right place. A commission could do that. It could also be responsible for the design of an insurance program, but it need not administer the plan itself; that decision could wait.

There were now three major, interrelated tasks: to prepare the legislation, to prepare a briefing document for the Legislature and the testimony to be presented to the Health Committee, and to participate in the work of the Federal-Provincial Committee on Health Insurance. For these purposes a new planning committee was struck. Mr. George Tattle, Health Department comptroller, was appointed chairman. Two other members were Mr. David Ogilvie of Blue Cross and Mr. Stanley Martin of the OHA, both of whom had attended the October conference. I continued as consultant, responsible for the drafting. The Planning Committee held regular meetings with Mr. Gathercole and less regular, but fairly frequent, meetings with Mr. Frost, Provincial Treasurer Dana Porter and Health Minister Phillips. As the date of the conference approached, several larger meetings were held with Deputy Provincial Treasurer Hugh Brown, Comptroller of Revenue Philip Clark, Comptroller of Finance Harold Walker, and representatives from the departments of Welfare and Municipal Affairs.

Because of the large expenditures involved, the preparation of cost estimates was a central concern. The original estimates in the Taylor Report were up-dated and refined and these were, in turn, carefully compared with cost estimates for all provinces that had just been completed and distributed by the research division of the Department of National Health and Welfare.

Both sets of estimates were made on the assumption that there would be immediate central controls on the number of beds to be approved for construction, but the Ontario estimates were based on the assumption of simultaneous introduction of out-patient diagnostic services, convalescent and chronic care benefits, and home care services. It emphasized that the estimates for the hospital care benefit would have to be increased substantially if these other benefits were not included.

Using the Ontario (utilization) method, the cost of the hospital insurance benefit, if the program were in operation in 1957, was estimated to be $141.8 million. The total program estimates are shown in Table 5:

In addition, there were estimates of yields of various rates of co-insurance, and various rates of premiums that would be required depending on whether the federal government's contribution was 60, 50, or 40 percent.

Armed with the proposals and cost estimates in a thirty-two-page briefing document, Provincial Treasurer Porter and Health Minister Phillips, and their advisers, arrived in Ottawa on Sunday, January 26, 1956 to attend the meeting of the Health Insurance Committee established by the October Conference.

STRATEGY III

In a dramatic move to press the federal government to move as far, as quickly, and as financially generously as possible, the Honourable Dana Porter released a press statement on the eve of the conference, outlining the Ontario position:

1. The meeting should plan the outline of a long-term national program to be developed in partnership between federal and provincial governments.

2. The program should have fairly uniform standards but should be flexible enough to let each province alter its various parts when and how it best suited each one.

3. Decision of one or more provinces not to proceed at this time should not hold up either the launching of a national plan or the granting of federal aid to provinces that have existing plans or are ready to introduce one.

4. The larger the federal share of the costs, the greater the equalization among the provinces. A 60 percent federal share of the estimated cost would be reasonable, provided the estimate were realistic.

TABLE 5

SUMMARY OF ESTIMATED PROGRAM COSTS (BASED ON ONTARIO
UTILIZATION AND PER DIEM COST ESTIMATES)

	1956	1957	1958	1959	1960
	($1000's)				
Total Costs:					
Active	$106,300	$120,400	$135,000	$150,300	$166,100
Convalescent	1,700	1,900	2,500	4,100	6,600
Chronic	12,100	13,400	15,000	17,500	20,900
Diagnostic services	16,000	16,400	16,800	17,200	17,600
Home care programs	5,300	5,500	5,600	5,700	5,900
Sub total	141,400	157,600	174,900	194,800	217,100
Sub total with 5% for administration	148,500	165,500	183,600	204,500	228,000
Mental hospitals	26,000	31,500	36,500	43,200	50,500
Tuberculosis sanatoria	7,000	7,000	7,000	7,000	7,000
Total	$181,500	$204,000	$227,100	$254,700	$285,500
Per Capita Cost:					
Active	$19.96	$22.05	$24.13	$26.23	$28.33
Convalescent	.32	.35	.45	.72	1.13
Chronic	2.27	2.45	2.68	3.05	3.56
Diagnostic services	3.00	3.00	3.00	3.00	3.00
Home care programs	1.00	1.00	1.00	1.00	1.00
Sub total	26.55	28.85	31.26	34.00	37.02
Sub total with 5% for administration	27.88	30.31	32.82	35.70	38.89
Mental hospitals	4.88	5.77	6.52	7.54	8.61
Tuberculosis sanatoria	1.31	1.28	1.25	1.22	1.19
Total	$34.07	$37.36	$40.59	$44.46	$48.69

SOURCE: Briefing document prepared for Ontario delegation, January 1956.

5. Part of the provincial share should be raised by personal tax premiums, and these should be made mandatory on all groups as soon as administrative machinery can be set up. Other parts of the provincial share should come from general revenues and co-insurance. Each province should determine how it allocates amounts among the three types.

6. Hospital care for the mentally ill and tuberculosis patients should be considered as insured benefits.

7. The federal government should share costs of administration at the same rate as costs of services.

8. A comprehensive hospital services program should be introduced first, covering diagnosis, hospital care and home care.[31]

It was clearly an attempt to influence any last-minute deliberations of the federal Cabinet.

Although the sessions of the conference were held *in camera*, the afternoon newspapers carried the full story of the Ontario proposals, with some comment by other ministers. Mr. Eric Martin, health minister for British Columbia, said that his government would be willing to accept an offer of fifty percent from the federal government provided the costs were calculated on the full costs in each province.[32] There was speculation that Ontario might reduce its demand for sixty percent to fifty percent, but that it, too, would insist on the calculation being based on Ontario's actual costs.[33]

The conference continued for four days with extensive reports from the three western provinces and Newfoundland on the operations of their respective hospital insurance programs.

Finally, on Thursday, at the afternoon session, the federal offer was simultaneously announced to the provincial delegates by Mr. Martin and in the House of Commons by the prime minister.

The federal offer was consistent with Mr. St. Laurent's and Mr. Martin's earlier policy declarations:

Its main points, in outline:

1. The federal government was willing to assist with technical support and financial assistance any provinces wishing to proceed with hospital insurance plans, as soon as a majority of provincial governments representing a majority of the Canadian people are ready to proceed.

2. Priority at this time should be given to diagnostic services and hospital care.

3. Provincial hospital plans (a) should make coverage universally available to all residents of the province; (b) include provision of specific diagnostic (laboratory and radiological) services to in-patients, and within an agreed period of time to out-patients; (c) limit co-insurance or "deterrent" charges so as to ensure that an excessive financial burden is not placed on patients at the time of receiving service.

4. The federal contribution would be a specified portion of normal operating and maintenance costs of hospital care at the standard ward level but would not include capital costs.

5. The federal contribution would not be made in respect of care in mental hospitals or tuberculosis sanatoria.

6. The federal contribution to each province in respect of its shareable costs would be· (a) twenty-five percent of the average *per capita* costs for hospital services in Canada as a whole; plus (b) twenty-five percent of the average *per capita* costs in the province itself multiplied by the number of insured persons in the province.

7. No contribution would be made in respect of provincial expenditures for the costs of administering a hospital insurance plan.

From the Ontario point of view it was both victory and defeat: victory to the extent that at last the federal government was committed to paying part of the costs of a hospital insurance program; defeat in that the federal share was less than sixty percent, indeed, for Ontario, less than half; there was also no provision for mental hospitals and tuberculosis sanatoria, nor for home care on which Ontario had placed heavy emphasis. In addition, administrative costs would be borne solely by the provinces. In the federal-provincial bargaining game these were losses of serious magnitude.

As Mr. Frost and his planning group analyzed the federal proposal, the two most serious issues were the uncertainty of federal participation attendant on the six provinces' requirement, and the interpretation of the *portmanteau* term, "universally available."

The requirement of six provinces meant Ontario and five others. But the "appointed day" for introducing a program would require a lead time of at least two years and, beyond a certain point in time—as on a trans-ocean flight—there would be a point of no return. If, at that point, the sixth province were still missing, Ontario would be placed in the position of having to go forward without federal cost sharing or of creating all the disruptions attendant on a decision to cancel. Both alternatives were equally (and totally) unacceptable.

The consequences of the term, "universally available," were serious. If it meant "compulsory" and obviously that was the federal intent, Mr. Frost's determination to follow a staged introduction would be thwarted. It was one thing for Ottawa to insist on immediate total coverage and quite another for Ontario. The federal government could sow the wind but it would be provincial governments that would reap the whirlwind if the administration encountered the foul-ups of the British Columbia plan.

The federal inputs into the policy process in Ontario had thus been both positive and negative—positive in its offer to share part of the costs, and negative in its creation of new constraints and new uncertainties. The fight for better terms would have to be continued, even if such efforts proved futile.

Despite the shortcomings of the federal offer (as assessed by Ontario),

136

they could not be used as an excuse for delay because of the initiatives already taken and the expectations created. The domestic strategy would have to be pursued without delay; the decision to create the commission must move forward rapidly.

The Planning Committee continued the preparation of material for the Legislative Committee and, with the assistance of Dr. Fred Evis, medical-legal consultant in the Health Department, completed the drafting of the legislation.

"An Act to establish the Hospital Services Commission of Ontario" was given first reading on March 5, 1956 and second reading on March 27. The Health Committee of the Legislature held six half-days of hearings commencing on March 14. The committee was comprised of forty-two members, of whom about thirty were in regular attendance, and was chaired by Dr. Matthew Dymond, later to become health minister. The Planning Committee had prepared a seventy-page briefing document for the legislators, and each member presented expert testimony on various aspects of the problems involved. Mr. Farquhar Oliver, Liberal leader, was a member of the committee, but Mr. Frost and Mr. MacDonald, CCF leader, were not; both, however, attended and participated fully in the discussions.

Mr. Frost opened the proceedings by reminding the members that:

We are anticipating and endeavouring to meet rising hospital costs in Ontario. They will undoubtedly have to be met, whether by a system of hospital insurance or some other way. ... When I say the cost, in 1956, for full population coverage, would be $190 million, that is what it is. ... When I say the problem is difficult, that does not mean we cannot do it. ... I would like you to get this problem in perspective, so that, through you, the people of Ontario will also get it in perspective. ... I am confident that it can be done and that we can arrive at a solution of how to do it.[34]

Mr. Farquhar Oliver was skeptical of the whole procedure.

The government has no Bill before us; it has no concrete idea as to how it would proceed to implement hospital insurance in this province, and what is more important, it has put before us no declaration that it has any intention in the foreseeable future of implementing a hospital insurance scheme. ... So actually what we are doing is going on a sort of "fishing expedition". ... We are operating in a vacuum.[35]

It was, indeed, an unusual role for a legislative committee, but on the issue of health insurance, it was not without precedent. It will be recalled that, thirteen years earlier, this was precisely the situation in the House of Commons—a committee examining a policy proposal that was not a government bill. It was part of Mr. Frost's strategy in building a consensus among a sufficient proportion of Ontario citizens that the time had come for the Government to act. At every point he stressed the difficulties, the costs, the administrative complexity, the risk of failure, the short-comings of the federal proposal, the inadequacy of existing insurance mechanisms, and the need for help from the medical profession and the hospitals.

He also used every opportunity to explain why Ontario could not make any such program mandatory from the beginning, and, therefore, the need for greater flexibility on the part of Ottawa. One important excerpt, reflecting his thinking, follows:

> If you could press a button and have all these people [the one-third not insured] pay their premiums, this plan would not present such great difficulties, but unfortunately there is no button you can press. . . . You must remember that to collect that premium, if the people do not pay and it is mandatory, you have to employ an army of bailiffs to chase up and down the streets of this fair province to get the people to pay $30 or $50, whatever the premium might be. That would be worse than the situation in Cyprus at the present time. . . . To make a plan of this sort feasible, you may have it partly mandatory, but it must also be partly permissive. Once you do that, then you do not need the bailiffs.[36]

It was frustrating for the opposition parties; there was not a detailed proposal with which they could grapple; they were almost unwittingly and unwillingly drawn in as participants in a problem-solving exercise.

In general, despite the opposition criticism that it had no health insurance bill before it, Mr. Frost skillfully kept the committee at the task he had set for it, of bringing the issues, difficulties, and costs into public debate. The newspaper and radio coverage was voluminous, and there is no doubt that the committee hearings performed their public education purpose.

The second major effect of the committee hearings was to provide an official forum for a number of interest groups to present their views. The major ones had already met privately with the three ministers concerned, and it is significant that the largest interest groups representative of consumers—farmers and labour—did not appear at all.

However, the inputs of a number of the interest groups offering testimony were important, and to these we now turn.

THE EXTERNAL CONTRIBUTIONS

1. *The Ontario Medical Association (OMA)*. In their prepared brief, the OMA Executive endorsed the commission form of administration, but it stated strongly that "medical services in the diagnostic field" should be considered separately from hospital care. It stressed that the bill should be amended to make provision for payment by the administering agency on a fee-for-service basis directly to the physicians responsible for providing the medical services. It then argued that the bill should also be amended so that citizens would be able to receive the designated diagnostic medical services whether provided by physicians in or out of hospitals.[37]

The OMA then criticized the proposals for assuming that a program should begin with mandatory coverage of the employed. Rather, it said, the Government should concern itself first with people who could not buy prepaid hospitalization care because (a) they could not afford it; and (b) they were not insurable.

Because the question of out-patient diagnostic services was to become a serious issue between the Government and the OMA, it is desirable to expand on their views respecting the diagnostic services. Their brief stated:

The physician should be paid directly by the administering agency, on an agreed fee-for-service basis for all services rendered. Those practising in the hospital will be required to reimburse the hospital for those expenses actually incurred with respect to space occupied, heat, light, building maintenance, expendable supplies, maintenance and depreciation of equipment. They will be required to provide staff sufficient to maintain an adequate standard of service and will be responsible for the remuneration of all members of their departments.

It is desirable that hospitals maintain their present equity in and control over their investment in equipment.

Assistance in the purchase of new equipment should be provided by the commission inasmuch as the amount expended will normally exceed the depreciation reserve due to technological advances and accelerated obsolescence.[38]

The effect of these requirements was somewhat alarming to at least two groups: the Planning Committee, already concerned with the administrative task of paying over a million hospital accounts a year, now faced with the prospect of adding to that several million more accounts for laboratory tests and x-rays; and the hospital representatives, thinking of leasing to radiologists and pathologists the entire diagnostic departments of their hospitals (which were important sources of revenue).

Mr. Frost, too, was obviously alarmed:

> Mark you, I only speak for myself, these experts have their own views on this subject, but my judgment is that in entering the field of diagnostic services, we should only go so far as is necessary to control hospital admissions. The views of Doctor Taylor and others may be different on this, but it would not be my desire to enter into the medical field in any way. I would prefer to stay out of it entirely, because of the implications and the cost.[39]

It was the first time he had publicly indicated why he was considering hospital care insurance but not medical care insurance.

There were further questions and elaborations of the OMA positions, including its strong endorsement of the home care program, stressing that home care services should also be available to a patient as an alternative to being admitted as an in-patient as well as to patients for whom home care would permit earlier discharge. This, OMA spokesmen said, would reduce incentives for unnecessary admission.

2. The Ontario Hospital Association (OHA). In the summer of 1955, the OHA Executive, taking notice of the publicity on the issue of health insurance, passed on July 25 a resolution that the Blue Cross Plan should be the carrier for any hospital insurance plan introduced in Ontario. It then appointed a committee to represent the OHA in any discussions with government. Later, the executive wrote to the premier offering to provide statistics and information, and to place both personnel and facilities at the disposal of the Government for this purpose. As a result, a meeting was held with the premier on September 29, at which time the services of Mr. Ogilvie and Mr. Martin were offered and accepted.

Despite the presence of these two on the planning committee, no indication was given to the OHA in the next six months of any role for Blue Cross, and the OHA executive took note of this at its meeting on March 13, at which it also gave final approval of the statement to be made to the health committee of the Legislature one week later.

The spokesman for the OHA was Mr. Arthur Swanson, executive secretary-treasurer. The statement was short. The OHA strongly endorsed the proposed commission, and asserted the desirability not only of the OHA being represented on it but of the chief administrative officer "being one with a broad experience and background in the field of hospital care." It supported strongly the proposal to remove the limitation on benefit days. It then countered the OMA position on diagnostic services: "... the Association would expect that no change would be effected in the traditional manner in which hospital services are provided, both for in- and out-patients, which include many ancillary services such as radiology, laboratory, etc., all of which are recognized as being part of a day of patient care."[40] The brief ended on a positive note: "We congratulate the government of the Province in the approach they are making and wish to place ourselves on record as offering to make available the complete facilities of the Association should they be needed."[41]

3. *The Canadian Life Insurance Officers' Association*. The president, Mr. F. W. Hill, the chairman of the association's Health Insurance Committee, and Mr. John Tuck, general counsel for the association, were the spokesmen. Other members of its executive were also present, and participated in the discussions. The basic position of the insurance industry was explained by Mr. Tuck:

> In framing a plan to aid in the financing of health costs it is not desirable, in the public interest, to establish a compulsory hospital insurance plan and to ignore the demonstrated ability and willingness of most of our people to insure themselves voluntarily with private health insurance agencies. Seventy per cent of the people of this province have done this at no cost to the government or the federal government or the municipal governments. This voluntary insurance is in many respects better than the proposed government plan. If government action is needed, it should supplement, not supplant, private insurance. . . .
> It is not necessary to destroy these private contracts to achieve a satisfactory method of financing the hospital expenses of the people of this province.[42]

In addition, he suggested that if the Government supplanted private hospital insurance, it might be under great pressure to upgrade its plan, and also to extend its insurance activities into the medical field. That would lead to strict government control of medical services and would result, in the view of many, in lower medical standards and as a brake on the advancement of medical science.

He then compared existing insurance with the proposed benefits:

> The proposed plan would provide, except in one respect, less cover [i.e., a lower range of benefits] than private plans . . . most of which provide semi-private cover. . . . Policyholders will not be happy to lose this extra protection.
> The one respect in which cover under the proposed plan would go beyond that provided in our contracts is the continuation of benefits for an unlimited period. Most insurance contracts now pay for 70 or more days of hospitalization. In 1951, 98.5 percent of hospital stays

were for less than 56 days. [He then asked], Is this one percent of cases best served by an insurance scheme? Might it not be more economical for governments to provide directly the necessary services for these people?[43]

He then elaborated on the rapid extension of insurance policies in their range of benefits, and the recent development of the "major medical" or "catastrophic" type of policy. Commenting on an earlier remark by Mr. Frost about "bailiffs collecting premiums," he pointed out that the companies in the association had 300 branch offices and 6,000 agents in Ontario available to merchandize and service this type of insurance efficiently and economically. He concluded:

Our contention therefore is that it would be unwise for the government to establish a plan that would involve it in doing things that can be done satisfactorily by private agencies. We recognize that some segments of the population, notably those people (some of whom are in the older age group) who have not the means to pay premiums, must be provided with hospital services. How to provide this care most economically is a real problem but we believe it is not beyond solution. However, we think it would be most unfortunate if the costs involved in duplicating the existing machinery serving the bulk of the population made it impossible to look after the hospital and medical requirements of those who need help.[44]

Mr. Tuck was then subjected to extensive questioning in which other members of his executive also participated. Replying to criticism that insurance contracts were frequently cancelled, he explained that group contracts which protected the bulk of their insured were not cancellable, and that a non-cancellable policy could be purchased by individuals.

Finally, Mr. Frost, for the first time, revealed his feelings about commercial insurance:

One of the great difficulties with private insurance is the fact that, first, there is a time limit which does not take care of catastrophes; and secondly that some companies at least have been pretty free with the cancellation clauses in their policies. I have had that experience myself, you see. [He had mentioned to the planning group that on his sixtieth birthday, two of his individual policies had been terminated.] They insure you and then the minute there is some trouble, while they will pay benefits for that particular illness, there is a rider attached to your policy, and that particular illness can never again be covered. . . . And then, again, when you reach a certain age, you are cut off.[45]

Mr. Tuck endeavoured to rebut these criticisms by citing the few complaints received by the superintendent of insurance, by the improvements that both competition and new insurance regulations were bringing about. He returned to his first query, whether it was necessary to dismantle the insurance system to handle the few long-stay chronic cases. Mr. Frost's response was that it would hardly be fair under an insurance plan to ask the Government to take all the bad cases.

Mr. H. L. Guy, also a member of the executive, ended the discussion by saying that the insurance companies would do their utmost to try and cooperate to mesh their services with whatever plan the Government might bring into effect.

4. *The Ontario Association of Accident and Health Underwriters.* This group represented what are generally referred to as the "sickness and accident" or "casualty" insurance companies, and the bulk of their coverage, as distinct from the life insurance companies, involved individual contracts. As expected, the association was opposed to government intervention in the free enterprise market. Their primary spokesman was Mr. John Ingle who addressed part of the brief to the basic question: "If people don't want to spend more money for medical care—proved by the fact that they don't do so voluntarily—how can we justify making them pay for it through governmental action?"[46]

Having concluded that such action was not justifiable, Mr. Ingle went on to state the case for the free enterprise approach.

It has been argued that if the government were to provide medical services, people would get more services for less money—but no one has yet found a way of giving people something for nothing. Government services are expensive.

On the other hand, many private medical plans furnish their services at cost and in all probability as cheaply as possible. Competition among the different plans tends to hold costs down to a minimum and it is very doubtful if the government could do the same job as cheaply— particularly a quality job.[47]

He then explained why the voluntary approach could not cover everyone:

Often one hears comments to the effect that not everyone can join a voluntary health plan and it is true that people with special handicaps cannot do so—but this is strictly for economic reasons. If such persons were admitted into a plan it would automatically raise the costs to a prohibitive level for those already covered, resulting in a benefit for the minority and a hardship for the majority, since due to the prohibitive cost the voluntary plans would be out of reach. There would also be a resistance on the part of the majority to such persons being admitted, for after all, why should they pay the medical bills of those far more likely to have an expensive illness than they are? The plans are generally set up to include people in the same health group in order that the costs to the voluntary health plan will not be too high. The likelihood of any one person in the group becoming sick or having an accident is supposed to be about the same. The chronically sick must be taken care of, of course, there is no question about that. But is a compulsory government health program the absolute answer to the problem?[48]

He then raised questions about the level of taxation that would be necessary, whether quality of services would continue, whether there were enough hospital beds, and proposed as a solution that the federal government should permit the individual tax-payer to deduct his premiums to voluntary agencies from his taxable income.

Mr. MacDonald, CCF leader, had obviously prepared for this presentation and he read from the Report of the Superintendent of Insurance the most recent figures on premiums collected and benefits paid out by four leading companies of the Association:

Travelers Insurance Co: premiums: $1,445,000; benefits: $883,000, or 61 percent of premiums.

Mutual Benefit Health and Accident Company: premiums $3,648,000; benefits: $2,105,000 or 56 percent.

Continental Casualty Company: premiums: $3,365,000; benefits: $1,414,000 or 42 percent.

Canada Health and Accident: premiums: $1,535,000; benefits: $607,000 or 39 percent.

I submit to you that we simply cannot entertain the prospect of insurance companies being involved as carriers in the providing of this basic coverage, because if we do, we will increase the cost of the plan which the Hon. Prime Minister emphasizes is very high already, by as much as 30 or 40 percent more, and if the Prime Minister's worries about finances are valid, he must really look at this one.[49]

With Mr. Ingles' claims that "private medical plans furnish their services at cost" having been somewhat deflated, Mr. John Tanti of Mutual Benefit came to his support in an endeavour to explain the high retention figures and, finally, under severe cross-examination, the following exchange took place:

Mr. Tanti: Just a minute, Mr. MacDonald. If the cost of health services is to be distributed evenly, let those who are uninsurable, let the government provide benefits for the uninsurable; in other words, we will insure the insurable.

Mr. Whicher: The "cream of the crop"?

Mr. Tanti: That is true. We will insure them and let the government provide for the uninsurable.

Mr. Frost: That sounds like a bad deal for the government.[50]

5. *The Ontario Chamber of Commerce.* The chamber did not appear before the committee but, later in 1956, presented a brief to the premier and members of his Cabinet, which was then printed in pamphlet form and widely distributed.

After a review of the "marked and far-reaching developments" (in voluntary insurance) over the past few years, the brief stressed that those not now covered by voluntary insurance fell into four categories: (a) indigents who are now provided with hospital care with the cost shared by the province and the municipalities; (b) uninsurables not covered by group plans and including a large percentage of older age groups; (c) remaining insurable groups that have voluntarily declined to purchase coverage or who have not been reached with satisfactory forms of coverage by voluntary agencies; and (d) coverage for long-protracted or catastrophic hospitalization costs not covered by existing plans which represented about one and a half percent of all hospitalizations.

As a result of this survey of the problem, "the Chamber is of the opinion that the further efforts of government, private agencies and free enterprise should be concentrated on the problem areas not presently covered to the satisfaction of all."[51]

The brief then listed the reasons for the opposition to a universal hospitalization plan:

1. The cost to the individual taxpayer of providing hospital care for himself and his family under a universal plan would be greatly increased.

2. Availability and standards of hospital care would not be improved along with the increased costs to the individual taxpayer.

3. The method of financing a universal plan, whether it be a combination of premiums plus supplementary taxation or by taxation alone (the end result of most government sponsored plans) or the way in which costs are shared between different levels of government, is in reality academic and mere juggling of figures. In the final analysis the taxpayer of Ontario will have to finance any Ontario plan.

4. In practice there are strict limitations to the total taxation that can be imposed by elected representatives in a democratic society.

5. If such a plan were adopted this would be a further large and irretraceable step on the road to socialized medicine.

6. The plan is unnecessary because better alternatives exist.

In its conclusion it stated the belief of the Chamber that Ontario's interest lay in exerting every effort to prevent the adoption of an unsound federal plan, and its conviction that suitable and adequate services could be provided under existing hospital plans.

THE POLICY—STAGE I

On March 28, 1956, the Hospital Services Commission Bill received third reading in the Legislature.[52] It created a commission with three primary functions:

1. To ensure the development throughout Ontario of a balanced and integrated system of hospitals and related health facilities.

2. To administer the Hospitals Act.

3. To administer a plan of hospital care insurance for Ontario.

To achieve these objectives, the commission was authorized to:

1. Approve the establishment of new and additional hospital facilities.

2. Approve the distribution of capital grants for hospital construction.

3. Administer any system of hospital care insurance, including diagnostic services, out-patient services, and home care services that may be established by the Lieutenant Governor in Council.

4. Determine the amounts to be paid to hospitals for approved services performed for insured patients under such a system.

5. Establish and operate institutes and centres for the training of hospital and related personnel.

6. Conduct surveys and research programs.

The first charge to the commission—the development of a balanced and integrated system of hospitals and facilities—emphasized the importance attached to the development of the services system. But the creation of the commission also fulfilled two other of Premier Frost's objectives: it was a major step in meeting public expectations heightened in part by his own declarations, and therefore a move to deflate the charges that he was stalling. The second purpose was to leave open the question of when a plan might be introduced and the form it would take, in order to maintain his bargaining position with the federal government.

The debate in the Legislature added little that was new to the discussion. Both opposition parties criticized the Government for its failure to act immediately on hospital insurance. In addition, Mr. MacDonald continued his criticism of any suggestion of deductible or co-insurance charges and endeavoured to deflate the "prohibitive cost" arguments by emphasizing that almost all the expenditures were already being made. Both agreed with the principle of the bill and were pleased to approve the action to set up an administrative agency. Mr. Wintermeyer, however, objected to the granting of such sweeping powers to an independent commission. A number of speakers were highly critical of what they considered inflated cost estimates, inferring an attempt to delay hospital insurance by frightening the public with high costs. Both parties claimed major credit for the progress achieved: the CCF with its Saskatchewan pioneering, and the Liberals in their association with the Liberal federal government's offer.

STRATEGY IV

The strategy continued on the two levels: the first, domestically, in the appointment of the commission, and the second, externally, in maintaining the pressure on Ottawa. On May 11, 1956 the premier announced three appointments to the commission. Mr. Arthur J. Swanson was named chairman. He had been superintendent of the Toronto Western Hospital for twenty-six years, and also served as executive secretary-treasurer of the Ontario Hospital Association. The other two were the Rev. John G. Fullerton, chairman of the Board of Governors of St. Joseph's Hospital in Toronto, and Dr. John B. Nielson, superintendent of the Hamilton General Hospital. All three were past-presidents of the Ontario Hospital Association.

The commission moved into newly renovated offices in the Legislative Building, hard by the office of Premier Frost. The Hospitals Division of the Department of Health was transferred to the commission.

Numerous steps were taken behind the scenes by Mr. Frost to ensure that there was no misunderstanding in Ottawa of his determination. One example was a request he made of me. While I was attending the conference in Ottawa, I was to meet with Mr. Stanley Knowles, health insurance critic of the CCF party. I was to assure him that Ontario's determination was firm and a first class program was the objective. I was to give Mr. Knowles any information he requested. Mr. Frost arranged the engagement by telephone and I spent a stimulating two hours with

147

Mr. Knowles answering his highly perceptive questions. In the end I think he was convinced of the determination of Mr. Frost who thereby gained another, if unusual, ally.

The possibility of successful negotiations with Ottawa began to dim, for in addition to its adamant stand on the details of the hospital insurance offer, the new federal tax-sharing proposals had fallen far short of Mr. Frost's target. It looked as if history might repeat itself, for it was the issue of tax agreements that had aborted the 1945 proposals. Would it happen again?

On June 8, Mr. Paul Martin met in Toronto with Mr. Frost, Mr. Porter, Dr. Phillips, and the members of the commission. The positions of each side were stated and restated, but Mr. Martin adhered strictly to the St. Laurent offer.[53]

Just how far apart they were became evident when Mr. Martin introduced his estimates in the House of Commons on July 26. There he reported on his talks with Mr. Frost as being "useful, helpful and co-operative." Observing that Ontario had established a Hospital Services Commission, he said, "It seems to me this would not be done if Ontario were not giving sympathetic consideration to the plan."[54]

On July 31, the *Toronto Globe and Mail* reported that Queen's Park officials had reacted negatively to Paul Martin's prediction that Ontario acceptance was near at hand.

> Premier Frost had made no secret of the fact that he believes the Federal Government has deliberately disregarded Ontario's submission for a more equitable share of tax revenues. Hence the money which should have been available to underwrite the cost of a hospital insurance scheme will be used for more pressing needs—schools, highways, and water resources. If the Premier is forced to choose between these essentials and a hospital insurance scheme there is no doubt at Queen's Park that hospital insurance will be relegated to the distant future.

On August 2, Mr. Frost reinforced this conclusion: "I don't intend, if I can help it," said the premier, "to place Ontario in an unsound financial position by imposing another huge financial burden on our taxpayers without being sure of our ground. The Federal proposals put through Parliament do not meet our requirements ... we're going to deal with financial fundamentals first."[55]

All of this was, of course, a political bargaining posture. The outcome of the tax agreement negotiations would have little or no financial effect on Ontario's share of the hospital insurance program, but the premier could not be faulted in using the stratagem to maintain the pressure on Ottawa.

On July 16, the commission held its first press conference.
Mr. Swanson made a number of announcements:

1. He could not "hazard a guess" as to when hospital insurance would
be introduced in Ontario. "The Commission," he said, "is now starting
to build the broad base which must exist before an insurance plan can
get under way."

2. One of the areas in which the commission was concentrating its
efforts was the development of rehabilitation centres, and the Workmen's
Compensation Rehabilitation Centre at Malton was being studied as a
model.

3. The commission was also studying the need for chronic care and
convalescent facilities, and the use of nursing homes.

4. There was a very serious shortage in Ontario of radiological and
laboratory technicians and medical record librarians, and the Commission was considering a training program for such personnel.[56]

On December 4, an important meeting was held by the premier and
the commission with representatives of the Ontario Hospital Association.
In September, the chairman of the commission, Mr. Swanson, had
written to the OHA, suggesting that they appoint three members to represent the association on a joint committee with the commission. This was
its first meeting. Mr. Frost introduced the discussion by referring to the
OHA as "partners in this great enterprise," and indicating that in one
form or another Blue Cross would be the carrier. The OHA spokesmen
said that they considered there were two alternatives: that Blue Cross
might serve as the agent of the Government, handling the entire program,
and its identity would not be changed substantially; or the entire Blue
Cross organization might be taken over as an "associated company" of
the Government working under the OHSC. Such an agency could no
longer carry the Blue Cross label.

The discussion began to focus on details. Mr. Frost said that it was
his intention to take over everything in the way of organization, but that
he would leave the Blue Cross reserve funds with the OHA.

The OHA mentioned that they were constructing a new building. Mr.
Frost requested them to continue, and also to make it expandable. When
it was indicated that additional adjoining land would be necessary and
might be obtainable, Mr. Frost called in the minister of public works and
directed him to begin expropriation proceedings to ensure that it would
be available.

The fact that seventy percent of Blue Cross subscribers had semi-private
coverage was raised and Mr. Frost indicated that Blue Cross should con-

149

tinue that coverage and that the necessary administrative arrangements would be made to enable it to do so. When asked about the launching date, Mr. Frost replied that he did not know; that decision was up to Ottawa.[57] It had been a very productive meeting, and the premier was obviously fortunate in the willingness of the OHA to cooperate.

The strategy in dealing with the federal government was also proceeding but, it appeared, not quite as successfully. On November 2, a meeting had been held in Toronto between Ontario representatives—Premier Frost, Dana Porter, Dr. Phillips and officials—and Dr. G. D. W. Cameron, deputy minister of national health and Dr. George Davidson, deputy minister of welfare. The Hon. Paul Martin was to have attended, but at the last moment was unable to do so. A full explanation of Ontario's proposal was given to the federal officials.

This was followed, four weeks later, by a meeting of the commission members with the same officials in Ottawa where the proposals were further elaborated, with much time being spent on Ontario's position with respect to mandatory coverage.

Two weeks later, on December 13, 1956, Premier Frost and the provincial treasurer met with Prime Minister St. Laurent in Ottawa. In addition to his presentation of the Ontario position, Mr. Frost gave Mr. St. Laurent a copy of the Ontario proposals and a covering letter (dated December 11) in which he restated the Ontario position and ended by saying that "time is of the essence and we should know by at least early in the new year whether the way is clear for us to proceed."[58]

On January 22, 1957, Mr. St. Laurent replied. The salient paragraph read as follows: "We are of the opinion that, provided the estimates of coverage given in your letter are in fact realized when the proposed scheme becomes effective, it could properly be considered as coming within the framework of the federal government's proposals. ... We would, of course, feel that some assurance on this point would need to be incorporated into the agreement between our governments on this subject."[59]

Mr. Frost was both frustrated and angry. He answered immediately in a long, five-page letter, singling out the quoted paragraph for first attack: "If this paragraph means that there would be no federal participation in our plan until we have reached 85 or 90 percent coverage, then it would seem to be a rejection of our proposal which has been discussed over several months."[60]

He then referred to his statement in the letter of December 11:

As a matter of fact, we have considered it desirable to obtain a coverage of from 85 to 90 percent of our people as soon as possible. There should be no misunderstanding on this point. We cannot guarantee an 85 or 90 percent coverage of our people on any date. Indeed at no time have we indicated that at the commencement of the plan, which we felt would be January 1, 1959, we could be assured of that coverage. . . . Our advisors and ourselves feel that broad coverage can be obtained and that we can achieve our objective of 85 to 90 percent, *and perhaps more, provided we do it in a sound way and provided we do not overburden the Commission and the insurance administration with impossible conditions.*[61]

Mr. St. Laurent replied four days later. He restated the federal position. He then said: "The 85 to 90 percent coverage which we mentioned and about which you express concern was the figure which you yourself mentioned in a context which we thought indicated that you expected to achieve this when your plan was established."[62]

But he now seemed, for the first time, to be willing to be more flexible, provided that further conditions were met:

We believe that if you feel you should not give assurance of being able to reach your figure of 85 percent by a certain stage, it should be clearly set out in our agreement that your plan will be universally available in fact as well as law and that your Commission will work without delay to obtain reasonably universal coverage. Moreover, we feel you should make public sufficient details of the plan you intend to offer, including the premium rates, the benefits, and other relevant conditions to enable us to satisfy Parliament that the plan you offer to the people of the Province will be sufficiently attractive to them as individuals to enable you, in fact, to achieve your 85% coverage in this largely voluntary plan within a stated relatively short period. I shall be glad to hear from you further, as it seems to me we are well on our way to reaching agreement on this matter.[63]

It was a concession, but at a price. The ready approval of the British Columbia and Saskatchewan plans was obviously straightforward; that of Alberta more complicated because of its provincial-municipal type of program. Newfoundland's acceptance of the federal offer, as one reporter observed, had been written out in long hand by Premier Smallwood on stationery of a Montreal hotel. But Ontario would have to meet special conditions. Before he could reply, Mr. Frost had now to attend to the domestic scene.

THE POLICY—STAGE II

It was noted above that, from the first two years of study, planning, and negotiations with the federal government, the first stage of the policy had

151

been the passage in 1956 of the legislation establishing the Hospital Services Commission. Another year of study, planning, and negotiations had now reached the point when the details of the program could be presented to the new Session of the Legislature, and incorporated into an expanded Health Services Commission Act. The second stage of decision making had arrived. It was time now to make public the full details of the proposed program. As one examines the extraordinary amount of attention already given to the issue by the mass media, it was surprising how much publicity the announcement received. All Ontario dailies headlined the proposals in large bold type, and devoted pages to its analysis. Apart from the fact of the announcement itself, there was little that was new. All of the principles and many of the details had been discussed a year earlier in the Health Committee of the Legislature. The main points were as follows:

Despite what it considers to be the limitations of the Federal offer, and in the expectation and hope that the Federal Government will change its policies on the points in question, the Government of Ontario submits the following proposal for a comprehensive hospital services program within the context of the Federal offer.

1. The introduction of a province-wide, universally available hospital care insurance program, with benefits to become available as soon as the administrative organization can be established and placed in operation following the reaching of agreement with the Federal government.

2. The Hospital Care Insurance Program will include as benefits, in-patient diagnostic services, standard ward care in active treatment hospitals, convalescent hospitals, and hospitals for the chronically ill, specified out-patient services, and either simultaneously or at a later date, diagnostic services on an out-patient basis.

3. The benefits are to be universally available to all residents of the province who have attained insured status by the payment of a personal premium. All persons in receipt of public assistance from the Government of Ontario will be accorded insured status. So-called medical indigents who are accepted as resident and indigent by a municipality will also be granted hospitalization at the expense of the Provincial Hospitalization Fund and the Municipalities, and the Municipalities will, in turn, be given unconditional grants from which these payments can be made.

In general the municipalities will be relieved of financial burdens incidental to this service:

(a) through an expected substantial reduction in the number of uninsured persons

(b) through the elimination of almost all hospital deficits.

4. The program will, from the beginning, be universally available to all residents of the province. Moreover, as it becomes feasible, membership will be made compulsory.

5. The provincial share of the costs of the program will be financed from a combination of:

(a) Payments by the Province from consolidated revenue fund;

(b) Premiums paid by or on behalf of the beneficiaries;

(c) Contributions by the Municipalities on behalf of resident indigent patients, to be offset by provincial unconditional grants.

6. Despite the refusal of the Federal Government to participate in the costs of care in mental hospitals or tuberculosis sanatoria, their services will be part of the basic plan, paid solely by Ontario.

The statement then listed three provisions of the federal cost-sharing formula which Ontario wanted changed:

1. Depreciation as a recognized and inescapable part of the cost of operating a hospital.

2. Administrative costs, also unavoidable in operating a hospital care insurance plan.

3. Co-insurance payments should be recognized, as they were by the Federal Government in 1945, as a form of provincial revenue to be considered as a shareable cost. [64]

The specific details of the proposal and supporting financial data were given to the members of the Legislature in a fifty-five-page memorandum. In introducing the legislation, Mr. Frost indicated that negotiations were going forward with the federal government but that he could not then comment on them. Then, obviously mindful of the fact that most of the opposition to his program came from among his own party supporters, Mr. Frost dealt with what he said were many statements made to him that the phenomenal growth of voluntary insurance made a government plan unnecessary. He said:

It is perfectly true that private insurers are very rapidly increasing their coverage in this province. But the coverage they are providing is only a partial coverage ... and I do not think that private insurers ever can meet the coverage that is required if we are to meet our objectives. ...

Present insurance coverage, desirable as it is, is simply not universally available; it is generally limited to the best risks. ... It is perfectly true that group coverages do include other than good risks, but individual policies only cover the best risks generally cancellable on illness. ... I may add that in many cases cancellations take place many years later and in fact at the very time the policy is needed. That is one of the objections and I point out to private insurers that they must face up to that fact. ... Again, premiums are generally increased at 60 years of age; and in most cases the coverage is not available after 65 years of age, except in group policies. ... Then again, present policies are limited as to length of stay in hospital. ... they do not, therefore, cover the catastrophic expense of hospital stay. ... It is very simple to say that Ontario has 3.5 million covered. We have 3.5 million people in this province who are partially covered, and they are partially covered only during the duration of the policy, and then because of certain things that enter into the matter they cease to be covered entirely. On the other hand, may I say that the private insurers have a very great part to play in this province—over and above the basic coverage—which is limited to standard ward care and all the things that go with it.... there are very many opportunities open to private insurance companies for the provision of supplementary benefits.[65]

He then presented and elaborated on the program outlined above, and concluded by saying: "This is the biggest business undertaking that this province has ever attempted in its 165 years of history. I emphasize again, as I have emphasized in the Memorandum which the House will consider, that it is only with good administration, unhampered by impossible conditions, that this plan can be made a distinct success."[66]

He was followed by Mr. Farquhar Oliver, Liberal leader, who, of course, found difficulty in attacking any of the elements of the proposed program (for the most vulnerable points stemmed from the federal Liberal policies), but he did criticize the long delay to January 1959, for the plan's introduction. He charged that the date had been selected on political grounds rather than, as Mr. Frost had claimed, on the basis of administrative requirements. Mr. Frost had been advised, he said, to "select an election date that is either a year and a half after the plan has been introduced on the assumption that the plan's success will be obvious or very soon after the plan has been introduced when the question of success or failure is still in doubt."[67] And, since 1959 would "in all probability" be an election year, "the Hon. Prime Minister had accepted [the advice] unquestionably."[68] Mr. Frost denied the charge.

Mr. MacDonald, the CCF Leader, then spoke at some length, scoring off the Liberals by suggesting that the federal (Liberal) government "now

154

is providing half the loaf [they offered in 1945] and they are even chiselling on half the loaf because they are not providing coverage for mental illness and tuberculosis." He then congratulated the prime minister "for putting into effect a plan which is modelled on the best one in the country [Saskatchewan]."

He then commented on Mr. Frost's statement explaining why voluntary insurance had not provided the answers but still had vast scope. "I listened to him [Mr. Frost] talking for all the world like a CCF man— because apparently some of the wolves behind the scene have been after him—he was apparently trying to pacify them, and trying to explain that the world is not coming to an end because the Tory party has betrayed them on what the Tory party has believed down the years. So let us have sympathy for the Prime Minister, because he is going to have a lot of foes behind him in trying to put this plan into effect [because] the Tories are 'Johnny-come-latelys' climbing on the bandwagon of something that the people of Canada have needed and wanted and sought, and on which they have been betrayed."[69]

The completed policy, the culmination of two years of staff work and political decisions, had been announced, and needed now only passage through the Legislature and agreement with the federal government to be converted into an operating program.

STRATEGY V

Mr. Frost replied on January 30 to Mr. St. Laurent's letter of January 28, again in a long letter, reminding the prime minister that "an interpretation of the term 'universally available' should not be imposed which in fact is not justified and could make the hospital insurance plan difficult and expensive and perhaps altogether impossible." "[Because of the great difficulties] a flexible plan system geared to our interpretation of universal availability should be used. This I am sure would meet every practical test that reasonable people could ask for and would completely justify federal and provincial participation."[70] It contained no new arguments but represented a strengthening of resolve.

Mr. St. Laurent replied on February 1, again restating the positions taken in the letter of January 28. But a way out of the impasse was hinted at: "I take it from your letter of the 30th that you are not yet ready to make public the details as to premiums which are necessary to reach a judgment on the attractiveness and probable coverage of your plan. I would suggest that as soon as your experts are ready, your Minister and officials might meet with Mr. Martin to discuss the details of your plan and the terms of a possible draft agreement for federal support of it."[71]

It was firm, yet it held out the possibility of compromise. On February

155

4, Mr. Frost sent a telegram to Mr. St. Laurent informing him that he "was quite prepared to have our Ministers concerned and our officials and experts sit in at once on a continuation of our conference." He also informed him that the telegram would be tabled in the Legislature with the other correspondence.[72]

The federal government had announced on January 2 that it would not introduce legislation in the current session to set up its proposed hospital insurance plan, the reason being that only three provinces had endorsed it.

There was also a suggestion emanating from Ottawa that Ontario could accelerate the introduction of the national plan by moving forward the launching date of the Ontario plan. Mr. Frost's response was that the federal government could expedite matters by removing the conditions respecting majority participation. "It can begin by contributing to B.C. and Saskatchewan which already have plans in action."[73]

The meeting between the two governments was scheduled for March 6. in Ottawa. On March 4, Mr. Dana Porter in his budget address, announced an unconditional grant of $1.00 *per capita* to municipalities to assist in meeting indigent hospital costs, with the condition that the grant would not become operative unless agreement had been reached with the federal government by the end of March.[74]

Questioned whether this was an ultimatum, Mr. Frost replied, "It is certain there must be an agreement before dissolution. If they don't come in before dissolution they won't come in after."[75]

But, even as he was speaking, action was being taken in Ottawa. As the Canadian Press reported, "The Liberal government, apparently reacting to Progressive Conservative charges that it is "bluffing" on its hospital insurance proposals, today initiated parliamentary action to get its scheme on the statute books."

On March 6, 1957, Mr. Porter, Dr. Phillips, Mr. Swanson, Mr. Gathercole, and I met with Mr. Martin and Health and Finance officials in Ottawa. By three o'clock, agreement had been reached and Mr. Martin and Mr. Porter issued a joint statement to that effect.[76] The major roadblock had been cleared.

But on the administrative level there was an almost overwhelming amount of work to be done: a decision on Blue Cross, appointment of commission personnel, the development of a budget-review system for determining hospital costs and *per diem* rates, the design of forms for registering beneficiaries in groups and as individuals, devising the most expeditious methods of enrolling and collecting from individuals, decisions on the degree of mandatory coverage at the beginning, further refinement of costs estimates based on the 1956 financial returns from hospitals now coming in, calculation of the premium rates and structure, agreement with the medical profession on diagnostic services, decisions on out-patient services, and, still, hard bargaining with the federal government on all the terms of the agreement. And there was much more.

On March 28, the amendments to the Ontario Hospital Services Commission Act were passed.[77] On April 12, the federal Hospital Insurance and Diagnostic Services Act was passed.[78] On July 9, a special meeting of the executive of the Ontario Hospital Association passed a resolution (1) that the OHA confine itself to the offering of Supplementary Hospital Coverage, and (2) that a plan for the orderly takeover of its staff and equipment by the commission be prepared and submitted to the Board of Directors.[79] On October 4, Mr. Swanson asked the OHA for the transfer of Mr. David Ogilvie to the commission as director of Hospital Insurance. The board agreed on October 8.[80] By the end of 1958, all Blue Cross employees not remaining to administer the Blue Cross supplementary benefit operations were transferred to the Ontario public service as employees of the commission.

In October, as consultant to the commission, I presented a report to the annual convention of the Ontario Hospital Association, outlining the principles and detailing the application of the "Master Plan" for hospital facilities.

On October 26, 1957, the premier announced further details of the program including the monthly premium rates.[81] These were set at $2.10 for a single person and $4.20 for a family. These rates included entitlement to benefits in tuberculosis sanatoria and mental hospitals. The plan was made compulsory for all employed persons in establishments having fifteen or more employees. Establishments of from six to fourteen employees could voluntarily apply as "mandatory groups" and once accepted also came under the mandatory provisions.

But largely because of opposition from the medical profession, out-patient diagnostic services were not included as a benefit, nor was there any further reference to home care.

On January 1, 1959, the Ontario Hospital Services Plan went into effect, with ninety-one percent of the population enrolled, and with federal sharing from the commencement. By the end of the year, 92.3 percent of the population were insured; by the end of 1960, the percentage had increased to over ninety-four percent.[82]

With the pioneering having been undertaken by Saskatchewan, British Columbia, and Alberta, Ontario's decision had tipped the scales sufficiently to make the nation-wide program possible.

Four years earlier, on March 23, 1955, Mr. Frost had said, "However, the question is not one of whether health insurance will come—come it must and will. The only question is—when is the right time for it?"

It had happened according to Premier Frost's time table. And there

157

was an election in 1959 as Mr. Oliver had predicted—"very soon after the plan had been introduced when the success or failure of the plan was still in doubt."

THE OUTCOMES

1. The Ontario Government had inaugurated a program of universally available hospital care insurance that greatly reduced the economic barrier to needed hospital services and also removed the threat of individual bankruptcy from unpredictable need for prolonged hospital care.

2. By assuming the leadership of those pressing the federal government in 1955 to fulfill at least part of its 1945 proposals, the Ontario government was clearly the determinative force that brought about the nation-wide system we now have. Had the Government not acted as it did, when it did, the alternative seems likely to have been what Mr. Frost warned, "a hodge-podge that no one will be able to disentangle."

3. By deciding not to introduce out-patient diagnostic services as a benefit simultaneously with the introduction of hospital insurance, the Government maintained its peace with the Ontario Medical Association, but it thereby, itself, contributed greatly to the demand for unnecessary admissions and the resulting demand for more active treatment beds then were genuinely needed for in-patient care.

4. By failing to act on the home care benefit proposal which it had strongly endorsed, the Ontario government failed to be as innovative in action as it had been in thought, and contributed again to the demand for unnecessary admission to, and unnecessarily prolonged stays in hospitals, with a waste of public funds and resources as a result.

5. To the surprise of most, and to the deep satisfaction of Premier Frost, the enrolment in the plan reached ninety-two percent in 1959 and over ninety-four percent in 1960, an outcome that attested to the universal need and desire for such protection.

6. By placing legal responsibility on the commission for the development of a balanced and integrated system of hospitals, it introduced a higher degree of rationality in the decision-making process on the location, size, and facilities of hospital resources than would otherwise likely have obtained.

7. Striking improvements occurred in hospital facilities, in quality of care, and in the equalization of wages and salaries of hospital employees with those for similar occupations in the population generally.

8. Major savings were achieved by municipalities through a sharp decline in non-insured indigent patients.

9. Despite the dire prediction of the consequences of state control, the interest and role of volunteers and the interest of the public generally in their hospitals expanded rather than diminished.

10. The long gestation period of planning, and the two year period devoted to expanding the administrative capability of Blue Cross resulted in the largest governmental administrative operation since the war going into effect smoothly and efficiently, and with less public outcry about administrative foul-ups than in almost any other province.

11. The commercial insurance companies lost the sales field of the standard ward benefit; the chief financial loss was to their insurance agents. Blue Cross continued to offer semi-private care benefits, and added others; today its operations exceed those of 1958.

12. The inclusion of mental hospital care as an insured benefit probably had as much psychological as financial effect, in that it undoubtedly contributed to reducing the stigma attached to admission to a psychiatric hospital.

13. By its actions that led the federal government to share in the costs of hospital insurance, Ontario thereby indirectly brought about the "windfall" of federal funds to Saskatchewan that enabled it to make the decision to introduce medical care insurance, and the cycle was re-started.

Chapter Four

The National Hospital Insurance Program:
The Case of the Reluctant Decision

IT WAS LATE on an April evening in 1957 and on Ottawa's Parliament Hill the long debate had ended. The Speaker put the main motion and the division bells began to ring. In one of those rare occasions, every member present that night in the House of Commons, representing four political parties, voted aye to adopt unanimously the motion on third reading of "Bill 320." Two days later, on April 12, almost as anti-climax, the Senate concurred with the same unanimity, and on May 1, the Hospital Insurance and Diagnostic Services Act was proclaimed the law of the land.

It had been a long time coming. It was thirty-eight years since health insurance had first appeared as a plank in the Liberal party platform, twelve years since the famous federal post-war reconstruction health insurance proposals, ten years since Saskatchewan had pioneered the first hospital services plan, and just over a year since the federal government had announced the proposals now incorporated in the new statute.

Most remarkable, however, was the unanimous vote (noteworthy not only by virtue of its rarity but also because it was misleading), for it obscured both the magnitude of the decision and the controversy in which it had been molded. Great events should be illuminated by high drama, but that element is missing when a decision is characterized by unanimous agreement rather than by conflict. Despite the absence of spectacle and theatrics, there was, nevertheless, an air of urgency in the House that spring night, a sense among the members of participating in a major decision of national policy, of launching a great social project affecting the life of every citizen as well as committing the people of Canada to the largest governmental expenditure for any program save defence. In the words of one member it was "a great social advance . . . the most constructive example in Canada to that time of those great legislative landmarks that are the products of political wisdom, social insight, and crystallized national conscience."[1]

It was indeed a great decision, and despite the unanimous vote, matched only by the conflict and apprehension that had preceded it. Experience with other hospital insurance plans had shown that, like all human institutions, the proposed program had enormous potential for success and an equal risk of failure. It could make available the highest quality of essential treatment, or squander hard-earned revenues on duplicated facilities, featherbedding personnel, and unnecessary care.

What made it especially hazardous from the federal point of view was that it was to be administered not by the federal government but by the provinces. The services were to be provided by independent parties—the hospitals, for the needs of second parties—the patients, as ordered by still other parties—their physicians. It was almost like signing blank cheques, leaving others to fill in the amounts. In substance, it was an unprecedented declaration of faith in the integrity and capability of hospitals, doctors, civil servants, and citizens to develop and use expensive resources wisely and prudently in the absence of the normal constraints of the market place.

Considering its humanitarian objectives, its potentialities, its implications, its risks, its costs, and its declaration of faith, it was a policy choice of the highest magnitude. Before analyzing the decision itself we shall examine first the background against which it was made.

THE BACKGROUND

With the collapse of the Dominion-Provincial Conference in 1946, the federal government's idealistic plans for post-war Canada were in disarray. So, too, was the financial position of most of the provinces. In the next two years decisions were taken to go at least part of the way with respect to taxation arrangements and health services. The first decision was to negotiate tax agreements with those provinces that wished to do so, and to separate entirely the earlier interdependence between the financial arrangements and the Green Book social security and health proposals. By 1947, tax agreements with seven provinces were in effect, with Ontario and Quebec the exceptions.

The second decision took longer. On December 10, 1946, Prime Minister Mackenzie King made a major change in the Health and Welfare portfolio by transferring Brooke Claxton, who had worked so assiduously on the Green Book Proposals, to the Defence Ministry and promoting Paul Martin from his position as secretary of state to minister of national health and welfare.

The new minister had been interested in health insurance even before his parliamentary career began in 1935, and had spoken on a number of occasions in the caucus on the party's long-standing commitment to and the importance of health insurance. Among those who knew the minister well there was no doubt of his dedication to the health proposals or that he would move ahead as rapidly as the Cabinet would permit. But the collapse of the 1945–46 conference had created a wave of pessimism among Cabinet members, dashing any earlier confidence in the possible success of major federal initiatives in fields of provincial jurisdiction. Moreover, as the nation grappled with the immediate problems of re-employment of service personnel and defence workers, those dreams of a better post-war world envisioned in the Green Book proposals seemed to be just that—only dreams.

Mr. Martin was determined, however, that as a new minister in the Health portfolio, he must make some progress. In January 1948, he had a long discussion with Prime Minister King and endeavoured to persuade him that he should not end his long career without at least initiating the program of health insurance which had been for so long a stated Liberal objective.[2] As the conversation continued, the maximum first step that Mr. King would agree upon was part of the 1945 proposals, the health grants.[3] After a number of drafts of a proposed statement prepared by Mr. Martin, and with strong support in the Cabinet from Justice Minister St. Laurent, on May 18 the prime minister announced in the House of Commons what came to be known as the national health grants program.[4]

The format of the grants followed the 1945 design, with two exceptions —one minor, the other major. Perhaps bowing to Mackenzie King's proclivity for caution, the former planning and organization grant (which hinted of action to come) was converted to the more neutral title of "health survey grant." The other was the hospital construction grant, a matching grant that replaced the loans for hospital construction proposed in 1945. The annual grants were as follows: general public health, $4,395,000; veneral disease control, $275,000; mental health, $4,000,000; tuberculosis control, $3,000,000; cancer control, $3,500,000; crippled children, $500,000; professional training, $500,000; public health research, $100,000 to be increased over five years to $500,000; and hospital construction, $13,000,000.

The health survey grant of $645,180 (including Newfoundland's share, added in 1949) was provided for three purposes: (1) to ensure the most effective use of the other health grants; (2) to plan the extension of hospital accommodation; (3) to plan the proper organization of hospital and medical care insurance. "These grants," said Mackenzie King, "represent the first stages in the development of a comprehensive health insurance plan for all Canada."[5]

For the provincial health departments, the grants were a welcome source of new funds. Here were revenues available for long-delayed health measures free from the annual battles with provincial finance officials who were, too frequently, still scrutinizing Health Department budget requests in terms of increments to the paltry depression and wartime appropriations. The full story of the impact of the health grants has never been told but it is fair to say that they did constitute, as Mackenzie King had described them, "the fundamental prerequisites of a nation-wide system of health insurance." One of the spin-off effects was that the meetings held in Ottawa to review annual expenditures and new proposals provided regularized opportunities for provincial and federal health officials to meet, compare ideas, report solutions to mutual problems, and exchange plans for new projects, on a scale never before known; the grants programs thus had a catalytic effect on nation-wide health services planning and development not anticipated when they were launched.

Most of the provinces assigned the health survey function to representative committees on which the health professions and the health department were represented. Since one of the intended tasks was to "plan the proper organization of hospital and medical care insurance" the committees helped to keep the issue very much in the forefront.

There was one other factor that helped to keep the issue in the public mind—the method of administration of the health grants. Provinces were required to submit specific proposals for Ottawa's approval for the expenditure of all funds. Every project grant to every province—and there were thousands of them—was announced by The Honourable Paul Martin. Few Cabinet ministers ever reaped such volumes of publicity from a single program. In fact, among journalists, the program was irreverently known as "milking Martin's millions." But in his many public addresses the minister never failed to refer to Mackenzie King's statement in describing the grants as "the first stage in the development of a comprehensive health insurance plan for all Canada," with the obvious inference that a second stage was imminent.

Shortly after the launching of the program, there occurred a remarkable change of key actors, both in Ottawa and Ontario, that was to create, as noted in chapter 3, an extraordinary impact on the shape of things to come. What had seemed to be legitimate theatre, playing out a fairly predictable scenario, now seemed to have become theatre of improvisation if not, in some cases, theatre of the absurd. Certainly new actors were creating new roles, the script was being changed, and the outcomes could not be anticipated.

Mackenzie King had finally decided to end his long prime ministership and his personal choice for successor fell on Louis St. Laurent, his minister of justice. Mr. St. Laurent reluctantly agreed to stand for nomination. The Liberal Convention elected him leader on the first ballot on August 7, 1948, and on November 15 he became prime minister. As one journalist observed, "When a man seeks an office it isn't news, but when an office seeks a man it is."[6] St. Laurent had become leader of his country without political commitments. As a former corporation lawyer (as Dale Thompson observes in his biography of Mr. St. Laurent) "[he] seemed hardly the man to lead the more impatient members of the party in what they considered was the true orientation of Canadian Liberalism, a sustained campaign of progress and reform . . . he believed in free enterprise as the most efficient means of assuring a high level of employment and prosperity . . . [and] he accepted social welfare legislation as a means of caring for the weaker members of society."[7] Government action to bring about a universal program of health insurance that would have the effect of removing the field from private enterprise would fit most uncomfortably within such philosophical parameters.

The second change of actor was the election of Mr. George Drew, then premier of Ontario, to leadership of the national Progressive-Conservative party. An implacable foe of Mr. Mackenzie King, Mr. Drew's political philosophy was clearly more in harmony with that of Mr. St. Laurent and he, too, favoured a private enterprise solution to the economic problems of health care.

The departure of Mr. Drew from Ontario led to actor change number three when, after a brief interregnum, Mr. Leslie Frost, the provincial treasurer, became premier of Ontario. His philosophy, too, accorded with that of both Mr. St. Laurent and Mr. Drew, but he had a much keener sense of the obligations of the largest and richest province in the design of Confederation than did Mr. Drew. He quickly moved, as Dale Thompson reports, to end the acrimonious relationship characterizing the King-Drew period. He wrote to Mr. St. Laurent to congratulate him on his election victory. Mr. St. Laurent immediately telephoned him and a few days later they met in Ottawa to talk, discovering that they held many views in common.[8]

In the 1949 federal election campaign, the new Liberal leader spoke primarily in generalities and made no firm commitment to health insurance. The party platform dealt with the issue in lukewarm terms: "The Liberal party stands for a national programme of social security . . . [which] will include a steady extension of insurance on a contributory basis to protect all citizens from loss of income and to provide for their old age [and] health insurance covering medical, dental, surgical and hospital health services on a contributory basis."[9]

The new Progressive Conservative leader, Mr. Drew, waged an aggressive campaign on a platform that had been hammered out at the leadership convention. The commitment to health insurance was also stated in general terms, without reference to how or when: "Adequate medical and hospital care will be provided for our people under a national health plan which will also include the most extensive preventative services."

The Cooperative Commonwealth Federation platform, as expected, contained a lengthy statement on health insurance, obviously greatly influenced by the experience in Saskatchewan. It said, in part: "The CCF believes that the Federal Government should take the leadership in, and assume the major responsibility for, the establishment of a comprehensive health service which will provide for all citizens full hospital, medical, dental and optical care, irrespective of their income."

The Social Credit party was also committed to health insurance but, again, in a different form. "A Social Credit Government would establish a non-contributory system of national health services to assure all citizens of access to necessary preventive medicine, medical and hospital care, free from any bureaucratic regimentation of patients, doctors, nurses or hospital authorities."

The results for the new prime minister were overwhelming. The Liberals obtained 190 seats, the Progress Conservatives forty-one (a loss of twenty-six), the CCF thirteen (a loss of fifteen), and Social Credit ten (a loss of three).

With such minor emphasis given to health insurance by either of the major parties, the results of a Gallup Poll[10] released shortly after the election seem paradoxical if one assumes some direct relationship between public opinion and the responses of political parties. The question was phrased: "Would you approve or disapprove of a National Health Plan whereby you would pay a flat rate each month and be assured of complete medical and hospital care by the Dominion Government?"

The responses (with the 1944 results for comparison) were:

	1949	1944
Approve	80%	80%
Disapprove	13	16
Undecided	7	4

The majority of four out of five supporting the proposal duplicated that of 1944. But it was obviously not reflected in the election mandate.

Between the health grants program of 1948 and the 1953 national elections, however, there were three new developments that were to affect the political scene with respect to health services. These were the hospital insurance plans of British Columbia and Alberta, and the joining in Confederation of Newfoundland with its cottage hospital system.

The British Columbia Hospital Insurance Service (BCHIS). The decision to introduce hospital insurance in British Columbia was taken in 1947[11] and the legislation was passed early in 1948.[12] The commissioner, Dr. J. M. Hershey and the executive director, Mr. Andrew Pitkethly, visited Regina to study the administration of the Saskatchewan plan in the following summer.

Because of the concentration of the B.C. population in the three cities of Vancouver, Victoria, and New Westminster, with a large part of the remainder of the population residing in unorganized territory, it was not feasible for B.C. to use the very efficient Saskatchewan municipal collection system. Moreover, although Blue Cross had been in operation since 1941, it had enrolled only 110,000 participants, and despite the fact that its equipment and many of its staff were employed by BCHIS, it was apparently impossible to expand the administrative system rapidly enough to permit payroll deduction collections of the premiums from all employed persons. B.C. was, therefore, the first government plan to confront the extremely difficult task of designing two collection systems for an entire population: by pay-roll deduction, and by what was termed in the few voluntary plans that were insuring individuals as "pay-direct." Because of the lack of foresight and appreciation on the part of the government of the magnitude of the administrative operation, the two collection systems had to be set up almost overnight. There was an additional factor exacerbating an already complex problem, for even in those businesses in which pay-roll deduction was or could have been introduced, the fact that much of the B.C. labour force was highly transient and seasonally-employed, made any system of monthly collection of premiums difficult to administer efficiently and accurately.

The combination of lack of advanced planning, inadequate time for training of new staff, and two complicated collection systems resulted in an administrative nightmare. Many were uninsured. Many who had paid premiums received no entitlement card; some who had not paid, did receive them; the change-of-employer and change-of-address procedures bogged down. (One beneficiary changed employers twelve times in one year). As time went by, the problem of arrears of unpaid taxes snowballed. By the summer of 1952, for example, a person could owe as much as $147.50 in addition to current premiums. The resentment of the delinquent taxpayers and of employers forced to act as tax-collectors grew exponentially.

A proportion of the uninsured were hospitalized and unable to pay their bills; hospitals' costs increased, as did their deficits. The public and the press responded with increasing criticism. The debates in the Legislature grew more acrimonious, leading to investigations, resignation of the commissioner, appointment of a formal Hospital Insurance Inquiry Board, transfer of the executive director, and resignation of the minister.

Under a new minister, Mr. Douglas Turnbull, who appointed a new commissioner, Mr. Lloyd Detwiller from the Finance Department, the situation began to improve. On April 1, 1951, co-insurance payments ranging from $2.00 to $3.50 per patient-day (depending upon the size of hospital) were imposed. The maximum for any one family was set at ten days' payment per year—creating yet another administrative problem. Despite the shortcomings of the premiums collection systems, the vast majority of hospital accounts were insured accounts: 86.2 percent in 1949, 85 percent in 1950, 83.7 percent in 1951, and 85 percent in 1953. (Approximately eight percent of all accounts were the responsibility of other agencies or legitimately self-paying patients).[13]

The imposition of co-insurance, together with premium increases in both 1950 and 1951, merely added fuel to the flames of public reaction to high premiums in general and the arrears question in particular. Added to the legislative and newspaper charges of inefficiency in the administration, and rumours of a split in the Liberal-Conservative Cabinet over the entire program, the net effect was to make hospital insurance the most bitterly emotional and controversial issue in the 1952 election campaign. The result was defeat of the Government.

The new Social Credit Government accepted a number of changes in policy that had been previously proposed. The six-months' prepayment and waiting period was abandoned, liability for and collection of arrears were officially abolished and thus, except for those persons subject to compulsory pay-roll deductions, participation in the plan became, in effect, voluntary. The co-insurance payment of $2.00–$3.50 per day to a maximum of ten days was abolished and replaced by a $1.00 per day charge, without limit. Rising hospital costs, which made insurance protection more desirable, and the removal of the liability for arrears brought over 30,000 new subscribers into the system. By early 1954, the system was working tolerably well. But on April 1, a new policy (on which the BCHIS commissioner had been neither consulted nor informed) was announced, abolishing the premiums for hospital insurance and increasing the social services retail sales tax from three to five percent. The "dollar-a-day" co-insurance was retained.

With the changed revenue system, all of the headaches, frustrations, waiting periods, pay-roll deductions, direct billings, uninsured hospital accounts, and three hundred BCHIS administrative and clerical positions were ended. The turmoil, bad publicity, and political repercussions of the *insurance* phase of BCHIS were over. Although the savings in administrative overhead were minimal (the increase in commissions to retailers for collecting the higher tax was not much less than the savings in administrative salaries), there was no doubt as to the greater efficiency of the system. Proof of residence for twelve months was all that was required for entitlement to insured hospital benefits.

Under a new commissioner, Mr. Donald Cox, and the assistant commissioner, Mr. Lloyd Detwiller, all efforts were now directed to the development of the hospitals system, improvement of standards, and refinement of the system of paying hospitals for insured services.

British Columbia had also paid part of the tuition costs in educating Canadian governments in the formulation of effective policies and administrative procedures in this most complex of the social insurances. It had demonstrated the danger of trying to import an administrative system from another jurisdiction differing in both its economic and political organizations. It had alerted other provinces to the necessity of a much longer lead time for planning and design of the program and for creating the policies of the administrative organization. But the popularity of the policy of universal prepayment, as distinct from criticism of its maladministration, could not be doubted. Like Regina, Victoria became a Mecca for health authorities in all other provinces in the mid-1950s as they prepared to introduce their own programs.

The Alberta system. With government-sponsored hospital care insurance plans operating in provinces on either side, it was not surprising that Alberta decided to introduce a program on July 1, 1950. Parts of a province-wide plan were already in effect. In 1944, the Alberta government had introduced a maternity hospitalization program providing standard ward care for all resident maternity cases, paid directly from the provincial treasury. Later, similar payments were made for all poliomyelitis cases. A hospitalization program for recipients of social assistance was introduced in 1950.

The new insurance system for the general population took the form not of a centrally administered program but of a patchwork system of provincially-subsidized, municipally-administered and -financed plans. The legislation provided that when a municipality had passed the required by-law, all ratepayers and their dependents were entitled to public ward accommodation in the local hospital with which the municipality had entered into a contract. All non-ratepayers (that is, tenants), could participate voluntarily in the plan by purchasing a hospital "ticket" at the low cost of $10 per year for an individual or a family. Because not all municipalities established local plans, the program was estimated to cover approximately seventy-five percent of the population by 1953.[14] Because the hospital was responsible for any deficit, and an arbitrary payment system based on five categories of hospitals practically ensured that many would have deficits, many municipalities were reluctant to make the decision. The Government then introduced indirect coercion. Without either legislative or order-in-council authority the health minister simply refused to approve construction grants to any hospital not in a municipal plan and this meant, of course, that the hospital was also denied the matching federal grant. It was, in effect, a form of compulsion, an instrument to which the Social Credit government had repeatedly said it was opposed.

The contrast between the effectiveness of the three plans in solving the twin problems of patients and of hospitals is obvious in the financial data on the sources of hospitals' income in 1954.[15] In that year, hospitals in British Columbia received seventy-three percent of all their income from the insurance system; in Saskatchewan, government payments were 85.7 percent of all income; in Alberta, however, only 38.6 percent of all hospital income came from the provincial government.

The Newfoundland cottage hospital system. When Newfoundland entered Confederation in 1949, it joined the ranks of British Columbia and Saskatchewan as a province with a hospital services plan. It was, in essence, what other Canadians would have called "state medicine" in that it provided services through provincially owned hospitals and physicians paid by salary. The service was limited to the isolated out-ports of Newfoundland. It provided services to those residents who paid an annual premium. Approximately forty-seven percent of the population were covered under this program.

By the end of 1950, four of the ten provinces had programs that covered, respectively, almost half, three quarters, and in B.C. and Saskatchewan, nearly the total, population. There were other influential developments.

The voluntary insurance movement. Of equal importance as background influencing the development of policy—from the point of view of timing and of the nature of the decisions made—was the rapid expansion of enrolment in the voluntary prepayment plans and the cooperatives and of those insuring through commercial insurance. In the two year period 1951–52, over a million more Canadians availed themselves of these forms of protection, bringing the total to 5.5 million.[16] The numbers covered and the annual increases for those years are shown in Table 6.

These increases gave credence to the assertions of the spokesmen for these agencies and for the medical profession and hospital associations that private enterprise could, indeed, fulfill the need except for those requiring government assistance.

TABLE 6

ESTIMATED ENROLMENT IN VOLUNTARY COMMERCIAL INSURANCE AND PREPAYMENT PLANS, 1950–52, BY TYPE OF PLAN AND BENEFIT.

Type of Insurer	Hospital Benefits			Surgical Benefits			Medical Benefits		
	1950	1951	1952	1950	1951	1952	1950	1951	1952
Insurance Companies									
Group Policies	1,269,000	1,635,000	1,870,000	1,242,000	1,670,000	1,926,000	526,000	800,000	1,094,000
Individual Policies	642,000	706,000	833,000	316,000	348,000	420,000	130,000	143,000	169,000
Blue Cross Plans	2,702,000	2,949,000	3,020,000	560,000	656,000	793,000	412,000	509,000	716,000
Medical Care Plans	55,000	70,000	60,000	662,000	871,000	1,084,000	661,000	871,000	1,084,000
Co-op Plans	82,000	134,000	160,000	14,000	20,000	46,000	4,000	5,000	10,000
Grand Totals	4,750,000	5,494,000	5,943,000	2,794,000	3,565,000	4,269,000	1,733,000	2,328,000	3,073,000
Less Estimated Duplication	319,000	390,000	450,000	208,000	267,000	311,000	88,000	124,000	166,000
Net Totals	4,431,000	5,104,000	5,493,000	2,586,000	3,298,000	3,958,000	1,645,000	2,204,000	2,907,000
Increase during Year		15.2%	7.6%		27.5%	20.0%		34.0%	31.9%
Percentage of Pop'n. Insured.	32.0%	35.9%	37.6%	18.7%	23.2%	27.1%	11.9%	15.5%	19.9%
Adjusted Population*	11,876,000	12,210,000	12,564,000						
Percentage of Adjusted Population Insured	37.3%	41.8%	43.7%						

*"Adjusted population" equals the population of Canada less that of British Columbia and Saskatchewan, where compulsory provincial government hospital care plans exist. No deduction has been made from "adjusted population" for the estimated 770,000 covered by government plans in Alberta and Newfoundland nor from the numbers with voluntary insurance for duplication with government plans.

SOURCE: Canadian Life Insurance Officers Association.

171

Among these developments, perhaps none was more significant than the creation by the medical profession-sponsored prepayment plans of a national agency which came to be called Trans-Canada Medical Plans (TCMP).[17] With the addition to membership of two other groups— Quebec Blue Cross and Maritime Hospital Services Association—TCMP was able to offer nation-wide coverage. Enrolment increased rapidly, from three-quarters of a million in 1951 to nearly 2.5 million in 1955. For this 15.2 percent of the Canadian population a service-type contract providing extensive medical care benefits and having the advantage of inter-provincial portability was now a reality.

A parallel major development that helped to create the new background was the rapid growth of commercial insurance. The commercial insurance field is serviced by two different types of companies, organized in two separate associations: the Canadian Life Insurance Officers Association (CLIOA) (now the Canadian Life Insurance Association) and the Association of Accident and Health Underwriters. Both types of companies sold group contracts but the casualty companies sold the bulk of individual policies. Both issued indemnity contracts which reimbursed their beneficiaries according to predetermined fee schedules.[18]

Commercial companies, in addition to selling contracts for hospital expense, typically separated medical from surgical benefits and insured each under separate contracts although, of course, both were frequently sold together. It is for this reason that the statistics of commercial insurance are reported in the two categories in Table 6.

In addition to these specialized contracts, in the early 1950s a number of companies began to offer insurance against potentially catastrophic expenses in contracts called "major medical." These could be purchased separately or "added on" to the basic contracts. They were characterized by a large deductible (much of which could be insured in a basic contract) and by a co-insurance payment of a percentage of the total charges above the deductible. The benefits were applicable to expenses for hospital care, and medical and surgical services.

There was aggressive competition among the various companies and, of course, between the companies and the voluntary prepayment plans. Each had one major advantage. The prepayment plans offered the advantages of a service type contract. The advantage for the insurance industry was that it typically "experience rated" its group contracts which meant that in competing for a contract for, say, hospital care, in a company with a high proportion of young, healthy adults, the commercial company could offer a premium considerably below that of Blue Cross which had a uniform rate for all groups.

It was a rapidly expanding industry as Table 6 indicates. Mr. Bruce Power, secretary of the CLIOA, said in an address in 1954: " . . . I should like to repeat that most of the developments in the field of voluntary health insurance have taken place during the short span of the last ten years. The business is a most dynamic one and many changes have already taken place during this period. . . . There are still many challenging difficulties to be tackled but it is a fact that each year sees a significant reduction in the number of Canadians for whom health costs are a serious problem."[19]

It was against this long background of the collapse of the 1945 federal provincial conference, the development of voluntary prepayment plans, the government programs of the western provinces, the changes in leadership of the two major parties, and the improving relationships between the federal government and the provinces, that the federal government enunciated and implemented the decision affecting the nation's hospital services and the manner of their payment.

ACTION IMPERATIVES

As we have seen in the brief overview above, the stage was being set for some kind of major action. It would be superficial to explain the federal decision by saying that the Liberals had made a promise in 1919 and an offer in 1945 and now were required to follow through. There were more fundamental reasons, involving the health of Canadians, the unequal capacities of the provinces to cope with the provision and financing of health services, and, finally, the pressures from provinces already administering programs of personal health services. Each of these contributed to the decision.

1. *Illness and its costs.* The circular effects of low income and illness have long been recognized, and statistical data from other countries were available as indirect supporting evidence. But in 1953 the Dominion Bureau of Statistics began to release analyses of the data collected during a year-long sickness survey, conducted in 1950–51, of a random sample of 40,000 households in Canada. Some of the results were staggering, particularly those relating to the volume of long-term illness. Equally striking was the statistical confirmation of the inequity among citizens in the distribution of the burden of both physical and mental illness and the financial impact of their costs.

2. *The volume of illness.* The survey defined illness in three categories. (i) "complaint periods," defined as departures from good health; (ii) "disability," requiring modification of a person's normal activity; and (iii) "bed rest or care." The survey revealed that 80.4 percent of the total population reported "complaint periods" in one year, with an average

173

of 2.2 such periods per year. The total number of complaint days were 705,400,000, the average complaint period thus lasting 23.7 days. "Disability" was more precisely measurable. The total number of periods of disability totalled 15,180,000, i.e., almost two per person. The number of disability days totalled 163,500,000, an average of 11.9 days per person. Only part of these disability days required bed care, but the totals for these were higher than had been expected. It was estimated that 6,580,000 persons, or forty-eight percent, reported a total of 11,100,000 periods of bed care totalling 76,800,000 days or an average of 5.6 bed days of care per person during the survey year. Some of these were in hospital. While Canadians prided themselves on being a healthy nation, the burden of illness was clearly enormous.

3. *The distribution of illness*. Even more serious was the inequitable distribution of disability among the various income groups, as Table 7 so dramatically confirms.

Apart from the fact that the low income group had almost twice as many disability days as high income groups, the difference between males and females is interesting. Males in the low income group had twice as many disability days as males in the medium income group and almost two and a half times as many as those in the lower high income group. But the pattern was not characteristic of females where disability days were much more uniform throughout all income groups.

4. *The distribution of expenditures*. The survey also collected expenditure data and these, too, reinforced in specific terms what was already generally accepted, that health expenditures are directly related to income. These data are summarized in Table 8.

TABLE 7

Estimated Average Number of Person Days of Disability per 1,000 Persons, by Sex and Income, Survey Year, 1950–51.

Income Group	Both Sexes	Male	Female
Total	12,105	12,269	11,938
Low income (under $1,500)	17,833	21,112	14,506
Medium income ($1,500–$2,999)	11,042	10,572	11,518
High income:			
Lower ($3,000–$4,999)	9,628	8,437	10,836
Upper (over $5,000)	11,384	11,143	11,630

Source: *Canadian Sickness Survey*, 1950–51.

TABLE 8

ESTIMATED AVERAGE EXPENDITURES ON HEALTH FOR ALL FAMILY
UNITS REPORTING EXPENDITURES, BY INCOME GROUP,
SURVEY YEAR 1950–51

Income Groups	Average Total	Prepayments for Plans	Direct Payment for Services
All incomes	95.00	41.00	69.00
Less than $1,500	58.10	25.00	48.40
$1,500–$2,999	95.90	40.00	66.10
$3,000–$4,999	122.00	48.70	79.40
$5,000 or more	163.80	57.00	119.90

SOURCE: *Canadian Sickness Survey*, 1950–51.

The proportion of all family units reporting health expenditures to-talled 86.4 percent. In other words, only ·one family in seven had no expenditures of any kind for health services or insurance during the survey year.

From the table it may be noted that: (a) the average expenditure for all families having expenditures for medical care was $95, but the average expenditure varied widely with income; (b) the lowest income group (less than $1,500 per year) spent an average of only $58.10 per family unit; (c) the low-middle income group ($1,500–$3,000) spent an average of $95.90; and (d) the highest income group ($5,000 or more) spent almost three times as much as the lowest income group, or an average of $163.80.

While the lowest income groups had more illness, it is evident that if the volume of medical care were measured by the amount of money spent for it, the volume purchased was greatest in the highest income groups.

Obviously, however, statistics of expenditures overlooked two impor-tant facts in the pricing of medical and hospital services; first, that high income patients may have paid more for the same services than did medium or low income patients, and second, that patients with little or no means may have paid nothing. It is impossible, therefore, to rely solely on ex-penditure data. On the other hand, neither can the statistics of services actually received by various income groups be relied on solely, for these are not related to variations in the amount of sickness sustained, on the average, by members of each income group. The only truly meaningful statistics are those that show volume of services in relation to volume of illness in each income group.

These were also collected by the survey. The incidence of need for services is expressed in "disability days" and the average volume of care received in respect of that illness is shown for each income group in Table 9.

Two important conclusions stem from these data. First, the low income groups received much less physicians' care, both in terms of the proportion of persons reporting such care, and also in terms of the average number of doctors' calls and clinic visits per person, than did the higher income groups.

The second apparent conclusion is that the hospital statistics do not seem to conform to the pattern, for the low income groups are reported as having received as many hospital days of care as the upper high income groups. The main reason for this, as the survey showed, is that males aged twenty-five to forty-four in the low income group were more prone to types of disability requiring relatively large amounts of hospital care—tuberculosis and accidents. If these two are removed, the pattern is sustained.

The sickness survey had thus given statistical measurements of what had already been known, that there is an inverse relationship between

TABLE 9

NUMBER OF UNITS OF HEALTH CARE REPORTED FOR SELECTED INCOME GROUPS, SURVEY YEAR 1950–51. (ESTIMATED AVERAGE NUMBER OF UNITS OF VARIOUS CLASSES OF HEALTH CARE PER 100 DISABILITY DAYS FOR EACH INCOME GROUP)

| | | | | High Income | |
	Total	Low Income	Medium Income	Lower	Upper
Physicians' services:					
Doctors' office calls	10.83	5.95	11.28	13.06	13.66
Doctors' home calls	4.36	2.18	4.10	5.63	6.77
Doctors' office and home calls	15.19	8.13	15.38	18.68	20.44
Clinic visits	1.34	0.65	1.44	1.76	1.27
Doctors' calls and clinic visits	16.53	8.78	16.82	20.44	21.71
Days of in-patient hospital care	14.41	14.11	15.53	12.32	14.27
Home nursing services:					
Visits of graduate nursing care	0.48	0.39	0.42	0.61[a]	
Days of non-graduate nursing care	0.55	0.49[a]	0.72[a]	0.27[a]	
Operations	0.38	0.22	0.35	0.50	0.56
Miscellaneous treatments	1.25	0.38[a]	1.22	1.84	

[a]Estimate below standard of accuracy.
SOURCE: *Canadian Sickness Survey*, No. 9, p. 29.

income and sickness and a direct relationship between income and volume of health care received. The combination of these two creates the economic problem of medical care.

5. *Provincial disparities.* These were of three kinds: (a) the level of health resources and services available to their respective populations; (b) the level of *per capita* expenditures on those resources and services, and (c) the levels of fiscal capacity to make expenditures. These factors, as they obtained in the 1950s, were analyzed in two studies published by the Canadian Tax Foundation.[20] The most relevant data from these studies will be considered here.

As Table 10 indicates, there were wide variations in the health resources available among the provinces. With respect to hospital beds, Canadians living in British Columbia had thirty-seven percent more beds available than did Canadians in New Brunswick and seventy percent more than did Canadians in Newfoundland. There were sixty-seven percent more hospital personnel available to Canadians in Saskatchewan than to those in Prince Edward Island. In British Columbia there was one doctor for

TABLE 10

MEASURES OF STANDARDS OF HEALTH AND HOSPITAL SERVICES,
PROVINCES OF CANADA

	Population Per Hospital Bed 1956	Patients Under Care % of Population 1956	Hospital Personnel % of Population 1951	Population Per Civilian Physician 1954	Population Per Dentist 1954
Nfld.	136	11.2	0.47	2,117	16,583
P.E.I.	78	17.2	0.60	1,280	3,182
N.S.	86	16.0	0.65	1,179	3,678
N.B.	110	17.4	0.64	1,436	4,973
Que.	98	12.4	0.62	1,005	3,570
Ont.	98	16.9	0.85	858	2,434
Man.	81	17.5	0.75	1,036	3,339
Sask.	85	23.7	1.01	1,168	4,368
Alta.	84	23.9	0.83	1,052	2,935
B.C.	80	19.3	0.86	777	2,416
Total	94	16.5	0.76	948	3,046

SOURCE: E. J. Hanson, *Fiscal Needs of the Canadian Provinces*, p. 32.

177

777 residents, in Ontario one for 858, in Quebec one for 1,005, in New Brunswick one for 1,436, and in Newfoundland, one for 2,117. The discrepancy ranged almost 100 percent between British Columbia and New Brunswick and 200 percent between British Columbia and Newfoundland. With respect to dentists the disparities were even greater.

Expenditures by provincial and municipal governments varied widely. The major differences, of course, were those between provinces having hospital insurance plans and those that did not, as Table 11 indicates. But even among those not yet involved with hospital insurance, the differences were large. In 1952, for example, Ontario *per capita* expenditures were thirty percent higher than Manitoba's and thirty-six percent higher than those of Prince Edward Island.

But of more significance was the proportion of average personal income of residents of the provinces required to sustain expenditures on those respective levels. These comparisons are shown in Table 12. Provincial *per capita* expenditures are indexed against the national average (100) and are then shown as a percentage of personal income for the years 1949, 1952, and 1956. In comparing the 1956 data, British Columbia spent fifty-four percent more than the national average and Prince

TABLE 11

COMBINED PROVINCIAL-MUNICIPAL EXPENDITURE ON HEALTH AND
HOSPITALS, PER CAPITA, 1952 AND 1956

	Per Capita 1952	Per Capita 1956	% Increase 1952–56
	$	$	
Nfld.	20.26	27.18	34
P.E.I.	12.91	18.54	43
N.S.	15.19	19.95	31
N.B.	16.16	20.03	24
Ont.	17.64	21.06	20
Man.	13.73	17.99	30
Sask.	39.41	47.85	21
Alta.	26.89	38.84	45
B.C.	39.00	42.03	8
Total	22.31	27.30	23

SOURCE: E. J. Hanson, *Fiscal Needs of the Canadian Provinces*, p. 34.

TABLE 12

COMBINED PROVINCIAL-MUNICIPAL EXPENDITURE ON HEALTH AND
HOSPITALS. INDEXES OF PER CAPITA EXPENDITURE AND PERCENTAGES
OF PERSONAL INCOME.

	Indexes Nine Provinces = 100			% of Personal Income		
	1949	1952	1956	1949	1952	1956
Nfld.	156	89	100	4.5	3.5	3.6
P.E.I.	95	57	68	2.4	1.8	2.3
N.S.	64	67	73	1.2	1.8	2.1
N.B.	58	71	73	1.2	2.1	2.2
Ont.	71	78	77	0.9	1.3	1.3
Man.	66	61	66	0.9	1.2	1.4
Sask.	166	173	174	2.3	2.7	3.4
Alta.	95	118	141	1.3	2.0	2.7
B.C.	230	172	154	2.7	2.7	2.5
Total[a]	100	100	100	1.3	1.7	1.8

[a]Eight-province average (excludes Newfoundland and Quebec).
SOURCE: E. J. Hanson, *Fiscal Needs of the Canadian Provinces*, p. 35.

Edward Island spent forty-three percent less. But to finance expenditures on that scale, British Columbia spent 2.5 percent of *per capita* income and Prince Edward Island spent 2.3 percent, an almost equal proportion for far fewer resources and services. Manitoba, on the other hand, spent thirty-four percent less than the national average, but allocated only 1.4 percent of income in doing so. It can be assumed that this was the result of political choice. (Quebec has been excluded from the calculations because a substantial proportion of services were provided by Catholic Orders, with a high level of contributed services. Quebec's expenditures were thirty-one percent below the national average.)

In final terms, the capacity of a province—in the absence of transfer payments from the federal government—to finance governmental goods and services rested on *per capita* income. Again, the figures vary by more than 100 percent, as shown in Tables 13 and 14.

It is the primary function of a national government in a federal system to think nationally. It must constantly address the question, "What in terms of living standards, and particularly in terms of public services, does it mean to be a Canadian citizen?" It was obvious that it meant

TABLE 13

PERSONAL INCOME PER CAPITA, PROVINCES OF CANADA 1952–56.
IN DOLLARS.

	1952	1953	1954	1955	1956	Average, 1952–56	Rank
Nfld.	586	632	653	682	749	660	10
P.E.I.	710	653	683	690	788	705	9
N.S.	847	891	902	918	971	908	7
N.B.	772	777	806	823	895	815	8
Que.	995	1,047	1,059	1,073	1,149	1,065	6
Ont.	1,410	1,459	1,446	1,504	1,594	1,483	2
Man.	1,170	1,166	1,126	1,191	1,325	1,196	5
Sask.	1,434	1,319	927	1,164	1,392	1,247	4
Alta.	1,365	1,357	1,239	1,292	1,456	1,342	3
B.C.	1,434	1,478	1,476	1,538	1,667	1,519	1
Total	1,203	1,235	1,205	1,257	1,361	1,252	

SOURCE: D.B.S. *National Accounts, Income and Expenditure, 1926–56* and *1958.*

TABLE 14

PERSONAL INCOME PER CAPITA, PROVINCES OF CANADA 1952–56.
INDEXES, AVERAGE FOR CANADA = 100.

	1952	1953	1954	1955	1956	Average 1952–56
Nfld.	49	51	54	54	55	53
P.E.I.	59	53	57	55	58	56
N.S.	70	72	75	73	71	73
N.B.	64	63	67	65	66	65
Que.	83	85	88	85	84	85
Ont.	117	118	120	120	117	118
Man.	97	94	93	95	97	96
Sask.	119	107	77	93	102	100
Alta.	113	110	103	103	107	107
B.C.	119	120	122	122	122	121
Total	100	100	100	100	100	100

SOURCE: E. J. Hanson, *Fiscal Needs of the Canadian Provinces*, p. 43.

different—indeed, far different—things province to province. Standards of resources and services that varied as much as two or even three times were clearly indefensible. Equally evident was the fact that the disparities could be overcome, or even ameliorated, in only one way—by federal participation in the financing of services with large infusions of nationally-collected funds.

6. *Provincial initiatives.* Every government is conscious of being at the focal point of myriad political forces making demands, offering advice, creating conflict, showering criticism, and a few, occasionally, assuring support. In the past, these forces have been mainly generated within the territorial jurisdiction of the government concerned. A provincial Cabinet looks out from the capitol building on a shifting mosaic of organized interest groups and provincial political parties whose demands and protests must be accommodated in such a way as to solve problems and achieve a maximum degree of political support.

In a federal state, the national government is at the centre of a much more complex array of forces. Not only must it deal with nationally organized interest groups and parties but it must also be concerned with the provinces on two distinct, but obviously related, levels—the provincial governments and the provincial political parties. For example, in the 1950s each of the four national parties in the House of Commons was affiliated with its counterparts in some or all of the provinces, and each party controlled one or more provincial governments. A federal Cabinet is forced, therefore, to anticipate the political consequences of its policies on its affiliated provincial parties, whether they are in the government or in opposition. This was well illustrated in chapter 3 where the position of the Ontario Liberal party was inextricably linked with the federal Liberal policy. The concern is even greater when the federal government deals with the provincial governments, both when its affiliate forms the government and when an opposition party is in control. A miniscule CCF party in opposition in Saskatchewan in 1944 was one thing; a CCF government with a hospital insurance program in place in 1947 was quite another. Provincial initiatives in policy areas that have current or future implications for the national jurisdiction must be seriously weighed.

The "mosaic" metaphor is frequently and aptly applied to the complex Canadian political scene. It was especially appropriate in 1940 when Ian Mackenzie had written in a memorandum to Mackenzie King, "these reforms are possible only when eight of the nine provincial governments are Liberal."[21] But in the post-war decade, the scene was less that of a mosaic and more that of a kaleidoscope. As we have seen, four provinces had varied programs in operation by 1950. Four provinces out of ten was not a majority but it was a minority that could not be ignored as these governments—and their affiliated party spokesmen in opposition in Ottawa—demanded that the federal Liberal party honour its 1945 offer of financial sharing. Step by provincial step, the pressures were mounting.

THE CONSTRAINTS

There were a number of barriers, limitations, legal restraints, and foreign policy considerations exacerbating the difficulties of the national government in making policy choices that would have some surety of success, both in terms of solving the problems and yielding support for the government. These included the federal system, the shortage of facilities, the costs, and the opposition of some provinces.

1. *The federal system.* If the federal government representing all Canadians was to develop a policy with the objective of ensuring that health services were available nation-wide on an equitable, prepaid basis, there were, theoretically, three options open to it: (a) It could seek a constitutional amendment enabling it to administer and finance a national plan; (b) It could increase the resources of the provinces by transfer payments enabling them to undertake programs on their own; (c) It could offer grants-in-aid on condition that programs of specified design be introduced, and in amounts large enough to induce the appropriate provincial responses.

Reasoned political analysis ruled out the first. True, consensus among the provinces in 1950 had enabled a national pension plan to be developed. But the differences in the impact on the autonomy of a province between an income maintenance program and a health program with its implications for community hospitals, provincially-based professions, provincial bureaucracies, and political credit for provincial parties, made any notion of a parallel solution in health services totally unrealistic. Alternative one was unacceptable.

Alternative two was feasible but highly dubious. Funds could be made available, but despite the nation-wide need as perceived in Ottawa, there was no assurance that every provincial government would give health services a similar priority. The funds might well end up in the form of what were thought to be more politically rewarding extensions of highways.

The third alternative, the choice that had been made in 1945, also had its shortcomings as the Royal Commission on Dominion-Provincial Relations had emphasized. It opened the federal government to the charge of distorting provincial priorities and of imposing its will on the provinces, and it also created a permanent moral and political commitment to a program over which the federal government might have little control. If this were the route to be selected, the policy would have to be designed so as to retain in federal hands as much control as possible.

Moreover, in Prime Minister St. Laurent's mind the federal system imposed yet another constraint, the unfairness of using tax revenues nationally collected from all citizens for the advantage of a minority of citizens in the event that only a minority of provinces accepted the offer. In his view, in a democracy majority interests must be served, unless the minority were identifiably disadvantaged members of society who needed government assistance. There could be no federal contribution for a minority of provinces having hospital insurance programs; there could, on the other hand, be federal aid to physically disabled persons, and that program he had not only supported but had initiated. A health insurance policy could become operative only if it enjoyed demonstrable majority support of both provinces and population.

2. *The inadequacy of facilities.* In Mr. St. Laurent's view the question whether the country as a whole, and certainly many parts of it, had hospital facilities adequate to meet the increased demand everyone anticipated that hospital insurance would create, loomed very large. His views were consistent with his legal background when he said, in 1952: "I do not feel that the government has the right to give Canadians contractual rights to hospital treatment until there is sufficient accommodation in the hospitals to enable the government to fulfill that obligation . . . I do not feel sure there is sufficient hospital space to enable all that would have contractual rights to receive hospital treatment."[22]

The proclaimed shortage of hospital facilities was a constraint on the policy of timing.

3. *The financial constraints.* The 1945 Green Book Proposals, it will be recalled, had been predicated on the transfer of major tax fields to the federal government. In the view of the federal government, failure to achieve agreement on the financial proposals had deprived it of the resources to underwrite the costs of the social welfare and health programs it had proposed and, as a consequence, the offer remained dormant.

With the departure of Premier Drew from Ontario to assume leadership of the national Progressive Conservative party and the succession to the premiership of Ontario of Mr. Leslie Frost, a new era of federal-provincial accord began between Ontario and Ottawa. There was thus renewed the possibility that the financial underpinnings of a new thrust for health insurance might be laid. But external forces were to intervene.

Canada had been obliged as a member of the United Nations to support that organization's efforts in the Korean war. That event in a small country on the other shore of the Pacific Ocean was to have extraordinary repercussions on Canadian domestic policy.

The tax agreements negotiated with eight of the ten provinces necessitated a conference in 1950 to achieve agreement on a new formula (that would, it was hoped, include the other two provinces—Ontario and Quebec) to take effect in 1952. For some of the provinces it meant a new opportunity to press for the health and social measures proposed in 1945. Fearful of the possible provincial demands, on the opening day of the conference Prime Minister St. Laurent deployed his most powerful artillery to shoot down any provincial expectations, calling on the secretary of state for external affairs to review the implications of the international situation, the minister of national defence for an indication of the increased burden on Canadian military resources, and the minister of finance to indicate what all this meant to the federal government in fiscal terms. "In 1945 when we hoped for and planned for a long period of peaceful development of our own country, the federal government laid before the provincial governments a comprehensive, integrated series of proposals. We do not feel that this would be an appropriate course in 1950 when we are faced with an entirely different perspective."[23]

The indicated consequences included a reduction of federal capital investment, the imposition of new direct taxes, and no changes in the tax agreements that would add to their over-all costs. He also referred to the health grants program, indicating that the minister of health "would be glad to receive suggestions for improvements in the program within the limits of the over-all commitment made in 1948."[24] There was one exception to the new austerity. Said Mr. St. Laurent: "There has been growing evidence that the public would be prepared to support and to pay for some system of contributory old age security."[25]

He concluded by stating that "the present is not a propitious time to make comprehensive proposals in other fields. ... I make no apology for asking my colleagues to supplement these observations of mine with additional details of the sombre background against which our deliberations will proceed."[26]

The triple salvos fired by ministers Pearson, Claxton, and Abbot had the desired effect. Only Premier Douglas of Saskatchewan had the temerity to point out that the current international situation was no reason for delaying the introduction of health insurance. "I submit that it will not cost any more, or but very little more, in the aggregate to provide health services for the people of Canada through health insurance programs than it is costing at the present time. People are now paying for health services. The only difference is that in a health insurance program the burden of paying for that health insurance is distributed over all of the population rather than falling on the people who have the misfortune to be ill."[27]

He then urged the setting up of a sub-conference that would examine and bring up to date the 1945 cost estimates prepared by the Heagerty Committee. But it was to no avail. There were other, higher priorities.

By 1955, defence expenditures had increased almost five-fold in five years, rising from 2.2 to 6.5 percent of gross national expenditures.[28] Between fiscal years 1949–50 and 1954–55, federal expenditures on health and social welfare almost doubled, from $738.8 million to $1,341.3 million. The major contributor to these increases was the new old age security program.[29]

In addition to the reality of enormous increases for defence and welfare measures, there was present in the Cabinet what might be termed a congenital apprehension about embarking on a program as large and as unpredictable in its long term costs as health insurance. The perennial response of at least some of his Cabinet colleagues to Mr. Martin's proposals was that a continuing commitment of such magnitude would leave no elbow room for the federal government to undertake anything else. Mr. Martin's response was, "Well, this has always been the case; it was the same when the first means-test old age pensions were discussed in 1925 and 1926. Everybody thought this would be the end; my goodness, how could we afford it?" As Mr. Martin observed, "I have never put forward a proposal as Minister of National Health and Welfare when this argument was not brought out, and it will always be brought out."[30]

4. *Provincial reaction.* As we have seen, certain provincial initiatives taken since 1945 were increasing the pressure for action. But, just as assuredly, the anticipated reactions of other provinces were constraints both on the shaping of a policy and of its timing. That Mr. Duplessis would oppose a national plan was certain, despite his agreement to a constitutional amendment to permit the development of a national program of old age security. Speaking to the 1951 annual meeting of l'Association des médecins de langue française du Canada, he said: "We are convinced of the practical impossibility of a compulsory health insurance plan which would turn physicians into civil servants."[31]

A year later he reaffirmed this attitude to a delegation representing the Quebec division of the Canadian Congress of Labour which had presented a brief to the Quebec cabinet urging national health insurance: "Health insurance is dangerous. It is not health insurance that will bring health. I have little confidence in assembly line cures." He ended his reply to the delegation by stating that he "had no intention of coming to an agreement with the federal government for setting up a national health insurance plan in the near future."[32]

Quebec's reaction was predictable. But what of the others? One of the major purposes of the health survey grant provided in 1948 was "to enable the provinces to plan the proper organization of hospital and medical insurance." In the mind of the minister of health, Mr. Martin, the expectation was that clear guidelines for provincial action would be developed.

Mr. Martin was to be disappointed. Only the reports from Alberta and Saskatchewan submitted proposals for health insurance substantially in conformance with the federal proposals of 1945.[33] The Ontario Survey Committee reported on the voluntary prepayment plans but made no recommendations for health insurance. The British Columbia report stressed the need for further study but recommended only that early consideration be given to a program for children. New Brunswick and Nova Scotia recommended that no government program be introduced until an adequate supply of hospital beds and trained personnel were available. The Nova Scotia report then went on, however, to suggest that the voluntary plans should be extended to cover the whole population by the simple device of providing government subsidies either to the services (hospitals, physicians) or directly to the prepayment plans whose premiums would then be within the reach of "almost all' persons. The inconsistency was ignored.

Three other provincial survey committees—those of New Brunswick, Prince Edward Island, and Manitoba—also recommended that voluntary plans should be encouraged and extended with the governments paying the premiums for those unable to pay. The medical and hospital association representatives on the survey committees had been successful in persuading the committees of the preferability of the new CMA-CHA policy. These recommendations by the survey committees did not, however, constitute government policy, as most of the ministers of health made clear in their letters transmitting the reports to Ottawa. But they did strengthen the CMA-CHA positions and emphasized the constraints within which a federal policy could be formulated. The survey reports thus both disappointed Mr. Martin and complicated his task. It is doubtful, however, that his disappointment was widely shared in the St. Laurent Cabinet in the early 1950s.

These and other lesser constraints reinforced Prime Minister St. Laurent's basic philosophy about the role of government in social programs. His attitude is well illustrated by his comment after a meeting with Premier Frost as late as January 1956. As Dale Thompson reports, "The two men agreed that political considerations were forcing them to advance too quickly, and that the first priority should be given to increasing hospital facilities; otherwise it would be impossible to cope with the increased demand for hospital care. After the Ontario Premier had left, St. Laurent emerged from his office, and commented in a bemused tone: 'You know, Mr. Frost doesn't like hospital insurance either.'"[34]

The significance of this observation in summing up the constraints on a health policy is apparent when it is recalled that two and a half years earlier, on May 1, 1953, Mr. Martin had announced that the hospital construction grant made available in 1948 had resulted in the construction of 46,000 new hospital beds, and the grant was cut in half.[35] One is tempted to add that, from the point of view of the minister of national health and welfare, an important constraint on the development of policy was the prime minister.

THE UNCERTAINTIES

1. *The costs.* The costs of a universal program were, as in all these major decisions, one of the important uncertainties. They were, however, far less uncertain now than they had been in all earlier examinations of the question. For the first time there were vast amounts of data available from the Blue Cross plans and from the universal plans of British Columbia and Saskatchewan. These data had been systematically analyzed by the research division of the Department of National Health and Welfare with adjustments made for the varying cost levels among the provinces. But, again, those estimates might hold up for only a brief time as the public became educated to a higher level of health services, and unit costs increased with improved standards of service and higher remuneration for health workers. Programs of this nature had a history of ignoring experts' predictions. Recent information (and misinformation) about the British National Health Service was used to challenge their reliability. The financial and statistical tables gave political leaders some comforting support but the worrying question of ultimate costs would not disappear.

2. *The medical profession and the hospitals.* A second uncertainty was the responses of the Canadian Medical and Hospital associations. Both had made a ninety degree turn in their policy: both still favoured health insurance but not if it were to be administered by the Government. How strong would their opposition be, and how much of it would be directed at the federal government? Ottawa might attempt to sidestep the issue by saying that the shape of the ten programs would be the responsibility of the provincial governments. On the other hand, to leave the essential design of the programs solely to the provinces could well frustrate any objective of the federal government that the result should be a "national"

plan in which all citizens were enrolled and those moving from one province to another be assured of full portability of equal benefits. The federal government would have to accept responsibility for the decision on the role of voluntary plans, and the implications of that were both serious and uncertain.

3. *The provinces.* Another uncertainty was the reaction of the provinces. Were they ready for so high a degree of what came to be called, "cooperative federalism"? Certainly, Premier Duplessis was not. And who knew how large a constitutional issue he could make of it? And if it were to be a national plan, would the provinces be willing to accept the amount of federal direction that would entail? True, the provincial health bureaucracies had accepted an inordinate degree of control in the administration of the health grants, but not without continuing criticism of their rigidities, red tape, and duplication of the auditing process. It was a moot point.

4. *The doubts.* Finally, there was that nagging question, "Could it be brought off?" Given the strong positions of the interest groups opposed to government action, the resistance of some provinces, and the sheer enormity of the undertaking, could an objective of such complexity be achieved so as to redound to the credit of the government and the party or would it simply engage them in unproductive and divisive controversy? And yet, the health grants program had yielded a high rate of political return, and the public opinion polls showed that the vast majority of the public was ready, if not eager. But the uncertainties remained.

THE EXTERNAL CONTRIBUTIONS

As the evidence of public interest in a national program mounted, so did the pressure in the House of Commons. In 1950, a committee of the House had been struck to examine the problems and issues in a program of old age security. Its work had paved the way for a constitutional amendment and forthcoming legislation. Several of its members agreed that it would be helpful if a similar committee were appointed to consider health insurance.

In February 1951, therefore, Mr. Stanley Knowles asked the health minister "if the government would consider setting up a parliamentary committee similar to the committee on old age security to study and report on the whole question of health insurance."[36] The Hon. Mr. Martin replied that "it is not the intention of the government to recommend the setting up of such a committee at the present time."[37]

Eight months later, at the opening of the Second Session of Parliament, Mr. Knowles asked the same question and received the same reply.[38] Mr. Knowles waited until June 1952 for a further assault. This time Mr. Martin replied: "We will examine the problem and in the regular session of 1952 I hope that we may be able—and I think I may go further than that and say that we are giving consideration to the matter—to set up a parliamentary committee to examine the whole problem."[39]

But nothing happened, and at the opening of Parliament in 1953 Mr. Knowles repeated his question yet again. Mr. Martin replied: "The government has come to the conclusion not to set up such a committee."[40]

There would be no parliamentary inquiry, but Mr. Martin's June 1952 statement indicating that there might be, had triggered responses among a number of interest groups who began the preparation of briefs in readiness for the anticipated public hearings. Some of these were presented to the Cabinet or the minister of health and others were made public through press releases and speeches. These were important inputs to the formulation of the policy.

1. *The Canadian Medical Association.* The CMA, as noted in chapter 3, had adopted a new policy that reversed its 1943 approval of a government-administered program and now committed its members to outright opposition to any such proposal and to support for the voluntary plan approach. It thus had two official statements: (i) its new policy, and (ii) its statement of principles that had accumulated over the years since 1934 and now bore little internal consistency. Simultaneously with its expanded support of the development and expansion of Trans-Canada Medical Plans (TCMP), it began to step up the activities of its Economics Committee. The first priority was a review of the two official statements of policy and principles. The drafts of the new statement were first approved by the Economics Committee and then submitted to the provincial divisions of the CMA for comment. Finally, at the 1955 meeting of Council, the new statement was approved as official policy:

On the question of health insurance, the CMA approves of the adoption of the principle of contributory health insurance ... [and] having seen demonstrated the successful application of the insurance principle in the establishment of the voluntary prepaid medical care plans, recommends the extension of these plans to cover all residents of Canada, with financial assistance from public funds where this is required; [and] recommends, where it becomes evident that the voluntary medical care plans cannot achieve adequate coverage, that provincial governments collaborate in the administrative and financial tasks of extending health insurance to all through the medium of the voluntary prepayment plans.[41]

The commitment to the 1949 policy of health insurance administered by the voluntary plans with governments subsidizing in whole or in part the premiums of those unable to pay was reaffirmed. It also strongly reasserted its long-held principle that if governments did become involved, health insurance should be administered by an independent, non-political commission.

The new statement also added a revised section concerning related services. "To assure economy and efficiency in the provision of services," it said:

(12) Hospitals, health departments and all other health agencies should coordinate their activities so as to provide their services more effectively and economically.

(13) Hospitals should be located and their facilities and size determined on a planned, regionalized basis.

(14) An adequate system of institutional facilities and services requires the balanced development of diagnostic facilities, active treatment general hospitals, rehabilitation centres, chronic care facilities (including mental and tuberculosis hospitals) and home care programs.

(15) Lay and professional organizations and government health agencies should participate in community, provincial and federal health planning activities.[42]

In the development of a nation-wide system of health services, much of the statement offered highly positive advice, particularly clause 14 emphasizing the importance of a balanced system of services ranging from diagnostic facilities through to home care programs.

There was one new element, however, that had not appeared in earlier statements. Previous documents had stated that methods of remuneration should be as agreed upon by representatives of the profession and the insuring agency. This was repeated, and a new section added: "In the provision of personal health services where the usual doctor-patient relationship exists, it is the view of the CMA that remuneration on a basis of fee for services rendered promotes high quality of medical care."[43]

Translated into bargaining demands by the provincial divisions of the CMA, it was to become a major issue as radiologists and pathologists, traditionally paid by hospitals on a salary or negotiated contract, insisted that they, too, be paid on a fee-for-service basis.

The most crucial influence of the CMA, however, was intensified opposition to a government-administered program. Each year, as enrolment of the member plans of TCMP increased, so did the confidence of the profession that the voluntary system might prevail. Although not as directly affected by hospital insurance as by any proposal for medical care, the CMA was concerned with the possibility of government-administered hospital insurance establishing precedents that would be difficult to reject if medical care insurance came later.

That the Government was fully aware of the CMA's policy and that some of its members, particularly the prime minister himself, were highly receptive to the voluntary approach, was indicated in 1951 shortly after the launching of TCMP. During the question period in the House of Commons on June 20, 1951, the prime minister was asked whether "the government has or will it give consideration to government participation in recent proposals of the Canadian Medical Association for national health insurance in Canada."[44]

The Prime Minister replied:

> The government as such has not yet given consideration to these recent proposals but I know . . . that several members of the government . . . myself included . . . have welcomed this further evidence of the concern of the medical profession in Canada to increase the efficiency and scope of their assistance to their fellow citizens in their traditional role of good Samaritans.
> If they can arrange to provide all Canadians with the medical care any of them may require from time to time on a prepaid basis, I am sure most of us will feel that is all to the good. I have no doubt that all levels of government will be most anxious to see them succeed in that undertaking and to consider with them what part those governments should take in helping to make the plan succeed and extend to the whole population.
> . . . I think it would be a most happy solution if the medical profession would assume the administration of and the responsibility for, a scheme that would provide prepaid medical attendance to any Canadian who needed it.[45]

It might well have been a happy solution for Mr. St. Laurent, but there was no brushing aside of the issue simply by his wishing success for the voluntary approach. Later in the day, Stanley Knowles (CCF) refocused the issue for the prime minister.

> I confess this attitude [of endorsing the CMA's proposals] struck me as a case of the Prime Minister's backing away from declared Liberal proposals. . . . I did not mind the Prime Minister congratulating the medical profession on any evidence of social responsibility that they may give, but I suggest that entirely apart from the views that we in this party hold, the Liberal party is already committed, and has been across the years, to the proposition that if we are going to have a

proper program of health insurance it must be administered in the name of all the people by their government.[46]

This public exchange not only illustrated the conflict within the Cabinet but highlighted one of the major policy choices the Government would have to make. It was obviously in the interest of the federal government to avoid a confrontation with the medical profession on the national level, but it was becoming increasingly evident that it could not avoid responsibility for the decision on the role, if any, that the voluntary plans would play.

2. *The Canadian Hospital Association.* The CHA, as noted above, submitted a brief to the minister in 1953 and added its weight to the CMA policy of restricting government action to subsidization of low income individuals to enable them to pay premiums to the voluntary Blue Cross plans.[47]

The brief also made a number of other important points.

(1) The specialized services now provided by a modern general active treatment hospital are necessarily expensive, and therefore such hospitals should be used only for those acutely ill patients who may benefit from such services.

(2) While this is true, the changing attitude to hospital care has increased community pressures for expanded hospital facilities. This demand for the services of the active treatment hospital has been accentuated by the development of the idea of prepaying for hospital services because, among the various alternative types of care which may be practicable for any given patient, it is natural to select the treatment for which payment has already been made.

(3) Unfortunately, this preoccupation with general hospital facilities has resulted in an almost complete ignoring of the needs for alternative types of care, such as convalescent hospitals, homes for the aged, or visiting-nurse services. Consequently, many general hospital facilities are being called upon to provide care which could adequately be given in much less expensive ways and in less expensive types of institutions.

The brief then underscored the potential danger of universal hospital insurance in these words: "By solving the economic problem of paying for general hospital care without solving the economic problems of other types of essential care, we are placing a treatment burden on general hospitals which does not properly belong to them and could be met less expensively in other ways."

It strengthened its case by drawing on the experience of the Blue Cross plans.

This experience clearly shows the need for careful scheduling of the various stages of a national health program. We are not counselling delay in the extension of hospital care insurance. We do believe that extension of hospital insurance without provision for such other services as care for long-term illness, for rehabilitation, for visiting home-nursing services, for out-patient services, is neither an economical use of limited resources nor even in the patient's, and therefore the community's, interest. We must make plans with boldness and imagination; but we must be certain that we have sorted out genuine needs and alternative methods of meeting such needs.

The brief then turned to the need for better planning in the development of facilities and the shortcomings in the rules governing the use of the federal hospital construction grant.

The grant, it said, should be increased to approximately one-third of the actual cost of construction; the facilities to which it could be applied should be expanded to include facilities other than beds; and the terms on which the grant was made available should be revised to take into consideration the fiscal capacity of the provinces to match the federal funds. It again emphasized the dangers in a limited approach: "The Association urges consideration by the federal government of the need for supplementing the National Health Program, in cooperation with the provinces, to include nursing homes, home-care programs, and homes for the aged."

3. *The Catholic Hospital Conference.* Although the Catholic Hospital Conference was affiliated with the Canadian Hospital Association it was probably even more concerned about the implications of a government program. One of its most definitive statements was that made at the June 1956 meeting attended by representatives of almost all of Canada's Roman Catholic hospitals. The president, Reverend Hector L. Bertrand, strongly urged the establishment of "a provincial health insurance scheme operated by private enterprise." He stressed four main points:

(1) In the light of papal pronouncements, we favour a health insurance scheme and we recommend it.

(2) This plan, if it can be put into practice and we believe it can, should be compulsory, contributory, and, preferably, operated by private enterprise.

(3) If a privately-operated scheme cannot be put into practice, we may have to settle for a state health insurance plan.

(4) If a state health insurance plan is inevitable this intervention must always and in each case respect the rights and privileges of the human person and safeguard the interests of private initiative insofar as this is possible.[48]

Because of its voluntary system of capital financing and its reliance on a large volume of contributed services, as the federal-provincial negotiations continued, the Catholic Hospital Conference made strong representations with respect to interest and depreciation, and recognition of the equity of paying the hospitals for the value of the contributed services.

4. *The Canadian Life Insurance Officers Association* (CLIOA). The insurance industry, like the CMA, had reversed its 1943 policy of support for a government program, and now exerted every effort to restrict the role of government to subsidy of individuals unable to pay commercial insurance premiums.

There were many important public addresses in 1954 typifying the industry's concerns and attitudes. One was given by Mr. William Anderson, vice president and managing director of North American Life Assurance Company, and one of the most knowledgeable experts in the field.[49]

Noting the rapid expansion of voluntary coverage, he asked: "Why then is there so much clamour for and persistent advocacy of compulsory measures in this field? Why do the platforms of the political parties and the overwhelming sentiments indicated by the Public Opinion Polls appear to favour 'Health Insurance' (so called) on a compulsory basis?" Part of the reason, he suggested, was the result of extravagant claims made on behalf of a governmental program.

> This rosy picture gains many adherents, some of them because of their sincere interest in better health and some because of uneasiness concerning the high and uncertain impact of health service costs on the family budget. Still others fall for the fallacy of free service or espouse and advocate compulsory health services as an attractive method of catching votes. What most people who favor compulsory health insurance fail to realize is that it is a Trojan horse. They fail to discern that under a superficially attractive exterior it hides the forces which will destroy their freedom of choice and import a full-fledged system of state medicine into their midst.... I fear and distrust those who

bring the "gift" of compulsory health insurance not only because it is compulsory but because it is not at all what it appears to be on the surface. I am convinced that it is not insurance at all but a deliberately designed and sugar coated illusion of insurance coverage—its purpose being the easy achievement of a system of state medicine as a major step towards complete socialism. However, I can sympathize with those who are taken in by this wolf in sheep's clothing since I regret to recall that it was only a decade ago that the life insurance companies and other interested groups went on record before a special Parliamentary committee as being in favor of a comprehensive and compulsory health insurance scheme for all people. As far as I am aware, all of the persons in the life insurance business who endorsed the life company views as then expressed have later recanted. Greater experience and familiarity with health insurance have bred a maturity of thought which concludes that compulsory health insurance cannot be separated from state medicine and socialism.

He then critically examined the voluntary plan approach. One of the problems was that premiums were set by the economic cost of the benefits provided and were not related to capacity of low income earners to pay. One possibility for meeting this problem, he suggested, was that employers might arrange that their employees' contributions be related to income. "This would mean that an employer would pay a higher share of the cost of the same coverage in the case of his lower income as compared with his higher income employees." (It was the same solution that the Royal Commission had discussed in 1940 and the Heagerty Committee had proposed in 1943.)

Another problem was that voluntary plans had not paid enough attention to those families that incurred truly catastrophic costs.

Unfortunately the voluntary plans have been much too concerned with the multiplicity of small costs which arise in the case of many families rather than the infrequent but very large costs which a small minority of families are forced to face. Indeed it may be argued that the voluntary plans have tended to become in too large measure a budgeting device for normal medical care costs rather than an insurance mechanism to offset extraordinary expense.

One of the factors militating against the voluntary approach was the impact of the federal income tax that enabled an individual to deduct expenditures in excess of three percent of income. Two regulations had a detrimental effect. The first was that payments made on behalf of the individual were deductible as well as those he made out of pocket. The result was that in the case of large bills, "the reimbursement to the individual together with the value of the tax exemption may exceed the costs incurred." The second was that premiums paid by the individual were not recognized as tax exemptions. There was not therefore, as in the United States, a tax inducement to join voluntary plans. He closed by expressing "the hope that the recently enunciated American attitude of encouragement to voluntary health insurance may find its counterpart within the councils of our own government."

This and many other similar addresses were of special importance in that they recognized the nature and magnitude of the problems but cogently argued for solutions that would build upon institutions already in place. Nor did the insurance spokesmen claim to offer total solutions but insisted that if government simply expanded its traditional role of assisting those in need, the combined efforts of free enterprise and government would go a long way towards that objective. It was a policy highly consistent with the personal philosophy of Prime Minister St. Laurent.

5. *The Canadian Chamber of Commerce.* As expected, the policy of the Canadian Chamber of Commerce parallelled and reinforced that of the CLIOA. Consideration of the issue had continued over a number of years and, in 1953, the Chamber announced its formal statement of policy.[50]

It took a positive approach to the national health grants program, believing "that these grants should be liberal as possible, bearing in mind that government revenues come from the people and that existing annual commitments for social welfare benefits are substantial and are increasing." On health insurance however, it was adamant:

> The Chamber is opposed to any form of compulsory health insurance or state medicine. So-called "free" health services would result in vastly increased demand upon them. Some of this increased demand will be to meet genuine need, but a good part of it will arise from persons demanding treatment as a right for imaginary ills or illnesses of no serious consequences which ordinarily do not require medical attention. It seems generally to be recognized that it is impossible to forecast with any accuracy the probable cost of a compulsory and comprehensive national health program, but it is inevitable that its costs would substantially exceed the amount spent today on health in Canada. The Chamber believes that the continued rapid growth of the various voluntary prepayment and insurance plans will soon result in the Canadian people being reasonably well covered against the costs of health services without sacrifice of individual responsibility. The only exception is the case of the indigent. The Chamber believes that the high standard of care now provided will be extended

in future to reach the whole of this group with the further development of health services on a voluntary basis, with government assistance.

The release of the statement, the publicity it generated, and the repeated reiteration of the policy by the ten provincial chambers added greatly to the support of the policy now endorsed by the CMA, the CHA, the CLIOA, and four provincial health survey committees.

6. *The Canadian Congress of Labour.* Both the Canadian Congress of Labour and the Trades and Labour Council had included strong support of health insurance in their annual briefs to the Canadian government. With their amalgamation in 1956 into one organization of over 1,000,000 members, their unified voice carried even greater force than had their separate submissions. On January 22, 1957, the new organization presented its first brief to the Cabinet and laid the heaviest emphasis on health insurance.[51] It called for early implementation of a Canada-wide program of health care, either by the federal government or jointly with the provinces, to cover preventive, diagnostic, curative, and rehabilitation services, including doctor and hospital charges. The submission of the provincial affiliates to provincial governments carried the same message, and even speeches by District Labour Council presidents advocating a national program were frequently reported in the press. Just how much influence these submissions and speeches carried is impossible to assess but the constant raising of the issue and the advocacy of a governmental solution contributed to the climate of opinion favouring government action.

7. *The Saskatchewan and British Columbia plans.* Quite apart from the political impact of the launching of the first two government plans by these provinces, important contributions to the national policy were made by the experience gained and some of the precedents set. Some of the more important of the inputs were the following.

(1) The practicability and the difficulties of universal coverage. Both plans had begun with compulsory payment of premiums. Both had used the courts to enforce payment. Saskatchewan, with its well organized municipal system, had had available an almost unique collection system. British Columbia, on the other hand, had been unable to achieve universal coverage despite the legal liability of all residents to pay the premiums. Finally, by abolishing premiums and increasing the sales tax, B.C. achieved universal coverage. It was therefore feasible for Ottawa to consider universal coverage as one of the conditions for its distribution of grants.

(2) Benefits. Both of the programs were of the "service," rather than the indemnity, type. Moreover both had abandoned the distinction used

197

by voluntary insurance between basic care benefits and the so-called "extras." Both had abandoned the limits on such extras as X-rays and laboratory tests, and had included in "a hospital day of care" the services that the hospital could offer, with the exception of the extra costs of semi-private and private room accommodation.

(3) The systems of paying hospitals. Saskatchewan was the first province to introduce a uniform system of accounting in hospitals, and British Columbia had quickly followed. Their initiatives were then followed by joint action by the Canadian Hospital Association, the Dominion Bureau of Statistics, and the Department of National Health and Welfare, to create the Canadian Hospital Accounting Manual (CHAM).

With a standardized package of benefits and uniform cost accounting procedures, it was possible to strike an all-inclusive daily rate which would meet the costs of providing the services to all insured patients. If the hospital collected at that rate from all other patients, it should achieve a balanced budget. This experience enabled the federal government both to lay down a standardized list of benefits, and to ascertain the costs on a standardized nation-wide accounting system.

(4) Quality control. Both provinces had created Hospital Standards divisions staffed by various professional experts who had three roles— (i) to inspect hospitals; (ii) to participate in the analysis of hospital budgets to ensure that the rates of payment were adequate to enable hospitals to maintain or raise standards; and (iii) to consult with the Hospital Planning Division in approving and assisting hospitals with their construction projects. Again, these precedents were incorporated in the requirements laid down by the federal government as conditions for its grants.

THE GOVERNMENT CONTRIBUTIONS

The contributions emanating from within the Government to the design of health insurance in Canada had commenced in 1940, it will be recalled from chapter 1, with the work of Dr. J. J. Heagerty at the direction of the minister, the Hon. Ian Mackenzie. That had expanded to an interdepartmental committee in 1942 and to a Cabinet committee in 1944. Their efforts, extending over five years, had produced two sets of proposals: (1) the model legislation drafted by the interdepartmental committee, later discarded, and (2) the 1945 health insurance offer of the Green Book proposals.

With the appointment of Mr. Paul Martin as health minister in 1946, there began a buildup of resources in the research division and in a new division of health insurance studies. Dr. Joseph Willard was appointed director of research in 1947 and gathered a team including Mr. John

Sparks, Dr. Lloyd Francis, Mr. John Osborne and Mr. William Mennie. Following the introduction of the health grants program in 1948, Dr. F. W. Jackson (then deputy minister of health in Manitoba) was appointed director of health insurance studies.

The research group began collecting and analyzing data from the voluntary and government programs on a continuing basis. As the provinces set up their health survey committees, the survey directors met regularly in Ottawa with these officers, the two deputy ministers, Dr. G. D. W. Cameron and Dr. George Davidson, and representatives of the Dominion Bureau of Statistics, to ensure that the provinces would collect their information in standardized form so that a national report could also be prepared and inter-provincial comparisons made. The contrast, in terms both of expanded personnel resources and vastly increased amounts of information and data for planning purposes, between the war period and the 1947–57 period, was extraordinary, and the work of the research staff was praised in the House of Commons even by opposition spokesmen. The effectiveness of the group was greatly enhanced, as in any government department, by its awareness that it was headed by a committed and knowledgeable minister.

As the debate on health insurance intensified during the 1953 election, the research staffs expanded their studies. A great many issues were examined, one of the most important being the question of benefits. It will be recalled that in 1945, a complete range of benefits had been proposed, to be introduced in two stages. General practititoner services were separated from specialist services and the first stage was to include, therefore, (a) general practitioner services; (b) hospital care; and (c) visiting nurse services. The second stage benefits were to include (a) specialist services; (b) other nursing services; (c) dental care; (d) pharmaceuticals; and (e) radiological and laboratory services.

These priorities were re-examined at length. It was obvious that with the pattern of comprehensive services set by the prepayment plans, no one could now suggest that general practitioner and specialist services be separated. In terms of positive health considerations and an economic use of resources, it would be wise to introduce medical services first. These were the first line of defence; the physical facilities necessary were already in place—the doctors' offices, clinics, and diagnostic facilities—although these would have to be rapidly expanded. Moreover, a far smaller proportion of the population had insurance against the cost of medical services than against that of hospital services.

Hospital services as an early benefit had two major attractions: it would solve the problem of those not now protected in some degree against the costs of hospital bills; it would also solve the problem of hospital deficits, mounting annually. But, if it were introduced first—and alone—there would be inevitable dangers of a misuse of services. "Hospitals" would need to be broadly defined to include convalescent and chronic care facilities.

Visiting Nurse services were an essential benefit. The Heagerty Committee had clearly seen the need to use the home when the hospital was not essential. These two benefits went hand-in-hand. The experience of such organizations as the Victorian Order of Nurses had shown the savings that would accrue from such a benefit at the earliest stage.

Dental care, proposed in 1945 as a benefit for "later stages"—no matter how high a priority it might be assigned in health terms—must still remain for a later stage. One single fact dictated that conclusion: there were simply not enough dentists. An alternative might be a children's dental care program, but there were probably not even enough dentists for that.

Pharmaceuticals as a benefit had merit, but the Heagerty Committee was correct in its judgement: it should come at a later stage. Moreover, Saskatchewan, with its drug benefit in its Social Assistance Medical Services Plan, was discovering it to be a very expensive program.

Radiological and laboratory services had been placed at the end of the 1945 list for later stages. The planning group rejected this priority rating summarily. An important reason was that this was one benefit which the director of health insurance studies advocated with almost missionary zeal. Dr. Fred Jackson had ensured that it was stage one of Manitoba's proposed program and a number of diagnostic units had been established outside Winnipeg, before he transferred to Ottawa.

And so the analyses were continued and the arguments pro and con set forth in position papers. The final decisions would be made by political leaders but all the options must be concisely stated and the probable outcomes set forth as fairly as expert knowledge and human judgement would permit.

But the merits and demerits of benefits, and the strategy of their timing were only one half of the equation. In a period of escalating defence expenditures, the costs of any proposed social program would weigh more heavily in the scale than usual. Moreover, of all the charges levelled against government programs, the most frequently used and most forcefully stated was their inevitably skyrocketing costs. Accordingly, the estimating of costs of each of the alternative benefits was recognized as the most important task of the planning group.

In addition to examining the data from the insuring agencies, the planning group analyzed the annual financial and statistical returns of all reporting hospitals, new hospital construction, wages and prices indices, changes in professional fees, and anticipated increases in numbers

of hospital personnel and in their rates of remuneration. All of these—
and other data—were analyzed and projected for each province.

These two aspects of the program, the benefits and the costs, are central
to any governmental decision and they lend themselves in more or less
degree to quantitative analysis and expression. But there were two other
major issues that were far more complex for they involved questions that
were at once philosophical, political, and practical.

The philosophical issues should be decided first for they would influence
all the others. What construct of values should underly the program?
Could a national program be compulsory, or had the bombardment of
public opinion by those opposed to a government program created a new
and now widely held antipathy to compulsion in any form? Was "anti-
compulsion" indeed a new social value held by a majority of Canadians?

If a major value held by Canadians was an increasing desire for fiscal
equity among provinces and regions, how could the federal legislation
and, particularly, the financial formula assist to that end? In other words,
should the health insurance formula contain an element of equalization
or was that a principle to be ignored in any specific program and negotiated
separately within the framework of the tax agreements?

The political element was pervasive and there was constant evaluation
of ideas in regular and informal meetings between the minister and his
deputies as well as between the minister, the prime minister, and the minister of finance. As the time for decision approached, the Cabinet and
caucus were also involved. The chief issue stemmed, of course, from the
constitutional jurisdiction of the provinces over health. Given the assumption that the federal government could state precisely the goals it
wished to achieve, and had clear cut program objectives to reach them,
what degree of federal intervention was possible in the 1950s? What would
the provinces tolerate?

The issue as it applied to health insurance was not new; it had been
fought out less than a decade before. Perhaps reflecting the sense of power
concentrated in wartime Ottawa in the early forties, Ian Mackenzie's
proposal presented to the House of Commons Select Committee on Social
Security was the ultimate expression of federal intervention in provincial
affairs. Not only had the proposal laid down the conditions in a draft
bill for the House of Commons; it drafted a model bill for the provinces.
In the revised version of 1944, it went even further. The model bill had
provided for administration by representative commissions; the 1944
amendment provided for the appointment of two federal representatives
to each province's commission. But when the issue began to be seriously
and formally discussed by the Cabinet, the concept of that degree of
federal control was rejected.

The final proposal simply said,
A province's participation in the plan would begin:

(1) Upon a province . . . presenting a plan, satisfactory to the Governor-in-Council, describing . . . the stages by which benefits will be provided and the full health insurance plan put into effect;

(2) Upon the province . . . making an agreement with the federal government to provide the initial benefits . . . within two years [and] provide for . . . a registration fee, for a registration, accounting and reporting system, for the costs of administration . . . to be paid by the province, and such other provisions and conditions as may be agreed to . . . "[52]

That was a proposal, of course, and we cannot know what "other provisions and conditions" might have been applied, but it implied that there would be at least informal federal standards against which a province's proposed program would be evaluated. Beginning in 1955, the debate again came alive. Should the 1945 policy be repeated or not?

Underlying the federal approach was the fact that it was to be a "national" program; every Canadian through direct and indirect taxes would contribute to one half of its cost and the federal government therefore had a half-share interest in the nature of the program in each province. The questions thus became: what degree of uniformity and what standards of quality should be nationally determined, and what degree and kinds of federal control would be necessary to achieve those standards? At the political level, as we have seen, the question was part of the entire context of federal-provincial power relationships in which the tax-sharing issue was of even greater consequence than health insurance—as it had been in 1945.

As the analyses and discussion continued, the conclusion was reached that a middle course between the two extremes of 1943 and 1945 should be steered. There could be no thought of imposing a model act on the provinces now (four had programs in action); on the other hand, the 1945 approach was too open and imprecise and invited every administrative disagreement to be raised to federal-provincial political conflict. It would be necessary, as a concomitant of its grant, for the federal government to impose a very substantial degree of control and supervision on the provinces.

Second only to the decisions about the nature of the program, the most crucial issue was that of the amount and method of distribution of the federal financial contribution. Chapter 1 revealed the travails of various committees exploring alternatives ten years earlier. The alternatives are probably limited only by civil servants' ingenuity and as one contemplates the myriad cost-sharing programs now in effect in Canada that commodity does not seem in short supply. But what were the desirable features of a financing formula?

There seems to have been a general assumption that the federal contribution should be a pre-determined percentage of the costs of the nation-wide program. In 1945 that percentage had been set at one-fifth of the *estimated per capita* cost plus one half the additional *actual* cost to a maximum federal contribution of sixty percent of the *estimated* cost. The *per capita* cost of hospital services in 1946 had been estimated to be $4.60. But sixty percent of the estimated cost can be quite different from sixty percent of the actual cost as Saskatchewan's experience one year later attested. Despite the shortage of beds and doctors, if it had entered into an agreement on those terms, it would have received less than forty percent of its actual costs from the federal government. Of course, this would have been better than a zero contribution, but it was far short of sixty percent.

If the principle of a percentage of costs were agreed upon, the question automatically following was: What should the percentage be? In 1945 the inducement needed to be very substantial, hence the sixty percent. In 1956 the pressures were coming from the other direction; the carrot need not be as large.

Given the still-glaring disparities among the provinces, there should be some element of equalization in the formula. It should also contain some intrinsic method of setting outside limits on the federal contribution. The 1945 proposal had endeavored to accomplish that by setting an annual *per capita* limit that was to hold for three years. But that formula had been designed in a period of strictly controlled wages and prices; now inflationary pressures were strong and, if it were to be a truly national cost-sharing arrangement, the provinces could not be expected to bear the total brunt of rising costs. The formula would have to provide for annual adjustments in the federal contribution related to rising costs.

This factor only made the equalizing objective more difficult. The pressure of costs of hospital equipment and supplies was nation-wide, and so were pressures increasing personnel costs which then approximated two-thirds of the total costs of operating a hospital. But those pressures varied from province to province. In the five years preceding 1955, for example, *per diem* costs in Canada had risen forty-one percent, but in British Columbia thirty-one percent and in Manitoba fifty percent. A formula would have to be flexible enough to meet these variations; i.e., the formula should take account of the costs in each province as well as of total costs in the nation as a whole.

The committee drafted and calculated various formulas, always concerned, at the ministerial level, of course, with whether the result when examined by the provinces would be acceptable to them.

THE STRATEGY OF IMPLEMENTATION

Again, as in chapter 3, because of the long time-span during which the Government was engaged with the issue, it is necessary to examine the overall strategy in stages, and between these stages to examine new inputs, withinputs, and outputs, as the process continued to its consummation. Indeed, underscoring the complexity of the process, the first stage of the strategy was directed not to implementation but to delay. This paradox will be examined first.

THE STRATEGY OF DELAY

The contradictory strategies of delay and of moving forward were a direct result of the opposing views within the Cabinet, reflecting, of course, the opposing opinions in the country as a whole. However, if the Gallup Poll of June 1949 was an accurate indication of the opinions held by the public (eighty percent in favour), then the minority was heavily over-represented in the Cabinet.

That there should be opposition within the Cabinet to yet another federal initiative was, however, understandable. Some members would be opposed in principle. Some would oppose the large financial commitment. Some, more cynical, would say that in the 1945 election social security proposals were necessary for a government grown unpopular under the weight of wartime restrictions, but now, safely reelected, no repetition of such proposals was required. Others, with greater political sensitivity, would argue that the collapse of the 1945 conference meant that the provinces, having been deprived of their revenues during the war and therefore of the substance of power, were in no mood to tolerate another federal intervention that would distort provincial priorities. The Government had been heavily criticized for its unilateral proposals in 1945 in the obvious fear that the federal government's domination in the federal-provincial scale, ill-gained because of the war, would be made permanent by grandiose federal programs in peacetime. These Cabinet members would argue that there were challenges enough facing Canada without added and certain conflict with the provinces. The Quebec members were especially concerned by the difficulties Mr. Duplessis' opposition would create. With the advent of the new leader, Mr. St. Laurent, the scales were tipped to a strategy of delay and the overwhelming electoral victory of the Liberals in 1949 gave credence to the tenability of that position.

THE STRATEGY OF CONDITIONAL RESPONSE

As we have seen, at the 1950 Federal-Provincial Conference, which might normally have presented the federal government with the need to take some form of positive action, the issue of health insurance was easily laid to rest. By 1953, however, it was not the provincial premiers who must be faced; it was the electorate. Given the strength of the opposing positions in the Cabinet, an election strategy would have to meet the following objectives: (1) It would have to maintain, if not enhance, the Liberal party's identification with a pro-health insurance policy; (2) It should not open the government to criticism for imposing its priorities on the provinces; (3) It should not only avoid any time commitment but should contribute to a postponement of any new demands on the federal treasury; (4) It should obtain as much electoral credit as possible from the health grants program; (5) It should remove the onus for action from the federal government and place it on the provinces.

The resulting compromise resolution in the Liberal party platform, melding these objectives, was stated as follows: "The Liberal party is committed to support a policy of contributory health insurance to be administered by the provinces when most of the provinces are ready to join in a nationwide scheme, and meanwhile to maintain and improve health grants to improve provincial health services."

What had been decided upon was a strategy of "conditional response" —the federal government would be committed to respond under certain conditions.

As the election of 1953 approached, however, Mr. Martin insisted that this was not enough, that at least some step, however small, must be taken. Because of the success of the health grants, particularly from a publicity point of view, it was decided to increase these, but at little or no cost. Three grants were announced: child and maternal health ($500,000 rising in annual increments to $2,000,000); medical rehabilitation ($1,000,000); and laboratory and radiological services ($4,329,000 rising to $7,000,000).[53] But to finance these, the hospital construction grant was cut in half ($13,000,000 to $6,700,000) on the grounds that the 46,000 new beds towards which the construction grant had made a contribution had achieved the Health Department's objective.

The 1953 election was fought even more vigorously than had been that of 1949. Both Mr. St. Laurent and Mr. Drew were now experienced and seasoned leaders, the acknowledged spokesmen of their parties. Mr. St. Laurent emphasized his government's achievements, spoke mainly in generalities, made no promises, and, in his references to health insurance, simply reiterated the party platform statement.

On this second time around, Mr. Drew was much more positive in his attacks on the Government and in putting forth the Progressive-Conservative platform. He issued a twelve-point manifesto in which a commitment was made to introduce a health insurance program through existing voluntary and commercial plans (and) without state medicine. The CCF 1953 platform statement was, if that were possible, even more vigorous than that of 1949. Only Social Credit made no reference to health insurance in its official platform. The major points referred almost exclusively to reforms of monetary and fiscal policy.

The final results of the election were: Liberals, 170 (a loss of twenty); Progressive Conservatives, fifty-one (a gain of ten); CCF, twenty-three (a gain of ten); Social Credit, fifteen (a gain of five). Although the Liberal seats had declined, the Government still held a very comfortable majority.

There could be satisfaction on the part of the majority of the Cabinet that the two strategies had proved complementary and had worked. The Liberal party's commitment to health insurance was intact and while the Government might be criticized for timidity and lack of action by some, it was seen by others as a party of pragmatists who recognized reality in dealing with provinces whose claims to independence were being heard in increasingly shrill voices. Furthermore, it looked as if the combined strategies could be successfully managed for a long time.

There was keen disappointment, however, among those members of the Cabinet and the caucus who felt a personal as well as a party commitment to health insurance. The failure to persuade the caucus and the extra-parliamentary party leaders to re-take the initiatives of 1945 meant that national health insurance would never be achieved until there were major changes in policies in at least two or three more provinces, and one of those would have to be Quebec or Ontario. Quebec could not be counted upon and it was in Ontario that the voluntary system was having its greatest success, muting the voices of many who in the past had been demanding government action.

But we have seen the build-up in favourable public opinion and the increasing press coverage of the issue in 1953, 1954, and 1955. For the federal government, 1955 would be critical, for in that year, a beginning would have to be made in renegotiating the tax agreements that would expire in 1957. That meant a conference with the provinces and that meant demands by the provinces, not only for improved fiscal terms, but for whatever else might seem of high priority to them.

The strategy of delay must be adhered to. The appropriate tactic would be to ensure that the question of health insurance did not appear on the agenda at all.

As part of his overall policy of improving relations with the provinces, the prime minister had decided that not only would there be a conference but that the provinces should share in shaping its program, and so, for the first time, the premiers were invited to come to Ottawa in April 1955 to agree upon an agenda for the main conference be held in October. This would give time for all governments to prepare their position papers and so expedite and make more fruitful the main conference's proceedings. It was a calculated risk but the advantages of provincial collaboration (after the lesson of 1945) appeared to outweigh the potential hazards of undesirable items on the agenda.

On April 26, 1955, the conference opened. Mr. St. Laurent reviewed the federal-provincial conferences of the preceding two decades, speaking at some length on the 1945 conference.

> The major proposals of 1945 were of a continuing nature and dealt with the main issues of financial concern to both the federal and provincial governments. . . . Despite a series of meetings over a period of nine months the conference was unable to reach agreement on these major proposals. As a result it was necessary to proceed subsequently to deal with those portions which could be implemented separately. When we review these major proposals of the 1945 conference, we find that a large proportion of them have been carried out; those that have not been implemented have been reconsidered from time to time and found to be inappropriate at the time, or impractical in the light of the further study that has been given the subject.[54]

To make certain that the provinces were aware of the financial constraints under which the federal government laboured, he emphasized again, as he had at the 1950 conference, the impact of the unsettled international situation and the associated defence expenditures it demanded. Although "the fighting has stopped" in the Korean war . . . "we [at this conference] must make our plans in the knowledge that we cannot foresee any really substantial reduction in defense expenditure during the next four or five years."[55]

He then referred to the progress in the tax agreements and in social security. Of the health insurance proposals he said: "[They] have only been implemented as far as the planning stage, and *the federal and most provincial governments have given higher priority* to other programs, including the increasing of the basic services and facilities which would be necessary to carry the load of a health insurance system."[56]

He then stated the federal government's new policy: "We believe that the proposals of 1945 are no longer suitable for our agenda in 1955."[57]

Later in his address, he reinforced his appeal for a restricted agenda: "The government of Canada believes that our conference is most likely to succeed if we plan to consider only a limited number of subjects of primary importance, leaving to subsequent meetings or to meetings of those Ministers primarily concerned, subjects that are more specialized or of less importance in our federal-provincial financial relationships."[58]

(Was health insurance more specialized or was it of less importance?)

He then indicated the agenda items as perceived from the vantage point of the national government. "The first subject . . . is that of future federal-provincial fiscal relations. . . . In addition, the federal government wishes to propose for consideration this year the question of assistance to the unemployed."

He ended his formal statement in these words: "The federal government is not now proposing any other items for inclusion on the agenda of our conference this year. We are prepared, of course, to consider whether other items should be included in the scope of this conference. We hope that the list can be kept to manageable proportions."[59]

It was a masterful performance: calm, objective, realistic, and controlled. The 1945 commitments had been ended; only two items were of importance, but even these must be dealt with in the light of a national economy currently burdened with heavy defence expenditures. The mood that he set was far closer to the pessimism he had engendered in opening the 1950 conference than to the optimism that had characterized that of 1945. But as he made his formal statement, there must have been a nagging thought in his mind that events were not as controllable as they appeared. There was no way of knowing what demands to expect from the provinces. Preparing for and facing a conference had become as burdensome and unpredictable as facing an election. And on this occasion there had been that unfortunate incident three weeks ago when Jack Pickersgill had been quoted as saying in a speech at Kitchener, Ontario, that health insurance would come "only if there was a change of government in Ontario." Pickersgill had explained in the Commons the next day that what he said was that health insurance "could not happen until the Ontario government adopted a new attitude."

Premier Frost had obviously been annoyed, if not angered, and one couldn't be sure what further reaction there would be. Maybe Pickersgill's speech and all those others given by Paul Martin emphasizing the policy of conditional response were having more effect than he had anticipated. He would soon know; it was now time for the traditional first speech by the premier of Ontario.

Premier Frost had no intention of permitting the federal government to restrict the agenda to two items; there were simply too many problems requiring joint federal-provincial action. He listed six: (1) The establishment of a federal-provincial Technical and Advisory Committee, to be composed of governmental advisers and, possibly, municipal representatives; (2) Fiscal arrangements between the federal and provincial governments; (3) Unemployment; (4) Health insurance; (5) Revision of the present federal health grants to allow more flexibility in their use; (6) Certain legislative or constitutional matters relating particularly to the operation of farm marketing plans.

Next to obtaining a fair deal for Ontario in the tax agreements, it was on item (4) that he was most determined. "This very important subject deserves the consideration of this conference. . . . It is generally recognized that any health insurance plan of a broad nature should have both federal and provincial participation. We suggest that the whole question be intensively studied with a view to . . . producing a sound, workable plan with which we could proceed."[60]

Prime Minister St. Laurent was as dismayed as the Hon. Paul Martin was inwardly jubilant. Mr. Duplessis could chide Mr. Frost: "I know that my friend Mr. Frost is not going to have an election this year, and did not make a speech in view of an election," but it was evident to the entire conference that Mr. Frost had adroitly returned the ball to the federal court and it was inconceivable that Ottawa could long avoid a specific response. The combined strategies of delay and conditional response had depended for their success on lack of further provincial initiatives. But here was the premier of the largest and wealthiest province insisting that this conference begin the preparations now.

Nor did it end with Mr. Frost. Mr. Campbell of Manitoba proposed: "The significance of current and future social security, welfare and health programs and the incidence of responsibility therefor."[61] Mr. Bennett of British Columbia offered: "That the proposals of Canada for health insurance embodying medical, hospital, dental and pharmaceutical services is a major and integral part of an effective social security program for the people of Canada, and insofar as possible, the proposals of Canada of August, 1945, should again be considered."[62]

Mr. Douglas stated: "I am reminded of the federal government's long-standing commitment to meet up to 60 percent of the cost of an approved provincial health plan. . . . we have gone far beyond that point in a Canadian health program which can be met adequately by the existing pattern of national health grants. The time for a further major advance is long overdue."[63]

And, finally, Mr. Manning of Alberta: "We also concur in the view expressed by some that the subject of public health and welfare should be included for discussion."[64]

Two premiers had specifically referred to the 1945 federal commitment which Mr. St. Laurent had been at pains to disavow. Only Mr. Duplessis had been helpful when he asked: "Mr. Chairman, would it be possible to have an agenda clear enough to be understood by everyone, short enough to cover the ground, and not too long to bring confusion?"[65] He met his own criteria by making no suggestions. The combined strategies of delay and of conditional response were now presenting the problem of the circus acrobat riding two horses that begin to veer off in different directions: one or the other must be abandoned.

But Mr. St. Laurent was not yet ready to abandon the strategy of delay. On the second morning of the conference, held *in camera*, the debate was both more informal and more aggressive. Mr. St. Laurent insisted that this was no time, with all the other governmental commitments, to place health insurance on the agenda. Mr. Frost, supported by the three western premiers, argued equally insistently that it was.

At noon, the federal delegation met in the prime minister's office to review strategy. There, the Hon. Paul Martin informed the prime minister that he did not believe that he (Mr. St. Laurent) was adhering to stated Liberal party policy and that if he continued to resist the health item, he (Mr. Martin) would have to resign as minister of national health and welfare.[66] Mr. St. Laurent finally moderated his stand and in the afternoon session compromised to the extent of agreeing that the issue should be listed on the forthcoming agenda under the general term, "Health and Welfare Services."

The newspapers interpreted the decision as a victory for the provinces. But it would still be possible to exercise delay: it would be the federal government that would define "most" in the Liberal party platform term, "most of the provinces."

The conference ended on the third afternoon and the delegates returned to their respective capitals to begin the extraordinary efforts of information gathering, analysis, endless committee meetings and, finally, preparation of bargaining positions and strategies for the October meeting.

In the midst of these preparations the opportunity arose for the provincial and federal deputy ministers of health to discuss their work in progress. This was at the regular annual meeting of the Dominion Council of Health, held on July 4, 1955.

The morning was spent on a discussion of the stages of a health insurance program and of which benefit or benefits would receive the highest priority. The federal officials, also for the first time, presented their latest cost estimates for the nation as a whole. These were:

Hospital Services—$312 million or ($19.60 *per capita*)
Diagnostic Services—$48 million (about $3.00 *per capita*)
Medical Services—$260 million (about $16.30 *per capita*)
Total—$620 million (about $39 *per capita*)[67]

Apart from the cost estimates, there was little that was new in the discussions. Each deputy minister felt constrained by the knowledge that his own minister was wrestling with just these questions and he, as deputy, must keep these considerations confidential. But there did seem to be developing a kind of undeclared consensus that in realistic political terms hospital care insurance was the likely first benefit.

In the period between April and October there were extensive discussions between the prime minister and the ministers of health and of finance, and in the Cabinet. Mr. St. Laurent had accepted the inevitable; the "first stage" of a national health insurance program—the health grants—had been played out over seven years and the second stage could no longer be politically or honourably avoided. Besides, there was the strong position maintained by Mr. Martin, and others in the Cabinet who supported his proposals. Some concessions must now be made. The Government must respond, but it must attach important conditions.

THE STRATEGY OF RESPONSE WITH CONDITIONS

At the convening of the main conference on October 3, 1955, Prime Minister St. Laurent again gave the opening address. He dealt first with the fiscal issues and then took up the health topic.

> We will also have occasion during our meeting this week to discuss the important question of health insurance. This is a matter, of course, which under our constitution falls squarely within provincial jurisdiction. The federal government does not wish to see this position altered; nor would it wish to be a party to a plan for health insurance which would require a constitutional change or federal interference in matters which are essentially of provincial concern.
>
> The federal government recognizes, however, that there may be circumstances in which it would be justified in offering to assist provincial governments in implementing health insurance plans designed and administered by the provinces. For a number of years, through the national health grants program, we have provided assistance in the development of a full network of basic health facilities and services fitted to the needs of the Canadian people. We recognize that the building up of these facilities through the national health program constitutes, in the words of my predecessor, Mr. King, "a fundamental prerequisite of a nationwide system of health insurance."

He reminded them of the Government's policy: "Under our federal system, to get health insurance started the people and the governments of the various provinces have to take the initiative in working out plans adapted to local conditions. We are ready to assist in a sensible and practical nationwide scheme, but that depends on satisfactory agreements with the provinces."[68]

He then asked what he considered to be the two important questions:

First: what are the stages by which further action by the provinces

211

in the field of health insurance might be considered feasible; what agreement can be reached among the provinces themselves as to the order of priority of the various services? Second: Under what circumstances would the federal government be justified in offering to assist provincial activities in the health insurance field?

"It has been suggested," he said, "that ... the next step to be taken might well be the provision of universal radiological and laboratory services."

On the second question, he observed:

In the view of the federal government the condition prerequisite to federal support of provincial programs in respect of health insurance is that it can reasonably be shown that the national rather than merely local or sectional interest is thereby being served.... in my view, so long as only one, two or three provinces, representing a distinct minority of the Canadian population, indicate their intention to proceed with health insurance, there can be little if any justification for the national government imposing taxes on all Canadian people to share the cost of health insurance in those provinces. But if there were a substantial majority of provincial governments, representing a substantial majority of the Canadian people who were prepared to embark upon provincially administered health insurance schemes involving no constitutional change or interference in provincial affairs ... then the federal government would be justified in participating in an increase in the capital assets of the Canadian people.[69]

It was a conciliatory manoeuvre and, coming at the beginning of the conference, signalled to the provinces that Mr. St. Laurent had changed his mind at least to some degree since the April conference. Nevertheless, the statement was carefully worded to protect the federal position. The term "most of the provinces" had now been defined as "a substantial majority of the provinces representing a substantial majority of the Canadian people." What was "substantial" in precise terms? Six provinces? Eight provinces? Sixty percent of the population? Seventy-five percent? The new terms could be construed to mean further delay through the imposition of impossible conditions. For the provinces there were major uncertainties ahead, despite the apparent shift in federal policy.

Again, the premier of Ontario was the first provincial spokesman. Mr. Frost continued the initiative he had taken at the April agenda meeting. He gave the first major indication of the direction he wished to go by saying: "The term health insurance is an all-embracing expression covering hospital services, diagnostic services and medical services. In regard to the first two, there is a very large uniformity of opinion. In regard to the third, there is not only disagreement but greater administrative difficulties. Accordingly, at this time our proposals relate to hospital and diagnostic services only."[70]

He then distributed to the conference members copies of five alternative proposals: (1) a plan for diagnostic services; (2) a home care program; (3) a catastrophic insurance proposal; (4) a hospital maternity care program; (5) a comprehensive hospital services plan to be implemented by stages.[71]

These proposals, he said, were submitted for purposes of study. "They are not submitted in any dogmatic sense. We are prepared to consider the proposals of any other government and indeed there may be proposals from others that we would consider more desirable than our own."

Mr. Duplessis, premier of Quebec, spoke next but limited his remarks to the fiscal issues, making his traditional case for the provinces' taxing authority—and therefore responsible government—to be safeguarded.

The next speaker was Premier Hicks of Nova Scotia who gave, for the first time, his government's views on health insurance.

Having discussed the tax agreements at length, he said: "Nova Scotia will give the most careful consideration to any plan which is proposed. The degree of participation by Nova Scotia, in any such plan must depend, of necessity, on the financial ability of Nova Scotia to finance any further services without imposing abnormal rates of taxation. This is a question which cannot be disassociated from the general question of federal-provincial financial relations."[72]

As expected, Premier Fleming of New Brunswick repeated the Maritime view: "[My government] strongly endorses the principle of health insurance. However, provinces with a low *per capita* income will require commensurately greater assistance from the federal government than the provinces with a high *per capita* income."[73]

Premier Campbell of Manitoba followed, taking the same line as the Maritime spokesmen:

We are most anxious to cooperate with Canada and our sister provinces in the fullest consideration and discussion of plans respecting national health insurance. In our view it is particularly fitting that the question of national health insurance be discussed at the same time as the matter of general financial arrangements, for the implementation of any such scheme—having as it does such tremendous implications for the various provincial treasuries—would, of course, require recognition in any agreement which may be reached on fiscal arrangements.[74]

Mr. Bennett, premier of British Columbia, responded, also as expected, with strong endorsement of a national program but with objections to the "substantial majority" concept.

> British Columbia recommends that any province which is willing to participate in a health program should not be retarded by the refusal of others to participate; . . . that this conference agree in principle upon the desirability of a health program adaptable to the requirements of the individual provinces; that such a plan make provision for medical, hospital, dental, and pharmaceutical services; and that the federal government share equally in the costs of such health programs to the extent that they have been or may be adopted by a province to meet its special requirements . . . [W]e will now enter into a program on a 50 percent basis with the national government.[75]

Premier Matheson of Prince Edward Island did not speak of health insurance specifically but simply included it in a general observation about national programs in general: "We view with some degree of caution any program that is financed jointly and equally where a program may be considered to be of national importance."[76]

Premier Douglas of Saskatchewan, again as expected, strongly endorsed national action, and he reminded the federal government of its 1945 commitment:

> In full expectation that [those] proposals would be honoured in due course, we in Saskatchewan proceeded to develop our own province-wide hospital insurance plan, and to pioneer as well in tax-supported medical care programs.
> In addition to joining with the provinces in establishing hospital insurance, in our view the federal government should be prepared to cooperate with any province desirous of setting up a medical care program, irrespective of whether or not it has proceeded with hospital coverage.[77]

He then referred to the Ontario proposals for hospital insurance and emphasized that Saskatchewan would be disappointed if the federal government indicated that was as far as it was prepared to go at this time.[78]

He concluded with a statement that was complementary to Mr. Frost's warnings about the hodgepodge that would be created in the absence of national action. He reminded them of Mackenzie King's famous statement in opening the 1945 conference that "the enemies we shall have to overcome will be on our own Canadian soil . . . in the guise of sickness, unemployment and want." He continued:

I cannot help but feel that lately there has been a lessening in our sense of national purpose. To some extent the vision which we had in 1945 has become blurred by sectionalism. Too often we have been pre-occupied with the fragments of a national program when we ought to have been concentrating on an overall comprehensive plan for the well-being and security of the Canadian people. It seems to me impor-tant that this gathering should return to the spirit and objectives of the 1945 Conference on Reconstruction.[79]

The final speakers were Premiers Manning of Alberta and Smallwood of Newfoundland, and both limited their remarks to the fiscal issues. The rest of the conference was held *in camera*.

At the end of the meeting, a communique was issued announcing the appointment of a committee of the conference, composed of the federal and provincial ministers of finance and health, which would meet at a later date to give more thorough and extensive consideration to the health insurance item.[80]

The provinces had exerted important influence on the timing and con-tent of the policy: there would have to be a decision; the first two benefits should be diagnostic services and hospital insurance, although Ontario had made a strong case for home care services. The federal contribution should be sixty percent although British Columbia had said that it would accept fifty percent. There had been strong pressure to include mental hospital and tuberculosis services.

For the federal government some of the uncertainties that had char-acterized its earlier consideration of the issue remained just that: Quebec was still opposed, and the Atlantic provinces and Manitoba although interested, were themselves uncertain. Whether they could participate would depend on the outcome of the negotiations on the fiscal agreements and the degree of subsidization in any cost-sharing formula that the fed-eral government proposed.

One uncertainty seemed to have been removed and yet one could not be sure. Ontario appeared determined, but Mr. Frost emphasized that his proposals had been put forth "for study." How strong was the com-mitment? British Columbia and Saskatchewan were committed, and Alberta appeared likely. Newfoundland was involved in a program covering part of its population, but could it afford its share of a program covering everyone?

For the provinces there were uncertainties as well: the costs, the formula, the benefits, the terms of an agreement, the number of provinces required for a "substantial" majority. The meeting of the committee scheduled for January would be all-important.

REFINING THE POLICY

With the announcement of the appointment of the federal-provincial committee, the federal government (with reluctance on the part of some ministers and the urging of others) had acknowledged that an offer of some dimension must be made to the provinces. The debate within the Cabinet therefore centred on the scope of the proposal to be made, again shaping up in a conflict between those insisting on the minimum and those supporting a more extensive program and less restrictive conditions.

In that combined vertical and horiziontal communications network that conveys political objectives and constraints from Cabinet members to senior officials and the legal, financial, and administrative realities from department officials back to Cabinet, the generalized and somewhat vague statements that had characterized the federal government's position to date were refined and made more specific: (1) The term "substantial majority" was refined by eliminating the word, "substantial." A majority of six would be acceptable; (2) "A majority of the population" would mean that either Quebec or Ontario must be included in the six; (3) It was agreed that of the alternative formulas for cost sharing, one should be selected that provided for some degree of equalization among the provinces; (4) It was agreed that the benefits would be limited to diagnostic services and hospital care; (5) It was agreed that a provincial plan must provide for and achieve universal coverage.

On January 1, 1956, Dr. Kenneth Charron succeeded Dr. F. W. Jackson as director of the Health Insurance Studies Division and his group and the research division continued their cost analyses and their calculations of the impact of alternative formulas on each of the provinces.

But Mr. Martin, despite the fact that the achievement of part of his long-held objective was in sight, was still concerned about opposition in the Cabinet. The lack of support had resulted, he felt, from the failure of other ministers, each too overwhelmed by his own ministry's concerns, to appreciate the importance attached by the provinces and the people to the problem of financing health services. He decided, therefore, to invite each member of the Cabinet to spend as much time as he could at the meeting of the Federal-Provincial Committee, which had been called for January 23, 1956. When the provincial representatives arrived at the Commons' Committee Room, they were surprised to see, seated immediately behind the chairman, a solid phalanx of Cabinet ministers from other departments.

For three and one half days, Mr. Martin skilfully drew from the delegates reviews of their health programs and, particularly, from the delegates from British Columbia and Saskatchewan, the nature, problems, and degrees of success of their hospital insurance plans. So great was the flow of information from the provinces that the delegates chatting over dinner surmised that the meeting was being used as much for the enlightenment of Mr. Martin's colleagues as it was to achieve agreement on precisely what should be done next.

But "Paul Martin's Seminar" could not go on indefinitely and, finally, at 2:30 p.m. on Thursday, Mr. Martin read a statement to the committee and Mr. St. Laurent announced in the House of Commons the federal offer to the provinces.

THE POLICY PROPOSAL

The federal government offered to pay one half of the national cost of diagnostic services and in-patient hospital care. The main points of the grant and of the conditions were as follows:

1. The federal government is willing to assist with technical support and financial assistance any provinces wishing to proceed with hospital insurance plans, as soon as a majority of provincial governments representing a majority of the Canadian people are ready to proceed.

2. Priority at this time should be given to diagnostic services and hospital care.

3. Provincial hospital plans (a) should make coverage universally available to all residents of the province; (b) include provision of specific diagnostic (laboratory and radiological) services to inpatients, and within an agreed period of time to outpatients; (c) limit co-insurance or "deterrent" charges so as to ensure that an excessive financial burden is not placed on patients at the time of receiving service.

4. The federal contribution would be a specified portion of normal operating and maintenance costs of hospital care at the standard ward level but would not include capital costs.

5. The federal contribution would not be made in respect of care in mental hospitals or tuberculosis sanatoria.

6. The federal contribution to each province in respect of its shareable costs would be: (a) 25 percent of the average *per capita* cost for hospital services in Canada as a whole; plus (b) 25 percent of the average *per capita* costs in the province itself multiplied by the number of insured persons in the province.

7. No contribution would be made in respect of provincial expenditures for the costs of administering a hospital insurance plan.

The strategy of delay had been forced to give way to the strategy of "response with conditions." Now the response had been made but the conditions were such as to ensure at least another year or perhaps even two years of delay. It would not be necessary to pass the enabling legislation until six provinces had indicated they were ready to proceed.

The delegates asked for clarification of a number of points, the meeting was adjourned, and the provincial ministers and their officials departed for their respective capitals to conduct the orthodontic analysis of examining this gift horse in the mouth.

The Hon. Paul Martin had a major stake in the provincial decisions. He had finally persuaded his Cabinet colleagues to fulfil part of the Liberal party's long-standing commitment, and they had done so, although minimally, and with very stringent conditions. If health insurance were as economically desirable and as politically attractive as Mr. Martin had always insisted, then to maintain his credibility in the Cabinet there should be an immediate and favourable response by the provinces.

But the required quota did not appear and, in fact, the controversy over hospital insurance seemed to expand as its prospects became more imminent. From its announcement in the first month of 1956 until the passage of the act sixteen months later, the hospital insurance offer never ceased to arouse controversial comment. Like a smoldering brush-fire there was always some smoke and some heat, and intermittently it flared up in brilliant flames of rhetoric, argument, charge, and counter-charge. Political parties, provincial ministers, hospital, medical, and insurance associations, the labour unions, and every newspaper editor and commentator in Canada defended, praised, criticized, or denounced some or all of it. It was too much, it was too little, it was too soon, it was overdue, it drained the federal treasury, it did not offer enough to the provinces, it was the road to socialism, it was the beginning of a new day, it would not represent any additional expenditure, it would bankrupt the nation, it would jam the hospitals, it was the only way to get more hospital beds.

A review of the newspaper editorial headings of the day reveals the confusion of tongues at the time: "it implies compulsion"—"it's not universal"—"ill-advised"—"the fairest remedy"—"road to chaos"—"many advantages"—"too much haste"—"do it now"—"remove the roadblock"—"supplement, don't supplant"—"year's biggest bargain"—"it won't be free"—"election bribery"—"a necessary solution"—"costs no more"—"the deceptive bargain"—"a welfare state"—"where is the end?"—"let's think this over."

THE STRATEGY OF ACCOMMODATION

But little was happening. Only three provinces had accepted the offer in principle—British Columbia, Alberta, and Saskatchewan. Ontario had set up a brief series of hearings by the Health Committee of the Legislature and had given a good deal of publicity to what it considered the defects in the federal offer. The committee hearings had been followed by legislation establishing the Ontario Hospital Services Commission, and although one of its responsibilities was to administer a plan of hospital care insurance for Ontario, no steps seemed to have been taken towards the implementation of such a program.

In June, Mr. Paul Martin visited Mr. Frost and the Hospital Services Commission in Toronto. There the Ontario case for changes in the proposal was restated in very emphatic terms. Ontario's key objections were the following: (1) the exclusion of hospital care in mental hospitals and tuberculosis sanatoria; (2) the fact that the total costs of administration were to the borne solely by the provinces; (3) the exclusion of depreciation and interest on capital debt as part of shareable costs; (4) the fact that Ottawa's share of Ontario's costs would be less than fifty percent; (5) the absence of a home care program; (6) the intention of the federal government to construe the term "universally available" as meaning universal coverage from the beginning; (7) the fact that there was no guarantee that, if Ontario launched its plan and there were not yet six participating provinces by that time, Ottawa would begin sharing at the plan's commencement.

Mr. Martin could be understanding, which he was; he could express sympathy, which he did. But he knew that he had extracted the last ounce of compromise from a reluctant Cabinet, and insisted that there was no possibility of changing the rules of the game at this stage. Ontario's plan would have to come "within the four corners" of the Ottawa offer.[81]

But there were also other forces for Mr. Martin to contend with. One was the extremely bad press the proposal was receiving in Manitoba. There, it seemed, the two leading dailies, the *Tribune* and the *Free Press*, were vying with each other to see which could be the more critical. This might have been expected of the *Tribune* but the *Free Press* had long been a Liberal party supporter and its editorials carried special influence among Liberals. So Mr. Martin visited the publishers and editors to try to reverse their editorial policy. The Canadian Medical Association, far more than the Hospital Association, was presenting difficulties. It was becoming increasingly concerned because of its radiologist and pathologist members who provided medical services in hospitals. But it was even more apprehensive of the precedent of the apparent rejection of the Blue Cross plans as vehicles for the administration of the provincial programs. And although Ontario's decision to appoint a representative commission to administer the program was a good omen, there was no assurance that other provinces would do so. That could set two bad precedents. So again Mr. Martin met with officials of the CMA to explain the importance to the medical profession of this new legislation.[82]

Despite the overwhelming advantages to the practising profession (and to their patients) of having all their patients insured for hospital costs, at the annual meeting of the CMA in Quebec in June 1956, "a resolution to the effect that the General Council (of the CMA) record a position favourable to the principle of universal hospital insurance was extensively debated and on a standing vote was defeated"[83]—a total reversal of its 1949 policy statement that hospital insurance should be the first objective.

Equally irritating, a former colleague and Mr. Martin's predecessor, Mr. Brooke Claxton, now spoke against the government's proposals. This was a major reversal for he had been the minister in charge of the Green Book proposals in 1945. Retired from politics, and now Canadian general manager for the Metropolitan Life Insurance Company, he argued that Canadians should pay for sickness and hospital insurance "out of their own means." Any plan a government advanced should "supplement the work of the insurance companies, not substitute for it."[84]

In addition to these and other critics outside Parliament, there was always the CCF gad-fly, Mr. Stanley Knowles, M. P., to keep the minister fully aware of the extent to which things seemed to be unravelling rather than coming together. In the House of Commons, July 27, 1956, there occurred one of many examples. The offer was then six months old.

Mr. Knowles said:

We are afraid that unless bold steps are taken by the government the proposals that were made last January may collect dust along with the Green Book proposals of 1945, the draft bill of 1944, the Marsh Report of 1943, a few speeches from the Throne in the forties, and the Liberal platform of 1919.

In six months three provinces have signified their readiness to come into the plan . . . but surely it must be evident that with this much time going by and no other province showing any indication that it is going to come into the plan, the time has come for the government to revise its proposals.[85]

By October, nine months after the offer had been made, Mr. Martin and his supporters in the Cabinet were worried. Reginald Hardy, reporting for *The Hamilton Spectator*, wrote on October 11, 1956,

There is now a feeling in official circles that time is running out and that if the plan is to be salvaged then some definite action must be taken. . . . What has happened, of course, is that the two big provinces have been waiting to see how the little ones jumped; and, in turn, the little provinces have been keeping an eye on Messrs. Frost and Duplessis. At any rate, Health and Welfare Minister Martin has become so concerned over the apathy of the seven provinces who have not yet declared themselves that he is going to engage in some very intensive "educating" of the Canadian public.

Mr. Martin made a special nation-wide appeal for the proposal on both the French and English television networks, and kept up his busy round of speeches at hospital, medical, and other conventions.

But time was also running out for Ontario. If the date of January 1, 1959, which Mr. Frost considered the earliest feasible time for launching, was to be met administratively, a critical path of decision making dictated that some decisions could not be postponed. The next session of the Legislature would begin about the end of January 1957, and legislation would have to be prepared for that. On the other hand, the longer Mr. Frost could delay, the greater became the pressure on Ottawa to be more flexible, particularly with respect to the issue of universal coverage and the date of commencement of cost sharing.

On December 13, 1956, Mr. Frost visited Mr. St. Laurent and Mr. Martin in Ottawa, bringing with him a complete statement of the Ontario program to be put before the Legislature in January and a covering letter in which he stressed that "time was of the essence and we should know early in the new year whether the way is clear for us to proceed."[86]

He insisted that Ontario could not make the program compulsory from the beginning but that he expected, but could not guarantee, an enrolment of at least eighty-five percent in the first year. The plan would meet the federal requirements of universal availability. Here was a province insisting on a voluntary plan notwithstanding the fact that it was the failure of the voluntary approach that had made a government plan necessary! On the second major issue, Mr. Frost was adamant that he would not launch the plan without assurance that Ottawa would share in the costs from the beginning. Mr. St. Laurent stressed that he was not justified in spending federal funds for less than universal coverage and that the six provinces' requirement for federal cost sharing could not be altered. Exceptions for one province could become precedents for the others. Nothing appeared to have been changed by that meeting.

On January 1, 1957, the *Toronto Star* reported another federal government decision that had the effect of stepping up the pressure on the uncommitted provinces: no legislation would be passed in the upcoming session of Parliament because only three provinces had indicated their acceptance of the offer. Because of the lead time required to develop an organization in preparation for a launching, lack of knowledge about the content of the proposed federal legislation and, therefore, of the nature of the required provincial legislation, greatly exacerbated the uncertainties for the provincial governments. For the provinces to make a decision to play in the game, they needed the rules. Ottawa was saying, in effect, that they would not get the rules until they had made a firm commitment to play.

Hard on the heels of this announcement, the *Toronto Globe and Mail* carried a story on February 5, 1957, clarifying the interpretation of the meaning of "plans in operation." The construction now placed was strict, indeed. It was not enough that there be a law; the plans must be in operation. That tended to reinforce the earlier report that there would be no legislation before an election.

On January 22, 1957—just one week before the opening of the Ontario Legislature—Mr. St. Laurent confirmed the federal stand in a letter to Mr. Frost: "We are of the opinion that, provided the estimates of coverage given in your letter are in fact realized when the proposed scheme becomes effective, it could properly be considered as coming within the framework of the federal government's proposals to the provinces of January, 1956. We would, of course, feel that some assurance on this point would need to be incorporated into the agreement between our governments on this subject."[87]

Mr. Frost's reply was immediate. Its salient point stated: "If this paragraph means that there would be no federal participation in our plan until we have reached 85 or 90 percent coverage, then it would seem to be a rejection of our proposal which has been discussed over several months. I cannot believe that this is intended, but the paragraph is certainly capable of that interpretation."[88]

Mr. St. Laurent was convinced of the correctness of the federal position, but he was also aware that a federal election was in the offing and that it might be difficult to explain to the electorate a failure to introduce the national plan because of his apparent obduracy. In his reply he restated the federal position and the changed conditions he was willing to accept.

I am confident you will realize on your side the problem which a plan of your type presents to us. We believe the test of being "universally available" in a province to which we are contributing is essential in order that all citizens in that province are able to take advantage of the contribution we are to make from general tax revenue. We feel that this availability must be real, not just theoretical; it must be administratively practicable as well as a matter of entitlement.

Secondly, we believe that to justify the very substantial contribution from our general tax revenue, the plan must not only be available to all but in fact be generally utilized. We believe that if you feel that you should not give assurance of being able to reach your figure of 85% by a certain stage, it should be clearly set forth in our agreement that your plan will be universally available in fact as well as law and that your Commission will work without delay to obtain reasonably universal coverage. Moreover, we feel that you should make public sufficient of the details of the plan you intend to offer . . . to enable us to satisfy Parliament that the plan you offer . . . will be sufficiently attractive to them as individuals to enable you, in fact, to achieve your 85% coverage in this largely voluntary plan within a stated relatively short period. I shall be glad to hear from you further, as it seems to me we are well on our way to reaching agreement on this matter.[89]

Mr. Frost's reply was received on January 31; it restated in strong terms the Ontario position, emphasizing that the federal interpretation of "universally available . . . could make the administration of the plan difficult and expensive, and perhaps altogether impossible." He ended the statement by committing the Hospital Services Commission to work without delay in every practicable way to obtain as wide coverage as possible.[90]

As Prime Minister St. Laurent and Mr. Martin reviewed the Ontario position once again, it could not be dissociated from the total nation-wide scene and dealt with in isolation. On the other hand, this was not a case of dealing with a small province nor, say, the eighth province to propose a plan. This province was the key to the entire strategy of implementation. But in health matters, negotiating with a province was perilously like negotiating with a sovereign state. It was true that now Mr. Frost appeared to want hospital insurance as much as did Mr. Martin, but in 1957 he did not need it as much as did the Liberals who must soon go to the country. It was also necessary to admit that in the implementation of the program it was provincial governments who ran the political risks if the programs malfunctioned.

And yet, Mr. Frost did not seem to them to appreciate the magnitude of his demands on the federal government which had to deal with uniformity and even-handedness with all of the provinces. He was asking for approval of a plan that would be essentially voluntary. To accept that concept and extend it to all provinces that chose the premiums method violated the fundamental principles underlying the national plan. True, two-thirds of Ontario's population were already insured. The question was whether a combination of publicity, low premiums, and an administratively convenient system would be enough to induce the other one-third to join. Mr. Frost was obviously convinced that it would, but not convinced enough that he would guarantee it. What he was asking was that Ottawa have the same faith he had. That might be a reasonable proposition with someone as seemingly committed as Mr. Frost. But, what would be the federal answer to other provinces who might argue for the same approach but have a lesser degree of commitment?

The political costs of a compromise with Mr. Frost could be high, but they were not certain to be high. On the other hand, failure to bring the plan to fruition after the great expectations engendered by the January 1956 offer and the hundreds of speeches made and articles written about it since, carried almost total certainty that the political embarrassment to the federal government would be great, and inevitably exploited by the opposition parties in an election year. The strategy of dealing with Mr. Frost would have to incorporate more compromise than seemed wise, and so there would have to be conditions attached that would maintain federal integrity and credibility in dealing both with the other provinces and in facing the electorate. Then all one could do was pray that Mr. Frost's faith in his voluntary approach was not misplaced.

Accordingly, the prime minister sent the following letter to Mr. Frost, setting forth the conditions and suggesting it was time for the ministers involved to negotiate the details:

> I welcome the assurances you give in your letter concerning the policy that your Hospital Commission will follow in regard to coverage. I also take from your letter that you would not see any objection to stating in our agreement that coverage will be available in fact as well as in law to all people in the province. . . .
>
> There remain the questions of detail concerning benefits, premiums and related matters that will enable us to form a judgement that the plan will in practice appeal to enough people to cause it to be utilized on a scale that would warrant support from the general tax revenues of Canada. . . .
>
> I take it from your letter of the 30th that you are not yet ready to make public the details as to premiums which are necessary to reach a judgement on the attractiveness and probable coverage of your plan. No doubt your experts are working on this. I would suggest that as soon as they are ready, your Minister and officials most directly concerned with the programme might meet with Mr. Martin and our officials to draft agreement for federal support of it.[91]

Mr. Frost replied by telegram on February 4 that he was "quite prepared to have our ministers concerned and our officials and experts sit in at once in a continuation of our conferences." It looked as if the impasse had been broken, but Mr. Martin had still to find two more provinces ready to make the commitment.

A mutually convenient date was negotiated by telephone and the Ontario ministers were invited to meet with their federal counterparts in Ottawa on March 6, 1957.

In the meantime, however, as Paul Martin and the prime minister continued their monitoring of the situation nation-wide and assessing it, increasingly, in the light of the prospects of an election, it became evident that the decision made at the beginning of January not to introduce the legislation in the current session was politically counter-productive. More and more newspaper commentators and spokesmen for such groups as labour were charging both governments with "buck-passing," "political passing game," "playing politics," "hedging," "weaseling again." This was not the image or the reality desirable at any time but especially not prior to an election campaign. Moreover, the delay in passing the legislation, as indicated earlier, increased the uncertainties of the provincial governments, making them even more reluctant to arrive at a decision. Accordingly, on March 5, the Government reversed itself and announced that the hospital insurance legislation would, after all, be introduced before adjournment, even though the requisite number of provinces had not signed on.

The following day, the Ontario delegation headed by Provincial Treasurer Dana Porter, and Health Minister Phillips met in Ottawa with Mr. Martin and Mr. Harris, the finance minister, and their advisers. By mid-afternoon agreement was announced in a joint statement.[92]

Ontario had indicated that it would make the plan mandatory for all employers having fifteen or more employees. In addition to "pay direct" individual enrolment, "mandatory groups" would be formed and if employers of six to fourteen employees wished to enroll as a group they could do so and the mandatory provisions would then apply. With this major commitment to the universal coverage objective, the federal government agreed to the Ontario definition of "universally available."

Mr. Martin indicated that if by the end of September the federal government had not concluded agreements with any of the provinces it would give consideration to arrangements which would place the province of Ontario in a position where it could begin its plan without any concern over the failure of other provinces to participate.[93]

Mr. Martin could, for the first time, feel a justifiable sense of elation. He would still have to find two more provinces but, in comparison with the negotiations with Ontario, that should not be too difficult. His next big hurdle was piloting the legislation through the House of Commons. There was no doubt about its ultimate passage but he would be facing some rough criticism.

THE POLICY ADOPTED BY PARLIAMENT

On March 25, just three weeks after his successful conclusion of negotiations with Ontario and one week after Newfoundland had accepted, bringing the total to five, Mr. Martin introduced a resolution into the House seeking authorization to introduce the hospital insurance legislation (Bill 320). The last stage in the output process had begun. Although there were some telling criticisms in the one-day debate, most of these were repeated later. Despite the criticisms, the resolution was readily approved, and the bill given first reading.

On April 4, Mr. Paul Martin moved second reading of "Bill 320 to authorize contributions by Canada in respect of programs administered by the provinces providing hospital insurance and laboratory and other services in aid of diagnosis." As in Ontario, where the proposal had been debated in the Health Committee before being introduced in the Legislature, the debate in the House on the actual bill had been preceded by "dress rehearsal" performances in the Committee on Estimates and on the resolution authorizing introduction. As a consequence, the parliamentary debate compensated with forensic eloquence for any lack of originality in the arguments. The chief objections and criticisms were seven in number.

1. Failure to include mental hospitals and tuberculosis sanatoria:

Dr. Blair [PC]: "We have a problem in mental disease in Canada that we will have to cope with some place, somehow. I do not like the fact that mental disease is not recognized because I feel it is a backward step."[94]

Mr. Nicholson [CCF]: "The Minister is still refusing to allow half the people in Canada who are sick to participate in what he described as an epoch-making step in the field of health."

Mr. Fleming [PC]: "The express exclusion from this scheme of patients in tuberculosis sanatoria and in hospitals for the mentally ill is a most unfortunate limitation. We as Her Majesty's loyal opposition have already expressed in the strongest terms our view that there is no justification whatever for the exclusion of these hospitals and institutions."

Mr. Diefenbaker [PC]: "Why are these hospitals and instititutions [for tuberculosis and mental illness] discriminated against? I say that the legislation is discriminatory in that it denies these institutions a right that should be theirs."

Mr. Martin [Lib.]: "No attempt is being made to discriminate against tuberculosis patients and those who suffer from mental illness. This

226

bill is designed to assist individuals in their individual hospital problems and not to subsidize provinces which are receiving assistance in other ways from the federal government."

2. Failure to include depreciation and interest as shareable costs:

Mr. Fulton [PC]: "Surely, then, a national hospital insurance scheme should provide for [all] hospital costs [including depreciation and interest] to be met on a national basis, on a uniform basis. Otherwise, how could it be called a national scheme?"

Mr. Martin [Lib.]: "[Because] the province[s] will generally be able to take advantage of moneys now paid under Blue Cross, under private contract schemes and under rural cooperative arrangements, the net economic burden on provincial general tax revenue in any one province will be considerably less than that assumed by the federal government .... So we say that as we are bearing the much greater burden it is not unreasonable to ask the provinces to take responsibility for considering ways and means for carrying this additional responsibility."

3. The requirement of six provinces should be removed:

Mr. Knowles [CCF]: Does the Minister realize that in his insistence upon six rather than five provinces he is really straining at a gnat? Does he realize that at the present time the five provinces which have agreed represent 56.3 percent of the population of Canada? One more province could be Prince Edward Island which would add six-tenths of one percent to the population of the agreeing provinces."

Mr. Hees [PC]: "The only block seems to be that a sixth province is required. Why that requirement was ever brought into negotiations I do not think any person can understand."

Mr. Martin [Lib.]: "If we had not insisted on a sixth province, we would not have had five now. What we are after is a nation-wide system."

Mr. Hees [PC]: "That is the strangest bit of arithmetic I have ever listened to. If we have six we will have seven, but if we do not require six we will have not any, or some such nonsense."

Mr. Martin [Lib.]: "The policy of the government is clear. We do not propose to use the money of the majority of the people of Canada to assist a province or group of provinces which represent a minority of the total population. That requirement is a very important one if we are to have a nation-wide system."

4. Administration costs should be included:

> *Mr. Hees* [PC]: "Administrative costs are very much a part of the cost of your plan.... these costs should be shared by the federal government."

> *Mr. Knowles* [CCF]: "I join with my friend the Hon. member for Lanark [Dr. Blair] in regretting that no provision has been made to include administration costs in the definition of shareable costs. After all, these are certainly part of the major costs of hospitalization in any province. We feel that they should be included."

5. The federal contribution is too low:

> *Mr. MacLean* [PC]: "In order that a proposal might be evolved that would be within the reach of the maritime provinces, I think consideration should be give to increasing the share of federal responsibility."

> *Mr. Knowles* [CCF]: "We feel that the percentage should be much higher than the 50 percent. When you pay for a portion of health or hospital care out of consolidated revenue you are drawing on those funds of the nation which most nearly approximate the principle of paying according to ability to pay. The contribution should be 80 percent rather than 50 percent."

6. It is only a partial and not a comprehensive plan:

> *Mr. Knowles* [CCF]: "So it is, Mr. Chairman, all down through the years the references made by the government have been to health insurance. Now we are getting just a portion, just an instalment, of a promise made 38 years ago."

> *Mr. Argue* [CCF]: "[In 1945] the government looked forward to an overall program of health insurance in which the federal government would pay approximately 60 percent of the cost of major health services. Instead we have a resolution covering a hospitalization plan only."

7. The veto power given to the provinces:

> This was an objection raised by Mr. Knowles in his attempt to remove the six-province requirement. "It does seem to me that this is a case of giving to certain other jurisdictions the power of veto over legislation of this sovereign parliament ... This bill can be passed ... yet it can remain on the statute books of Canada without ever coming into actual effect because of the right of veto written into this clause." He then tried one more tactic which he put in the form of a question:

Has the minister considered the position in which he will be if a month from now there is still no sixth province? Suppose he feels he would like to recommend to his colleagues in the cabinet that the plan be put into effect. Is he aware of the fact he is not able to do so because of the very rigid requirement for six provinces which he has put into this legislation? Should he not give himself and his government, for the few weeks more they will still be the government, freedom of action with regard to this matter?

Despite this endeavour to be of assistance to the minister, Mr. Martin simply replied, "As we will be the government not only for the next four weeks but for the next four years I have no worries on that score."

Mr. Knowles made one more effort.

"[This provision] makes it possible for federal implementation of this legislation to be delayed. That has been the sorriest part of health insurance so far as the Liberal party is concerned over the years, namely, delay. Yet now when at long last we have this bill before us there is in it a clause . . . which makes it possible for a province like my province of Manitoba to veto this legislation of the federal parliament."

These were the major criticisms. At the same time, while arguing for amendments that would, in their opinion, improve the measure, all parties had words of commendation for the legislation:

Mr. Diefenbaker [PC]: "[It is a] bill which we hope will soon be implemented and become the law of the land. We in the opposition throughout the years have favoured this type of legislation."

Mr. Knowles [CCF]: "This matter is of equal if not greater importance than any subject which could be dealt with by a legislative body in this country. It deals with the health of our people and proposes a forward step in social concern for that health. Therefore we shall support the resolution."

Mr. Shaw [SC]: "We heartily endorse the basic principle of this resolution."

Mr. Martin [Lib.]: "This is, for all of us in this house, an historic occasion. In all the years I have been in this house I have had no greater feeling of satisfaction than at this very moment. Never has the government, and I am sure others in this house, had such a feeling of complete conviction as to the vital importance of the legislative action we are now proposing."

And so, as the roll-call vote was taken on that historic evening of April 10, every member in the House voted "aye" and as the *Toronto Globe and Mail* reported: "To tumultous applause, the Commons tonight gave third and final reading to the proposed national hospital insurance plan. Cheers echoed through the Chamber as the House voted formally 165 to 0 for the scheme. Prolongued desk-thumping broke as Prime Minister St. Laurent rose to vote. More applause greeted Health Minister Martin, Opposition Leader Diefenbaker, Mr. Knowles and Mr. Hansell as they voted in their turn."[95]

On April 12, the bill was passed by unanimous vote in the Senate. On May 1, the act was proclaimed the law of the land. There would still be delay—more than a year—before there was an operating program. But on April 17, five days after the Senate had acted, Premier Matheson of Prince Edward Island announced that his province intended to sign an agreement.[96] The combined strategies of delay and of conditional response had run their course and given way to the strategy of accommodation. The offer had been made and it would now be necessary to wait and see whether the new conditions would be met.

The Hospital Insurance and Diagnostic Services Act was, indeed, an historic measure and not alone because of its own substantial history. It was the largest governmental undertaking since the war and it would require federal-provincial cooperation on a scale never before known. It had been characterized by extraordinary controversy, not only on the question of whether it should happen at all, but in its timing, scope, nature, and shape. It bore the marks of the deep conflicts within the Cabinet in which it had been conceived and of the turbulent and critical environment in which it emerged.

Its basic features were outlined above in the discussion of the federal government's offer of January 1956. The act passed in April 1957 provided both more substance and greater specificity, and the order-in-council containing the regulations passed in February 1958, provided the final details.

The degree of control was extraordinary. Every essential requirement for the operation of a program was prescribed by the federal government. The provincial government would have to establish a hospitals planning division; it must license, inspect, and supervise hospitals and maintain adequate standards; it must approve hospital budgets; it must approve the purchase of furniture and equipment by hospitals; it must collect the prescribed statistics and submit the required reports; and the province must make insured services available to all on uniform terms and conditions.

The "uniform terms and conditions" requirement effectively prevented any province from adopting the CMA-CHA-CLIOA proposal of subsidizing individuals to enable them to pay the premiums of the voluntary plans. Any program that required means-testing a part of the population would obviously not be available on "equal terms and conditions."

It was a tough contract that the provinces were required to sign. The combination of Mr. Martin and the prime minister had been extraordinarily successful in managing a delicately balanced strategy. In the first stage there had been the conflict between delay and action; next there had been the necessity to balance action with appropriate conditions.

And so, one by one the agreements were signed. The first was with Ontario and the negotiations extended over a number of weeks. Again, it was the most important for it would be setting precedents for all the others. In the midst of the negotiations with Ontario, the election intervened. To the dismay of the Liberals and the surprise of almost everyone else, the Government was defeated and the Progressive Conservatives under Mr. Diefenbaker obtained a plurality but not a majority of seats. The party standings were: Progressive-Conservatives 112 (a gain of sixty-one); Liberals 105 (a loss of sixty-five); CCF twenty-five (a gain of two); Social Credit nineteen (a gain of four); other four (a loss of two).

THE STRATEGY OF THE FORMER OPPOSITION

There was great speculation among governments and in the press on whether the new Government would accelerate the hospital insurance program and about the extent to which it would correct those defects which it had so vigorously opposed. But it is a truism that in our system of government no problem appears in the same light once an opposition member becomes a minister of the Crown. For every improvement in benefits he advocated while in opposition, he must now realistically count the costs.

Prime Minister Diefenbaker, anxious in his minority position to establish the credibility of his Cabinet as a worthy government, convoked on November 25 another federal-provincial conference. Its primary purpose was similar to that of the Agenda Conference in April 1955. It was called in the prime minister's words "to seek your ideas and your proposals,"[97] and he assured the premiers that in these conferences the federal and provincial governments "parley as equals, equally concerned to provide to those we represent, the best government and the best fruits of government."[98] It was an auspicious beginning. In the course of his remarks, the prime minister made two references to hospital insurance. Reviewing the past arguments about the "six province" rule, he informed the conference that "unless the provinces expressed strong reasons to the contrary," his government proposed to amend the Hospital Insurance Act to remove the six provinces' clause and to substitute for it an earlier and more definite date for commencement of the plan.

His second offer was a hollow one, indeed, and clearly represented an attempt to save face over an about face. He indicated that he and his colleagues "had no objection to providing for inclusion of mental hospitals and tuberculosis sanatoria which have been estimated will cost $68 million to begin with ... but we wish to make clear that whatever is offered to provincial treasuries in this manner cannot be provided in other forms, and in particular must be taken into consideration in any revision of the Tax Sharing Arrangements Act."[99]

What one hand giveth the other hand taketh away.

With a new government listening and, in the case of hospital insurance, serving almost in the role of an appeals court, several provinces did make a last-ditch appeal to what they hoped would be more sympathetic ears.

Mr. Frost made no mention of hospital insurance in his opening statement, nor did Mr. Duplessis. The latter delivered in effect a lecture on the constitution, in which the hospital plan was lumped in an attack on all grants programs whereby one government raises the funds and another government spends them, and he quoted from Laurier and King to confirm that it was an "unsound principle" and a "vicious system."[100]

Mr. Campbell of Manitoba was therefore the first to mention the issue and he asked for inclusion of mental and tuberculosis services, interest and depreciation on buildings, and the costs of administration as shareable costs. He emphasized the importance of timing and the need for an immediate statement of federal policy. "Until we know what action the federal government proposes to take on these questions we cannot further develop our plans with any degree of certainty."[101]

Mr. Hicks of Nova Scotia pointed out that Nova Scotia was committed, and the people would welcome it, but he was, as the date of commencement neared, increasingly concerned about its cost. "... The financing of it may and I think does present a serious problem for all provinces and particularly for what I might call the poor provinces. We are here again faced with the question of the financial capacity of each province to provide a national standard of service."[102]

Mr. Bennett, too, was already committed; but he wanted more. The entire 1945 list of benefits should be available for cost sharing and "implemented step by step as experience dictates to the provinces concerned."[103] And federal funds should be available to two or three provinces without any suggestion of a minimum of six.

Mr. Douglas followed up Mr. Bennett's arguments on timing of federal participation. Referring to a press report of a statement by Mr. Frost that "Ottawa should throw out the restrictions and proceed on the basis of dealing with single provinces," he said that was the Saskatchewan view as well. He closed his statement with these words: "Therefore, we are proposing, Mr. Prime Minister, that your government take whatever steps are necessary to bring about federal participation in the hospital insurance plan, with payments commencing January 1, 1958, in those provinces having plans in operation."[104]

Mr. Manning was one of those who did not mention hospital insurance as such, but like Mr. Duplessis, he pointed to some fundamental weaknesses in both the tax rental agreements and grant-in-aid programs. He reviewed the objections to the conditional grant-in-aid: they work the greatest hardship on those provinces most in need of financial assistance; they penalize provinces whose standards are already higher than those proposed by the national government, and the projects are determined by the federal government.

As a result of this practice, policy with respect to an increasing number of programs in fields of provincial jurisdiction is more and more being determined at the federal level with the provincial governments being left no alternative but to forego this form of federal assistance entirely or accept the project as proposed notwithstanding the fact that it may embody features on which the province might prefer to spend less or do without entirely in order to give priority to some other project which, having regard to the needs of its people, it considers more essential and urgent. In our opinion, the ramifications of this practice should be seriously considered by this conference.[105]

It was a point of view that would be increasingly heard in the years ahead, but the momentum for the largest grant-in-aid program ever designed in Canada was not to be countered at this late date and, indeed, Alberta had already given its commitment to join.

There were no new demands at the conference; all had been made before. Two changes had been made by the new government: the six provinces rule would be changed and an earlier start was therefore probable, and the provinces could include mental and tuberculosis services, but any federal contribution in that respect would be subtracted from any increases in the tax-sharing arrangements. It wasn't much, but for those provinces having programs in operation an earlier starting date would be something.

On June 26, 1958, the Diefenbaker government amended the Hospital Insurance Act enabling the program to begin on July 1, 1958. No other changes to the Martin design were made, and no province took up the option of including mental and tuberculosis services.

On July 1, 1958, five provinces—Newfoundland, Manitoba, Saskatchewan, Alberta, and British Columbia—had programs in operation eligible for federal cost sharing. Nova Scotia, New Brunswick, and Ontario introduced their programs on January 1, 1959. Prince Edward Island's plan began on October 1, 1959. Quebec's plan began on January 1, 1961.

It was eleven and a half years since Saskatchewan had pioneered, alone. And, although Paul Martin, like Moses, was denied the opportunity of leading his people into the promised land, nevertheless, his dream—shared by M. J. Coldwell and Stanley Knowles—was now a reality.

THE OUTCOMES

1. With the irresistible offer of federal cost-sharing, six provinces that had not previously been involved in hospital insurance launched programs meeting the federal conditions. With uniform definitions of residency, the same waiting periods for eligibility of new residents, and uniform benefits, ten provincial plans were melded into the reality of a national program. By 1961 almost the total population of Canada was entitled to the same comprehensive hospital care benefits enjoyed by the people of Saskatchewan and British Columbia for over a decade.

2. Contrary to most predictions, there was no grand rush to the hospitals. In fact, the annual rates of increase in days per 1,000 population declined. From 1953 to 1958, the annual rate of increase had been two percent. From 1958 to 1962 the rate was 1.7 percent, and from 1962 on the rate has been 1.1 percent per year.[106] The main increase in hospital utilization had occurred *before* the national program.

3. The combination of hospital construction grants and voluntary insurance followed by the universal hospital insurance program enabled Canada to increase enormously its hospital resources. The total number of hospital beds was more than doubled and, taking into account population growth, the beds available to citizens were increased by fifty-five percent. The objective of equalizing resources among the provinces was partly achieved in that provinces with a low bed-population ratio were brought up to a level of six or more beds per thousand population. (See Table 15) New Brunswick had the largest relative increase (from 3.9 to 7.1 per 1,000, a gain of 3.2 beds per 1,000). Quebec and Alberta had the next largest increase, 3.0 beds per 1,000. Quebec's increase brought it from the lowest ratio in Canada to just under the new average of 7.0 beds per 1,000. But Alberta, with 6.1 in 1954, expanded its supply to 9.1 beds per 1,000. Saskatchewan with 5.9 per 1,000 in 1954, increased its ratio to 8.4 per 1,000. Part of the explanation in these two provinces lies in the combination of a major shift of population from rural to urban centres and the difficulty, politically, of closing or even reducing the size of hospitals.

234

TABLE 15

NUMBER OF HOSPITAL BEDS AND HOSPITAL BEDS PER 1,000 POPULATION, CANADA AND THE PROVINCES 1954 AND 1971, COMPARED.

	1954		1971		Increase	
Province	No. of Beds	Beds/ 1,000	No. of Beds	Beds/ 1,000	No. of Beds	Beds/ 1,000
Newfoundland	4,737	4.4	3,119	6.0	1,482	1.6
Prince Edward Island	636	6.1	690	6.2	54	.1
Nova Scotia	3,164	4.7	5,223	6.6	2,059	1.9
New Brunswick	2,118	3.9	4,489	7.1	2,371	3.2
Quebec	15,702	3.6	39,715	6.6	24,013	3.0
Ontario	22,260	4.4	51,975	6.7	29,715	2.3
Manitoba	3,672	4.4	7,135	7.2	3,463	2.8
Saskatchewan	5,181	5.9	7,779	8.4	2,598	2.5
Alberta	6,361	6.1	14,810	9.1	8,449	3.0
British Columbia	7,098	5.6	14,402	6.6	7,304	1.0
Canada	67,929	4.5	149,337	7.0	81,408	2.5

SOURCE: Dominion Bureau of Statistics, *Hospital Statistics* 1954 and 1971.

4. The program achieved its primary objectives of meeting hospitals' operating costs and protecting individuals and families from financially crippling hospital bills. But the policy decision to introduce hospital care as the first insured benefit made the program unnecessarily expensive. Although the provinces had agreed in 1955 that out-patient and in-patient services should be introduced simultaneously, and the federal government had responded accordingly, most of the provincial governments—through failure to reach agreement with the medical profession—did not introduce the out-patient benefit until their medical care insurance programs began operating a decade later. That, and the fact that the benefits did not extend to nursing homes and home care programs, resulted in the provision of a substantial volume of services in high cost general hospitals that could have been provided at lower cost by other means.

5. The decision of the federal government not to include mental hospitals in the cost-sharing program had, in the end, a salutary effect, as provinces added psychiatric wards to general hospitals where the costs were shareable. This contributed immeasurably to bringing the treatment of mental illness into the main stream of health care.

6. Although it is difficult to make judgements with respect to changes

in quality over time (and perhaps impossible for the non-medically train- ed), nevertheless it seems reasonable to assert that there has been a marked improvement in the quality of care arising from the increased resources made available through the hospital insurance program. Probably the most important indicator is the number of hospitals accredited by the Canadian Council on Hospital Accreditation. In 1954, 284 hospitals were accredited; by 1974 that number had increased to 615.

7. The financing formula which was intended to provide some degree of equalization by providing a higher proportion of costs in low-cost provinces than in high-cost provinces, proved to be a fairly rough instru- ment, since provincial *per capita* costs were imperfectly correlated with *per capita* income. As Table 16 reveals, the federal contribution to the Atlantic provinces in 1971 ranged from fifty-three percent for New Bruns- wick to sixty percent for both Prince Edward Island and Newfoundland. Ontario received forty-nine percent, as predicted. But there were sur- prising shifts from the estimates in the other provinces. British Columbia, predicted to receive forty-five percent, was, by 1971, receiving fifty-four percent; Alberta received fifty percent rather than the predicted forty-six percent; the contribution to Saskatchewan increased from a predicted forty-seven percent to 52.5 percent; and that to Quebec declined from an estimated fifty-three percent to forty-seven percent in 1971, when it had the highest *per capita* cost of all the provinces, despite the fact that it had the lowest utilization rates in the country.

The anomaly in the formula became more apparent as *per capita* costs increased, and the gap in the actual *per capita* payments to the provinces widened. By 1971, *per capita* payments from the national treasury to subsidize Canadians residing in Ontario with the highest *per capita* income were $8.35 (almost twenty percent) higher than to Canadians residing in Newfoundland with the lowest *per capita* income.[107]

8. Although British Columbia had abolished premiums and begun financing its program through an increase in the retail sales tax in 1954, it seems reasonable to say that an unanticipated outcome of the national program was the extent to which the provinces ultimately abandoned the "insurance" or "premiums" system. By 1973, only one province— Ontario—continued to require the payment of premiums as a condition for entitlement to hospital care benefits; in all the others, proof of *bona fide* residence was the only requirement. Their programs were financed from general revenues collected through various combinations of income tax, sales tax, and, in one case, property tax. In those provinces, therefore, they are no longer "social insurance" programs and are more accurately described as "hospital services" programs.

TABLE 16

PROVINCIAL PER CAPITA COSTS OF HOSPITAL INSURANCE, FEDERAL PER CAPITA CONTRIBUTIONS, AND FEDERAL PERCENTAGE CONTRIBUTIONS, 1956 ESTIMATES AND 1961 AND 1971 ACTUAL, COMPARED.[1]

Province	1956 Estimates			1961 Actual			1971 Actual		
	Per Capita Cost	Federal Contribution	Federal Share %	Per Capita Cost	Federal Contribution	Federal Share %	Per Capita cost	Federal Contribution	Federal Share %
Newfoundland	$12.19	$ 8.77	72	$19.53	$12.88	65.9	$72.78	$43.54	59.8
Prince Edward Island	14.26	9.27	65	23.00	13.74	59.7	71.67	43.26	60
New Brunswick	16.76	9.89	59	32.72	16.17	49.4	90.53	47.98	53
Nova Scotia	17.91	10.21	57	28.32	15.07	53.2	86.14	46.88	54.4
Quebec	20.58	10.91	53	26.99	14.74	54.6	111.74	53.34	47
Ontario	24.02	11.77	49	35.03	16.75	45.5	104.91	51.57	49
Manitoba	21.98	11.21	51	33.49	16.36	48.7	92.24	48.41	52.5
Saskatchewan	36.00	12.22	47	38.81	17.69	44.1	91.87	48.32	52.5
Alberta	26.86	12.36	46	35.00	15.72	44.9	100.83	50.56	50
British Columbia	28.53	12.84	45	34.27	16.14	47.1	86.60	47.00	54
Canada	22.98	11.49	50	31.98	15.99	50	101.42	50.71	50

[1] 1961 was the first year in which all provinces participated.

SOURCE: House of Commons *Debates*, March 25, 1957, p. 2678; Department of National Health and Welfare, *Annual Reports*, 1963 and 1973.

9. With the contribution by the Government of Canada of forty-five percent of the cost of the Saskatchewan Hospital Services Plan, the Saskatchewan government was able to introduce its long-delayed medical care insurance program. The long battle that characterized the introduction of a national program of hospital services insurance was now to be repeated over the next decade, as the nation grappled with the issue of medical care insurance.

Chapter Five

The Saskatchewan Medical Care
Insurance Plan:
The Decision to Pioneer Again

FOR THE SECOND TIME in the unfolding drama of health insurance in Canada, the action shifted from the main plot to a sub-plot, the scene again set in the province of Saskatchewan. The chief governmental actors were those who had also participated in Act II, although, as we shall see, midway through this act, a major change occurred in the lead role. The other starring roles were taken, however, by an entirely new set of actors, the leaders of the Saskatchewan medical profession.

The act opened on the evening of December 16, 1959, with the premier announcing on a radio broadcast the Government's decision to proceed with the launching of a provincial medical care insurance program. The major gap in the health services spectrum was now to be closed; and although opposition was expected to be formidable, no one foresaw the magnitude of the conflict ahead, nor how high in social and political terms the costs of the confrontation would be. What began as a sub-plot would turn out to be a major development in the long and complex scenario.

When the announcement was made, the CCF party had been in office over fifteen years. There was, therefore, an extensive background against which the decision was finally taken, and which is essential to an analysis of the policy decision.

THE BACKGROUND

The major theme running through the background was, of course, the relationship between the medical profession and the Government, just as it was, more obviously, the centre of the drama once the decision was taken. That relationship can be conceptualized in a number of ways. It can be viewed as the connection between a government and a powerful interest group in a democratic society, as I have done elsewhere.[1] It can be assessed, as Professor Seymour Lipsett has done, as the typical dilemma of all socialist governments confronting socially necessary "vested interests" while constrained from strong action by the need to maintain a democratic majority.[2] It can also be viewed as the relationship between a public government and a private government, a concept that will be analyzed later.

To fully appreciate what occurred during the first CCF period in Saskatchewan, it is necessary to examine, first, how the medical profession conceived its role and, second, how it perceived its relationship to government before the CCF came to power.

There was then no medical school in Saskatchewan so that with the exception of those who had been born there and had returned after completing their studies elsewhere, the entire profession had immigrated to the province, with the majority coming from the medical schools of Manitoba, eastern Canada, and the United Kingdom.[3]

The conditions for medical practice, as for other occupations, were far from attractive, with hostile climate, poor roads, inadequate facilities, and few amenities. In comparison with their confreres in other provinces, Saskatchewan doctors, too, were pioneers. That pioneering ethos, infusing the other attributes of an elite profession, had created both strong bonds among members and a sense of collective responsibility. The spirit of cooperation that imbued most Saskatchewan residents was also characteristic of most of the profession which prided itself on its enlightened attitude towards organized means for solving problems. The profession had helped in the establishment of the Anti-Tuberculosis League; it was a report of a College committee that led to the Government's creation of the Cancer Commission on which the College was represented; in sharp contrast to the rest of North America, a high proportion of physicians had salaried contracts in the municipal doctor plans; individual doctors had been active in helping to organize Union Hospital districts, and were, of course, among the leaders in developing hospital facilities.

With the provincial government's activities restricted to the traditional public health functions, the profession saw itself as the one agency in Saskatchewan collectively responsible for medical care. This responsibility was not limited to the actual practice of medicine, for both informal groups

240

and formal College committees had spent many hours studying health insurance, which they favoured, and state medicine, which they opposed. Saskatchewan had been the only division of the CMA to propose that government introduce "state-aided" health insurance, and it had done so in 1933, a full year before the publication of the CMA's Report on Medical Economics setting forth the principles on which health insurance should be organized. In 1939, a group of Regina doctors organized one of the earliest profession-sponsored prepayment plans. All of these actions were seen simply as evidence of the Saskatchewan profession's advanced position on medical economic affairs and the exercise of its collective public responsibility. As the president of the College pointed out in 1943, the purpose of setting up a health insurance committee to make an intensive study of the federal proposals was to ensure "that there will be a medical body well enough qualified to confer with *and direct* any Provincial Health Insurance Commission."[4]

One other factor contributed to both the profession's solidarity and its sense of responsibility for the "domain" of medical care. In 1936, chiefly because of the overhead expense of two offices and declining membership in the voluntary Saskatchewan Medical Association, it was decided that the association should be amalgamated with the College. The members of the council thus added to their duties those of the directors of the association and the registrar assumed the duties of an association secretary.[5]

The College, with compulsory membership, thus became the Saskatchewan division of the CMA. The College council was the only body in Canada serving the dual functions of regulating the medical profession in the public interest and speaking as the voice of organized medicine in promoting the profession's interests.

Two statements in the early 1940s reveal both the profession's deep concern about prospective political action, and its determination to control any such intervention through the device of the so-called independent, non-political commission. As an outcome of its response to Dr. Heagerty's 1941 invitation to the CMA for advice, the College passed for the second time a resolution endorsing "state-aided" health insurance, "provided that the administration of such an arrangement is put into the hands of a non-political independent commission on which the medical profession is adequately represented by *its own representatives elected by and responsible only to the College.*"[6]

The second statement appears in the 1944 report of the Health Insurance Committee in which it comments on the Heagerty draft proposals.

... the question of health insurance ... is of such magnitude and so important, that were the profession to make a false step or adopt a wrong attitude either in matters of procedure or policy, irreparable harm might be done. On the other hand one can hardly expect that Government would be a party to the destruction of medicine or the profession.

The Commission will obviously have a majority of non-medical members, and the danger exists that the profession may be jettisoned. . . . it is hoped that the strength of the Medical Advisory Board . . . will result in the Health Insurance Commission not violating our rights, our liberty, or our well-being.[7]

It was not only the threat of governmental action that was disquieting; there was concern about public opinion generally. In considering a public relations program in 1943, the committee noted: "For some time now in certain sources, a great deal of abuse has been directed against the profession. . . . We all know that, individually, the Doctor is everyone's friend, but as a group we are regarded as anything but that."[8] It appeared that the self-image of the profession as being the most advanced in Canada in its attitudes toward and support for joint profession-public actions to improve and extend health services was not fully shared by all the public.

It is obvious that the profession feared involvement with government, and to those knowledgeable about the corruption and patronage of the Liberal political machine in Saskatchewan as detailed in Escott Reid's classic study, and confirmed in follow-up studies by Lipsett and Smith,[9] there were reasons for their concern. On the other hand, the insistence on administration by an independent, corporate body on which they were "adequately represented by representatives elected by and responsible only to the College" implied either a lack of understanding of the basic principles of responsible government or a major attack upon it. Such a commission would have been simply a committee of delegates who would have had to check back for instructions from their respective organizations and would have been, therefore, incapable of administering a program, and impossible to hold accountable. Nevertheless, in the political milieu in which the profession lived, the desire was fully understandable.

Despite these misgivings, the College's brief to the Saskatchewan Legislature's Select Committee on Social Security in 1943 was positive:

Some organized scheme or plan, state-aided, appears to be essential. . . . voluntary plans and cooperative associations have their place but they cannot reach the masses. . . . while we are firmly of the opinion that any scheme of health insurance should provide for the patient a free choice of his medical attendant where practicable, and services should be paid for on a reasonable and agreed fee-for-service rendered basis, we do think the scheme can be combined with something equivalent to the present Municipal Doctor Plan, with payment on a combined salary and fee basis.[10]

The brief concluded with a strong note of cooperation: "You have our assurance that if a plan of health insurance along the lines indicated in our submission is eventually adopted, we will cooperate with the Legislature or with any body set up to work out details."[11]

As we have seen, however, the outcome of the Legislative Committee's hearings was the passage of a health insurance act in the dying days of the Liberal-dominated Legislature, without warning, or consultation, or provision for an independent commission with College membership.[12] That episode greatly exacerbated the fears of the profession. In his presidential address a year later, Dr. R. W. Kirkby summed up the effects of the Liberal government's action on the Saskatchewan profession. "The health insurance Bill was a bombshell to us. Great concern was felt throughout the profession and we immediately took steps to protect ourselves . . . It was foisted on us without notice . . . many of us lost a lot of faith in politicians as a result."[13]

In short, if a political party that reflected the profession's own "establishment" values could not be trusted, what might be expected from a farmer-dominated party of socialist reformers? A legacy from the past to the new CCF government was, therefore, a vastly increased apprehension on the part of the profession as to what government might do.

It was not surprising that the profession, with sole responsibility for the provision of medical care, and, in its view, having the only expertise in the province on organized health programs, should view with alarm the electoral victory of a party that was *saying* that not only traditional public health, but the whole range of health services, was a matter of public interest, but also *would form a government* committed to taking the initiative in the organization and financing of programs. It was also natural that it would view with suspicion any so-called experts from outside the province unfamiliar with the indigenous ways of an open, pioneering society that led all Canada in prepaid medical care.

Despite their apprehension that their worst fears might now be realized, the formal relations between the College and the new Government began cordially. Following the election in June 1944, President Kirkby invited the premier to meet the council at the Hotel Saskatchewan in Regina on the afternoon of August 23. The president complimented Mr. Douglas on his accession to office and offered the cooperation and assistance of the profession in the developments that lay ahead.[14] The conversation gradually turned to specific matters and Mr. Douglas indicated his strong commitment to provide health services to those receiving pensions and

243

other welfare payments. The physicians agreed that this group required special consideration. Methods of administration of a program and the probable costs were explored.

The differences in their ideological approaches began to surface and, finally, just before 6 p.m., when the premier was to leave to attend another meeting, he was challenged to come back later in the evening to explore further the views of the profession on health insurance. Mr. Douglas agreed.

Despite their differences in philosophy, during that single evening the basic understandings on the operation and the costs of the social assistance medical care program were agreed upon. The premier offered, and the profession agreed to accept, $9.50 *per capita* (the Heagerty estimate) on a one-year experimental basis, and the premier agreed that the Government would also pay costs of administration.

Further discussions were held on details. On September 13, the premier made a formal offer[15] which was accepted by the College on October 1, 1944.[16] Similar agreements were made with other health professions and the Hospital Association. The first comprehensive social assistance health services program in Canada went into effect on January 1, 1945.[17]

Thus, in this first encounter, accommodation had been surprisingly easy. There were, of course, no losers in the bargain: everybody gained —doctors received fees on behalf of indigent patients; fee-for-service payment was unchallenged; patients (and their relatives) were freed of responsibility for payment; municipalities were relieved of many of the costs of indigent care; and the right of the Government to administer a medical care program was acknowledged. Moreover, political credit would redound to the Government and the party.

But the agreement did not deal with the main issue, a universal health insurance program.

As we saw in chapter 2, the Government's second action was to appoint Dr. Henry Sigerist as a commissioner to survey health needs in the province and provide a series of explicit objectives and priorities. Dr. Mindel Sheps, a member of the CCF party, was appointed secretary of the Sigerist Commission. Dr. Lloyd Brown, chairman of the College's Health Insurance Committee, was appointed as one of the technical experts advising Dr. Sigerist. The major recommendations of the Sigerist Commission were outlined in chapter 2, the most important being that a permanent Health Services Planning Commission be established. At a special session of the Legislature, the Health Services Act was passed, creating the commission and authorizing, among other matters, payment for health services "for such classes of persons as might be designated by the Lieutenant Governor in Council."[18]

Although the College council had raised the question of an independent, non-political commission with the premier during the August meeting at the Hotel Saskatchewan, the Government did not adopt that model for its Planning Commission. Instead, the commission was comprised of four members: Mr. C. C. Gibson, who was, until his appointment, superintendent of the Regina General Hospital, and who also became director of the Hospitals Division of the Department of Public Health, Mr. T. H. McLeod, an economist and a member of the recently-created Economic Advisory and Planning Board, Dr. C. F. W. Hames, deputy minister of public health, and Dr. Mindel Sheps, secretary. Although the College was asked for nominations for the chairmanship, no names were forthcoming, and the position was left vacant for fifteen months at which time (February 1946) Dr. Cecil Sheps (husband of Dr. Mindel Sheps), was appointed acting chairman.

The Health Services Act had also authorized the appointment of an advisory committee to the commission. The Advisory Committee (ultimately comprised of thirty-one members) was appointed, and held its first meeting on March 2, 1945. The two representatives of the College of Physicians and Surgeons were Drs. J. F. C. Anderson and C. J. Houston.

The first confrontation. As discussed earlier, despite the apprehensions of the profession, the relations between the College and the new government had begun amicably. Examination of the sixteen-year period between 1944 and 1960 reveals a kind of ebb and flow in those relationships with important episodes of disagreement approximately every five years, the first in 1945 and the fourth, and most serious, beginning in 1959.

As noted in chapter 2, immediately following its appointment in 1944, the new Health Services Planning Committee began the preparation of a series of policy memoranda for consideration by the minister. The first of these was a Report on Regional Health Services. It will be recalled that the concept of regionalized health services had been worked out in detail by the Heagerty Committee with the collaboration of the CMA in 1942. The HSPC simply adopted this approach. It will also be recalled that certain members of the CMA General Council, during the special meeting called in 1943 to debate the Heagerty proposals, had endorsed the capitation method of paying general practitioners. Later, in the same year the Saskatchewan College had stated that "We think the scheme can be combined with something equivalent to the Municipal Doctor Plan, with payment on a combined salary and fee basis."[19]

The report, therefore, proposed three basic policies:

1. The division of the province into health regions that would be democratically established following local petition and voter approval. With their boards composed of representative of municipalities within the regional boundaries.

2. The regionalized medical care system would be based on "group practice and diagnostic centres" at the regional centre and, where population warranted, groups of two, three, or four doctors at district centres.

3. The general practitioner service would be a salaried service (built upon the existing municipal doctor programs) which would allow the institution of a retirement pension program, paid holiday time, and paid leave for post-graduate work. The provision of the basic general practitioner service would be "a minimum and a beginning."[20]

The report was presented to the Advisory Committee at its meeting on March 2, 1945, chaired by the premier in his capacity as minister of health. With the supporting evidence mentioned above, the commission members and, presumably, the premier, were unprepared for the immediate and negative response from the College. A meeting with the premier was requested by the College and scheduled two weeks later. Significantly, the premier was accompanied by the deputy minister, Dr. Hames, but by no other member of the HSPC.

The discussions were lengthy and covered a variety of issues.[21] The profession maintained that there was no serious gap between the objectives of the Government and those of the profession; the major difference was in the proposed mode of administration. The committee accepted subsidy of doctors in remote areas, but opposed grants which could or might be used "as a means of coercion to force a salaried system of medical care in rural areas." There was one discordant voice in the College delegation, that of Dr. R. K. Johnston, a municipal doctor. He reported, as chairman of the Municipal Doctor Committee, that in a survey he had conducted, seventy-one municipal doctors "were almost 100 percent for a practice consisting of municipal contract work [salary] and outside practice [fees for major surgery], and that on the whole they favoured the municipal work as it was now operated." But his voice was lost in the committee committed, as it was, to fee-for-service.[22]

The committee indicated its lack of confidence in the HSPC and, particularly, in the secretary (who was from outside the province). The premier replied that he desired the chairman to be a medical doctor sympathetic to both the Government and the medical profession. He stated that it was the Government's policy to provide state-aided health insurance for the cities and municipal doctor plans in rural areas. He pointed out that an independent commission was not possible because the spending of tax revenues must be under a department of government directly responsible to the Legislature.

The committee recommended a hospitalization plan and subsidies for voluntary medical plans. The premier replied that he was working on the first, but that the second would not be satisfactory because under voluntary plans many would not be covered. The committee emphasized that the proposals of the HSPC were unacceptable. The three basic issues that were to be in conflict over the next fifteen years were now clear.

1. *The method of payment.* The HSPC (primarily the secretary Dr. Mindel Sheps), and Dr. C. G. Sheps (informally, prior to his appointment as acting chairman in 1946) had stressed to the premier the dangers in the fee-for-service method. Such a system "would continue the worst features of private medical practice with its emphasis on curative rather than preventive medicine; and that doctors might overcharge the government through unnecessary surgical operations."[23]

Despite Dr. R. K. Johnston's survey of the opinions of municipal doctors, the official College position endorsed fee-for-service and opposed the salary method as "state medicine" that would make civil servants of the profession. Even the municipal doctors, it was pointed out, were paid on a fee-for-service basis for major surgery.

2. *The independent, non-political commission.* The view of the HSPC was stated as follows: "The formulation of any policy that might be termed 'state medicine' must be the duty of the Department of Public Health. . . . it alone is responsible to the people, and it alone has the sanction of the law to make its policies effective."[24] Its real reason for opposition, says Professor Lipsett, was that it "feared that such an 'independent' body would be dominated by physicians who were hostile to the objectives of the plan and would therefore oppose measures that might jeopardize their own interests."[25]

The College's case for an independent commission has been noted above: its fear of "machine politics," its conviction of its superior expertise in health needs and the delivery of health services in Saskatchewan, and the CMA principles endorsed in the Heagerty Committee's draft legislation.

3. *Regionalization.* The HSPC saw in a regional system greater opportunities for building up resources of facilities and personnel outside Regina and Saskatoon, increased citizen participation, and a more rationalized system of health services delivery.

The College, on the other hand, saw in a regionalized system reduced mobility of patients, and a teacher-schoolboard relationship with elected boards that would have no representatives of the profession.

It is also obvious that a policy of decentralization, with certain specialists at regional centres, would have reduced the flow of referred patients to

Regina and Saskatoon. Moreover, if regional boards negotiated contracts with regional medical societies, the political control by the College of the system as a whole would have been seriously fragmented.

As the premier and the Cabinet weighed the situation and assessed the opposition of the College, it was concluded that the over-riding concern was the severe shortage of physicians in Saskatchewan, augmented by the warnings of the College that the introduction of a system as radical as that proposed by the commission would not only deter many doctors from coming but cause others to leave. This threat appears to have been the dominating factor affecting many of the Government's decisions.

Despite the impasse, the HSPC continued during the summer of 1945 with the organization of two demonstration health regions. The first of these, based on Swift Current, was characterized by unusually able local leadership, and immediately on its formation as Health Region No. 1, with Mr. Stewart Robertson as secretary, the board decided to launch both a hospital and a medical care insurance plan. Health Region No. 3, based on Weyburn, decided to introduce a region-wide hospital insurance plan only. The council of the College became alarmed at the action of the Swift Current board, considering this an end-run, by-passing the College, and at one stage the registrar, Dr. J. G. K. Lindsay, sent a letter to each of the doctors in the region, suggesting that they "decline to attend" a meeting with the regional health officer.[26] However, the negotiations between the board and the local medical society continued.

On July 29, 1945, the College's Health Services Committee (the Health Insurance Committee re-named) met to consider the regional developments, and decided that the time had come to press its case with the premier. Interestingly, since the event triggering the meeting was action being taken in a largely rural area to build upon several municipal doctor plans to create a regional program, the College committee selected to meet with the Government was composed of four specialists, one from Saskatoon, and three from the largest clinic in Regina. This group met with the premier on August 15, and again on September 18, each time pressing for an independent commission and opposing regional organization.

The "independent commission" issue was one of the most serious and complex problems to be faced by the Government, for it was in Saskatchewan that the question was first confronted in realistic terms. It will be recalled from chapter 1 that the idea of a non-political independent commission representative of those receiving services, those providing the services, and the Government, was first adopted as one of the main principles of the CMA in 1934. In 1942, as the Heagerty Committee was preparing its report, that idea was also strongly supported by the spokesmen for labour and farmers on the grounds that if such a body on which they would be represented were not created, the health insurance plan would be dominated by the medical profession. Accordingly, the draft legislation provided for a representative commission, with a medical doctor as chairman. That draft had been prepared by federal civil servants. In 1945, when the federal Cabinet made its offer to the provinces, the proposed model act was abandoned, forcing each provincial medical association to make its case to the provincial government. There the proposal would be examined, not only by a committee of civil servants, but by a government directly concerned about the degree of authority it could delegate to an "independent" commission and still retain sufficient control so that the minister and the Cabinet remained fully responsible to the Legislature. Saskatchewan, was, therefore, the first provincial government to confront the hard task of defining that very complex relationship (and, worse, in its first year in office).

In response to the strong demands of the College at the August and September meetings, and acutely aware of the shortage and the mobility of physicians, the premier finally wrote a letter to the College that was to be regarded by the profession almost as its Magna Carta.[27] The premier qualified his statement by indicating that in the light of "the slow progress that is being made in the Dominion-Provincial Conference [the health insurance proposals had been made on August 6, 1945, that is, about six weeks earlier]...a final decision need not be taken immediately.... further discussions would be of mutual benefit and no hasty decision need be taken in this matter."

"That being so, it would seem to me that the following general principles have been agreed upon." (There then followed two pages of text containing eleven points, of which only the most salient are summarized here.)

1. That a health insurance scheme in the Province of Saskatchewan shall be administered by a Commission which shall be free from political interference and influence.

2. That this Commission shall be representative of the public, those giving the service, and the Government.

3. The Commission shall have sufficient power and jurisdiction to enable it to establish and to administer a plan which will provide the best possible health insurance plan for the people of this province.

4. The powers of the Commission shall be as follows: (a) The Commission shall have all powers necessary to carry out the objects of the Act and administer the health insurance plan in Saskatchewan; (b) While the government is responsible for placing policy before the Commission and for matters of finance, collections, disbursements, audit and reports,

the Commission shall nevertheless be independent in the manner and detail of the mechanics necessary to carry this policy into effect and to obtain the objectives desired by the Act.

5. In so far as the medical profession is concerned, the Commission shall refer to the medical advisory committee the following matters, and take action thereon as the medical advisory committee recommends: (b) The general character of the agreement and arrangements whereunder the profession will provide medical services.

6. Negotiations regarding the rights and conditions of practice of and for physicians . . . shall be conducted between the Commission and . . . the College of Physicians and Surgeons.

He then repeated his invitation that a negotiating committee be appointed . . . "in order that we may arrive at a mutually satisfactory agreement regarding these matters."

Granted the premier's caveats, it appeared that the profession had won its basic demands. The key concession was acceptance of an independent, non-political commission with substantial authority, but equally important was the agreement that the College would negotiate for the profession on such matters as "arrangements whereunder the profession will provide medical service." This meant that the threat of fragmentation of the profession through negotiations with regional boards was ended, as was any threat to the fee-for-service method of payment.

Dr. J. Lloyd Brown happily observed that the new government now stood for "health insurance rather than state medicine."[28] But, as we shall see later, there also appeared to be some in the Government who felt that the premier's letter had compromised too greatly the principles of responsible government.

A number of other developments contributed to an improvement in relations. On July 1, 1946, Dr. Frederick D. Mott replaced Dr. C. G. Sheps as chairman of HSPC. Although an American citizen, Dr. Mott was a graduate of McGill Medical School. He was also recognized as an outstanding expert on the provision of medical care for rural populations based on his experience with the U.S. Public Health Service and on his recently published book (co-authored with Dr. Milton Roemer), *Rural Health and Medical Care*.[29] As a result of the collapse of the Dominion-Provincial Conference the issue of medical care insurance appeared to subside, and this was reinforced in Saskatchewan by the preoccupation of the Government with the introduction of the hospital care insurance program.

Both parties therefore concentrated on their respective policies: the

Government its public medical care programs, and the profession, the voluntary plans. A brief review of these will be helpful at this point.

Two medical care programs, in addition to the municipal doctor plans and the cancer program, were the prime government showpieces. These were the Swift Current program and the social assistance medical care benefit.

The Swift Current experiment. Swift Current Health Region No. 1, located in the south west corner of Saskatchewan, had a mainly rural population of approximately 50,000, based on the city of Swift Current with a population of 6,400. When the program began, in 1946, there were nineteen physicians; by 1950 the number was thirty-five—almost double. It was financed by a combination of premiums and property tax, with a subsidy from the provincial government of approximately ten percent. What did the profession say of it?

In 1949, Dr. Howden, a practitioner in the region, in a paper presented to the annual meeting of the College, asked "How does the practice of medicine in a region like this differ from private practice?" His answer: "Aside from the economic aspects there is fundamentally little difference in doctor-patient relationships, type of practice and so on. As there is free choice of doctor and patient, and as the work is done on a 'fee-for-service' basis, there has been almost no disruption of the present personalized system of private practice."[30]

The then deputy secretary of the CMA, Dr. Arthur Kelly, wrote a comprehensive review of the program in 1948. His conclusion after long discussions with the medical doctors both within and without the region was as follows: "An observer ... gathers the impression that here is a successful experiment in the large-scale provision of medical care, courageously applied, efficiently managed, and remarkably free from attempts to make the facts fit preconceived ideas, financial or otherwise."[31]

But perhaps the most surprising assessment came from Dr. J. Lloyd Brown, perennial chairman of the Health Services Committee, who presented a comprehensive paper on the Swift Current program at the June 1949 meeting of the British Commonwealth Medical Conference in Saskatoon.

Dr. Brown outlined the main characteristics of the program, noted its close adherence to the health insurance principles of the Canadian Medical Association, and then observed:

In [this] experimental scheme, one finds a rather sound system in effect. The people are receiving a high quality of medical care and the doctors, though hard-worked, are reasonably happy and providing good co-operation.

251

When other Health Regions are formed in the Province it will envision more central control and authority at a provincial level for proper coordination of Health Region problems.

Every encouragement should be given to the people of this Region in continuing the excellent experimental effort they are so courageously undertaking. Much of the experience gained will be of inestimable value in consideration of any provincial or dominion-wide scheme of Health Service, which may subsequently be put into effect.[32]

These comments were clearly inconsistent with the policy of the College with respect to regionalization which Dr. Brown had helped to formulate, but it was clear that Swift Current had become more than an "experiment."

The social assistance medical services plan. It will be recalled that the profession cooperated with extraordinary speed in the development of the health services program for recipients of social assistance. It was the first Saskatchewan program to operate on the "ceiling" principle of payment. As noted above, the profession agreed to use, on an experimental basis in the first year, the Heagerty Committee cost estimate of $9.50 *per capita*. Physicians submitted their accounts according to the fee schedule. The initial payment was fifty percent and at the end of the year the balance in the fund was prorated according to the accounts submitted. Doctors' accounts were assessed by the Medical Assessment Board, three physicians nominated by the College and appointed and paid by the Government.

It was accepted by the profession that the recipients of this program were non-self supporting and, when patients, would have been unable to pay full fees. In the first year, the percentage of accounts paid was 77.5 percent, and in 1946, fifty-nine percent. Beginning in 1949 a new agreement provided for a new contract schedule of fees, and a *per capita* payment of $12.00. The program was administered by the Medical Services Division of the Department of Health.

The voluntary prepayment plans. The municipal doctor plans, described in chapter 2, had proved a relatively effective means for attracting a physician and for insuring residents where a majority of sixty percent of the ratepayers approved the necessary by-law. In a province where cooperative organizations were so widely used for a great variety of purposes, it was not surprising that residents of municipalities where the requisite sixty percent could not be obtained should seek other means. In 1938, just a year after the first voluntary prepayment plans were launched in Ontario,[33] the Mutual Medical and Hospital Benefit Act was passed, enabling any group of ten or more individuals to organize a plan.[34] But, more important, in the following year, municipal legislation was amended permitting the payment of premiums by non-property owners. The family maximum established for any combination of annual land tax and personal tax was set at $50.

The Regina Mutual, sponsored by a Regina Cooperative, was unsuccessful in negotiating a contract with the Regina Medical Society and thereupon began to make plans to establish a clinic with salaried physicians. When this, too, failed, it provided coverage for services obtained through the physician of choice and its enrolment began to increase fairly rapidly.

The Saskatoon Mutual was launched with 167 members and achieved an enrolment of 16,000 by 1946 when it began to lose ground because of financial difficulties and competition from the newly established Medical Services Inc. (Saskatoon) sponsored by the profession.

Obviously worried by the consumers' initiatives, a group of Regina physicians later in 1939 launched Medical Services, Inc. (Regina). Its objectives were declared to be limited to "the purpose of obtaining statistics on the actual costs of providing a fundamental and sound medical and hospital service" and its growth was very slow, reaching only 2,000 in the next nine years. In 1949, the Regina Mutual plan and Medical Services, Inc. (Regina) were amalgamated under the name, Group Medical Services (GMS).

By 1950 the two profession-controlled plans dominated the voluntary scene. Medical Service, Inc. (Saskatoon) had enrolled 35,000 and GMS (Regina) 12,000. Commercial companies also provided indemnity contracts with varying ranges of benefits.[35]

Several features of the profession-sponsored plans are important. (a) All plans in Canada offered at least one comprehensive contract that included home and office calls. (b) Most of the plans were of the "service" rather than the "indemnity" type, that is the physician billed the plan directly for his fee, rather than billing the patient. (c) Until 1959 (in Saskatchewan) no plan charged a utilization fee at time of receiving service. (d) There was, except in Ontario, very little "extra-billing," the payment by the plan in accordance with the fee schedule being generally accepted as payment in full. (e) The prepayment plan institutionalized the profession's preference for payment by fee-for-service. This is not to say that all of these policies were universally endorsed by all the profession; many of its members argued for utilization fees, for abandoning home and office calls as benefits, for no restrictions on extra-billing and for indemnity contracts, but their voices did not prevail.

The public plans in Saskatchewan, on the other hand, exhibited a number of other characteristics: salaried service in the municipal doctor plans, "ceiling principle" (that is, a fund of a fixed amount) in the social assistance plan, both ceiling principle and utilization fees in the Swift Current program, and perhaps most important, more difficulty in negotiating fee schedule increases with the public plans than with the physician-controlled prepayment plans.

In 1949, as noted in chapter 4, there were nine profession-sponsored plans operating in Canada, and their enrolments were rapidly increasing. The success of the plans led the CMA to re-examine its famous 1943 policy. The decision to change that policy was ratified by the CMA Council in June 1949, at the annual meeting held in Saskatoon, at which Dr. J. F. C. Anderson of Saskatoon became president of the CMA. The profession continued to endorse the principle of health insurance but withdrew its support of plans organized and financed by government.[36]

As noted above, The Saskatchewan College had proposed "state-aided health insurance" to the provincial government in 1933, and had re-affirmed that policy in 1942 and 1943. It had done so, again, in 1948. It was clearly at odds with the new policy of the CMA, despite the fact that Dr. J. F. C. Anderson was the incoming president of the CMA, and this prompted a major debate at the annual meeting of the Saskatchewan College in October 1949. Following the lengthy discussion, the 1948 resolution was re-endorsed and ordered to be forwarded to the government.[37]

Following his cross-Canada tour of the provincial divisions, Dr. Anderson's presidential report was published in the *Canadian Medical Association Journal* in January 1950.

It was interesting to note the differences in health insurance awareness in the various provinces. In some there would appear to be little present demand on the part of the people for any government-sponsored health insurance scheme, with little or no advocacy from the provincial government, and hence no real general concern throughout the profession in those provinces. . . . The situation, as one travels west, is very different. Here groups representing the people have actively advocated Government medical plans. The Governments are actively interested in Government Health Insurance and the Province is definitely committed to its introduction. The profession in both British Columbia and Saskatchewan seem much more ready to accept some form of compulsory Health Insurance, and have already accepted compulsory hospitalization in principle and practice (although objecting to its timing and some of its administrative practices)."[38]

The observations in this report were remarkable and could probably have come only from a CMA president practising in Saskatchewan:

1. Government advocacy of health insurance was a consequence of "groups representing the people [who] have actively advocated Government medical plans" [and not, as more conventional CMA wisdom had it, because of wily politicians buying the public's votes with its own money].

2. The Province of Saskatchewan was definitely committed to its introduction.

3. The profession in British Columbia and Saskatchewan appeared much more ready [than the other Divisions of the CMA] to accept some form of compulsory Health Insurance.

(It is interesting to speculate that if the Government had introduced medical care insurance in 1949 or 1950, in line with the commitments in the Douglas letter of 1945, a universal plan would have had the profession's approval and full cooperation. What happened in the short space of ten years?)

It was also in this period—1949–1951—that two major developments occurred, one positive, and the other negative to such degree that it may well be thought of as the second confrontation.

The first was the experience of the Health Survey Committee. It will be recalled from chapter 4 that Health Minister Paul Martin had finally persuaded Prime Minister Mackenzie King to introduce in 1948 the health grants program which included the health survey grant. Following extensive negotiation with the College over the terms of reference, the Saskatchewan Health Survey Committee was appointed on January 11, 1949.[39] Its membership included two representatives of the College of Physicians and Surgeons, one each from the dental and nursing professions, the hospital association, rural and urban municipalities, farmers, farm women, labour, and two from the HSPC (the chairman and the research director). Dr. C. J. Houston and the registrar, Dr. Gordon Ferguson, represented the College.

The committee held twenty-five meetings over a period of two years and, though representing such diverse groups, submitted a unanimously-endorsed two-volume report with 115 recommendations respecting health services and forty-five concerning hospitals, together with a master plan for the location, size, and facilities of all hospitals in the province.[40] Its central recommendation was the following:

A comprehensive health insurance program should be undertaken in Saskatchewan at the earliest possible date. This health insurance program should be integrated with and built upon existing health programs which should be extended, modified, and co-ordinated as required, to the end that adequate health care of high quality shall be available to all residents of the province on the basis of need and without regard to individual ability to pay.[41]

The Health Services Committee of the College held a special meeting to determine its reactions to the report. In general, the comments were favourable. The main recommendations were approved with the caveat, "provided they are interpreted in conformity with the 1951 resolution of the College which endorsed the CMA resolution of 1949."[42]

The health survey report was an important event as well as document.[43] Apart from its substantive recommendations, perhaps its most important contribution was the demonstration that representatives of the professions, the public, and the Government could seriously and frankly tackle major issues and come to a consensus on solutions. This result was highlighted by Dr. C. J. Houston in his report to the annual meeting of the College in September 1951: "I trust that you will find much of interest as you peruse the Survey Report but the work of the Committee has a second and perhaps even greater significance. It has established a precedent in working out health matters. *It has proved that a widely representative type of Commission can work.*"[44]

Unfortunately, from the profession's point of view, the positive effects of the Survey Committee experience were simultaneously being threatened by a change in the Cabinet.

The second confrontation. The second confrontation was triggered by Mr. Douglas's decision that he could no longer carry the Health portfolio in addition to the premiership. He appointed as his successor Mr. T. J. Bentley, who had experience as a farmer, Saskatchewan wheat pool executive, and member of Parliament.

Concerned about the new minister's degree of commitment to the principles enunciated in the premier's 1945 letter, the chairman of the Health Services Committee, Dr. J. L. Brown and the registrar met with Mr. Bentley on March 13, 1950 to probe his reaction.[45] The minister acknowledged that he did not favour commission administration, but would take up the matter with the Cabinet. There thus began the second analysis and debate on precisely what the concept of an "independent, non-political commission" really meant.

The minister asked for specific answers to such questions as "What would be the degree of responsibility which the Commission would have to the Minister?" "Who would be considered to be ultimately responsible for the medical plan?" "How would the matter of personnel for the program be handled?" "What so-called public health functions would be considered as not falling within the jurisdiction of the Commission?"[46]

He followed this with an offer to the College of a proposal then being discussed by the Health Survey Committee that the HSPC (five civil servants) be expanded to represent the public and the professions.

On April 14, the College replied with a lengthy statement substantially reiterating its long-held views on an independent commission.[47] This letter was discussed on January 6, 1951, by the College's Health Services Committee with the premier and Mr. Bentley. The committee had insisted that the premier be present because of its alarm over what it considered to be the intentions of the new minister to by-pass the firm commitments of the premier given in 1945. Because of the high level policies to be discussed, no permanent officials were present.[48]

The key question, put by Dr. Houston, was: "We wish to know if the Government still supports the principle of administration ... by a so-called independent non-political type of Commission, ... previously endorsed by the Premier; ... it has been intimated that the Government, or some of its Members, wish to alter that status."

It was a long and repetitive debate. The Government's position was that if by "non-political" and "independent" the College meant "free from patronage or the influence of CCF politics," then the Government was in agreement. However, if they meant a completely autonomous body with authority to tax the people without responsibility (to the minister), then the Government could not agree. The College's position was that the Government would be responsible for policy and the commission would be responsible for carrying out Government policy. Obviously, the real question was, "Who shall control?" with each side suspicious of the other.

What gradually emerged was the premier's view that, in the absence of federal action, there was no pressing necessity to make a decision. A committee should, therefore, be struck further to refine the respective roles of commission and government. This was agreed to. Dr. Houston concluded the meeting by stating his disappointment at what he considered a change of heart with respect to the 1945 commitment and his fear of what such a change presaged for the future.

The minister wrote to the College in January proposing the addition of representatives of the public and professions to the HSPC, and asking them again for their views in respect of the authority of the proposed commission.[49]

Periodic discussions continued and, in 1954, the newly-designed HSPC was established but, in the meantime, the Health Department and commission administrative functions had been integrated in a reorganized

Health Department, with the chairman of the commission becoming deputy minister, while retaining his position as chairman of the commission.[50] The commission, in the process, reverted to its original status as a planning and advisory body. The new regulations required that the commission meet at least five times annually, but by 1959, as a result primarily of the deteriorating relations between the Government and the profession, it met not at all.[51]

The third confrontation. Two related developments serve as background to the third confrontation. The first was the rapid expansion in the 1950–55 period of the profession-sponsored prepayment plans and of commercial insurance. By 1955, the two Saskatchewan plans had achieved a combined enrolment of 185,000 and an additional 53,000 had some degree of commercial insurance protection. Moreover, despite the fact that such contracts contravened the law, both MSI (Saskatoon) and GMS had negotiated contracts with some sixty rural and village municipalities (whose enrolments are included in the above figures).

This growth had an extraordinary impact on the leaders of the organized profession as they saw a real possibility rather than, as in 1951, simply a vague hope that their plans offered a politically and economically viable alternative to government action.

Although extending health services had been referred to in the 1952 election campaign (in which the CCF had increased its majority in the Legislature from thirty-one to forty-two members), a health program had not been a major issue. As noted above, the Planning Commission had been expanded to include professional and public members but no new programs had been proposed. In 1955, however, after extensive discussions (apparently unknown to the HSPC) between Health Department officials and the boards of a number of health regions, it was announced in September that referenda would be held in four regions (subsequently, two withdrew the proposal) on proposed regional medical care programs based on the Swift Current model. Following the announcement, physicians practising in the regions received letters from the respective boards inviting comments on the proposed programs.

Being taken wholly by surprise, once again the College mobilized for immediate action, with the Health Services Committee meeting in Saskatoon on September 11. There, the basic complaints were reviewed and a counter-strategy devised.

It was agreed that the two profession-sponsored plans should act as one unit in making a joint proposal to each of the two boards; that the regional boards should be shown the facts and shortcomings of the proposed schemes; that the profession should "act as a whole" and individual doctors and groups should not act on their own without the full approval of the official body, and that each practising physician in the province should "be given the opportunity of providing a written undertaking to make no separate agreement without the approval of the College."[52] It was also decided that the time had come for a meeting with the premier and the minister of health.

That meeting was held on October 22, 1955. The written brief[53] stressed the profession's complaints: the bypassing of the profession in the regional proposals, the propagandizing of the Swift Current model as an ideal solution when it was, in fact, unacceptable to the profession,[54] and the refusal of the Government to amend its legislation to facilitate the expansion of the voluntary plans. The specific charges were that "every known device was employed by these representatives [of the Health Department] to isolate the well-meaning public citizens on these boards from obtaining proper consultation and full information." Among the charges levelled against the regional proposals were that they restricted freedom of choice of doctor, interfered with highest standards of quality, prevented interlocking possibilities with other health schemes, encouraged restricted regional thinking, would result in a hodgepodge of schemes lacking uniformity, had no representation on the boards of those providing the services, envisioned an unlimited amount of services for a limited fund, were based on incomplete and entirely misleading statistics, understated the costs of administration, and "contained many other premises."

The opposing positions were clearly demarcated and strongly stated. The profession was not encouraged by the ensuing four-hour discussion. A week later, the chairman of the Coordinating Committee wrote to all doctors in the province informing them of the committee's conclusions arising from the meeting: "1. The government is endorsing the Proposed Plan fully. 2. They will attempt to have it adopted irrespective of any consultation with the medical profession. 3. The Premier was not well informed about the whole thing and several of his facts were entirely incorrect. 4. The government will not willingly support a voluntary plan type of service."[55]

The battle lines were now drawn and the profession prepared for the encounter. The letter concluded: "May your Committee once again stress the vital importance of united action by the profession. Many thanks for the steady stream of letters of support. ... never have they been more unanimous. Keep up the good work and your Committee will not let you down."

The committee did not. The College quickly mobilized the doctors in the two health regions (No. 2 and No. 4) that were about to vote. Every major organization in the two areas was contacted, public speeches were made, discussions were held with municipal leaders and Health Board members, and every avenue of publicity, including that generated by the profession-sponsored prepayment plans, was used as fully as possible.

The result was an overwhelming defeat for the proposed regional medical care plans by a margin of six-to-one in one region, and three-to-one in the other. There were several factors (including the certainty of increased taxes) accounting for the rejection, but there is no doubt of the contribution of the physicians' campaign to the result and of their recognition that they had become a strong political force.[56] It was a dress rehearsal for five years later.

The chief lesson emerging from confrontation number three was a heightened awareness of the potential role of the doctor-sponsored plans. This prompted redoubled efforts to expand that role with aggressive salesmanship and the unification of the two plans into one province-wide organization. Because the role of the profession-sponsored plans was to become the central issue in the 1960 confrontation, it will be instructive to examine their development in Saskatchewan in more depth.

Some of the background, as seen from within the profession, is contained in a confidential 3,000 word paper[57] entitled "The Development of Medically Sponsored Prepaid Medical Care in Saskatchewan," presented to a joint meeting of the boards of directors and senior executives of the two plans in Regina in February 1951.

The paper reviewed the developments of the voluntary plans, noting that MSI (Saskatoon) had been established as a result of the growing threat of the Saskatoon Mutual Plan which had begun "to grow in strength to a sufficient degree to completely cast aside the advice and support of organized medicine and, along with what appeared to be strong offers of assistance from the Provincial Government, threatened to completely jeopardize the future of prepaid medical care in the province and the welfare of the profession in general." A few months after the establishment of MSI (Saskatoon) representatives of the two Saskatchewan plans attended the first conference on voluntary plans called by the executive of the Canadian Medical Association in Winnipeg, in June 1947. The paper commented on that meeting in these words:

> The spirit of opinion prevailing at this conference was that, on the political side at least, voluntary prepaid medical plans were racing against time and that any move by the medical profession as such to take the lead in the development of medically sponsored prepaid medical care on a voluntary basis was both urgent and desirable. It was the threat of a compulsory plan in B.C. in 1935 that brought the profession in that province to its feet in one organized group to sponsor B.C. Medical Services Associated; it was the threat in Saskatoon which

led to the setting up of MSI, and it was the general demand throughout the country which was having an influence on the political atmosphere, which made the development of these medically sponsored plans a matter of urgency.

As a result of this meeting (the paper continued), a joint committee was established in the autumn of 1947; it examined the possibilities of the two agencies coming together under the MSI (Saskatoon) charter, but legal counsel advised that a new charter should be obtained. In December 1948, the minister of health, Mr. Douglas, rejected a request for a province-wide charter, saying he felt that their objectives could be achieved under their existing charters. As a result of the ensuing delays, Medical Services Regina combined in 1949 with the cooperative-sponsored Regina Mutual to become Group Medical Services.

In reviewing the situation as it had developed to 1951, the paper concluded: "The development of prepayment plans has taken place with the primary purpose in mind of providing a sound method for residents of the Province for prepaying their health needs and thereby eliminating a demand for government-sponsored, compulsory health insurance."

Efforts directed towards amalgamation continued, with substantial success in making more uniform the benefits provided and premiums charged in the two plans. But the will to amalgamate never seemed to be fully able to overcome the natural inertia or apathy of two bureaucratic organizations, although as we have seen in the battle over the health region development in 1955, a single proposal was made by the two plans.

As a result of aggressive salesmanship, new nation-wide contracts negotiated by Trans-Canada Medical Plans, the development of individual enrolment contracts, and strong emphasis on community plans to replace municipal doctor contracts, the two profession-sponsored plans added significantly to their total enrolment. By 1959, MSI (Saskatoon) insured 217,000 under its various contracts and GMS had reached a total of 91,000. The mutual (Co-op) plans, on the other hand, whose development had spurred the profession to sponsor its own plans, had virtually disappeared. Only the Saskatoon Mutual remained, and its enrolment had shrunk to a little over 5,000.[58]

As noted in chapter 3, the resurgence of health insurance as an issue in federal-provincial relations in 1955 had added further impetus to locally-generated reasons for the College to reexamine its policies. This need was reinforced in very practical terms by the 1956 federal announcement of hospital insurance which included in-patient and out-patient benefits that would directly involve, as a minimum, all pathologists and radiologists. But what raised the whole issue from academic to real-life terms was, as the committee's discussions emphasized, the fact that "a federal supported hospital plan put into effect, due to the expressed wish of the provinces ... could mean a contribution to Saskatchewan of 10 to 12 million dollars by 1958."[59] It could be assumed that this sum would be available for a government medical care program.

In 1957, the College was asked by the CMA what it considered to be the essential requirements in the event of a universal hospital, diagnostic, and medical care program. The College reiterated its strong support of administration by voluntary plans with subsidy by government of low income earners and then listed the stages by which health services should be initiated.[60]

The order of priorities envisaged by the College was based on the premise that the Government ought first to do well what it was already doing before it embarked on any new programs. Its sequence of priorities was, therefore, as follows:[61]

1. Public Health measures; 2. Adequate provision for General Hospital beds; 3. Adequate and proper care for the mentally ill; 4. Care of the aged and chronics; 5. Rehabilitation; 6. Benefits. Re: appliances; 7. Provision of laboratory and x-ray services; 8. Medical and dental care; 9. Ophthalmological benefits; 10. Drug benefits.

Obviously, the Government and the College were far apart in their health services priorities. Not only that, but the success of the profession-sponsored plans which embodied or institutionalized the profession's policies had the effect of exacerbating the strains in profession-government relationships in the two major programs administered by the Government. While not of such consequence as to rise to the level of confrontation, they were serious issues and irritations that resulted in hardening policy positions.

The first was the always smoldering issue of an independent commission. It became increasingly clear that the 1954 reform fell far short of the demands of the profession for an "independent, non-political" commission with powers over both administration and finance. And what seemed its most serious defect, as indicated by the episode of the 1955 health region plebiscites, was that membership on the commission did not seem to give the profession the forewarning of imminent government decisions that it had expected nor even any real sense of participating in policy formulation of any consequence.

The second, reinforcing the first, was the continuing refusal of the Government to turn over to the College the entire responsibility for administering the social assistance medical care benefit, as had been done in four other provinces. It remained the position of the Government that it could not abdicate its responsibility for the management of public funds by annually turning over to the College a half-million dollars with no authority over actual payments.

The third issue was the application of the "ceiling principle" in both programs. Such a system, the profession argued, was based on the unfair premise that there should be a fixed total fund from which to pay for an undetermined volume of services. This concept had been formalized in the 1945 Dominion proposals, offering the provinces sixty percent of a fixed *per capita* sum of $9.50 for physicians' services, and this had been the figure accepted by the College in the original, experimental contract negotiated for the social assistance program in 1944.

Its second application had been accepted in the Swift Current program in 1957 when an increasing number of physicians and an increasing volume of services had converged head on with serious drought conditions and therefore constrained revenues. The compromise had been acceptance of a fixed maximum fund by the Swift Current medical society and the imposition of utilization fees for home and office calls by the board.

While it is not certain that the ceiling principle has any permanent effect in controlling rising costs, what it does achieve, however, is the objective of all paying agencies, whether private or governmental: a known, fixed amount which can be budgeted, either through premiums or taxes, for the ensuing fiscal year.

By 1957 the College had apparently come to the conclusion that the ceiling principle in these two programs was an undesirable precedent in case a province-wide program should be introduced. Accordingly, the College informed the Government in January 1957 that for the following year the contract must provide for fee-for-service payments (at a rate of fifty percent) without a *per capita* limit.[62]

In March 1958, the Government replied that it was not prepared to accept any change, but would increase the *per capita* payment to $21.00. The College refused and informed the Government that if it did not accept the principle of paying on a "straight fee-for-service" basis at fifty percent of the 1957 contract fee schedule, the program would be ended.[63] The Government finally acquiesced. Although the number of recipients declined slightly, total payments to physicians increased from $510,400 to $569,400, not quite reaching the average $21.00 *per capita* that had been offered.

In the same period, The Swift Current Medical Society gave notice to the regional board that the principle of a negotiated fund from which fee payments were made on a pro-rated basis was no longer acceptable. The board accepted and so the ceiling principle was abandoned there also.

As the Government now thought about the CCF's health program commitments, it was obvious that what now looked as the halcyon days of 1948 and 1951 were over. Not only had attitudes and policies changed; what was most remarkable was the extent of the political power that the College now wielded and the concerted means by which it coordinated and exercised this power. The explanation for part of this phenomenon, not experienced in such degree in other provinces, lay, as do so many problems confronted by governments, in the legacy of history.

The medical profession in Canada is legally organized through the provincial Colleges of Physicians and Surgeons, an institution that is itself a lineal descendant of the mediaeval guilds.[64] Provincial legislation establishing the Colleges confers upon them governmental powers. The purpose is two-fold: (1) to protect the public by prescribing the qualifications of practitioners, licensing annually those so qualified, and providing penalties for those who violate the standards or for those who practise medicine without being licensed; (2) to delegate the responsibility of administering the act to those to whom it applies. By virtue of such legislation, such groups are referred to as self-governing professions, but it is clear that in exercising these functions on behalf of the public, the Colleges are, in fact, quasi-governmental agencies exercising functions that the Government might well exercise itself.[65]

In addition, like all other such groups, the profession is organized to protect and promote its own interests, through the national Canadian Medical Association (organized in 1867) and its ten provincial divisions. These divisions can best be designated as the political arm of the profession in the respective provinces. Among their functions are fee schedules, negotiation of contracts with prepayment agencies and government departments, scientific and other programs for their annual conferences, public relations, and the like.[66] In all provinces but Saskatchewan, Alberta, and New Brunswick, membership in the association was voluntary. For example, in Ontario in 1959, out of approximately 8,000 physicians registered with the College, about 5,700 were paid-up members of the Ontario Medical Association. In Alberta and New Brunswick, payment of the license fee to the College automatically provided membership in the separately organized association.

But, in Saskatchewan, the two roles were combined. That is, the council of the College, whose primary function was to exercise the governmental responsibility of protecting the public interest was composed of precisely the same members whose duty it was to enhance and protect the interests of the profession. From the point of view of the practitioner, his annual license fees of $150 were also his membership dues in his professional association. In contrast with his Ontario counterpart, he had no choice; membership in the political arm of the Saskatchewan profession was universal and compulsory.

The union of these two bodies in Saskatchewan had a number of effects. Through universal membership, the association was assured of adequate revenues from the compulsory annual licence fee. No physician could "opt out" by simply not paying his association dues. This meant that it was much more difficult to register dissent from an association policy; one could not simply "vote with one's feet" by electing not to join or continue membership. But most serious of all, it completely obscured what should have been that distinct line when the collective medical body was acting in its own, rather than in the public, interest.[67]

However, it also seems clear that it was not alone the combining of these two roles in one organization and one council that accounted for the extraordinary political influence of the College.

What had emerged over the years in Saskatchewan was, in essence, a unique "private government"—the College of Physicians and Surgeons. Its legal base rested on the Medical Profession Act. Its economic base lay in the profession's control of the expanding prepayment plans for which it determined the policies respecting enrolment, benefits, method of payment, and, to a large extent, the amount of payment. It was unique in that, unlike other private governments, membership was not voluntary. As Grant McConnell states in the chapter on "Private Government" in his book, *Private Power and American Democracy*, "Equally important in defining a private government is the individual member's right to resign. Resignation is the individual's ultimate recourse and the element that distinguishes the private association from the public body."[68]

The College thus resembled the state in which the only alternative to jurisdiction of the Government is to emigrate from the territory. In fact, in July 1962, a *Montreal Star* editorial called it "a state within a state."[69] One can push the analogy too far but one could say that there were in Saskatchewan two governments in the field of health, a private and a public one, each with its own legislature, cabinet, bureaucracy, revenue system, territorial domain, and political ideology. Any action on the part of one to occupy the territory of the other was certain to invite conflict.

That certainty had been enhanced by yet another major change that had occurred within the Saskatchewan medical profession—the composition of its membership. With increasing resources being allocated to medical services, more doctors had settled in the province. But the major difference was that a large proportion of the newcomers had immigrated from Great Britain—the so-called "refugees from the National Health Service."

The most frequently heard reasons for leaving Britain were the "evils" of a government administered health service. In the late 1950s the *Saskatchewan Medical Quarterly* regularly published articles and letters by expatriates critical of the National Health Service. By 1960, recent British immigrants accounted for about one-third of the 750 practising physicians

265

in the province. The forces opposed to any government program were greatly strengthened by this unprecedented influx of new immigrants.

Scanning the political horizon early in 1959, therefore, the Government viewed a turbulent scene. An election—and therefore the time for decision—was approaching. The Government and the caucus were mindful of their long-standing commitment, and painfully aware of the changed environment. It was true that the whole concept of government sponsorship of health services had received new impetus as a result of federal action launching the national hospital insurance program. That alone had given new confidence to public medical care supporters. But it had also drawn together and therefore strengthened all those who were opposed to any further extension of government action. Any advance by any provincial government would be hazardous and, for Saskatchewan, especially so. Nevertheless, in a three-day special meeting of Cabinet in November 1959, the decision for medicare was made,[70] and publicly announced in a radio broadcast on December 16, 1959. Why was the decision made?

THE ACTION IMPERATIVES

1. As suggested above, the primary reason for action was a philosophical commitment to the concept that, as with basic education, access to health services is a fundamental human right tempered only by the resources of the community as a whole to finance them. In practice, the philosophy entails a societal obligation to ensure that services are available and to remove, insofar as possible, the financial barriers to their essential use. This had been accomplished only partially. One-third of the population had no insurance or prepayment protection of any kind against the costs of medical services.[71] For undetermined numbers of others, protection was inadequate and, for many, very expensive.

2. The physician shortage, although less acute than in 1944, was still serious. The physician-population ratio in Canada as a whole in 1960 was 1:879. But among the provinces, despite all its public expenditures on health and hospital services, Saskatchewan ranked sixth, with a ratio of 1:1019 and the urban-rural discrepancy in distribution, noted in chapter 2, had increased.[72]

3. The Swift Current region medical plan, despite its many shortcomings, was acknowledged both by physicians practising under it and the people it serviced to be successful as a universal, tax-financed program. It had attracted a higher ratio of doctors-to-population than any other rural part of Saskatchewan. On the other hand, two subsequent attempts to extend the regional concept had failed, due largely to the political

opposition by the profession to any expansion of regional organization and resistance by farmers to an increase in taxes. A province-wide, centrally-financed plan, therefore, seemed the only means of giving some hope of expanding the supply of physicians, particularly in the vast areas outside Regina and Saskatoon.

4. The CCF policy emphasis during the 1950s had been necessarily concentrated on economic growth; further developments in social services policy depended on broadening the economic base, or on some new revenue source. The introduction of the national hospital insurance program had provided precisely what was necessary—the federal subsidy to Saskatchewan in 1959–60 totalled $13.3 million. Here was a revenue resource that obviously belonged to the health sector.

5. The Canadian Medical Association, with its political stethoscopes sensing public opinion in the country, was fully alert to the rising tide of interest in health insurance, so much so, that in December 1960, it advised Prime Minister Diefenbaker that a royal commission should be established to investigate the whole broad area of health services.[73] Health insurance was in the air. The burden of health costs for many Canadians was increasing. The existence of a problem was not at issue; but both its nature and the desirable solution were controversial.

6. There was also a fundamental need of the CCF to refurbish its image as a party that met basic human needs, that ensured, in the premier's words, "the dignity of the individual ... the undeniable right of every person to health, opportunity, and freedom."[74] With the relative decline in the party's popular support in the election of 1956 it was essential that another bold, imaginative thrust, comparable to the hospital plan of 1947, should be made.

Given the Government's basic philosophy, its fifteen-year unfulfilled commitment, the general climate of public opinion favourable to health insurance, the "windfall" revenues made available by the contribution of federal funds to the hospital plan, and the need for the CCF movement to recapture the idealistic thrust of the mid-forties, it was now time to achieve the long-delayed goal.

THE CONSTRAINTS

As the Government considered the possible ways in which a health service might be organized, the doctors paid, and the program financed, it became increasingly clear that in all three aspects the options available to it were extremely limited.

267

1. As the Government observed the increasing experience in the United States—for example, in the Health Insurance Plan of New York, the Kaiser plans on the West Coast, and Group Health in Washington, D.C. —they felt confirmed in their view that medical care of superior quality could best be delivered through regionally-organized, group practice clinics paid on the capitation system.

But such options were closed. The profession had successfully opposed regional organization in 1945; only the "experiment" in Swift Current had been tolerated, and in 1955 it had been condemned. With respect to payment, a proposal for any method other than fee-for-service would clearly be futile. The development of the prepayment plans, controlled by the profession, had irrevocably institutionalized that one payment method.

2. Moreover, no system could be operated without the cooperation of the physicians and, since Saskatchewan was not the most attractive place in Canada—or in North America—in which to practise under the best of systems, and physicians were both extremely mobile and, in Saskatchewan, chronically in short supply, it was obvious that any proposal must be acceptable to the organized profession.

There was more. It was not enough that the program be acceptable; in conformance with commitments to the College, representatives of the profession must also be engaged in its planning. But since, in recent statements the profession had declared that a government program was neither desirable nor necessary, what would be its positive contribution to a plan to which it was opposed? Its participation in the planning could be expected, therefore, to constitute another constraint on the development of a government policy.

3. There would be yet another. It was the increasing awareness that the fragmentation of health programs, the separate institutionalizing in distinct bureaucracies of public health, of mental health, of hospital services, and of prepayment plans, created serious problems of gaps, overlapping duplication, wasteful administrative costs, and discontinuities in the individual's access to services. Since 1934 the profession had insisted on the separation of medical care from all other programs (chiefly to protect a medical insurance fund from being raided by competing programs) and on its administration by an independent commission. The premier's letter of 1945 accepting the commission form of administration was still regarded by the profession as a firm commitment. No options were open here; a "non-political, independent" commission would have to be proposed. Moreover, as a dozen years of argument affirmed, there would be disagreement on the precise powers to be granted to it.

4. As in most political decisions, timing was also a constraint. In chronological terms, the issue appeared to be the same as in 1945 when the hospital legislation was being considered. But, in fact, the situation was very different. Because of the need to involve the profession and other interest groups in the planning stage, the gestation period would be greatly protracted. There was no hope, as in 1948, of going into the forthcoming election with a successful accomplishment at which to point with pride. Despite the long-term recognition of the CCF's commitment to health services, any proposal would be, unavoidably, an election issue.

5. Finally, there was the chronic constraint of limited revenues. Despite the federal contribution to hospital insurance, the costs of that program were rising rapidly, as were demands for increased financial assistance to hospital capital costs. These had to be weighed in relationship to the competing demands from all other government programs.

Taken together, the constraints left little room for preferred choices. Realism demanded doing the best with what existed within the limited resources available and the institutional patterns already established.

THE UNCERTAINTIES

1. *The costs.* There was some uncertainty about costs as there is about most public programs, but it was less than in the case of the hospital plan fifteen years earlier. For now there were the two prepayment plans and the Swift Current program, and their cost data could be supplemented by the comprehensive statistics of the social assistance medical care plan. The uncertainties about costs lay in two areas: (a) The open-ended nature of the demand for and supply of medical services provided under a fee-for-service system intrinsically creates uncertainty; and (b) If doctors refused to practise within the system and insisted on billing in excess of the schedule of fees authorized for reimbursement, how much would this add to the total medical bill paid by Saskatchewan residents?

2. *Public reaction.* A second major uncertainty arose from the constraint of timing, noted above, that forced the Government to go into the election with medicare as an issue rather than as an operating program. But *what would be* the reaction of the public? This was not 1944 when the entire CCF program, with health services as a major proposal, had been strongly endorsed. Now, two-thirds of the population had varying degrees of protection; now, the doctor-shortage had been partly alleviated; now, instead of endorsing a government program, the doctors were saying that it was unnecessary. How strong would be the effect on public opinion of

269

the doctors' opposition? What compromises would be necessary? And to think of the unthinkable, what if they simply refused to participate, and many of them leave permanently? The prospects were anything but reassuring.

3. *The Press.* The conclusion to be drawn from (2) was that only an extraordinarily vigorous election campaign could possibly provide a strong base from which to negotiate. But the uncertainty here was the power or influence of the press. Practically all the daily and weekly newspapers in the province, except the CCF's own weekly, *The Commonwealth*—read in the main only by the faithful—could be counted upon to oppose any proposal for a government-operated plan. Could this opposition be overcome through the channels of radio, television, and public meetings? It was a moot point.

4. *The Liberal strategy.* Yet another force was unpredictable—the public reaction to the Saskatchewan Liberal party's new approach, endorsing medicare in principle but asserting that it should be introduced only after the degree of public demand had been ascertained by a province-wide referendum. At the same time, the provincial Liberals were also in a slightly ambivalent position for the national Liberals had been responsible for the national hospital insurance program and, now in opposition, were pressing the Diefenbaker government for action on medicare. Mr. Ross Thatcher, the Liberal leader of the opposition, was aware of this and used it as an argument for delay. Speaking in the Legislature on February 14, 1961, he said, "Most people seem to agree that a Federal election will come within a year and a half. No matter which party is elected then, it would seem that in the very near future a national prepaid medical scheme will be introduced right across Canada."[75]

The Liberal strategy, therefore, had two potential results: First, the Saskatchewan Liberals could offer the voter a reasonable, though unspecified, alternative to the CCF proposal. If the national Liberals should be returned to power in Ottawa and introduce a federal medicare program, it would provide a financial boon to Saskatchewan's already hard-pressed revenues, easing the burden of medical services. Second, the Liberal policy could be marshalled as a strong argument against a repetition of the 1945 hospital plan decision "to go it alone."

Taken together, these and other uncertainties of lesser consequence presaged a hazardous outcome. But the stakes were high, and fulfillment of the CCF party's commitment could no longer be delayed.

GOVERNMENT PLANNING

Ever since the decline in its public support evidenced in the 1956 election, the Government had been conscious of the fact that its enforced pre-occupation with economic growth during the fifties had resulted in its over-all program being only marginally different from those of "the old-line parties." It was also sensitive to the fact that after fifteen years in office with substantially the same leadership, it was being accused of lack of innovative ideas and enthusiasm for new programs. If the party were to continue to be a "third force" in Canada to be reckoned with, and if it were to regain its appeal as a party of ideals, there would need to be a return to first principles. It was this recognition that the premier manifested in the Throne Speech debate in the Legislature in 1960.

> The measure of abundance and greatness [of this province] is not just its farms, uranium mines, oil wells, factories, or its steel mills. These things are means to an end and not an end in themselves. In the final analysis the greatness of this province will depend on the extent to which we are able to divert a reasonable share of wealth production ... to raise the standard of living of our people, and to give them a reasonable security against old age, against sickness and other catastrophes.[76]

To begin the translation of this awareness that extraordinary new thrusts must be made in several social program areas, the Cabinet held a three-day conference on planning and budgeting with its Economic Advisory and Planning Board in April 1959. The basic purposes of the meeting were two: to appraise the Government's existing programs; and to plan new directions for future action. A great many areas were examined, and several committees were struck to study and report back.[77]

As a result of this review, it was decided that prime consideration should be given to a province-wide comprehensive medical care program as the next major step. The inter-departmental committee appointed to determine the appropriate course for planning was chaired by Dr. Burns Roth and included officials from Health, Treasury, Welfare, and Municipal Affairs: Dr. Vincent Matthews, Dr. Murray Acker, Thomas Shoyama, David Levin, A. W. Johnson, Meyer Brownstone, and William Hardy.

The Cabinet directive to the committee provided broad guidelines: the program should be universal and comprehensive, financed through a combination of sales taxes and premiums, and, while basically provincial in its orientation, should leave as much responsibility as would be practical to the health regions. The committee was requested to complete its studies by the next meeting of the conference in November at which time, "if the committee's proposals are acceptable, consideration will then be given to establishing a public committee to discuss a medical care insurance program for the province."[78]

The Inter-Departmental Committee, like its prototypes in Ottawa and other provinces, prepared as a first step a comprehensive analysis of existing prepayment plans, examining thoroughly the range of their services, their costs, and their good and bad points. Of the municipal doctor plans, it concluded: "Experience with the different plans would seem to show that where the physician is on salary there is some dissatisfaction with the quality of care. Where the agreement is on a fee-for-service basis, municipalities complain of overservicing."[79]

The examination of the profession-sponsored plans revealed higher *per capita* costs and the imposition of exclusions and waiting periods for individual subscribers. In the case of MSI (Saskatoon), which had operated at a deficit for the preceding two years, new policies had been adopted providing for it to pay only fifty percent of the cost of home and office calls, a maximum of $35 for diagnostic services, and for limits of five days for nursing services and of $10 for physiotherapy treatments. The deterrent charges and other limitations had been decided upon as an alternative to a twenty-eight percent increase in premiums which would have had the result, as the medical director of MSI (Saskatoon) said, that "you end up by pricing yourself out of the market."[80] These changes, the report observed, "may mean that the [MSI] program has ceased to be comprehensive medical care insurance."

The report also noted the inconsistency in the profession's insistence on voluntary enrolment and the preference of MSI (Saskatoon) for compulsory participation by all the residents of a municipality under the enabling municipal by-law.

The report then examined the payments for medical services by the various programs and plans and by patients.

In comparison with the rest of Canada, the data showed that payments under public programs in Saskatchewan were considerably higher than in the country as a whole, while payments under voluntary prepayment and patient residual payments were proportionately lower. It also showed that while only one-third of the population lacked insurance, nevertheless, direct payments by patients accounted for over forty-five percent of physician income indicating the shortfall of insurance payments.

Examination of taxation statistics indicated that physicians' incomes in the prairie provinces in the preceding twelve years had been consistently higher than the Canadian average, and that while in 1946 Saskatchewan physicians' incomes had been the lowest of the three prairie provinces, from 1954 to 1957 they had been the highest.

Following forty pages of review and analysis of the existing systems and programs, the committee outlined for consideration a section on objectives and scope of a province-wide program. The single underlying

TABLE 17
ESTIMATED PAYMENTS TO ACTIVE CIVILIAN PHYSICIANS, BY REVENUE
SOURCE, SASKATCHEWAN, 1957.

Total Payments		$14,200,000
Public Medical Care Programs		1,685,000
Swift Current	$ 650,000	
Municipal Programs	$1,045,000	
Special Provincial Programs		1,272,500
Pub. Assist.; Cancer;		
Psychiatric; Soc. Welfare; T.B.		
Special Federal Programs		320,800
DVA; Armed Forces,		
Indians and Eskimos		
Workmen's Compensation Board		330,000
Voluntary Prepayment Plans		4,081,985
Voluntary non-profit	$3,690,985	
Commercial	391,000	
Direct Patient Payments		6,509,715

SOURCE: Saskatchewan Interdepartmental Committee, *Report*, 1959.

objective should be "to apply the maximum knowledge of modern medical science for the prevention of disease and the care of the sick and disabled without regard for any individual's inability to pay for needed services."[81] This objective implied:

1. the principle of prepayment through the complete transfer of medical care expenditures from the private to the public sector ... and the distribution of the costs over the entire population in accordance with ability to pay.

2. the inclusion of the entire population within the framework of the program is important not only for the achievement of the financial objectives but to assure equal access to care for urban and rural dwellers, persons in all occupational groups, and for those in low, medium, or high incomes.

3. phased development of comprehensive services. The health services of the future should be comprehensive, embracing community health and individual health, preventive and curative. Because of initial shortages in health personnel, facilities, or economic resources it may be necessary to develop a completely comprehensive program by stages.

4. legislative and administrative measures designed to promote a high

quality of medical care. A major organizational measure which leads to the promotion of medical care of high quality is the provision of services by means of group practice arrangements.

5. major emphasis on measures of prevention ... medical practitioners who have been occupied almost exclusively with the treatment of diseases must be encouraged to participate in preventive programs and apply preventive measures to personal health care.

6. maintenance of public and governmental responsibility. In a democratic society based upon democratic social institutions, the final responsibility for the program must rest with the legislature and the government. Thus the statutory basis for the program and the general operating and financial policies cannot be shifted to a voluntary or quasi-public body.

7. promotion of regionalization consistent with economy and efficiency. A province-wide program demands provincial planning and unified general policies. At the same time it is highly desirable to achieve the participation of local government.

8. promotion of professional education and training.

9. measures to enhance research activities.

10. promotion of health through public education.

With these objectives, the committee examined the services that should be included as benefits and those that should be phased in at a later date. Physicians' services were, of course, the highest priority, with optical, dental, pharmaceutical, home care, and chiropody services to be considered for later inclusion.

On the question of administration, the committee examined in both philosophical and practical terms the distribution of functions to be exercised by the provincial government and by regional boards. With a predilection for as much local control and responsibility as possible, the committee nevertheless concluded that a high degree of province-wide uniformity was essential in some aspects of the program. These included: determining the content of the program, negotiating the method and amount of payment, payment of accounts, statistics and research, and collection of revenues. Regional boards should be responsible for developing ancillary programs, providing diagnostic facilities and group practice centres, and facilitating educational programs.

The committee also prepared estimates of costs based on the proposed scale of benefits and on the data summarized in Table 17. Assuming population increases of 2.5 percent per annum, and expenditure increases of four percent per annum, the total cost for 1961 was estimated at

$17,704,050, or a *per capita* cost of $19.50.[82] To this sum it would be necessary to add an estimated five percent for administration, or $885,000.

There was one other benefit that had potential for conflict, the provision of diagnostic services. On the basis of Swift Current experience, these were estimated to cost approximately $2.50 *per capita*. It was suggested by the committee that these might be provided through the hospital services plan in which case their costs would be shareable under the federal Hospital Insurance Act.

The committee recommended that the program be financed by a combination of a personal tax plus a contribution from general revenues.

In the final section of the report, the committee summarized the functions of an advisory committee: to advise the Government on the design of the program; to serve as a sounding board for the views of the Government, the health professions, and the public in many areas of organization of services which are still indefinite and unresolved; to focus attention on the needs and problems of each group; to serve as a forum which would force each agency to examine its premises and arguments. Because knowledge about the best design for medical care programs and the most effective way of meeting health needs is shared by many groups in the community, the committee believed that such a body could gather, assess, and modify many of these ideas and, with this information, advise the Government, the health professions, and the public on rational program development.

Despite the obvious failure of the expanded Health Services Planning Commission, the planning group clearly envisaged an advisory committee as having extremely important functions, but ultimate decision-making powers as viewed by the College of Physicians and Surgeons as inhering in a "non-political, independent" commission were not among them.

At the November Cabinet-Planning Board conference, the Interdepartmental Committee Report served as the basis for a lengthy and thoroughgoing discussion. The question of timing was given special consideration by the Cabinet. There would need to be a period of at least twelve months for the appointment, deliberations, and report of the Public Advisory Planning Committee; sufficient time to establish the administrative organization; and perhaps a year's notice to voluntary and other plans to wind up their operations. It was the general view that the target date could not be set earlier than July 1961 and it might possibly require extension to a date later in 1961 or January 1, 1962. It was an extremely tight schedule, a short "critical path," and, unfortunately for the Government, the process would involve factors over which it had little or no control.

Accordingly, it was decided that a representative public advisory planning committee on medical care should be appointed as soon as

275

possible, with a dead-line for its final report the end of 1960, and with sufficient flexibility in establishing the program any time between July 1, 1961 and January 1, 1962. The unusual importance of this projected launching date will become evident later. The Cabinet was obviously inordinately optimistic about its ability to time the staging of events, as subsequent experience was to prove.

The Cabinet then directed the committee and the minister to: 1. present terms of reference for the advisory committee; 2. appoint the committee before the end of the year; 3. draft a proposed bill for Cabinet considera- tion; 4. continue studies during the interim period; 5. give consideration to producing an edited version of the committee report for distribution to members of the Legislature.[83]

On November 27, 1959, the deputy minister forwarded to the minister a preliminary draft bill for the Cabinet's consideration.[84] Its major outline and most of its provisions followed closely the Saskatchewan Hospitaliza- tion Act, with some clauses borrowed from the federal Hospital Insurance Act. Those sections which differed necessarily from those acts were in harmony with the decisions of the Cabinet-Planning Board Conference and, so far as possible, with the principles enunciated by the Canadian Medical Association. As a draft, it was expected, of course, that it would go through numerous Cabinet revisions and be further revised as a result of any recommendations of the Advisory Committee that differed sub- stantially from the draft.

Although the work of the Interdepartmental Committee had gone for- ward with all deliberate speed, developments in the external environment had not been proceeding as harmoniously. Signals were already indicating difficulties ahead. They had begun, in fact, about six months earlier, with the premier's first announcement of the Government's intentions.

STRATEGY I

In the process of implementing the decision taken in April 1959 (a period extending just over three years), six stages of the over-all strategy can be discerned. The first stage was the announcement of the decision and the appointment of two committees.

The opening shot in what was to become the most embittered election campaign in Saskatchewan history was fired on April 29, 1959. Premier Douglas, speaking in a by-election in the Kinistino constituency, an- nounced—shortly after the Cabinet decision at the Cabinet-Planning Board conference—that his Government would proceed with a compre- hensive medical care insurance plan that would cover the entire popula- tion.

Three days later, the registrar of the College, Dr. George Peacock, wrote to say "your planning could have considerable impact on the practice of medicine in this province and, as such we would be most appreciative if you would favor us with some indication of what your proposed plans consist."[85]

On May 1, the premier replied, indicating that as soon as its own studies had reached a point where concrete proposals could be considered, it was "the Government's intention to call in representatives of those giving the services and of the general public in order that we may have the benefit of their advice before any policy decisions are made. . . . I can assure you that . . . it is the Government's intention to have the fullest possible consultation with those most vitally concerned."[86]

The 1959 Fall convention of the College provided the first opportunity for the profession to respond to the premier's announcement. The leaders of the profession were aware not only of the Interdepartmental Committee but also that a draft bill had already been submitted to the minister. Indeed, part of the Government's continuing problem in executing both its strategy and tactics resulted from the communications system available to the College. Within hours, sometimes minutes, of a meeting of the commission or of a senior committee, or even of Cabinet, the College's strategists were informed. Occasionally, but apparently with less frequency and certainty, the Government, too, received intelligence from sources inside the council.[87] Now, the College leaders were angry, for they felt the earlier promises of full consultation had not been kept.[88] Discussion of the College's response in the event of the threatened government action was the meeting's primary concern. As a warning to the Government, the following resolution was unanimously passed:

Whereas, we the members of the College of Physicians and Surgeons of Saskatchewan know that medical care has always been readily available to the public regardless of its ability to pay, and that no one has ever been denied medical attention because of his financial position, and

Whereas, recently much publicity has been given to the possibility of the introduction of a plan for a compulsory Government controlled province wide medical care plan, and

Whereas, we firmly believe the standards of medical services to the people will deteriorate under such a system, and

Whereas we feel that some misunderstanding of the profession's position on this matter may exist, Therefore be it resolved, that we, the members of the College of Physicians and Surgeons of Saskatchewan oppose the introduction of a compulsory Government controlled Province wide medical care plan and declare our support of, and the extension of health and sickness benefits through indemnity and service plans.[89]

The next response was the premier's—three weeks after the Cabinet-Planning Board conference had made its extensive review. Speaking on a provincial affairs radio broadcast on December 16, he outlined the Government's decision "to embark upon a comprehensive medical care program that will cover all our people."[90]

He then stated the basic principles which the Government believed to be sound:

1. The prepayment principle; 2. Universal coverage; 3. High quality of service; 4. A government-sponsored program administered by a public body responsible to the legislature and, through it, to the entire population; 5. [It must be in] a form that is acceptable both to those providing the service and those receiving it.

He also announced the intention of appointing a representative committee to recommend to the Government a medical care insurance scheme which would best suit Saskatchewan's needs.

With the dramatic escalation of a long-term government commitment to the status of imminent legislative action, the College took immediate steps to reinforce its October declaration by issuing another detailed policy statement defining the parameters within which government action might take place. The document was entitled "Rights and responsibilities of individual citizens and medical practitioners on all matters governing medical care."[91]

It is a lengthy statement but because of its importance in setting forth not only the rights and responsibilities of the profession but also those of citizens, it contributes greatly to an understanding of the cataclysmic events that were to follow. In essence, it was a declaration on the part of the private government of the profession to the Government and people of Saskatchewan that it was prescribing unilaterally the rules of the game. The statement follows:

The College of Physicians and Surgeons of Saskatchewan believes that the preservation of the basic freedoms and democratic rights of the individual is necessary to insure medical services satisfactory to the people of Saskatchewan.

The maintenance of health by the prevention and/or treatment of disease is the primary concern of the medical profession and of fundamental importance to all citizens of Saskatchewan.

The people of Saskatchewan as recipients of physicians' services, and the members of the medical profession as providers of physicians' services, have certain rights and responsibilities which must be respected if a satisfactory medical service is to be continued.

"The people of Saskatchewan as the recipients of physicians' services have the right to determine:

1. whether or not they wish to prepay the cost of physicians' services
2. the insuring company or agency
3. the comprehensiveness of coverage.

The individual citizen must have the following rights and responsibilities:

1. freedom of choice of doctor.
2. freedom of choice of hospital within the limits of safety to others.
3. freedom of recourse to the courts in all disputes with whatever party.
4. freedom to choose the method by which he will pay or prepay his medical care.

The medical profession acknowledges its privilege and duty to care for the health needs of the citizens of Saskatchewan regardless of race, color, creed or ability to pay. As providers of physicians' services, the medical profession must have the right and in the public interest, the responsibility to:

1. ensure that a high standard of medical care is maintained.
2. have its composite opinion considered by those responsible for legislation in the health field.
3. refuse to participate in any plan which in its opinion is not conducive to a continuing high standard of medical care.
4. evaluate the worth of its services and retain the principle of fee for service wherever and whenever possible.
5. maintain mediation committees to deal with complaints, from whatever source, be they medical, ethical or economic and respect the recommendations made by these committees.

The individual physician must have the right to:

1. freedom of choice of location of practice.
2. freedom of choice of patient except in an emergency.
3. choose whether or not to become a participating physician in any insurance plan.
4. determine his method of remuneration.
5. treat his patients in and out of hospital within the limits of his competence as judged by his confreres without interference by laymen.

When the statement is examined in detail, there are few points with which many would quarrel, and many that both citizen and patient would support. Citizens might object that they are not simply "recipients"; not only do they finance the services, they are the sole reason for the services to exist. They might also object that, in this category of "recipient," their choice of methods of payment is restricted; they are not permitted to choose, as one of their democratic rights, to make their payments through their elected government; they can choose only a "company" or an "agency."

The original draft of this statement had been prepared by the executive of the Ontario Medical Association and submitted to its council in 1959. Because of the imminent publication of a new policy statement by the Canadian Medical Association, it was decided that the OMA statement should not be released.

The Saskatchewan version of the statement differed substantially from the OMA draft which gave the people of Ontario more options by declaring that they have the right to determine: (i) whether or not they wish to prepay the cost of medical services; (ii) whether prepayment will be made on a voluntary or mandatory basis; (iii) the degree of financial participation by government in any plan of prepayment; (iv) the comprehensiveness of any plan.[92]

The Saskatchewan College declaration, in contrast, denied these rights to citizens and thereby greatly restricted the potential role of government. Its issuance at a critical stage of negotiations on the terms of reference of the Advisory Committee not only revealed the very wide gap between the College and the Government but served notice of further conflict to come.

For the Government, with the decision to act now being taken, time was of the essence. In setting up the Advisory Committee, the minister, in keeping with the predetermined timetable, indicated that he wanted a report by December 31, 1960. For the profession, faced with the Government's policy declaration, delay was one of the primary strategies. Since the College had to assume that a public committee in which it would have only three of ten members might well endorse the Government's proposal, it recognized that it might be trapped in a series of recommendations to which it was fundamentally opposed. At first, the College refused to participate, but, as a result of behind-the-scenes conversations with D. B. Rogers, editor of the *Regina Leader-Post*, the College was persuaded that, from a public relations point of view, this position had become untenable.[93] On January 18, 1960, the College informed the minister that it was prepared to name its representatives if the terms of reference were amended, and if changes were made in the composition of the committee. The strategy was to expand the field of investigation far beyond the issue of medical services to include, among others, the public need of health care, the scope of benefits essential to providing such care, the means by which existing services would be integrated into any new plan, methods of remuneration, and relationships between the professional self-governing groups and administrative commissions. The College was thus insisting that the public inquiry be addressed to *its order of priorities, rather than to the Government's*. It was also providing an agenda for a two or three year project.

At a meeting of the College committee with Premier Douglas and Health Minister Walter Erb on January 26, it was agreed that the terms of reference should be expanded, that the five principles enunciated by Douglas should be relegated to the preamble, and that two more members should be added to the Advisory Committee: a representative of the Chamber of Commerce and one from the Saskatchewan Federation of Labour.

Delaying tactics continued,[94] but, finally, on April 25, the committee and its membership were announced.

The members of the Planning Committee were as follows: Representing the public: Dr. Walter P. Thompson, former president of the University of Saskatchewan, (chairman), Mrs. Beatrice Trew, and Mr. Cliff H. Whiting; representing the College, Dr. J. F. C. Anderson, Dr. E. W. Barootes, and Dr. C. J. Houston; representing the College of Medicine, University of Saskatchewan, Dr. Irwin Hilliard; representing the Saskatchewan Chamber of Commerce, Mr. Donald McPherson; representing the Saskatchewan Federation of Labour, Mr. Walter Smishek; and representing the Government, Mr. T. J. Bentley (former minister of health), Dr. V. L. Matthews, and Dr. F. B. Roth, the deputy minister of health. The secretary was Mr. John E. Sparks.

The Committee began its studies of the expanded agenda. In part, it was an up-dating of the work of the health survey committee of 1949–51 in that it was examining the same issues. But there was a difference, for now the consensus was gone and the prospects of change were immediate. Even as the College reluctantly acquiesced in the appointment of its representatives, it was preparing for what it considered to be the political battle of its life—the June 1960 provincial election.

The College council assessed its members $100 to wage its publicity campaign against the Government's medical care program. About 600 of the province's 900 doctors paid the fee and, later, the CMA, with some doubts about the wisdom of the strategy, contributed $35,000. Public relations offices were set up in Regina and Saskatoon and consultants were employed. The College position was supported by the Liberal party, as well as by other groups—the Pharmaceutical and Dental associations, and the Chamber of Commerce.

It is not the purpose of this analysis to examine the details of the 1960 election, except to say that by its intervention and its expensive propaganda campaign, the College succeeded in making medicare the major issue of the election. By its acceptance of CMA funds, it was the first of the parties to enlist support from outside the province.

In a four-party contest, it was probably inevitable that any party, whether obtaining a majority or a plurality of seats would do so on the basis of a minority vote. Such was the case. The CCF increased its seats to thirty-eight of the fifty-four in the Legislature. Its popular vote totalled forty percent. The Liberals received thirty-three percent, the Conservatives fourteen percent, and Social Credit twelve percent. Neither of the latter two elected any members.

What was to be read into the results? The College contended that the election which had virtually been converted to a referendum on medicare, had indicated majority opposition to the Government's policy. But, called on the telephone by a reporter at his home in Toronto in the early hours of June 9, Dr. Arthur D. Kelly, the general secretary of the Canadian Medical Association stated, as his personal opinion, "This is a democracy. ... our efforts will now be bent on avoiding the defects we see in government plans elsewhere."[95]

But the Saskatchewan College did not interpret the election in this light and began to re-plan its strategy to prevent the Government's policy from coming into effect. Obviously, one of the most potentially effective devices was that of delay, and this could be used legitimately because the Government had bowed to the College's insistence that the terms of reference of the Advisory Planning Committee on Medical Care (note the specificity of the title which the Government insisted on retaining) be broadened to include the entire spectrum of health services, and not simply medical care insurance, as the Government had wanted. As the committee's deliberations dragged on into the fourteenth month (six months beyond the original schedule, and with no end in sight) the Government decided that it could brook no further delay.

There were two internal reasons for this. The first was the Government's own credibility; it had been elected with a commitment to medicare which must be fulfilled. The second was that within three years there would be another election, and the program must be introduced, be "de-bugged," and be seen to be operating successfully before that date. In the meantime, however, a third and external reason—not present when the original timetable had been established—had been introduced. That was the formation of the New Democratic Party, and the possibility of Tommy Douglas becoming its leader.

As the recent biographer of Tommy Douglas makes clear, Douglas had favoured the formation of the new party but had resisted suggestions that he stand for the leadership, feeling that his ties were with Saskatchewan. In February 1961 he had discussed the question with the caucus;

later he discussed it with his Weyburn constituency association, and then later, with M. J. Coldwell. Finally, by June 18, he decided to let his name stand, although he would "do no barnstorming."[96]

There were two major effects of the formation of the new party and Douglas's acceptance of the leadership candidacy. The first, noted above, was the renewed determination with respect to medicare to adhere, as far as possible, to the original timetable. The second was that there was now a third extra-provincial force interested in the outcome of the medicare issue in Saskatchewan, the New Democratic Party, which would obviously benefit from its success. The two other external forces were, of course, the Canadian Medical Association and the insurance industry, both concerned with its defeat. It is interesting to speculate that if there had been no external "allies" on either side, the resolution of the conflict might have been more amicably achieved; but such was not to be the case.

On June 21, 1961, that is, a few days after Douglas's decision to stand for leadership of the NDP, he directed the Hon. Walter Erb, minister of health, to write to Dr. Thompson, asking for an "interim report" so that the Government could introduce "enabling legislation couched in general terms, to be prepared and introduced in the Legislature at the Fall Session."[97]

The College knew, of course, that a draft bill had been prepared months earlier. It was also fully aware of the desire of the founders of the new party to have a successfully operating medicare program in Saskatchewan to help launch the NDP—and Tommy Douglas—on their way.

Despite the opposition of the representatives of the College and the Chamber of Commerce, the Thompson Committee responded with an interim report on September 25, 1961. It included recommendations of the majority for a program providing universal coverage and a comprehensive range of medical service benefits, financed by a subsidized premium which could be met by all self-supporting persons, and administered by a public commission, responsible to the Government through the minister of public health.[98]

The three College representatives, supported by the Chamber of Commerce member, submitted a memorandum of dissent, arguing for the CMA policy of subsidizing low-income individuals and families to obtain coverage through existing voluntary agencies.

The representative of the Federation of Labour, Walter Smishek,[99] submitted a thirteen-page dissent, recommending payment of physicians by salary, and financing by means of the income tax, and opposing deterrent fees, premiums, and administration by a commission.

The Thompson Committee, like other such commissions of inquiry, had served as a filter of ideas and views from briefs and presentations of many organizations and individuals. It had not, obviously, been able to reconcile the highly divergent points of view. In order to come to some accommodation, the small majority had chosen a middle road: it had rejected the College and insurance industry philosophy on the one hand and the Federation of Labour position on the other. In addition to the positive recommendations of the majority, the report also transmitted to the Government what it didn't really want to hear: confirmation that the opposition of the medical profession to the original Douglas principles was unyielding.

Now nine months behind its original schedule, convinced that much of this delay had been deliberately contrived by the profession's representatives on the Thompson Committee, and with the premier's departure now imminent, the decision on timing was made even more hazardous by another College stratagem.

Aware, through its representatives, that the Thompson Committee majority report would not be endorsing its policies, the College reinforced its long-standing insistence that no legislative action be taken without direct, prior clearance with the profession, by passing at the September 1961 convention the following resolution: "... it is essential that the findings and recommendations of the Thompson Committee should be submitted to the College of Physicians and Surgeons, and before any legislative action to implement any part of the findings of the Thompson Committee, the College should be informed of such legislation."[100]

The choices for the Government were both hard. To consult further was to ensure unacceptable delay; not to consult was to be further damned. Apparently feeling that nothing more was to be gained, that not much more could be lost, that all the constructive solutions were now in, and with a special session of the Legislature already called to accommodate recent changes in the federal Income Tax Act, the Government by-passed the College. It concentrated in this last, critical period on weighing the internal and external proposals, accepting some, rejecting some, modifying others, and melding the sundry pieces until the Saskatchewan Medical Care Insurance Bill was ready for introduction in the Legislature. It embodied the principles enunciated by the premier in December 1959, almost two years earlier, that is, all but one: it was not "acceptable to those providing the services."

THE POLICY

Fifteen years after the first universal hospital insurance legislation in North America in 1946, its companion piece, the first universal medical care insurance act, had been finally proclaimed law. In terms of the health service needs of the province, as well as in the increased difficulties of bringing the plan to fruition, it had been an unfortunate and expensive delay.

What did the legislation provide? The act was called The Saskatchewan Medical Care Insurance Act and sub-titled, "An Act to provide for Payment for Services rendered to Certain Persons by Physicians and Certain other Persons."[101] Its basic intent, therefore, was to pay for services. The administration was placed in a commission of not fewer than six nor more than eight members, including the deputy minister of health, and of whom at least two others, not including the chairman, were to be physicians. The commission was authorized "to establish and administer a plan of medical care insurance for the residents of Saskatchewan and the improvement of the quality of the insured services provided under such a plan." In addition, there was to be an advisory council representative of professional and other interested organizations having unusually important powers in that it was required to be consulted by the commission or the minister on any matter that substantially affected the operation of the plan and, in addition, it was authorized on its own initiative to propose improvements, extensions, restrictions, or modifications of the plan. There was also to be a medical advisory committee composed of physicians approved by the College.

The program was to be universal and compulsory, i.e., every resident was required to register himself and, if any, his dependents. A resident became a beneficiary, i.e., entitled to insured services, by paying the premiums for the current year (plus arrears, if any).

Insured services were defined as services of physicians and surgeons in the office, hospital, or home. The acceptance of payment by a physician was deemed to be payment in full for the services rendered, with the exception that when a patient had not been referred to him, a specialist was entitled to charge the difference between the general practitioner and the specialist fee in the College's official fee schedule.

The patient was guaranteed freedom of choice in the selection of his physician and the physician the right to free acceptance or rejection of a patient.

In the only reference to the method of financing, the lieutenant governor in council was authorized to provide for the levying and collection of a premium to be paid by or on behalf of every resident.

Also included were clauses providing for assurance of secrecy with respect to reports, for the establishment of an appeal procedure, and authorization for the Government to enter into any agreement with the Government of Canada with respect to insured services.

The act concluded, in standard form, with authorization for the commission to make regulations, subject to approval by the lieutenant governor in council, with respect to a number of subjects for the purpose of establishing and administering the plan of medical care insurance. In summary, these included:

(a) arrangements for payments to physicians and other persons providing services; (b) lists of persons entitled to receive payments (after consultation with the appropriate professional body); (c) rates of payment; (d) manner and form for submission of accounts; (e) manner and form in which payments were to be made; (f) identification of beneficiaries; (g) the terms and conditions on which physicians and other persons were to provide insured services to beneficiaries; (h) information to be obtained; (i) meetings and conduct of business of the commission; (j) appointment of committees and sub-committees; (k) remuneration of members of committees; (l) the maintenance and improvement of the quality of the services provided under the act to the end that the highest possible standards of services would be achieved: (m) generally for the carrying out of the provisions of the act according to their true intent.

To the legislative draftsmen, the authorization for the issuing of regulations appeared straightforward. Legislative draftsmen are cautious by nature. Their predilection is to use legal phraseology that has stood the test of acceptance by the courts. These regulations were no exception, most of the terminology being borrowed from the legislation establishing the Saskatchewan Hospital Services Plan and the federal Hospital Insurance Act. It came as a shock to them that the College would, as we shall see, interpret their standardized phraseology as posing threats to the profession, especially Section (g) referring to "terms and conditions"— a term borrowed from the federal Hospital Insurance Act.

Changing the actors. With the introduction of the medicare legislation Tommy Douglas had crossed off the last item with which he could deal of his unfinished agenda for Saskatchewan. He had now to take up his responsibilities as leader of the New Democratic Party to which he had been elected at the founding convention in August. He was succeeded by the Hon. Woodrow S. Lloyd who had served as minister of education and provincial treasurer. The political styles of the two men were strikingly different but there is no impression of any difference in their dedication to the medical care objective. Mr. Lloyd was sworn in as premier on November 7 and, with his new mandate, his first major decision was to make an important change in the Cabinet by transferring Mr. W. G. Davies to the Health Ministry and Mr. Erb to Mr. Davies' previous post as minister of public works. It was clearly a demotion for Mr. Erb which was to have serious consequences, but it was a decision that Mr. Douglas had been avoiding for some time.[102] Mr. Davies had been the executive director of the Saskatchewan Federation of Labour, and a member of the Health Survey Committee in 1949–51. He was not, therefore, unfamiliar with either the major issues or the influential personnel.

In addition to these changes at the political level, time was running out in the tenure of Dr. F. B. Roth as deputy minister of health, for he had announced a year earlier his decision to accept an appointment at the University of Toronto at the end of June 1962. He was to be succeeded by Dr. Vincent L. Matthews, then assistant deputy minister, and a member of the Thompson Committee. It was a critical time for such major changes, particularly when the leadership of the College was coalescing more strongly in the face of the apparent finality of the legislative decision on medicare.

STRATEGY II

As noted in other chapters, because of the long preparatory period required for the introduction of complex programs, the strategy of implementation moves forward simultaneously with the preparation of the legislation. It is necessary, therefore, to go back in time to the Cabinet meeting on June 20, 1961, which marked the beginning of the second stage of the strategy of implementation. The first decision, noted above, was to request an interim report on medical care insurance from the Thompson Committee. Lengthy discussion in Cabinet led to the issuing of a directive to the Health Department to make plans for the following: 1. the operation of the program beginning January 1, 1962, that is, in just over six months; 2. collection of the premiums beginning November 1, 1961, that is, in just over four months; 3. the introduction of a pay-roll deduction system; 4. submission of data to the Treasury Board with respect to estimated costs and sources of revenue; 5. immediate recruitment of administrative personnel.[103]

These steps were to be taken on the assumption that the last possible data for final decisions required for implementation of the program would be no later than October 15, 1961.[104]

As we have seen, the premier's decision to stand for leadership of the NDP had reinforced his determination to adhere to the original timetable, despite the intervening delay. Subsequent events were to show that the timetable was now unrealistic—particularly the assumption that premiums could be collected beginning November 1, if final decisions were postponed to as late as October 15.

Moreover, there were new problems. The uncertainties and constraints surrounding the problem of financing the massive new program were discussed earlier. But now fate seemed to have intervened in a cruel and untimely way. Everyone—Government, doctors, and public—knew that only the lack of financial resources had delayed the introduction of the program for fifteen years. Then, in 1958, there had benevolently appeared the federal grant for hospital insurance, freeing a large block of provincial funds; and so the decision was made. In the intervening two years since the decision, however, serious drought and economic recession had resulted for the first time in its sixteen years of office, in a forecast deficit of $5 million for the ensuing (1961–62) fiscal year. Moreover, the expenditures on hospital insurance were rising rapidly and new capital requirements for hospitals would have to be found. There was now no budgetary cushion whatever from which any subsidization of the new program could be made. The total cost would have to be financed (as it would have been at any time during the 1950s) from new revenues. Moreover, if, as the Government had consistently said, the amount of any premium was to be kept within the financial capacity of the vast majority of the population, recourse to other tax sources would be unavoidable, and these should be taxes having the least possible regressive effect. To avoid the impact of using a single source only, a combination of four taxes was finally decided upon:

1. Premiums of $12 for individuals and $24 for families, with a calculated yield of $ 6,000,000.
2. An increase of six points in the income tax (approximately one percent of taxable income) expected to yield $ 3,600,000.
3. An increase of one percent in the corporation income tax, expected to yield approximately $ 1,000,000.
4. An increase from three percent to five percent in the retail sales tax, to yield, for health services, an additional $14,000,000.

The increases in existing taxes, it was decided, should go into effect on January 1, 1962. But by September it was recognized that the collection of premiums in the fall of 1961 was impracticable. It was therefore decided that the collection of these would be postponed until September 1962, to provide insurance coverage for the second year.[105]

With the passage of the act, and the selection of the new minister, the most urgent action was the appointment of the representative commission. This task was begun as soon as the new minister had had an opportunity to become acquainted with his responsibilities and his senior personnel. Wishing to comply with the College's statement of principles that medical representatives were to be selected by the College, on November 28 Mr. Davies telephoned Dr. Dalgleish, the president, to arrange a meeting with the College representatives.[106] Dr. Dalgleish informed him that in his colleagues' opinion, they could not meet. This was followed by a letter from the minister conveying the same request, and suggesting December 12 or 16 as a meeting date.[107] Dr. Dalgleish's reply reiterated the council's refusal to cooperate, citing the failure of the Government to discuss the medical care legislation in advance.[108] He did say, however, that the council would meet to discuss the health needs of the people and proposed an agenda that resembled the College's agenda for the Thompson Committee in 1960.[109] The minister replied that while he would be willing to discuss these items on a suitable occasion, the Medical Care Insurance Act was a matter of pressing and primary importance.[110] The impasse had begun.

With the "appointed day" having been postponed to April 1, further delay was impossible, and the commission was appointed on January 5. No suitable physician being available, the chairman was not a medical doctor but a senior government finance official, Mr. Donald Tansley. The deputy minister of health, Dr. F. B. Both, served *ex officio*. A professor of medicine, Dr. Samuel Wolfe, and a practising physician in Prince Albert, Dr. O. K. Hjertas, who had once served as secretary of the Health Services Planning Commission, and later as medical health officer in the Swift Current region, were the only medical doctors who would accept appointment. The commission was immediately attacked by Dr. Dalgleish and by spokesmen for the Liberal party.

Despite the refusal of the College to negotiate with the Government, both parties were presented with a new public arena in which to restate their respective positions. The occasion was the Regina public hearings of the Royal Commission on Health Services. The Hall Commission was now into its fourth month of hearings, having held meetings in six provinces.

The Government's brief was presented on January 22. The statement outlined its philosophy with respect to health services as a basic right, asserting that "Health services must be viewed as public services which can be best planned, organized, administered, and financed by governments."[111] It urged the federal government to introduce a program of medical care insurance paralleling the hospital insurance plan, and for which it should assume at least sixty percent of the costs. It specifically rejected the government-subsidy-of-private-plans approach because of a lack of control of premiums and of expenditures on benefits, the means test requirements, the amount of subsidies required, and the resulting distortion in the allocation and development of health resources.

The College brief consisted mainly of a review of the priorities and arguments it had presented to the Thompson Committee and included its original and supplementary briefs to that body. It then discussed developments since that report, including the passage of the act in November with all its shortcomings. It also repeated the October 17, 1961 resolution affirming the refusal of the College to accept a government controlled medical scheme. In its conclusion, the College stated clearly the recourse it would have if the Government persisted: "If the Government of the province implements the Saskatchewan Medical Care Insurance Act, the medical profession must continue to oppose it. Therefore we can not agree to render service under the plan. We would, however, continue to treat our patients in accordance with our capabilities. *We would presume that patients presenting receipts of payment would be able to obtain reimbursement from the insurance program.*"[112]

It was indeed a far cry from the Government's hopes for a service type plan, and it revealed the College's strategy in the event of the Government's perseverance.

The positions of the two parties were not new to the Royal Commission; the CMA and Insurance Association briefs and those of the labour union had reinforced these opposing policies in every capital city since the tour began. But in Regina witnesses were more adamant, the arguments more forceful, the tension higher, and the sense of immediacy more poignant.

The hearings, however, helped not at all in bringing the parties together, and so, with the Government's appointment of the Medical Care Insurance Commission, the strategy of implementation had reached the end of the second stage.

STRATEGY III

With the announcement of the commission, actions to create the administrative organization and appoint personnel accelerated. In contrast to 1946 when expertise in hospital insurance administration in Saskatchewan was non-existent, in 1962 not only were there experts in the Government familiar with all the tasks to be done, but for some functions the organization was already in place. Since the collection of the medical insurance tax was to be combined with collection of the hospital services tax, the registration and collection machinery of SHSP would serve both. With respect to the payment of physicians' fees, the medical services division of the department had been processing over one-half million dollars of accounts each year. What was needed was a forty-fold increase in its processing capacity.

The only local source of additional qualified personnel was, of course, the staffs of the two physician-sponsored prepayment plans. Their personnel were alerted to the employment opportunities in the commission through advertisements pointedly directed to people "with health insurance administrative experience." What looked, from the commission's point of view, as simply an obvious solution both for the commission which needed help and for the employees of prepayment plans about to become redundant, was, from the College's point of view, diabolical raiding of their employees in agencies for which the College had plans for expansion. It appeared as simply another overt action by the Government in the campaign to cancel the College's hard-won gains.

Almost one month was engaged by the new commission in planning and preparing for the administrative tasks to begin on April 1, so it was not until February 8, 1962, that, in the delicate matter of attempted negotiations, the commission picked up where the minister had left off by requesting an early meeting with the Council. Two weeks later, Dr. Dalgleish replied, citing a bill of particulars in which the Government had acted unilaterally, ending with the passage of the Medical Care Insurance Act as a form of "civil conscription."[113] [Since the commission was the bastard progeny of an illegitimate act, the College declined to recognize it.

Deprived of access to medical representatives through the official channel, the commission fell back on what it considered its only alternative, a letter to each practising physician. This proved abortive, with many replies reminding the chairman that in trade-union negotiations such an approach, by-passing the elected spokesmen, would be held unethical.[114]

With the College maintaining a policy of "non-recognition" of the commission (a not unknown strategy in relations between hostile governments), the initiative for negotiations had necessarily to revert to the minister. On March 2, Mr. Davies wrote to Dr. Dalgleish, reminding him that since the Legislature was now in session, the Government was prepared to make changes in the act to meet the profession's objections, but not to repeal it.[115] Two weeks later, Dr. Dalgleish replied, again citing a list of grievances, and asking whether expected changes in the act would permit implementation of the profession's proposals.[116] On March 22, Mr. Davies wrote again, restating the Government's position that the Medical Care Insurance Act was now law and that the latest possible date for changes was March 28, and inviting the College to meet on that date.[117]

In the meantime, however (on March 2), the minister had made two announcements, both of major importance. The first was that out-patient diagnostic services would be provided through the Hospital Services Plan. The reason for this decision was that the costs of hospital-based out-patient diagnostic services would be shared by the federal government under the Hospital Insurance and Diagnostic Services Act. Over $500,000 in federal grants were at stake here. But it also meant antagonizing the radiologists and pathologists over the question of paying for similar services in doctors' offices. Since 1958, diagnostic out-patient services had been a controversial issue in every province from Quebec west, and all of the governments had avoided a confrontation by not introducing them as benefits.

The second decision was to have consequences that were great, complex, and immeasurable. In its month-long review of its administrative responsibilities and in its planning to meet them, the commission had finally come to the conclusion that "the sheer administrative task" of setting up the program could not be accomplished by April.

The minister had been so informed, and after anguished discussions, the Cabinet had acquiesced. The parallel problem in launching hospital insurance and the contrasting response in December 1946 will be recalled.[118] Then, T. C. Douglas had insisted that despite the administrative difficulties, the dead-line must be met. This time the Cabinet capitulated to the arguments of the administrators, although it is impossible to know how much weight to attach to the fact that up to this time attempts to negotiate with the College had been wholly frustrated. The postponement until July 1, as will be seen later, was to create extraordinary problems for the Government by giving opposition forces three additional months in which to mobilize.

By now, however, the College's strategy of refusing to negotiate had to undergo serious reappraisal; there was a limit to the public's understanding of the doctors' refusal even to talk, despite the apparent degree of success of the College in stalling operations and contributing to a general public impression of a faltering of purpose in the Government through its postponement a second time of the plan's inaugural date. Moreover, the March 22 invitation had proposed an "open agenda." A meeting would provide another forum in which to urge the College's priorities and the subsidization of membership in voluntary plans. The attendant publicity would also likely be helpful. It was decided to accept the invitation.

The meetings took place, as proposed, on March 28 and continued on April 1 and, briefly, on April 11. Following the first two meetings, a letter from the premier, and a "memorandum" from the College delivered on April 11, formalized the results of the discussions.

The Government's proposed concessions included removal of concern, "if such there is," about possible interference with professional standards and professional independence; provision for new mechanisms in arriving at fair and equitable physician remuneration; provision for appeal procedures; the appointment of additional medical members to the commission, and, for the first time, *a major concession to consider changes whereby the physician need not accept payment directly from the commission.*[119]

It is difficult to overemphasize—from the Government's point of view

—the magnitude of this concession. When fee-for-service is the method of payment in a prepayment plan, the system preferred by the insured and the insuring agency—and, indeed, by a majority of physicians[120]— is that the physician bills the insuring agency according to an official fee schedule, is paid directly by the agency, and accepts that payment as payment in full. The obligation is met by one transaction. This was the method (the service contract) that had been introduced and adopted by the profession in all of its own prepayment plans. It had also been accepted by the profession that since the prepayment plans were serving as their collection agency, thus reducing both their losses from bad accounts and their collection costs, it was reasonable to accept a reduction in the rendered fee listed in the fee schedule, by an amount that varied, typically, from ten percent (in Ontario) to fifteen percent (in Saskatchewan).

Obviously, the Government also preferred this method. But, from its point of view, there was another major issue quite apart from the far greater convenience to patients of the service contract method. In such a program the Government acts as an intermediary. On the one hand it negotiates a fee schedule. The Government also accepts responsibility for all the administration costs. It agrees to pay, say, eighty-five percent of all accounts as payment in full and estimates what the total will be. It then levies a tax—or taxes—to raise the estimated, required funds. But, if a large proportion of physicians—or all, as proposed by the Saskatchewan College—practise outside the plan and are entitled to bill their patients directly for amounts determined by them, there is no known limit on the total levy that citizens must pay for medical care. Carried to an extreme, the principle of "extra-billing" could be such as to defeat the purpose of insurance (for example, some specialists in Toronto charge 200 percent of the OMA schedule).

Yet another issue arises from this transition from one system to another. Under conditions of private practice, without insurance, physicians typically applied the "sliding scale of fees" principle by charging the wealthy more and the poor less for a specified service. Under an insurance system permitting "extra-billing," the same principle could apply. The Saskatchewan College, for example, declared that it "would not make [extra] charges to indigent groups," implying that extra charges would be made to non-indigents. But the charging of a higher income patient an additional fee means that he is charged twice; it is his higher taxes that have already made it possible for the doctor to receive the standard fee on behalf of his low income and indigent patients. The result is a form of double taxation, a kind of "double dipping."

The Saskatchewan government was therefore deeply concerned not only with the greater inconvenience, and the higher costs of administration, but even more by the potential increase in total medical costs that a reimbursement system might entail. A ten percent extra-billing charge by all doctors, for example, could add up to $2,000,000 to the total cost paid by Saskatchewan residents. Nonetheless, it appeared to be a price that would have to be paid for a principle about to be abandoned. And so the concession was offered on April 4. The Government had now accepted the system which the College had explained to the Royal Commission it would use as a defensive strategy if the Government persisted with its medical care insurance plan.

One week later, the College replied. It rejected outright the Government's concessions: "The minor amendments do not fundamentally change the legislation.... this Act is completely unacceptable to the profession."[121] As an alternative the College offered as "*the final concession which we can make*" a proposal through which insurance would be universally available through existing or new prepayment plans; that a registration board would function (through the provincial auditor) as an approval body; that government would pay the premiums for indigents; that all other insured persons would be subsidized by the government; that, in addition, each approved agency would determine and charge the premiums it required; that patients would pay their accounts directly to their doctors and would receive a refund of a major portion (unstated) of the expense incurred, but no additional charges would be made to indigents.[122]

The gulf between the two positions had greatly widened, for while the Government's proposals now incorporated even more completely the CMA principles,[123] the plan proposed by the College as an alternative was, if anything, more unattractive than anything previously proposed; in fact it was a highly retrograde step from the prepayment plans currently operating. It was administratively cumbersome. It left the total bill for medical care wholly uncontrollable. The amounts to be paid by the patient would be unknown since the proposal stated only that the patient would be reimbursed a "major portion" of the expenses incurred. What was "a major portion?" At the same time, there was no control on premiums to be charged by the approved agencies nor on amounts of co-insurance they might impose.

When the council returned to meet with the Government on April 10, having spent the entire weekend reworking its proposal, it was evident that the Government had made up its mind that further negotiations on "non-negotiable" issues would be fruitless. Mimeographed press releases had been prepared, and the meeting with the council was peremptorily ended after the premier had read his statement to the members.

The council was angry over its treatment, particularly over the refusal even to discuss the results of the weekend's work, and the arbitrary way in which the meeting had been terminated. It was the low point of trust in the Government and the high point of frustration and anger to that date.[124]

The Government rejected the alternative for seven stated reasons:

1. that it required the repudiation of the commission; 2. that the Government would have no part in determining the total amount the people would pay; 3. that it would leave to the private agencies the full right to set premiums, co-insurance charges, or extra-billing; 4. that no government operating agency would be permitted; 5. that there was no indication whether the Swift Current Plan would continue; 6. that indigents would be identified and dealt with in a special way; 7. that permitting a large number of private plans strikes at the root of the insurance principle based on substantially the whole population.[125]

The statement concluded, "It is the intention of the Government to proceed to introduce a medical care insurance plan designed to meet the needs of our citizens."

Stage three had seen the commission ignored, the Government forced to postpone the "appointed day," and the refusal of the College to cooperate in any way with the administration of the act despite the major concession and the other commitments.

For the Government, it was the point of no return. Either it capitulated or it put on a bold front, prepared for the launching, and hoped for the best. It chose the second course; high as the political costs might be, they appeared less than the costs of capitulating. That would be to admit that in a contest between a public and a private government, the public government could lose. With its convictions as to its mandate as a duly elected majority government, and that it was acting in accordance with the rules of democratic, responsible government, this was to think of the unthinkable.

But at the same time, to even contemplate that the profession might withdraw services—that they might strike—that, too, was to think of the unthinkable, and so the Government did not think about it.[126] As the premier said in the Legislature on April 11: "It is the Government's belief that doctors will carry on treating their patients and accepting remuneration on the same basis as they have been doing for years in Government-sponsored plans such as treatment for cancer. This, we believe, will give the plan an opportunity to prove that it will not affect their professional freedom nor lower the standard of their service. On the contrary, we believe it will give doctors an opportunity of a type they have never had to beneficially influence the practice of medicine in Saskatchewan."[127]

Stage four began, from the point of view of the Government, in an emotional state of intense frustration, born of a new conviction, as Badgley and Wolfe comment, "that the medical profession and its supporters are prepared to do everything in their power to subvert the law. It [the Government] then acted unwisely, angrily, and against many of its own advisers."[128]

With the mounting distrust on both sides, the Government was concerned that the reimbursement method it had offered the College would result in a great deal of "extra-billing" and that patients would find themselves only partly insured. The commission's authority in such situations appeared to be unclear in the act. Accordingly, on April 12, the Government introduced minor amendments to clarify certain sections and added to the act a new provision similar to a clause in both MSI (Saskatoon) and GMS contracts, granting the commission authority to act as an agent for insured persons in respect of payment for services.[129]

The intensity of the reaction of the profession and the press was totally unexpected. "Peacetime conscription," "abrogation of civil rights," were charged.[130] The premier's explanation that the provision also appeared in the Saskatoon Medical Services contract and was already implicit in the act had little effect. Nor did his charge that editorial interpretations were "inflammatory distortion."[131] The mood of the profession ensured a suspicious and hostile attitude towards any change not clearly a major concession. The amendments were passed by the Legislature with the Liberal party opposed.[132]

The commission accepted that there would be no dialogue with the profession but there were certain formalities that had to be observed. Accordingly, on April 21, the chairman wrote to the president of the College, Dr. Dalgleish, informing him that the administrative organization was now established, procedures were being finalized, and drafting of regulations was nearing completion. He then outlined the proposed payment policies, modelled on those of the physicians' prepayment plans *with the additional option of the physician billing the patient.*[133] He proposed that the commission and the College meet on May 7.[134] The council of the College did not deign to reply.

On May 24, the chairman of the commission wrote to the registrar to consult the College, in compliance with the act, on the approved lists of physicians and of specialists to be paid in accordance with the respective general practitioner and specialist fee schedules.[135] The response of the registrar in his letter on June 1 was, apparently, uncooperative, and the chairman replied, referring to the registrar's legal responsibilities to provide such lists.[136]

Meanwhile, as the commission geared itself for the July 1 launching, the scene shifted once again to the political level. One week after its short meeting with Cabinet on April 12, the College announced that a two-day meeting of all doctors would be held in Regina on May 3 and 4. The premier requested, and was granted, an opportunity to address the meeting, which was attended by two-thirds of the province's physicians.

The mood of the meeting was almost unanimously defiant, and the self-confidence of the profession was greatly reinforced by a critically significant event, the defection from the Government ranks and the CCF party of the former minister of health, Mr. Walter Erb.[137] The announcement came after a stirring and passionate address by the vice-president of the College, Dr. E. W. Barootes, and immediately before the introduction of the premier. Its effect was electrifying; the citadel was beginning to crumble.

Few spokesmen have ever confronted a more unreceptive audience as this former school superintendent, now government leader, addressed the profession. His speech was a low-key review of events to that date, an elaboration of the program, and a firm declaration by the Government to administer the plan in such a way as not to interfere with the doctors' professional freedom. He ended with an appeal to their rational judgement, hoping that a calm, unemotional assessment would conclude that the program, as proposed, would meet the objectives of both profession and public: "My appeal is to what has been termed 'the ancient wisdom of your profession.' We seek not to change the ends of medicine. We do seek to find ways and means to adapt the financing of medicare to 20th century society and the legitimate expectations of that society. In this, the 'ancient mission' need not be lost. Its achievement can be advanced. I invite you to join in a bold attempt to consolidate past gains and to move towards new horizons in the field of medical care."[138]

Rational goals, courageously expressed, could neither legitimize the Government's actions in the doctors' minds nor abate in any way the rising confidence of the profession that in solidarity it would triumph. A near unanimous standing vote was the response to the president's question as to who would oppose the medicare plan and refuse to act under it.[139]

As the College leaders now reappraised the impasse, there appeared to be four options open to it.

1. To accept the act and practise medicine as the commission dictated, which would gradually erode away the freedom of practice and would ultimately result in low-quality medical care.

2. To test the legislation in the courts, but legal advisers said there was little chance of success.

3. To leave the province for more favourable areas where one could practise with freedom and peace of mind, but many doctors were reluctant to do this as they were well established in practice and had their families to consider.

4. To protest to the Government by withdrawing normal medical services. This seemed to be the only road left open if the doctors were not going to succumb to the act.[140]

The fourth was decided to be the only tenable course, and the meeting passed resolutions instructing the council to make plans for the establishment of an emergency service in selected hospitals on July 1 when all doctors' offices would be closed. The two parties were now on a collision course.

STRATEGY V

It was now time for the Government to think realistically about the heretofore unthinkable—a doctors' strike. The commission, on the other hand, had not only begun to think about it but had also begun preparations. It had already made plans for recruiting doctors from other countries. On May 4, the second day of the doctors' mass meeting, advertisements appeared in British newspapers, and Dr. Sam Wolfe, member of the commission, flew to London to begin interviewing candidates for vacant rural practices and to ascertain the possibilities of temporary recruitment in the event of withdrawal of services.[141] By June 17, arrangements had been made for an airlift, and a news-item carried by Reuter's reported that a dozen British doctors were willing to go, without regard to the merits of the issue, but feeling "that a strike can only bring discredit to the whole profession."[142]

Meanwhile a newly organized pressure group—the Keep Our Doctors Committees (KODC's)—was generating enormous volumes of publicity.[143] These committees had started when a group of four women in Regina had been warned by their physicians that they would not be treated after July 1 if they were members of the Government's plan, and therefore decided to act. The movement spread to other centres and quickly recruited "opposition politicians, druggists, dentists, conservative businessmen, the medical profession, and everyone with a grievance against the government."[144] On May 30, a cavalcade of approximately 900 people in 400 automobiles converged on Regina to meet the premier with petitions containing 46,000 names. The premier met with 100 of them and urged them to work through their local MLA's. This was interpreted as a snubbing of what they considered their legitimate right of access to Government and added to both their hostility and their renewed efforts.[145]

The most significant effect of the KODC's was that they provided a means by which Liberal, and some Conservative and Social Credit party members could coalesce on a single issue as they could not normally do. Their press releases were constant sources of news and were given generous space in most of the newspapers of the province.

A strike of doctors? In Canada? Impossible! As indicated earlier, that had been the Government's view. It had been unthinkable; now the prospect was real. What were its resources to meet the crisis, and what others might be called upon, or created? What actions must be taken?

1. There were approximately 110 physicians employed in full time health services (e.g. regional medical health officers, staffs of the mental hospitals) or in administrative positions. Some of these might be seconded to hospitals not included in the emergency service.

2. Fortunately, there was the Air Ambulance Service, perhaps the most valued public service ever introduced by the Government. It would need to be augmented by private aircraft. The necessary directives were given. The service could readily transport patients, if necessary, to hospitals in neighbouring provinces or states.

3. The profession would need to be warned of its legal responsibilities to patients which, as Professor Tollefson emphasizes, are clear: "When a doctor has accepted a patient who requires the continual services of a physician, the doctor cannot, without the patient's consent, withdraw his services unless the patient has a reasonable opportunity to obtain suitable alternative services."[146]

4. Doctors were leaving. Others would have to be found. The recruiting campaign had already begun and would need to be accelerated.

5. Back-to-work legislation. This option was never seriously considered. Apparently, the idea surfaced that the Government might ask the federal government to invoke civil defence legislation to force the doctors to provide service after July 1. On June 7, Health Minister Davies said the Government had given "no serious consideration" to this possibility. "The feeling all along is that we don't want to threaten or talk about compelling legislation, we want to discuss and reach an agreement."[147]

Of all these, the recruiting of physicians from outside the province on a temporary basis would be, if successful, the most effective means of alleviating the emergency situation. Indeed, with the actual and announced departures of doctors, the publicity given to the offers of sale of large medical clinics in both Regina and Saskatoon, and the advertisements of doctors' homes for sale, the recruiters would also have to seek candidates for permanent positions.

But as the preparations for crisis continued and the opposition protests mounted, the Government was dealt another serious blow by what became virtually an externally imposed referendum on the legislation—the federal election on June 18, 1962. Wrote Pat O'Dwyer in the *Ottawa Journal*: "Saskatchewan voters, aroused to a frenzy due to fear of losing their doctors, will use the federal franchise as a virtual referendum in the provincial medicare crisis."[148]

It became especially significant because Tommy Douglas, the new NDP leader, had chosen to run in Regina, a seat the Progressive Conservatives had captured in 1958 with a 2–1 majority and 24,400 votes.

If the profession had made medicare the central issue in the 1960 provincial election, it was Douglas who made it the issue in the federal election in 1962. The opposition parties in Saskatchewan responded in full force, with several Liberal and Progressive Conservative constituency organizations deciding not to run two candidates in order to consolidate the anti-NDP forces.

For Woodrow Lloyd and his CCF government, the timing of the federal election could not have been more damaging. These were the Diefenbaker years in the West. In 1958, Conservatives won forty-seven of forty-eight seats in the prairie provinces; in 1962 they retained forty-two of them while losing eighty-two seats nationwide. It might therefore be argued that the Diefenbaker sweep in Saskatchewan would have occurred in any event (owing largely to Agriculture Minister Hamilton's foreign wheat sales) and that the medicare issue was irrelevant. But that was not the interpretation in the press. It was not Diefenbaker's victory; it was medicare's defeat. And what made it so crystal clear was that Tommy Douglas, the new leader of the NDP and father of medicare, was defeated in the capital city where he had so long governed as premier.[149]

Even David Lewis, secretary of the new party, and just elected, blamed the medicare battle for Douglas's defeat,[150] and a *Toronto Star* editorial, "A Blow Against Medical Plan," accepted that "Douglas had been beaten by mothers fearful . . . of a denial of medical attention for their children."[151]

Premier Lloyd did his best to deflect the damage. "As far as the medicare plan goes," he commented, "the results of a federal election can in no way be significant."[152]

The jubilation of the Canadian Medical Association, with its leaders assembled in Winnipeg at their annual meeting, was matched only by that of the publishers and editors of the Saskatchewan press. In his presidential address on June 17, Dr. Gerald Halpenny stated that in the medical insurance impasse in Saskatchewan, "patients, the doctor, and the profession would all suffer. I can only hope, that the unscrupulous politicians will also suffer very severely for their reckless gambling with the welfare of the citizens whom they claim to represent." The legislation, he said, made the commission "the sole provider of medical services. Our colleagues in Saskatchewan have received the unanimous support of every provincial Division across Canada . . . and . . . [we] are ready to come to their aid, if assistance should prove necessary."[153]

While this impassioned call to arms was delivered for the dual purpose of influencing public opinion and reinforcing professional solidarity, the behind-the-scenes discussions of the profession's position by the CMA executive members were far more calm and deliberate. Dr. Dalgleish presented a comprehensive and politically sensitive assessment of the situation:

> This government . . . is so dedicated and firmly committed to the rigid course they have adopted that they would probably be willing to sacrifice the future of their own political party, the reputation of the medical profession and the quality of future medical care in Saskatchewan. . . . It is inevitable that some of the forces engaged in this dispute will have to give way in the very near future, and it is not likely that either faction will achieve a clean-cut victory.
>
> As yet, however, there has been no indication that the Saskatchewan government is willing to consider any significant, acceptable changes in their existing legislation, to which they appear to be more firmly committed. *Over the past two and a half years, the public in that province seems to have accepted and approved of the fact that they will be provided with some form of plan for comprehensive, all-inclusive medical care insurance.* None of the groups that have advocated delay, mediation and discussion of the disputed features of the Saskatchewan Medical Care Insurance Act have given any indication that this legislation should be completely withdrawn.[154]

Despite this sobering review, or perhaps because of it, it was not surprising that the Saskatchewan division had the support of the CMA. The members of the Saskatchewan division were now, by the turn of fate, the shock troops fighting the battle for the entire profession. As the *Toronto Globe and Mail* observed: "The battle being waged is merely the opening round in a war over government medical insurance which may spread to the entire continent."[155] Elsewhere there appeared little opposition to, and in some provinces even strong indications of support for, the CMA subsidization policy. Only in Saskatchewan was there actual legislation that would effectively wind up the operations of the profession-sponsored prepayment plans. The Saskatchewan government was being confronted not only by the Saskatchewan doctors, but by a profession united nation-wide. To the new uncertainties about the actual extent of the Government's wavering support there was added the certainty of the profession's determination and of its apparently growing strength.

With burgeoning confidence stimulated by the reinforcing effects of a large conclave and the exhilarating results of the election, the profession took the offensive. Dr. Halpenny sent a telegram[156] calling for "immediate discussions" between the Saskatchewan profession and the Government (a meeting sought by the Government for a month and already being arranged through the good offices of the Saskatchewan Hospital Association).[157]

Dr. Dalgleish reiterated the appeal for a meeting, saying that "the onus is on the government and it is the responsibility of the government to have discussions with the profession in a plan acceptable to all of us."[158] Now with victory clearly in sight, it was time for the final confrontation with an obviously discredited and weakened government.

Senior officers of the Saskatchewan Hospital Association, alarmed at the prospects of the closing of all hospitals except emergency centres, and encouraged to do so in an earlier letter from the premier, had begun to act in the role of mediator, meeting first with the Government on June 11. On June 19, the day after the federal election, the executive of the Hospital Association again met with the premier and other ministers and officials for a three-hour review of the situation and a canvassing of alternative courses of action. These discussions (and others) culminated in arrangements for a meeting between the council of the College and the Cabinet on June 22.[159]

The decision to meet was widely approved by the press. The *Saskatoon Star Phoenix*, for example, which had been strongly anti-government to this point, emphasized in a long editorial on June 22 the need for compromise and good will, adding that "Implementation of the Act should have been delayed until discussions could have resumed. This is a mark against the government. . . . The doctors on their part, now that the Act has been passed by the Legislature, cannot expect an unequivocal repeal of the legislation."

The editorial then referred to Premier Lloyd's offer to develop health care on a regional basis: "Here may be the answer. . . . after all, the Swift Current doctors found it satisfactory and so did the public—over a 15 year period. . . . The government has shown a willingness to depart from its original rigid conception of a medical care plan. The college now has a similar opportunity to resolve all the difficulties."

With the hopes and fears of so many riding on the outcomes, the meeting began in an atmosphere sated with tension. Both parties were aware of the high stakes and the potentially tragic consequences of their decisions. Despite the basic mutual distrust, the discussion was frank, serious, and polite. There was clear recognition that time was running out, that the image of a profession and the credibility of a Government, as well as the kind, and the availability, of a program of health services, lay in the balance.[160]

The Government remained firm in its conviction that with its major concession permitting doctors to practise outside the act on a reimbursement basis it had effectively drawn the teeth from the charge that the act was civil conscription. It was equally convinced that the College's multi-carrier proposal precluded any possibility of achieving the advantages of a universal program which could become an integral part of a genuine health services system. Convinced of the rightness of its policy and its legitimacy as the representative government of the people, it was nonetheless fully aware of the adamant stand of nearly the total profession, the mounting opposition engendered by the KODC's and the hostile press, and the damage to its apparent strength by the federal election results. On the other hand, major organizations representing labour, farmers, teachers, and churches, together with individual letters numbering in the thousands,[161] provided moral and political support just when it was most needed. The Government was obviously beleaguered; but its objectives were clear, its strategy perhaps lacking in balance and its past tactics not always productive, but its continuing, though less vocal support (when weighed against the stridency of the voices of those opposed), sharpened its resolve to see the commitment through. It was now or never.

The College council, for its part, was highly confident. The KODC's had generated public support far in excess of expectations, the routing of every CCF-NDP Saskatchewan candidate in the federal election only a week before—including T. C. Douglas, the instigator of medicare—all on top of the defection of the former minister of health, had provided ample evidence that many people were changing their minds, that the Government was, indeed, on the ropes, and that a united profession having two major weapons at hand—the exodus threat, and a withdrawal of services—could achieve the accommodation it sought. The primary objective was to preserve the prepayment plans intact; some degree of government intervention and regulation might be tolerated as a short-run sacrifice but with the demise of an already tottering government, the plans could then be unshackled and assume again their proper role in the more congenial environment of a friendly government. They must be preserved, no matter what the cost. The meeting, therefore, was a confrontation of two groups of men, each convinced of the legitimacy of its role, the rightness of its goals, and of its power to achieve them.

The Government presented a lengthy memorandum[162] summarizing the concessions it had made or was now willing to make. They included the changes desired by the College to ensure protection of professional freedom; a reiteration of the earlier proposal of the right of physicians to practise outside the plan, and willingness to discuss regional administration along the lines already negotiated and concluded with the Swift Current health region. The memorandum ended with a proposal for a mediator as had been suggested by the Hospital Association.

The College responded with the case for its multi-carrier approach, as proposed originally in its submission to the Thompson Committee and modified by the Barootes revision of April 4.

The premier, buttressing his position with quotations from the Thompson Committee, replied that the Government could not accept that concept under any circumstances. He then referred to the great distance the Government had gone in accepting the reimbursement principle proposed in the College brief which meant that every doctor had the option to— and therefore any or all could—practise outside the act.

The council responded that this principle would split the profession— those within and those outside the act—and this was also completely unacceptable. The profession wanted an act it could endorse (as it had its own prepayment plans); therefore the present act and the commission must go; "as a very minimum" the appointed day must be postponed until at least September by which time an act could be devised with which the College could agree.[163] The reply to this was that delay was futile; obviously the College would come up with the same position, and the same issues would remain.

Two other ideas were explored. The first was a total reimbursement plan rather than one that offered doctors an option of dealing directly with the commission. The Government rejected this, saying that each doctor should have that option, and of course wanting to have as large a proportion of the population as possible insured under the service plan arrangements. The other was the case for regionalization. It is difficult to assess how seriously this was pressed. The Government, it will be recalled, believed ideologically in the regional concept but had finally rejected it on both financial and administrative grounds. The profession had rejected the regional concept since it had been first proposed in 1945. But now the regional concept might serve as a basis for a different solution. If the Swift Current health region (as a public "body corporate") could be designated an "agent" of the Medical Care Insurance Commission (MCIC), then why not other corporations (such as MSI (Saskatoon))? The Government's response was that the region could not meet the CMA's principle no. 11 that "any board, commission or agency set up to administer any medical insurance program" must have "fiscal authority or autonomy." Since the program was to be financed by provincial taxes, only the Government had fiscal authority and autonomy.

The premier then proposed that the council take immediately to its College members a three-point Government commitment:

1. To provide through regulation for any doctor to practise outside the act, with the suggestion that the council advise all members to remain outside until they were individually satisfied. (The health minister added that since the Government preferred the service-type plan, it would do everything it could to make practice under the act attractive.)

2. To meet regularly with the council representatives to consider any other changes; and

3. A written commitment to "enshrine" in the act all agreed-upon changes. Given that the act would not apply to physicians who did not want it to apply to them, it was, the premier stressed, an offer based on principles the profession could accept with dignity.

At this point it appeared that a break-through might be reached. The president of the College, Dr. Dalgleish, said that he could take this proposal to his Health Services Committee this week; if (only) the Government had made this proposal at the May 3 meeting the doctors would not have had to beg for postponement.[164] But the possibility vanished as another spokesman immediately declared that this act would not be bought by the doctors, that the proposal offered no encouragement at all for the doctors to change their minds.

There was then a short break during which the parties obviously re-examined the course of the discussions, and replanned their strategy. On resumption of the meeting, President Dalgleish restated the profession's position that it was the act that stood in the way. Would the Government not give more consideration to the College's multi-carrier proposals?

The premier replied that the College's position had not changed, that it was incompatible with the Government's position but, as for changes in the present act, he would be prepared to go over them clause by clause. He then went on to restate the earlier offer, emphasizing again that the act would not apply to any physician who did not want it to.

After fruitless restatements by both sides, the meeting adjourned for dinner.

On the council's return at 8:15, the president made a statement that the Government had today presented the council with much more material to be studied, notably on reimbursement.[165] Yet the Government had asked the profession to accept these changes without legislative assurances that this method was possible. All that the profession could say was that the proposal would be accepted for further study.

The meeting ended at 10:35 and the Cabinet turned its attention to tho nature of the press release. With a withdrawal of services about to begin, the people must know why their government had acted as it did. The council members were obviously deeply involved in a similar exercise.

On Monday, the College presented for the first time a statement of its detailed criticisms of the act.[166] All the major issues had already been raised but two new criticisms were presented: the size of the advisory council and the provision for a medical advisory council, the latter being held to be unnecessary in a medical *insurance* plan.

On Tuesday, the premier forwarded his commentary on the College's objections.[167] The reply was conciliatory, and restated the Government's willingness to make the necessary changes. The commentary concluded with a long paragraph emphasizing the functioning and merits of the reimbursement plan. A copy of the memorandum was dispatched to every physician in the province.

As the hours ticked on, frantic efforts were made by other groups to induce the parties to continue negotiations, the Saskatchewan Hospital Association being joined by the leaders of the urban and rural municipal associations'. But the position of both sides remained fixed. At 12:01 a.m., July 1, 1962, the withdrawal of services began.

The news editor of CFQC-TV, William Cameron, described the tension in Saskatchewan in late June:

> The plains of Saskatchewan bring forth men and women who learn early what it is to know struggle and discomfort. By her very nature, Saskatchewan must produce a combative people. Controversy is as natural to them as their fierce love of the forbidding wilderness which they have tamed. But never has there been a greater controversy than this. All over Saskatchewan, her sons are taking sides as never before. And, like the cloud of an oncoming Saskatchewan dust storm, and with equal power to strike fear into Saskatchewan hearts, there looms ever larger the date that all Saskatchewan dreads—July 1.[168]

Stage five of the strategy of implementation had been characterized by extraordinary attempts by the Government to dissuade the profession from withdrawing services. It had made a major concession that compromised seriously its service-plan ideal. It had publicly committed itself to legislative changes that would enable any doctor to practise outside the act; it had changed the regulations and committed itself to incorporate those changes in the legislation. But these had not been enough, for while doctors could, indeed, practise as "privately" as they had done before any system of prepayment (but now with assurance of payment of all accounts), the coming into force of the act would mean the abandonment of the profession-sponsored prepayment plans.

It meant the relinquishing of a major part of the territorial domain of the College's private government. If the plans were completely dismantled, there would be no hope of their revival under a friendly public government. This was a prospect not to be accepted, and so the ultimate weapons—the permanent exodus of some, and the withdrawal of services of most, physicians—were brought into action.

Stage five of the Government's strategy to implement its program had failed. The issue now was, as Premier Lloyd had said earlier, "whether the people of Saskatchewan shall be governed by a democratically elected legislature, or by a small, highly organized group."[169]

STRATEGY VI

The question of whether the defeat was permanent or temporary now clearly hung in the balance, the outcome dependent on which side emerged the stronger in what most observers saw as a "contest of wills." Both parties recognized the critical and determining role of public opinion and expanded their publicity campaigns to generate support. Both held daily press conferences for a corps of newspaper, radio, and television reporters that each day increased as more "foreign" correspondents arrived on the scene.

But how was public opinion to be judged? How were support and opposition to be weighed? For there were many "publics" and there were all shades of opinions. As the long weekend came to a close, the editorial pronouncements flashed across the wires and were amplified by radio and television. The national press of Canada, as might be expected, divided along three lines: those who were critical of the Government, those critical of the profession, and those who pronounced "a plague on both your houses."

The *Ottawa Citizen* (July 3) was critical not only of the doctors' strike action but of "their attempting to throw all possible obstacles in the way of an eventual solution" by their insistence that "there can be no further negotiations until this unjust and monopolistic act is withdrawn." The *Citizen* saw the national CMA as responsible and called on it to give leadership in the public interest.

The *Montreal Star* (July 3) viewed the College as setting up "a state within a state, making its own laws and ignoring those of the state itself."

The Montreal *Le Devoir* (July 3) blamed the profession: "It is the medical profession that refuses to negotiate. It demands that the law be repealed. What government could obey a similar "diktat" without giving up as a government? What the doctors of Saskatchewan win from the legislature—if they win—they will pay for dearly in prestige and moral authority."

The *Toronto Globe and Mail* (July 4) declared: "The doctors of Saskatchewan have taken an action which is not open to any individual or any group within a democracy. They have deliberately decided to disobey a law of that Province, a law duly enacted by a duly elected Government of the people.... Such action cannot be condoned in a law-abiding community."

The *Toronto Daily Star*, long known for its pro-health insurance stand, was, as expected, highly critical of the profession, and most concerned for the long-term effect on health insurance legislation. The *Star* (July 6) summed up its views in these words:

> It is this principle of government insurance against the costs of illness that the Saskatchewan College of Physicians and Surgeons is really fighting.... It is clear, however, that they are prepared to use ruthless methods to get their way. Nothing in the history of the roughest trade unions rivals this attempt, by a respected professional society, to use the sick and injured as hostages in a political battle.
>
> If the college wins its fight by these unfair means, the cause of adequate health insurance in North America may be set back by as much as a decade. That is why reactionaries, in and out of the medical profession, are rallying to the support of the striking doctors—including many who normally oppose all strikes.
>
> This makes it all the more essential that the public in Canada and the United States should understand the real issue in the struggle.

The *Kingston Whig-Standard* (July 6), also favourable to health insurance, saw the problem in the monolithic organization of the profession: "It would probably be a salutary thing if the individual doctors began standing on their own feet for a change and shook off the dictatorship of their professional associations. Few doctors, in Saskatchewan or anywhere else, would dare stand up and say what they really thought about any professional problem unless their words had been approved in advance by their association."

But there were other eastern newspapers critical of the Government. The *Halifax Chronicle-Herald* (July 4), for example, stated: "The refusal of the majority of Saskatchewan's doctors to practise under the Medical Care Insurance act is understandable.

To our knowledge, no other class of citizens in Canada today is required, as are doctors by this statute, to work exclusively for the state under terms and conditions laid down by the state."

This view was echoed by the *Quebec Chronicle-Telegraph* (July 4): "The doctors of Saskatchewan are fighting a battle of vital importance to the freedom of every Canadian. For what is really at stake here are all the personal rights that have been won for us gradually through the years."

The *Toronto Telegram* (July 4) also saw it as an issue of control of the profession: "If the new Saskatchewan law were concerned only with medical insurance, that is, how the patient pays and how the doctor receives payment, there would be room for negotiation.... But the [Premier] Lloyd scheme of Medicare in Saskatchewan goes far beyond this. It removes from the medical profession the control of the doctors and transfers it to the government."

Also, in the East, there were newspapers critical of both. *The Ottawa Journal* (July 4), was one example: "All the arguments from the government as well as the profession, the mutual shifting of responsibility, do not change this fact: both the government and the doctors have failed the people whom they are dedicated to serve."

Closer to home, in the neighbouring western provinces, the editorial comment was similar.

The *Vancouver Province* (July 4) was the most restrained, recognizing the very complex moral struggle in Saskatchewan:

It is easy to take sides in the Saskatchewan Medicare argument; it is not so easy to be certain that it is completely the right side....

We have come to expect medical attention—immediate attention if we need it badly—as an inalienable right of a member of a civilized society. We find it difficult—if not impossible—to condone the idea of what is being called, perhaps unfairly, a medical "strike."....

On the other hand there is the widespread recognition that the doctors, as members of what we call a free society, have their rights to defend.

Only one thing in the Saskatchewan dispute seems beyond argument: This is no way to start a medical care plan. Other governments please note.

The *Winnipeg Free Press* (July 4) laid the responsibility for the impasse on the profession: "The Saskatchewan government appeared to be ready to go a considerable way toward meeting the stated objections of the doctors toward the plan. The Doctors' refusal to move from their previously held position can only lead to a widespread loss of public confidence in the sincerity of their stated motives."

The *Lethbridge Herald* (July 4), on the other hand, placed major responsibility on the Government: "The doctors of Saskatchewan have a responsibility to the people. But so does Premier Lloyd, and his is even greater. He should acknowledge it and suspend the plan. There would be no disgrace in doing so, and he would reveal himself a greater man than if he pursues his present course."

Most of the other leading papers, however, while condemning the legislation, placed the blame on both parties.

The *Victoria Colonist* (July 4): "One reads with distaste and dismay in fact that doctors are on strike. One had never thought that at any pinch members of the medical profession would withhold the humanitarian gift that is laid solemnly in their hands. Equal blame for this distressing situation must be placed on the Saskatchewan government. It had at least a month's warning of what would happen when its medicare plan came into effect."

The *Calgary Herald* (July 5): "Regardless of the complex and tangled series of events that led to its being called, the Saskatchewan doctors' strike can mean nothing but suffering for the people of the province, shock for other Canadians, and frustration in the fight against state medicine.

It is true that the government has used brute legislative force to adopt a program that can only, in the end, indenture a highly respected profession to government service.

It is true that the plan will ultimately lower medical standards, and tragically, it is true that the plan was not needed in the first place. Saskatchewan's cases of social inequity in terms of medical care could have been solved by much gentler government action.

But that time has passed and the plan is law and in effect.

Whether the doctor likes it or not, he has been placed on a pedestal by his fellow beings. For the doctor to step down now and use the people who enshrined him as pawns in a bigger game, is to run the risk of winning lasting public enmity. . . .

This strike must end, and the doctors must end it."

Interestingly, there was more emphasis in the West on the proper channels of protest: recourse to the courts.

The *Winnipeg Tribune* (July 4): "Saskatchewan doctors have begun to challenge the province's medicare scheme in the courts.

This is the proper and democratic course for doctors to pursue. . . .

The Saskatchewan doctors' strike has muddied the situation by raising two additional basic issues; first, should any group in the community defy a law because members of the group do not agree with it; second, if the community has to step in and restrain the use of the strike weapon by police, firemen, utility workers and railwaymen for the common good, is not care of the sick an equally essential service?

. . . The courts and the ballot box are the effective means of securing redress for grievances in a democratic society. Victory gained outside these traditional means could prove short-lived and costly."

On balance, Canadian press opinion outside Saskatchewan was decidedly against the College's position, most taking the view that the legislation, whether good or bad, was, nevertheless, law and must be obeyed. The alternative, if open to the medical profession, was open to all, and that road led to anarchy.

What of the foreign press?

In general, the major British dailies were critical of the profession:

The Observer (July 6): " ... the medical situation in Saskatchewan is more than a [doctors'] strike, it is a mutiny."

The Daily Mail (July 4): " ... when doctors strike and neglect patients, the voice of humanity protests. That this could happen in Britain is so inconceivable that we regard Saskatchewan with astonishment and sadness."

In the United States, the issue was more relevant, for the United States Senate was in the process of debating (and defeating) President Kennedy's medicare program for the aged.

The Washington Post (July 19) was the most critical of the profession:

Whatever the merits of Saskatchewan's new medical care act, the strike staged by doctors throughout the Province is indefensible.

... a strike by doctors is a betrayal of their profession. It reduces medicine to the level of a business. Worse, it desecrates the Hippocratic Oath which consecrates doctors to use their art for the benefit of the sick. ... In every sense of the word, this strike is bad medicine.

One other source of opinion obviously carried great weight with both parties—outstanding physicians and important medical journals.

Dr. James Howard Means of the Harvard Medical School wrote a much publicized letter to Premier Lloyd in which he stated, "I think the behaviour of the striking doctors is reprehensible."[170] Dr. Richard Ford, professor of legal medicine at Harvard, long known as an opponent of socialized medicine, also stated: "It is my opinion that no doctor has the right to strike in the present crisis in Saskatchewan."[171] And Dr. Albert Sabin, discoverer of the oral polio vaccine, categorized the strike as "contrary to everything the practice of medicine stands for."[172]

Lancet, an independent medical journal, which had initially refused to carry the advertisements for the commission, on July 9 reversed that decision and commented editorially: "Withdrawal organized for political ends is, we think, wrong. ... [The doctors' action] is an alien procedure, out of keeping with the character of any profession, and especially that of medicine."

There were, of course, far more statements by other medical leaders supporting the Saskatchewan College stand.

But those were the assessments of the national and international press, and however much encouragement the Government was inclined to take from them, the paramount point was that, in the main, these did not reach Saskatchewan voters. At home, where press opinion would have its major impact on government's supporters and detractors— and the independents in between—the reaction was universally critical of the Government.

The *Moose Jaw Times-Herald* (July 3) was typical. July 1 was "The Day that Freedom Died in Saskatchewan." The overriding issue was:

How far does the good of the community require the limitation of the rights of the individual and the community?

This is the vital question that points like a dagger at the heart of every citizen of this province, and to reveal to them what it means when a democracy is transformed by act of a government into a dictatorship. All over the world individual freedoms are seen to be in jeopardy. The people of Saskatchewan have lived in the happy thought that it could not happen to them, but it has. . . .

Truly it was a sorry day Sunday, July 1st, 1962. A day that will be marked with a black blotch on the calendar as the day when freedom died.

The *Yorkton Enterprise* was one of the most vociferous in its defence of the College's position:

It [the medicare act] is not designed for the good of the people as a whole! If the government honestly seeks to provide medical care services for all people why did it summarily discard all suggestions made to the Thompson commission which did not measure up to its own totalitarian ideas?

If the doctors were to go ahead and accept the so-called concessions offered by the government without those concessions being made law by the Legislature they would then be denying their generations of service and beliefs. They would put themselves and generations yet to come right under the control of a government that worships power above people.

These [doctors] are not men who have a "callous disregard for the welfare of the people," but are men whose every waking hour is dedicated to this welfare. This action of the doctors in providing medical emergency service and refusing normal service is not a vindictive thing—it is an action taken with great reluctance in an effort to protect the people from even greater inroads on their freedom at some future date.

If the doctors lose their freedom to practice then we can anticipate the government's infringing on the rights of all other professional and business groups as they find it expedient. This is why the doctors are asking the government to repeal this iniquitous act, to forget political implications and seriously consider the welfare of the people.

The *Regina Leader Post* and the *Saskatoon Star-Phoenix* (the province's two largest dailies, both owned by the Sifton Press) were, of course, the most influential. Both papers were opposed to the compulsory aspects of the program:

The *Regina Leader Post* (July 4): " ... There is not the slightest doubt but that the central issue in this whole dispute has been compulsion. ... There was no remotest justification for this government—which was returned to power on a minority vote—to try to enforce its will in this arbitrary way."

Saskatoon Star-Phoenix (July 4): "Compulsion or coercion of Saskatchewan's doctors remains and should be removed."

On the national and international scene the doctors had clearly been placed in a dilemma. By using the device of withdrawal of services—termed, almost everywhere, a strike—they had made that action, rather than the act itself, the central issue. And, because they had refused to accept the concessions, including the right to practise outside the act, it was they who appeared the more obdurate. At home, however, where the issues were seen in more personalized terms, as CCF politicians against Liberals, as socialist philosophy versus free enterprise, as government coercion forcing the exodus of doctors, the Government could only hope that the more favourable external views might have some impact.

As the press conferences of the two parties continued their daily pattern, the conflicting interpretations of Saskatchewan reporters and the "foreign" reporters became more apparent. On July 9, one reporter, Don McGillvray, reported that "there is a growing complaint among doctors that the outside press is treating their case unsympathetically" and that on Saturday the Regina Chamber of Commerce held a cocktail party for reporters which "turned out to be a press conference at which members of the Chamber explained the doctors' actions."[173] He then noted that Government supporters had the opposite feeling, that the local press wasn't giving them a fair show and had been buying space in local newspapers to reprint articles written from Saskatchewan by outside papers.

As the crisis continued, Saskatchewan newspaper editorials took the offensive. A *Weyburn Review* (July 12) editorial was typical: "Perhaps the medicare legislation looks less ferocious to people who are not ruled by a government dedicated to the destruction of our economic system. . . . Some of the comments from afar, however, display a remarkable ignorance of what is happening in Saskatchewan."

The sixth stage in the strategy of implementation began, as we have noted, with the Government's having to manage its side of a strike situation. No provincial government in Canada had ever faced such a crisis in peacetime, with fear almost universal, and with the lives of some citizens obviously in jeopardy. Moreover, if deaths attributable to the situation did occur, no one could be certain where the blame would be laid. The highest objective was to get back to the negotiating table, but the immediate task was to ensure that no citizen suffered unduly. This meant more active recruiting for the emergency, a hard decision, invoking as it would, all the emotional overtones of "strike-breaking"—anathema to a Government now associated with the labour movement of Canada. But this was no ordinary strike against the public interest; human lives were involved, and every means must be taken to protect them.

The Commissioners were relieved to find, however, that outside Saskatchewan, the "strike breaker" fear was, for the most part, irrelevant, as editorials and even some medical spokesmen, as we have seen, condemned the act of disobedience of the law. By June 24, the recruiting drive in England had reached the point of signing contracts with physicians and arranging their air-lift to Saskatchewan. A number arrived even before the July 1 deadline.

At the beginning, 240 doctors staffed the emergency service in thirty-four hospitals, about thirty-five others were estimated to be cooperating with the plan, while still others continued to practise for ethical reasons. An estimated 250 went, as usual, on holidays. It was this group that posed the never-to-be answered question: If the plan had gone into effect on April 1, how many of these might have continued in practice as a matter of conscience rather than on July 1 going as usual on vacation? That number could never be known, but whatever it was, it was one of the high costs of that postponement decision.

The second task was to renew the enthusiasm of supporters and respond positively to the increasingly vociferous and demanding outcries of the KOD committees. Their success or failure in mobilizing opposition could well determine the outcome.

The KODC's held rallies at various points in the province and planned as their climactic event a mammoth rally on the Legislature grounds in Regina on July 11. The premier spoke out on July 9, counselling against mass meetings "that cannot contribute to a solution of the problem," but the plans went forward with advertisements in the press, and co-operation by dentists, pharmacists, and merchants whose places of business were closed so that employees, clients, and customers could attend.

On July 11, the automobiles began to pour in. The leaders carried a petition (that had appeared the day before in full-page newspaper advertisements) declaring that "no ruler in a free society may coerce a minority group of citizens . . . nor discriminate against them in their profession . . . the Government alone is responsible . . . we protest the dictatorial provisions of the Act . . . and . . . paid mercenaries from abroad."

But it proved to be anti-climactic. Instead of the forty to fifty thousand forecast by KODC leaders, only four to five thousand appeared.[174] The tide of pro-doctor opinion had begun to ebb. It was, as Badgley and Wolfe said, the "beginning of the end."[175]

The recruiting of doctors from Britain, other parts of Canada, and even from the USA, accelerated, reaching a total of 110.[176] The number of hospitals providing emergency services increased by twenty-five, and some doctors, mainly in the rural areas, were returning. The 200 physicians providing the emergency services in the original thirty-four hospitals were gradually becoming exhausted, and on July 20, College spokesmen said that the emergency service physicians had declined to 190. Obviously, for those on duty, there were limits to their physical capacity, no matter how highly motivated they might be.

The stalemate was complete, but in the first week of the summer holiday season, communications began that were to provide the key to an unlocking of the impasse. Mr. Don McPherson, a Regina lawyer, had been campaign manager of the Regina Progressive Conservative candidate, Ken More, who had defeated T.C. Douglas on June 18. He now felt that it was time for some behind-the-scenes negotiations. He called the Hon. Mr. Blakeney, the provincial treasurer, and explained his proposal to contact a key member of the College council. If he returned with proposals or conditions, could he reach the minister immediately by phone and would these then be immediately transmitted to the Cabinet? Positive assurances were given. He then invited Dr. J. F. C. Anderson to his summer cottage, and there over several days he reviewed in the light of his own legal experience the provisions of the act and the (amended) regulations and proposals of the Government.[177]

During their discussions, telephone calls (from a telephone a mile away) were made by McPherson to Blakeney and Anderson to the College. The fundamental issue was, from the College's point of view, the retention of the prepayment plans, MSI (Saskatoon) and GMS, and finally there emerged as a possible compromise solution (a suggestion already made to and dismissed by the Government), that insured persons be entitled to assign their "payment rights" to the approved prepayment plan of their choice, that is, the commission would transmit its payments to designated prepayment plans which would pay the doctor. It would be a major concession by the College for it meant that the plans would no longer have (with respect to medical services) the right to raise revenue through premiums and obviously a "private government" without "fiscal authority and autonomy" (the CMA's phrase) would be as devoid of power as a public government without independent authority to levy taxes. On the other hand, it would represent a major gain for those doctors unalterably opposed to having any contact whatever with the Government or its commission. On the Government's part the cost was equally great for by perpetuating a fragmented payment system it precluded the development of a unified and integrated health delivery system, including the further development of the regional concept. At the same time, it would go a long way towards achieving a major government objective: providing for the great majority of the people the advantages of the "service type" plan.

Other strategies were discussed by the two men, of course, but the most significant effect of McPherson's intervention was that a possible compromise proposal was now being discussed at the highest levels. The drama now needed only the presence of a new catalyst for a resolution of the conflict.

The Cabinet Strategy Committee weighed alternative strategies and tactics with respect to the Macpherson compromise as well as other proposals.

Their conclusion was that they should select an "informal negotiator" who would be authorized to discuss matters with McPherson and Robertson (the College's solicitor), but who would *not* be authorized to speak *for* the Government. If these informal negotiations resulted in a plan that was mutually agreeable, a mediator could be chosen who "miraculously" would come up with a proposal that was mutually acceptable.

The alternative to this course of action would be a decision to stand firm and reject the McPherson overtures. This would require a careful calculation of the Government's ability to provide adequate medical services (over and above the emergency services) for what could be a relatively prolonged period. This, it seemed to the committee, would be essential to the maintenance of adequate public support for a "stand-firm" position.[178] Their analysis was then taken to the full Cabinet. One of the committee's scenarios had called for a miracle worker. It would be yet another week before he would appear on the scene.

On July 4, Premier Lloyd had left on a secret mission to Toronto and Montreal to discuss strategy with national New Democratic Party leaders, including the constitutional expert, Dr. Frank Scott of McGill Faculty of Law. He was also in touch with Lord Taylor, a medical doctor who had assisted in the launching of the British National Health Service and been granted a lifetime peerage by the Labour government. He had visited Saskatchewan in 1946 just as the Hospital Services Plan was being developed, and so had some knowledge of the province and of the CCF government's health policies.

He had been contacted in early June by Graham Spry, agent-general for Saskatchewan in London, and a friend since the war years when both had worked for an organization known as PEP—Political and Economic Planning—which developed a large number of policy position papers for the U.K. government during and immediately after the war.[179] Spry had forwarded to Lord Taylor a copy of Premier Lloyd's speech to the Saskatchewan doctors, which he did not read. A few days later Spry brought with him to the House of Lords, Dr. Sam Wolfe, then in London to recruit doctors. They discussed a copy of the MCI Act and Taylor immediately reacted unfavourably to Clause 49 (1) g which, as he said, "could be interpreted as giving the MCIC the power to direct doctors in the way they should do their work." He wrote to Premier Lloyd to express this view and, as well, expressed the same objections in a letter to *Lancet*, the British medical journal.[180] A few days later he advised Dr. Wolfe to advertise in the major daily papers since the official medical journals would not publish his advertisements.

On July 4, Lord Taylor received the letter from Premier Lloyd asking him to come to Saskatchewan to help. He agreed, on condition that the Government pay his expenses, pay him no fee, but provide a week's fishing at the conclusion of his visit.

It was not for twelve days, however, until July 16, that he was able to leave England. In the meantime, there had been a press conference with Canadian reporters in which he endeavoured "to build up a picture of myself which would prove acceptable to the doctors of Saskatchewan, ... that although I was being invited by the Government, my interest was in fair play all around." Mindful of the communications network among doctors around the world, he also made sure that the doctors in Britain were reasonably favourable to his going. Conversations with the editor of *Lancet* and the secretary of the British Medical Association led to the necessary endorsements. A cablegram to Dr. Arthur Kelly, general secretary of the CMA, elicited the reply that he hoped to see Taylor in Saskatoon. So far, so good.

His first contact in Canada was Mr. George Cadbury, at the Toronto Airport. Cadbury had been chairman of the Saskatchewan Government Economic Advisory and Planning Board, and he readily filled him in on a broad range of issues, emphasizing the Government's objectives. Taylor made it clear in this exchange that he was convinced that "professional men seem to need the stimulus of self-employment if they are to do their best work;" that "lay control is not acceptable unless there is no alternative;" and that "I suspected that co-operative consumer-controlled medical clinics were not generally compatible with the highest standards of medical practice." Since the community clinics then being developed in Saskatchewan were very much in the news, his reaction was that he would have to persuade the Saskatchewan government not to impose them by law and also to convince the doctors that it was safe to permit such clinics to exist.

It is useful to summarize some of Taylor's key observations as he analyzed the situation following his first conversations with the Government, and the profession with whom he established immediate relations.

On the Government's proposal: "The plan itself was a good one; it was based on the principles of universal prepayment for medical care, universal coverage, fee-for-service payment, and a single Commission to administer."

On Government strategy: "Unfortunately the bill introducing the scheme was not properly discussed with the profession and was thrust through the Legislature in a hurry because of the impending move of Mr. Douglas from provincial to federal politics."

On the doctors: "The Government had built up a remarkably fine hospital service. At first the doctors had been reluctant participants; but soon they were co-operating to the full and they themselves had created two voluntary insurance schemes ... the doctors were willing to see these medically-administered schemes extended. What they objected to was a universal scheme which would abolish their independent schemes and provide them with only a single pay-master. It was this belief—that they were to be forcibly enrolled as Civil Servants—rather than any real anxiety about finance which caused them to refuse to co-operate."

On the Government objectives: "The Government on the other hand, was sincere in its determination to ensure that the people of the province should all receive the best possible medical care, without financial burden at the time of illness and without any taint of charity."

After meeting with the doctors on the emergency service in the Regina General Hospital, he said, "As I had expected, they differed in no respect from other good doctors anywhere else in the English-speaking world. They were obviously fine men but they were puzzled and worried about what had hit them. They knew little of politics and had no love of politicians. They knew that professional freedom was essential, if they were to do their work properly. They believed it was in danger, but they could not say precisely where the danger lay."

"The American Medical Association was at this time hysterically opposed to Medicare; and it endeavoured, not without some success, to communicate its hysteria to the doctors and the public in Saskatchewan. ... I think it would be fair to say that, despite its good will, the Government was quite ignorant of the pattern of thought of the ordinary medical practitioner. Its members could not conceive of people who did not believe in collective action, who ·were resolutely opposed to public control, and who believed that even the most benign of civil services would all too soon turn into a dangerous tyranny."

Having talked with both sides in the controversy in Regina, on Tuesday evening he travelled to Saskatoon.

There were other important developments on that Tuesday. One was the beginning of hearings on an application for an injunction against the Medical Care Insurance Commission, launched by the vice-president of the KODC and Dr. L. M. Brand of Saskatoon.[181] A second was the announcement that Dr. J. F. C. Anderson, chairman of the Council's Steering Committee and former president of the CMA, was flying to the U.K. to make an appeal on behalf of Saskatchewan doctors at the annual meeting of the British Medical Association.[182] The third was the announcement of the appointment of Mr. Justice Harold Thompson, a retired judge, as a one-man royal commission to investigate complaints of discrimination in the granting of hospital privileges to newly-arrived doctors.[183] The Government had previously announced its appointment of Harold Hansen of St. Paul, Minnesota, a lawyer of international reputation and general counsel for the Association of Co-operative Medical Plans in the United States, to advise the Government and to aid the royal commissioner.[184]

There were other arrivals. The "Sub-Committee on Saskatchewan" of the executive of the Canadian Medical Association had met on the weekend in Ottawa, and both the president, Dr. William Wigle, and the general secretary, Dr. Arthur Kelly, arrived in Saskatoon with senior officers of the association to assist their confreres.[185]

That same evening, two other groups also wrestled with aspects of the issue. The first was composed of delegates from a number of the mushrooming community health clinics—now estimated at between thirty and forty—being organized and four in actual operation, meeting in Saskatoon to form the Saskatchewan Council for Community Health Services.[186] The second group, however, was even more important—

the delegates to the annual CCF Convention, who were even then debating resolutions supporting the medicare plan and recommending the curtailment of the licensing powers of the College of Physicians and Surgeons.[187]

The coincidence that the CCF Annual Convention was scheduled for Saskatoon in the third week of July 1962 was a fortunate stroke of fate for it meant that the Cabinet would be in the same city as the council of the College. Both groups had been in almost constant session since the first of the month, but now they would be only three blocks apart. If there were to be communications at all, and there had to be, the opportunities were obviously greatly enhanced. But the coincidence provided even more: an opportunity for the CCF-NDP to act as host to a spokesman for the College—a kind of reciprocal hospitality, as it were, for Premier Lloyd's address to the doctors. The initiative had come from the College by telegram and had been agreed to. Dr. Dalgleish had been selected as spokesman. The substance of his address had already been passed to the Government in a letter of July 14 which, added to the proposals informally received, suggested a slight easing from the July 1 position. It proposed: 1. that operation of the Medical Care Act be suspended for a limited and specified period of time. 2. during that period, discussion and negotiations between the Government and the College would continue. 3. if agreement were reached on amendments to the Act, satisfactory to both parties, the amendments to be enacted at a Special Session of the Legislature.[183]

Premier Lloyd replied on July 17 stating that "the only new feature we are able to detect is that you would like the Act suspended for a *limited and specified time* rather than for an *indefinite period*. In considering this we asked ourselves the rather obvious question, 'What would happen if no agreement were reached at the end of the specified time period?' An obvious next move could be for the College to request an end of the time period . . . . there is really no new feature."[189] He then repeated that doctors could practise outside the act now, that some were doing so, and that for them, and any others who chose to do so, the act was already suspended. "The Government is concerned that your members have not accepted the fact that they are free to practise privately."[190]

Following this written exchange, both Premier Lloyd and Dr. Dalgleish addressed the convention on Wednesday.

Premier Lloyd's speech dealt solely with the medical care plan. As a new party leader he had been engrossed in a political battle more serious than that ever faced by a provincial premier until eight years later when the new Bourassa government of Quebec confronted a similar situation He was now reporting on his stewardship to the party supporters, cogni zant from the numerous resolutions submitted that there were many who were critical of the extent of concessions already made.

320

He rejected suspension of the act, or the calling of an election, raised the issue of the use of its power by the College, emphasized that the issue was not the Medical Care Act alone, but "the democratic process." He ventured that "there are those who are concerned not that the medical care insurance plan will not work but that it will work too well . . . they realize that satisfaction is contagious, that Canadian public opinion is on the move in this direction and areas beyond are watching carefully the Saskatchewan scene."[191]

He reasserted, as expected, the right of doctors to practise outside the act, and that a return to normal services could be accompanied by a special session of the Legislature.

It set the background for the speech by Dr. Dalgleish in the afternoon session. He made the three proposals set forth in the July 14 letter. He emphasized that "it is still the College's belief that the best way to achieve a solution . . . is to suspend the Act and have doctors resume normal service . . . but the College has decided to shift its stand in an attempt to settle the issue."[192]

But in elaborating on this proposal, it was stressed that amendments would have to include: 1. A doctor who chooses may practise outside the Act without any provisions of the Act applying to him; 2. Medical services provided outside the Act could not be insured services under the Act; 3. A beneficiary be allowed to assign to any agency his right to payment from MCIC; 4. The Commission would not differentiate between services for which a refund was requested and services for which direct payment was made to a doctor; 5. Private agencies would be recognized as collectors of the amount of premium levied by the Commission.

At the conclusion of his address which was politely, if not enthusiastically, received, Dr. Dalgleish returned to the Medical Arts Building where he and the other members of council received their distinguished guest, Lord Taylor.

Dr. Kelly's description, written almost immediately after the event, of how Lord Taylor ingratiated himself is instructive not only on the attainment of agreement in this case but for all would-be mediators:[193] "The consensus of professional opinion was cool if not adverse to this relatively unknown government adviser and it must be admitted at this time and in the climate of Saskatchewan any friend of government would be suspect."

After some other remarks, Kelly goes on:

Although the guest could not be classified as a mediator, he immediately began to act as one. He told the Council what he had learned in his brief stay in Saskatchewan and very skillfully dissected the essentials of Dr. Dalgleish's speech [which he had just heard]. He said that as a doctor he was in favour of the new proposals which established the useful function of the prepaid plans and that he would endeavour to convince the Premier and the Cabinet of their merits. As a politician he doubted that government would agree to the plans acting as tax collectors and advised the Council not to press the point. By sheer force of an attractive and aggressive personality he rapidly reached the stage where Council was agreeing to his transmission of the doctors' case to Government and after two hours of discussion he departed to do just that.

The following day he reported back that after a good deal of argument he had persuaded the Cabinet to accept the concept that the medically sponsored prepaid plans could continue to function under the Medical Care Insurance Act.

"This," says Dr. Kelly, "I regard as a triumph of diplomacy because I was not at all optimistic that the Government would concede anything in this area."

Lord Taylor thus appeared to agree on the fundamental contention of the profession that the prepayment plans must remain in operation, and on which the Government would have to compromise. This, of course, was part of the solution proposed earlier by McPherson, and which the Cabinet Strategy Committee had already analyzed. Taylor does not say whether he had been informed of these earlier proposals. But he does say, at this point: "To jump ahead for a moment. The following morning the Government agreed to this proposal [to retain a payment role for the plans], and from then on a very different atmosphere began to prevail."[194]

Lord Taylor, not having been appointed a mediator, with two strikes against him since he was a socialist politician and had come at the invitation of the Government, and only one positive credential, that he was also a practising medical doctor, began gradually to be trusted by a majority of the council. He thus assumed the role of an intermediary, striding back and forth along the three short blocks between the two hostile forces, the one encamped in the Bessborough Hotel and the other in the Medical Arts Building, the latter still up for sale.

Recognizing that the doctors "were ready at the drop of a hat to put the worst possible interpretation on anything which the Government might say," he "quickly decided that since the doctors and the Government were, in effect, speaking different languages, it was vital for them not to meet. If they did there were bound to be misunderstandings and, at once, the fighting would start all over again. So I had to keep them apart at all costs, until final agreement had been reached."

And this he did, labouring indefatigably for five days, reporting, explaining, interpreting, persuading, cajoling, even threatening to leave, weaving through all of it large measures of wit, humour, and histrionics.

By Friday, he had prepared a draft of an agreement, and this became the basis for detailed negotiations. Assisting him were five officials: Tim Lee, secretary of the Cabinet, Tommy Shoyama, chairman of the Economic Advisory and Planning Board, Don Tansley, chairman of MCIC, A. W. Johnson, deputy provincial treasurer, and R. G. Ellis, legal counsel for the Health Department. This draft was then discussed and finally approved by Cabinet.

He then took it to the College council where line by line it was discussed, debated, and changes proposed, with the College solicitor, Mr. Robertson, having the same difficulties in getting explicit instructions. Back again to the Bessborough to review the new demands and get precise counter proposals and rewording. As Taylor makes clear, it was slow going.

By Saturday night, it appeared hopeless and Taylor prepared to depart, but was persuaded by Dr. Dalgleish to stay. By Sunday night he felt they were ready to sign, but advised them to sleep on it over-night. Early Monday morning he was informed that they were ready, and the agreement was formally signed. Taylor tried to obtain more drama for the event by having a public ceremony but "they [the doctors] had the feeling that they were making concessions in signing the agreement at all, and some of them retained considerable doubts in their minds. To sign the document in public was more than they could stomach."[195]

And so, on July 23, after twenty-three days of a withdrawal of services, and eight days of intensive negotiations, the Saskatoon Agreement was signed, and the Saskatchewan Medical Care Insurance program—in greatly modified form—became an accomplished fact. As befitting an agreement concluded between two hostile governments, both Lord Taylor in his reminiscent article, and Dr. Arthur Kelly in his, refer to the agreement as "a treaty."

But as is well known, a more accurate term would have been "a cease-fire."

It is unnecessary here to present a detailed analysis of the agreement. That has been brilliantly done from a legal point of view by Tollefson and from the mediator's point of view by Taylor. The purpose here is to examine the effect of the accepted compromises on the Government's policy objectives. It will be useful, however, to summarize the main points, bearing in mind that, as Taylor observes, "the objective was to find a way of combining publicly supported universal coverage with the true essentials of professional freedom." It is a long document because Lord Taylor had two objectives: (1) to be as certain as humanly possible that there would be no misunderstanding and (2) to convince the supporters on both sides that neither set of negotiators had "sold out."

There was one major concession by each party that enabled the rest to follow. The council accepted the Government's position that the medicare plan must be universal and compulsory and that the Government would be the sole collector of revenues and the disburser of payments (i.e., responsible for the function of assessing medical accounts); the Government accepted the College's position that the voluntary prepayment plans be retained as billing and payment conduits for those doctors who did not wish to deal directly with the commission. The "agency" concept included the two profession-sponsored plans, the Saskatoon Mutual Plan, and Health Region no. 1 (and such other regional plans as might be established).

As Taylor says, they were to act as a barrier between the Government and the individual doctor, ensuring that he did not have a single paymaster with overtones of becoming a civil servant.

These arrangements thus provided four ways in which a doctor could choose to practise and, accordingly, four choices for the patient:

1. The doctor may choose direct payments from the commission which he accepts as payment in full. These payments may be fee-for-service, salary, or a combination.

2. The doctor may practise partly or entirely in association with one or more of the voluntary agencies. For such of his patients who are enrolled with such agencies, he will submit bills at the agreed upon rate (eighty-five percent of the minimum fee schedule). The agency will transmit the account to the commission which will pay the agency which, in turn, will pay the doctor, who will accept the payment as payment in full.

3. The doctor may practise partly, largely, or entirely outside any voluntary agency and not be enrolled for direct payment by the commission. He will bill patients entirely at his own discretion. He is required to submit an itemized bill to the patient containing the information normally given to a voluntary agency. In this case the patient must claim reimbursement from the commission and pay any difference between the doctor's fee and eighty-five percent of the minimum schedule.

4. The doctor may choose to practise entirely for private fees, provided that his patients also agreed to seek no reimbursement. The patient must agree in advance and no itemized statement is required.

The existence and possible further development of community health services associations was accepted. It was recognized that there might be places where few or no doctors were enrolled for direct payment by the commission. The remedy was in the hands of citizens themselves, with advice, if desired, from the commission, but the citizens' role must be restricted to that of landlord.

In furtherance of this hands-off-role, it was also agreed that the legislation would provide that the Government had no intention of establishing a full-time salaried government medical service.

The Swift Current regional plan would continue, but the Government felt that the time was not yet ripe to reach decisions with respect to the role of regional boards in other health regions. Any further decisions on their role would be taken only after consultation with the regional boards and with the College but should other regional boards become approved agencies, such developments would not prejudice the activities of existing agencies within such regions.

The commission was limited to the function of reimbursing patients, paying directly doctors enrolled with it, and paying to voluntary agencies bills submitted on behalf of their subscribers. The commission was not intended to administer a provincial medical service. All sections of the act relating to maintenance and improvement of quality of care were removed.

The Medical Care Commission was expanded by adding three medical members, one a general practitioner, one a specialist, and one a representative of university medicine.

In the event of disagreement in negotiations over the fee schedule, provision was to be made for mediation and binding arbitration.[196]

The Government agreed that the commission would cease recruiting doctors except for those needed in under-doctored areas.

With the signing of the Agreement, the withdrawal of services officially came to an end. Doctors manning the emergency services returned to their respective practices; many others returned from their normal July vacations; others did not return at all; most of the hospitals re-established normal operation; and the Government began preparations for a special one-day session of the Legislature to incorporate the terms of the agreement in the Medical Care Insurance Act.

But the peaceful convalescence that Lord Taylor had prescribed was too much to expect, for the trauma had been too serious, the emotional wounds too deep, the dislocations too severe, the compromises too galling, the loss of trust too great, for any speedy reconciliation and recovery to occur. Continuing, deep-seated suspicion clouded every action or statement by either party.

A total of sixty-eight doctors had left the province, some of them highly qualified specialists. Many of the British doctors on temporary contracts remained, a handful of them now without assignments. Despite the appointment of a royal commission to examine charges of discrimination in granting hospital privileges, similar new charges continued to be made.[197]

The growing threat to the established profession was the developing community clinic movement. By the end of July it was reported that clinics had been established in five centres, final arrangements were being made in ten more, and fifteen other associations were being organized, almost all to be staffed with recently recruited British doctors.[198] Their development ensured a continuation of bitter division in the ranks of physicians, and among citizens and neighbours in the communities involved, as well as a firm conviction in the College that they were government inspired.

For almost a year the dispute over the method of paying radiologists and pathologists festered as an open sore and not until June 5, 1963 did the Government concede that, at an additional cost of one-half million dollars annually (in lost federal revenues), it would have to accede to these specialists' demands.

To the strategists of the Liberal, Conservative, and Social Credit parties, it was apparent that the CCF administration had run its course. After nearly two decades in office, with only one change in leadership, and only minor changes in Cabinet membership, it was obvious that, quite apart from medicare, the accumulation of political debits now exceeded credits. As the three parties planned their strategies and deployed their resources for the 1964 election, informal agreements were made not to run candidates in every constituency in order to consolidate the opposition votes. Although several constituency results were challenged because of the slim majorities, and the CCF-NDP retained the same percentage of votes it had received in 1960, the Liberals under Ross Thatcher won a majority of the seats on election day, April 22, 1964, and a new Government took over.

Six weeks later, the Royal Commission on Health Services, appointed by a Conservative government at the behest of the Canadian Medical Association three years earlier, issued Volume I of its Report. The commission rejected outright the subsidy method so strongly fought for by the profession, and unanimously endorsed a plan fundamentally the same as the original Saskatchewan government proposals. But it was obviously small comfort to those who had gone down to defeat. Legislative monuments to the past are not particularly attractive alternatives to the exercise of government responsibilities.

The entire battle had been a tragic episode, polarizing the society in a manner never before, and not again to be, experienced by any Canadian province until the autumn of 1970 in Quebec. As an editorial in the *Canadian Medical Association Journal*[199] stated on July 28, 1962: "Those who are unfamiliar with the detailed history of events surrounding the encounters between the Saskatchewan doctors and their government can have no adequate understanding of the deep and powerful undercurrents of distrust and suspicion that bear on all relations between these two opposing forces."

Although the agreement had been signed, with major concessions on both sides, it was manifest that the College had not really accepted even the drastically modified medicare act, and that the Government was unhappy with the structure resulting from the compromises it had made.

On the day following the agreement, the *Toronto Telegram*, which had consistently supported the College editorially, reported in an article headlined "MDs Won't Drop Guard" that "the CMA made it plain it is not giving up its fight against socialized medicare ... and served notice that the profession hopes for the defeat of the CCF-NDP government. 'The whole thing might be changed in the next election,' said Dr. Glenn Sawyer, general secretary of the Ontario Medical Association."

The *Edmonton Journal*, also critical of the Government, reported the same day: "Doctors Claim Medical Pact Retreat Only." "The battle may be over," it continued, "but the war is still on. Although it is difficult to assess just who won the medical care dispute, one thing is certain: Saskatchewan doctors have not dropped their opposition to the government-sponsored plan. The doctors say they have made a strategic retreat. They are going to continue fighting Premier Woodrow Lloyd's medical care plan. They may even wreck it."

In March 1963, a statement of policy was issued in the *Saskatchewan Medical Quarterly*: "We must be cognizant, of course, of the fact that we must live with the Medical Care Insurance Act for the time being."[200] Clearly, the hope was that with the decline in fortunes of the NDP, a new Liberal government would be formed which would restore the prepayment plans to their former roles and enable them to insure the total population through subsidies of those with low incomes.

OUTCOMES[201]

What were the outcomes of a policy to which a commitment had first been made in 1944 and which had required eighteen years to bring to fruition?

1. There was established, for the first time in any province or state in North America, a universal, tax-supported medical care insurance plan administered by public authority.

327

2. For the people of Saskatchewan the economic barrier to medical services and the fear of financially crippling medical bills had been banished. Also eliminated were the commercial insurance concepts of deductibles, non-insurable conditions, limitations with respect to age, employment, or membership in groups, and experience rating—all the devices that protect insurance funds but frequently at the expense of individual hardship.

3. The new program retained, as one option, the physician-controlled plans as agencies for the transmitting of doctors' accounts and doctors' payments and granted them authority to act as insuring agencies for a variety of supplementary benefits. By accepting this role for the prepayment plans, the Government had relinquished any possibility of developing a regionalized system of health services as had been envisioned since 1945. Thus, although the profession had lost its near-monopoly control of the medical care prepayment system, the agreement had frozen the status quo in the profession-preferred mold.

4. The CCF party of Saskatchewan had achieved one of the major objectives to which it had been committed since its inception. But it did so at a cost of polarizing Saskatchewan society to a greater extent than did any of its other social policies. Although it is impossible to ascribe political defeat to any single cause, it seems reasonable to assume that this polarization served as a catalyst in uniting the opposition forces sufficiently to defeat the Government in 1964 and prevent its return until 1971. Despite its defeat of the CCF, the new Liberal government accepted the medicare program and did not, as many expected, and the College of Physicians and Surgeons had hoped, restore the prepayment plans to their former roles.[202]

5. The fact that such a program was in being, and therefore proved feasible—even though achieved at high political cost—was to have an important influence on the then-sitting Royal Commission on Health Services. The commission's recommendations gave medical care insurance the highest priority for action by the Canadian government and proposed a program parallel to national hospital insurance and similar to the Saskatchewan program.

6. The Saskatchewan decision moved the subject of health insurance forward on the political agenda of the federal government and all the provinces. Three provincial governments—British Columbia, Alberta, and Ontario—almost immediately introduced medicare plans that conformed to the proposals of the medical profession and the insurance industry.

7. For the first time in Canada there had been an organized withdrawal of services (most observers called it a strike) of the most essential service group in society for a political rather than an economic objective. As a host of observers asked, What did this mean for the democratic process? If the most prestigious elite group in society could, with impunity, flout the law, what did the law mean? And how many other organized groups providing essential services would follow suit?

8. The private government of the profession had lost its revenue system. That had been expropriated by the Government. From now on fee levels and percentage of fee payments would have to be negotiated with the Government rather than with the profession's own prepayment plans. Nor could such issues as co-insurance be unilaterally determined by the profession. It is impossible, of course, to guess what physician incomes in Saskatchewan might have been if the Government plan had not been introduced. But, with the plan, the increases were dramatic, with an increase of thirty-five percent in 1963 over 1960 (1961 and 1962 were atypical) bringing Saskatchewan doctors to first place among all the provinces, and $3,400 above the Canadian average.[203]

9. One unexpected by-product of the withdrawal of services was the community clinic movement. It gained substantial support in a number of communities, was moderately successful in a few, caused major dissension in most of these, and, over time, began to wane. By 1974 only two clinics, cast in the original mould, continued to function successfully.

10. The immediate effect on medical manpower was very serious; a net loss of sixty-eight doctors was reported in the first seven months of 1962. By the end of 1963, 260 physicians who had been in practice in 1961 were no longer in Saskatchewan. This contrasted with an average pre-1960 experience of ninety-two registrants annually and sixty removals from the register through retirement, death, or departure from the province.[204]

On the other hand, by June 1963, the number of physicians had increased to the level of January, eighteen months earlier, and by June 1964, had increased by another sixty-two, bringing the physician-population ratio to its highest-ever level.[205]

11. The preference of the physicians in Saskatchewan not to deal directly with the commission and the reluctance of potential patients to run the risk of being "extra-billed" through the reimbursement method led to an extraordinary increase in enrolment in the prepayment plans—from 290,000 in June 1962, to over 530,000 by the end of 1963. These "subscribers" thus were assured of the service-type benefit contract and of additional benefits insured by the plans.

12. In 1963, the proportion of doctors billing the commission directly was minimal, amounting to only 21.5 percent. By 1970, this proportion had increased to 51.5 percent, with the proportion channelled through the prepayment plans declining from sixty-eight percent to 40.5 percent.

13. For the Canadian organized profession as a whole, the Saskatchewan episode had created a serious breach in its Trans-Canada Medical Plans structure. One province was now gone, but that could be considered "a fluke of history" for it was the only province to have a socialist government. No serious threat appeared elsewhere. But it *had* happened and there were lessons to be learned. One of those who gave the matter serious consideration was Dr. William Wigle, the new CMA president. In an article in the *CMA Journal*, he wrote:

> The medical profession must be impressed with the fact that a large segment of the population want to prepay their medical care completely. It is also obvious that many people would have no objections to the funds being raised by taxation.
>
> We in the profession must face these issues and act in accordance with our beliefs. *The prepayment of medical care in all its phases—the collection of funds, administration and the payment for the services—must be more diligently studied and controlled by the profession or it will be done by someone else.*
>
> The details of how these ends may be achieved must be the immediate responsibility of the profession in Canada, and the programs must be developed, debated and adopted with determination and unity, within the next few months.[206]

It was a ringing call to the profession to reinforce the private governmental structure it had created to prevent any further breach in the system. And it made very clear its fear of, and determination to exclude, any other influence in the arrangements the profession controlled.

Chapter Six

The National Medicare Program:
Policymaking and Minority Government

AS THE FIRST SCENE of the next major act of the health insurance scenario opened on July 19, 1965, the audience might well have felt again a sense of *déjà vu*. There was the same setting: a committee room of the House of Commons; the scene: another federal-provincial conference; the leading roles: also the same, the prime minister and the ten provincial premiers. The time, however, was different—ten years since the conference that had produced the hospital insurance program, twenty years since the federal offer to the provinces in 1945. Moreover, the tolls of time, the vagaries of elections, and the caprice of politics had introduced a host of new actors into the cast. Lester Pearson had replaced Louis St. Laurent; Robarts had replaced Frost; Lesage had replaced Duplessis; Stanfield, Hicks; Fleming, Robichaud; Roblin, Campbell; Shaw, Matheson; and Thatcher, Douglas. Only three premiers had been present at the 1955 conference: Manning, Smallwood, and Bennett. What was especially significant was that six of those eight new actors reflected changes in the parties forming their respective governments.

But just before the action began, one could not help being intrigued by the timing of these great events. Why were great decisions about health services made every ten years? For decades, Canadian national politics had operated on a circadian rhythm timed to the traditional four-to-five-year election cycle. Crests of governmental activity peaked just before and just after elections and troughed at the half way point, providing a four-to-five-year period for attention to the Government's agenda. But since World War II a new factor has been introduced. Negotiations of the tax agreements, requiring a federal-provincial conference every five years, had disrupted that regularized ebb and flow of political pressure. Now, in addition to the normal confrontations with the opposition in the House, the Government must face external, organized demands twice in a lustrum. Louis St. Laurent, for example, had faced the electorate in 1949, the provinces in 1950, the electorate in 1953, the provinces in 1955, and the electorate again in 1957. The intervals between peaks of high pressure had been reduced by half. There was now no surcease in the process of meeting concentrated external pressures, for two rhythmic patterns were functioning, each on a different chronological wave length. To make matters worse, the appearance of minority governments had completely disrupted the traditional cycle of elections, so that even the fortuitous intersecting of the two wave-patterns in the St. Laurent period—elections and conferences alternating one to two years apart—was unlikely to recur. Ministers and senior officials seemed to plunge from an election to a federal-provincial conference or from a conference to an election. The good old days when government could count on four years to fulfill election commitments (or hope that the electorate would forget them) were now past. Not only had the tempo increased, but the cadence had been lost.

The conference just opening was no exception, for although it was only two years since the last election, rumours were rife that the days of the Pearson minority government were numbered. The outcomes of this meeting might well hasten its end.

The main theme of the conference had been signalled in the Throne Speech in April: "My Government will at an early date meet with the Governments of the Provinces in order to discuss with them ways in which federal and provincial action can most effectively contribute to programs that will provide health services to Canadians on a comprehensive basis."[1]

The prime minister, as is the custom, was the first to speak, and he quickly came to "the provision of health services ... the item of our agenda which is the most important of all."[2] He elaborated on the subject and ended by saying, "Accordingly, I repeat that it is now the responsibility of the federal government to cooperate with the provinces in making medicare financially possible for all Canadians. The government accepts that responsibility."[3]

The contrast between the position taken by Prime Minister Pearson and that by Louis St. Laurent could not have been greater. In the twenty-year period, 1945–1965, the Liberal government's policy on health services had turned full circle—from initiation to reluctant acquiescence to initiation. The decision for medicare had been made, a decision of enormous consequences, engaged in such high controversy that it made the battle for hospital insurance look like a contest between farm teams. Before analyzing why and how the decision was made, it is necessary to review briefly the environment in which it occurred.

THE BACKGROUND

It had been, without doubt, the most turbulent period in Canadian politics in a generation. The Progressive Conservatives under John Diefenbaker had assumed power as a minority government in 1957; they had then won in 1958 the largest majority ever enjoyed by a Canadian party, and had lost it to become again, briefly, a minority government that lasted from June 1962, to April 1963. The Liberals had come back to power—but they, too, lacked a majority, the results being Liberals, 129 (a gain of thirty); Conservatives, ninety-five (a loss of twenty-one, and down from 208 in 1958); New Democratic Party, seventeen (a loss of two); and Social Credit, twenty-four (a loss of six).

The minority government had now to confront a host of issues—defence policy on the acceptance of nuclear warheads being the most contentious and the deepening financial crisis the most serious—and begin action on the two major election promises of pensions and medicare.[4] There was, of course, some reason for optimism on the latter issues, for the NDP could be counted on to support both of these programs in principle. Their votes, combined with the Liberals, would outweigh the combination of Progressive Conservatives and Social Credit.

The main thrusts of these declarations of Liberal policy had been hammered out at a study conference on national problems, sponsored by the National Liberal Federation, at Queen's University in September 1960. There, documents on social security measures prepared by Maurice Lamontagne and Tom Kent had been heatedly debated and the issues focused. Shortly after, Mr. Walter Gordon became chairman of the policy committee set up to prepare for a national Liberal rally to be held in Ottawa in January 1961. There, among a great many other resolutions, that on health insurance was strongly endorsed, and emerged in the 1962 platform in these words: "[A Liberal government will] establish, in co-operation with the provinces, a medical care plan for all Canadians." The same wording was used in the platform of 1963.

The Progressive Conservative platform of 1963 made no reference to health insurance. After all, the party could claim credit for having appointed a royal commission to examine the entire issue of health services and it could stand pat until that body had reported. Nor did the Social Credit platform mention the issue. That party did seem, however, to be echoing the policy of the Canadian Medical Association and the insurance industry. Its last plank stated: "Creeping Socialism Will Be Halted: The

State will assume its rightful responsibility to provide adequately enough for those unable to provide for themselves."

The NDP, under Tommy Douglas, had made medicare its primary issue in the 1962 campaign, as we saw in chapter 5. Both the commitment and the emphasis were repeated in 1963, with the platform statement strongly rejecting the CMA subsidization policy.

What was unique in the new configuration of political forces was that the man who had been chairman of the Policy Committee, and then chairman of the Liberal Campaign Committee, was Mr. Walter Gordon. He and Mr. Keith Davey had been key members of the team revitalizing the Liberal party organization and forcing it to develop a coherent set of new policies that would, it was hoped, produce a majority Liberal government. Now, as minister of finance, he was the first to hold that office who genuinely believed in a national health insurance program. It was to make a difference.

The Liberal party and the NDP were not the only associations that had achieved consensus on the question of the future course of health insurance in Canada. The second group of inputs came from the Canadian Medical Association and its new comrade-in-arms, the insurance industry of Canada. As noted in preceding chapters, the role of the organized medical profession had become increasingly important. Its influence was powerful not simply because no medicare plan could work without its cooperation but because of the variety of ways in which its influence was exerted.[5] Doctors' views were expounded to patients, friends, journalists, and local members of Parliament; medical leaders had easy access to ministers of health (many of whom were medical doctors) and their deputies (most of whom were also M.D.'s), as well as to premiers and prime ministers. CMA policy statements were sent to all members of Parliament and all provincial legislators. As we shall see, by 1963 its policies were accepted by some provincial governments which were legislating them into law and arguing for them at federal-provincial conferences. But even more persuasive than all persuasion was demonstration: eleven profession-sponsored prepayment plans that incorporated the policies and principles to which the profession had become so firmly wedded.

In comparison with the American Medical Association, the attitudes of the CMA were remarkably enlightened. In 1943, the CMA had not only declared a policy favouring the principle of health insurance but had endorsed clause by clause a proposed bill to launch a national program. By 1949, in the vacuum created by the failure of governments to act on the 1945 proposals, the profession had sponsored a number of prepayment plans and their beginning success had prompted a change in that policy. The CMA still strongly supported health insurance for everyone, but the route should be one that limited the role of government to the subsidization of the premiums of those who could not afford to make their own payments to the voluntary agencies. That policy had been reaffirmed and strengthened by subsequent statements in 1955 and 1960. But the cataclysmic events in Saskatchewan—the re-election of the Douglas government in 1960 and its imminent passage of the Medical Care Insurance Act—seemed to demand that the CMA take some further action to forestall the possibility of government medical care insurance again becoming a political football at either the provincial or federal level. There must be some way of inserting into the decision-making process a larger element of calm, deliberate, and rational judgement, safe from the intervention of "politics." Accordingly, at the 1960 meeting of the CMA, the council, "taking account of the fact that all major Federal Political parties are interested in medical services insurance on a tax-supported basis," resolved: "That . . . the CMA Executive . . . approach the Federal Government to ask them to establish a committee to study the existing and projected health needs and health resources of Canada; and to study methods of ensuring the highest standard of health care for all citizens of Canada, bearing in mind the CMA Statement on Medical Services Insurance."[6]

The letter conveying the recommendation was forwarded to Prime Minister Diefenbaker on December 12, 1960, and on December 21, Mr. Diefenbaker responded by announcing that a royal commission would be appointed.[7] By his decision, the prime minister may well have assumed that he had removed the issue of health insurance from his active agenda for the next three years. In any event, he had enhanced the confidence of the CMA that the decisions on health insurance would be made rationally by an independent commission and not be distorted by the pulling and hauling of politics.

Meanwhile the CMA and its provincial divisions had pressed forward in the development of the prepayment plans, and the CMA, particularly, strongly supported the development of a national coordinating body, Trans-Canada Medical Plans (TCMP).[8]

In chapter 5 the concept of a "private government" as distinct from the public government of the province was used in analyzing the functions of the Saskatchewan College of Physicians and Surgeons. The concept is also useful here, for what the CMA was attempting to do was to persuade the provincial plans to enter into a "federal" relationship with a newly created organization having a national thrust. Indeed, as the records of early meetings reveal, the discussions were not unlike those of a federal-provincial conference as they attempted to reconcile national objectives with provincial realities. The first meeting to consider a national coordinating body was convened by the CMA in 1947 in Winnipeg with representatives of six plans attending. Four years of negotiations brought the announcement on June 18, 1951, by Dr. Norman Gosse, president of the

CMA, of the formation of Trans-Canada Medical Services (changed in 1955 to TCM Plans), with seven cooperating plans.[9]

The objective of those sponsoring TCMP was to limit its membership to plans sponsored and controlled by the respective provincial divisions of the CMA. But there was no physician-sponsored plan in Quebec and in the maritime provinces there were two organizations: Maritime Medical Care sponsored by the profession in Nova Scotia, and Maritime Blue Cross-Blue Shield which sold both hospital and medical care insurance, and was endorsed by the doctors in New Brunswick and Prince Edward Island. Finally, the CMA came to recognize the impossibility of achieving nation-wide coverage solely through plans its divisions controlled. The by-laws of TCMP were therefore amended in 1955 to state that "The Plan shall be sponsored, endorsed, approved or designated by a provincial medical association as a plan acceptable to its standards in such provinces." Both Quebec Blue Cross and Maritime Blue Cross became approved members under the expanded definition.

A national federation was now in being and there were nation-wide groups and others located in two or more provinces needing to be serviced. The railway workers, dependants of members of the armed services, and even the federal civil servants themselves, were in that category, and for whom TCMP would be competing with the commercial insurance companies. But TCMP was composed of plans that were not only provincially incorporated and thus limited to provincial boundaries but they were also "provincial" in their outlook, a result, no doubt, of their having been designed to meet local conditions, and having contractual relations with local doctors. There was, accordingly, as C. Howard Shillington (the former executive director of TCMP) reveals in his book, *The Road to Medicare*, "the continual fear of some plans that the national association would become the master rather than the servant of the plans."[10] Although the objective was to develop a national uniform contract, it was never possible to achieve that goal. All TCMP could offer was coverage through a dozen provincial plans with some differences in the benefits and the premiums. It could, however, assure portability of coverage for members of groups moving to another province. In the competition with the insurance companies for the three large groups mentioned above, TCMP was selected only by the railway workers and that contract almost broke up TCMP, as Ontario's Physicians Services Inc. refused to act as a provincial carrier.[11]

Nevertheless, enrolment in the voluntary plans continued to increase, as did the numbers insured through commercial insurance. By 1965 when the Pearson government was giving its most serious thought to a government plan, almost five million were insured in some degree under commercial insurance and over 5.6 million were covered under the profession-sponsored or -approved plans that were members of TCMP.

In 1959, the 118 companies selling health insurance benefits formed a national organization, paralleling that of TCMP, named the Canadian Health Insurance Association (CHIA). Mr. Shillington stated their objective as follows: "Taking a cue from the medically sponsored plans, it would seem that one of the first objectives of the new organization was to woo the doctors to a favorable attitude toward the pattern of insurance coverage which the industry followed, namely, indemnity, with, in most cases, patient participation (deductibles and coinsurance) and with no contractual relationship or obligation on the part of the doctor."[12]

Mr. Shillington assessed this strategy as follows: "If one might be permitted to guess that the industry gave careful consideration to its choice of methods to woo the doctors' support, it must be admitted that it chose well in seizing upon the spectre of possible government interference in the future of medical care insurance. Certainly no other weapon could have caught the attention of the average doctor faster than the fear of what might happen under government insurance."[13]

The next step the industry took was to bring the two organizations together. Although Mr. Shillington indicates that some of the TCMP plans were suspicious of the industry's motives, with urging by the CMA, TCMP joined the Canadian Health Insurance Association to form the Canadian Conference on Health Care in 1960.

At the first meeting of the new conference in 1961, the insurance industry spokesmen urged that the discussions concentrate on voluntary insurance as an alternative to a government plan.[14] As Mr. Shillington reports:

It was suggested that the members of the conference had a common purpose to make adequate health care available to all Canadians. A strong plea was made that government insurance was imminent, that it represented a giant monolith, and that doctors would be prisoners of such bureaucratic operation which would, thereafter, completely control the purse strings and dictate the terms of service. Related to this whole approach was the theme that the doctors' only protection lay in the retention of multiple insurance organizations in the health field and for this reason, every support should be given to the insurance companies who were fighting the profession's battle as much as were the sponsored plans.[15]

Thus, the profession was ideologically and politically joined with the insurance industry in its opposition to a government program while at the same time its sponsored prepayment plans were locked in strong competition with those same companies.

Events were moving in the direction that the Canadian Conference desired, owing in large measure to the expanding publicity given to the policy by the conference and its members. In specific terms, the role of government had been reduced to (1) paying the full costs of services for those in receipt of continuing welfare support, and (2) subsidizing those whose incomes fell below a threshold calculated on their taxable incomes (as verified by their income tax returns).

On the basis of surveys conducted in British Columbia and Alberta, the CMA estimated that those whose incomes were such as to require subsidy included three categories:

1. About twenty-five percent were indigent and needed full subsidy.

2. Those receiving incomes below the income tax threshold who already had insurance, estimated at twenty-five percent.

3. Approximately one-half of the non-taxable income earners who would require partial subsidy.

The CMA estimated that "at the maximum, approximately three million persons would qualify for consideration."[16]

As the Royal Commission travelled across the country in 1961 and 1962, it heard this policy urged upon it in at least thirty-five briefs submitted by the CMA and each of its divisions, by all the prepayment plans, and by spokesmen for the insurance industry and the chambers of commerce. However, not only was the commission hearing the message, but so were three provincial governments—Alberta, British Columbia, and Ontario.

The Alberta government, as we noted in chapter 4, had loudly proclaimed its opposition to a universal government plan on the grounds that it involved compulsion. Unlike Saskatchewan, Alberta did not levy a compulsory premium for its hospital insurance program, financing it from general revenues. But these, of course, were accumulated from compulsory taxes, including an ear-marked provincial tax of four mills on property.

The policy was clearly enunciated in the brief to the Royal Commission on Health Services by the minister of health of Alberta, Dr. J. Donovan Ross, who said his government was opposed to any program of state medical care "which removes all direct individual financial responsibility; so-called socialized health and medical services are incompatible with the rights and responsibilities inherent in a free and democratic society."[17]

Near the end of 1962—five months after neighbouring Saskatchewan's venture began, Premier Manning announced that a medicare program would be introduced at the next session. This was confirmed in the Throne Speech in February 1963, and the necessary legislation was introduced on March 11 to enable the Government to pay individual subsidies to assist low income earners to obtain voluntary insurance either through Medical Services Inc. (Alberta), or through insurance companies. The policy was a clear victory for the CMA-CHIA leaders with whom the details of the program had been worked out. It was expected that between 250,000 and 300,000 would apply. The government subsidy would vary from one-third of the premiums (for those with taxable incomes up to $500) to one-half of the premiums (for those with no taxable income), and this would entail government expenditures estimated to be between four and six million dollars. All details were to be left for decision by regulations, and the announcement of these was to be postponed until after the intervening election.

On June 16, the program details were announced at a press conference at which the plan was lauded by the premier and by CMA and CHIA spokesmen. Dr. Ross said that it would give Canadians a program they could set along side "the socialistic type of program" in operation in Saskatchewan.[18]

The range of benefits which insuring agencies must provide was set forth, as well as the maximum premiums permitted. The authorized maximum premium rates (with MSI premiums shown in brackets) were: single, $63.00 ($54.00); family of two, $116.00 ($114.00); family of three or more, $159.00 ($144.00). These maxima, therefore, constituted a green signal light for new unilateral increases in premiums which would automatically result in increased payments from the Treasury. Stress was placed on the fact that there was no means test. Subsidy would be obtained following a statutory declaration of the preceding year's income.[19]

Three agencies were established: (1) the Directorate, representative of the government, MSI, the College of Physicians and Surgeons, and the insurance companies, to give advice to the minister and to handle disputes between policy holders and the carriers; (2) a similarly representative assessment committee to mediate disputes between physicians and carriers; (3) a non-profit corporation, Alberta Medical Carriers, Inc., to be a clearing agency for the carriers in order to pool the high risks in the population. The medical profession and the insurance carriers (about thirty companies qualified for approval in the program) were aware that the Alberta program had to succeed or there would undoubtedly be continuing and irresistible demands across the country for a program modelled on that of Saskatchewan.[20]

Two weeks beyond the enrolment target date of October 1, only 100,000 had applied for subsidies. The application period was extended. By March when the minister reported to the Legislature, an estimated total of

1,100,000 Albertans (of a total estimated population of 1,300,000) were insured, and of these 150,000 (out of the estimated 300,000 eligible) were subsidized.

In the summer of 1964 as Premier Manning and Dr. Ross criticised the Hall Commission's "welfare state-ism," there were growing criticisms of "Manningcare" as the journalists labelled it. Two were serious: (1) that the reason only forty percent of those estimated to be eligible for subsidy were in fact protected was the inability to pay the high premiums; and (2) that the income tax threshold wasn't fair in that wealthy farmers making heavy purchases of equipment could qualify (by depreciation and tax allowances) for subsidy while a worker with dependants earning as little as $3,500 a year could not.

Despite the high proportion of the population not insured under the program, it was a policy from which Dr. Ross would not depart.

The second major break-through for the CMA-CHIA policy occurred in Ontario. Late in April 1963, in the closing days of the legislative session, the minister of health, Dr. Matthew Dymond, introduced the government medicare bill, providing for a plan to assist anyone to subscribe to one of the non-profit plans or to become insured by an insurance company. Enrolment would be voluntary, maximum premiums would be established, all insurance contracts would be "guaranteed renewable," that is, non-cancellable by the insurance company by reason of age, chronic ill-health, etc., and doctors would deal with patients or insuring agencies as they chose. Two standard contracts would be offered, the second at lower premiums and requiring deductibles and co-insurance payments.[21] It also provided for Medical Carriers Inc. a re-insuring agency, to handle bad risks. The proposal was vehemently attacked by the Liberals and NDP as "leaning over backward to be of assistance to the insurance companies," and "a 100 percent capitulation to the insurance companies and the medical profession."[22]

The bill was not passed at that session and in August 1963, an investigating committee, chaired by Dr. W. G. Hagey, the president of the University of Waterloo, was appointed to conduct public hearings on the proposal. The majority of the committee endorsed the principles of the bill without reservation and added suggestions for covering the indigent and subsidizing the medically indigent.[23] As was to be expected, the labour member filed a minority report, calling for the adoption of a Saskatchewan-type medicare program. Ontario, he said, could afford the best, and he stated categorically, "the interests of the insurance industry should not be of greater concern than the well-being of the people themselves."[24]

As a result of the criticism in the Legislature and in the media, the bill was amended in January 1966 in such a way as to end the participation of the voluntary plans and the insurance companies in the task of insuring the low income and high risk groups. Instead, the Government established the Ontario Medical Services Insurance Plan (OMSIP) to insure individuals and to subsidize those who needed assistance according to the insurance industry proposed income tax thresholds.

With the 585,000 covered by OMSIP in 1966, and 6,154,000 insured through voluntary methods, the insurance industry placed great emphasis on the fact that 95.2 percent of the population of Ontario had some form of protection—without a universal government program.

The cost to the Ontario government, met from consolidated revenues, amounted in fiscal year, 1967–68 to approximately $55 million (including welfare recipients).[25]

In British Columbia, the pattern was similar to that of Ontario. At first, the Government appeared to lean toward the subsidization of individuals and families who could not afford the prepayment plan and insurance company premiums. After extensive discussions with the profession and the insuring agencies, the Government established its own agency, the B.C. Medical Plan (BCMP), to insure those who could not afford to obtain group coverage. The income tax thresholds were used in determining eligibility for subsidy. The reason given by Dr. Peter Banks, then president of the B.C. Medical Association, for the decision, was that subsidization of individuals through the various insuring agencies would be "cumbersome, and potentially dangerous to the independence of the plans."[26]

Three provinces had now acted in such a way as to leave the majority of the population who could afford voluntary insurance to the private sector while government paid part or all of the cost for "the poor risks." For Ontario, the policy on hospital insurance had been turned 180 degrees. It will be recalled from chapter 3 that it was just such a division of public and private responsibility that Prime Minister Frost had rejected when it had been proposed in the Legislative Committee. "That," Mr. Frost had said, "sounds like a bad deal for the government."[27]

As we have seen, the election in Saskatchewan had triggered an extraordinary range of developments in health insurance: a compulsory plan in Saskatchewan, quick responses by three other provinces to insure the "uninsurable" while leaving the general field to voluntary agencies, and the extraordinary responses of those agencies in extending their coverage as widely as possible. But all the issues now became focused in the long-awaited Report of the Royal Commission on Health Services (RCHS).

Following Prime Minister Diefenbaker's announcement in December 1960, that he would appoint a commission, there was considerable delay in activating it. It was not until March 1961, that the appointment of the chairman was announced, and not until June that Mr. Diefenbaker informed the House of Commons of the other six members.[28] The chairman, Emmett M. Hall, chief justice of Saskatchewan, was a life-long friend of Mr. Diefenbaker, both having graduated from the University of Saskatchewan College of Law in 1919. Two were medical doctors (both English-speaking), Dr. David Baltzan of Saskatoon and Dr. Arthur van Wart of Fredericton, a past president of the Canadian Medical Association. Dean Alice Girard of the University of Montreal School of Nursing was the only woman and the only native French-speaking member. The other three members were Dr. Leslie Strachan, a dentist from London and former president of the Ontario Dental Association, Mr. Wallace McCutcheon, an industrialist, and Dr. O. J. Firestone, an economist. Professor Bernard Blishen was appointed research director, Dr, Pierre Jobin, medical consultant, and M. G. Taylor, research consultant.

On August 9, 1962, Senator McCutcheon was appointed to the Government and thereupon resigned his membership on the commission.

Following three months of hearings, the study of scores of special reports, travel to other countries, and lengthy deliberations, the commission released its report on June 19, 1964, just short of three years since its appointment, and just three days before the annual meeting of the CMA. It was signed by all six remaining members.

Its recommendations can best be understood in terms of the stated "Objective."

As we examined the hundreds of briefs with their thousands of recommendations we were impressed with the fact that the field of health services illustrates, perhaps better than any other, the paradox of our age, which is, of course, the enormous gap between our scientific knowledge and skills on the one hand, and our organizational and financial arrangements to apply them to the needs of men, on the other.

What the Commission recommends is that in Canada this gap be closed, that as a nation we now take the necessary legislative, organizational and financial decisions to make all the fruits of the health sciences available to all our residents without hindrance of any kind. All our recommendations are directed toward this objective.[29]

The commission then went on to state that "this goal should be incorporated in a declaration of purpose," and recommended that a "Health Charter" it had drafted "be accepted as an objective of national policy for Canada."[30] The essence of the Health Charter was the following:

The achievement of the highest possible health standards for all our people must become a primary objective of national policy and a cohesive factor contributing to national unity, involving individual and community responsibilities and actions. This objective can best be achieved through a comprehensive, universal Health Services Programme for the Canadian people,

IMPLEMENTED in accordance with Canada's evolving constitutional arrangements;

BASED upon freedom of choice, and upon free and self-governing professions;

FINANCED through prepayment arrangements;

ACCOMPLISHED through the full cooperation of the general public, the health professions, voluntary agencies, all political parties and governments, federal, provincial, and municipal;

DIRECTED towards the most effective use of the nation's health resources to attain the highest possible levels of physical and mental well-being.[31]

There then followed eight sub-sections defining and expanding upon the terms used in the main statement. For example, "full cooperation" was said to mean:

(a) the responsibility of the individual to observe good health practices and use available health services prudently;

(b) the responsibility of the individual to allocate a reasonable share of his income (by way of taxes or premiums or both) for health purposes;

(c) the methods of remuneration of health personnel—fee-for-service, salary or other arrangements—and the rates thereof should be as agreed upon by the professional associations and the administrative agencies and not by arbitrary decision, with an appeal procedure in the event of inability to agree;

(d) the maintenance of the close relationship between those who provide and those who receive health services, maintaining the confidential nature of that relationship;

(e) the provision of educational facilities of the highest standards and the removal of the financial barriers to education and training to enable all those capable and desirous of so doing to pursue health service careers;

(f) the adequate support of health research and its application;

(g) the necessity of retaining and developing further the indispensable work of voluntary agencies in the health care field;

(h) the efforts to improve the quality and availability of health services must be supplemented by a wide range of other measures concerned with such matters as housing, nutrition, cigarette smoking, water and air pollution, motor vehicle and other accidents, alcoholism, and drug addiction;

(i) the development of representative health planning agencies at all levels of government, federal, provincial, regional and municipal, and integration of health planning.[32]

And, lest this prescription should sound utopian, the commission then said: "This is what Canada and the provinces working together should do. It is not an idealist's dream but a practical program within Canada's ability, financially and practically, as subsequent chapters will show. It is what Canadians ought to strive for and expect through their governments. They should not be content with less."[33]

It was an extraordinary call for action coming as it did from a prestigious royal commission. Nor did the commission stop there. It stressed that "all these matters [on which it had made recommendations] will require careful planning and the fullest cooperation at all levels of government and with the health professions. It follows that the advisory and planning councils we recommend in Chapter 2 should be agreed upon and chosen following a Federal-Provincial Health Conference *which we urge should be called within six months* by the Federal Government."[34]

It then defined, again, the flexible system it had in mind. "We do not suggest that the various provincial programs be required to conform to any rigid pattern, but to qualify for federal support they need to provide, in whatever manner may be chosen, universal coverage in the province regardless of age or condition, or ability to pay, upon uniform terms and conditions, and to adhere to the basic inclusive features of each of the programs recommended."[35]

This statement of objectives was reinforced by the strategic importance of its first recommendation:

1. That the Federal Government enter into agreement with the provinces to provide grants on a fiscal need formula to assist the provinces to introduce and operate comprehensive, universal, provincial programs of personal health services, with similar arrangements for the Yukon and the Northwest Territories. The programs should consist of the following services, with the provinces exercising the right to determine the order of priority of each service and the timing of its introduction:

Medical Services

Dental Services for children, expectant mothers, and public assistance recipients

Prescription Drug Services

Optical Services, for children and public assistance recipients
Prosthetic Services
Home Care Services[36]

By its insistence on "uniform terms and conditions" (a term borrowed from the federal Hospital Insurance Act) the commission had rejected the subsidization policy of the CMA-CHIA, for if 3,000,000 Canadians were subjected to a means test while the rest were not, obviously the terms and conditions would not be uniform. However, it appears that the commission did not reject the subsidization route as much on the grounds of principle as on the more pragmatic tests of administrative and financial feasibility.

The commission's position was based on an analysis of how much the citizen could be expected to allocate from current income to the *entire range* of health services. The CMA-CHIA proposal was concerned with personal expenditures on physicians' services only. The commission was required to take the broader view since it was looking to the time when all health services would be paid for on a regularized, budgetary basis.

Using current data on hospital insurance premiums, the premiums in the most comprehensive voluntary prepayment plans for medical services, current experience of voluntary drug prepayment plans, and the best available estimates for optical, nursing, and other services, the total annual average health budget for an individual if all services were prepaid was estimated to be $125.40 and for a family, $345.60, which, for purposes of this discussion will be rounded to $125 and $350, respectively.[37]

It will be recalled that the CMA-CHIA policy used the income tax exemption threshold as the cut-off point for determining whether an individual or a family would be entitled to subsidy. It estimated that three million people (or, more correctly, individual income earners and family heads representing 3,000,000 persons) would need to be considered for subsidy.

As the commission examined this income tax exemption "threshold" concept, it concluded that it was irrelevant as a yardstick for determining the need for subsidy. It decided that the fundamental question was: "What percentage of his or her annual income can an income earner consistently allocate on a regular prepayment basis to a full range of health services?" It then turned to consumer expenditure surveys as a guide in making what must be an arbitrary value judgement, on the assumption that what consumers *will* allocate is probably closely related to what they *are currently* paying. Surveys showed that at low, medium, and medium-high income levels, people consistently allocated about four percent of income to health services.[38]

But, said the commission, responsible political leaders might decide that on a fully prepaid basis, in the interests of improved health, the limit might be set at five, six, or even, perhaps, at seven percent. (Note that an increase from four to five percent would represent a twenty-five percent increase in national expenditures on personal health services.)

If it is assumed that five percent is a reasonable percentage of income to allocate to a full range of health services, and that no one should pay more, then all individuals whose incomes are below $2,500 and all families earning less than $7,000 would be entitled to subsidy. (That is, five percent of $7,000 would be equal to the $350 annual cost.) If the six or seven percent thresholds were decided upon the income threshold would drop proportionately. Using the latest available income distribution data, the commission calculated that with alternative cut-off points of five, six, and seven percent, the percentage of all income earners requiring subsidy would be respectively 73.8 percent, 63 percent and 53.8 percent. In population terms in 1962 this would have meant fourteen, twelve, or ten million persons, respectively, who would have had to be means tested. If the proportion of income allocated to health services were to remain at the current four percent, approximately one million more income earners would be eligible for subsidy.

Giving full weight to both the philosophical arguments and the practical administrative requirements, the commission recommended a federal subsidy of provincial publicly-administered programs. Its reasoning was stated as follows:

1. That the method of subsidy should be one that subsidizes the insurance fund rather than one that subsidizes individuals.

2. That reliance on the method of voluntary insurance would be unnecessarily slow and inevitably incomplete.

3. That the number of individuals who would require subsidy to meet total health services costs is so large that no government could impose the means test procedure on so many citizens, or would be justified in establishing a system requiring so much unnecessary administration. The health services will make enough demands on our resources. We must not waste them.

4. That, so far as the issue of compulsion is concerned, we believe that as long as decisions of this kind are made by democratically elected legislatures, as long as they provide only basic essentials (for example, standard ward hospital care) and assure citizens free choice of physician and hospital and free choice of additional items against which they may insure through private arrangements, then we have confidence that our democratic ideals will not only be protected, but, in fact, more

fully realized. It is of great significance for a democratic society such as ours that the Hospital Insurance and Diagnostic Services Act was passed by an unanimous vote of the House of Commons representing all political parties.

5. That the health insurance fund in each province should be administered by one agency in order to achieve full integration in effective planning of *all* health services, and thus to obtain the most efficient administration of all sectors of the proposed health services program. We have recommended that the existing hospital insurance program be administered by the same agency in each province as administers all personal health services. This necessarily means rejection of any proposal that the one phase of health services, namely payment of physician's services, be administered by a separate agency.[39]

The rejection of the CMA's subsidization policy by the Royal Commission was bitter medicine for the profession. The report had been released just three days before the annual meeting of the CMA in Vancouver and, of course, totally dominated all non-scientific discussion at the conference. It was almost impossible to believe that the commission, which had been appointed at its request, would not have almost automatically perceived the superior wisdom of the CMA approach. The CMA had seen the commission as a means of removing "consideration of health and health insurance from the hectic arena of political controversy" on the grounds that "a heated and emotionally charged election campaign in which contesting parties are faced with the urge to outdo each other in the attractiveness of their projected programs, scarcely provides the ideal atmosphere for dispassionate and objective consideration of the future pattern of health care in this country."[40]

A royal commission had given "dispassionate and objective consideration to the future pattern of health care" and had reached the same conclusion that the profession feared would emerge from the "hectic arena of political controversy." Moreover, during the years of the commission's deliberations, the health insurance issue had not subsided in the political arena; indeed, the issue was being more widely and heatedly debated than ever before. The report would add fuel to the fire and undoubtedly accelerate the date of decision.

The report of the RCHS was a major challenge to the profession's policy of maintaining control of the distribution system of medical services. The commission's questioning of the underlying principle of means testing those who could not afford the premiums of the voluntary plans as being both inherently undemocratic, and administratively inefficient, was an attack on what had become an article of faith for the profession within the doctrines of individual freedom and the free enterprise system.[41] In addition to pragmatic arguments, the commission had clearly used a stigma to beat a dogma. The perdurance of the profession's "private governments" (TCMP now being a federated system) clearly depended on the outcome of what was shaping up as an ideological war.

The profession's leaders surveyed the terrain and began to replan their strategy. Despite the psychological and political blows delivered by the commission, it was, after all, simply an advisory body, appointed by a Conservative government and the Liberal government might not accept all of the advice. Moreover, there were extremely encouraging signs among a number of provincial governments, where the constitutional jurisdiction on health matters lay. Alberta had given the lead, adopting wholeheartedly both the profession's philosophy and its sponsored prepayment plan as one of the carriers. Now British Columbia and Ontario were joining the ranks of the converted. With three of the four most powerful provincial governments adopting the CMA-CHIA policy, the odds in favour of the market economy approach and against the political economy philosophy endorsed by the commission had shifted most favourably. A massive effort must now be made to ensure that nothing interfered with this progress in provincial decision making to implement the CMA-CHIA policy.

Despite the CMA's apparent early confidence in the commission, nevertheless, it had launched in 1962 the most intensive study in its history of the whole field of medical economics. In addition to expanding the work of its Standing Committee on Economics, and its Committee on Prepaid Medical Plans, the Executive Committee set up two more committees: the Special Committee on Policy, and the Special Committee to Adapt the Australian Plan of Medical Services to Canadian Conditions. The Australian plan had a number of features attractive to some of the profession's leaders: it was voluntary, used a variety of carriers, and operated on the indemnity principle with substantial part-payments by patients.

As these committees were completing their work, the Royal Commission reported. It was impossible at the Vancouver meeting of the CMA to deal adequately with so voluminous a document and so momentous an issue. But time was running out, as the Liberal party's 1962 and 1963 election commitments attested. For the second time in its history, the CMA decided to convoke a special meeting of council to deal with the issue of health insurance. It scheduled the meeting for January 1965—twenty-two years after the 1943 special meeting—its purpose to reverse irrevocably that regrettable decision taken amidst the emotional overtones of war when, in Macaulay's words, "none were for the party and all were for the state."

The Executive Committee had prepared a synthesis of the reports of its four committees and presented to the meeting their essence in a series of eighty statements to be adopted as resolutions, or received for information.

Excerpts from the *Transactions* of that important meeting highlight the debate on the main ideological themes and provide us with deeper insight into the profession's thinking.[42]

19. Volume I of the Report of the Royal Commission presents us with proposals in the field of health insurance which differ radically from our preferred approach. . . . The Report presents a case for the transfer of expenditures for all health services from the private to the public sector of the economy and in so doing it has undertaken to demolish many of our arguments on medical services insurance which the profession advanced in its submissions during the public hearings.

24. We have stated our belief that a tax-supported, compulsory program of medical services insurance is neither necessary nor desirable. In our society citizens accept many aspects of compulsion for the good of the community. In public health and particularly in the field of hospital insurance we function under a system which is state-operated, tax-supported and in many respects compulsory. However, it appears that compulsory controls which are inherent in a single source of funds are capable of restricting progress in hospital function. We feel that a single source of funds with compulsory controls could similarly restrict progress in medical services.

25. The Royal Commission in advancing its compulsory, tax-supported, state-operated medical services proposal, appears not to have envisaged any exception to the universality portrayed. . . . We declare that the individual physician must have the right to practise privately outside any arrangements and that the individual subscriber should have the right to avail himself of services from such a physician without loss of benefits.

51. The right of the medical profession to establish the worth of its services has been one of our cherished privileges and for many years it has been a function of provincial medical organizations to establish, modify and amend tariffs of medical fees. These provincial schedules were originally designed to provide a guide to physicians in respect of charges for professional services when the patient was himself paying the account and were capable of adjustment to meet the economic circumstances of the individual. In some instances the schedules were regarded as minimum average tariffs and it was assumed that they applied to a patient who represented the mythical average of the

economic community. With the growth of prepayment agencies these schedules became the bases upon which doctors are remunerated from a pool of subscribers' money. It is inherent in the collective approach to the payment of doctors by fee-for-service that the amount of the fee should be established and the effect of schedule changes on premium structures is well known.

59. We are therefore confronted with a clash of ideologies and it is our view that it surely represents exaggeration to magnify the difficulties to the degree that a compulsory, tax-supported system is presented as a preferable alternative, principally on grounds of administrative simplicity. The mainstay of the profession's proposal for the extension of medical and health services under voluntary auspices is that the costs for the self-supporting should remain in the private sector of the economy and that public funds should be employed to subsidize the indigent completely and the marginal income classes to the extent of their need. We believe this concept to be valid, acceptable to Canadians generally and consonant with what we regard as the true responsibility of governments in this field.

70. As realists we should be aware of the attractiveness of the philosophical concept that people should be financed by governments to the best of medical care in unlimited amount. This concept is eloquently stated in the Report of the Royal Commission on Health Services and it may prove to be beguiling to our fellow citizens and to the governments which represent them. We have a duty to proclaim what we believe to be a superior method, not in our own interest, but for the continued progress of medicine and for the ultimate benefit of our patients.

78. The Royal Commission on Health Services has presented us with an exhaustive and most valuable appraisal of Canada's health needs and resources. The fact that we cannot agree with the Commission's recommendations on the best method of insuring personal health services does not detract from our admiration and support of other features of the Commission's work.

A number of subordinate issues was also considered at that historic meeting. Apparently the Committee on Prepaid Plans had been influenced by the CHIA whose member companies sold many indemnity policies limited to in-hospital medical and surgical services. These, said the committee, should be available as an alternative to the comprehensive range of benefits, in order to provide consumers with a choice:

44. "If premiums for first-dollar coverage become excessively high, the alternative of the less expensive patient participation plans will gain in popular favour. There should, however, be available to subscribers a

clear-cut choice between plans of equal comprehensiveness, one on a first-dollar basis and the other with deductibles and co-insurance."

A second issue was the stress placed on the dangers of all the funds coming from a provincial government, from an agency, therefore, that would not have "fiscal authority and autonomy." This had been a cardinal principle of the CMA since 1934. It was restated in these terms at the Special Meeting:

33. The Royal Commission further envisages that the administration of the services which it proposes should be undertaken provincially by a representative Commission, which would also assume administration of the hospital insurance program. Our experience to date with provincial Commissions administering this latter program suggests that they lack fiscal authority, that the decision to increase premiums or taxes is in the last analysis a political decision and before such a decision is reached the service may be adversely affected.

34. Under the system of voluntary medical insurance which pertains in this country the carriers have fiscal authority and autonomy, and the elements of competition and the value of their offering influence their exercise of such authority. In the public sector similar autonomy and authority are vested in school boards in many provinces. If health services in their broadest sense should ever be financed by taxation such fiscal autonomy will be essential, if only to protect the interests of all elements of the health services in the face of all other government expenditures.

The committee had referred to the autonomy of school boards. It also had experience with Workmen's Compensation boards that were able to impose levies on employers to meet the costs of medical services. It might also have referred to the Swift Current region plan. These, too, had "fiscal authority and autonomy."

It is difficult to assess the practicality of this strongly held belief. The idea seemed to have been that a special fund would be exempt from normal constraints and, particularly, as would be the case if controlled by provincial governments, not subject to competition with other priorities. But, obviously, this was wishful thinking. Even under conditions of private practice there were limits on physicians' incomes, on the size of the "pool" from which they were derived, else, why were incomes of physicians lower in New Brunswick than in Toronto? Moreover, even in the prepayment plans which the profession controlled limits were imposed by the market, as prepayment plan executives warned the fee committees of the danger of increasing fees beyond the point where the plan's premiums would be competitive with those of the insurance companies. Nevertheless, this fear of what would happen to medical incomes if appropriations for health purposes were to be made by governments facing a host of competing demands remained a matter of grave concern.

With its policy clarified and its resolve strengthened by the provincial developments and the consensus achieved at the special meeting, the executive stepped up its publicity campaign, and arranged for a meeting with the minister of health in Ottawa. The meeting was scheduled for May 25, 1965; but to enable Prime Minister Pearson to attend, it was postponed to June 9.[43]

It was against this background of political instability, intense political party rivalry, Royal Commission findings and recommendations, increasing public interest in medical care insurance, continuing expansion of the prepayment plans, the decisions of Alberta, Ontario, and British Columbia to establish subsidized programs, and the increasing aggressiveness of the CMA and the CHIA in pursuit of their subsidization policy, that the Pearson government made its decision. Why was it made?

THE ACTION IMPERATIVES

The background outlined above highlighted a number of factors contributing to the Government's decision, but it will be useful to recapitulate these and refer to others that were also instrumental in the final choice.

The major factor was the long-term commitment of the Liberal party to health insurance. That had been first undertaken in the party platform of 1919. It had been followed by the 1945 Green Book proposals which identified health insurance not only with the party but, for the first time, with a Liberal Government. Although Prime Minister St. Laurent had declared in 1955 that the 1945 offer was no longer valid, there was clearly in the minds of Canadians who thought about it at all—and members of Parliament thought about it a good deal—the sense that the commitment must some day be redeemed. This feeling had been strengthened of course by the introduction of national hospital insurance ten years before. That event created, in a sense, the "other shoe" syndrome: when would it be dropped? Hospital insurance had been highly successful; when would its twin—medicare—be adopted? Somehow, it had become a natural, normal expectation that awaited only the time when a special concatenation of political forces, public attitudes, and determined leadership would reach the necessary "critical mass" and the dream would be realized. Those elements were present, as never before, in 1965.

The defeat of the Liberals in 1957 had led to the selection of Lester Pearson as leader and the infusion of new personalities with more progressive ideas into the leadership cadre. The commitment to health insurance had never been more assertively stated than in the election campaigns of 1962 and 1963. Now the party was in office, and, on inviting Miss Judy LaMarsh to join the Cabinet as minister of national health and welfare, the prime minister informed her that she would "be responsible for the Pension and Medicare programs and would have to 'fight the Minister of Finance' for money for them."[44] But, as she observed, "considering the extent of Walter Gordon's commitment to these programs as campaign chief *that* fight wouldn't be too tough!"[45]

For those within the Cabinet and caucus committed to health insurance, the report of the Royal Commission came not only as a surprise but as a rallying cry of support. Not only did it highlight the unmet needs, document and assess the resources, and through its dramatic formulation of a "Health Charter for Canadians" enunciate the goals to be achieved, but by the very scope and vigour of its recommendations the report became, itself, a force galvanizing the nation to action.

For a modern industrialized nation, the unmet needs were prodigious: still high infant mortality; high incidence of illness; inadequate supply of trained personnel; general lack of insurance and inadequacy of much of it; inequitable distribution of expenditures on health services; and, the disparate financial capacities of the provinces to act. The report documented them all.

Moreover, there was now that expanding threat on the Left from the New Democratic Party with its show-piece, the Saskatchewan medicare plan, demonstrating that medicare was as feasible and effective as hospital insurance and equally desirable. True, the birth-pangs of Saskatchewan medicare had been horrendous; the Government that had sponsored it had been toppled; but it was obvious that the new Government had embraced it and would not dream of dismantling it.[46] By 1965, the Saskatchewan example was, like Banquo's ghost, a constant spectre at every Liberal Cabinet meeting when medicare was discussed. Stanley Knowles, now reinforced by Tommy Douglas, never let the Government forget it. Although the Diefenbaker government had introduced no legislation while it was in office, its leaders could at least claim paternity of the Royal Commission that had moved public opinion so far forward and they could, and some of them did, chide the Government for its failure to respond.

In addition to party obligation, however, and all the rational reasons adduced by the Royal Commission for government action, the main thrust came from that handful of new progressive leaders in the Cabinet: Judy LaMarsh, Walter Gordon, Allan McEachen, Maurice Lamontagne, and, following the election of 1965, Jean Marchand. In addition, with extraordinary influence, there was Tom Kent "whose speech to the Kingston Conference 'Towards a Philosophy of Social Security' contained many of the more radical ideas that became the Liberal Government's policies."[47] Kent had been appointed assistant to the prime minister and "coordinator of programs." And then there was the Rt. Hon. Lester Pearson whose basic humanitarian philosophy embraced medicare and ensured his support, but who, as in so many other controversial issues, found it difficult to maintain a consistent thrust towards an agreed-upon goal.

The leadership was now present, the needs, as documented by the Royal Commission, were great, the goals were defined, and a rough road map was at hand. It was time to act.

THE CONSTRAINTS

Government policy making is never simple but in a federal state on an issue in any way involving the constituent provinces it takes on additional complexity, particularly when the policy area falls within the jurisdiction of the provinces as health insurance has been assumed to do.

Even when the constitutional question has been legally settled—in this case, through the right of the federal government to proceed under its blanket power to spend—to all the normal problems created by competing demands and pressures of interest groups, there are added the political realities of the differing policy positions of the ten provincial governments. Their positions are equally complex for not only do their views represent the distillations of the pressures of their respective dominant interest groups, their program priorities and financial resources, but, as well, the survival needs and expansionist desires of their respective bureaucracies. Moreover, these differences could not be resolved in the normal hierarchical processes of the typical system-sub-system relationship (as, for example, a provincial government dealing with its municipalities) but, rather, in the changing political environment of the sixties, required negotiations between near equals "akin to those of effective international diplomacy."[48]

For, coinciding with the emergence of the new autonomy-seeking Quebec under Premier Lesage, the Liberal government in Ottawa found itself also confronting other provincial governments with strong, determined leaders backed by solid and seemingly impregnable majorities. With the provinces no longer content to accept Ottawa largesse if it meant accepting Ottawa's dictates, clearly the centralization-decentralization pendulum had reached its apogee and was commencing its back-swing to the provinces, and despite the frequent references to the advancement of cooperative federalism, the competitive and, sometimes, hostile nature of the relationship in the sixties was yearly being reinforced.[49]

An electoral commitment to a national constituency and the corresponding expectations of the national electorate for federal action in a field of provincial jurisdiction posed a dilemma that had been solved before, but the omens for its resolution now were increasingly dark. Two major concessions had been shaped by the shifting equilibrium: the decision to permit Quebec to receive corporation income tax credits (or "points" as they came to be called) in lieu of direct payments to its universities via the Canadian University Foundation; and the acceptance of Quebec's right to establish an independent, though coordinated, pension plan that paralleled the Canada Pension Plan despite Ottawa's original intent to establish one unified national system.

But even these major concessions were not enough to satisfy the resurgent provincial forces.

Another constraint was the growing opposition to "shared-cost" programs. The term "shared-cost" programs which has increasingly come into the language of "officialese" is not in fact as precise as the original term it is replacing—"the conditional grant-in-aid"—in that it removes from its intrinsic meaning any concept of "conditions"; on the other hand, the term "shared-cost" may convey better than does the word, "grant," the notion that there is no pre-determined limit on the amount of the funds forthcoming. In any event it was the imposed conditions that, it was claimed, eroded provincial autonomy and distorted priorities, that had become increasingly repugnant to the provinces. One of the outstanding examples was the set of condition imposed in the agreements signed under the Hospital Insurance Act which among other things required the provinces to introduce a comprehensive system of standards setting, licensing, and inspection of hospitals. It was a highly desirable requirement, which some provinces had previously undertaken, but *it was imposed.*

The first concerted, formal attack on the grant-in-aid mechanism occurred at the 1960 Federal-Provincial Conference and was led by the dynamic new premier of Quebec, Jean Lesage, and strongly supported by Premier Manning of Alberta. Although the federal government did not immediately respond officially, the Liberal party (then in opposition) in its 1961 policy statement introduced the idea of federal withdrawal from permanently established programs and of the possibility of a province contracting out without the penalty of losing the federal funds.[50] At the 1963 Federal-Provincial Conference, with the Liberals back in power, new proposals were suggested, and at the 1964 Conference, formally made, to meet the first objection by providing for a province's "opting out" on condition that the program be maintained and the transferability of benefits interprovincially be continued.[51]

There was another disturbing element in the equation of the federal system. The continuous expansion of equalization payments, whether imbedded in the basic taxation agreements or incorporated in specific programs, was clearly creating growing resentment, not officially express-ed, over the amount of transfer payments flowing through the federal treasury from wealthy to less wealthy provinces. The dilemma of the national government, therefore, in fulfilling the commitments made to a national constituency in a field of provincial jurisdiction was, as stated above, by no means new, but the limitations on its options for meeting those expectations were new—or at least, greater—and obviously required not only imagination but a sharper sensitivity to provincial values, atti-tudes, goals, and resources.

THE UNCERTAINTIES

With the growing opposition of the medical profession, business, and some provincial governments, for a minority government the prospects were most uncertain. There were several disturbing factors.

1. *The cost.* The cost of the national medicare program could reason-ably be estimated for the first year, based on the experience of several of the comprehensive medical service plans and the highest fee schedules in such provinces as Ontario and Alberta, and on the experience in Saskat-chewan. The Royal Commission had made projections but if the formula were to be open-ended (i.e., a sharing of expenditures determined by the provinces, as the hospital insurance formula was), there could be no assurance of what, say, in five years, the provinces' collective demands on the federal treasury would be. From the federal point of view a fixed annual *per capita* grant (as had been proposed in 1945–46) would be greatly preferable. But there was little likelihood of provincial acceptance of that gambit which would simply transfer the total burden of unpre-dictable cost overruns to them.

2. *The provinces' response.* There was great uncertainty on this ques-tion. The low-revenue provinces could probably be counted on to support the move so long as a major equalization factor was included in the cost-sharing formula. Alberta could be counted upon to reject a proposal involving any degree of compulsion. Ontario had introduced medicare legislation but it had delayed its passage until a commission could examine it in public hearings. Quebec had already declared for an independent program. Given the new mood of the provinces any proposal of any kind would find its opponents.[52]

3. *New sources of revenue.* Given the state of the budget, new revenues would almost certainly be required. But with taxpayer resistance at a new high, and the question of a comprehensive restructuring of the revenue

system under consideration by the Carter Royal Commission, again there was uncertainty as to the best course, or whether indeed there was any acceptable course.

4. *Physicians' cooperation.* The Saskatchewan doctors' withdrawal of services had clearly demonstrated how far the profession would go in opposing measures it did not like. Though it was true that the brunt of such similar confrontations as might occur would be borne by provincial administrations (and the onus by provincial parties) no political credit would redound to the federal government (or to the national Liberal party) if it was its actions that had triggered the confrontation.

5. *The business community response.* Here, again, was an uncertainty of unpredictable dimensions, depending upon the nature of the policy adopted. If the policy were supportive of the insurance industry, the business community would be content; if it were not, the political side effects could be serious. They might not be too serious for the Government, but they certainly would be for the Liberal party[53] at election time; and for a party governing with a minority the effects might well be disastrous. For a minority government, the uncertainties were extreme, indeed. But if the proposal could be brought off successfully, not only would it be a statutory landmark, worthy in itself to commemorate the Centennial, but it would also redound to the political credit of the Liberal party. The gamble must be taken.

THE EXTERNAL CONTRIBUTIONS

In the background discussion, the policy proposals of the Canadian Medical Association and the Canadian Health Insurance Association were duly noted and there is no doubt that great weight was attached to their views. These inputs need not be repeated here.

There were, in addition, other powerful interest groups whose contributions were important. The stand adopted by the CMA and CHIA came under strong attack from the two largest organizations speaking for consumers: the Canadian Labour Congress and the Canadian Federation of Agriculture. They spoke from different levels of experience with the insuring of physicians' services: a high proportion of union members were already insured through collective bargaining agreements, whereas the members of the agricultural industry were typical of those who had least access to group prepayment at rates reasonably related to their incomes. Their submissions to the Royal Commission on Health Services reflected their differences.

The Canadian Labour Congress. The brief of the Canadian Labour Congress (CLC) rejected outright the idea that the issue was "insurance" or that the private sector marketplace could meet Canadians' health needs. These could best be looked after, it claimed, by a public health program that was "comprehensive in scope, universally available without regard to means, equitably financed, free of co-insurance, deductibles or other financial deterrents, and having a representative Advisory Council, and its administration precluding control or undue influence by any interest group."[54]

Its most salient contention was that *insurance* was not the main issue. Accepting that prepayment plans had been helpful, the CLC argued that they were simply a convenient technique for the budgeting of health care costs, and that the real issue was that health care should be thought of as a public service. Simple tinkering with the status quo by an extension of prepayment was not good enough. It then condemned the fee-for-service ("piecework") system, emphasized the shortcomings of the prepayments plans ("answerable to organized medicine and not to consumers"), attacked the whole concept of means-testing, and criticized the CMA proposal for subsidizing voluntary plans as creating a monopoly of health service producers—a policy contrary to the public interest.

Each of these points, and a number of others, including organization, financing, costs, and manpower needs, were elaborated upon in an extraordinarily comprehensive and well documented submission, the emphasis centring on the inadequacy of a patchwork system. "It is not the array of different types of personnel and services that we wish to stress. It is their disarray that matters; the fact that these services are by and large uncoordinated, fragmented, and all too often unrelated."

"We favour a system of public health care that will be universal in application and comprehensive in coverage. We favour a system that will present no economic barrier between the service and those who need it. We are opposed to any provision which will require some people to submit themselves to a means test in order to obtain service. We look to a system of health care that will be regarded as a public service and not as an insurance mechanism. We consider that the public health care program is one of the major remaining gaps that need to be filled in our social security system."

The Canadian Federation of Agriculture. The submission of the Canadian Federation of Agriculture (CFA) was not as comprehensive as the CLC brief, but it was similar in that its recommendations were the result of decisions that had been taken by local, provincial, and national conventions. It also exuded a kind of grass roots integrity. The people on whose behalf it was presented had the greatest grievances—the shortages of facilities and personnel, the low incomes, the great distances to services, and the absence of any real opportunity to be insured at a reasonable cost. Its major recommendation was: "Resolved that the Canadian Federation of Agriculture support measures to obtain a complete prepaid national health insurance plan under provincial and Federal government sponsorship and control to give full medical and surgical care at a premium that the lowest income group can reasonably afford."[55]

The federation reminded the commission that these views had been held ever since its first submission to the House of Commons Committee on Social Security in 1943. It, too, saw the weaknesses in the present fragmentation of services and strongly recommended that "the Commission give particular attention to and recommend ways of achieving the coordinated planning of all services and conditions related to health—preventive, curative, nutritional and social—so that as far as possible the physical and mental health of the people shall be preserved, protected and improved on all fronts."

On the major issues of voluntary versus public plans, its response was a low-key questioning rather than a bold statement of certitudes, reminding the commission that in human affairs dogmatic assertions give no surety of real solutions. On this issue the CFA stated that "it seems to [us] that the essential difference in these two concepts is this: the voluntary plan approach however elaborated or supplemented, leaves very much in the hands of the medical profession the question of administration of most of the plans, of remuneration, of control of misuse, of organization of medical services, of coordination with public health services, and so on. The governmental approach, even on a fee-for-service basis, does open up an avenue of review by government . . . of some of these things and the continuing interest and responsibility of government in others, all in the interests of the effectiveness and reasonable economy of the services given on behalf of the consumer. . . . We may confidently say, on behalf of our members, that they do not see what is wrong with the injection into this great and vital area of service—that is, medical care—an element of public responsibility not only for ensuring universal coverage, but for how the job is done and how much is paid to have it done. The view that involvement of the state is destructive of the freedom of the medical profession, and an ultimate threat to its professional integrity, seems to us to be really a cynical one. It assumes a degree of irresponsibility on the part of the public and a crassness of motivation on the part of the medical profession that does not seem to our people to be acceptable. We would not for a moment deny or underrate the great importance of maintaining, in the medical profession, very high standards of integrity, professional competence, and ideals of public service . . . we do not see how or why universal medical insurance, governmentally established and administered, should destroy these things. Rather, it should provide an economic basis on which to build new and improved standards of service and responsibility. . . . Universal Medicare insurance, financed by moderate premiums, supplemented by Federal and Provincial government tax revenues, can be and should be a very big step in this direction. Achievement of this involves redistribution of income, as between individuals, between areas, and between provinces."

Perhaps equally interesting, coming from a sector of the population beset with fluctuating incomes and uncertain prospects, a good deal of emphasis was given to the use of premiums as a revenue device.

Still other policy ideas were contributed by the provinces. References have already been made to a number of these, but it will be useful to summarize them here.

The first was, of course, Saskatchewan medicare. It had demonstrated that a universal, comprehensive government plan was feasible but that it carried grave political risk. Universality and comprehensiveness were clearly achievable goals. Saskatchewan also contributed to the policy questions of paying physicians and using the prepayment plans.

There was, however, an additional input at the national level from the Saskatchewan plan and that was, of course, that it had been introduced by a CCF government whose party had recently formed the NDP and whose seventeen members in the House of Commons never failed to remind Parliament of their accomplishments. The NDP also had another input to make, its precise weight impossible to assess: a minority Liberal government would need the NDP votes to have its policy adopted and, by virtue of occupying this critical bargaining position, the NDP obviously would not endorse any proposal that ran counter to its fundamental principles.

Alberta, too, as has been discussed above, had influences to bring to bear on the policy. In addition to its objections to all shared-cost programs, the Social Credit government had taken a philosophical stand strongly opposed to universal health insurance on the grounds that it involved compulsion. Alberta had acted on that philosophy and now had in operation a program that involved the medical profession and the insurance industry in the heart of the action.

Ontario was also in the process of adopting the CMA-CHIA policy and could be expected to argue strongly for that approach in a federal-provincial conference.

THE INTERNAL CONTRIBUTIONS

In addition to the prime minister, two other ministers, those of National

Health and Welfare, and of Finance, were primarily involved in the medicare issue. For a brief period of a little over two years, for the first time in the history of health insurance in Canada, both ministers were in favour of the project, in the persons of Judy LaMarsh and Walter Gordon. Also, for the first time, there was genuine enthusiasm in the Prime Minister's Office, with Tom Kent serving a liaison function and, when necessary, as a catalyst or expediter. As we shall see, the situation was to return to normal when the actors changed in December 1965, with Mitchell Sharp becoming minister of finance and Allan McEachen health minister.

The Health Department, it appears, was as surprised by the range, vigour, and direction of the Royal Commission recommendations as the medical profession itself (and, one may assume, far more delighted). But, unlike a royal commission which publishes its recommendations, folds its tents and silently steals away, a government department has a continuing responsibility for every proposal that is translated into policy; the response is therefore invariably less bold and infinitely more concerned with outcomes, whether predictable or fortuitous.

The Health Department established fourteen committees to analyze the various sections of the report, evaluate them, and comment on the feasibility of the proposals and their relationships to on-going programs of the department and its long-range planning.[56] The Royal Commission on Health Services, although exposed by Alberta and Ontario to some aspects of provincial displeasure with federal-provincial relations had not, it became clear, been fully cognizant of either the range or depth of provincial feelings. The commission had found relatively little criticism of the hospital insurance program and obviously assumed that medicare, if implemented, would be designed along the same lines and enjoy the same acceptance. The Health Department Committee on medicare, too, feeling comfortable with the familiar, envisaged a federal medicare structure closely paralleling the hospital insurance model. And in her frequent sessions with the committee, these proposals were fully supported by Miss LaMarsh. The proposal was then submitted to the prime minister who immediately appointed a committee of senior officials from the Health and Finance departments and from the Privy Council Office.[57]

The addition of the Privy Council and Finance officials added new perspective to the discussions. With his extraordinary diplomatic skills, the prime minister was probably more alert to the changing nature of federal-provincial relations than anyone else in the Cabinet. It was clear that if all Canadians were to be insured, federal leadership was essential. In the past, national standards had been established by the federal government's use of the conditional grant-in-aid. Both the Royal Commission and the Health Department had recommended that model. The prime minister was aware that there was now no possibility that such a circumscribing model would be acceptable to the provinces. There began, therefore, an intensive examination of shared-cost program designs that would comport with the rising provincial impatience with federally-imposed restraints and yet impair in no way future opportunities for federal initiatives. It was a complex issue which would yield to resolution only after intensive analysis, endless meetings of officials and ministers, testing for viable options, and issue finally in a formal statement by the minister of finance in 1966. But a medicare policy could not wait. It was necessary, therefore, to design an *ad hoc* arrangement that would meet immediate exigencies but not proscribe or prejudice a long-term general policy.

Clearly, the requirements under the Hospital Insurance Act of a formal agreement and provision for detailed federal auditing of provincial accounts were no longer tolerable. The proposal would have to be based on a general understanding of what a medicare program was, an agreement only on general principles on which a provincial plan would be erected.

Accordingly, in the interdepartmental committee, "principles" or "criteria" were examined, rejected, refined, and reduced to the absolute minimum, until four remained: comprehensive, universal, publicly administered, and portable. Gone would be the need for written agreements and for federal audit, that irritant and symbol of provincial subordination. It was simplicity itself. Not a federal program, but ten provincial programs that together with federal sharing would aggregate to a national program of uniform minimum standards for all Canadians.

There was one more fundamental solution to be sought, a cost-sharing formula that would also accord with the new realities. A fixed *per capita* amount, similar to the proposals of 1945 would be preferable from the federal point of view but unacceptable to the provinces. A second possibility was the formula of the hospital insurance plan. But, if the new federal stance obviated the possibility of individual agreements and federal audits, then, to be consistent, the federal government must be equally oblivious to individual provincial program costs. In short, the hospital insurance formula was unacceptable precisely because one-half of the federal contribution was geared to each province's *per capita* cost. The only alternative seemed to be a single national figure, applied equally to all. That, of course, was the national *per capita* cost. If the federal government paid one-half of that amount on behalf of every insured person, calculations indicated that that figure would contribute less than half the cost in the wealthier provinces and up to eighty percent in the poorer provinces. It would be a serendipitous outcome that all (or almost all) would applaud.

THE STRATEGY OF IMPLEMENTATION I

By the end of 1964, the minority government of Lester Pearson was a beleaguered force. Rocked by scandals, almost paranoid from the incessant leaks of policy discussions and reports of dissension among ministers, demoralized by the puerile feud between the leader of the opposition and the prime minister, and fatigued by the long drawn out negotiations with Quebec over the pension plan and the protracted flag debate in Parliament, the Cabinet appeared to lurch from crisis to crisis.

The Christmas recess had provided a welcome respite and, as Denis Smith reports, "There was a new mood of urgency and firmness in the Prime Minister's leadership."[58] On January 27, 1965, the prime minister wrote to members of the Cabinet requesting advice on legislation that should be mentioned in the Speech from the Throne. He asked for "an attractive and constructive program" which would be "striking enough to help shift the focus of political attention away from Opposition attempts to harry us on other matters which may be smaller in substance but larger in politics."[59] He reminded them that by the beginning of the session two out of three social measures in the election platform would have been implemented: extended family allowances and the pension plan. The third was medicare. On this he said, "I do not think we can plan to take that on, at least in any comprehensive way, in 1965. But we do need to make some plans for dealing with the greatest needs in this area."[60]

Mr. Gordon replied on February 1, stating that he agreed that medicare could not be enacted in 1965, but urging that the speech should contain "some mention or reference to medicare" to remind the public of the Government's commitment.[61]

Accordingly, the Speech from the Throne contained a commitment to call a conference of the provinces (as had been recommended by the Royal Commission) to discuss health services for all Canadians.[62] The first step of the strategy was thus decided. The proposal would be made in the first instance in the most general terms, to avoid the possibility that immediate waves of opposition to specific details would capsize the proposal before a firm launching could be made. To ward off any unpredicted attack, it was decided to send a reconnaissance team of senior health officials to each of the provincial capitals to discuss the matter with the ministers of health and ascertain what the reaction to a federal initiative would be.[63]

The senior officials reported that all of the provinces ranked "high among their objectives the establishment of a health services plan."[64] There were, of course, considerable differences as to the type of plan favoured. What was equally evident was the variation in the capacities of the provinces to finance the health services which they considered essential. The situation had not changed much since 1955.[65] The brief discussions, almost solely with health ministers and health officials, had been encouraging, but obviously there had been an oversight. No views were obtained from finance ministers and premiers.

On June 9, as scheduled, the prime minister, and the health and finance ministers met with the Canadian Medical Association's advisory committee to the federal government. The committee re-stated its opposition to a compulsory, comprehensive plan with a single source of funds. It stressed that physicians should have the right to opt out of any plan, the patient also having the right to opt out without loss of benefits; it also stressed the difficulties in any extension of out-patient benefits under the Hospital Insurance Act. It re-affirmed its endorsement of the programs developed and being developed in Alberta, British Columbia, and Ontario, and offered to discuss similar proposals with the prime minister and his colleagues at any time.[66]

The committee reported back to CMA council that it had received a sympathetic hearing and had conveyed to the Cabinet members views which it felt would be considered at the Federal-Provincial Conference. It did not, however, receive any indication of imminent action by the federal government, despite the fact that a federal-provincial conference on the subject had already been called.[67]

And now, on July 19, the conference, as described at the beginning of the chapter, was about to open.

The prime minister's introduction was most diplomatic. The federal government would not impose its views on the provinces, rather "it is now the responsibility of the Federal government to cooperate with the provinces in making Medicare financially possible for all Canadians. The government accepts that responsibility."[68]

To disabuse the provinces of any ideas of federal domination, the prime minister said, "I am not proposing a new shared-cost program....in the case of Medicare I believe it is appropriate and possible to proceed by another route. The Federal Government, subject of course to Parliamentary approval, will support provincial Medicare plans by means of a fiscal contribution of predetermined size."

Of course, the federal government did have conditions. But they must not be presented as such. The prime minister therefore said, "This proposal does not require detailed agreements governing the Medicare plan. It calls only for a general Federal-Provincial *understanding* as to the nature of the health programs which will make a Federal government believe that there are four criteria on which such an understanding should be based."

The four "criteria"—or "principles" as they were called—were as follows:

First, the scope of benefits should be, broadly speaking, all the services provided by physicians, both general practitioners and specialists.

Secondly, the plan should be universal. That is to say, it should cover all residents of a province on uniform terms and conditions. Since the basic reason for a Federal contribution is to make Medicare possible for all Canadians, it would hardly be logical to bring a Federal contribution into play for plans not aimed at universal coverage.

Thirdly, I think it will readily be agreed that a Federal contribution can properly be made available only to a plan which is publicly administered, either directly by the provincial government or by a provincial non-profit agency.

Fourthly, I think it is important to recognize the mobility of Canadians; each provincial plan should therefore provide full transferability of benefits when people are absent from the province or when they move their homes to another province.

There then came the first acknowledgement that new federal taxes would be required, in addition to any that provincial governments might find it necessary to levy in transferring medical services payment from the private to the public sector: "The Federal and Provincial governments together will have to raise the revenue needed for Medicare, or else reduce other expenditures. No one, I am sure, would assume that these costs could be added to budget deficits, which must be determined according to economic circumstances and responsible fiscal policy."

Taking cognizance also of the Hall Commission recommendations that there be massive expenditures on facilities and personnel training, the prime minister announced the proposal for a Health Resources Fund which would be concentrated on medical schools and teaching hospitals.

In view of the conflicts that were to come, the response of the provinces was extraordinarily low-key. Ontario did not respond to the specific proposal at all but commented on the need for developments in mental health, reorganization of health grants, and increases in hospital construction grants.[69]

Quebec reiterated its previous stand:

When our plan is introduced, it will be operated outside any joint Federal-Provincial program in line with our general policy of opting out in all areas within our competence. Quebec's decision in this matter rests on the acceptance of our obligations to our citizens and on the necessity to exercise our rights; it is not guided by any desire for isolation; it is still less connected with any strategy aimed at inducing each province to establish a program completely different from that of the others, which would make it relatively easy for private interests apprehensive about Medicare to play one province against another in order to postpone, or even prevent, its introduction in Canada....in fact, Medicare may be one subject on which there is most agreement among Canadians generally, regardless of their ethnic origin. The Federal government can make it easier for provinces to exercise their constitutional powers, for example, by rectifying the present system of sharing revenue sources in Canada.[70]

New Brunswick fully endorsed the policy statement but emphasized that "our ability, and the ability of several other provinces is limited, not by desire or intelligence, but by dollars and cents."[71]

Manitoba indicated that the provision of health services was high on a list of priorities in that province. It reminded the conference that seventy-two percent of its population were now insured and that five years earlier Manitoba had introduced a medicare program for recipients of social assistance. "We hope before long to extend the application of Medicare and both the non-profit and other types of health insurance coverage continue to grow vigorously in the province. Our policy is to work ultimately toward a comprehensive and universally available health insurance plan relating to the principle of need with government assistance being made available to those who are unable to provide this protection from their own resources."[72] Manitoba was clearly siding with Alberta in the kind of program that it wanted.

Saskatchewan, with a program already in operation, was of course pleased with the proposal but emphasized "that the extension of health services should be undertaken only when positive steps are taken by all governments, the medical profession, hospital boards, and the public to effectively control the level of hospital and medical costs." Saskatchewan was speaking from experience and the words were to echo for many years.

And so, with minimum debate, and no outright opposition, the conference adjourned.

The resolution of a governmental policy is rarely if ever final. Despite a minister's reluctance "to open up an act" for minor adjustment, the Queen's Printer's office is annually deluged with revisions to decisions embodied in earlier statutes. In the majority of government policies, the decisions are announced with the introduction of the legislation in the House and, if the Government has a majority, with the exception of minor revisions forced by the opposition, the basic policy will remain substantially unaltered. But, as with hospital insurance a decade earlier, the annoucement of the medicare proposal a year in advance of its passage as an act permitted, if it did not invite, continuing attacks on the policy. What we are concerned with in this section, therefore, are the decisions the Government adopted in meeting these pressures and the modifications, if any, to the basic policies incorporated in the proposal. In other words, to what extent did the "politics of strategy" affect the policies of the measure? If compromises were forced, these were changes in policy; if a demand for change was resisted, it was a decision to reaffirm the original policy.

The next stage in the strategy was dictated in large measure by five factors: (1) The minority position of the Liberal government, after, as well as before, the election in November 1965;[73] (2) The increasing opposition from the insurance industry and the medical profession; (3) The growing resistance among several of the provinces to the principles underlying the federal plan; (4) The increasing seriousness of the state of the economy in the face of rising inflation and the budgetary deficits of the federal government; (5) The increasingly vocal support of the Liberal party for the proposal, constantly reinforced by the NDP.

The seeming harmony of the 1965 Conference at which medicare was proposed was deceptive for, once the interested parties began to read between the lines of the generalities in which the principles were couched, the newspapers and electronic media gave vast coverage to the issue of medicare and the mounting opposition to it. The election campaign itself focused a great deal of public attention on the issue as did a four-day conference in Ottawa in November when representatives of twenty-one Labour, Welfare, and Church groups met to discuss a health charter for Canadians.[74]

It was true, however, that the election results—a gain of only two seats for the Liberals—had not demonstrated a major out-cry by Canadian voters for medicare and this was reinforced later by a poll[75] conducted by the Canadian Institute of Public Opinion in September 1965, which produced the following results:

Question: "Do you think the medicare program should be a compulsory one in which every Canadian would have to join, or do you think it should be a voluntary plan, in which Canadians themselves could decide whether or not to join?"

The responses:

	Compulsory	Voluntary	Undecided
Total	41%	52%	7%
East	40%	50%	10%
Quebec	47%	46%	7%
Ontario	40%	54%	6%
West	45%	51%	4%

That except in Quebec slightly over half the respondents preferred a voluntary approach was not lost on the decision makers.

In September 1965, the B.C. medical plan came into effect, adopting the CMA-CHIA policy of subsidizing those whose incomes fell below the income tax threshold but establishing a governmental agency to insure all individuals and families—as distinct from groups—whether requiring subsidy or not.

The Ontario plan, modelled on Alberta's, was unveiled in the Legislature on January 28, 1966, and provided subsidies for those who obtained private insurance if their taxable incomes were below $1,000. It was estimated that twenty-five percent of the population would qualify.

The Alberta voluntary plan completed its first year. And although 200,000 people were still uninsured (approximately one-half of them low income earners eligible for subsidy), the determination of the Government to oppose Ottawa's format seemed to rise exponentially.

The Ontario legislative debates on Bill 6 (OMSIP) were a dress rehearsal for the national debates to come, for here, in contrast to Alberta, a strong opposition of Liberals and NDP conducted a vigorous attack on the Ontario insurance company-oriented policy. Premier Robarts defended his program as being "designed to meet our financial capabilities for the moment and to help those who need it most" and clearly Ontario was moving on the assumption that its program could meet the four federal criteria.[76]

THE POLICY

The broad outlines of the policy that emerged from the great variety of inputs from interest groups and provinces, from the new stresses in the federal-provincial relationships, and the withinputs developed through the interaction of the bureaucracy and the political leaders had been presented to the Federal-Provincial Conference in July 1965. Now, late in the session of 1966, time was running out, if the program were to be introduced, as planned, to coincide with Canada's Centennial on July 1, 1967.

The critical stage had been reached when the legislation must be presented to and piloted through the Commons. But, since the conference, there had been a remarkable change in the key actors. Judy LaMarsh had been replaced by Alan MacEachen as health minister and Walter Gordon had been succeeded by Mitchell Sharp. Miss LaMarsh remained in the Cabinet as secretary of state but Walter Gordon was now a back bencher, his forum the caucus and his public speeches. Mr. MacEachen was as determined to see medicare enacted as had been Miss LaMarsh, but the switch from Gordon to Sharp meant that Finance had reverted to its traditional position of opposition to medicare. It was a crucial change.

As the draft legislation cleared Cabinet before introduction in the House, the only opposition to be raised even by Mr. Sharp was whether the timing was right in view of the inflation threats. The decision was to proceed.

The details of the act followed the "principles" laid down earlier.[77] However, the bill revealed two new policies. The financial base on which the federal share would be calculated would be the "national" *per capita* costs calculated on the costs in *participating* provinces rather than in all provinces. This would mean adjusting the national figure each time another province came into the program. It would also probably mean a smaller federal contribution until Ontario with its large population and high costs entered into the calculations.

The second new policy involved an enlargement of the definition of "publicly administered." Private insurance companies could serve as carriers provided that no profits accrued to the company, their books were open to public audit, and their administration was responsible to the provincial government. This was an obvious shift in strategy to placate Alberta and Ontario and enable British Columbia with a half-dozen voluntary plans to qualify immediately.

In view of the strength of the opposition, and the minority position of the Government, the outputs were extraordinarily bold. There was an obvious, and justified, assumption that support would be forthcoming from the NDP, whatever the position of the other opposition parties.

STRATEGY II

It had been the hope of the minister that the second reading could take place before the summer recess, but the session had run out and the postponement provided more time for opposition forces to mobilize. The Government could take some heart from the fact that the official opposition was divided, too, Mr. Dinsdale saying, "we heartily endorse it" and Mr. Fulton condemning it as "heavy handed and ruthless, financial blackmail . . . not cooperative federalism [but] . . . dictatorial federalism of the worst sort."[78]

The parliamentary debate and the accompanying publicity on the details of the program resulted in a massive reinforcement or snowballing effect as the opponents of the proposal took advantage of the parliamentary recess that permitted a last-ditch offensive. A focal point for the opposition was the regularly-scheduled Provincial Premiers Conference held in Toronto on August 1 and 2. So strident were the tones, so angry the voices, so vehement the opposition, that one journalist summed up: "The Federal government's proposed legislation lies torn, tattered and politically rejected."[79] And another said, "But in the end, they [the provinces] did gang up on Ottawa so surely and thoroughly the whole future of Medicare is now in the balance."[80]

The chief objections were universality and rejection of the policy of subsidizing those voluntarily enrolled in private insurance companies and prepayment plans. The attacks in some leading newspapers were buttressed by ignorance or deliberate attempts to mislead. In one article, the *Toronto Telegram*[81] said that under federal medicare:

1. "[There would be] almost certainly no cheaper premiums."
   (False, if the fifty percent federal contribution were used by the province for the intended purpose);

2. "Ontario subsidizes OMSIP to the extent of $70 million and the extra money from Ottawa ... couldn't be used to wipe out this deficit."
   (False; this is precisely what the federal contribution was for);

3. "Employers usually pay some part of the premiums. If the employers dropped out—they don't directly pay any part of OMSIP premiums [irrelevant because OMSIP insured individuals]; the employee with Government help would be left to pay the lot."
   (False; since employers' contributions were invariably locked into union contracts).

There was also in this period constant reiteration of that blatantly false myth that Ontario, which provides half of federal revenues, would therefore pay half of the national costs. Ontario, of course, pays nothing to Ottawa; taxes are paid to Ottawa by Canadian citizens who happen to reside on a piece of Canadian territory called Ontario and much of whose high incomes is generated in other provinces and funnelled into head offices in Toronto through a highly centralized economic system.[82]

It was clear that the messages were getting through to the Cabinet. On August 4, 1966, in a brief discussion with newsmen,[83] Prime Minister Pearson gave the first official hint of financial concerns, saying that in the face of rising inflation[84] he had directed his ministers to cut back on government spending, but reaffirmed July 1, 1967 as the starting date for medicare, although stating it was not a deadline in the sense that all provinces must come in at that time. (Many in the Cabinet were hoping they wouldn't.) He also indicated he would be willing, as the Premiers' Conference had demanded, to hold a further federal-provincial conference on the subject. Moreover, the press was reporting a widening split in the

Cabinet. Winters and Sharp, with reputedly a majority following in the Cabinet, but not including the prime minister, were marshalling their forces in opposition to MacEachen and LaMarsh in Cabinet and Walter Gordon in the caucus to change the launching from the promised symbolic date of July 1, 1967, to July 1968.

On September 7, the second and more direct hint of delay appeared. Asked on a CBC public affairs program if the new austerity program in government would delay medicare, Mr. Sharp replied, "Well, I don't know," adding that a decision had not been made.[85] Nevertheless, he announced the postponement the next day in the House of Commons in his capacity as acting prime minister while Pearson was abroad in the United Kingdom attending a Commonwealth Prime Ministers' Conference. The resulting furor in the party was matched only by the jubilation of medicare opponents and critics. Health Minister MacEachen considered resigning from the Cabinet. Marchand informed MacEachen that if he did so, they would leave together.[86] On September 15, Walter Gordon attacked the Government's policy of delay in a speech in Port Arthur: "The argument that medicare should be put off in order to combat inflation will not stand up upon reflection. On the other hand the decision is being hailed as a great victory by those who are opposed to medicare in any form at any time. I believe that Parliament should proceed with the medicare legislation this fall and be prepared to implement it as soon as it has been accepted by a number of provinces."[87]

In her colourful language, Judy LaMarsh described the reaction to the Sharp decision in one part of the public: "The opponents of medicare smelled an ally. They came out from their lairs again: the medical profession, the provinces, medical care insurers, all of them. They renewed their vehement objections to the program. Sharp thus, very early in the Leadership race (as yet not even openly declared), put the Medicare question in issue."[88]

Almost all of Canada's leading newspapers, except the *Toronto Daily Star* and the *Ottawa Citizen*, endorsed the decision as a responsible move, and it was obvious that this action by Finance Minister Sharp strengthened the federal government's position in persuading the provinces at the upcoming Finance Ministers' Conference that restraint was essential in an over-heated economy. But at a conference of Liberal M.P.'s, Ontario Liberal MPP's, and a covey of party workers held in Peterborough over the weekend, the consternation, disappointment, and resentment over Sharp's power play in the prime minister's absence were resoundingly voiced. Said Leonard Shifrin, editor of a party newspaper, "The cheque the Liberals first wrote in 1919 has been bouncing ever since." Angry that a decision of such import had been taken without caucus consultation, young leaders, several of them parliamentary under-secretaries (including

Trudeau, Marchand, Munro, MacDonald, Basford, Pelletier, and Gray), sent a telegram to the prime minister demanding a caucus meeting.

The meeting of caucus was held on October 4. It was a stormy affair. As Peter Newman reports, the Government's stand was attacked by Lamontagne, Munro, Macaluso, Gordon, Faulkner, and Trudeau.[89] Judy LaMarsh described her role as follows:

> There was considerable danger that we would be unable to convince enough members in the House to vote for an amendment to postpone the date of implementation.
>
> I was convinced by this time that we would have to postpone the date of implementation until 1968 although I had originally chosen July 1, 1967 for its Centennial significance. I did my best to rally the Caucus by reminding them that no one had more of a stake in the legislation than I (the current minister appearing to have abandoned ship), and I intended to support one year's suspension, providing no further playing about with the legislation was countenanced.[90]

As Peter Newman has reported: "Mr. Pearson entered the argument to say that the medicare postponement had been his decision and that if the caucus did not agree with it they had better plan on a leadership convention."[91]

As Miss LaMarsh reports, "The Caucus went along and subsequently, Sharp as Minister of Finance clearly put the Government behind the delay, pitted against Walter Gordon who was not even a member of Cabinet. The party [at the Liberal Convention in Ottawa on October 10–12] had perforce to go along too."[92] But the party did not go along without insisting that July 1, 1968, be the latest date, and that there would be an earlier start if economic factors turned favourable.[93]

However, with this decision, there came a very critical attack from the most unlikely source: the president of the CMA who called the delay "a betrayal of Canada's needy people."[94] The strategy of the CMA was clear. If it could gain acceptance of its policy for a program for the needy based on a means test, the result might be the abandonment of the Government's universal plan.

On October 13, second reading on the medicare bill began, once again under the direction of Mr. MacEachen. It was a tense and courageous performance. A minister in a minority government, itself divided, facing strong criticism in the caucus, opposition in the business community and the professions, rejection of the proposal by the most populous provinces, aware of his near-decision to resign and the opposition's continuing contention that he should, MacEachen masterfully parried the attacks and piloted the bill. And, of course, he had the support of the NDP with Tommy Douglas' castigations of the Conservatives' "tin-cup medicare."[95]

On October 17 a CMA delegation,[96] acting on its earlier criticism, met with Mr. MacEachen to urge the Government to introduce a program for the medically indigent, protesting that the decision to postpone would deprive five million people of help they needed. This was a sixty-six percent increase over the number they had stated would need help in their brief to the Royal Commission on Health Services.

Although most of the opposition was directed towards thwarting the bill, one result of opposition criticism and pressure was acceptance by the Government of a policy change easing the addition of future benefits. The Government had originally felt that additional benefits should be adopted only after parliamentary approval. Because some members of the opposition were demanding the immediate inclusion of optometrists' and dentists' services, a compromise provided that if provincial legislation were first enacted such benefits could be added by the more flexible method of order-in-council.[97]

On October 25, after eight days of acrimonious debate, the bill passed second reading with only ten Conservatives and eleven others from Social Credit, Creditistes, and Independents opposed.

On December 8, the bill was given third reading in the House and, despite an impressive and eloquent argument by David Lewis of the NDP that the original starting date be reinstated, was finally passed by a vote of 177 to two.[98]

The debate in the Senate was brief and the act was passed on December 16, 1966. Five days later it received Royal Assent. The interested observer might justifiably have assumed that the long battle for national medical care insurance was ended, that in the Cabinet the issue had been settled. It would have been a naive assumption. The Hon. Mitchell Sharp, some provinces, the providers and the insurers of services had not given up. Whether the program would be launched or the landmark piece of legislation remain an inoperative statute still lay in doubt.

The argument for further delay—or even outright abandonment—hinged on the worsening financial position of the federal government. As finance minister, Walter Gordon had been able not only to bring the budget into relative balance but had even managed a small tax cut. For fiscal year 1966–67 Finance Minister Sharp had forecast a deficit of $150 million; it actually turned out to be $428 million despite a substantial tax increase. For fiscal year 1967–68, he forecast a budget deficit of $750 million.[99]

On October 24, 1967, Mr. Sharp announced that he favoured a supplementary tax-raising budget and a postponement of the July 1968 starting date of medicare.[100] Now back in the Cabinet in an ill-defined role as president of the Privy Council, Walter Gordon argued that the situation was more a political than an economic crisis. It was "a crisis of confidence in the government, the result of the party's defeatism, its confusion on medicare, foreign investment, the Carter Report, and government spending and uncertainty about the future leadership of the party."[101]

But an even more serious threat was revealed at the Federal-Provincial Meeting of Finance Ministers on November 16 and 17. There, Mr. Sharp took the initiative by presenting his revised estimate of the cost of medicare at $1 billion. As the *Globe and Mail* reported, "He appeared to put the estimate of the cost of medicare in the most dramatic—and frightening —terms possible" and, on questioning, said that he "did not know what Canadians were now spending on health insurance under voluntary and provincial plans."[102] The provincial finance ministers generally welcomed the proposal for another delay and some demanded it.

Mr. Sharp then acted to capitalize on this support. An emergency meeting of Cabinet was called for Monday morning, November 20. On Sunday Benson told Gordon that "Sharp is against Medicare and that it will be dead forever if deferred now."[103]

Sharp presented his case to the meeting. Gordon responded by telling the Cabinet that "the collective decision on medicare must be respected and not undermined."[104] After lengthy debate, the medicare launching date remained unchanged.

In the first week of January the financial situation worsened. On January 6, Edgar Benson informed Gordon that "Mike [Pearson] was worried both by the financial situation and the exchange rate and about what he should say about medicare. He [had] told Benson he had made a mistake about the latter subject."[105]

Mistake or not, it had been that group who had coalesced behind the leadership of Lester Pearson and, with his support, had brought medicare to Canada: Walter Gordon, Tom Kent, Keith Davey, Judy LaMarsh, Alan MacEachen, Maurice Lamontagne, and, later, Jean Marchand, and Edgar Benson. Their coming together had revitalized the Liberal party in its doldrum days in opposition and, among other important enactments, they had fulfilled a fifty-year Liberal commitment to health insurance. They were both challenged to that objective and supported in its achievement by Tommy Douglas and Stanley Knowles and their small band of NDP supporters. The final vote in the House of Commons—177 ayes to two nays—almost reaching the unanimous vote on hospital insurance ten years earlier, undoubtedly reflected the recognition of the Canadian people that a new system must come into being.

THE OUTCOMES

1. Unlike the case of hospital insurance, there was no minimum requirement of a majority of the provinces agreeing to the program before the

federal contributions could be made. Accordingly, on the inaugural date of July 1, 1968, only two provinces, Saskatchewan and British Columbia, qualified. Three more, Newfoundland, Nova Scotia, and Manitoba, commenced at the beginning of the fiscal year, April 1969. The others followed in this order: Alberta, July 1, 1969; Ontario, October 1, 1969; Quebec, November 1, 1970; Prince Edward Island, December 1, 1970; and New Brunswick, January 1, 1971. The Northwest Territories' plan began on April 1, 1971 and the Yukon program on April 1, 1972.

The first outcome was, therefore, achievement of the Liberal party's 1919 election promise formalized in the federal government's commitment at the 1965 Federal-Provincial Conference to "cooperate with the provinces in making Medicare financially possible for all Canadians." This was the federal view and was probably so construed by Saskatchewan and British Columbia. It could scarcely have been so interpreted by Ontario and Alberta, for the political costs to them of their "cooperation" were large, and they and some others considered the arrangement less "cooperation" than coercive "political blackmail." But whatever the political and economic costs that would impinge upon other provincial priorities, ten provincial programs with portable benefits finally came into being and a national plan was born. Such is the power of the federal purse even in areas outside its constitutional jurisdiction. The price which the federal government was to pay, however, both politically and economically, was also high.

2. The federal government was forced to raise new revenues and after examining and weighing numerous options, a new tax (called the social development tax—graduated to incomes up to $6,000 and constant thereafter), was decided upon. It, too, embittered still more the provincial governments, several of which were already, or considering, utilizing the same revenue source.

3. The political costs were primarily the worsening of federal-provincial relations at a time when unusual amity was needed in order that the scheduled reconsideration of the constitution might occur in a calm atmosphere of cordiality and trust rather than in the turmoil of financial strain and political recrimination. The extreme statement of provincial attitudes to both the medicare plan and the social development tax was uttered in total exasperation by Premier Robarts of Ontario: "Medicare is a glowing example of a Machiavellian scheme that is in my humble opinion one of the greatest political frauds that has been perpetrated on the people of this country. The position is this: you are taxing our people in Ontario to the tune of $225 million a year to pay for a plan for which we get nothing because it has a low priority in our plans for Ontario."[106] Only Premier Bennett had the temerity to say that Robarts was wrong.

4. Three provinces fought hard battles to obtain concessions even after the act was passed. Alberta, opposed to compulsion, found it necessary to abandon its insurance company consortium. So personally opposed to federal intervention was the health minister, Dr. Ross, that on the announcement of Alberta's decision to participate, he resigned the post he had held for twelve years.

In Ontario, consideration was given over a long period of time to the future role of Physicians' Services Incorporated and, finally, concluding that there was no real contribution to be made in serving simply as a post-office, PSI ceased its prepayment operations on October 1, 1968, when the Ontario plan began.

But the insurance industry operations in Ontario medicare were another matter. Given the basic philosophy of OMSIP, it was not to be expected that the insurance companies would be summarily dropped from their place in the administration. They were, of course, reduced to serving as post-offices and deprived of their profits from medicare contracts. Their inclusion in the administration caused an enormous amount of duplication and an unnecessary additional administration cost. They were phased out in 1972.

The Quebec battle had two objectives: to stay out of the plan and, when it was clear that that was impossible, to force Ottawa to hand over to Quebec the revenues from the social development tax collected from residents of that province before the Quebec plan began. For the period July 1, 1968 to November 1970, when Quebec's plan commenced, the amount was estimated to be approximately $160 million. With his new, large majority in the House of Commons, Prime Minister Trudeau was not inclined to accept the Quebec argument and so, finally, that demand ceased to be made.

The British Columbia plan adaptations were fairly easy to make since the insurance industry had had a relatively insignificant part in insuring medical benefits in that province and the non-profit prepayment plans could, with minor changes, be readily designated as "publicly-administered." It was necessary only to have personnel responsible to the Medicare Commission assess all medical bills and audit financial statements.

The Atlantic provinces confronted similar, complex problems of creating new administrative agencies, dealing with the existing prepayment plans, and finding new sources of revenue. Their difficulties were only partly ameliorated by the favourable terms of the financing formula.

5. The drain on the federal treasury occasioned by the new medicare expenditures and unusually rapid increases in hospital insurance costs necessitated in the view of federal finance officials a cut-back in other health expenditures. The decision was made, therefore, to phase out most

of the national health grants program and to stretch out the allocations from the health resources fund.

6. The transfer of medicare financing from the marketplace to the public sector resulted (in part, as planned) in an increase in Canadian expenditures on health services. The main reasons were the end of uncollectable medical accounts and the virtual ending of courtesy service, the steady increase in the population, the rapid increase in the physician-population ratio, increases in the unit costs of services, expanding technology, and increased utilization resulting from such changes as age distribution of the population, increases in the proportion of the population living in urban areas, improved education, and inflation generally. The increases have been, in fact, greater then those envisaged by the Royal Commission on Health Services which had recommended increased expenditures to meet clearly observable unmet needs and improve inadequate resources of personnel and facilities.

The federal government had reacted to its lack of control of expenditures by offering new proposals to the provinces. These having failed, it unilaterally announced in 1975 upper limits on the percentage increases of hospital and medical care insurance costs that it would share, and gave the required five-year notice of termination of the Hospital Insurance Agreements. Finally, by the passage of the Established Programs Financing Act in 1977, responsibility for the program was transferred to the provinces. Income tax points and unconditional payments to be adjusted in accordance with GNP were also transferred to the provinces. The conditional grant-in-aid system as a device to introduce and finance health insurance had run its course in just two decades.

As indicated above, all the provinces but Saskatchewan encountered varying degrees of difficulty in meeting the federal conditions in order to obtain the federal largesse. But, without doubt, the experience of Quebec was the most dramatic, highlighting the complexity of decision making in a federal state, especially under conditions threatening domestic upheaval.

To that analysis we shall now turn.

Chapter Seven

Quebec Medicare:
*Policy Formulation in Conflict and Crisis**

THE FINAL MAJOR ACT of the thirty year drama of national health insurance had reached its climax on the inaugural date of the federal medical care insurance program—July 1, 1968. The drama would not be complete, however, until eight more sub-plots—the provincial government decisions —had been resolved. Saskatchewan and British Columbia had qualified with only minor adjustments to their existing programs. In all the other provinces, as noted in chapter 6, there were serious political decisions to be faced, complex administrative arrangements to be made, and new revenue sources to be found. The decisions in Alberta and Ontario, for example, were especially difficult, involving as they did choices on whether and, if so, how to use the insurance companies and prepayment plans.

It was the Quebec sub-plot, however, that was to become the most conflict-ridden, and therefore the most politically perilous, of all. Commencing with disagreement with the federal government, it rose to crisis proportions with the specialists' withdrawal of services, and reached its climax as medicare became inextricably bound up with, and its dénouement greatly influenced by, an even greater crisis—the kidnapping of a foreign diplomat, murder of a Cabinet minister, and a federal government finding of "apprehended insurrection." It surpassed in magnitude even the crisis of Saskatchewan eight years earlier.

*This chapter is a revised version of an article that appeared in *Canadian Public Administration* vol. 15, no. 2.

Before beginning the analysis of the Quebec medicare decision, it is necessary to review the background against which the scenario unfolded.

THE BACKGROUND

One of the major reasons for the complexity of the medicare issue confronting the Government of Quebec was the continuing conflict with the Government in Ottawa as Quebec's aspirations of the sixties clashed with the seemingly immutable realities of the federal relationship. An analogy is that of a nation both conducting a vigorous foreign policy in the wake of foreign initiatives, and confronting related domestic needs on an unprecedented scale and within the confines of a very limited time frame. As in similar crisis situations elsewhere, one sometimes senses that the main actors performed as if beset from within and beleagured from without, as the not-so-tranquil Quebec revolution generated its own mass expectations and Ottawa dangled an irresistible offer—on its own terms.

Accordingly, overriding all program objectives of the provincial government, two major goals dominated Quebec's strategies and negotiations in this period: (1) complete autonomy in all areas of provincial jurisdiction, including not only new developments in domestic programs and international cultural relations but also a transfer to Quebec of the control and financing of all shared-cost programs in any way related to social and cultural development; and, as necessarily following, (2) the fiscal capacity to finance the programs independently of Ottawa's conditional grants systems.

In 1966 Premier Johnson stated Quebec's position in these terms:

Specifically what does Quebec want? As a sovereign state of a nation it wants free rein to make its own decisions affecting the growth of its citizens as human beings (i.e., education, social security, and health in all respects) through economic development (i.e., the forging of any economic and financial tool deemed necessary) through cultural fulfillment (which takes in not only arts and literature but the French language as well) and the presence abroad of the Quebec community (i.e., relations with certain countries and international organizations).[1]

In Professor Ramsay Cook's assessment, these interrelated constitutional objectives had become of such primary importance that early in the sixties they overtook "debate and action in the field of social and economic reform."[2] But medicare, clearly, was an exception, for in its domestic application it involved changes of such sweeping magnitude that it resulted in a government crisis. In its constitutional implications, it resembled from Quebec's point of view the last telling blow of a wounded lion, the final imposition of one more federally initiated program. Eventually the Government in Ottawa recognized that that particular policy position could never again be occupied; as Prime Minister Trudeau was to say four years later to Quebec's finance minister: "Mr. Dozois, you will never have another Medicare, I promise you that."[3]

But these "national" objectives of Quebec ran counter to four federal government objectives: (1) The necessity of maintaining a direct federal "presence" with Canadian citizens, which could not be limited simply to imposing federal taxes to subsidize provincially-administered programs for which provincial governments presumably received the political credit; (2) The desirability—indeed, in Ottawa's view, the necessity—of maintaining national standards and portability of program rights even in programs such as hospital insurance in which a "contracting out" privilege might be granted after the program had been in operation for some time; (3) The retention of strategic fiscal control of the economy, an objective that would be weakened by outright transfer to the provinces of large spending programs and their accompanying income tax "points"; (4) And, finally—as a Liberal government—fulfillment of a commitment made by the party in 1919 and constantly reiterated thereafter to develop a program of *national* health insurance.

In this contest of wills for *deux nations* or one, or some viable point on the spectrum in between, Quebec had won three clear victories, each of such importance and embodying such principles as to indicate that the last had been seen of the typical grant-in-aid program in which Ottawa provided half the funds but all, or most, of the rules, and thus imposed its scale of priorities upon provincial objectives and budget allocations. These three, all familiar to Quebecologists, were: (1) The Barrette-Diefenbaker compromise on university grants in 1960 when the federal government agreed to a tax abatement of corporation income tax to Quebec in lieu of direct grants (via the Canadian Universities Foundation) to universities; (In 1967 this exception was adopted as policy applying to all provinces.) (2) The victory on the pension plan in which Quebec was able to establish its right to separate control, direction, and funding of a social program earlier characterized by the federal government as a national objective; (3) The adoption by Ottawa of a policy of the right of the provinces to "contract out" of existing shared-cost programs in the Established Programmes (Interim Arrangements) Act, 1965 whereby the provinces could receive the federal compensation under well-established joint programs in the form of a federal tax abatement rather than in cash payments.[4]

These decisions thus not only represented important mile-stones in Quebec's self-realization but reflected, as well, a general, albeit slow and sometimes grudging, change in opinion in Ottawa in its difficult balancing act of simultaneously maintaining control of its national responsibilities and acting as a "distributor of indulgences to state units."[5]

Indeed, they represented more—victories that embodied precedents for two fundamental principles: (1) a national objective could be achieved by separate but joint (and integrated) action: the pension plan; (2) provinces could "contract out" or "opt out" of established programs: hospital insurance.[6]

It was within this context that, at the 1965 Federal-Provincial Conference, Prime Minister Pearson proposed the medicare measure that was to climax his parliamentary achievements. As described in chapter 6, only the dedication of a few ministers explains its accomplishment, for not since the pipeline controversy of 1957 had a legislative measure of such explosive potential been proposed. The prime minister was extraordinarily diplomatic in his introduction. It was, he told the provincial delegates, an offer that fulfilled the Canadian government's responsibilities for cooperation with the provinces to achieve agreed-upon national standards, but it was *not* to be a typical conditional grant-in-aid program: "in the case of Medicare it is appropriate and possible to proceed by another route."[7] He then enumerated four principles that in the federal view should obtain: comprehensive services, universal coverage of all residents, public administration, and transferability of benefits for residents moving from one province to another. In addition, the federal government would "support provincial Medicare plans by means of a fiscal contribution of pre-determined size" (later set at fifty percent of the national *per capita* cost multiplied by the insured population in the respective provinces).[8]

From the federal vantage point, "principles" may not be "conditions," but in the application at the provincial level the distinction became blurred indeed. The distinction was, in fact, academic, for the "principles" were to give rise to problems and difficulties for the provinces greater than did the "conditions" of any other shared-cost program. How Quebec would respond to the federal initiative was predetermined by the policies it had already adopted in seeking the objectives of greater independence in its decision making within the federal system.

The other major element in the background that was to figure so prominently in the drama was, of course, the medical profession. In the early sixties, the organization of the medical profession of Quebec was highly fragmented. The largest single body was L'Association des médecins de langue française, comprising most of the French-speaking doctors, which was primarily interested in scientific and cultural affairs. The second was the Quebec division of the Canadian Medical Association, a relatively small group, a majority of whose members were English-speaking physicians in Montreal. The third was the College of Physicians and Surgeons (referred to, in Quebec, as a "corporation"), the body created by statute to regulate the profession with respect to admission, standards of qualifications, and professional conduct, and to take disciplinary measures when necessary. Its primary function was, as in all other provinces, protection of the public. Its mandate came from the Legislature.

In the absence of any other single unified voice to speak for the profession, however, the College had assumed activities that were not authorized by the legislation, particularly, consideration of the economics of medical care,[9] and had gone so far as to present a brief to the Castonguay Commission favouring health insurance in principle but "with minimum government intervention."[10]

In 1961 in recognition of their lower economic status and (in the major centres) lack of access to hospital beds, a group of general practitioners decided to organize under the syndicate law which, after extensive study of its operation in France, had been passed in Quebec in 1944.[11] The general practitioners began their organization in various Quebec regions under the leadership of Dr. Guy Laporte, who was succeeded in 1965 by Dr. Gerard Hamel. The regional organizations were grouped in the Fédération des médecins omnipraticiens du Québec (FMOQ) in 1965 and by 1966 represented approximately sixty percent of all general practitioners. During the same year the Fédération des médecins spécialistes du Québec was also launched, and Dr. Raymond Robillard became its first president.[12]

Three agencies were now paramount in the Quebec medical scene: the College of Physicians and Surgeons, and the two federations incorporated under the Syndicates Act to represent the interests of the profession.[13]

The power to be exercised by these respective agencies was later to become a major issue of conflict with the Government but, equally important, the two syndicates representing the profession came to have divergent views. The general practitioners supported the principle of universal health insurance and the specialists were adamant in their view, which coincided with those of the insurance industry, the Canadian Medical Association, and other business and industry spokesmen—that the role of government should be to subsidize those who could not afford private insurance.[14]

In addition to the fragmentation of the profession there were other aspects of the health system largely created by the specialists that would be vitally important in the Government's consideration of any proposed changes to that system.

The majority of the specialists in Quebec were graduates of three medical schools, Laval, Montreal, and McGill. The specialist achieved his qualifications through a minimum of eleven years' education and residency training, where the competition among individuals was prolonged and intense, and recognition of achievement was based on individual decisions and actions taken in respect of other individuals, the patients.

The world of the specialist as a social system was highly differentiated from that of the political and business decision maker.[15] The emphasis on individualism and individual responsibility was enhanced by the fiduciary relationship between the physician and his patient, in which the physician determined the fee he would charge based not only on the intrinsic relative worth of the specific medical "act" but also on the patient's ability to pay. Through this custom (known as the "sliding scale of fees") the physician performed a "Robin Hood" function as he provided low cost or free medical care to the poor who were obviously subsidized by his high charges to the rich. Once established in his practice with appointments to one or more hospitals in which his access to a number of beds for his patients was assured, the specialist in his functioning as "economic man," as distinct from his humanitarian role as healer, was clearly a prime example of the independent business entrepreneur. Moreover, he worked within a closed system, that is, the profession as a whole functioned as a state-maintained monopoly, guarded by the profession-controlled College of Physicians and Surgeons which regulated qualifications for entry to the system and meted out such disciplinary measures as were deemed necessary.

In addition, and particularly as it manifested itself in his association with hospitals, he had had an extraordinary influence in the development of the system, for as the Castonguay Report stated, "decisions relating to fixed assets and especially those involving the establishment of new services are still taken within the hospital, by virtue of the dynamism and personal interest of those who are there."[16] The improvements in the facilities, the advanced technology, the emphasis on standards, the striving for accreditation could not have been achieved and maintained without the leadership of the members of the profession. In short, the personal commitment, dedication, long preparation, and involvement engendered in the specialist an understandably proprietary attitude towards the system.

Added to the doctor's high sense of dedication and individual responsibility and his key role in the development of the system were the social attributions of prestige and influence. Until the 1960s the doctor's social position in Quebec had been second only to that of the priest. With the secularization of Quebec society in the 1960s he became, as a professional, number one.[17]

The fact that there was no large-scale profession-sponsored prepayment plan meant that Quebec doctors were late in coming to grips with new forces of change. For a prepayment plan introduces new factors: (1) there is a fee schedule with a known, fixed charge for each act;[18] (2) there is an assessment committee of a practitioner's colleagues which may ask for a medical justification for the medical act for which he is billing; (3) the practitioner becomes aware that he no longer performs the "Robin Hood" function; he can now ignore the income status of his patient because some other mechanism (in private prepayment plans, usually the employer contribution, and in public plans, the subsidy from general revenues) enables him to receive his full fee on behalf of low income patients, and the case for high fees from the rich disappears. With the imminent introduction of universal medicare, the Quebec practitioner was being required to adapt overnight to a system that his fellow professionals in other provinces had learned to live with for over two decades.

In addition, there seemed in Quebec a lack of awareness by the profession of the consumer revolution taking place everywhere, as students rebelled against their universities, consumers demanded manufacturers' responsibility, and citizens' groups challenged and demanded participation in all forms of decision making that affected their lives.[19]

The Castonguay Commission summarized the situation as follows:

> The organization of health services of the "closed system" or "medical model" type surely involves advantages: it allows greater autonomy of the system and better control of the formulation of objectives, with regard to personnel and the accomplishment of tasks. However, this type of organization lends itself to well-founded criticism, in our view: it is accused of being insensitive to the real needs of the people and not sufficiently flexible to modify its objectives and adapt its services to the socio-economic changes of the contemporary world.[20]

Former Health Minister Jean-Paul Cloutier expressed it this way: "There are many people asking themselves about the aptitude of professional associations to evolve rapidly and adapt to the new requirements of a society which wants to open up certain areas of activity and exercise a kind of surveillance which could produce beneficial effects."[21]

The profession, of course, had not been unaware of change, particularly of the role of government as an agent of change, for it had seen the impact of government hospital insurance on the hospitals. Although the hospital plan had achieved its primary objective of removing for patients the economic barrier to essential hospital care, there was a good deal of evidence that despite notable advances the Government had not entirely fulfilled its role as partner to the hospitals.[22] There had thus been little in the hospital insurance or social assistance medical care programs to counteract an almost innate distrust of politicians and government by the profession, or to persuade its members that any contemplated further extension of the Government's role in the health field would have salutary results for the profession. Nor was it to be expected that the profession would act any differently from any other minority group in the face of impending major changes externally imposed. It would seek to control those changes to forestall any threatened deprivation of its rights and perquisites.

It was in this turbulent environment, confronting an external government determined to intervene in the Quebec jurisdiction and powerful interest groups on the domestic scene, that the Quebec government was forced to determine its policy, create its strategy, and then act.

As in some of the preceding chapters, it is necessary to begin with consideration of the first stage of the strategy before examining the other elements in the policy formulation.

STRATEGY I

As noted above, the policy governing the strategy with respect to the federal offer of medicare had already been determined. The offer must be rejected. At the 1965 Conference, Premier Lesage replied to Prime Minister Pearson in these words: "We firmly intend to provide our citizens with a comprehensive medical insurance plan. . . . it will be operated outside any joint Federal-Provincial program; the Federal Government can make it easier for provinces to exercise their constitutional power by (say) releasing a number of points of the tax on personal or corporate income tax to provinces intending to set up their own comprehensive medicare plan."[23]

Following the conference, Premier Lesage set events in motion. He appointed Mr. Eric Kierans minister of health, announced that a limited plan of health insurance would be introduced the following year, and set up a research committee chaired by an actuary, Claude Castonguay, to begin studies on health services and health insurance in Quebec. Unfortunately, his plans for action came to a premature end with the return to power of the Union Nationale party in the election of June 1966, under the leadership of Daniel Johnson.

Despite the change in government there appeared no concomitant change in the basic strategy. One of Premier Johnson's first major actions was the appointment of a commission of inquiry in November 1966, with, again, Claude Castonguay as chairman, its mission to examine and make recommendations on the entire field of health and social welfare.

With the release of the committee's first volume in 1967, the need for government action was now more apparent than ever.

As in all other provinces, the Report of the Hall Commission in 1964, with its unexpected and bold recommendations for a provincially administered, national program of medical care insurance, parallel to hospital insurance, had a major impact on public opinion in Quebec and on the Government. The Castonguay Commission studied carefully the findings and recommendations of the Hall Report, and reinforced this massive material with public hearings and studies conducted by its own staff. It adopted some of the Royal Commission recommendations, rejected others, and proposed new directions and new designs for the delivery of health services in Quebec. Its major impact was to make even stronger the case for medicare in Quebec and thereby stimulated both public expectations and government consideration. The major arguments were: (1) Health indices gave a picture of greater need and lesser access to health services than in most other provinces. For example, the infant mortality rate was much higher than the average and life expectancy was lower.[24] (2) A high proportion of the population were in low income categories. Because of the well-known circular relationship between illness and poverty, only extraordinary governmental initiatives could hope to break the links. (3) A relatively low proportion of the population carried any form of private insurance. Despite an increase of over fifty percent in the number insured in the preceding ten years, the 1964 total represented only 43.1 percent of the population, and, as in other provinces, left out the "older citizens, rural groups, and people with low incomes who do not have insurance but whose need for health services is greater."[25] (4) The high unemployment rates not only reduced incomes for expenditure on health services but also, in many cases, resulted in family heads and single wage earners losing their group insurance coverage when they became jobless. (5) There existed a serious shortage of general practitioners and health facilities, combined with serious maldistribution of both facilities and personnel. In short, the same major factors that had resulted in a recommendation for universal health insurance by the Hall Commission for Canada as a whole were seen by the Castonguay Commission to prevail in Quebec with even greater immediacy, and it recommended, therefore, "that a complete and universal health insurance plan be established in Quebec."[26] (6) And then—of no small consequence— there was that constant factor in the background, the federal offer of one-half of the cost of a program that would meet its four principles,

an amount estimated at a minimum of $105 million for Quebec in the
first year.

As the Johnson administration examined the situation, there was no
doubt that the federal carrot was attractive, the Castonguay objectives a
noble ideal, and the rationale highly persuasive. However, the constraints
on precipitate action were real. (1) The conditions of the federal offer,
unless they could be drastically modified, contained both constitutional
and political implications that bordered on the unacceptable. To bow
now to the federally imposed conditions would represent a retreat from
the rapid evolution toward a more independent role for Quebec in the
federal system. (2) Domestically, the offer threatened the financial underpinnings of a host of competing demands for government action—all of
high priority and all with high price tags—and all this in the face of
annually mounting deficits.[27] The tax base of the Quebec economy was
limited; its retail sales tax was the highest and its personal and corporation
income taxes among the highest in Canada. (3) Moreover, as noted above,
the general shortage of health facilities and personnel was, to a degree,
simultaneously a reason for acting and for not acting. To create universal
potential demand through universal health insurance is to create universal
expectations; should the demand be postponed until the supply had been
increased, or should immediate demand be relied upon to create an adequate supply? (4) A fourth constraint was the opposition of powerful
bodies: the Quebec division of the Canadian Manufacturers' Association,
the Quebec Chamber of Commerce, the insurance industry, and the
Federation of Medical Specialists of Quebec.

These were formidable factors forcing caution and at the same time
demanding restraint, wisdom, and political sagacity.

In addition to the constraints, there were still other factors with unknown potential that also dictated caution.

1. *The total costs.* Both the federal government and the Castonguay
Committee had made extensive estimates of costs but their reliability
for Quebec was still in doubt. Not only were the un-met needs of those who
were uninsured unknown, but also the actual payments that would have
to be made to physicians were still very uncertain, and their impact on
an already over-extended budget unpredictable.

2. *The Ottawa response.* A second uncertainty was the degree of flexibility at Ottawa. Given Quebec's already strong feelings on self-determination, the growing resistance to the federal proposals by Ontario and Alberta, and the principle of "contracting out" that Ottawa had accepted, what were the chances of adopting partial measures that would meet the needs of the highest priority group, those with low incomes? Or what about a policy that would permit subsidizing low-income individuals insured through existing agencies, as strongly pressed by the insurance industry and the medical profession? But the Ottawa response would be most uncertain.

3. *The response of the medical profession.* This posed the greatest uncertainty of all. There was some encouragement in the policy of the Federation of General Practitioners favouring a government program. But that was more than offset by the more determined opposition of the more powerful specialists' federation. In the summer of 1967 the power of the specialists had been forcefully manifested. In August, 205 radiologists withdrew all but emergency services, breaking off negotiations being conducted under the hospital insurance program. Their action was supported on September 1 by 2,300 specialists who refused to participate any longer in the social assistance medical plan begun eighteen months before.[28] The dispute was finally ended when the Government agreed to extend payment for radiologists' services in their private offices and to authorize a general fee increase.[29]

Their success in that *contestation* had clearly demonstrated to the specialists their new found strength in the federation. To the Government it was a harbinger of what might happen if it introduced a program contrary to the CMA subsidization policy which the specialists strongly endorsed.[30] The cooperation of the profession on terms compatible with the Government's objectives was very much in doubt.

4. *Finances.* There were two other uncertainties, both having to do with financing. The Castonguay Committee had recommended that a universal program be financed by an increase in the personal income tax of 1.0 percent (with exemptions for single persons of $2,000 and for families of $4,000). But the Union Nationale government knew that the rising cost of education (whose benefits also were long-term while the costs were immediate) had been an important factor in Lesage's defeat and Johnson's victory. The whole idea of public education had been pushed beyond public acceptance. Would compulsory health insurance engender similar negative reactions?

The second financial problem arose because the Castonguay Committee had recommended a contribution to the health insurance fund of approximately $90 million from provincial revenues. But the current budget was already running a deficit of $136.5 million and required extensive borrowing.[31]

STRATEGY II

The release of the Castonguay Report on August 29, 1967, created a wave of public enthusiasm: the newspapers headlined the recommendations and quoted Jean Lesage, the Liberal opposition leader, as approving all of them.[32] Claude Ryan, editor of *Le Devoir*, warmly endorsed the report, noting that under private schemes the rich are better taken care of than the poor, and commending especially the idea of creating an independent health insurance board that would be outside party politics.[33] Eric Kierans, former Liberal health minister, said: "With a report like that the Johnson Government would have a hard time facing the Liberal Opposition."[34] The minister of health favoured a universal scheme because of the paramount importance of health.[35] The political pressures for action were mounting.

But no policy issue is quite as straightforward and clear cut for a Cabinet charged with the responsibility of governing as it is for either a royal commission or an opposition party. Moreover, the Johnson cabinet appeared divided. That had been revealed by Health Minister Cloutier in a press interview when he said, "I will make myself the defender of the *Report* in Cabinet."[36] Weighing the needs and demands, the constraints and uncertainties, the costs and benefits, Premier Johnson responded by following the cautious line of the Throne Speech. Instead of launching a universal plan at this time, he reaffirmed the Government's decision to begin the program by adopting measures that would come to the aid of those classes of society most in need of help. He then took two delaying actions: he referred the report to a group of government experts for financial analysis and to the Health Committee of the Assembly for general consideration.[37] That would give time for further government analysis and planning and postpone a final decision until the opening of the Assembly in 1968.

But the public debate on health insurance did not abate, and the media were filled with the controversial statements of its supporters and critics and the stories out of Ottawa of further attempts by Finance Minister Sharp to have medicare postponed yet again,[38] and of his warning that taxes would have to be increased to finance it. In January 1968, a public opinion poll had a special message for the government of Quebec.[39] The question and the results were as follows:

As you may know, the minister of finance has announced that taxes will have to be increased to pay for Ottawa's medicare program. Under these circumstances, which of these statements comes closest to the way you, yourself, feel about it?

	National	Quebec	Ontario	West
Federal government should bring in medicare as promised	55%	64%	49%	55%
Medicare should be postponed	19%	20%	19%	19%
Medicare should be dropped	19%	12%	23%	19%
Can't say	7%	4%	9%	7%

Despite the stated premise of the question that medicare would signal an increase in taxes, two out of three Quebec voters were in favour of the national plan, a proportion nine percentage points higher than the national average.

It was now time to be definite and specific. The Throne Speech announced, therefore, that the Government would "establish, by degrees, a comprehensive sickness insurance program, geared to the resources of the Quebec economy and to the means of tax-payers. In order not to impose too heavy a burden, it will begin by increasing its assistance to those in greatest need."[40]

However, as the Government thought about its strategy vis-à-vis Ottawa, it was obvious that major changes were occurring there. A new leader of the Liberal party, Pierre Elliott Trudeau, had become prime minister and an election was in the offing. Might that bring about a change in policy, a more flexible approach to the provinces?

And so the July 1, 1968 inaugural date of the federal medicare program came and went; Quebec was not in, nor were seven other provinces. Only Saskatchewan and British Columbia were charter members.

In the fall came the third change of lead actor in Quebec. On September 26, Jean-Jacques Bertrand became premier, following the death of the Hon. Daniel Johnson. The elements of uncertainty were increased as the new leader tested the throttles of power.

The new Trudeau government soon indicated its policy on medicare, and it dashed all of Quebec's hopes for increased flexibility. In his fall budget, Finance Minister Benson imposed an increase of two percent in the income tax (to a maximum of $120) and, with seeming perversity, named it the "social development" tax.[41] The action exacerbated tensions between the federal and provincial governments as never before. The provincial reaction was one of frustration and anger. By separating the two percent surtax from the regular income tax, the federal government prevented the provinces from sharing in its proceeds. Moreover, calling it a social development tax was, they said, a fiction that deceived no one; it was in fact a health insurance tax,[42] a direct levy to finance expenditures in a field of provincial jurisdiction, which not only flouted the spirit of the constitution but also made it difficult or impossible for the provinces to have recourse to the same field.[43] (Indeed, for these same reasons Premier George Drew had inveighed against federal invasion of the field of direct taxation at the Dominion-Provincial Conference in 1946.)[44] In Saskatchewan and Manitoba, it made more visible the provinces' special income taxes for medical care. In Quebec, where the Castonguay Committee had recommended a one percent income tax levy, the political costs of such a course were clearly multiplied by Ottawa's action. Finally, by levying the tax on all Canadian citizens, it increased the already heavy pressure on provincial governments to act on medicare and accept the federal priorities and principles.

Premier Bertrand[45] protested that "We cannot tolerate that the Federal government should feel free to levy additional taxes on our citizens in order to finance programmes outside Quebec which we know to fall within provincial jurisdiction."[46] Ontario's Treasurer McNaughton, demanded "that this money be turned back to us unequivocally . . . so that we may embark upon our own course of public medicare at an appropriate time."[47] Other provinces were no less adamant, and federal-provincial amity fell to its lowest point in years.

THE INTERNAL CONTRIBUTIONS

The finance and health officials of the Quebec government had been studying medical care insurance program alternatives and their costs since the 1965 Conference and, since late 1967, the continuing volumes of the Castonguay Committee Report. The frustrating element was the degree of dependence on outside forces that would limit the choices.

As the 1969 session of the Assembly progressed, the dilemma for Quebec became increasingly acute. The shape of domestic decisions depended upon the outcome of its external negotiations with Ottawa, and despite strong parallel stands by both Ontario and Alberta, the federal government with its recently acquired large majority in the Commons, and especially its success in Quebec, was in no mood to compromise. Demands by Quebec that the federal government turn over to it the entire proceeds from the (in Quebec's view, unconstitutional) social development tax so that it could independently finance any program of its own design, fell on deaf ears. Premier Bertrand had earlier stated the unhappy dilemma that his government faced all along:

Ottawa has placed us in a position where we might be one of the last provinces to sign. . . . Either Quebec joins the programme, and thus flies squarely in the face of the Canadian constitution, or else we do not join up and thus deprive our people of a lot of money to which they have the right. What does one do in a case like this? Don't we have to be realistic and make the best of the situation, that is, sign the agreement with Ottawa, counting on its being the last time?[48]

Some of the press, however, described the Government's internal concerns in different terms. The *Quebec Chronicle-Telegraph* editorialized: "The real answer to Quebec's sudden change of attitude must be sought elsewhere. . . . the Union Nationale is aware it has a provincial election on its hands. . . . Mr. Bertrand wants to make sure of a sweeping mandate. . . . What better way to do this than by blaming all of Quebec's troubles on Ottawa. . . . Quebec does not want medicare but Ottawa has forced its hands. . . . So whether Quebec likes it or not, medicare is going to come to the province."[49]

In this dilemma, Quebec developed an ingenious case. It had already opted out of one program—hospital insurance—which it was continuing to operate with federal approval. The federal medicare legislation permitted either federal withdrawal or provincial contracting out at the end of five years.[50] Moreover, the federal government had said that this was not a shared-cost program like past programs, and did not involve any continuing intervention in provincial decision making by the federal government.

Seeing this evidence of increasing latitude in the federal arrangements, Quebec officials wondered if the five-year provision could be shaken. What was immutable about a five-year period? Why not design the program to meet federal approval one day, and opt out the next? The twin objectives of national standards and provincial self-determination would both be achieved. It was a good ploy, but it didn't work; Ottawa wouldn't buy it.

If the announced target date of July 1, 1970 were to be met (and an election platform reinforced), for the Quebec government the eleventh hour had arrived.

By April, continuing reassessments of the situation in the light of the refusal of the federal government to accede to Quebec's demand for a return to it of the $110 million income surtaxes expected to be collected in Quebec led to the inevitable choice. In his budget address on April 29, 1969, Finance Minister Dozois announced that the Government would introduce a universal and public medical care plan. "The Minister of Health will be responsible for obtaining fiscal compensation from the Federal government to enable us to introduce our own health insurance plan."[51]

Accordingly, as the first step, on June 13, the Assembly passed an act establishing the Quebec Health Insurance Board, composed of twelve representatives of health professions, workers, employers, and government departments.[52]

With the establishment of the board, the administrative machinery could be created while the necessary negotiations and the designing of the program continued. At this point, we shall review the external factors that contributed to that design.

THE EXTERNAL CONTRIBUTIONS

The inputs were many and varied, and, as in any political issue, a substantial number were in conflict.

1. The articulated public demand was very strong, expressed most vociferously by the "common front" of the unions (CNTU and QFL), the teachers (CEQ), and the farmers (CFU). Their briefs to the Castonguay Committee had demanded an end to the professional corporations, the introduction of state medicine along the lines of the British National Health Service, salaried service rather than fee-for-service, and financing through the graduated income tax.[53] Their demands seemed to be supported by the public opinion polls indicating a willingness of citizens to pay the additional taxes required for the benefits of a program.

2. Since the cooperation of the physicians was indispensable the principles enunciated by the medical syndicates were of great influence. The Federation of General Practitioners had expressed its approval of health insurance in general terms, but the Federation of Specialists demanded that three major conditions be met: (a) The right of a physician to practise outside the program and to bill directly his patient for his fees, and the right of the patients to be reimbursed by the plan at the established rates (the "opting out" principle); (b) Control of all aspects of professional practice through the Quebec College of Physicians and Surgeons; (c) A negotiated fee schedule bearing some reasonable relationship to that established by the Ontario Medical Association.

3. There was strong opposition from the Quebec Manufacturers' Association, the Quebec Chamber of Commerce, and the insurance industry. The insurance industry recognized, of course, that acceptance of the federal conditions would eliminate their sales of basic medical insurance, although there might remain a possibility of participation in the administration of the program, as in Ontario. But if a limited provincial plan providing subsidies to individuals were adopted, a much larger role for the insurance industry would follow. They therefore opposed the federal proposal and urged acceptance of the specialists' policies.

4. The recommendations of the Castonguay Committee were also extremely influential. These emphasized universal coverage, financing by means of a one percent income tax and provincial general revenues, the right of practitioners to "opt out" but not of their patients to be reimbursed, and a rationalization of the health services delivery system (or non-system) through regionalization and development of poly-clinics.

5. The federal government exerted influence through its requirements of universal coverage, comprehensive range of medical services, administration by a public body (or by publicly supervised non-profit agencies), and portability of insured status among provinces. Of these four conditions, that requiring universal coverage presented the most serious policy difference from the Quebec interim position and, as the second requirement appeared in the federal legislation, it too opened up possibilities of major disagreement. Conditions three and four, however, requiring administration through a public agency and transferability of benefits, presented no obstacles other than that of principle—that the federal government should not be dictating conditions at all.

6. And last, but certainly not least, there were the opposition parties, the Liberals anxious to make a come-back, and the lusty eight-member Parti Québécois, its leader in the Assembly a practising physician, Dr. Camille Laurin, pressing for immediate action. It was an interesting reversal of the roles of government and opposition from those in the Saskatchewan medicare battle, for the Liberal and PQ spokesmen constantly criticized the delay in introducing a comprehensive, universal program.

As the inputs were analyzed and evaluated, it was not only the diversity of the conflicting views that was glaringly apparent; it was also what they shared in common: their absolute rigidity. The federal *conditions*, euphemistically called *principles*, were immutable; the demands of the common front strident; and the policies of the specialists adamant. It would require consummate political skill to find a solution that met all the conditions without alienating some powerful body of public opinion.

THE POLICY

On March 10, 1970, the Union Nationale Government introduced the Health Insurance Act (Bill 8) which received unanimous approval on first reading.

The act reflected primarily the inputs from the federal legislation and the Castonguay Committee. It was universal, comprehensive, and portable, and it was assigned to the Health Insurance Board for administration. There were two fundamental differences from all other provincial plans: it would be financed by a 0.8 percent income tax and a 0.8 percent payroll tax on employers; and health professionals would be able to opt out but if they did so their patients would not be reimbursed for any part of their fees.

Despite its aspirations for independent action, the Quebec government, as in every other province, had found the lure of the federal offer of one-half the cost of the program impossible to ignore, and it had therefore accepted the financial contribution—and all the accompanying conditions.

STRATEGY III

By now, however, time had run out for the Union Nationale Government; the election must be called. Thus, before the medicare bill could be debated and passed, Premier Bertrand announced the election date of April 29. With the dissolution of the Assembly, Bill 8 died. Whether the Government's policy of delay in coming to a decision on medicare contributed to its defeat is unclear, but on this issue at least it had given the appearance of a government unable to make up its mind. It is a fatal image when the opposition forces are strong.

The election (and the pre-election Liberal leadership convention) presented three surprises: the choice of Robert Bourassa as leader of the Liberal party; the decisive defeat of the Union Nationale party in the election, and the successful entrance into politics of Claude Castonguay, chairman of the Committee of Inquiry into Social Services (from which he resigned), and his appointment as minister of health. Castonguay was to emerge as one of the strongest men in the Cabinet and, as a result of his actuarial training and his experience with the committee, he was patently one of the most knowledgeable men in the field of health services, their delivery and financing, and their problems.

He embarked immediately upon a comprehensive policy review of the original Union Nationale bill, re-examining from the beginning the policy inputs and particularly those aspects dealing with the cooperation of the professions. The revised bill was presented to the Legislature on June 25.

THE REVISED POLICY

In general, the new bill duplicated that proposed by the Union Nationale on March 10. But as a result of negotiations with the medical syndicates one concession was offered: a maximum of three percent of physicians in any specialty and three percent in any one of Quebec's administrative regions would be permitted to opt out, with their patients being reimbursed up to a maximum of seventy-five percent of the established fee schedule.

On the other hand, in line with the committee recommendations, there were new proposals for a five-member committee to resolve disputes between practising physicians and the Health Insurance Board: two members were to represent the profession, two the Government, and the chairman was to be independent of the Government but not a member of the profession. The board was also given the authority to inquire into "any matter within its competence" and in doing so had the power and immunities of commissioners under the Public Inquiries Act. The program was to come into operation upon agreement with the syndicates. In presenting the measure, the minister also reaffirmed his confidence in the validity of the committee's earlier cost estimates.

FEEDBACK FROM THE ENVIRONMENT

The changes brought immediate critical response: The specialists directed their strongest attack on the limitation of three percent on those who could opt out. That should be a right of *all* physicians; they criticized severely the proposal for a committee to resolve disputes on the grounds that all aspects of professional practice should remain under the control of the College of Physicians and Surgeons. An equally strong and diametrically opposed barrage came from a "united front" of the unions (CNTU and QEL), teachers (CEQ) and farmers (CFU).[54] The unions opposed "the evasions, inadequacies and injustices" of the bill which they believed was written to accord with doctors' whims, offering scant coverage, and perpetuating the *privilèges intolérables* of the doctors.[55] Specifically, they attacked the opting-out provision, which they said involved the risk of producing two categories of doctors, one for the rich and one for the poor. They also wanted the scheme to be financed by a progressive levy rather than a constant percentage; stronger supervisory bodies; and much wider coverage, including dentures, drugs, and eyeglasses.[56]

The only answers to the entire problem, the common front claimed, were: (a) abolition of the "corporations" currently negotiating on behalf of the professions;[57] (b) introduction of a British-style system of state medicine rather than medical care insurance; (c) remuneration of all professionals providing service by salary rather than by fee-for-service; (d) creation of a crown corporation to manufacture and distribute pharmaceuticals. This attack on the legislation was made at a press conference at which it was announced that a province-wide campaign would be launched through public meetings and the distribution of hundreds of thousands of pamphlets criticizing the act and proposing the above alternatives.[58] To these criticisms were added those of the opposition parties. Jean-Paul Cloutier, former Union Nationale health minister, said that the withdrawal clause could cause enormous difficulties in practice, particularly in areas where there were few specialists or even general practitioners.[59] It was, in the view of most opposition critics, a "sell out" to the profession. Dr. Camille Laurin, health spokesman for the Parti Québécois, contended that while opting out was permitted in other provinces, the younger members of the profession understood that Quebec had special needs which precluded its use in that province. "We must conclude that this clause is the result of secret negotiations, an article made to measure for the benefit of certain prima donnas whose temper should be calmed in order not to affect the functioning of the public system."[60] Jean-Paul Cloutier also argued that the bill tipped the scales in favour of the doctors by placing all control of professional activities solely in the hands of the professional syndicates.[61]

Caught in the crossfire between the specialists protesting that the three percent was too small and the unions and opposition parties that it should be wholly removed, Castonguay agreed that the legislation had serious shortcomings that could be later overcome; the essential task was to get the main program underway so as not to deprive taxpayers of the benefits.[62]

He felt that few physicians would, in fact, opt out, and added a veiled threat that there were other means of assuring that the population would receive the kind of medical care to which it was entitled: "for instance, hospitals are financed from public funds and doctors like working in them. In such circumstances [as withdrawal of large numbers of physicians] can the government remain passive?"[63] But he remained conciliatory in tone, observing that "the quality of medicine is never decided by legislation and if we go beyond certain points in our attitudes, we can affect adversely the motivation of the profession and the quality of its work."[64]

Bill 8 passed second reading on July 9, and was referred to the Health Committee for clause by clause consideration. While the legislative process continued, preparations for implementing the program were of course already underway.

STRATEGY IV

The strategy now concentrated on the stage of implementation. There were many tasks in launching a program of such magnitude, but the major concerns were registration of the population, revenues, and the conclusion of agreements with the professions.

1. *Registration of the population.* The Quebec Health Insurance Board

(QHIB) had been established by the Act of June 1969. Its president, Mr. Robert Després, had immediately begun the task of establishing administrative objectives, recruiting senior personnel, and making feasibility studies of data processing equipment. Despite the indecision at Cabinet level whether the program would be universal or limited in its enrolment as the negotiations continued with Ottawa, the instructions to QHIB had been, "Be ready for a universal plan by July 1, 1970."

It was a prodigious task to accomplish in so short a time, although fortunately from the point of view of the complexity of the administrative problems, it was never contemplated that the program should be operated through a hundred or more insurance companies as was done in Ontario. However, with unusually competent management, the task was accomplished. More than four million Quebec residents were first contacted in a registration campaign made possible by data collected from existing registers. This was followed by newspaper advertisements providing application forms. By June 9, 4,500,000 were registered; by June 30, the organization was ready to roll.[65]

From July 1 on, a major problem for the QHIB management was one of staff morale. The entire effort had been planned on critical-path strategy for July 1, but from then until November 1, the target date was a moving one, and as the target receded, morale declined, despite "dry runs" using the accounts of the medical assistance program.[66] An innovation in medical care insurance administration in Canada was the issuance of plastic cards (similar to credit cards) to all beneficiaries and the supplying of all doctors' offices with automatic imprinters (which with delightful French-Canadian humour became known as "Castonguettes") to reduce errors in transcribing identification numbers of both physicians and patients.

2. *Revenue collection.* It was unnecessary for the QHIB to establish an agency for revenue collecting since the contributions were to be collected by the Quebec revenue department. The revenue collection was, in fact, one aspect of the program with which the QHIB was only indirectly concerned, since the act provided that benefits were not contingent upon payment of the tax as they typically are in provinces financing by means of premiums.

3. *Negotiations with the professions.* Five organizations were involved: the Federation of Medical Specialists; the Federation of General Practitioners; the Dental Surgeons; the Professional Association of Optometrists; the Association of Oral Surgeons. With the optometrists, negotiations were reasonably straightforward. They wanted to participate, and the major items to be agreed upon were fees, services to be insured, general

standards of competence, and competence for such special services as adjustment of contact lenses.

Negotiations with the dental syndicate were difficult since the policy intent was to limit dental services to those performed by dental surgeons requiring specialized operating equipment available only in hospitals. But the Quebec Dental Surgeons Association requested the removal of this limitation since the majority of hospitals outside the main centres were not specially equipped, and unless patients travelled long distances, it was for them an unrealizable benefit. In addition, they claimed, it placed an artificial distinction between what a patient had to pay for and what could be obtained as an insured benefit.

Negotiations with the medical profession were of another order. Although the medicare bill had passed second reading unanimously, the Health Committee, to which it was referred for clause by clause deliberation, became the new battle arena for all the criticisms levelled at its provisions from all sides of the political spectrum as well as from the professions and the public. Although not by choice. The committee had decided to hear no more public representations, but on July 8 the "common front" of the four major unions created a "confrontation" by crashing the committee meeting and demanding that their views be heard. It was then decided to grant the professions the same opportunity. Although the discussions were of a generally high order, it was now becoming clear that the lines were crystallizing: on the one side the unions, the opposition parties, and the government, and on the other the specialists, with the FMOQ playing a fairly neutral and constructive role.[67] The opting out provision was clearly the key issue: the unions threatened a strike if it were not withdrawn; the specialists said they would not sign an agreement if it were not greatly expanded.[68]

In the midst of these deliberations, the debate was given new thrust by the release of Volume VII of the Castonguay (now Nepveu) Committee Report, dealing with the relationship of government to all the professions that had been granted or were requesting self-governing status. The analysis paralleled that of the Ontario Committee on the Healing Arts, but went beyond the latter to include, for example, engineering and architecture, and concluded:

> The notion of professions which guided the edification of our professional law owes less to the survival of Middle Ages corporatism than to the ideas of liberal society on State intervention, to the fearful attitudes of Quebec's population with respect to the State and to the ideologies and interests of social groups (lawyers, notaries, doctors) who traditionally have taken over the legislative function in Quebec. At least, it is difficult to explain in any other way the sometimes ex-

aggerated tendency of the Quebec state to entrust its own rules to corporations [that is, professions].[69]

What the specialists saw was not only a change in the equilibrium of their present system—all fees to be predetermined, coming from a single, monitoring source and a restructuring of the independent relationship of the College of Physicians and Surgeons to government—but as well, if the Castonguay Report were adopted, perhaps a complete change in the system of fees payment itself.

Their first encounter with the Government was not reassuring. After sporadic discussions[70] in the spring of 1970 between the syndicates and the minister of health and his senior officials (discussions which the specialists considered wholly unsatisfactory), the Union Nationale government had introduced Bill 8 which included provisions differing substantially from the specialists' views. By the time it became necessary to consult with the new Liberal government, interest had been compounded on the legacy of distrust.

The deprivations which the profession perceived in the bill were three: (a) loss of opportunity (viewed as a "right") to deal financially only with the patient rather than with the insurance system and to charge fees in excess of the government rates, an option provided in other provinces; (b) deprivation of self-government of the profession as a result of certain powers given to the Health Insurance Board which appeared to have the potential to remove control over strictly professional matters from the College of Physicians and Surgeons;[71] (c) deprivation of income because of expected insufficient appropriations for the insurance fund.

INTERNAL POLICY REVIEW

Aware of the extraordinary array of strong and conflicting views now before it, the Government conducted a thorough-going reappraisal of its policies incorporated in the bill. The three percent opting out provision clearly satisfied no one. On the other hand, given the income levels of Quebec residents, a system in which any substantial number of physicians might opt out could add seriously to the financial cost of medical care and thereby compromise the objectives of the entire program.[72] To permit no opting out carried with it an unpredictable cost that might reach terrifying proportions: the exodus of an uncertain number of the most highly qualified specialists in Quebec. It might be a relatively small number, but the English-speaking specialists were highly mobile as were most of the French-speaking specialists who were bilingual.[73]

The issue of controls by the College was coloured by (1) the new philosophy of the Castonguay Committee respecting relations of the Govern-

CHAPTER SEVEN

ment to all professions,[74] (2) the tacit recognition that the College had not rigorously fulfilled its mandate to guard the public interest, and (3) the experience with claims evaluation under the medical welfare program. Former Health Minister Cloutier expressed it this way, "We were very conscious when we drafted our own Bill of the need to regulate professional activities more closely; we had learned our lesson during the administration of the Medical Assistance Act ... as a result of the dissatisfaction felt by the Health Department and the Medical Assistance Board [occasioned by] the slowness and lack of severity of the decisions of the College of Physicians and Surgeons."[75] There was also grave concern that it would be irresponsible to undertake payment of $300 million of public funds to any group without some greater degree of financial control than was possible through existing mechanisms.

On the issue of the level of payments, there were conflicting realities. The primary one, as has been discussed, was the limitation of the province's economy, its tax potential, and the budget. The second was that in recent years physicians' incomes in Quebec had consistently averaged between fourteen to sixteen percent less than those in Ontario[76] despite the fact that the physician-population ratio in Quebec was approximately fifteen percent lower than in Ontario. Or, expressed in another way, *per capita* expenditures on medical care in Quebec were twenty-six percent less than in Ontario.[77] In the interests of improving the supply of physicians it would be desirable to close the income gap as much as possible; but equally important was the realistic acceptance of current budgetary constraints.

Weighing the options, the Government came to the conclusion that, in the long run, the risk of a major exodus was less than the alternative of permitting what might well be widespread opting out of the program. Accordingly, when the bill was returned to the Assembly the "opting out" clause remained, but the provision for three percent to opt out *with reimbursement of their patients* was removed. For all practical purposes this foreclosed the possibility of opting out. The powers of the Health Insurance Board to deal with disputes over payments was retained, but the issue of the level of payment was left open.

The bill was passed on July 10, 1970, by a vote of fifty to eighteen, being opposed only by the Créditistes on the principle of compulsion. When it would become law now depended on negotiations with the health professions; but from their point of view the Government had declared, in effect, the contentious issues non-negotiable.

The classic bargaining situation now obtained, the confrontation of two organizational systems with differing objectives but interdependent needs.[78] Because the delay of the program and the outcome of the

402

conflict were of such unusual public concern, both parties were critically aware of the powerful role that public opinion would play in the outcome. In the strategy of both, publicity would be a major weapon.

In addition to its publicity campaign the other stages of the specialists' strategy would be negotiation, partial withdrawal of services, full withdrawal. The Government's scenario would progress through negotiation, mediation, Health Committee hearings, and a special session of the National Assembly to launch the program without the syndicate's agreement. Each side had powerful ultimate weapons: the specialists could refuse delivery of their services, indispensable to the program; the Government could resort to back-to-work legislation which had effectively ended the teachers' strike in 1969. Both of these would be violent, crude uses of power with unpredictable costs and uncertain outcomes.[79]

By July 21, in the view of the specialists, the negotiation stage had failed. The appeal to public opinion had now to be expanded and accelerated to force the Government to compromise. Dr. Robillard, in a press interview, acknowledged that he was leading a saturation public information campaign in what he termed "an heroic attempt" to force the Government to backtrack without facing a strike.[80]

The difficulty for the specialists was not only the absence of strong, organized allies (as the Saskatchewan College had had in the Liberals and Conservatives), but also basic disagreement within the profession, as the Federation of General Practitioners continued its separate negotiations. The specialists had two audiences: the general public, to be reached through the media, and their patients. It was also essential that the profession itself be informed and united.

The campaign, financed from a war chest variously quoted as amounting to as much as $500,000,[81] was waged among these groups simultaneously. A group of twenty-seven (later expanded to fifty) specialists began tours of the province concentrating on hospitals and their medical staffs and on interviews with the local media. Thousands of pamphlets were distributed; Dr. Robillard published his book, *Medicare, the MDs and You!*,[82] a lucid and persuasive statement of the specialists' position; wives of specialists became an active force, holding hundreds of kaffee klatches and making thousands of phone calls. "The specialists are in revolt against this law" (Dr. Raymond Robillard, quoted by Claude Ryan in *Le Devoir*, July 22, 1970). Claude Ryan argued that that attitude was inadmissible: the law had been passed, an expression of the sovereign will of the people, and the specialists were bound by it like everybody else. "The specialists have a right to get angry," said Jean Pellerin, "but not to scare the people with strike threats."[83] Dr. Robillard said it was not up to him to call a strike: "If the impasse continues, only the members of the Federation can decide whether there will be a strike."[84] The "common front" of unions and citizens' committees used explosive language about the specialists' "blackmail."[85]

On the positive side, the campaign emphasized freedom, liberty, quality of care, and the evil of "conscription" in a democratic society. But inescapably fear became the main ingredient: fear of government interference in the practice of medicine, fear among doctors and their wives of a decline in standard of living, fear among patients that the services would be cut off, fear among the public that the number of doctors in Quebec would seriously decline.[86]

The specialists' publicity campaign reached its climax on August 27 with a massive rally in the Maurice Richard Arena. Approximately 4,500 people attended. Leading medical spokesmen from France, Belgium, the UK, USA, Saskatchewan, and Ontario, the president of the Canadian Medical Association, as well as Dr. Robillard, dramatized the threats to liberty, freedom, quality of care,[87] and the rights of the patient[88] that the act constituted. Perhaps the most ominous statements were those of Dr. Richard Wilbur, assistant executive vice-president of the American Medical Association, who said there was, in fact, a shortage of 50,000 doctors in the United States, and of the representatives from Belgium and Saskatchewan who claimed that their strikes had been successful. The term "Japanese strike" was heard more frequently, referring to a total withdrawal of services by the medical profession in Japan in 1961.

At the end of the rally, 98.5 percent of the 1,500 specialists present voted in favour of the following resolutions: "Resolved that the QFMS defend the professional freedoms of the physician and especially his therapeutic freedom and his right to opt out of the medical insurance plan without loss of benefits for the patient." "Resolved that the QFMS use all means necessary to this end and resort to a confrontation if necessary." The second resolution was construed by all to mean, of course, a strike.[89]

In assessing its policy position, the Government could not ignore the new inputs resulting from the specialists' strategy and it also had to take cognizance of public opinion as expressed in the press. By its very intensity the specialists' campaign evoked such descriptions as "blackmail" and "terrorist tactics."[90] In a calmer vein, René Lévesque cited the authority of Mr. Justice Hall for the important point that organized medicine derives its powers from the state, and the fact that the state has granted it a monopoly on such an indispensable service involves the responsibility to make that service available.[91] La Presse felt that the specialists' extremism would cost them dearly in the eyes of the public, although the personal dependence of individuals upon their doctors' skills would influence their judgement; a workable compromise must be sought.[92] The Montreal Star criticized the importation of foreign spokesmen to address the specialists' meeting, and compared such outside interference with the ill-advised statements of Generals Norstad and de Gaulle.[93]

But the Quebec press interpretations gave little guidance towards a decision and out-of-province comments were even more ambivalent. The *Toronto Daily Star* (long known for its pro-health insurance stand) saw the stance of the specialists in a negative light:

> The medical specialists held a big meeting yesterday. Strike meetings are a form of witchcraft. The people attending the meeting believe that if they shout, sing, applaud and exhort each other loudly enough, they will cast a spell that will assure their cause of success.
>
> They force Premier Bourassa and his government to negotiate under the gun. No government can give in to the threats of a small group in society and stay long in power. If the Quebec doctors believe that the threat of a strike will improve their bargaining position, they are wrong. If they finally do go on strike, their strike will be broken.[94]

On the other hand, Richard Purser writing in the *Ottawa Journal* concluded: "... and the ultimate reason the government cannot win is that an effort to break a strike means a flight of doctors from the province. . . . the doctors can leave but [the government] can't."[95]

The specialists' position became weakened, however, and the input from their campaign correspondingly lessened as they lost support of the other health professions. The president of the optometrists had already denounced the specialists' campaign as retrograde and suggested that the $500,000 could be better used re-training some of their members.[96] A split between the specialists and the general practitioners came out into the open when the latters' president, Dr. Gerard Hamel, said: "We never wanted to wash the medical profession's dirty linen in public," but that he had to defend the Fédération des médecins omnipraticiens du Québec (FMOQ) against attacks which the specialists had applauded. He said the general practitioners preferred fair and adequate income, obtained through negotiation, to the practice of making up for deficiencies by extra charges on their richer patients. The FMOQ claimed that it was more concerned with the great majority who would take part in the program than with the tiny minority who intend to opt out.[97] On the other hand, spokesmen for the young generation of specialists in training —the interns' and residents' syndicate—supported the specialists' stand.[98]

But the conflict proceeded along its seemingly inexorable path as if some master hand had drafted the scenario and the actors were playing their roles toward a predetermined finale.

On September 10, Dr. Robillard announced the specialists' ultimatum: if the deadlock in negotiations was not broken in fifteen days "there would be a confrontation."[99] Premier Bourassa again denounced their stand as political blackmail, and said "it is absolutely clear that the government cannot tolerate any situation whatever in which the population might suffer because of this type of confrontation."[100]

On September 11, the health minister announced the appointment of a conciliator, Judge André Montpetit, adding that if he were unsuccessful the Health Committee of the National Assembly would be reconvened, and if necessary the Assembly itself. He also scored the "fear" and "poison" propaganda being used by the specialists in their campaign: their charges of "government-imposed socialistic-communism, of deterioration in the quality of health care of patients who would be unattended, of a flight of physicians." None of these he felt would, in the event, prove to be true.[101]

By September 15 the specialists had prepared a twenty-two page document restating their case and the arguments for it (which came to be referred to as their "white paper"). It has the appearance, like the camel, of having been put together by a committee, for parts of it are articulate, strongly buttressed arguments (most of which have already been considered here). In other parts it suggests an intemperate emotional outburst certain to infuriate the Government[102] and to reduce the doctors' credibility with the public: it refers to the civil service as lacking in responsibility and competence, and to politicians without necessary preparation who in their "dark ignorance" are led "by those who govern them" (i.e., the senior civil servants). "The government intends to install state medicine of a socialist-bureaucratic type."[103]

On September 25, following a meeting with the premier, Dr. Robillard withdrew from the mediation proceedings and the premier announced that the issue would now be transferred to the Health Committee of the Assembly. But now issue three, the rates of remuneration, seemed to have become the key stumbling block. Dr. Robillard reported to the press that "the government's position on opting out *and on monetary arrangements* now are crystallized . . . . as a result all efforts at conciliation are at an end."[104] And in *Le Devoir*, Claude Ryan pointed to remuneration as the real roadblock.[105]

On Sunday and Monday (September 27 and 28) the Cabinet held lengthy special meetings and maintained its stand, as one journalist reported, "in spite of relentless pressure by the specialists through Dr. Robillard,"[106] except for a new compromise on opting out. Instead of two categories of doctors there would be three: (1) *les engagés:* those who opt in and collect their fees in full from the QHIB; (2) *les désengagés:* those who opt out but agree to charge no more than the authorized fees to their patients who would then be reimbursed in full;[107] (3) *les non-*

participants: those who do not participate at all, charge their self-determined fees and whose patients would not be reimbursed any amount.

On Thursday, October 1, the Health Committee of the Legislature began its hearings. Meanwhile the specialists entered stage two of their strategy. Dr. Robillard announced in Montreal that twenty percent of the specialists had already gone on strike. Simultaneously the president of the College of Physicians and Surgeons announced that the College reached agreement with the minister on the respective powers of the College and the Health Insurance Board.[108] This was obviously a successful "end-run" play by the Government with the College, by-passing the Federation of Specialists.

At the committee hearings, the specialists were conspicuous by their absence but the three other involved groups—dentists, optometrists, and general practitioners—emphasized that negotiations were proceeding satisfactorily, if slowly.[109]

The committee sent a special invitation to Dr. Robillard but a reply by telegram to Premier Bourassa from Robillard stated that the federation council was convinced that the Government had no intention of changing its position. "Under these circumstances the legislative committee gives no hope of solution."[110] Some considered the reply contemptuous.[111]

At the Tuesday afternoon meeting the federation sent two representatives, Dr. Léger, secretary of the federation, and a lawyer, who explained the federation's position, answered no questions, and handed over the "white paper."[112]

Reviewing the week's events, the *Montreal Star* editorialized: "If public education was the aim of last week's sessions of the National Assembly's Health Committee they could hardly have been more successful . . . . there was no longer any doubt where the chief blame for the bitter dispute over Medicare lay. By his latest and unfortunately quite typical, act of contempt, Dr. Raymond Robillard made it quite clear who was blocking the road to agreement."[113] The committee adjourned.

By Monday, October 5, the withdrawal of services had accelerated with approximately one-quarter of the specialists manning emergency services in relay teams; most of the others had left the province. The Government now decided to change its policy on the level of remuneration, and the premier offered to increase the health insurance fund by $20 million, an average of over $3,000 per physician.[114] In view of the breakdown of the Health Committee's efforts, the premier announced a special meeting of the National Assembly for Monday, October 12, to amend the medicare act to include the proposals now offered, including an interim fee schedule.[115]

On Thursday, October 8, at 8:00 a.m., the specialists began a full-fledged strike, maintaining only limited emergency services in thirty-eight hospitals. The issue, as the *Montreal Star* saw it was quite simple: "Who will govern?"[116]

By now, however, medicare had lost its first place concern in the Government's deliberations and its monopoly of headlines and prime time in the media. For on Monday, October 5, at 8:00 a.m., in the midst of strenuous efforts to assess the impact of a strike and assure the protection of the lives of those dangerously ill, with the Government seeking desperately for sane decisions, the word flashed that James Cross, the British trade commissioner, had been kidnapped and held for exorbitant ransom by the "Liberation Cell" of the Front de Libération du Québec (FLQ). And as the week wore on and communiqués were issued by the kidnappers, the atmosphere grew more tense. Then, to compound the crisis, on Saturday, the premier's deputy, Labour Minister Pierre Laporte, was kidnapped by the "Chenier Cell." On Monday, October 12, lawyers were designated to negotiate with the FLQ.[117] Under these pressures the scheduled National Assembly meeting to consider medicare was postponed.

The specialists' council met to consider its position and decided that the crisis had no bearing on their case.[118] Following their meeting Dr. Robillard announced: "Though we deplore the current events and consider the kidnappings of Messrs Cross and Laporte unfortunate we believe the situation does not affect our position one way or the other.... I can assure you we will not take advantage of the situation."[119]

The editorial response to this statement was one of incredulity: were the specialists in tune with the real world? As the *Montreal Star* commented, "that statement, of course, is just another example of the social vacuum in which the leaders of the specialists have been operating since Medicare became an issue."[120]

Over Tuesday, as rumours ran rampant, tensions grew, and the army was ordered to guard strategic buildings and VIPs in Ottawa, the specialists reconsidered their decision and offered a truce, but—still distrustful—only on condition that the opting out issue would still be negotiable and that any fee schedule established by the legislation would be subject to negotiation and retroactive application.[121] This conditional offer was seen, apparently, not as a patriotic response but simply as taking advantage of a public emergency, and the Government refused.[122]

On Wednesday the pressures on the specialists mounted: the Quebec Hospital Association, the Association of Medical Directors, and the Association des médecins de langue française begged them to call off their strike;[123] the College of Physicians and Surgeons sent a telegram calling on all physicians and surgeons to go back to work immediately, basing its demand on the reports it had received about the actual availability of medical care in the hospitals of Quebec;[124] the opposition Parti Québécois appealed for an immediate return to work, charging that the strike was endangering the lives of many;[125] medical students at the University of Sherbrooke denounced the specialists' strike.[126] There had been a threat from the "Nelson Cell" of the FLQ to kidnap a doctor if the strike were not ended by Wednesday,[127] and this was, understandably, a serious matter; Dr. Robillard became *introuvable*[128] and armed guards protected the headquarters of the Federation of Medical Specialists of Quebec and doctors on call.

On Thursday, October 15, as rumours of threatened insurrection mounted, armed forces were called in and, together with all municipal police, placed under control of the Quebec Provincial Police. The Cabinet was meeting in a day-long emergency session to deal with the crisis of the kidnappings; at 9:00 p.m. they made their final offer to the FLQ with a demand for a reply by 3:00 o'clock the following morning. Simultaneously the National Assembly met, and in a twelve-hour session, authorized medicare for November 1, whether or not the specialists agreed. They also removed surveillance of the doctors' professional activities from the Health Insurance Board, provided for the three categories of opted-in, opted-out, and non-participating physicians, and—most important—ordered the specialists back to work.[129] Their session ended in the early morning of Friday, October 16, minutes ahead of the 4:00 a.m. proclamation by the federal government, at the request of the Quebec government, of the War Measures Act which outlawed the FLQ and suspended normal due process with respect to search, seizure, arrest, and detention.

Despite the appeals of the Government, the press, the hospital association, the College of Physicians and Surgeons and the general practitioners, and the deteriorating situation in the emergency hospitals, the specialists remained adamant; no less than three-quarters of their members were already outside the province, and they were receiving fully publicized support from the Ontario Medical Association and the CMA. At a meeting at CMA headquarters in Ottawa on Friday night approximately 600 specialists decided by voice vote unanimously not to comply. Phone calls were placed to all other members (mostly in Lake Placid and Toronto) to attend a meeting in Ottawa on Sunday.

As the debate raged there may have been some members listening in a side room to the voice of Prime Minister Trudeau eloquently reminding his countrymen of the fragility of a democratic society when citizens flout the law: "Freedom and personal security are safeguarded by laws; those laws must be respected in order to be effective . . . . those who would defy the law and ignore the opportunities available to them to right their wrongs and satisfy their claims will receive no hearing from this government. We shall ensure that the laws passed by Parliament are worthy of respect. We shall also ensure that those laws are respected." The irony of the situation could not have been lost.

On Saturday, as the specialists converged on Ottawa, the Canadian Medical Association publicly entered the fray for the first time to represent the specialists who were uncertain of the legal consequences of making statements of their own. Speaking for the specialists of Quebec who had "been conscripted, muzzled, and threatened with jail," President D. L. Kippen castigated "this highly oppressive piece of legislation [which] appears to be without precedent and deserves to be unreservedly condemned by all those who value liberty and freedom. No Canadian legislation—civil, industrial, or labour—has ever applied such severe restriction on the civil rights and liberties of individuals."[130]

This, of course, is incorrect. Bill 41 simply repeated, almost verbatim, the similar provisons of an act ordering teachers to return to work in October 1969,[131] and of Bill 38 ordering construction workers back to work in August 1970.[132] But no one in the medical profession had spoken out on either of those occasions against "such severe restrictions on the civil rights and liberties of individuals." Nor did spokesmen for the profession see those events as they saw their own. As the CMA *Bulletin* editorialized: "If it [the government] is successful in forcing compliance on that group [the specialists], it may only be a matter of time until other professions and groups are subjugated in the same manner. When that occurs, if it is allowed to occur, the end result will be a police state."[133]

By Sunday, however, with the discovery of the murder of Pierre Laporte, with demonstrations expected in the streets, with rumour rife, and public anxiety of near panic proportions, they saw that the time had come to end the strike and obey the law. In a meeting of over 1500 specialists at CMA headquarters in Ottawa, guarded by the army, with attitudes and opinions still deeply divided, and aware that they were now throwing away their trump card, the specialists voted to return; but under protest. With the president, Dr. D. L. Kippen, still serving as spokesman, the CMA issued a press release at 7:00 p.m. Sunday: "In view of overnight events and information received regarding possible emergency medical requirements, the FMSQ and the CMA encouraged physicians to return to their practices immediately. The reaction to Bill 41 which forces physicians back . . . and automatically classifies all those who refuse as criminals, varies from shock, disbelief, to disgust and outright rage. These men are not returning to work because Mr. Bourassa has demanded it."[134]

On November 1, 1970—four months behind its own schedule, twenty-eight months behind Ottawa's—Quebec's medicare program went into effect. Immediately there arose many of the administrative and operational problems that seem inevitable in programs involving some form of communication on paper between millions of people and an administrative agency. Because of anticipated delays in processing an average of 85,000 accounts a day, doctors were entitled to draw up to $2,000 a month in advance payments, and 3778 took advantage of the arrangement. In the first month the reject rate of claims due to errors or insufficient information was 37.35 percent. This reached a peak of 54.74 percent in January. By July 1971, the percentage of rejects had declined to 27.4 percent or close to the forecast of twenty-five percent which is functional for this type of computerized operation. There were long delays in doctors' offices and hospital out-patient departments, but those seem in the main to have been accepted as inevitable by patients who recognized a backlog of needs that only now could be translated into effective demand.

The reaction of the specialists was mixed, and without more exhaustive research, impossible to assess fully.[135] The return to work was a humbling experience,[136] only partly assuaged by the notion that compliance was due to the emergency and not to the government fiat. Among some specialists the initial response was one of petulance, it is even said that patients (who were guilty of voting the culprit politicians into office) were deliberately inconvenienced and delayed, but their general reaction was one of calm acceptance, and therefore that folly was abandoned. A second response was what one would expect of a leading profession: more attention was paid to the Castonguay Report and there was an increasing acceptance of both its findings of inadequacies in the health delivery system and of its goals for future development.[137] The federation itself established a consulting agency[138] to initiate and assist in the development of poly-clinics. Hospital medical staffs undertook ways and means of rationalizing and removing duplication of services in hospitals. (For example, two major hospitals in Quebec City amalgamated both their medical staffs and boards of trustees.) Some specialists emigrated, but the actual count is difficult to make since Quebec College registration may be maintained by a non-resident. At McGill medical school, as of August 1971, sixty-six full-time and part-time faculty out of a total faculty of about 1,000 had resigned since 1970, about twice the normal attrition rate.[139] The net increase of registered physicians in Quebec in 1971 over 1970 was 313 compared with a net increase of 242 in 1970.[140] In any event the exodus was less than expected by the Government and far less than feared by the public. In 1974 seventy physicians were non-participating, but only seven were *désengagés*, that is, billing the patients direct for the same fee they would bill the Health Insurance Board.[141]

THE OUTCOMES

Not all the outcomes can be known, and some, such as the effect on the health of Quebec residents, cannot be ascertained for some time to come, but others are visible.

1. Quebec residents have had removed whatever economic barrier intervened between their medical need and their access to care. That barrier was both incalculable and in dispute. The medical profession would argue that their sliding scale of fees system barred no one; spokesmen for the public would argue that the very act of asking for free or cut-rate services inhibited thousands until need was desperate.

2. Contrary to expectations, the volume of services provided to residents declined in the short run. The "before" and "after" studies by Enterline, et al[142] revealed a decline of 7.5 percent in the number of office, home, clinic, and hospital calls. Home visits dropped by almost two-thirds, while office calls increased by thirty-two percent. Even more surprising, the average work day of a physician decreased by one and one-half hours. Average waiting time increased from 5.3 to 10.2 days, with the largest increases in higher income groups. Considerable increase in utilization of physicians' services by persons in lower income groups took place. One of the major conclusions of the Enterline team was: "Of particular significance is the increased frequency with which physicians were seen for a series of common and important medical symptoms. This suggests that the removal of the economic barriers to medical care may actually improve the general level of health of the population."[143]

3. There was an increase in taxes on income earners above the $2,000 and $4,000 exemption thresholds with respect to the Quebec tax, and above $1,000 and $2,000 with respect to the federal social development tax while it was in effect. It was absorbed into the regular income tax in 1972.

4. There was an initial loss of some outstanding professional talent, particularly in the specialties of anaesthesia, radiology, pathology, and psychiatry, while at the same time there were substantial increases in physicians' incomes. More physicians were attracted to Quebec in 1971 than in 1970, and the improvement in the physician-population ratio has continued.

5. The traumatic effects of the strike on the public and of the back-to-work order on the specialists are both subjective and incalculable; only time can heal the relationship between the profession and the Government and restore the image of the profession, although this latter may be accelerated by the removal of money from the doctor-patient relationship.

6. Because of the open-endedness of the financial commitment the Government will be increasingly impelled to examine ways and means

of controlling costs without reducing quality, and this is likely to create continuing conflict with the health professions.

7. A new bureaucracy has been created, and therefore a new thrust will be given to expansion of health programs, with annual proposals for new undertakings and budget increases.

8. The effect on the people of the refusal to obey the law by society's most prestigious elite may be to further weaken respect for law as did the widespread violation of Prohibition in the United States; if it is generally believed that this strategy won for the specialists concessions not otherwise obtainable, others may be induced to use the same methods, and the ultimate recourse of restoration of the status quo by government fiat may well become an increasingly common, less remarkable phenomenon.

9. The strong policy stance of the Quebec government vis-à-vis the federal government has undoubtedly terminated the conditional grant-in-aid as an acceptable device in imposing national priorities on the provinces—certainly as far as Quebec is concerned.

10. The quality, vision, and imagination of the Castonguay Committee Report, which served as a major source of idea inputs in the policy process, has established a new standard for all government departments in Quebec and for many health commissions and departments in Canada. Its systems approach provides a fundamental new thrust in the analysis of existing programs and of means for their improvement.

11. The advanced management philosophy, organization, and administrative processes of the Health Insurance Board should, similarly, have a highly salutary effect on many other administrative agencies in the Quebec government, and other health insurance agencies in Canada will undoubtedly be adopting some of their innovations in their own operations.

12. It is true that in the execution of its strategy of implementation there were some advantages for the Government in the fact that the profession was divided. In the long run, this division is likely to prove a serious impediment in the development of an integrated health service through poly-clinics as envisioned in the Castonguay Report. It would seem equally desirable from the profession's point of view that there be a single organization to represent its interests.

Chapter Eight

Reflections

WE HAVE BEEN CONCERNED throughout this work with two major themes: the substance of the decisions that created and shaped the health insurance system in Canada, and the process by which the decisions were made. Let us reflect on these in turn.

THE HEALTH INSURANCE PROGRAMS

As these words are being written, the Canadian health insurance system, whose tortuous history generated so much federal-provincial conflict, is being drastically altered by the passage of the Established Programs Financing Act.[1] In a sense the new arrangements mark the end of the *national* program as the format of the conditional-grant-in-aid is abandoned. Federal funds will continue to be made available but the amounts will be adjusted to increases in Gross National Product rather than to actual costs of the health services programs. At the same time, the basic hospital and medical services will continue to be available on uniform terms and conditions, so that from the point of view of the insured resident there will appear to be no major changes. The federal government will continue to monitor the system and have the authority to withhold funds if national standards are not maintained, but the provinces will gain more flexibility in the organization and mix of insured services.

This *volte face* must appear as a vindication of the doubts of the Rowell-Sirois Royal Commission as to the practicality of the conditional grant-in-aid and the "joint administration of activities" it required.[2] And yet, had the federal government not acted to establish and share in the costs of national programs, there can be little doubt that hundreds of thousands, if not millions, of Canadians would still be unprotected against health care costs. Nor would the low income provinces have been able to provide the levels of services that the federal funds made possible.

In addition to reflecting on how different the outcomes might have been in the absence of federal decisions, it is also interesting to speculate on "what-might-have-been" if alternative policies had been chosen. Would the outcomes have been different? There are several examples.

What if the health insurance proposals of 1943–45 (the Mackenzie-Heagerty design) had been accepted by the provinces? The likelihood is that the program would have had the full endorsement of the medical profession and the insurance industry, thus avoiding confrontations whose deleterious effects still mar our society. Other battles would also have been avoided, for the model act of 1944 provided that provincial programs be administered by an independent, non-political, representative commission that (strange as it may seem) would also have had two senior federal officials as members. Within each province, all health services would have been administered by one agency. As the CMA assumed in its 1934 Report on Economics, there would have been a fixed fund from which doctors would have been paid by capitation, pro-rated fee-for-service, or salary. The federal share of costs was also fixed, i.e., sixty percent of the *estimated* costs as determined by federal statisticians and accountants. Because the cost figures were to be revised only every three years, provinces would have been solely responsible for cost over-runs.

The most distinctive difference would have been in the design of the delivery system. Each province was to have been organized into administrative health regions responsible for providing both preventive and treatment services, with a regional medical officer having a broad range of powers to advise local practitioners and to monitor and improve quality of care. Each person would have selected a practitioner and remained on that list until selection of another doctor had been made. What was envisaged, obviously, was a much more directed and coordinated system than was actually adopted. With a "list system" it seems reasonable to judge that one different outcome would have been a more equitable distribution of general practitioners throughout the nation. Whether the system would have provided higher quality of care, lower hospital utilization, more emphasis on preventive services, and lower costs, one can only speculate, but mechanisms would have been created to give more control on the deployment of resources than in the present system.

On the other hand, it seems likely that the Mackenzie-Heagerty design would have produced even more federal-provincial confrontations than has the present system, primarily over the cost-sharing formula. And for precisely the same reasons that the low income provinces are wary of the

416

1977 changes—their failure to maintain a consistent federal share of rising costs in the future.

Yet another fork in the road when a different choice might have produced different outcomes occurred in Saskatchewan in 1945. What if Premier Douglas had acted on the advice of his Health Services Planning Commission to introduce a medical care program, with general practitioners paid by salary, as the first step in a comprehensive program? Given the opposition of the specialists documented in chapter 5, it might well have resulted in the confrontation of 1962 taking place in 1945 or 1946. Would the profession have been as determined and united as it was in 1962? It would, of course, have lacked the institutional base of the prepayment plans. Would an active government recruiting campaign directed both to returning veterans from the armed forces medical services (accustomed to salary) and to doctors in Britain, have been able to find replacements for those who threated to leave? There are some, like Professor S. M. Lipsett (who was studying the CCF in Saskatchewan at the time), who believe that it could have been brought off successfully.[3] Had that policy option been implemented, it is obvious that, in some parts of Canada, at least, the design of the delivery system might well have been vastly different. On the other hand, it is possible that the experiment might have failed and the fee-for-service system reverted to. We shall never know.

Or, take the hospital construction policy. What if, instead of the 1948 hospital construction grant that catalyzed the construction of 46,000 hospital beds in five years, one half of the grant had been allocated to facilities for group practice clinics with incentives for physicians to practise in them? Again, we can never know, but one could argue that the volume of hospital care and therefore the cost of health services would have been less.

Or, what if the priorities had been re-ordered? What difference would it have made if medical care had been introduced first, in 1958? All governments had been warned of the dangers of hospital insurance. Yet, only hospital insurance and diagnostic services could be wrung from a reluctant federal cabinet by the Hon. Paul Martin. Was this an example of Herbert Simon's contention that "satisficing" (i.e., finding a course of action that is "good enough") rather than "maximization" is the objective of the politician in contrast to the businessman? It seems reasonable to conclude that had the most rational choice been made, then medical services and hospital outpatient services would have been the first programs. It seems likely that a more economical pattern of utilization of services would have resulted.

Another alternative scenario is intriguing. It will be recalled that the (Hall) Royal Commission on Health Services issued a unanimous report recommending a government administered program. It will also be recalled that Senator McCutcheon had resigned from the commission on his appointment to the Cabinet. From his public statements criticizing the report on its release, it seems reasonable to believe that the report would have been substantially different had he remained, or even that a minority report would have been filed. It is even conceivable that a majority of four—McCutcheon, the two physicians, and the dentist— might have supported the CMA-CHIA policy on subsidization.

That scenario leads to the next question: If a majority of the Royal Commission had recommended against a government-administered program and in favour of the CMA and the insurance industry solution, and the Government had accepted it, how different would our system have been? As the British Columbia and Ontario experience suggests, there would probably be two systems: voluntary plans and commercial insurance coverage for groups, and a government administered program for individuals and those needing financial assistance. On the basis of the Alberta experience, there would possibly be several hundred thousand Canadians not insured. Based on experience in the USA it is not likely that the total expenditure on health services would be any less, while the costs of administration would undoubtedly be more. On the other hand, a much smaller share of Canada's total health care expenditures would be flowing through the public sector, and this reduction in the size of the stakes in contention between the federal and provincial governments might well have meant lesser strains on their relationships.

Of a different order is the question of the role of Saskatchewan. Why was Saskatchewan's contribution to the entire process so important, making as it did, two of the six determinative decisions? Only comprehensive comparative analyses with controls on the important variables might adequately explain the differences in Saskatchewan that account for the initiatives taken there. Although Saskatchewan shares characteristics with all provinces, and other regional characteristics with Alberta and Manitoba, there were important differences. These included: the precarious underpinnings of the one-crop economy and the severity of the depression; the geography of the province that yielded a uniformly thin distribution of population in small rural municipalities and urban centres; the high proportion of citizens serving as local government councillors and school trustees together with the extraordinary number of cooperative associations that also contributed to widespread citizen participation in policy making and reinforced an orientation directed to collective action to solve mutual problems; and, finally, the formation of the CCF party, with its strong ideological commitment to social security measures and its unusually large membership that ensured widespread public debate. But even all these would not tell us how much weight to allocate to that elusive and unquantifiable variable, the quality of leadership.[4]

Another phenomenon in the process commanding attention is the role and power of interest groups. Only in the last few years have we become aware of the increasing power of organized professions providing essential services. The shocks administered to the body politic by the withdrawal of all but emergency services by two provincial medical associations cannot be accurately assessed, but they were traumatic. As more recent experience—strikes by teachers,nurses, professors, social workers —attests, the Saskatchewan and Quebec episodes were early demonstrations of the increasing difficulty of governing complex, pluralistic, democratic societies. One cannot reflect on these confrontations and the resulting "overloading" of government without concern for the capacity of the democratic process to survive.

But the other side of the coin also raises grave concerns. And that is the quality of the services provided by the human services professions, whether they be doctors, dentists, nurses, social workers, teachers. Quality is clearly a fragile attribute of human services. It depends not only on competence but also in large measure on individual morale, on how one feels about the system, on how confident one can feel about one's career and the conditions surrounding its pursuit. When, for example, governments act without notice or adequate consultation to introduce drastic changes or cuts in resources, morale is seriously lowered and, inevitably and perhaps unconsciously, quality is adversely affected.

At the same time as one considers the power and influence of organized and determined interest groups, one cannot overlook the contributions to the development of the Canadian health insurance system made by the voluntary prepayment plans (and, to a lesser degree, the insurance industry). Not only did they popularize the whole concept of prepaid health services but they created the administrative organizations and developed the administrative procedures and sophisticated equipment to make the system function. They pioneered in the concept of the service contract, educated hospitals and doctors to acceptance of a "third party" interest in fees, rates, and quality of services, and educated the public to acceptance of the payment of premiums for health purposes, thereby providing a ready-made tax source for governments.

The reactions of the leaders of voluntary prepayment plans to the government takeover were undoubtedly mixed, but interviews with many of them suggest that any unhappiness was heavily counterweighted by the knowledge that government action was extending to all what they had struggled to bring to many. It was, at once, a tribute to their ideals and an extension of their goals.

And, finally, the study raises the question of the "allocation of values."

419

In the preface, reference was made to Easton's definition of the functions of government as being "predominantly oriented toward the authoritative allocation of values in a society." Since competing values (and competition for values in the economic sense) were, as we have seen, at the heart of the conflicts that characterized the introduction of health insurance in Canada, it is interesting to reflect on just what some of those new values were. Among the most important were the following:

1. That health services be available to all Canadians on equal terms and conditions. Obviously, this is a value easier to legislate than to accomplish, given the still-prevailing, though less inequitable, maldistribution of physicians. But at least there is no longer a direct financial barrier to access to essential services.

2. That the indignities of the means test, with its accompanying harrassment by municipal relief inspectors demanding reimbursement, no longer be imposed on the medically indigent.

3. That the costs of health services for the indigent be assumed by the senior governments and not by municipal governments where the heaviest burdens were likely to occur in municipalities least able to pay. The two programs thus ended more than three and one half centuries of Elizabethan Poor Law tradition.

4. That the costs of health services no longer be borne primarily by the sick and those able to obtain voluntary insurance but by all income earners, roughly in accordance with ability to pay.

5. That the "Robin Hood" function of equalizing health care costs to patients, performed in the past by physicians through the "sliding scale of fees" principle, be accomplished through the tax system.

6. That the programs be administered by public agencies, accountable to legislatures and electors.

One could continue to reflect on many other aspects of the development of the health insurance system but these emerge as the most significant.

We shall now consider the policy-making process.

THE POLICY PROCESS

If one were to ask why Canada has a universal, government-operated health insurance program, the answer was probably best stated by the then general secretary of the Canadian Medical Association, Dr. T. C. Routley, in a nation-wide radio broadcast in 1943. "Health insurance appears to be inevitable for Canada because the people want it."[5] But if one accepts his judgement, then one cannot fail to be impressed by the length of time it took for the desire to be transformed into operating programs. As long ago as 1919, the idea had received sufficient support to become a stated plank in the Liberal party platform. But it was to take another half-century—almost two generations—for health insurance to become a nation-wide reality.

Professor Kenneth Bryden has chronicled a similar time-table for the "developmental process" in the achievement of old age pensions.[6] Both programs were responses to similar economic problems created by the rapid urbanization and industrialization of Canadian society. And both encountered the same kind of resistance—characterized by Bryden as being "grounded in the market ethos." Both the insurance industry and organized medicine framed the issues in terms of free enterprise versus "socialized medicine," with the claims that not only would the medical profession lose its professional autonomy and the public its freedom of choice, but that government health insurance would open the floodgates to socialism. The strength of the forces opposed to change is evident in the public opinion polls indicating that from 1944 to the middles sixties, eighty percent of the population were in favour of a national health insurance program.

This study adapted the systems analysis model as an analytic tool, and it has enabled us to delineate and examine the interactions among the inputs from interest groups, parties, and public opinion, the withinputs of the decision-making (or conversion) process of government, the outputs of policy and strategy, and the outcomes, or impact on the environment. It has also revealed the crucial role of "feedback" and therefore the importance of the government's sensory system.

As useful as I believe this model to be, it may be helpful to reflect briefly on other models for the additional insight they may give to the policy process we have examined. We shall look first at the two models of decision making analyzed by Charles E. Lindblom in his classic article, "The Science of Muddling Through,"[7] and elaborated upon in later works.[8] The standard model Lindblom calls *the rational comprehensive* method. In this model, the decision-maker (1) identifies his problem; (2) clarifies his goals, ranking them in order of importance; (3) lists all possible policies for achieving them; (4) assesses the costs and benefits of each alternative policy; (5) selects the appropriate policy or policies calculated to bring the greatest benefits and the least disadvantages.[9]

This model, so logical in theory, is, according to Lindblom, impossible to follow in practice, and for several reasons: the difficulty of obtaining agreement on goals and values, and therefore of achieving consensus on means; the prohibitive costs of obtaining all relevant information and making all relevant analyses; and, not least, man's limited problem-solving capacity.

As a consequence, what policy makers actually do is follow the model that Lindblom calls *successive limited comparisons* or *disjointed incrementalism*. By this he means that policy makers consider only those policies whose known or expected consequences differ only marginally from the status quo, and only those policies whose known or expected consequences differ only incrementally from each other, and make their choice among policies by ranking in order of preference the increments by which social states differ.[10]

The characteristics, therefore, of the method of disjointed incrementalism are the following: (1) selection of value goals and empirical analysis of the needed action are not distinct from one another but are closely intertwined; (2) since means and ends are not distinct, means-end analysis is often inappropriate or limited; (3) the test of a "good" policy is typically that various analysts find themselves agreeing on a policy; (4) analysis is drastically limited.[11]

At first glance, the evidence in these seven case studies appears to comport with the incrementalist model. As one examines the fifty-year period, noting that municipal medical and hospital care plans were followed by voluntary plans, which were followed by the Saskatchewan Hospital Services Plan, and then the B.C. Plan, and then the federal decisions, and so on, one is impressed by the incrementalist thesis, for each decision does seem to be an increment to and an extension of an earlier series of decisions.

But, if one examines each of the decisions by itself, considering it from the point of view of the government making it, then none was a simple incremental decision, for each was something very large, new, and different, commanding different kinds of resources on an unprecedented scale, introducing new and complex relationships with powerful interest groups, requiring new revenues, affecting every citizen, and presenting exceedingly risky political consequences. Not only did the proposed new policies represent quantum leaps from the status quo but the alternatives that were considered differed radically from each other, ranging from government subsidies to the poor to enable them to insure through a voluntary agency to state medicine with doctors on salary. As noted above, these decisions introduced fundamentally new values, and were so recognized by the actors participating in the process.[12]

Despite Lindblom's criticisms of the rational model, the extent to which the pattern of decision making in several of our cases can be said to have approximated its requirements is quite remarkable. There was unusual consensus on objectives, although wide differences of opinion about means; there was wide search for alternative solutions, although admittedly, not of all possible alternatives. There was also extensive concern with consequences of each alternative. And, finally, there was rational choice within the perceived constraints. What we find, therefore, are elements of both the rational and the incremental models.

The writer who has best synthesized these elements is Amitai Etzioni in what he calls the "mixed scanning" model.[13] In this model the analyst distinguishes between fundamental or "contextuating" decisions which differ substantially from existing policy and the incremental or minor decisions made daily. When an issue or problem becomes serious enough, the policy makers engage in "scanning" for alternative solutions. The scanning will be "mixed" in that only a very few alternatives will be seriously examined. This model is therefore both less comprehensive than the rational model and more encompassing than the incremental model. Since Etzioni's model makes more explicit acknowledgment of fundamental decisions than does Lindblom's, it appears to accord more realistically with the experience examined here.

There are two other models, also designed as responses to the short-comings of the rational model. These were used by Graham Allison in his analysis of the Cuban missile crisis.[14] The first he calls the organiza-tional process model. "Governments," he points out, "consist of a con-glomerate of semi-feudal, loosely-allied organizations, each with a substantial life of its own."[15] It is through organizations (departments, Privy Council Office, Prime Minister's Office, Treasury Board, Finance Department, Statistics Canada) that problems are perceived, information is processed to define alternatives and estimate consequences, and that government acts as these organizations process their routines. "Govern-ment behaviour can therefore be understood . . . less as deliberate choice of leaders and more as *outputs* of large organizations functioning according to standard patterns of behaviour."[16]

Allison's "organizational process" model sheds light on some of the decisions examined here, but not on all, for in most of our cases, there was no existing organization whose routine outputs would have yielded a health insurance policy. The policy was introduced by politicans and not by an established government organization. There is one exception. It seems reasonable to conclude that the 1945 decision would be illustra-tive of Allison's concept of policy as organizational output. It will be recalled that Ian Mackenzie had been minister of defence when he was transferred to Pensions and National Health. There he found a division of Public Health Services, whose director, Dr. J. J. Heagerty, had given a good deal of thought to health insurance and had collected a great deal of information about it. Within four months Mackenzie wrote to the prime minister proposing the immediate introduction of a national health insurance program. It seems reasonable to conclude that Mackenzie did not bring the health insurance policy with him, but that the bureaucracy—small as it was—was the source. Subsequent events are also illuminated by the Allison organizational process model. When the proposal was rejected by Cabinet, Dr. Heagerty, with the support of the minister, began to develop external pressure groups by inviting fourteen organizations to assist in preparing legislation. As the development of a government policy moved beyond the confines of the Health Department,[17] the representatives of other organizations—the Dominion Bureau of Statistics, the Actuarial Division of Trade and Commerce, and the Department of Finance—clearly made contributions consonant with their respective information bases and standard operating procedures. The Department of Finance, for example (with the one exception of the two-year period when Walter Gordon was minister) maintained a consistent policy over the thirty-year period, illustrating again that where one stands depends upon where one sits.

Although other examples come to mind of the roles of bureaucratic organizations *qua* organizations, in the series of cases examined here, the Allison organizational process model does not appear as helpful as his second alternative, "Bureaucratic Politics."

Allison introduces this model in these words:

> The leaders who sit on top of organizations are not a monolithic group. Rather, each is, in his own right, a player in a central, competitive game. The name of the game is bureaucratic politics: bargaining along regularized channels among players positioned hierarchically within the government. In contrast with [the rational] Model, the bureaucratic political model sees no unitary actor but rather many actors as players who focus ... on many diverse problems ... in terms of no consistent set of strategic objectives but rather according to various conceptions of national, organizational and personal goals, making government decisions not by rational choice but by the pulling and hauling of politics.
>
> The decisions and actions of government are essentially ... political outcomes: outcomes in the sense that what happens is not chosen as a solution to a problem but rather results from compromise, coalition, competition, and confusion among government officials who see different faces of an issue; political in the sense that the activity from which the outcomes emerge is best characterized by bargaining.[18]

Although the cabinet system provides far more centralized control of decision making than does the American presidential-congressional system, nevertheless, the seven decisions are replete with experiences to which the bureaucratic politics model adds new insights. The influence of W. C. Clarke, strong enough in his role as deputy minister of finance, to thwart the minister of health in 1943; the proposal of C. D. Howe at the 1946 Conference to abandon the health grants, which the Health Department officials considered the indispensable foundations of an improved health system, in exchange for the federal government giving up the gasoline tax (which the Cabinet Committee and Mackenzie King accepted); the hauling and pulling within the Pearson cabinet that nearly aborted medicare and did force important amendments.

Unfortunately for the researcher on Canadian government, in the cabinet system most of these conflicts and their attendant bargaining take place behind closed doors, and only occasionally and usually long after the events do iceberg tips break through the sea of secrecy hinting at the bureaucratic politics beneath.

Both of Allison's models are related to yet another typology—that which distinguishes between "allocative" (or substantive) policies (e.g., health policy, defence policy, etc.) and "positional policies," described by Peter Aucoin as follows:

> Positional, as opposed to allocative, policies refer to those outputs which affect the structuring of influence in the conversion system. A good deal of political activity by individuals and groups is related not so much to securing (at least in the short run) an allocation of desired values but rather the attainment of desired positions vis-à-vis other individuals or groups. What is sought is a share of the coercive abilities of the government.[19]

There are many examples of positional policies in these cases. Indeed, one of the major issues between the medical profession and governments focused on the question of positional policy. That was the insistence of the profession that health insurance be administered by an independent commission on which they would be represented. This arrangement would have ensured that the influence the profession exerted on the formulation of policy would have been continued in its execution. The proposal of the federal government (in the draft act of 1944) to appoint two members to the health insurance commission in each province was a similar stratagem. There were, of course, many examples of the importance of the "structuring of influence" in the development of the policies we have examined: the creation of the Health Services Planning Commission in Saskatchewan in 1944; the relationship of the Office of the Provincial Economist and the Ontario Premier's Office that enabled George Gathercole to have daily contact with Mr. Frost, a premier supremely in control of his cabinet; Mr. Frost's decision to ensure the support of the Ontario

Hospital Association by creating the Hospital Services Commission and appointing three past-presidents of the OHA as its chairman and first members; the establishment of the Saskatchewan Medical Care Insurance Commission in an attempt to win medical profession cooperation, and its boycotting by the College; the position of Tom Kent in Prime Minister Pearson's office and his relationship with the minister of finance, Walter Gordon;[20] the use, by Ian Mackenzie, of the Dominion Council of Health to develop consensus among the provincial deputy ministers of health and the representatives of the health professions and the public; Diefenbaker's appointment of the Royal Commission on Health Services in 1961.

All of these illustrate the importance of the structuring of influence on policy outputs, and the relevance of the concept of positional policies.

But even given the elements of chance inherent in the organizational process, bureaucratic politics, and "positional" models, as well as our awareness that (in Allison's words) "compromise, coalition, competition, and confusion among government officials" characterize the policy process, it remains remarkable how rational were the outputs of the political bargaining on health insurance. For the legislative acts were well-conceived means to pre-determined ends and had a high degree of inner logic and consistency. The explanation must surely lie in the fact that there are far fewer leverage points in the Canadian than in the American system, that one minister is responsible, and that only one committee of Parliament, the Cabinet, is ultimately responsible.

Finally, in reflecting on the policy process, one is impressed by the contributions to government policy decisions of dedicated and committed political leaders. Ian Mackenzie, Tommy Douglas, Paul Martin, Leslie Frost, Woodrow Lloyd, Walter Gordon, Judy LaMarsh, Alan MacEachen, Lester Pearson, Claude Castonguay, and others used their positions of authority, influence, and power to make choices about alternative futures for Canada. They were assisted by similarly committed leaders, like Stanley Knowles, not in positions of authority, but in the opposition, where they could inform, needle, prod, and criticize, and keep the issue very much alive. For several of them, the personal costs were high, but the values for which they fought were idealistic, humane, and compassionate, reducing risk and fear and expanding confidence, hope, and freedom.

Notes

Notes to the Preface

1. M. G. Taylor, "The Saskatchewan Hospital Services Plan" Ph.D. diss., University of California, Berkeley, 1949, (mimeo).

2. David Easton, *A Systems Analysis of Political Life* (New York: Wiley, 1965), and David Easton, *A Framework for Political Analysis* (Englewood Cliffs, New Jersey: Prentice-Hall, 1965).

3. Daniel Katz and Robert L. Kahn, *The Social Psychology of Organizations* (New York: Wiley, 1966).

4. Ira Sharkansky, *Public Administration* (Chicago: Markham, 1970).

5. Easton, *A Framework for Political Analysis*, p. 50.

6. See, particularly, Richard Simeon, *Federal-Provincial Diplomacy* (Toronto: University of Toronto Press, 1972) and Donald V. Smiley, *Canada In Question: Federalism in the Seventies* (Toronto: McGraw Hill Ryerson, 1975).

Notes to Chapter One

1. The federal government was represented by Prime Minister Mackenzie King, C. D. Howe, Louis St. Laurent, and J. L. Ilsley; the provinces by George A. Drew, Maurice L. Duplessis, A. S. MacMillan, J. B. McNair, Stewart S. Garson, John Hart, J. Walter Jones, T. C. Douglas, and E. C. Manning.

2. Dominion-Provincial Conference (1945) *Plenary Conference Discussions*, p. 7.

3. Ibid., p. 59.

4. *Canadian Medical Association Journal* XXVIII (June 1933): 671.

5. *Canadian Medical Association Journal* XXIX (November 1933): 55–556.

6. Advisory Committee on Health Insurance, *Report*, pp. xi–xxii.

7. Ibid.

8. Canadian Medical Association, Committee on Economics, *Report*, 1934, p. 6.

9. For a review of Health Insurance Developments in Canada to 1948 see the first 110 pages of M. G. Taylor, "The Saskatchewan Hospital Services Plan," PhD diss., University of California, Berkeley, 1949 (mimeo). For a brief discussion of the B. C. attempt by one who was deeply involved, see H. M. Cassidy, *Public Health and Welfare Reorganization in Canada* (Toronto: Ryerson, 1945), pp. 52–53, 90–92.

10. Ibid., pp. 43–50.

11. M. G. Taylor, "Provincial Social Assistance Medical Care Plans in Canada," *American Journal of Public Health* (June 1954): 750–59.

12. Royal Commission on Dominion-Provincial Relations, *Report*, Book II, p. 42.

13. Ibid., p. 36.

14. H. B. McKinnon to Mackenzie King, December 19, 1942 (*Mackenzie King Papers*).

15. Mackenzie King to H. B. McKinnon, January 4, 1943 (*Mackenzie King Papers*).

16. J. W. Pickersgill, *The Mackenzie King Record, Vol. I: 1939–1944* (Toronto: University of Toronto Press, 1960), p. 476.

17. Ibid.

18. Ibid.

19. Ibid.

20. Ibid., p. 564.

21. Royal Commission on Dominion-Provincial Relations, *Report*, Book II, p. 83.

22. Ibid., p. 33.

23. Ibid., p. 35.

24. Ibid., p. 39.

25. Ibid., p. 40.

26. Ibid., pp. 42–43.

27. Ibid., p. 43.

28. Ibid.

29. Ibid.

30. Donald V. Smiley, *Conditional Grants and Canadian Federalism* (Toronto: Canadian Tax Foundation, 1963), p. 6.

31. *Mackenzie King Diary*, January 15, 1941.

32. Ibid., March 26, 1941.

33. Ibid., March 24, 1942.

34. Pickersgill, *The Mackenzie King Record, Vol. I*, pp. 25–27.

35. Ian Mackenzie to Mackenzie King, December 27, 1939 (*Mackenzie King Papers*).

36. Mackenzie King to Ian Mackenzie, January 5, 1940 (*Mackenzie King Papers*).

37. Advisory Committee on Health Insurance, *Report*, 1943, pp. xi–xxii.

38. The organizations consulted were: The Canadian Dental Association, Canadian Hospital Council, Canadian Life Insurance Officers Association, Canadian Medical Association, Canadian Nurses Association, Canadian Pharmaceuti-

cal Association, Canadian Public Health Association, Catholic Hospital Council of Canada, Catholic Women's League of Canada, Federated Women's Institutes of Canada, La Federation des femmes canadiennes françaises, National Council of Women, Trade and Labour Congress of Canada, Canadian Federation of Agriculture, Canadian Labour Congress.

39. Order-in-Council P.C. 836, February 5, 1942.

40. Sir William Beveridge, *Social Insurance and Allied Services* (New York: Macmillan, 1942).

41. L. C. Marsh, *Report on Social Security for Canada* (Ottawa: King's Printer, 1943), p. 144.

42. Ian Mackenzie to Mackenzie King, January 20, 1943 (*Mackenzie King Papers*).

43. Economic Advisory Committee, *Report*, January 20, 1943 (*Mackenzie King Papers*).

44. Ibid.

45. Letter from Ian Mackenzie to Mackenzie King, January 20, 1943 (*Mackenzie King Papers*).

46. *Mackenzie King Diary*, January 22, 1943.

47. House of Commons. Special Committee on Social Security, *Minutes of Proceedings and Evidence, No. 1*, Tuesday, March 16, 1943.

48. The Physical Fitness Act was promulgated on November 1, 1943.

49. Special Committee on Social Security, *Proceedings*, p. 30.

50. Ibid., p. 107.

51. Canadian Medical Association, Committee on Economics, *Report*, 1934.

52. Ibid., p. 4.

53. Ibid.

54. Ibid., pp. 4–6.

55. Ibid., pp. 37–38.

56. Canadian Medical Association, Special Meeting of General Council, *Transactions*, January 18–19, 1943 (mimeo).

57. Ibid.

58. Ibid.

59. Ibid.

60. Ibid.

61. House of Commons. Special Committee on Social Security, 1943, *Proceedings*, p. 141.

62. Ibid., p. 143.

63. Ibid., p. 144.

64. Ibid., p. 145.

65. Ibid., p. 144.

66. Ibid., p. 145.

67. Ibid., p. 175.

68. Ibid., p. 180.

69. Ibid., p. 242.

70. Ibid., p. 242.

71. Ibid., pp. 515–16.

72. Ibid., p. 516.

73. Ibid.

74. Ibid., p. 520.

75. Ibid., p. 521.

76. Ibid., p. 331.

77. Ibid., p. 285.

78. Ibid., p. 291.

79. Ibid., p. 292.

80. Ibid., p. 366.

81. Ibid., p. 367.

82. Ibid., No. 28, p. iv.

83. Ian Mackenzie to Mackenzie King, August 19, 1943 (*Mackenzie King Papers*).

84. Interim Report of the Committee on Health Insurance Finance, December 28, 1943 (*Brooke Claxton Papers*).

85. Ibid.

86. Ibid.

87. Report of the meeting of provincial ministers and deputy ministers of health, Ottawa, May 10–12, 1944, Special Committee, *Proceedings*, pp. 275–76.

88. Letter from George Drew to Mackenzie King, January 7, 1944 (*Mackenzie King Papers*).

89. Memorandum by Claxton for Cabinet Committee, February 17, 1945 (*Brooke Claxton Papers*).

90. Speech from the Throne, House of Commons *Debates*, January 27, 1944.

91. Memorandum, Brooke Claxton to prime minister, January 22, 1944 (*Brooke Claxton Papers*).

92. Memorandum from J. W. Pickersgill to the prime minister, annotated by Mackenzie King, February 14, 1944 (*Mackenzie King Papers*).

93. Notes for the agenda for the meeting of the Cabinet Committee, February 17, 1944 (*Brooke Claxton Papers*).

94. Minutes of Cabinet Committee, Feb. 17, 1944 (*Brooke Claxton Papers*).

95. Secretariat Progress Report, May 3, 1944 (*Brooke Claxton Papers*).

96. *Mackenzie King Diary*, July 22, 1944.

97. Minutes of Cabinet Committee Meeting, August 3, 1944 (*Brooke Claxton Papers*).

98. House of Commons *Debates*, August 14, 1944, p. 6649.

99. Ibid.

100. *Mackenzie King Papers*.

101. *Mackenzie King Diary*, July 19, 1944.

102. On this period, see J. W. Pickersgill and D. F. Forster *The Mackenzie King Record, 1944–45* (Toronto: University of Toronto Press, 1968), vol. II, chaps, IX, X. See also J. L. Granatstein's study of the Conservative Party, *The Politics of Survival* (Toronto: University of Toronto Press, 1967).

103. *Mackenzie King Papers*.

104. Ibid.

105. Ibid.

106. All the political party platform quotations used in this study are taken

from D. Owen Corrigan's invaluable compendium, *Canadian Party Platforms 1867–1968* (Toronto: Copp Clark, 1968) and will not be further cited.

107. *Toronto Daily Star*, April 5, 1945.

108. *Mackenzie King Papers*.

109. A. D. P. Heeney, memorandum for the prime minister, June 20, 1945 (*Mackenzie King Papers*).

110. Cabinet Committee on Dominion-Provincial Relations, June 20, 1945.

111. Pickersgill and Forster, II, p. 449.

112. Memorandum, Brooke Claxton to Mackenzie King, July 27, 1945 (*Brooke Claxton Papers*).

113. *Mackenzie King Diary*, August 5, 1945.

114. Dominion-Provincial Conference, 1945 *Proceedings*, p. 59.

115. Ibid., p. 5.

116. Ibid., pp. 89–95.

117. Ibid., p. 113.

118. Ibid., p. 117.

119. Secret memorandum by Alex Skelton reporting on provincial visits, October 28–November 19, 1945 (*Mackenzie King Papers*).

120. Dominion-Provincial Conference, Co-ordinating Committee, *Proceedings*, November 26, 1945, p. 197.

121. Minutes of Cabinet Committee on Dominion-Provincial Relations, Report of Working Committee on Health Insurance, January 4, 1946 (*Mackenzie King Papers*).

122. Dominion-Provincial Conference, 1945, *Proceedings*, p. 227.

123. Ibid., pp. 247–48.

124. Ibid., pp. 253–309.

125. Ibid., pp. 270–278.

126. J. W. Pickersgill and D. F. Forster, *The Mackenzie King Record, 1945–46* (Toronto: University of Toronto Press, 1970). Vol. III, p. 25.

127. Ibid.

128. Ibid.

129. Ibid.

130. Ibid.

131. Pickersgill also suggests that Mackenzie King neither understood nor accepted "the Keynesian arguments for the use of central fiscal and monetary policies as economic stabilizers." Ibid., p. 203.

132. Dominion-Provincial Conference, 1945, *Proceedings*, p. 328.

133. Ibid., pp. 362–63.

134. *Mackenzie King Diary*, April 28, 1946.

135. Dominion-Provincial Conference, 1946, *Proceedings*, pp. 383–87.

136. Ibid., p. 398.

137. Ibid., p. 574.

138. *Mackenzie King Diary*, May 1, 1946.

139. Dominion-Provincial Conference, 1945, *Proceedings*, p. 574.

140. Ibid., pp. 583–624.

141. Ibid., p. 621.

142. *Mackenzie King Diary*, May 3, 1946.

143. Dominion-Provincial Conference, 1945, *Proceedings*, p. 621.

Notes to Chapter Two

1. S. M. Lipsett, *Agrarian Socialism* (Berkeley: University of California Press, 1950).

2. C. Rufus Rorem, *The Municipal Doctor System in Rural Saskatchewan*, Publication No. 11 of the Committee on the Costs of Medical Care (Chicago: University of Chicago Press, 1931). See also, The Committee on Economics of the College of Physicians and Surgeons of Saskatchewan, "The Municipal Doctor in Saskatchewan," *Saskatchewan Medical Quarterly*, 2, 8 (October 1938): 12–15; R. K. Johnston, "We like Municipal Contract Practice!" *The Canadian Doctor* (May 1938): 17–19; C. M. Thomas, "The Municipal Doctor Scheme," *Canadian Medical Association Journal* 51 (July 1944): 64–68; Committee on Medical Economics of the Canadian Medical Association, *The Municipal Doctor* (Bulletin No. 5).

3. Rorem, p. 13.

4. Statutes of Saskatchewan, 1916, C. 21, Section 28.

5. Ibid., 1934–35, C. 28, Section 7, and C. 29, Section 15.

6. Ibid., 1932, C. 28, Section 14.

7. Ibid., 1937, C. 30, Section 9.

8. Ibid., 1939, C. 55.

9. See the statement of the Canadian Medical Association Committee on Economics at the 1946 Annual Meeting. 77th Annual Meeting, *Transactions*, p. 37.

10. Statutes of Saskatchewan, 1916, C. 12; ibid., 1917, C. 9; ibid., 1947, The Act Respecting Union Hospitals, C. 108.

11. F. D. Mott, M. D., "Hospital Services in Saskatchewan," *American Journal of Public Health*, 37 (December 1947): 1539–44.

12. Statutes of Saskatchewan, 1909, C. 87, The Rural Municipalities Act, Section 193.

13. Survey undertaken in 1948 by the Health Services Planning Commission.

14. Statutes of Saskatchewan., 1918–19, C. 100, Section 2. (Emphasis added.)

15. Ibid., 1927, C. 67, The Union Hospital Act, Section 2.

16. Ibid., 1936, C. 37, The Village Act, Section 236; ibid., C. 36, The Town Act, Section 8.

17. Ibid., 1934–35, C. 30, Section 245.

18. Saskatchewan Legislative Assembly, Select Special Committee on Social Security, brief of the Department of Public Health, p. 14.

19. Statutes of Saskatchewan, 1938, C. 24.

20. Saskatchewan Health Survey *Report*, 1951, pp. 213–18.

21. Saskatchewan. Urban Municipalities Association, 1933 Annual Convention, *Proceedings*, p. 52.

22. Saskatchewan Association of Rural Municipalities, 29th Annual Convention, 1934, *Report of Proceedings*, p. 38.

23. See above p. 5.

24. SARM, Thirty-first Annual Convention, 1936, *Report of Proceedings*, p. 46.

25. Saskatchewan Legislative Assembly, *Verbatim Report of Address by J. M. Uhrich, M. D.*, January 28, 1935, p. 23.

26. Ibid., p. 28.

27. Canada. Royal Commission on Dominion-Provincial Relations, *Report*, Book I, pp. 121–22.

28. D. McHenry, *The Third Force in Canada* (Toronto: Oxford University Press, 1950).

29. Saskatchewan Department of Public Health, *Annual Report*, 1942, p. 12.

30. *Saskatchewan Legislative Journal*, March 26, 1942.

31. Ibid., March 2, 1943, p. 31.

32. Saskatchewan Legislative Assembly, Select Special Committee on Social Security and Health Services, *First Report*, April 12, 1943, p. 6.

33. Ibid., p. 8.

34. Order-in-Council, 1134/13, October 14, 1943.

35. Saskatchewan Legislative Assembly, Inter-sessional Committee, *Minutes and Proceedings*, November 18, 1943, p. 1.

36. *Saskatchewan Legislative Journal*, February 18, 1944, p. 5.

37. Saskatchewan, Select Committee on Social Security, *Minutes and Proceedings*, p. 13.

38. Statutes of Saskatchewan, 1944, An Act Respecting Health Insurance, C. 76, Section 11.

39. College of Physicians and Surgeons, Committee on Health Insurance, *Minutes of Meeting*, April 2, 1944.

40. Ibid.

41. *Saskatchewan Medical Quarterly*, 8, 4 (December 1944): 7.

42. *Regina Leader Post*, April 1, 1944. An interesting parallel event occurred twenty-six years later when the Union Nationale Government of Quebec introduced a medicare act in March 1970 and immediately called an election, in which it, too, was defeated.

43. Ibid., June 16, 1944.

44. Canadian Medical Procurement and Assignment Board, *National Health Survey*, 1945, p. 20, Table VI.

45. Ibid.

46. Ibid., p. 27.

47. Government of Canada, *Health Reference Book*, 1948, p. 88.

48. Ibid., p. 32.

49. Ibid., p. 33.

50. *Regina Leader Post*, April 2, 1954. For an appraisal of Tommy Douglas's role in bringing health insurance to Saskatchewan, see J. T. McLeod, "Health, Wealth, and Politics," in L. Lapierre and J. T. McLeod (eds.), *Essays on the Left* (Toronto: McClelland and Stewart, 1971).

51. Personal correspondence to the writer.

52. Saskatchewan, *Health Survey Report*, I, p. 219.

53. Report of the Saskatchewan Department of Public Health, 1933, p. 7.

54. *Canadian Medical Association Journal*, 28 (June 1933): 671.

55. *Saskatchewan Medical Quarterly*, 6, 1 (April 1942): 52.

56. College of Physicans and Surgeons of Saskatchewan, "Submission to Select Committee of the Legislative Assembly" (March 1943), reprinted in *Saskatchewan Medical Quarterly*, 8, 1 (March 1944): 13–19.

57. Ibid.

58. Saskatchewan Hospital Association, Annual Convention, 1935, *Report*, pp. 18–22.

59. Ibid., 1936, *Report*, pp. 98–105.

60. SARM, 39th Annual Convention, *Proceedings*, March 1944.

61. Ibid.

62. House of Commons. Special Committee on Social Security, *Proceedings*, 1944, p. 237.

63. The League had also issued in 1940 a pamphlet entitled, *Plan for State Medicine and Hospitalization*.

64. Ibid.

65. Escott Reid, "The Saskatchewan Liberal Machine before 1929," *Canadian Journal of Economics and Political Science*, 11, 1 (February 1936): 21–40, reprinted in Norman Ward and Duff Stafford, *Politics in Saskatchewan* (Toronto: Longman's, 1968), pp. 93–104. That it had not changed for the better is indicated in S. M. Lipsett, *Agrarian Socialism*, chap. XII, and in David Smith, *Prairie Liberalism* (Toronto: University of Toronto Press, 1975).

66. Lipsett, *Agrarian Socialism*, p. 313.

67. T. C. Douglas, Address to the Saskatchewan Hospital Association, November 9, 1945 (T. C. Douglas *Papers*).

68. See chap. 5, pp. 243–44 for further details.

69. Saskatchewan. Order-in-Council 1013/44. There was a good deal of criticism later that a professor of the history of medicine—known for his book on Soviet medicine—had been chosen rather than an expert in health services organization and administration. Two observations about the report may be made. The first is that, despite the incredibly short period in which it was prepared, it was, according to Professor Milton Roemer of UCLA, one of the most advanced health services reports of its time, giving some idea of the state of the art of health planning in the early 1940s. The second is that, after a very distinguished career, Dr. Sigerist wrote in his diary in 1950: "There are two situations in life that are close to happiness. One is when the immediate future looks bright" (he cites being in Paris at the age of twenty as an example). "The other is when you have that warm feeling of having accomplished a job well." He cites two examples, one being "in 1944 when I came back from Saskatchewan."

70. Dr. J. Lloyd Brown (chairman of the College's Health Services Committee), J. L. Connell, D. D. S., Mrs. Ann Heffel, R. N., and Mr. C. C. Gibson. Dr. Mindel Sheps was appointed secretary.

71. Saskatchewan Health Services Survey Commission, *Report of the Commissioner*, October 4, 1944.

72. Statutes of Saskatchewan, 1944 (Second Session), The Health Services Act, C. 51, Section 5.

73. Health Services Planning Commission (Saskatchewan), Memorandum re Free Hospitalization, Aug. 30, 1945.

74. M. G. Taylor, *Administration of Health Insurance in Canada* (Toronto:

Oxford University Press, 1956), p. 136.

75. Dr. Harvey Agnew, "A 'Units of Credit' System for the Payment of Hospitals," *The Canadian Hospital* (November 1943): 44. For a further discussion of the system, see the symposium in *Hospitals* (January 1944) and the reply by Dr. Agnew in the succeeding (February) issue.

76. For an analysis of related experience in paying hospitals, see M. G. Taylor, *Administration of Health Insurance*, pp. 153–67.

77. Memorandum from the Premier's Office, November 29, 1944.

78. Letter from chairman, Medical Advisory Committee, to the Hon. T. C. Douglas, February 17, 1947.

79. For a brief analysis of the reorganization, see M. G. Taylor, "Some Administrative Aspects of the Integration of Health Services," *Canadian Journal of Public Health*, (August 1951): 329–35.

80. Mr. G. W. Myers became executive director on the return of Dr. Rosenfeld to the USA on September 1, 1948.

81. En route from Berkeley to a post at the University of Toronto, I visited the plan on January 19, 1947. Although the staff were working under highly adverse conditions, their morale appeared extraordinarily high, all seeming to be inspired and excited by the challenge of the new enterprise.

82. Royal Commission on Health Services, *Report*, p. 301.

83. A Study by Odin Anderson and J. H. Feldman, *Family Medical Costs and Voluntary Health Insurance* (Chicago: University of Chicago Press, 1956), showed that in the U.S., too, rural residents, on becoming insured, reverse their previous pattern of receiving fewer services than urban residents and do, in fact, begin to receive more.

84. This was in sharp contrast to the experience of B.C. which introduced a premium-financed plan in 1949. It was one if not the main issue defeating the Government in 1952. In Saskatchewan, the plan became popular before it became expensive; in B.C., it was expensive before it was popular.

Notes to Chapter Three

1. Federal-Provincial Conference 1955, Preliminary Meeting, *Proceedings*, pp. 2–9.

2. Ibid., pp. 12–15.

3. M. G. Taylor, "Government Planning: The Federal-Provincial Health Survey Reports," *Canadian Journal of Economics and Political Science* XIX; 4 (November 1953): 501–10.

4. Canadian Medical Association, Statement of Policy, 1949.

5. See below, pp. 141–46.

6. M. G. Taylor, "Confidential Report on Health Insurance for the Ontario Government," 1954 (mimeo).

7. Ibid., pp. 13–15.

8. Joint Committee on Health Insurance

9. *Taylor Report*, pp. 48–50.

10. Ibid., p. 45.

11. Ibid., p. 39.

12. Federal-Provincial Conference, 1955, *Proceedings*, p 22.

13. Personal conversation with Mr. Gathercole.

14. Ontario Legislature, *Debates*, March 23, 1955, p. 1144.

15. Ibid., p. 1147.

16. Ibid., p. 1148.

17. Ibid., p. 1135.

18. Personal letter from George Gathercole, September 20, 1975.

19. *Toronto Globe and Mail*, April 5, 1955.

20. *House of Commons Debates*, April 6, 1955, p. 2862.

21. Ibid., p. 2863.

22. Federal-Provincial Conference, 1955, Preliminary Meeting, *Proceedings*, p. 7.

23. Ibid., pp. 14–15.

24. M. G. Taylor, "Program Design and Evaluation: The Ontario Hospital Services Plan," *Canadian Journal of Public Health*, 50, 4 (April 1959): 136–43.

25. Ibid.

26. Ibid., p. 140.

27. Federal-Provincial Conference, 1955, *Proceedings*, p. 8.

28. Ibid., pp. 8–9.

29. Ibid., p. 21.

30. Ibid.

31. *Toronto Globe and Mail*, January 23, 1956.

32. *Ottawa Citizen*, January 23, 1956.

33. Ibid.

34. "Stenographic Report of the Meetings of the Standing Committee on Health," March 14, 1956, pp. 3–7.

35. Ibid, pp. 7–8.

36. Ibid., pp. 82–83.

37. Ibid., p. 96.

38. Ibid., p. 102.

39. Ibid.

40. Ibid., pp. 113–14.

41. Ibid.

42. Ibid., pp. 130–38.

43. Ibid., p. 132.

44. Ibid., p. 133.

45. Ibid., p. 137.

46. Ibid., p. 168.

47. Ibid., p. 170.

48. Ibid., p. 171.

49. Ibid., p. 175.

50. Ibid., p. 177.

51. Chamber of Commerce of Ontario. Statement on Health Insurance, 1956.

52. Statutes of Ontario, 1956, C. 31.

53. Personal notes. In June 1956, I was asked to serve as consultant to the commission, with one responsibility, that of setting up a research division within

the commission. Mr. Ronald Verbrugge was transferred from the Provincial Economist's Office to the commission and continued his work on financial matters. Miss Isabel Boyd was appointed to assist in the research for the development of an overall Master Plan for hospital facilities.

54. *Toronto Globe and Mail*, July 27, 1956.

55. *Windsor Star*, August 3, 1956.

56. *Toronto Globe and Mail*, August 3, 1956.

57. Personal notes.

58. Letter, Mr. Frost to Mr. St. Laurent, December 11, 1956, correspondence tabled in House of Commons and Ontario Legislature, February 4, 1957 (mimeo).

59. Letter, Mr. St. Laurent to Mr. Frost, January 22, 1957.

60. Letter, Mr. Frost to Mr. St. Laurent, January 24, 1957.

61. Letter, Mr. Frost to Mr. St. Laurent, January 24, 1957 (emphasis in original).

62. Letter, Mr. St. Laurent to Mr. Frost, January 28, 1957.

63. Letter, Mr. St. Laurent to Mr. Frost, January 28, 1957.

64. Ontario Legislature, *Debates*, January 29, 1957, pp. 19–25.

65. Ibid.

66. Ibid., pp. 25–26.

67. Ibid., pp. 30–31. The quotation is from the author's book, *The Administration of Health Insurance in Canada*, copies of which, at Mr. Frost's direction, were distributed to all members of the Legislature.

68. Ontario Legislature, *Debates*, January 29, 1957, p. 33.

69. Ibid., p. 35.

70. Letter, Mr. Leslie Frost to Mr. St. Laurent, January 28, 1957.

71. Ibid., Letter, Mr. St. Laurent to Mr. Leslie Frost, February 1, 1957.

72. Telegram, Mr. Frost to Mr. St. Laurent, February 4, 1957.

73. *Toronto Globe and Mail*, February 6, 1957.

74. Ontario Legislature, *Debates*, March 4, 1957.

75. *Toronto Globe and Mail*, March 5, 1957.

76. Ibid., March 7, 1957.

77. Statutes of Ontario, 1957, C. 46.

78. Statutes of Canada, 1957, C.

79. Ontario Hospital Association, Minutes of Meeting of Executive Committee, July 9, 1957.

80. Ibid., Oct. 8, 1957.

81. *Toronto Star*, October 26, 1957.

82. Ontario Hospital Services Commission, *Annual Report*, 1960.

Notes to Chapter Four

1. House of Commons *Debates*, April 10, 1957, p. 3367 (Mr. Elmer Philpott).

2. Personal interview with Mr. Martin, June 21, 1971.

3. See above, p. 21.

4. House of Commons *Debates*, May 14, 1948, p. 3933.

5. Ibid., p. 3932.

6. L. G. Bernard, quoted in Dale Thompson, *Louis St. Laurent, Canadian* (Toronto: Macmillan, 1967), p. 241.

7. Ibid. p. 242.

8. Ibid., p. 276.

9. This and the following platform references are from D. Owen Carrigan, *Canadian Party Platforms 1867–1968* (Toronto: Copp Clark, 1968).

10. Reported in *Toronto Daily Star*, July 13, 1949.

11. Personal interviews with the minister of health, the Honourable George Pearson, in 1947, 1948, and 1949, and with senior BCHIS officials.

12. Statutes of British Columbia, 1948, C. 88.

13. M. G. Taylor, *The Financial Aspects of Health Insurance* (Toronto: Canadian Tax Foundation, 1958).

14. Ibid. pp. 57–73.

15. Ibid.

16. Joint Committee (of the insurance industry), *Financing Health Services in Canada* (Toronto: The Committee, 1954).

17. C. Howard Shillington, *The Road to Medicare in Canada* (Toronto: Del Graphics Publishing Co., 1972).

18. Carman A. Naylor, "Recent Developments in Group Insurance," Address to the Third Canadian Medical Care Conference, June 1, 1956 (mimeo).

19. Paper presented to the First Medical Conference, 1954.

20. Eric J. Hanson, *Fiscal Needs of the Canadian Provinces* (Toronto: Canadian Tax Foundation, 1961) and M. G. Taylor, *Financial Aspects of Health Insurance* (Toronto: Canadian Tax Foundation, 1968).

21. See above, p. 16.

22. *Toronto Globe and Mail*, September 2, 1952.

23. Conference of Federal and Provincial Governments, *Proceedings*, December 4–7, 1950, p. 5.

24. Ibid., p. 9.

25. Ibid., p. 8.

26. Ibid., p. 9.

27. Ibid., p. 53.

28. Dominion Bureau of Statistics, *National Accounts, Income and Expenditure, 1929–1956*.

29. Department of National Health and Welfare, *Social Security Series*, memorandum no. 16.

30. Personal interview.

31. Reported in *Montreal Star*, October 5, 1951.

32. Reported in *Quebec Chronicle Telegraph*, December 10, 1952.

33. M. G. Taylor, "Government Planning: The Health Survey Reports," *Canadian Journal of Economics and Political Science* XIX, 4 (November 1953): 501–10.

34. Thompson, *Louis St. Laurent*, p. 413.

35. House of Commons *Debates*, May 1, 1953, p. 4680.

36. Ibid., February 7, 1951, p. 155.

37. Ibid.

38. Ibid., October 24, 1951.

39. Ibid., June 21, 1952, p. 4462.

40. Ibid., February 19, 1953, p. 18.

41. Canadian Medical Association, *Policy Statement*, June 1955.

42. Ibid.

43. Ibid.

44. House of Commons *Debates*, June 20, 1951, p. 4348.

45. Ibid., pp. 4348–49.

46. Ibid., pp. 4386–87.

47. Canadian Hospital Association, "Brief on Health Insurance, 1953." (mimeo).

48. *The Montreal Gazette*, June 26, 1956.

49. William Anderson, Address to Annual Meeting, North American Life Assurance Co., 1954.

50. Canadian Chamber of Commerce, Statement of Policy on Health Insurance, 1953.

51. Reported in *Toronto Star*, January 23, 1957.

52. Dominion-Provincial Conference, 1945, *Proceedings*, p. 91.

53. Department of National Health and Welfare, *Report on the National Health Grants Program*, (1962) p. 38.

54. Federal-Provincial Conference, 1955, Preliminary Meeting, *Proceedings*, April 26, 1955, pp. 3–4.

55. Ibid., p. 6.

56. Ibid., p. 5. (Emphasis added.)

57. Ibid., p. 6.

58. Ibid., p.7.

59. Ibid., p. 11.

60. Ibid., pp. 11–77.

61. Ibid., p. 31.

62. Ibid., p. 37.

63. Ibid., p. 47.

64. Ibid., p. 50.

65. Ibid., p. 19.

66. Interview with Mr. Paul Martin.

67. Official summary of the meeting of provincial health officers and advisors, July 4, 1955.

68. Federal-Provincial Conference, 1955, *Proceedings* (October 3, 1955), pp. 3–4.

69. Ibid., pp. 8–9.

70. Ibid., p. 23.

71. Ibid., p. 25.

72. Ibid., p. 58.

73. Ibid., p. 66.

74. Ibid., pp. 85–86.

75. Ibid., p. 92.

76. Ibid., p. 98.

77. Ibid., p. 106.

78. Ibid., p. 107.

79. Ibid., p. 110.

80. Reported in *Ottawa Citizen*, October 5, 1955

81. Personal notes.

82. Interview with Mr. Paul Martin.

83. Canadian Medical Association, 89th Annual Meeting *Transactions*, June 1956, p. 25.

84. Reported in *The Montreal Gazette*, April 11, 1956.

85. House of Commons *Debates*, July 27, 1956, pp. 6557–58.

86. Letter, Mr. Frost to Mr. St. Laurent, December 11, 1956, correspondence tabled in House of Commons and Ontario Legislature, February 4, 1957 (mimeo).

87. Letter, Mr. St. Laurent to Mr. Frost, January 22, 1957.

88. Letter, Mr. Frost to Mr. St. Laurent, January 24, 1957.

89. Letter, Mr. St. Laurent to Mr. Frost, January 28, 1957.

90. Letter, Mr. Frost to Mr. St. Laurent, January 30, 1957.

91. Mr. St. Laurent to Mr. Leslie Frost, February 1, 1957.

92. Reported in *Toronto Globe and Mail*, March 6, 1957.

93. House of Commons *Debates*, December 21, 1957, p. 2719.

94. These quotations are from the House of Commons *Debates*, March 26, April 4, April 8, and April 10, 1957. In the interest of brevity some of the statements have been condensed.

95. Reported in *Toronto Globe and Mail*, April 11, 1957.

96. Reported in *Toronto Star*, April 17, 1957.

97. Federal-Provincial Conference, *Proceedings* (November 25 and 26, 1957), p.8.

98. Ibid., p. 9.

99. Ibid., p. 10.

100. Ibid., p. 23.

101. Ibid., p. 51.

102. Ibid., p. 34.

103. Ibid., p. 65.

104. Ibid., p. 85.

105. Ibid., pp. 94–95.

106. R. G. Evans, "Beyond the Medical Market Place," in Spyros Andreopoulos (ed.), *National Health Insurance* (New York: Wiley, 1976), p. 146.

107. For a more detailed discussion, see Eric J. Hanson, *The Public Finance Aspects of Health Services* (Ottawa: Queen's Printer, 1964), pp. 116–22.

Notes to Chapter Five

1. M. G. Taylor, "The Role of the Medical Profession in the Formulation and Execution of Public Policy," *The Canadian Journal of Economics and Political Science* XXV, 1 (February 1960): 108–27.

2. S. M. Lipsett, *Agrarian Socialism* (Berkeley: University of California Press, 1950).

3. Saskatchewan, Health Survey Committee, *Report*, vol. I (Regina: Queen's Printer, 1951), pp. 149–51.

4. *Saskatchewan Medical Quarterly* 7, 4 (December 1943): 13. (Emphasis added.)

5. Statutes of Saskatchewan 1937, C. 69. See also, D. M. Baltzan in *Foreword* to the first issue of the *Saskatchewan Medical Quarterly* (April 1937).

6. *Saskatchewan Medical Quarterly*, 6, 1 (April 1942): 52. (Emphasis added.)

7. College of Physicians and Surgeons *Bulletin No. 3* (1943).

8. Ibid.

9. Escott Reid, "The Saskatchewan Liberal Machine Before 1929," *Canadian Journal of Economics and Political Science*, 11, 1 (February 1936): 21–40; S. M. Lipsett, *Agrarian Socialism* (chap. XII); and David Smith, *Prairie Liberalism* (Toronto: University of Toronto Press, 1975).

10. College of Physicians and Surgeons, Submission to Select Committee of the Legislative Assembly (March 1943).

11. Ibid.

12. See above, p. 77.

13. *Saskatchewan Medical Quarterly*, 8, 4 (December 1944): 7.

14. Personal correspondence from Dr. C. J. Houston, of Yorkton, who was a member of the executive at the time.

15. T. C. Douglas to registrar, September 13, 1944. (T. C. Douglas *Papers*).

16. R. W. Kirkby to T. C. Douglas, October 1, 1944. (T. C. Douglas *Papers*).

17. See above, pp. 87–88.

18. Statutes of Saskatchewan, 1944, 2nd Sess., C. 51.

19. College of Physicians and Surgeons, Submission to Select Committee of the Legislative Assembly (March 1943).

20. Health Services Planning Commission, "Report on Regional Health Services," March 1945, (mimeo.)

21. A summary of the discussion appears in the *Saskatchewan Medical Quarterly*, 9, 2 (May 1945): 14–21.

22. Ibid.

23. S. M. Lipsett, *Agrarian Socialism*, p. 293.

24. Health Services Planning Commission *Report*, Part II, p. 2.

25. Lipsett, *Agrarian Socialism*, pp. 290–91.

26. Letter from the registrar to physicians in Health Region No. I, December 24, 1945 (T. C. Douglas *Papers*).

27. T. C. Douglas to Dr. J. L. Brown, September 19, 1945 (T. C. Douglas *Papers*).

28. J. L. Brown to T. C. Douglas (undated). (T. C. Douglas *Papers*).

29. F. D. Mott, and M. I. Roemer, *Rural Health and Medical Care* (New York: McGraw-Hill, 1948).

30. C. P. G. Howden, M.D., "The Swift Current Program," *Saskatchewan Medical Quarterly* 13, 4 (December 1949).

31. A. D. Kelly, "The Swift Current Experiment," *Canadian Medical Association Journal* (1948): 406–511.

32. Dr. J. Lloyd Brown, "Swift Current Health Insurance Scheme," *Saskatchewan Medical Quarterly*, 13, 2 (July 1949): 251–58.

33. Associated Medical Services and Windsor Medical Services.

34. Revised Statutes of Saskatchewan, 1938, C. 24.

35. Health Survey Committee, *Report*, 1951, vol. I, p. 215.

36. Canadian Medical Association, Statement of Policy, 1949.

37. *Saskatchewan Medical Quarterly*, 13, 4 (December 1949): 249 ff.

38. Report of Dr. J. F. C. Anderson, president of the Canadian Medical Association "Regional Meetings of the CMA," *Canadian Medical Association Journal*, 62, 1 (January 1950): 94.

39. Saskatchewan. Order-in-Council 74/49.

40. Saskatchewan Health Survey Committee, *Report*, vols. I and II (Regina: Queen's Printer, 1951).

41. Ibid., p. 225.

42. *Saskatchewan Medical Quarterly*, 16, 1 (April 1952): 91.

43. Ken MacTaggart, describing the report as "exhaustive," said, "The Saskatchewan Survey has often been called the classic of such projects." Ken MacTaggart, *The First Decade* (Ottawa: The Canadian Medical Association, 1973).

44. C. J. Houston, in *Saskatchewan Medical Quarterly*, 15, 4 (December 1951): 626.

45. "Memorandum for File," March 13, 1950. (T. C. Douglas *Papers*).

46. Ibid.

47. J. L. Brown to Hon. T. J. Bentley, April 14, 1950. (T. C. Douglas *Papers*).

48. Meeting with Medical Advisory Committee of the College of Physicians and Surgeons, Saturday, January 5, 1951, *Verbatim Notes*. (T. C. Douglas *Papers*).

49. *Saskatchewan Medical Quarterly*, 15, 1 (April 1951): 537–38.

50. M. G. Taylor, "Some Administrative Aspects of the Integration of Health Services," *Canadian Journal of Public Health* (August 1951): 329–35.

51. Personal interviews.

52. Resumé of Special Meeting of Central Health Services Committee, September 11, 1955, *Saskatchewan Medical Quarterly* 19, 4 (December 1955): 140–44.

53. Brief of the Medical Advisory Committee of Seven, October 22, 1955. (T. C. Douglas *Papers*).

54. It is difficult to reconcile these views with those expressed in 1949 by Drs. Brown and Howden. See above, pp. 251–52.

55. Letter from chairman of Coordinating Committee, Dr. J. L. Brown, to all Saskatchewan doctors, October 31, 1955. (T. C. Douglas *Papers*).

56. *Saskatchewan Medical Quarterly*, 20, 2 (September 1956): 107–13

57. The paper is unsigned but from the context it can be assumed that it was presented by either the executive director or the medical director of Medical Services Incorporated, Saskatoon.

58. Saskatchewan. Advisory Planning Committee on Medical Care, *Interim Report* (1961), pp. 17–19.

59. *Saskatchewan Medical Quarterly*, 21, 2 (September 1957): 90.

60. Ibid.

61. Ibid., pp. 89–90.

62. *Saskatchewan Medical Quarterly* 22, 2 (September 1958): 82–83.

63. Ibid., p. 84.

64. For a description of the development of the "College" and "Association" functions, see M. G. Taylor, "The Role of the Medical Profession in the Formulation and Execution of Public Policy."

65. In Quebec and Ontario, in the 70's, legislation has been passed to introduce a wider degree of public participation in this "self-governing" process. In this connection, see Ontario Committee on the Healing Arts, *Report*, Vol. III, and J. T. McLeod (ed.), *Essays on the Left* (Toronto: Queen's Printer, 1970), pp. 86–89.

66. Alberta is another exception; despite the existence of a separate association, negotiations with the Government on economic matters are conducted by the College. For a more detailed analysis of the public interest of much of this work, see M. G. Taylor, "The Role of the Medical Profession."

67. The Royal Commission on Health Services (chaired by the former chief justice of Saskatchewan) was very concerned about this conflict of interest in one body. It recommended "That in all provinces the College of Physicians and Surgeons be separately organized from the provincial Division of the Canadian Medical Association and that the power of all provincial medical licensing agencies be extended to give them sufficient authority to ensure that medical and surgical practice is of high quality." Royal Commission on Health Services *Report* (1964), vol. I, pp. 31–34.

The Ontario Royal Commission on Civil Rights quoted with approval the following (1966) statement of the General Medical Council of England: "The general duty of the Council is to protect the public, in particular by supervising and improving medical education. . . . The Council is not an association or union for protecting professional interest." (p. 1162).

68. The concept of private government had been extensively treated in the literature, beginning with Charles E. Merriam's *Public and Private Government* (New Haven: Yale University Press, 1944). Other analyses include: "Professional Associations as Governments," chap. 4 of Corinne Gilb, *Hidden Hierarchies* (New York: Harper and Row, 1966); Lane Lancaster, "The Legal Status of 'Private' Organizations Exercising Governmental Powers," *Southwestern Social Science Quarterly*, 15 (1935): 325–26; Grant McConnell, "Private Government," in *Private Power and American Democracy* (New York: Alfred A. Knopf, 1966); and Sanford Lakoff, *Private Government* (London: Scott Foresman and Co., 1973).

69. *Montreal Star*, July 5, 1962.

70. Cabinet Conference on Planning and Budgeting, *Minutes*. (T. C. Douglas *Papers*).

71. Advisory Planning Committee on Medical Care, *Report*, p. 26. This report indicates that forty percent of the population were insured through prepayment plans and commercial insurance; twenty-seven percent through public plans. This included 107,000 covered by municipal doctor plans which, as we have seen, varied widely in the range of services insured.

72. Ibid., p. 219.

73. See chap. 6, p. 335.

74. T. C. Douglas, Throne Speech Debate. Saskatchewan Legislative Assembly, *Debates*. April 17, 1960.

75. *Regina Leader Post*, February 15, 1961.

76. T. C. Douglas, Throne Speech Debate, April 17, 1960.

77. Conference on Planning and Budgeting, April 20–23, 1959, *Minutes* (T. C.

Douglas *Papers*). The issues discussed included education, welfare, pensions, cultural and recreational services, water facilities, rural telephones, highways and municipal roads, rural electrification, industrial development and, of course, medical care insurance. The policies that emerged from the six months' planning process were outlined in a 1960 election campaign document entitled, "Modern Living."

78. Ibid.

79. Saskatchewan. Interdepartmental Committee, *Proposals for a Medical Care Program for Saskatchewan*, p. 30. (T. C. Douglas *Papers*).

80. W. B. Tufts, M.D., "Principles of Co-insurance." Address to Saskatchewan Medical Convention, October 22, 1959.

81. Interdepartmental Committee, *Proposals*, p. 42.

82. Ibid., p. 68.

83. Memorandum, November 26, 1959. (T. C. Douglas *Papers*).

84. Memorandum, Dr. F. B. Roth to Hon. J. Walter Erb, November 27, 1959. (T. C. Douglas *Papers*).

85. G. W. Peacock to T. C. Douglas, April 28, 1959. (T. C. Douglas *Papers*).

86. T. C. Douglas to G. W. Peacock, May 1, 1959. (T. C. Douglas *Papers*).

87. Personal interviews.

88. Personal interviews.

89. *Saskatchewan Medical Quarterly*, 25, 4 (December 1959): 281–82.

90. Copy of radio address. (T. C. Douglas *Papers*).

91. Council of the College of Physicians and Surgeons of Saskatchewan, *Statement of Policy*, March 2, 1960.

92. OMA, *Report to Council*, 1959.

93. Personal interview.

94. For details, see Ken MacTaggart, *The First Decade*.

95. *Toronto Star*, June 10, 1960.

96. Doris French Shackleton, *Tommy Douglas* (Toronto: McClelland and Stewart, 1975), pp. 225–26.

97. *Interim Report of the Advisory Planning Committee on Medical Care* (September 25, 1961), p. 5.

98. Ibid., p. 59.

99. Nine years later, on the return of the NDP to power, he became minister of health.

100. *Saskatchewan Medical Quarterly*, 25, 3 (September 1961): 177.

101. Statutes of Saskatchewan, 1962 (Second Seesion), C. 1.

102. See F. R. Badgley and Samual Wolfe, *Doctors' Strike* (Toronto: MacMillan, 1967), p. 40.

103. Cabinet Minute No. 856, June 20, 1961.

104. For unexplained reasons that clearly reflect on the minister (Mr. Erb), much of this assignment was not carried out by the department. Consequently, when the Thompson Committee Report was received, there were only four weeks in which to finalize these decisions and prepare the final draft of the legislation.

105. Address of Hon. W. S. Lloyd, provincial treasurer, in the Saskatchewan Legislature, October 20, 1961.

106. E. A. Tollefson, *Bitter Medicine* (Saskatoon: Modern Press, 1964), p. 88.

107. W. G. Davies to H. D. Dalgleish, December 4, 1961. (Woodrow Lloyd *Papers*).

108. H. D. Dalgleish to W. G. Davies, December 12, 1961. (Woodrow Lloyd *Papers*).

109. See above, pp. 281–82.

110. W. G. Davies to H. D. Dalgleish, January 5, 1962.

111. Royal Commission on Health Services, *Hearings*, January 22, 1962. Dr. C. J. Houston saw this statement as the crux of the issue. "On the one side are those who seek to preserve professional freedom. On the other side [are those who espouse this] dogma. . . . it implied complete subservience to the stare [and the destruction] of professional freedom and indeed all freedom." *A Family Doctor's Reaction to the Medical Care Crisis* (private publication).

112. Royal Commission on Health Services, *Hearings*, January 23, 1962.

113. The term "civil conscription" had been used by the Australian High Court in declaring the Australian plan unconstitutional, but Tollefson maintains that this argument is unfounded in the Canadian constitution. See. E. A. Tollefson, *Bitter Medicine*, p. 93.

114. See excerpts in Badgley and Wolfe, *Doctors' Strike*, pp. 85–87.

115. W. G. Davies to H. D. Dalgleish, March 2, 1962. (W. S. Lloyd *Papers*).

116. Referred to in W. G. Davies to H. D. Dalgleish, March 22, 1962. (W. S. Lloyd *Papers*).

117. Ibid.

118. See above p. 290.

119. Statement of Premier Lloyd to meeting, March 28, 1962. (W. S. Lloyd *Papers*). Emphasis added.

120. In an extensive survey of physicians by the Canadian Medical Association in 1960, eighty-seven percent of participating physicians accepted plan payments as payment in full; in dealing with insurance companies, sixty-eight percent preferred to be paid directly by the company (CMA *Transactions*, 1960), p. 13.

121. Council of the College, Memorandum, April 11, 1962. (W. S. Lloyd *Papers*).

122. Ibid. Emphasis added.

123. See Tollefson, *Bitter Medicine*, p. 98.

124. Personal interviews.

125. Woodrow S. Lloyd, *Statement to the Saskatchewan Legislature*, April 12, 1962. (W. S. Lloyd *Papers*).

126. A. W. Johnson, "Biography of a Government: Policy Formulation in the Government of Saskatchewan 1955–62," Ph.D. diss., Harvard University, 1963, ch. XI.

127. W. S. Lloyd, quoted in *Regina Leader Post*, April 11, 1962.

128. Badgley and Wolfe, *Doctors' Strike*, p. 47.

129. Statement of Premier W. S. Lloyd, Saskatchewan Legislative Assembly, April 12, 1962. (W. S. Lloyd *Papers*). Professor Tollefson believes that the clause was "politically expedient and legally wider than necessary." (E. A Tollefson, *Bitter Medicine*, p. 101.)

130. *Regina Leader Post*, April 13, 1962.

131. Ibid.

132. *Statutes of Saskatchewan*, chap. 68, 1962.

133. D. D. Tansley to H. D. Dalgleish, April 21, 1962. (W. S. Lloyd *Papers*). Emphasis added, as this alternative became increasingly important in the strategy.

134. Ibid.

135. D. D. Tansley to G. Peacock, May 24, 1962. (W. S. Lloyd *Papers*).

136. Copy of the registrar's letter is not available, but the chairman's reply said: "Although we have noted the contents of your letter, we will continue to consult with the College." D. D. Tansley to Dr. G. W. Peacock, June 8, 1962. (W. S. Lloyd *Papers*).

137. *Regina Leader Post*, May 3, 1962.

138. Address of W. S. Lloyd to College of Physicians and Surgeons, May 3, 1962. (W. S. Lloyd *Papers*).

139. *Regina Leader Post*, May 3, 1962.

140. A. F. W. Peart, M.D., "The Medical Viewpoint," *American Journal of Public Health*, 5, 53 (May 1963): 724–28.

141. *Regina Leader Post*, May 5, 1962.

142. *Regina Leader Post*, June 17, 1962.

143. A. M. Mohamed, "Keep Our Doctors Committees in the Saskatchewan Medicare Controversy" (M. A. thesis, University of Saskatchewan, Saskatoon, 1964.)

144. Badgley and Wolfe, *Doctors' Strike*, p. 52.

145. *Regina Leader Post*, May 31, 1962.

146. E. A. Tollefson, *Bitter Medicine*, p. 148.

147. *Saskatoon Star Phoenix*, June 7, 1962.

148. June 15, 1962.

149. *Regina Leader Post*, June 19, 1962.

150. Ibid.

151. *Toronto Star*, June 19, 1962.

152. *Regina Leader Post*, June 19, 1962.

153. *Winnipeg Tribune*, June 18, 1962.

154. *Report* of the meeting of the Canadian Medical Association executive, 95th Annual Meeting of the CMA, *Canadian Medical Association Journal* (July 21, 1962), pp. 142–3 (Emphasis added.)

155. June 21, 1962.

156. *Saskatoon Star Phoenix*, June 20, 1962.

157. Ibid.

158. Ibid.

159. *Regina Leader Post*, June 20.

160. "Notes of Meeting between Cabinet and the Council of the College of Physicians and Surgeons," June 22, 1962 (handwritten notes). (W. S. Lloyd *Papers*).

161. I read only a hundred or so of these (in the Lloyd *Papers*), most of them handwritten, but they constituted an outpouring of hope and personal encouragement unique in an era increasingly cynical of the relationship between representatives and electors. Of course, not all letters were supportive! At the same time College spokesmen reported that letters to the College were running twenty-five to one in favour of the College stand.

162. "Statement of Government to College of Physicians and Surgeons, June 22, 1962." (W. S. Lloyd *Papers*).

163. This recurring phrase meant, of course, conferring veto power on the profession. The College would have argued that the last of Douglas's five principles ("acceptable to the profession") meant exactly that.

164. "Notes of Meeting," June 22. 1962 (W. S. Lloyd *Papers*). p. 52.

165. There may have been more to this argument than first appears. In the survey of physicians' opinions referred to above, the CMA Committee on Prepaid Plans, commenting on the responses to a question on reimbursement, said: "Your committee feels that lack of experience in Canada with reimbursement methods made this question not well understood and that many doctors regarded it of doubtful practicability." Canadian Medical Association, *Transactions*, 1960, p. 13.

166. Council of the College of Physicians and Surgeons, "Criticisms of the Saskatchewan Medical Insurance Act," June 25, 1962.

167. Government commentary on the document entitled, "Criticisms of the Saskatchewan Medical Insurance Act," June 26, 1962. (W. S. Lloyd *Papers*).

168. *Canadian Forum*, July 1962, p. 3.

169. *Regina Leader Post*, June 3, 1962.

170. *Toronto Star*, July 4, 1962.

171. Ibid.

172. *Canadian Press*, July 9, 1962.

173. *Medicine Hat News*, July 9, 1962.

174. The *Toronto Telegram*, favourable to the College, editorialized on July 12, "The doctors of Saskatchewan may have to be rescued from their so-called friends, if the performance of the Keep-Our-Doctors movement is any indication."

175. Badgley and Wolfe, *Doctors' Strike*, p. 65.

176. *Regina Leader Post*, July 15, 1962.

177. Personal Interviews.

178. This section is based on a summary of discussions of the Cabinet Strategy Committee (undated, but clearly in the second week of July). (W. S. Lloyd *Papers*).

179. Lord Taylor, "Saskatchewan Adventure," *Canadian Medical Association Journal* 110, 6 (March 1974): 725. This is a remarkable report on his role as mediator, expanded from a seventeen-page memorandum he dictated just before leaving Regina in 1962. (W. S. Lloyd *Papers*).

180. Ibid., p. 726.

181. *Regina Leader Post*, July 17, 1962.

182. Ibid.

183. Ibid., July 18, 1962.

184. Ibid., July 5.

185. Ibid., July 18, 1962.

186. *Saskatoon Star Phoenix*, July 18, 1962.

187. Ibid.

188. H. D. Dalgleish to W. S. Lloyd, July 14, 1962. (W. S. Lloyd *Papers*).

189. W. S. Lloyd to H. D. Dalgleish, July 17, 1962. (W. S. Lloyd *Papers*).

190. Ibid.

191. *Regina Leader Post*, July 18.

192. *Saskatoon Star Phoenix*, July 19, 1962.

193. A. D. Kelly, M.D., "Saskatchewan Solomon," *Canadian Medical Association Journal* (August 25, 1962): 416–17.

194. Lord Taylor, "Saskatchewan Adventure," 110, 7, *Canadian Medical Association Journal*: 835.

195. Ibid., May 1974, p. 1102.

196. Four days after the signing, at the request of the College, a supplement to the agreement was signed, removing the compulsory arbitration provision. Lord Taylor regards this as a loss to the profession.

197. Report of the Honourable Mr. Justice Mervyn Wood, December 11, 1963.

198. *Regina Leader Post*, July 30, 1962.

199. *Canadian Medical Association Journal* 87 (July 28 1962): 190.

200. *Saskatchewan Medical Quarterly* 27, 1 (April 1963): 12–13. (Italics added.)

201. For an elaboration of outcomes, see Badgley and Wolfe, *Doctors' Strike*, chap. VII; Arnold Swanson, "Some Effects of Medicare on Hospitals in Saskatchewan," *Canadian Hospital* 42, 11 (November 1965): 50–53; E. A. Tollefson, *Bitter Medicine*, chap. VII; W. P. Thompson, "Saskatchewan Doctors' Opinions of Medicare," *Canadian Medical Association Journal* 93 (October 30, 1965): 971–76; and Ken MacTaggart, *The First Decade*.

202. David Smith, *Prairie Liberalism*, pp. 296–97.

203. This pattern did not continue. Whereas in the period 1960–65, Saskatchewan's average annual increases were the highest in Canada, in the latter half of the sixties, as national medicare came into being, Saskatchewan physicians fell to ninth place.

204. H. L. Portnuff, "Review of Medical Loss," College of Physicians and Surgeons, *News Letter*, December 1963.

205. R. A. Spasoff and S. Wolfe, "Trends in the Supply and Distribution of Physicians in Saskatchewan," *Canadian Medical Association Journal* 92 (March 6, 1965): 523–28.

206. W. W. Wigle, M.D., "Saskatchewan Before, During and After," *Canadian Medical Association Journal*, 87 (September 8, 1962): 574–75.

Notes to Chapter Six

1. House of Commons *Debates*, April 5, 1965, pp. 2–3.

2. Federal-Provincial Conference, July 19–22, 1965, *Proceedings*, p. 15.

3. Ibid., p. 16.

4. On this period see: Denis Smith, *Gentle Patriot: A Political Biography of Walter Gordon* (Edmonton: Hurtig, 1975); Lester B. Pearson, *Memoirs*, Vol. III (Toronto: University of Toronto Press, 1975); Peter C. Newman, *The Distemper of Our Times* (Toronto: McClelland and Stewart, 1973); Judy LaMarsh, *A Bird in a Gilded Cage* (Toronto: McClelland and Stewart, 1969); Walter Gordon, *A Political Memoir* (Toronto: McClelland and Stewart, 1977).

5. M. G. Taylor, "The Role of the Medical Profession in the Formulation and Execution of Public Policy," *Canadian Journal of Economics and Political Science* XXV, 1 (February 1960): 108–27.

6. Report of Committee on Economics in *Transactions* of the 94th Annual meeting of the Canadian Medical Association (June 19–21, 1961), p. 29.

7. House of Commons *Debates*, December 21, 1960, pp. 1023–24.

8. C. Howard Shillington, *The Road to Medicare* (Toronto: Del Graphics, 1972). For a comparative study of the two types of plans, see Theodore I. Goldberg, "Trade-Union Interest in Medical Care and Voluntary Insurance," Ph.D. thesis, University of Toronto, 1962.

9. *Toronto Globe and Mail*, June 19, 1951.

10. C. Howard Shillington, *Road to Medicare*, pp. 113–14.

11. Ibid., p. 114.

12. Ibid., p. 138.

13. Ibid.

14. Ibid., p. 139.

15. Ibid., pp. 140–41.

16. Submission of the Canadian Medical Association to the Royal Commission on Health Services, 1961, p. 75.

17. Government of the Province of Alberta, Submission to the Royal Commission on Health Services.

18. *Edmonton Journal*, June 29, 1963.

19. This method of income determination has one defect in that the current year's entitlement to subsidy is calculated on last year's income, and incomes can fluctuate substantially from year to year.

20. *Edmonton Journal*, June 29, 1963.

21. Ontario Legislature, An Act Respecting Medical Services Insurance, Bill 163, 1963.

22. Ontario Legislature *Debates*, April 25, 1963, pp. 2776–83.

23. Report of the Medical Services Insurance (Hagey) Committee, 1963.

24. Ibid.

25. Ontario, *Public Accounts*, 1967.

26. Shillington, *Road to Medicare*, p. 126.

27. See above, p. 145.

28. House of Commons *Debates*, June 20, 1961, p. 6600.

29. The Royal Commission on Health Services, *Report*, p. 10.

30. Ibid.

31. Ibid., p. 11.

32. Ibid., p. 12.

33. Ibid., p. 13.

34. Ibid., pp. 14–15.

35. Ibid., p. 15.

36. Ibid., p. 19.

37. Ibid., pp. 734–36.

38. See, for example, Dominion Bureau of Statistics, *Urban Family Expenditures, 1959* (Ottawa: Queen's Printer, 1963), p. 20 ff.

39. The Royal Commission on Health Services, *Report*, pp. 743–44.

40. Excerpts from a *Canadian Medical Association Journal* editorial, January 14, 1961, pp. 116–17.

41. For an extended discussion of the ideological basis of the confrontation, see Bernard Blishen, *Doctors and Doctrines* (Toronto: University of Toronto Press, 1969).

42. Canadian Medical Association, *Transactions of a Special Meeting of the General Council*, January 29–30, 1965, p. 7.

43. Ibid., p. 14.

44. Judy La Marsh, *Bird in a Gilded Cage*, p. 48.

45. Ibid.

46. David Smith, *Prairie Liberalism*, pp. 296–97.

47. Peter Newman, *Distemper of Our Times*, p. 65.

48. D. V. Smiley, "Public Administration and Canadian Federalism," *Canadian Public Administration* V: 3 (September 1964): 374.

49. See Neil Caplan, "Some Factors Affecting the Resolution of a Federal-Provincial Conflict," *Canadian Journal of Political Science* II, 2 (June 1969): 173–86; and Richard Simeon, *Federal Provincial Diplomacy* (Toronto: University of Toronto Press, 1972).

50. Liberal party platform, 1961. These developments are also admirably discussed by Smiley in "Public Administration and Canadian Federalism."

51. The changes were embodied in the Established Programs (Interim Arrangements) Act, 1965.

52. In this period, other issues were providing the same kinds of uncertainties: pension plan, welfare sharing, off-shore mineral rights, etc.

53. In the minds of many Liberals, these two in the post-war years had become indistinguishable.

54. Canadian Labour Congress, submission to the Royal Commission on Health Services, May 1962.

55. Canadian Federation of Agriculture, submission to the Royal Commission on Health Services, May 1962.

56. Personal interviews.

57. Personal interviews.

58. Denis Smith, *Gentle Patriot*, p. 215.

59. Ibid.

60. Ibid., p. 216.

61. Ibid.

62. House of Commons *Debates*, April 5, 1965.

63. Federal-Provincial Conference, 1965, *Proceedings*, p. 16.

64. Ibid.

65. See above, pp. 177–81.

66. Canadian Medical Association, *Transactions*, 1965, p. 14.

67. Ibid.

68. Federal-Provincial Conference, 1965, *Proceedings*, pp. 15–18.

69. Ibid., pp. 29–30.

70. Ibid., pp. 54–56.

71. Ibid., pp. 62–64.

72. Ibid., p. 74.

73. The party standings following the election (with pre-election standings in brackets) were: Progressive Conservatives, 97 (95); Liberals, 131 (129); National

Democratic Party, 21 (17); Social Credit, 5 (24); Creditiste, 9; Other, 2.

74. "Health Services in Canada": Report of a working conference on the implications of a health charter for Canadians, Ottawa, November 28–December 1, 1965.

75. *Toronto Daily Star*, February 10, 1966.

76. Ontario Legislature, *Debates*, February 18, 1966, p. 700.

77. Statutes of Canada, 1966–67, C. 64.

78. House of Commons *Debates*, July 12, 1966, p. 7601.

79. *Toronto Daily Star*, August 3, 1966.

80. *Toronto Telegram*, August 6, 1966.

81. Ibid.

82. Personally, I have paid income taxes to the federal government while residing at different times in four provinces. To suggest in each of these cases that B.C., Alberta, Saskatchewan, or Ontario was "contributing to Ottawa" is nonsense.

83. *Toronto Telegram*, August 4, 1966.

84. All financial critics, inside and outside of Parliament, were sounding the alarms on inflation. See, e.g., *Financial Times*, August, 8, 1966.

85. *Toronto Globe and Mail*, September 8, 1966.

86. Peter Newman, *Distemper of Our Times*, p. 412.

87. Denis Smith, *Gentle Patriot*, p. 290.

88. Judy LaMarsh, *Bird in a Gilded Cage*, p. 340.

89. Peter Newman, *Distemper of Our Times*, p. 413.

90. Judy LaMarsh, *Bird in a Gilded Cage*, p. 339.

91. Peter Newman, *Distemper of our Times*, p. 413.

92. Judy LaMarsh, *Bird in a Gilded Cage*, p. 339.

93. Denis Smith, *Gentle Patriot*, p. 291.

94. *Winnipeg Free Press*, October 13, 1966.

95. *Toronto Globe and Mail*, October 18, 1966.

96. House of Commons *Debates*, October 19, 1966.

97. Revised Statutes of Canada, chap. 64, sect. 4 (3), p. 566. Medical Care Act, 1966.

98. House of Commons *Debates*, December 8, 1966.

99. Denis Smith, *Gentle Patriot*, p. 333.

100. *Toronto Globe and Mail*, October 25, 1967.

101. Denis Smith, *Gentle Patriot*, p. 333.

102. *Toronto Globe and Mail*, November 18, 1967.

103. Denis Smith, *Gentle Patriot*, p. 336.

104. Ibid.

105. Ibid., pp. 338–39.

106. Constitutional Conference, *Proceedings*, February 10, 1969.

Notes to Chapter Seven

1. Statement of The Hon. Daniel Johnson, 4th meeting of the Tax Structure Committee, Ottawa, September 14, 1966. See also the chapter by Daniel Johnson,

"Canada and Quebec," in Isaiah Litvak, *The Nation Keepers* (Toronto: McGraw Hill, 1967).

2. Ramsay Cook, *The Maple Leaf Forever* (Toronto: Macmillan, 1971), p. 86.

3. Constitutional Conference, February 1969, *Verbatim Record*, p. 648.

4. The proposal for contracting out was made at the Federal–Provincial Conference of 1964. When the same subject was discussed at the 1965 conference, Quebec pledged not to change the structure or the functioning of services already provided for in joint programs from which it wishes to opt out. Federal-Provincial Conference, 1965, *Proceedings*, p. 18.

5. Aaron Wildavsky, in Austin Ranney, ed., *Political Science and Public Policy* (Chicago: Markham, 1968), p. 63.

6. As later Quebec arguments were to show, what were not settled were the questions of the meaning of "established" and of how soon contracting out could occur after "establishment."

7. Federal-Provincial Conference, 1965, *Proceedings*, p. 15.

8. Ibid.

9. This paralleled the activities of the College of Physicians and Surgeons in Saskatchewan up to the latter part of the sixties when a separate organization— the association—was created. See M. G. Taylor, "The Role of the Medical Profession in the Formulation and Execution of Public Policy," *Canadian Journal of Economics and Political Science* XXV, 1 (February 1960): 108–27.

10. Brief of the College of Physicians and Surgeons to the Committee of Inquiry on Health and Social Services, mimeo, 1967, pp. 9–12.

11. Revised Statutes of Quebec, Professional Syndicates Act, 1944, chap. 146.

12. Thirty-one medical specialties are recognized by the Quebec College of Physicians and Surgeons as compared with fifty-one in the United States. Each became organized as a syndicate and combined in the federation.

13. Jules Deschenes, "The Professionals in Contemporary Quebec," *Bar Association Review* (1967): 69–80.

14. Briefs of the FMS and FMOQ to the Committee of Inquiry on Health and Social Services.

15. See Oswald Hall, "Half Medical Man, Half Administrator: An Occupational Dilemma, " *Canadian Public Administration*, II, 4 (December 1959): 185– 94 and "The Informal Organization of the Medical Profession, *Canadian Journal of Economics and Political Science* 12, 1 (February 1946): 30–44; B. R. Blishen, *Doctors and Doctrines* (Toronto: University of Toronto Press, 1969), chap. IV, "The Organization of Practice."

16. Committee of Inquiry on Health and Social Services, *Report* (Quebec: Government of Quebec, 1967) vol. IV, tome 1, p. 91.

17. P. C. Pineo and John Porter, "Occupational Prestige in Canada," *Canadian Review of Sociology and Anthropology*, IV, 1 (February 1967): 24–40. (Although the position does not represent a professional group, the provincial premier in Quebec ranks seventy-five points ahead.)

18. A fee schedule for prepayment purposes on a "service contract" basis was introduced by the specialists in 1967 in the administration of the medical assistance plan but applied, of course, to only a fraction of the population. (See, in this connection, Raymond Robillard, *Medicare, the MDs and You!* (Montreal: Robil-

lard, 1970), pp. 43–49.

19. See Marie R. Haug and Marvin B. Sussman, "Professional Autonomy and the Revolt of the Client," *Social Problems* (Fall, 1969): 153–61, and Corrine Gilb, *Hidden Hierarchies: Professions and Government* (New York: Harper and Row, 1966).

20. Committee of Inquiry on Health and Social Services, *Report*, vol. IV, tome 2, p. 26.

21. *Montreal Star*, July 3, 1970.

22. As the Castonguay Committee put it: "the dissatisfaction of the hospital authorities vis-à-vis relations with the Department of Health appeared constant. They deplored the absence of mechanisms to discuss institutional objectives, to assist in establishment of standards, to finance research into hospital administration, in brief to bring about efficient management, taking into account the overall needs of the people.... we conclude that this dissatisfaction is, in large measure, founded." Committee of Inquiry on Health and Social Services, *Report*, vol. IV, Part II, tome 1, pp. 91–92. The Castonguay Report is one of the outstanding health reports produced in Canada. Much of the credit is due Dr. Jacques Brunet, now deputy minister, and Dr. Sidney Lee, then professor of public health at Harvard University, now on the Faculty of Medicine at McGill. See his recent article on the Commission, "Quebec's Health Services in a Period of Dynamic Change," *Hospital Administration in Canada*," (January 1977): 13, 18, 23, 24, 47.

23. Federal-Provincial Conference, 1965, *Proceedings*, p. 54.

24. Committee of Inquiry on Health and Social Services, *Report*, vol. I p. 41.

25. Ibid., p. 258.

26. Ibid., p. 46. The Government had already taken the initial step by introducing in 1967 a medical assistance plan which provided medical services to 340,000 people receiving regular forms of public assistance. Successful negotiations were conducted with the two syndicates representing the profession and a fee schedule agreed upon. One effect of this program was to increase the demands of other low income groups, and these were expressed, particularly by the unions who relentlessly pressed their case before the Castonguay Committee and in their annual meetings with the Cabinet as well as in the media generally.

27. *Provincial Finances* (Toronto: Canadian Tax Foundation, 1967, 1968, 1969).

28. Their strategy was outlined by Dr. Robillard as follows: "We stopped billing the Medical Assistance Plan but instead billed the patient from whom however we never asked money but just asked to bill the government and pay us when and if they ever got the money." (Personal letter to author, Sept. 1, 1971.)

29. With the new 1967 contract with the general practitioners, the Government instituted a dues check-off system on behalf of the syndicate. In that year membership reached about three-fourths of registered general practitioners. There were charges of sell-out to the Government but in 1971 the specialists also obtained the check-off privilege.

30. Brief of the Federation of Medical Specialists to the Committee of Inquiry, mimeo, 1967.

31. *Provincial Finances* (Toronto: Canadian Tax Foundation, 1967).

32. *Montreal Star*, August 29, 1967.

33. "La création d'une régie autonome sera ... un excellent moyen de prévenir l'infiltration du virus de la partisanerie politique dans le mécanisme des décisions." Claude Ryan in *Le Devoir* (Montreal), August 28, 1967.

34. *Toronto Daily Star*, August 26, 1967.

35. "La santé ou la manque de santé constitue définitivement la question la plus urgente touchant la famille." M. Jean-Paul Cloutier, quoted in *La Presse* (Montreal), August 29, 1967.

36. *Montreal Star*, August 29, 1967.

37. *Le Devoir* (Montreal), August 30, 1967.

38. See above pp. 370–74.

39. *Montreal Star*, January 27, 1968 (poll taken November, 1967).

40. Quebec National Assembly, *Debates*, February 20, 1968, p. 4.

41. Ronald Robertson, "October Revolution: The Budget, 1968," *Canadian Tax Journal*, XVI, 6 (November–December 1968): 425–38.

42. "It is public knowledge that this income surtax is intended to finance the medicare scheme." Finance Minister Paul Dozois, budget speech, National Assembly, *Debates*, April 29, 1969, p. 50.

43. Dominion-Provincial Conference, *Proceedings* (Ottawa: Queen's Printer, 1946), p. 12.

44. Ibid., p. 121.

45. Jean-Jacques Bertrand succeeded The Hon. Daniel Johnson as premier of Quebec, following the latter's death on September 26, 1968.

46. Federal-Provincial Conference of ministers of finance and provincial treasurers (November 4–5, 1968), *Proceedings* (Ottawa: Queen's Printer, 1968), p. 14.

47. Ibid., p. 11.

48. *Le Devoir* (Montreal), April 9, 1969.

49. Editorial, *Quebec Chronicle-Telegraph*, April 10, 1969.

50. The Medical Care Act (1966), chap. 64. s. 8.

51. Finance Minister Dozois, budget speech, National Assembly, *Debates*, April 29, 1969, p. 50.

52. Bill 30, Quebec Health Insurance Board Act, June 13, 1969.

53. See their respective briefs to the Committee of Inquiry on Health and Social Services.

54. "Quatre grandes centrales syndicales du Québec viennent de former un front commun afin d'obtenir du gouvernement un régime d'assurance-maladie qui profite réellement à la population, a annoncé hier lors d'une conférence de presse M. Michel Chartrand," *L'Action* (Quebec City), June 26, 1970.

55. *Le Devoir* (Montreal), June 30, 1970.

56. Ibid.

57. This is incorrect: the syndicates (and not the "corporations" or colleges) were negotiating for the professions.

58. *Quebec Chronicle-Telegraph*, June 30, 1970.

59. *Le Soleil* (Quebec), July 3, 1970; *Le Devoir* (Montreal), July 6, 1970.

60. *Montreal Star*, July 3, 1970.

61. *Le Devoir* (Montreal), July 3, 1970.

62. *Montreal Star*, July 3, 1970.

63. Ibid.

64. Ibid. In a televised debate with labour leaders Castonguay said that the legislation was breaking new ground and much would be learned from experience, but he could not accept the unions' contention that doctors should be treated just the same as other unionized workers (*Montréal-Matin*, July 6, 1970).

65. M. Serge de la Rochelle (public relations director, QHIB): "Nous serons prêts pour le ler juillet; si le gouvernement quel qu'il soit, ne l'est pas, c'est une autre chose." *Le Soleil* (Quebec), April 1, 1970.

66. When I visited the QHIB headquarters in April 1971, morale had obviously been restored: productivity in processing units was extraordinarily high, in some cases fifty percent above typical norms.

67. See the brief of the FMOQ presented on July 3, 1970.

68. *Montreal Star*, July 10, 1970; *Le Devoir* (Montreal), July 10, 1970.

69. Committee of Inquiry on Health and Social Services, *Report*, part 5, vol. VII, tome I, *The Profession and Society*, pp. 24, 33.

70. *Montreal Star*, March 11, 1970; *La Presse* (Montreal), March 12, 1970; *Le Nouvelliste* (Trois Rivières), March 12, 1970.

71. Section 18(b) of the Health Insurance Act provided as follows: "in the exercise of its powers, the Board may, by itself or any persons appointed by it, inquire into any matter within its competence. It may also in the same manner hold any inquiry necessary for the purposes of Section 37 of the Health Insurance Act. For such purposes, the Board and every such person shall have the powers and immunities of commissioners appointed under the Public Inquiry Commission Act." This was considered by the profession as meaning that such commissioners would be entitled to investigate anything having to do with professional practice.

72. This, of course, was a highly contentious point: the specialists claimed that very few would in fact opt out, whereas some observers believed that large numbers would do so: "il faut prévoir que la 'vaste majorité' des médecins seront non-engagés," (*La Presse* (Montreal) October 2, 1970). The essential point the specialists emphasized, as other provincial medical associations had also done, was the need for a "private sector" operating beside the "public sector" which would serve, among other things, as a "safety valve" in a monopsony situation.

73. French-Canadian physicians' mobility was, of course, less influenced by competence in English than by the attachment of the specialist and his family to the Quebec milieu.

74. Embodied in Bill 250, November 1971.

75. *Montreal Star*, July 3, 1970.

76. In 1962 Quebec physicians' net earnings averaged 16.9 percent less than in Ontario (Department of National Health and Welfare, *Earnings of Physicians in Canada, 1957–65*). In 1968, after the introduction of OMSIP the difference had risen to twenty-four percent (Dominion Bureau of Statistics, *1968 Taxable Returns by Provinces and Occupation*).

77. In 1968 taxation year DBS *Taxable Returns by Province and Occupation* showed total income for medical doctors and surgeons in Ontario of $223,399,000, and in Quebec of $123,469,000.

78. See Thomas Schelling, *The Strategy of Conflict* (New York: Oxford Univer-

sity Press, 1963), pp. 21–53; Alan Coddington, *Theories of the Bargaining Process* (London: George Allen and Unwin, 1968; John G. Cross, *The Economics of Bargaining* (New York: Basic Books, 1969).

79. "Il s'agit pour les spécialistes de combattre une loi par la violence—tout aussi brutale et injustifiable, et potentiellement bien plus coûteuse que celle des bombes," René Lévesque in *Journal de Québec*, July 24, 1970; and on the other side: "the coercive and punitive nature of the emergency legislation to end the strike ..." *Montreal Gazette*, October 17, 1970.

81. This figure was frequently referred to in the press but there are no available data to indicate what the amount was.

82. Raymond Robillard, *Medicare, the MDs and You!*

83. Jean Pellerin in *La Presse* (Montreal), August 11, 1970.

84. Fred Poland in the *Montreal Star*, August 15, 1970.

85. "Le chantage crapuleux des médecins spécialistes qui ne pensent qu'à s'enrichir au détriment des petits salariés et refusent de se mettre au service de la population du Québec" Claude Masson in *La Presse* (Montreal), August 24, 1970.

86. Expectant mothers were especially vulnerable. One of the main by-products of the campaign was, as Dr. Robillard said, "an unusual demand for care.... patients have begun to wonder whether the doctor they have been used to will soon not be available" (quoted in *Montreal Star*, August 28, 1970). He also characterized the campaign with patients as "moral persuasion."

87. The *Toronto Globe and Mail* correspondent reported that while in the arena the speeches dealt with "state medicine, bureaucratic meddling, freedom to opt out, quality health care, sacred professional principles, conscription of doctors ..." In the corridors the discussions "dealt with a less complicated topic—money" (*Toronto Globe and Mail*, August 28, 1970).

88. Denial of the right of the doctor to opt out was presented as a denial of the basic freedom of the patient to seek care from the doctor of his choice without the penalty of not being reimbursed for any part of the fee he was charged, rather than as a denial of the right of the specialists to additional income.

89. Louis LaBerge, president of the QFL said that if the doctors strike, a back-to-work law should be passed immediately. Dr. Robillard later observed, "It is very amusing that the CNTU and the QFL should want special legislation imposed on the doctors after opposing such legislation in the construction industry," (*Toronto Daily Star*, August 28, 1970).

90. E.g. in *Le Devoir* (Montreal), August 10; *La Presse* (Montreal), August 24; *Journal de Québec*, July 24.

91. *Le Journal de Montréal*, August 29, 1970.

92. "Mais il ne faut pas oublier que l'humanité qui défile dans le cabinet du spécialiste ne vient pas présenter des ultimatums mais quémander le bien le plus précieux sur cette terre: la santé" (*La Presse* (Montreal), August 27, 1970).

93. *Montreal Star*, August 26, 1970.

94. *Toronto Daily Star*, August 27, 1970.

95. *Ottawa Journal*, September 4, 1970.

96. *Toronto Daily Star*, August 22, 1970.

97. *La Presse* (Montreal), September 3, 1970.

98. *Toronto Telegram*, September 26, 1970.
99. *La Presse* (Montreal), September 10, 1970.
100. *Le Devoir* (Montreal), September 11, 1970.
101. Ibid., September 12, 1970.
102. For a discussion of some of the rules said to govern relationships between groups seeking an accommodation see, F. C. Ikle, *How Nations Negotiate* (New York: Harper and Row, 1964), p. 144 ff.
103. Federation of Medical Specialists of Quebec, "Medicare Bill 8" (September 15, 1970), mimeo.
104. *Montreal Star*, September 28, 1970.
105. "... si le gouvernement voulait adopter en matière de rémunération une attitude moins géométrique ... il serait possible aux deux parties de rouvrir sans délai le dialogue" (*Le Devoir* (Montreal), October 2, 1970).
106. Dominic Clift in the *Montreal Star*, September 30, 1970.
107. This position is in fact voluntarily maintained by a substantial number of physicians in Manitoba who wish to deal directly with their patients but who accept eighty-five percent of the schedule as payment in full. Their administrative costs are higher.
108. *Le Devoir* (Montreal), October 2, 1970.
109. *Montreal Star*, October 2, 1970.
110. Ibid.
111. "Négligeant avec une impertinence sans précédent 'l'invitation expresse' qui leur avait été lancée la veille, les médecins-spécialistes ne se sont pas davantage présentés devant la Commission" (Normand Girard in *Le Soleil* (Quebec), October 3, 1970).
112. *Montreal Star*, October 1, 1970. The federation's council was aware of the negative public relations impact that this performance would have. But they felt that there was no other way of dramatizing their total frustration.
113. *Montreal Star*, October 5, 1970. See also editorial in *Le Devoir* (Montreal), October 3, 1970.
114. *Toronto Daily Star*, October 6, 1970.
115. The reason that the general practitioners were not directly negotiating on fees was that it had been agreed by the Government that there would be only one fee schedule; any up-grading won by the specialists would apply to the general practitioners.
116. *Montreal Star*, October 8, 1970.
117. For a day-by-day chronicle of the kidnapping crisis, see George Radwanski and Kendall Windeyer, *No Mandate but Terror* (Toronto: Simon and Schuster, 1970).
118. But, of course, it did. Claude Ryan brought out at least one way in which the two events were seen to be linked. "Those doctors who heard the FLQ manifesto read on television Thursday night will not have been able to avoid being impressed by the flagrant contrast between the state of affairs denounced by the FLQ and the position which doctors occupy in our society. The FLQ's methods must be condemned. But we shall not easily escape the rage that burns in thousands of hearts at the sight of inequalities like those from which doctors, among others, benefit. In the face of the defiance predicted for tomorrow, we can scarcely

wring our hands today over the fate of a group that displays such arrogance towards the rest of society" (Claude Ryan in *Le Devoir* (Montreal), Saturday, October 10, 1970).

119. *Montreal Star*, October 12, 1970. With hindsight it is reasonable to conclude that the specialists missed an extraordinary opportunity to achieve a massive reversal of public opinion. If, in the growing climate of fear and near-panic immediately following the second kidnapping, they had decided to return as a patriotic duty and as a demonstration of their commitment to law and order, the Government would inevitably have been forced to compromise even further.

120. Ibid., October 13, 1970.

121. *Le Devoir* (Montreal), October 14, 1970.

122. Ibid.

123. *La Presse* (Montreal), October 17, 1970.

124. *Montréal-Matin*, October 15, 1970.

125. *Le Devoir* (Montreal), October 14, 1970.

126. *La Presse* (Montreal), October 14, 1970.

127. *Le Devoir* (Montreal), October 14, 1970.

128. *La Presse* (Montreal), October 13, 1970.

129. Bill 41 provided for fines of up to $500 a day or imprisonment for practitioners and from $5000 to $50,000 for officers for every day the specialists remained on strike after October 17. It is interesting to note that the Castonguay Committee had recommended a procedure for negotiation of agreements and settlement of disputes which recognized a right to strike and withdraw all but emergency service. "On the other hand, there would be no question of declaring these services 'essential' and to oblige the workers to provide the services under threat of injunction. Recent experience demonstrates this procedure does not always give the results expected." (Committee of Inquiry on Health and Social Services, *Report*, vol. I, p. 147).

130. CMA, *Special Bulletin*, October 19, 1970, p. 6.

131. Revised Statutes of Ontario, chap. 68, October 23, 1969.

132. Quebec National Assembly, Bill 38, An Act Respecting the Construction Industry (August 8, 1970). An important distinction is made by Dr. Robillard in that in the other episodes the Government was intervening between employers and employees and in this case dealing with an independent, self-governing profession (personal communication, September 1, 1970).

133. CMA, *Bulletin*, p. 6. But the editor of the *Ontario Medical Review* saw the connection. In the November issue he raised the question: "This makes us wonder how many physicians protested when the civil rights of the groups which preceded them were violated by specific legislation applicable to them. The lesson here must be that the medical profession cannot isolate itself from the problems of other citizens if it is to expect support of those citizens in its time of difficulty." Given the generally conservative attitudes of established elites, it is likely that the profession had viewed the Government's actions with respect to teachers and construction workers as justifiable restorations of law and order.

134. *Montreal Star*, October 19, 1970. The day before, the president of the CMA had also issued a press release in which he said, "The CMA recognizes that at this particular point in Canadian history matters of even greater concern

demand the attention of the Canadian communications media and the public. We can only request your assistance to adequately voice our protest—not only in defense of the medical specialists of Quebec as citizens, *but to help protect free enterprise* [italics added] and one of the finest health care systems in the world." This statement perhaps reveals more than any other that the medical spokemen still did not comprehend what the conflict was really about; for the Castonguay Committee *Report* (as well as the Hall Commission *Report*) had made it abundantly clear that the provision of medical services was no longer "free enterprise," as this statement indicates: "It is definitely recognized throughout the world, and Canada and Quebec in particular, that the State must intervene progressively in the field of public health and health insurance. The maintenance of the people's health more and more is accepted as a collective responsibility. This is not surprising since it must be admitted that without vigorous State action, the right to health would remain a purely theoretical notion, without any real content" (Committee of Inquiry on Health and Social Services, *Report*, vol. IV, tome 1, p. 30, par. 78).

135. This section is based on interviews with specialists (some of whom are expatriates), government leaders, and journalists.

136. There is an interesting parallel between the reaction of the specialists to the back-to-work order and of the management of the privately owned hydroelectric utilities in Quebec before their take-over in 1962: "It can't happen here!"

137. Dr. Robillard's book, *Medicare, the MDs and You!*, contains a chapter on future goals and patterns highly compatible with those of the Castonguay Committee.

138. Ibid., p. 103.

139. Personal communication from Dr. Maurice McGregor, dean of McGill medical school, November 1971.

140. Personal correspondence with the registrar of the College of Physicians and Surgeons. The most serious losses were from all accounts among radiologists, anaesthetists, and psychiatrists.

141. Quebec Health Insurance Board, *Fifth Annual Report* (1974).

142. Philip E. Enterline, Allison McDonald, J. Corbett McDonald, Nicholas Steinmetz, "The Distribution of Medical Services Before and After 'Free' Medical Care," *Medical Care*, 11, 4 (July–August, 1973): 269–86; "Effects of 'Free' Medical Care on Medical Practice—The Quebec Experience," *New England Journal of Medicine*, 288, 22 (May 31, 1973): 1152–55.

143. Ibid.

Notes to Chapter Eight

1. House of Commons, Bill C-37 (March 7, 1977).

2. See above, p. 12.

3. Personal conversations.

4. In his analyses of federal and provincial governmental outputs, David Falcone has concluded that government policies are mainly influenced by three factors: increasing population, industrialization, and urbanization. But none of

these seems to explain the two major policy decisions in Saskatchewan. See David J. Falcone, "Legislative Change and Output Change" (Ph. D. dissertation, Duke University, 1974); David Falcone and William Mishler, "Legislative Determinants of Provincial Health Policy," a paper presented at the 1972 annual meeting of the Canadian Political Science Association. On the distributional aspects of health insurance, see Rod Fraser, "The Distributional Impact of Government Funded Health Care," in *A Research Agenda in Health Care Economics* (Ontario Economic Council, Working Paper 3, 1975), and Pranlal Manga, "A Benefit Incidence Analysis of Public Medical and Hospital Insurance in Ontario" (Ph. D. thesis, University of Toronto, 1976).

5. T. C. Routley, "Health Insurance for Canadians." (Text of a radio broadcast, September 17, 1943, reprinted in full in *Saskatchewan Medical Quarterly*, 17, 4 (December 1953), pp. 27–32.

6. Kenneth Bryden, *Old Age Pensions and Policy-Making in Canada* (Montreal: McGill-Queen's University Press, 1974), pp. 5–7.

7. Charles Lindblom, "The Science of Muddling Through," *Public Administration Review*, 19 (Spring 1959): 79–88.

8. Charles Lindblom, *The Policy Making Process* (Englewood Cliffs, N.J.: Prentice-Hall, 1968), and David Braybrooke and Charles Lindblom, *A Strategy of Decision* (New York: The Free Press, 1970).

9. Lindblom, *The Policy Making Process*, p. 13. See also Ira Sharkansky, *Public Administration* (Chicago: Markham, 1970), pp. 37–70.

10. Lindblom, "The Science of Muddling Through," p. 81.

11. Ibid.

12. Peter Aucoin, "Theory and Research in the Study of Policy-Making," in G. Bruce Doern and Peter Aucoin (eds.), *The Structures of Policy Making in Canada* (Toronto: Macmillan, 1971).

13. A. Etzioni (ed.), *Readings on Modern Organization* (Englewood Cliffs, N. J.: Prentice-Hall, 1969), pp. 154–65.

14. Graham T. Allison, "Conceptual Models and The Cuban Missile Crisis," *American Political Science Review*, LXIII, 3 (September 1969): 689–718.

15. Ibid., p. 698.

16. Ibid.

17. For a more recent analysis of the process, see Hubert L. Laframboise, "Moving a Proposal to a Positive Decision: A Case History of the Invisible Process," *Optimum*, IV, 3 (1973): 31–41.

18. Allison, *Conceptual Models*, p. 708.

19. Peter Aucoin, "Theory and Research in Public Policy-Making," pp. 23–27.

20. G. Bruce Doern, in G. B. Doern and P. Aucoin (eds.), *The Structures of Policy Making*, p. 51.

Index

Committee of Inquiry on Health and
Social Services, 453n22. *See also*
Castonguay Report
Committee on the Costs of Medical
Care (US), 23
Committee on Post-War Reconstruc-
tion, 17
Community Health Clinics (Saskat-
chewan), 326
Conditional grant-in-aid: views of
Royal Commission on Dominion-
Provincial Relations, 12; opposi-
tion to, by Alberta, 355; by Quebec,
355; abandonment in national
health insurance, 377, 415–16
Conversion process, xiv
Cook, Ramsay, 380, 452n2
Cooperative Commonwealth Federa-
tion (national), 8; elections (1945),
47; health insurance policy (1953),
166; forms New Democratic Party,
282–83
Cooperative Commonwealth Federa-
tion (Saskatchewan). *See* Saskat-
chewan Cooperative Common-
wealth Federation
Corporations (Quebec). *See* Quebec
College of Physicians and Surgeons
Corrigan, D. Owen, 430n106
Council for Community Health
Services (Saskatchewan), 319
Cowling, Alfred, 124
Cox, Donald, 169
Crerar, T. A., 40, 42
Cross, John G., 455n78
Cross, James, 408

Dalgleish, H. D.: negotiations re
medicare commission, 288–29, 291,
296; report to CMA Executive,
301–2; address to CCF Conven-
tion, 320–21; negotiations on
Saskatoon Agreement, 321–23
Davey, Keith, 374
Davidson, George F., 150, 199
Davies, William G., minister of
health, 286, 291, 299
de la Rochelle, Serge, 455n65
Depression: effect on health care, 5–6
Deschenes, Jules, 452n13
Després, Robert, 399
Detwiller, Lloyd, 168–69

Diefenbaker, John: prime minister
(1957), 231; elections (1962), 300;
elections (1963), 333; appointment
of Royal Commission on Health
Services, 335; use of Royal Commission device, 426
Dinsdale, Walter, 369
Doern, G. B., 460n20
Dominion Council of Health, 5;
meeting (1942), 16; opposition to
independent commissions, 22–23;
meeting (1955), 210
Dominion-Provincial Conference
(1941), 12; failure, 12; Mackenzie
King's views on, 12, 13
Dominion-Provincial Conference
(1945–46), 1–3, 49–66; George
Drew proposal (1944), 39; risks in
holding, 39; Cabinet Committee
on, 40–44; postponement, 44;
federal proposals, 52–55, 163–64;
Co-ordinating Committee of, 55–
56, 57–61, 62, 63; Economic Committee, 57; Alex Skelton survey of
provincial governments, 56–57;
Ontario proposals, 58–59; Saskatchewan proposals, 59–60; Quebec
proposals, 62–63; collapse, 66;
Mackenzie King's views on, 61,
63, 66. *See also* Federal-Provincial
Conferences
Douglas, Thomas C., 65; commitment to health insurance, 79–80,
87; hospital insurance strategy,
98–101, 103, 105; Federal-Provincial Conference (1950), 184–
85; Federal-Provincial Conference
(1955), 209, 214, 232; first meeting
with Saskatchewan College of Physicians and Surgeons, 243–44;
letter to College (1945), 249–50;
objectives, 271; announces medicare program (1959), 276; announces principles, 278; becomes
leader of NDP, 283; resignation as
premier, 286, 292; electoral defeat,
300; in opposition, 353, 374, 417,
426
Dozois, Paul, 381; announces Quebec
medicare, 393, 454n42
Drew, George: urges Dominion-Provincial Conference (1944), 39; op-

tem, 170
Newman, Peter, 372, 448n4
Nova Scotia, 186, 213, 333, 336, 375

O'Dwyer, Pat, 300
Ogilvie, David, 130, 132, 157
Old age security, 185, 421
Oliver, Farquhar, 137, 154
Ontario Association of Accident and Health underwriters, 143–45
Ontario Blue Cross, 112–15
Ontario Chamber of Commerce, 145–46
Ontario elections (1955), 158
Ontario Health Survey Report, 110
Ontario Hospital Association: hospital insurance policy (1955), 140–41; negotiations with Premier Frost, 149–50, 157
Ontario hospitals (1953), resources, 110; indigent hospital care, 111; maintenance grants, 111; costs, 111–12; revenues, 111–12; utilization, 115–17
Ontario Hospital Services Commission: established, 137, 146; appointment of members, 147; negotiations with Ontario Hospital Association, 149–50; announces Hospital Services Plan, 152–53; and structuring of influence, 425
Ontario Hospital Services Plan: planning, 127–30; Taylor Report, 127–28; objectives, 129; cost estimates, 134; characteristics, 152–53; premiums, 157; takeover of Blue Cross, 157; program launched, 157
Ontario Legislature, Committee on Health, 137
Ontario Medical Association: policy re hospital insurance (1956), 139–40; draft statement of rights and responsibilities, 280; support of Quebec specialists, 409
Ontario Medical Services Insurance Plan, 340–41, 368
Ontario Welfare Board (1935), 6
Osborne, John, 199

Parti Québécois, 409
Patterson, W. J.: postpones 1943 Saskatchewan election, 74; ap-

points Committee on Social Security (1943), 75–76
Peacock, George, 277
Pearson, Lester: secretary of state for external affairs, 184; prime minister, 331; health policy, 333–34, 353–54; and conditional grants, 361–62; minority government, 363; Throne Speech (1965), 363; meeting with CMA, 364; Federal Provincial Conference (1965), 364–66; faces Cabinet opposition, 370–72; delays medicare, 372; doubts on medicare 374; leadership role of, 426; 448n4
Peart, A.F.W., 446n140
Pellerin, Jean, 403
Pensions and National Health, Department of, 3
Phair, J. T., 128
Phillips, MacKinnon, Ontario minister of health, 123, 150, 225
Philpott, Elmer, 437n1
Physicians' Services Inc. (Ontario), 336, 376
Pickersgill, Jack W., 125, 208, 428n16, 430nn92,102
Pineo, P. C., 452n17
Pitkethly, Andrew, 167
Planning and Organization Grant (1945), 51
Poland, Fred, 456n84
Porter, Dana, Ontario treasurer, 132; meeting with Prime Minister St. Laurent, 150; completes negotiations with Paul Martin, 156
Porter, John, 452n17
Portnuff, H. L., 448n204
Powell, E. R., 85
Power, Bruce, 172–73
Prince Edward Island, 177–78, 179, 186, 214, 236, 336, 375
Private government, 265, 443n68
Progressive Conservative party. See National Progressive Conservative party
Provincial Premiers Conference (1966), 369–70
Purser, Richard, 405

Quebec: university grants, 355; Quebec Pension Plan, 355, 381; attack

469

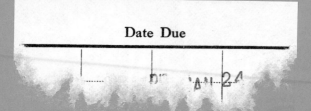